Accounting Theory & Policy

A Reader

Accounting Theory & Policy

A Reader

Robert Bloom
School of Business Administration
College of William and Mary

Pieter T. Elgers
School of Business Administration
University of Massachusetts

HARCOURT BRACE JOVANOVICH, PUBLISHERS
San Diego   New York   Chicago   Atlanta   Washington, D.C.
London   Sydney   Toronto

Library of Congress Catalog Card Number: 80-82576

ISBN: 0-15-500477-8

PREFACE

Our aim in compiling this reader has been to provide an up-to-date and comprehensive set of readings in accounting theory for the upper-level undergraduate and graduate accounting student. The articles in this volume have a conceptual and pragmatic flavor, emphasizing the application of theory to practice.

There is a risk of rapid obsolescence for any compilation of current research articles. Moreover, instructors of accounting theory courses, present company included, tend to be highly idiosyncratic in the design of the accounting theory course. Nevertheless, we have been led by several convictions to the preparation of this volume. First, there is a need for a collection of readings that reflects the recent, thorough reassessment by accounting researchers and accounting policy-makers of the role of accounting theory in the setting of accounting standards. This reassessment has enabled a broadening of the domain of accounting theory as well as a sharper delineation of the limits of accounting theory in the policy-making process. Specifically, accounting policy decisions are increasingly acknowledged to be matters of social choice, involving a possible trade-off of the interests of one group against those of another group. From this perspective, accounting policies may be viewed appropriately as outcomes of a political process, and the arguments for or against a given policy may be phrased legitimately in terms of "whose ox gets gored." Accordingly, whether a given method of accounting is consistent with an underlying theory of income or value may not be a compelling argument in the policy debate. This appreciation of the insufficiency of traditional accounting theory has been accompanied by a broadening of the body of theory relevant to accounting, to include theories in welfare economics, political science, human information processing, macroeconomics, finance, and other areas pertinent to assessing the consequences of accounting rules.

Second, the organization of this book and the selection and sequence of articles has enabled us to express our personal, if not original, view of structure in accounting theory. If a coherent body of accounting theory has been developed to allow either the rationalization or the criticism of present accounting practice, then it should be possible to reveal the structure of that body of accounting theory by an orderly progression. This progression should move from (a) consideration of the basic nature of accounting theories (for example, as compared to theories in the physical or social sciences) to (b) the articulation of criteria by which competing accounting theories might be validated or discarded, then to (c) the appraisal of various comprehensive theories, and finally to (d) the resolution of disputes such as those listed in the current agenda of the Financial Accounting Standards Board (FASB). It will not surprise many of our readers to learn that the progression outlined here has not been smoothly accomplished in this volume, reflecting in our judgment the present state of theorizing in accounting.

In sum, the papers included in this collection are likely to impress upon the reader that accounting theory is necessary though insufficient in the accounting policy-making process; that new theories and empirical findings in related fields have important implications for both the subject matter and the methodology of accounting theory; and finally that a formidable task awaits the accounting theorist attempting to apply a coherent frame of reference to the enlightenment of current accounting controversies.

Earlier versions of this set of readings have been used as the primary text in an M.B.A. elective course in accounting theory as well as a senior undergraduate accounting theory seminar. The M.B.A. course has stressed the first three parts of the outline. The undergraduate course, while incorporating selected portions of the earlier readings, has emphasized Parts III, IV, and V of the outline. Thus, while some instructors may desire to supplement this collection of readings with their own favored pieces from the periodical literature, and perhaps to revise the content of Part V ("Other Current Issues") to reflect changes in the FASB agenda, we believe that this collection will provide a useful basic or supplementary text for several years beyond its publication date.

This book begins with the basic foundations of accounting theory and policy, setting the stage for later coverage of specific issues. Part I focuses on the nature of accounting policy decisions and surveys the research strategies available for aiding accounting policy decisions. This section helps to define the role of accounting theory (or a priori research). Part II explores approaches to accounting theory, criteria for the evaluation of accounting-policy standards, implications for accounting policy of market efficiency and portfolio theory, and the issue of materiality. Part III deals with the nature of accounting income, the problem of allocation in income measurement, and various proposed alternatives to historical cost accounting. Part IV is concerned with extensions in corporate accounting disclosures: forecast reporting, human asset accounting, and social reporting. Finally, Part V examines such other specific issues from recent FASB agendas as solvency and liquidity, accounting recognition criteria and executory contracts, and intangible assets.

We selected the articles for this volume essentially in terms of how provocative and stimulating they were rather than for their compatibility with our own views. Length was not a critical factor in the selection process, because we were looking for significant contributions to accounting thought. Pronouncements of the Financial Accounting Standards Board and the Accounting Principles Board are not included in this volume under the assumption that the reader has access to a collection of such material. For other articles dealing with topics covered in this book, the reader should refer to the selection bibliographies.

The editors gratefully acknowledge the helpful comments furnished by the following professors on the outline for this book: Richard E. Baker, Northern Illinois University; Ahmed Belkaoui, University of Chicago; James Boatsman, Oklahoma State University; John W. Cook, Georgia State University; Joel S. Demski, Stanford University; Edgar O. Edwards, Rice University; Bob Keeny,

Guilford College; Philip E. Meyer, Boston University; Maurice Moonitz, University of California at Berkeley; Richard L. Pannell, American Institute of CPAs and Fairleigh Dickinson University; Richard A. Samuelson, San Diego State University; David Solomons, University of Pennsylvania; Keith Stanga, University of Tennessee; and Gary Sundem, University of Washington. Our debt of gratitude extends to the authors of each of the articles contained in this volume and to the various academic and professional journals in which these articles originally appeared for permitting us to reprint the selections. We also appreciate the typing and administrative assistance provided by Patrice Richman and Glynis Gray at the College of William and Mary.

Robert Bloom, Williamsburg, Virginia
Pieter T. Elgers, Amherst, Massachusetts
April 1980

CONTENTS

III/INCOME MEASUREMENT, ASSET VALUATION, AND CHANGING PRICES

IV/EXPANSION IN THE CONTENTS OF ACCOUNTING REPORTS

V/OTHER CURRENT ISSUES

I/INTRODUCTION: THE ROLE OF ACCOUNTING THEORY IN POLICY FORMULATION*

This book focuses on accounting theory and policy in a decision-making context, fully exposing readers to the dilemmas confronted by the accounting-policy decision makers—the Financial Accounting Standards Board and the Securities and Exchange Commission. Accounting theory is not an end per se. Theories reflect either descriptive or prescriptive behavior, the way individuals or firms actually do or should act. Accounting policy consists of developing accounting standards guided by a basic theoretical framework of financial reporting. It is important to understand accounting theory with an eye to examining accounting-policy decisions, which have economic, political, and social consequences.

In the sole article of this part, May and Sundem (1976) provide a way of examining the accounting policy-setting process. They contend that the most auspicious benefit of accounting-policy research is to assist in the formulation of theories for policy choices. Viewing such choices in a social context, May and Sundem point to the role of political organizations like the Financial Accounting Standards Board and the Securities and Exchange Commission in affecting social welfare. In light of our ignorance of individual and collective decision-making processes, a social ordering of accounting policies cannot be set forth according to the authors. Nevertheless, May and Sundem discuss various research strategies which may help to enlighten the policy decision. These strategies include security price-based research, a priori research, sensitivity of accounting time series, modeling individual and aggregate decision making, and behavioral research with regard to empirical studies on the association of accounting data with security prices.

*The editors advise reading the preface before proceeding further in the book.

Research for Accounting Policy: An Overview

ROBERT G. MAY AND GARY L. SUNDEM

A significant amount of accounting research is devoted to questions of accounting (financial reporting) policy. Such research is addressed to the alternative models, measurement rules and disclosure requirements that are or might be applied in current financial reporting by business enterprises. Such research accounts for much of the combined research efforts sponsored or undertaken by institutions such as the AICPA and FASB as well as for much of the independent academic research in accounting.

The purpose of this paper is to offer a model for organizing one's thoughts and efforts directed toward the process of accounting policy making and related research strategies. The motivation for attempting such a task is a conviction that results from individual accounting research studies must be interpreted as interrelated building blocks for accounting policy decisions. As Gonedes and Dopuch [1974] showed, virtually no research strategy used by accounting researchers to date is capable of selecting the most socially desirable accounting alternative. However, because Gonedes and Dopuch applied such a demanding performance criterion to accounting research (i.e., achieving a social ranking of alternatives), they leave an impression of great pessimism. Yet, as will be evident later, the most promising use of any given research strategy (data source) in the area of financial reporting policy is not in selecting optimal alternatives; rather, it is in contributing, *along with all other available strategies,* to developing theories that then may be used by policy makers to settle specific issues.

The paper begins with a description of accounting policy making as a social choice process. This discussion contains a brief enumeration of certain implications of the social choice dimension of accounting policy making; the second section presents a model for interpretation of research for accounting policy making; and the third section discusses the potential contributions of various research strategies.

ACCOUNTING POLICY DECISIONS AS SOCIAL CHOICES

For nearly half a century, the accounting profession has been concerned with forming accounting policy, i.e., deciding which measurement and reporting alternatives are acceptable and which are not. From the time the first standard audit report in 1933 referred to "accepted principles of accounting" [Rosenfield, 1964], the profession has taken upon itself the task of deciding what is accept-

The authors would like to thank the participants of the accounting colloquia at the University of Washington and Oklahoma State University for their helpful comments on earlier drafts.

Robert G. May and Gary L. Sundem, "Research for Accounting Policy: An Overview," October 1976, pp. 747–763. Reprinted by permission of *The Accounting Review.*

able. The Committee on Accounting Procedure (1939–1959), The Accounting Principles Board (1959–1973) and the Financial Accounting Standards Board (1973–) have had major policy-making responsibility. Yet, after all of these years of policy making, the procedures for policy formulation are not always well understood.

Before proceeding to a detailed discussion of policy decisions, it is necessary to distinguish between accounting theories and accounting policy [Ijiri, 1975, pp. 9–11]. An accounting theory is a descriptive or predictive model whose validity is independent of the acceptance of any goal structure. Though *assumed* goals may be part of such a model, research relating to a theory or model of accounting does not require acceptance of the assumed goals as necessarily desirable or undesirable. On the other hand, accounting policy requires a commitment to goals and, therefore, requires a policy maker to make value judgments. Policy decisions presumably are based on *both* an understanding of accounting theories *and* acceptance of a set of goals. Research relating to accounting policy decisions must recognize and discern the aspect of the policy-making process at issue.

For the moment, we will discuss the unique aspect of accounting policy, namely, goal formulation. Several recent attempts have been made to delineate the goals or objectives of financial accounting [e.g., Arthur Anderson & Co.; 1972; Study Group on the Objectives of Financial Statements, 1973; Defliese, 1973; and Accounting Standards Steering Committee, 1975]. Since the selection of a set of goals is inherently a value judgment, most debate about sets of goals is a debate about whose value judgments are best. This is an insoluable problem, as value judgments are neither right nor wrong, true nor false. The resolution of the problem of selection of goals must be solved by general agreement, not by proof of correctness. Therefore, the first step in a logical process of policy formulation is to obtain general agreement on the goal of financial accounting.

The statements of goals of financial accounting made to date suffer from two major problems: (1) they have not received general acceptance and (2) they do not provide a basis for selecting among alternative policies. For instance, a recent statement of goals asserts that "the basic objective of financial statements is to provide information useful for making economic decisions" [Study Group of the Objectives of Financial Statements, 1973, p. 13]. However, this is not a statement of a goal of financial statements, but merely a delineation of the domain of accounting policy decisions. That is, it states *what* accounting policy makers are to be concerned with, but it does not state *how* comparisons among alternative policies are to be made.

We suggest that an objective of maximization of social welfare (which may be implied, though not stated, in the above objective) is a necessary addition to the above goal statement.[1] While this is admittedly our value judgment, such a goal seems to provide a criterion for policy decisions and, to our knowledge, no one has expressed disagreement with it as an objective. In a letter to the AICPA, the SEC has expressed concern that accounting policy decisions be "consistent with the public interest" [Burton, 1973, p. 271]. Indeed, the Securities Acts clearly were motivated by a desire to prevent recurrence of the socially deleterious events surrounding the crash and ensuing Great Depression. More-

---

[1]See Committee on Concepts and Standards; External Financial Reports [1975, pp. 42–44] for more details.

over, the U. S. Congress has intervened in accounting policy decisions at least once, in the investment tax credit decision, when it felt that an accounting policy decision was not in the public interest. Since accounting policy decisions that apparently are not consistent with the public interest can be reversed by a higher authority, it is apparent that either accounting policy makers (the SEC-FASB) at least must appear to pursue a social welfare criterion or have their power consistently preempted by the legislature, which presumably applies such a criterion. Thus, the political environment of accounting policy formulation implies acceptance of a social welfare criterion for accounting policy decisions as social choices.

It is possible for accounting policy decisions to be made by each individual or firm producing a financial statement, in the same way that policy decisions concerning any other economic commodity are made. A demand for accounting information exists because individuals wish to improve their investment decisions. This private demand would lead to production and sale of financial statements.

Although general public policy would apply (e.g., general antitrust policy would apply to the industry structures that evolved in the production and sale of private financial information about business enterprises), no special public accounting policy would be necessary to satisfy demand for financial information on the part of individuals. Research in financial accounting could contribute to such a laissez-faire environment by producing microeconomic information (e.g., predicting individual costs and benefits), similar to cost and market research relevant to the production and distribution of other goods and services.

But accounting information may have public value apart from its private value [Fama and Laffer, 1971; Hirshleifer, 1971; and Demski, 1974a]. Because accounting information may influence individual investor's assessments and, through these assessments, the structure of security prices, therefore the information may influence the distribution of costs of capital among firms and, through that distribution, the allocation of capital to various uses in the economy. The possibilities of both production and consumption externalities in information generation imply that regulation of accounting information production may lead to an allocation of resources that is pareto superior to that achieved by a free-market equilibrium allocation. Moreover, changes in information production induced by regulation may alter the value of securities portfolios and, through those values, the distribution of wealth among individuals. Either one or both of these potential influences adds a social value dimension to the regulation of financial accounting information.

A necessary (but not sufficient) condition for regulation to create a socially *better* allocation of resources and/or distribution of wealth is that it *at least* be capable of producing a *different* allocation and/or distribution than would be attained in a free market.[2] There are several reasons that this condition may

---

[2]The social desirability of any piece of *regulation* will depend on the amount of and ownership of resources used to decide on and enforce the regulation as well as the reallocation of resources and redistribution of wealth brought about by the regulation. Henceforth, we will not be concerned about the desirability of any particular regulation, but we will accept the result that regulation is potentially desirable. The dilemma of comparing the social desirability of alternative *allocations* is discussed in Demski [1974a, pp. 227–228].

be met. First, regulation can impose production of information on entities with comparative advantages in producing the information (usually perceived to be the business enterprise in the case of financial accounting information). However, these entities do not necessarily have a private incentive to do so. In this way, it may be possible to alter the information set employed privately by investors in forming their preferences for various securities by altering the distribution of costs of information [May and Sundem, 1973]. Such alterations may affect resource allocation and wealth distribution directly by changing the production opportunities of other (external) information suppliers, even though their effect on the security price structure is minimal. Second, since optimal investment strategies imply interfirm comparisons, some external economies in information processing may be achievable through imposition of certain uniformities in financial accounting information produced. This may mean lower costs of acquiring information for investors and other decision makers. Third, to the extent that a policy apparatus lessens the probability of major financial scandals, it may contribute to the general perception of risk *over a vast number of risky investments* and, therefore, the level of savings and investment in the economy as a whole.

Accounting information is like many other commodities produced in our economy today: the private market for such information is modified by explicit public policy (regulation) decisions. The decisions to produce and consume accounting information are influenced by the FASB, SEC and other regulatory bodies. As noted earlier, in practice as well as in theory, the social welfare impact of accounting reports apparently is recognized. Therefore it is no surprise that the FASB is a political body and, consequently, that the process of selecting acceptable accounting alternatives is a political process. If the social welfare impact of accounting policy decisions were ignored, the basis for the existence of a regulatory body would disappear. Therefore, the FASB must consider explicitly political (i.e., social welfare) aspects as well as accounting theory and research in its decisions.

In a democratic-capitalist society, it is virtually unassailable in principle that social policy should be sensitive to individual preferences.[3] However, Demski [1973] has shown that, in general, the characteristics of accounting information per se (e.g., relevance, objectivity) do not reflect the preferences of individuals affected by the use of the information. This implies that policy makers must go beyond comparing alternative policies regarding the degree to which their outputs conform to certain purely technical or aesthetic standards, e.g., "true economic value," "true income," relevance and objectivity. That is, accounting policy makers must employ a decision model that is sensitive to individual preferences. Such a decision model is called a collective choice rule.

Unfortunately, selection of a collective choice rule is complicated by two very formidable difficulties. First, it has been proven that it is impossible to

[3]This notion was expressed most succinctly by Quirk and Saposnik as follows:

"In principle, one could conceive of a whole host of theories of welfare economics, based upon differing sets of value judgments concerning the manner in which the term "desirable" state of the economy or economic system should be defined; in practice, essentially all of modern welfare economics is based upon one fundamental ethical postulate. To borrow Samuelson's phrase: In evaluating states of the economy, *individuals' preferences are to count.*" [1968, p. 104].

construct a collective choice rule that satisfies even a minimal set of general conditions.[4] Second, notwithstanding the impossibility of constructing a completely satisfactory collective choice rule, it seems reasonable to assert further that it is extraordinarily costly, if not impossible, to construct a social decision-making system that could assess the consequences for and preferences of every individual who might be affected by a given accounting policy decision.[5]

Clearly, the above discussion presents a paradox. On the one hand, we would like to have a systematic way for accounting policy makers to choose among alternatives based on individual preferences. At the same time, no such systematic way exists that satisfies even a relatively few desirable properties. Moreover, as a practical matter only limited knowledge of individual preferences is feasible.

One way to face this challenge is to explore applications to accounting of the concepts of social choice that have evolved in welfare economics and decision theory. Some initial efforts in this direction were Demski [1974a and 1974b], Gonedes and Dopuch [1974] and May and Sundem [1976], but the issues are far too formidable to resolve here. Research into the selection of an appropriate collective choice rule for accounting policy decisions is one of the most difficult tasks facing accounting researchers. We will proceed on the assumption that no satisfactory resolution of the issues will abandon completely the ethical judgment that *individuals' preferences are to count* in accounting policy decisions.

A MODEL FOR ACCOUNTING POLICY DECISIONS

Our model of accounting policy decisions now has a goal—maximization of social welfare—and a social decision process employing some collective choice rule (currently, the FASB with their operating procedures) for selecting among accounting alternatives. This section completes the model by describing the framework for research in accounting theories to support the accounting policy decisions. This framework is shown in Figure 1; this figure provides the basis for the subsequent discussion of potentials for and limitations of accounting research.

Notice that Figure 1 is subdivided (by the dotted lines) into several sectors, including (1) business firms and auditors, (2) individuals, (3) markets and (4) accounting policy makers. These sectors are not meant to be mutually exclusive in the sense that no individual may be represented in more than one. Rather, they are intended to represent individuals in various distinguishable roles relevant to the discussion. Notice that there is a counterclockwise flow in the figure. This represents the general direction of impetus or influence in the accounting policy-making process, at least in principle, and necessarily abstracts

---

[4]Arrow's original proof, which applies to collective choice rules that represent orderings of social states, first appeared in Arrow [1951]. Arrow's theorem was first cited in the accounting literature by Demski [1974a]. The conditions, the proof and its implications are described in very readable style in the unstarred (non-mathematical) chapters of Sen [1970] and in Quirk and Saposnik [1968, Chapter 4].

[5]A social decision-making system, as the term is used here, is intended to include a collective choice rule plus the necessary institutional apparatus to implement the rule.

FIGURE 1
The Accounting Policy-Making Process

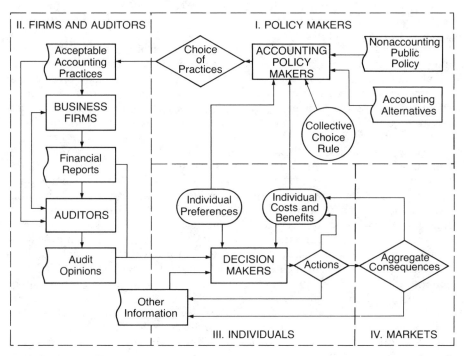

from the many potential countercurrents and forces. We will discuss each of the four sectors individually, indicating briefly some of the kinds of research that are appropriate for that part of the policy process. Then we will discuss the overall framework of accounting research for policy decisions.

Sector I represents the formal accounting policy decision system. Accounting policy makers are shown explicitly, but there is no implication that they must exert an influence on the choice of accounting practices allowed. They could allow a laissez-faire environment to exist, with financial accounting statements treated as a nonregulated commodity. However, the potential social welfare impacts of these statements and the current institutional structure suggest that some regulation is likely, so the framework is more consistent with the existence of specific accounting policy makers with some power to enforce their policy decisions. It is also consistent with the current political environment within which the FASB and SEC operate—one in which accounting policy decisions must be acceptable to a broad set of individuals and not merely consistent with "accounting theory."

Accounting policy makers must specify the set of acceptable accounting practices, which depends on the collective choice rule and social decision system they use (which were discussed in the previous section). It also depends on the accounting alternatives available; development and refinement of these alternatives is an important area for research. Nonaccounting public policy is also an important input. An often neglected area of research is how accounting policy fits into an overall public policy framework. (See, e.g., Committee on Concepts and Standards: External Financial Reports [1975], p. 43.) Other inputs relate to feedback on the impacts of policy decisions on individuals which will be discussed in more detail later.

Section II of Figure 1 traces through the effect of policy decisions on financial statements, including auditors' opinions. A first step in predicting ultimate consequences of policy decisions is to predict their effect on financial statements. Therefore a priori research, which predicts the financial statement effects of alternative measurement and reporting rules, can be an important research contribution. And, where possible, empirical research confirming or describing actual financial statement effects is probably even more helpful.

Sector III consists of all individuals in society, each of whom makes consumption and investment decisions. We arbitrarily could divide these individuals into three categories: (1) those who produce and/or audit financial statements or other information, (2) those who use financial statement and other data in their decision making and (3) those who do not use any investment-relevant information. Most accounting research makes these divisions and concentrates only on *users* of financial statement data. This is a major simplification that is not necessarily desirable. Only if the extra cost of a complete analysis is greater than the benefit achieved is such simplification desirable. So, in our general framework we include *all* individuals whose welfare can conceivably be affected by accounting policy in this sector. Thus, this sector may include individuals who act in the capacities of enterprise management and independent auditors or, for that matter, public policy makers in the other sectors.

Individuals use information, including, but by no means limited to, financial statements and auditors' opinions, in making consumption and investment decisions. Tracing through the effect of financial reports on individual actions is an important area of accounting research. Such research may examine directly the influence of financial reports on actions. Or, it may assess the influence on predictions of the feasibility and consequences (costs and benefits) of various courses of action, and perhaps to a lesser extent, any influence on preferences. Further, the effects of financial reports cannot be restricted to their influence on only traditional investment decisions. For example, one effect of available financial reports may be to stimulate decision makers to produce other information, either for their own or others' consumption.

Direct effects of financial reports on individual actions may be assessed by examining the decisions of users of the data. But secondary effects, some due possibly to the presence of information or decision alternatives that would not exist in the absence of financial reports, may affect the action of nonusers as well.

Sector IV, markets, highlights even more effects on nonusers of financial reports. Individual consumption and investment decisions in the aggregate generate equilibrium market prices. These, in turn, influence the allocation of resources and distribution of wealth in the economy. While virtually all investment decision makers may act rationally on the assumption that their individual transactions cannot affect prices, in the aggregate many such decision makers, taking similar actions, may change prices. Similarly, a decision by one individual to seek or produce information to supplement or complement what appears in financial reports supplied by firms may only affect that individual. On the other hand, many decision makers making similar conclusions may create sufficient demand to stimulate the emergence of a new firm or industry specializing in production of such information.

When such aggregate effects take place, not only are they not necessarily taken into account (predicted) by the many individual decision makers whose collective actions cause them, but also they may touch the lives of many individuals whose actions did not contribute in the least to their occurrence. For example, when the relative price of a security changes, the wealth levels of all holders of that security change, even though some holders chose to hold the security at both the former and the present prices.

Three primary areas of research are relevant in the market sector: (1) determine the method by which individual actions combine to yield equilibrium prices, (2) develop descriptive models of equilibrium prices with accounting numbers among the explanatory variables and (3) determine the effects of different sets of equilibrium prices on resource allocation and wealth distribution. Researchers in finance and economics probably have a competitive advantage over accounting researchers in areas 1 and 3, but it is still necessary for accountants to be aware of research in these areas and to apply that research to accounting problems. Moreover, area 2 may not stimulate much interest among researchers in finance and economics.

Combining the individuals and markets sectors, we can see the ultimate consequences of accounting policy decisions. If a social welfare criterion is accepted, these policy decisions ideally should be judged on (1) their aggregate consequences, (2) the effect on individual costs and benefits implied by these consequences and (3) the preferences of individuals for alternate possible consequences. Prediction of these elements is part of the policy-making process and completes the circle in Figure 1.

An overview of Figure 1 gives several insights into potential directions for accounting research. Most important is the fact that with our current state of knowledge about decision processes, markets and collective choice, it is impossible to derive a definitive social ordering (or partial ordering) of accounting alternatives. No one piece of research can do that, and none should claim to. Gonedes and Dopuch [1974] correctly criticize many studies for making such a claim. Yet, research studies do not have to provide a social ranking to be helpful to policy makers. Any research that increases our understanding of any of the relationships in Figure 1 can provide a benefit. We should not despair because accounting research cannot provide conclusive evidence about the optimal set of allowable accounting practices. Rather, we should focus our research effort on producing information that is useful to policy makers in their decision process, including information that may help them revise their process.

Given the present political and institutional structure (including an implied but not necessarily well-specified collective choice rule and sensitivity to non-accounting public policy), the two primary inputs to policy decisions are: (1) forecasts of the *consequences to individuals* of policy alternatives and (2) forecasts of *individual preferences* over those consequences. The role of research in support of actual policy decisions is *not one of selecting the best alternatives*. Rather, it is one of forecasting or producing information for forecasting consequences for and preferences of individuals. It is generally impossible to construct a social decision-making system that possesses all of even a minimal set of desirable characteristics: therefore, it is also impossible to construct *conclu-*

sive accounting research strategies (methods) for determining optimum accounting policies—without first assuming away the collective choice dimension. (See Beaver and Demski, [1974], pp. 175–176; or Gonedes and Dopuch, [1974], pp. 78–80).

To forecast consequences and preferences, researchers must specify the level of analysis. Demski [1974a, pp. 222] has suggested use of a complete general equilibrium analysis of alternative accounting policies, specified in terms of the individual ". . . consumptions schedules to which they give rise." However, the suggestion would seem to apply only to the general theoretical level rather than the specific policy-decision (operational) level. Under present technology, it is clearly infeasible to consider the consequences and preferences over those consequences of each possible variation on accounting policy for each individual in society who is potentially affected. Moreover, it is doubtful that policy makers could comprehend the full set of tradeoffs of costs and benefits over all affected individuals. Yet, if it is generally accepted that a market (laissez-faire) system for accounting information is inadequate, policy decisions must be made. This implies that although a sensitivity to individual preferences may be desirable, it is one of the things that inevitably will be traded off to some degree in favor of tractability and efficiency in any practicable policy-making process.[6] Most likely, information (research) produced for accounting policy decisions will consist of evidence relevant to predictions of consequences of various policy alternatives for various groups of *similarly affected individuals*, along with evidence relevant to predictions of the preferences (or at least the direction of preferences) *of the same groups* for such consequences.

In considering the sources and methods of obtaining such data, another important implication of the accounting policy-making process (as depicted in Figure 1) should be emphasized. The introduction of aggregate effects of direct individual actions (sector IV of Figure 1) is a reminder that not all consequences can be predicted at the individual decision-maker level. Aggregate or market effects (e.g., price changes) are spillover effects of direct actions taken by individuals. Such spillover effects may have consequences for other individuals who have not contributed directly to their occurrence. Thus, for instance, the set of relevant expected consequences and preferences for a given accounting policy decision includes the expected consequences for and preferences of *nonusers as well as users* of accounting information.[7]

RESEARCH STRATEGIES: SOME EXAMPLES

We have used the framework in Figure 1 to point out some potentially fruitful areas for accounting research. In this section we use the framework to examine some specific existing research strategies. The framework will allow us to assess both the potential and limitations of these strategies.

[6]Demski seems to agree implicitly with this implication in acknowledging the value of research efforts that may help ". . . simplify the consequence domain . . ." in Beaver and Demski [1974, p. 176].

[7]In essence, this is a rejection of the approach used, in part, in Study Group on the Objectives of Financial Statements [1973], pp. 17–20, where the objectives of financial statements are referenced to their presumed usefulness to typical investors and creditors.

The inability of research strategies generally to provide conclusive evidence for significant policy problems takes us back to Figure 1 with the question: "What avenues are available to help policy makers predict consequences, particularly aggregate consequences, of major policy alternatives?" It is of considerable importance that Figure 1 depicts a *linked process* from the use of acceptable accounting alternatives in financial reporting (sector II) through the aggregate consequences of the use of the resulting information by individual decision makers (sector IV), finally leading to the individual costs and benefits associated with those aggregate consequences (upper right of sector III.).

In principle, policy makers should be able to trace the implications of any given policy alternative through each link in the process. In practice, of course, this is hardly possible to any satisfactory degree because of the lack of a comprehensive and cohesive theory or set of theories descriptive of the behavior of the process in each stage. Of particular significance are: (1) the absence of a theory of individual investment decision making, based, at least in part, on accounting information and (2) the absence of a theory which explains equilibrium market prices, at least in part, in terms of accounting variables and which is consistent with the theory of individual decision behavior. Mutually consistent theories of individual equilibria and market equilibria have been put forth in the finance literature in recent years (i.e., portfolio theory and capital asset pricing theory), but these theories are nonspecific as to how observable forms of information, such as available accounting information, influence individual decisions and the structure of market equilibrium prices.

The challenge of developing such accounting-specific theories of individual and market behavior is formidable. Moreover, the demands of the task probably cannot be met without employment of virtually all research tools and methods presently in use by accounting researchers (and, perhaps, some yet to be developed). This is the basic theme of the remainder of the paper.

Before reviewing several potentially productive research strategies, an additional comment is in order. Some people may argue that the individual investment decision level is irrelevant for accounting policy making since the latter inherently is oriented toward aggregate consequences. For instance, in a recent critique of various research strategies (vis-a-vis accounting policy decisions), Gonedes and Dopuch [1974, p. 106] made the following statement specifically aimed at lab/field research studies:

> Specifically, given an efficient capital market, studies of the behavior of particular types of investors (e.g., 'average' investors or 'financial analysts') are not likely to lead to reliable generalizations about the relationship between the production of accounting information and capital market equilibrium. To see this, recall that, within a competitive market, market behavior is a function of the interaction among rivalrous price takers. The attainment of equilibrium in such a market is induced by the workings of the system as a whole, or *aggregate* market behavior, and not by the actions of particular individuals.

We do not disagree with this description of how market equilibria obtain—which perhaps makes it appear paradoxical that previously we pinpointed as significant the absence of a theory of *individual* investment decision making incorporating accounting variables. Actually, we see no inherent conflict as long as theories of individual behavior are not themselves taken to be ideal predictors of market behavior. A predictive theory of capital market equilibria could, of course, be constructed without regard to individual decision making, but there is no intrinsic superiority to such an approach. Moreover, although individual actions are not necessarily one-for-one with competitive market phenomena, there is no inherent reason suggesting that theories predicting market phenomena *cannot* be constructed based on theories of individual "rivalrous price-taking" behavior. Indeed, precisely because market equilibria are established (at least as manifest by observable exchange prices) by the interactions of individuals, this approach would seem to be very promising a priori. Yet another reason to pursue a theory of individual decision making is that, as Figure 1 depicts, the consequences for individuals of altering accounting policy are jointly a function of individual action and aggregate or market actions.

A Priori Research

Before accounting policy makers can choose among alternatives in accounting, alternatives must exist from which to choose. So, an important precedent to accounting policy decisions is research that specifies alternative measurement and reporting possibilities. Included in this research is the development of accounting models such as price-level-adjusted models, replacement cost models and exit value models. Also included is research into methods of measurement and reporting that are potentially applicable within any of these models. While this research itself cannot provide evidence on the desirability of various models or measurement methods, it can direct empirical investigations into the most promising areas.

A priori research also may be useful in constructing potential models of behavior at all major points in Figure 1. Such a priori models will be especially helpful in developing testable hypotheses regarding the effects of accounting variables on individual decisions and on market equilibria.

Predictive-Ability Research

One specific potentially fruitful avenue for accounting research is investigation into the relationship between accounting signals and the distributional properties of future returns from investments in firms' securities to which decision makers' preferences are presumably sensitive. The types of investigations include such things as studies of the time-series properties of accounting numbers and tests of predictive ability.

Early in the history of empirical research in accounting, Beaver, Kennelly and Voss [1968] introduced the predictive ability criterion. Hakansson [1973, p. 160], among others, expressed a belief that the criterion was well suited to research problems in accounting—particularly as a building block in a decision theoretic approach.

However, the predictive-ability criterion is not without its faults. Greenball [1971] pointed out: (1) that studies of predictive ability are really joint tests of the outputs of alternative accounting methods and the particular prediction model(s) selected and (2) that such tests are irrelevant for assessing the potential of various accounting methods to serve nonprediction-oriented decisions (e.g., performance measurement). Similarly, Gonedes and Dopuch [1974, p. 109] observe that there ". . . remains the question about whether . . . predictive ability is a sufficient basis for selecting from alternative accounting techniques."

However, these limitations should not be taken as fatal flaws, since, as pointed out earlier, no research technique consistently will produce conclusions as to the relative social "desirability" of accounting alternatives. If the predictive-ability criterion and other criteria for examining the time-series properties of accounting alternatives are used and interpreted judiciously, they offer a potential contribution, albeit a limited one, to research for accounting policy making. This potential is present because, as is evident in Figure 1, all consequences of accounting policy (other than the direct production-related consequences of imposing the policy on firms and auditors) come through the use of the outputs in decisions—some of which inevitably will hinge on *predicted* values of relevant variables.

Sensitivity of Accounting Time-Series to Policy Alternatives

A largely neglected (in recent times), but potentially profitable, avenue of accounting research is investigating the degree to which actual accounting time series may be expected to differ under various accounting alternatives, given observable or even assumed or simulated environmental conditions under which firms operate. Although unappealing as a sole basis of choices among accounting alternatives, such investigations can make a potentially important, though perhaps prosaic, contribution—particularly when integrated with the predictive ability and basic time series approaches mentioned in the preceding section. In the linked sequence leading to predictions of consequences of policy alternatives depicted in Figure 1, every link contributes to the ultimate objective. Moreover, since predictions of the effects of alternatives on accounting outputs is the first substantive step in predicting consequences, it has special implications for the efficiency of the *applied policy-making process*. That is, considerable savings potentially may be realized if the prediction process stops at this point in those cases where the alternatives being considered show no potentially significant differences in accounting outputs. However, again we must emphasize the importance of a cohesive theory covering the entire chain. "Significance" must be gauged in terms of possible ultimate consequences of the alternatives at the end of the chain in order for a cutoff decision to be appropriate at the accounting output prediction stage.[8]

Modeling Individual Decision Making

Upon reflection, the most serious limitation of studies of time-series properties and/or predictive ability is the lack of criteria within those research strategies for determining (1) what constitutes variables worthy of prediction and (2) what constitutes significantly different predictive ability (or other char-

---

[8]This is another way of saying that statistical significance and behavioral or economic significance are not the same.

acteristic) of accounting outputs under different policy alternatives.[9] This again emphasizes the importance of employing such strategies within the fuller context depicted in Figure 1. The principal direct source of criteria for time-series and predictive-ability studies is a theory or model of individual investment decision making under uncertainty—specified, at least in part, in terms of accounting variables.

The central method in deriving such a model would be the application of decision theory similar to the way it has been applied in finance in recent years. However, there is an important distinction. Since the investment decision essentially boils down to a tradeoff between present and future consumption (usually in the form of claims to the intermediate good, cash), it is obvious that present and future consumption (cash) streams are the variables of interest to an investor—not historical accounting variables per se. Thus the challenge to accounting in modeling the investment decision is to specify how and which accounting variables that satisfy the constraints of a public reporting environment in which management and investor goals are potentially incongruent relate to the variables to which investor preferences are sensitive. Of course, this is precisely the problem implied by time-series and predictive-ability research—which brings out a virtually unavoidable interaction between model building and time-series and predictive-ability efforts.

Behavioral Research

To date, most behavioral research aimed at financial accounting has been oriented toward testing the so-called functional fixation hypothesis [Ijiri, Jaedicke and Knight, 1966] in lab or field environments controlled to various degrees, i.e., testing subjects' decision sensitivity to alternative accounting measurement rules, e.g., FIFO versus LIFO [see Gonedes and Dopuch, 1974, Exhibit 1, p. 107 for a list of such studies through 1973]. Such studies are in general highly susceptible to criticism, particularly for lack of external validity, i.e., failure to sufficiently simulate conditions under which actual investment decisions are made so that few, if any, valid generalizations can be drawn from the results [Gonedes and Dopuch, 1974, pp. 104–106]. Aside from such methodological problems, there are also the issues of whether the way individuals actually use information should influence financial reporting policy and, therefore, whether actual information processing is a fruitful subject for research aimed at policy making.

Clearly if research for accounting policy making were aimed strictly at constructing normative theory, the relevance of such studies could be questioned quite legitimately. However, if our earlier conclusion is accepted that the purpose of research for accounting policy is aimed at constructing theories enabling policy makers to predict consequences of policy alternatives, then studies concerned with how individuals process information, and, specifically, how they process accounting-type signals, take on considerable potential relevance. Of course, this potential relevance is also dependent upon acceptance of the rel-

[9]A third major limitation pointed out by Greenball [1971] is the dependence of predictive-ability tests on prediction models selected. However, this limitation can be ameliorated by fairly exhaustive replications over the set of plausible prediction models available under a given state of technology.

evance of a theory of individual, as opposed to purely aggregate, investment decision making for which we made a case earlier. Its importance is limited by the fact that nonusers as well as users of financial statements are affected by accounting policy decisions.

Modeling Aggregate Market Behavior

Moving to sector IV, the market sector, from sector III, the individual decision sector, in Figure 1 we can observe that general equilibrium analysis, or even more limited theoretical work into equilibrium in the capital markets, has a potential contribution to make. For even if a satisfactory theory of individual decision making based on accounting information can be developed, there remains the problem of predicting the aggregate effects of individual decisions, which are also conditional on accounting information.

Bearing in mind that presumably "individual preferences are to count" in accounting policy choices, general equilibrium analysis, in which aggregate phenomena, e.g., equilibrium prices and quantities traded, are derived from a model in which individuals and their preferences are represented, would seem to be a preferred methodology [Demski, 1974a]. However, due to the dimensionality problem noted earlier associated with representing each individual, firm, etc., in one model, as a practical matter traditional macroeconomic methods, which typically operate only on aggregate variables and, often, in a partial equilibrium mode, may be more promising.

Security Price-Based Research

Recently, much hope was placed in the security price structure as a source of direct evidence for determining optimum accounting policy, based on the apparent fair-game efficiency [Fama, 1970] of the market with respect to publicly available information. The basic objective of this research was to identify the set of accounting practices that would produce financial reports that were most highly associated with the security price structure. Most methods of measuring association may be described in general terms by (1), where R_{jt} is the observed rate of return for security j over time period t. R_{mt} is the corresponding rate of return on the market portfolio (usually represented by some broad-gauged index), A_{jt} is the cumulative record of accounting data about firm j as of time t and g' is the selected measure of association (e.g., the now-familiar API) between unexpected increments in firms' accounting records and unexpected changes (not explained by market changes) in firms' securities prices:

$$R_{jt} - E(R_{jt}|R_{mt}) = g'[A_{jt} - E(A_{jt}|A_{jt-1})]. \tag{1}$$

In terms of Figure 1, this measure of association relates the output of sector II, financial reports, with the aggregate consequences of sector IV. But Figure 1 highlights some potential problems with this research strategy.

First, this method can be applied only when the effect of accounting alternatives on financial reports is known (i.e., when A_{jt} is known for each alternative). Research identifying accounting alternatives and predicting the effects of these alternatives on financial reports is a necessary adjunct to security price-based research.

A second concern is the measurement problems caused by "leapfrogging" from accounting outputs to aggregate market consequences; this treats the territory between (i.e., individual decision making and the process or phenomenon of aggregation) as a "black box." Any alleged association is based on a chain of causation: (1) from unanticipated accounting signals (new information) through their impact on individual expectations, (2) from individual expectation changes through individual actions and (3) from individual actions to their impact on aggregate supply and demand for securities which would imply price changes. Confidence in the associations developed, especially predicting continuing associations of the same type, would be much greater if there were a well-developed theory describing at least some of these links. Research into opening up the black box in sector III of Figure 1 seems to be an important supporting factor for security price-based research.

A third class of problems, closely related to the black-box aspects of security price research to date, relates to the treatment and effects of "other information." The effect of nonaccounting information on prices is surrogated by R_{mt}, so that the effects of the data in individual firms' financial reports can be isolated. This created two potential problems: (1) other information may have an impact not adequately reflected by R_{mt} and (2) market-wide effects of accounting reporting practice may be reflected in R_{mt} and thus not identified as an effect of the accounting policy. In addition, accounting policy may affect the economic availability of other information; thus, the full impact of accounting policy cannot be reflected in the association between accounting outputs and security prices [May and Sundem, 1973]. This is especially true if data from a nonextant accounting policy is being associated with extant prices.

The fourth major problem with security price-based research is that it stops at aggregate consequences, not relating these consequences to individual costs and benefits or preferences. Gonedes and Dopuch [1974, pp. 48–75] show that only under various combinations of very limiting assumptions do the prices of firms' securities reflect the ex ante values to investors of information production decisions of management. Since it is hard to conceive of any real situations where these assumptions hold, security price-based research has little potential for assessing the desirability of accounting alternatives.

Despite these limitations, security price-based research does have some potential value by providing a measure of the relative effects on prices of alternative accounting policies (see Gonedes and Dopuch [1974, p. 76]). However, even to provide this benefit, security price-based research must overcome the several measurement problems mentioned earlier. Most important is the bias present in association measures when accounting policy decisions involve choices between the status quo and potentially costly alternatives [May and Sundem, 1973]. Unfortunately, the majority of nontrivial accounting policy decisions involve such choices. In those cases, the only way presently available to divine information about the potential relative effects on security prices of heretofore undisclosed costly alternatives is to experiment—a strategy most policy makers would be loathe to attempt.

On a more positive note, not all accounting policy decisions involve highly costly but previously unreported alternatives. For instance, there may be questions of whether the status quo policy of requiring costly reporting under multiple alternatives by certain firms should be continued, e.g., whether firms should continue to be required to report fully diluted earnings per share as well as primary earnings per share figures. The apparent marginal contribution to market estimates of securities' expected returns and risks of one such alternative, given that extant reporting policy requires reporting of both alternatives, conceivably can be tested using security price data (see Sundem, Felix and Ramanathan [1975]). Similar strategies apply to alternatives that are not all included in current mandatory reporting requirements—*provided* excluded alternatives are known to be available to market participants at virtually zero acquisition costs (as in Beaver and Dukes [1972]).

On an additional positive note, it should be pointed out that measures of the effects of accounting changes have potential value in ex post evaluation of actual policy decisions. Since accounting policy decisions, like other decisions, involve uncertain future consequences, knowledge of errors in prediction in one case may lead to refinements of predictions in other cases. That is, if an alteration in accounting policy is adopted based on policy maker's predictions of expected changes in relative securities' prices, confirmation of whether such changes take place subsequently as expected is potentially valuable in refining policy makers' models for predicting consequences of policy alternatives. In effect, what holds for policy makers' predictions holds as well for theory verification, i.e., the security price structure is a potentially valuable source of data for verification of proposed theories of equilibrium prices, specified in terms of accounting variables.

In conclusion, security price-based research encompasses only part of the policy-making process. As such, it cannot provide a social ranking of alternatives. But it does make an important link in the process. If measurement problems can be overcome so that confidence can be placed in that link, this type of research potentially has a contribution to make.

CONCLUSION

We could continue with additional examples of research methods that by themselves will not yield results that directly bear on the desirability of accounting alternatives but can serve as building blocks in a complete view of accounting policy decisions. However, by now our main point should be clear. With our present state of technology in accounting research, there is no research method that will identify the most desirable accounting policy alternative. Nor is there any great likelihood that such a method will emerge, given the social choice dimension of accounting policy making. But there are many research methods that can provide data useful to accounting policy makers who must predict consequences of accounting alternatives and preferences over those consequences. The results of such research should not be put forth as conclusive support for any accounting alternative; neither should it be rejected because it is not able to provide such conclusive support.

This paper does not support the usefulness of any piece of accounting research that might be attempted. Such research still must be carefully designed and carried out. We do not propose any methods of judging the internal validity of research designs. But, given that a research study has internal validity, we propose a framework in which its external validity can be examined. By identifying the aspects of the accounting policy-making process in Figure 1 that are being examined, both the potential contributions and the limitations of research projects readily can be identified. We hope this provides an interpretative framework for accounting research, such that: (1) contributions are not ignored, (2) unwarranted generalizations are minimized because they are no longer perceived as necessary to justify the research effort and (3) accounting research will be more productive in general due to greater complementarity among individual research efforts.

REFERENCES

Accounting Standards Steering Committee. *The Corporate Report* (Accounting Standards Steering Committee, 1975).

Arrow, K. J., *Social Choice and Individual Values* 1st edition (John Wiley and Sons, 1951: 2nd edition Yale University Press, 1963).

Arthur Andersen & Co., *Objectives of Financial Statements for Business Enterprises* (Arthur Andersen & Co., 1972).

Beaver, W. H. and J. S. Demski, "The Nature of Financial Accounting Objectives: A Summary and Synthesis," *Studies on Financial Objectives 1974*. Supplement to Volume 12 of the *Journal of Accounting Research*.

———, and R. E. Dukes, "Interperiod Tax Allocation, Earnings and Expectations, and the Behavior of Security Prices," *The Accounting Review* (April 1972), pp. 320–332.

———, J. W. Kennelly and W. M. Voss, "Predictive Ability as a Criterion for the Evaluation of Accounting Data," *The Accounting Review* (October 1968), pp. 675–683.

Burton, J. C., "The SEC and the Accounting Profession: Responsibility, Authority, and Progress," in R. Sterling, *Institutional Issues in Public Accounting* (Scholars Book Co., 1973), pp. 265–275.

Committee on Concepts and Standards: External Financial Reports, "Objectives of Financial Statements: An Evaluation," Supplement to *The Accounting Review* (1975), pp. 41–49.

Defliese, P. L., *The Objectives of Financial Accounting* (Coopers and Lybrand, 1973).

Demski, J. S., "The General Impossibility of Normative Accounting Standards," *The Accounting Review* (October 1973), pp. 718–723.

———, "The Choice among Financial Reporting Alternatives," *The Accounting Review* (April 1974a), pp. 231–232.

———, "The Value of Financial Accounting" (Unpublished paper, Stanford University, Graduate School of Business, 1974b).

Dopuch, N., and L. Revsine, eds., *Accounting Research 1960–1970: A Critical Evaluation* (University of Illinois, 1973).

Fama, E. F., "Efficient Capital Markets: A Review of Theory and Empirical Work," *Journal of Finance* (May 1970), pp. 383–417.

———, and L. Laffer, "Information and Capital Markets," *Journal of Business* (July 1971), pp. 289–298.

———, and M. H. Miller, *The Theory of Finance* (Holt, Rinehart and Winston, 1972).

Gonedes, N., and N. Dopuch, "Capital Market Equilibrium, Information Production, and Selecting Accounting Techniques: Theoretical Framework and Review of Empirical Work," *Studies on Financial Accounting Objectives: 1974*, Supplement to Volume 12 of the *Journal of Accounting Research*.

Greenball, M., "The Predictive Ability Criterion: Its Relevance in Evaluating Accounting Data," *Abacus* (June 1971), pp. 1–7.

Hirshleifer, H.: "The Private and Social Value of Information and the Reward to Inventive Activity," *American Economic Review* (September 1971), pp. 561–574.

Ijiri, Y., *Theory of Accounting Measurement* (American Accounting Association, 1975).

———, R. Jaedicke and Kenneth E. Knight, "The Effects of Accounting Alternatives on Management Decisions," in Jaedicke *et al.*, eds., *Research in Accounting Measurement* (American Accounting Association, 1966), pp. 186–199.

May, R. G. and G. L. Sundem, "Cost of Information and Security Prices: Market Association Tests and Accounting Policy Decisions," *The Accounting Review* (January 1973), pp. 80–94.

———, "Cost of Information and Security Prices: A Reply," *The Accounting Review* (October 1974), pp. 791–793.

———, "Accounting Policy Decisions as Social Choices" (Unpublished paper, University of Washington, Seattle, 1976).

Quirk, J. and R. Saposnik, *Introduction to General Equilibrium Theory and Welfare Economics* (McGraw-Hill, 1968).

Rosenfield, P. H., "The Auditors Standard Report Can Be Improved," *Journal of Accountancy* (October 1964), pp. 53–59.

Sen, A. K., *Collective Choice and Social Welfare* (Holden-Day, 1970).

Study Group on the Objectives of Financial Statements. *Objectives of Financial Statements* (AICPA, 1973).

Sundem, G. L., W. L. Felix and K. V. Ramanathan, "The Information Content of Earnings Per Share" (Unpublished paper, University of Washington, 1976).

II/FOUNDATIONS

The papers included in Part II provide a frame of reference for evaluating the specific accounting theories, both global and piecemeal, treated in the later parts of this book.

Section A, entitled "Nature of Accounting Theory," includes five papers addressing problems in defining the subject matter and methodology of accounting theory. Each of the authors offers a different perspective concerning the reasons for disputes among accounting theorists, and attempts to explain the reasons for the alleged failure of accounting theory to importantly affect accounting policy.

The initial paper by Brief (1975) offers a historical perspective on current accounting controversies, and suggests that perennial accounting disputes are rooted in uncertainty about the future. Brief argues that providing direct forecasts of cash flows and other future-oriented information in financial reports might cause the concept of profit to become obsolete as a measure of past performance or as a predictor of future performance. If the concept of profit becomes obsolete, then theoretical debates concerning accounting concepts of income and value also lose importance.

Sorter (1969) argues that the many and varied uses of accounting data, as well as the array of decision models presently in use (and from a normative view, the variety of "correct" decision models, many of which are still undeveloped) make it impossible to produce income and asset numbers that are optimal for the wide range of users. As an alternative, Sorter proposes an "events" theory under which accountants would provide "information about relevant economic events that allows users to generate their own input values for their own decision models." Stated differently, the conventional accounting emphasis on income and valuation may entail a serious loss of information to users. As a result, the valuations and aggregations generated by the accountant may be less useful than disaggregated data.

The papers by Wells (1976) and by Peasnell (1978) differ on their views of the similarity of accounting theory to theories in the physical sciences. Wells argues that accounting theories are similar to scientific theories, except that they deal with financial rather than physical phenomena. This leads Wells to interpret the current apparent disarray in accounting theory as a war of competing paradigms, which is a prerequisite and a harbinger of theoretical progress. Peasnell argues that accounting should be conceived of as a service activity,

21

rather than a science, and that the varieties of accounting theories do not represent competing paradigms, but rather reflect a gradual widening in the scope of accounting theory.

The final selection is by Sterling (1970) and provides a review of empirical theories in general, as a framework for assessing theories in accounting. Sterling argues that the problem in accounting is not conflicting theories about the same subject matter, but rather theories concerned with different subject matters. The view of accounting as a measurement-communication process suggests that because accounting models are simply the inputs to decision models, it is the decision theories that need empirical confirmation.

Section B is entitled "Objectives of Financial Statements" and contains assessments of two recent attempts by the accounting profession to define the objectives of financial accounting. Anton's (1976) paper attempts to place the objectives contained in the AICPA's Trueblood Report (1973) in a hierarchical structure, and is directed at providing a clear description, rather than an evaluation, of that document. By contrast, Dopuch and Sunder (1980) provide a critical review of FASB's Statement of Financial Accounting Concepts No. 1 (1978). This document, as well as predecessor documents, is judged to be a failure, because it is unlikely to aid in the resolution of specific accounting issues. The authors develop a suggested set of modest objectives for the FASB, primarily directed toward achieving compromise solutions to accounting issues, based on consideration of the interests of affected groups in society.

Section C is entitled "Evaluation of Accounting Policy Decisions," and addresses the question of how to rank competing accounting methods. The three papers in this section present criteria by which financial accounting policies may be judged. Beaver, Kennelly, and Voss (1968) argue that alternative accounting measurements are similarl to competing scientific hypotheses, and thus may be evaluated based upon their ability to predict events of interest to decision makers. The authors caution that this predictive ability criterion is not to be interpreted as an indiscriminate search for a method of accounting which maximizes some measure of statistical association. Accounting theory has an important role to play, because theory provides an explanation why a given association exists, and enables the researcher to generalize from the sample data to a new set of observations.

Solomons (1978) examines the role that politics should play in the accounting policy process. While acknowledging various ways in which accounting numbers may have economic impact, Solomons argues that if accounting is ". . . used to achieve other than purely measurement ends, faith in it would be destroyed," and describes the proper function of accounting as "financial cartography." This implies to Solomons that the job of accountants is to present "the facts" in as neutral a fashion as possible, and that the use of such facts for achieving economic policy objectives should be left to others.

Zeff (1978) suggests that the recent prominence of arguments based on the economic consequences of accounting standards reflects a veritable revolution in accounting thought. The FASB must be expected to consider the possible adverse economic consequences of its proposed actions, though accounting principles of fair presentation should continue to be the basic foundations for accounting policy decisions.

The following section concerns the implications of market efficiency and modern portfolio theory for accounting policy. Beaver (1974) develops a set of objectives for the FASB based upon a large body of empirical research suggesting that security markets are reasonably "efficient" in the sense that publicly available information is quickly and unbiasedly reflected in securities prices. Beaver's interpretation of this evidence suggests that many current controversies are "much ado about nothing;" the substantive questions in accounting concern what information should be disclosed, and whether accounting statements are the best medium for disclosing this information.

In the second paper in this section, Beaver (1978) examines current trends in corporate disclosure with respect to: (1) the objectives of disclosure, (2) the nature of the disclosure process, (3) methods for evaluating the desirability of further disclosure, and (4) the concept of materiality. The paper calls for the infusion of one additional trend, an economic perspective, to corporate disclosure decisions.

The last section of this part is entitled "The Problem of Materiality" and contains one article by Bernstein (1967), who surveys accounting practice and reports wide variations among accountants in making materiality judgements. Arguing that guidelines to materiality decisions are essential, Bernstein suggests a border zone of ten to fifteen percent of net income be adopted because such a zone leaves room for individual judgment, and also seems to represent the thinking of many accountants.

II-A / NATURE OF ACCOUNTING THEORY

The Accountant's Responsibility in Historical Perspective

RICHARD P. BRIEF

Several years ago it was reported (*The New York Times*, January 4, 1972) that many accountants, "like victims of an earthquake or the fist of Joe Frazier, . . . wander dazedly asking what happened; where did the force come from; why wasn't it foreseen; how could it have been avoided . . .?" The article elaborated on the current state of the profession, indicating that "now, from within the profession itself, revolt is brewing. . . . And for more than 100,000 accountants themselves, the preservation of their professional credibility could not have higher significance. This credibility is under attack in the Congress, in the courts and within the profession itself." This revolt is not new. It has been brewing for nearly 100 years.

One way to gain insight into the vexing and unsettled questions connected with the responsibility of accountants is to approach the subject from an historical perspective. In the pages that follow we examine nineteenth and early twentieth century thought on various topics which have been, and continue to be, of concern to accountants. It will become evident that "history repeats itself" and that most of the basic problems considered by accountants now are also those which have perplexed the profession for nearly a century. Thus despite all the changes in the business environment, controversy within the accounting profession today has remarkable similarities to the discussion taking place decades ago. Why do certain accounting problems appear to be perennial and why has regulation and legislation apparently not solved many of the fundamental disputes in accounting?

The thesis of this study is that accounting controversy persists because profit calculations involve "uncertainty about the future." Legislation and regulation cannot reduce this controversy because they cannot eliminate the ele-

The original version of this paper was written while the author was a Visiting Professor of Finance, Dartmouth College. It was presented at the annual meeting of the American Accounting Association in August, 1974, during a session sponsored by the Academy of Accounting Historians. Comments and suggestions by the discussants, Professor David Green, Jr. and Mr. Leonard Spacek, and by Mr. Walter Oliphant, Professor Louis Goldberg, and the reviewers of *The Accounting Review* changed the manuscript in important ways. Their help is appreciated. In addition, some of the ideas expressed in this paper are a joint product of several years of discussion with my colleague, Professor Joel Owen. Research support was provided by the Tuck Associates Program, Dartmouth College, and it is gratefully acknowledged. Naturally, the author is solely responsible for this paper.

Richard P. Brief, "The Accountant's Responsibility in Historical Perspective," *The Accounting Review*, April 1975, pp. 285–297. Reprinted by permission of *The Accounting Review*.

ment of uncertainty from the problem of profit determination. Consequently, until the subject of uncertainty is given a central position in accounting theory, the problems recognized in earlier times will continue to be deferred to later generations for resolution.

The paper is divided into three sections. The first surveys accounting thought on the subjects of disclosure and alternative techniques and questions concerning the scope of audit and audit certificate. Although there has been an enormous amount of legislation and regulation in these areas, many of today's problems are no different from those which preoccupied the profession during the last century. In the second section, the attitude toward the accountant's responsibility for forecasts and estimates is examined. Historically, an effort was made to minimize uncertainty-related problems by arguing that the accountant's main responsibilities was for "prosaic facts" and "dry realities." The third section concludes that this emphasis on the past rather than the future conflicts with the idea of profit as a return for risk bearing. However, the modern corporate concept of profit is a product of lawyers, not of accountants, and legislation governing the payment of dividends has had a significant impact on the development of accounting.

LEGISLATION AND PROBLEMS OF THE ACCOUNTANT'S RESPONSIBILITY

This section considers two broad topics relating to the accountant's responsibility: full disclosure and alternative techniques and the scope of the audit and audit certificate. Nineteenth century accountants were concerned with the improvement of practice in these areas and many of them, like their twentieth century counterparts, advocated more effective regulation to reduce the degrees of freedom in accounting behavior. The profession was almost unanimous in its belief that accountants should take the lead in promulgating reform. However, there was a diversity of opinion on the specific changes in practice that were needed and some cautioned that certain kinds of regulation would have undesirable consequences.

Full Disclosure and Alternative Techniques

In the last quarter of the nineteenth century debate over the interpretation of the legal requirement that "dividends must not be paid out of capital" and the determination of "profits available for dividends" were inextricably connected to the depreciation problem and other familiar subjects (Brief, 1970). During this period accountants attempted for the first time to formulate theory, to codify methodology, and to clarify their responsibility. The development of accounting was marked by angry argument, caustic rhetoric, and more important, a very sophisticated and penetrating dialogue on a wide range of subjects.

Underlying much of the debate was the belief that reported profits had an effect on investor behavior. The nature of this relationship was boldly and sarcastically described in 1837 (*Railway Magazine*, p. 2): "Let it only be seen by six months working of that line [Grand Junction] that a profit will accrue to proprietors of 8 or 10 percent per annum and there is little hazard in predicting that other lines of great intercourse will be amply supported." Thus, when a railroad charged £14,625 to capital and paid a dividend by arguing that "the efficiency and the value of the engines have been materially increased" after the severe winter of 1838, the sufficiency of disclosure and capitalization policy were criticized by the *Railway Magazine*, which stated: "a more puny and meagre document we have never witnessed" (1838, p. 189). The subject of accounting error, its economic effect, and the accountant's responsibility for this error were a source of continuing argument throughout the period (Brief, 1965).

Many accountants advocated that the profession should take the lead in writing new legislation to improve business practices. One writer put it this way (*The Accountant*, December 12, 1885):

> Is there a single word in the whole of the Acts restraining the payment of dividends out of capital? There is not; what is said seems to amount to this, that the payment of dividends out of capital can be made. . . . What are accountants doing towards drawing up formal suggestions on this and other equally important points on which the Companies Acts are notoriously at fault? Not going to sleep, let us hope.

In addition, a very competitive attitude towards others, notably lawyers, also is observed in the profession's formative years. This attitude is illustrated by the common complaint that "Existing law is deplorably defective, and . . . the Chartered Accountants acting through their Institute should be the first to move in the matter, and not allow the work to be done, and the honour to be appropriated by other and less capable hands" (*The Accountant*, December 19, 1885)

At an early date *The Accountant* (April 30, 1881) stated that "If a balance sheet be correct although condensed he [the auditor] is bound to sign it" because the auditor should not publicly disagree with management. But *The Accountant* also advocated full disclosure of the amounts charged to depreciation, the method of valuation, etc.:

> A shareholder is entitled to know, not what is the true value of his shares, for that in most instances is a matter of opinion, but *how* the value of fixed assets has been estimated—whether at cost, at a valuation . . . , or otherwise, and what sums have been placed in reserve or written off for depreciation, running out of leases or other decreases in value . . .

However, although the editor argues that "Much of the information . . . might be given if the legislature made its publication compulsory upon all," he also believed that "it is difficult to enforce full information without committing an act of injustice towards companies, as opposed to private concerns, which need never print any balance-sheets" (June 4, 1881).

Although many accountants, in the nineteenth century as in the twentieth, argued that legislation which increases the amount of disclosure in financial statements and reduces the number of alternative methods is a desirable goal, others, like the editor of *The Accountant*, also considered some of the undesirable by-products of achieving these objectives. The extreme position was that "as I don't approve of too much grandmotherly legislation in a free country where a people should learn from their own experience how to take care of themselves, I don't approve of the State preventing undertakings being floated with an inducement of this sort" [returning interest on capital during construction] (*The Accountant*, December 4, 1886). In the same vein, when the editor of *The Accountant* discussed (October 8, 1881) the balance sheet of John Crossley and Son, Limited, which was criticized on the basis of inadequate disclosure by the

Citizen newspaper, he reasoned, in effect, that inadequate disclosure would increase a firm's cost of capital:

> Here, indeed, the entire assets are lumped together in one line, and we infer that no outsider is expected to take shares; in fact, none but a semi-private concern would issue such a balance sheet. Any ordinary company would assuredly separate its freehold and plant, its stock-in-trade, its book-debts, and its cash, though it might include "minerals" perhaps with freeholds. The *et cetera* at the end of the liabilities means the reserves, no doubt, against discounts, bad debts and any other drawbacks. But the true answer of the public to such a balance sheet, however respectably audited, is to respectfully let the company's shares alone. *We therefore, consider that the "dissatisfied shareholder" must be deemed a goose.* (italics added)

Dicksee, doubtless the most influential nineteenth century accountant, also questioned the effect of legislating accounting practices (*The Accountant*, March 1, 1902):

> ... even with regard to such important questions as the value of assets, provision for depreciation, the assessments of profits earned, and the distribution of unrealised profits, the Courts have shown a marvelous disinclination [to provide] principles for the safe guidance of the auditor. ... No doubt it has acted wisely in adopting this course, however, because any attempt to state explicitly what the duties of auditors are in all cases would afford the best possible excuse in such cases for the insufficiency of the audit that has been performed.

And seventeen years earlier Matheson, responding to a criticism of failing to specify exact methods in his book on depreciation, had the same apprehensive attitude about fixed rules (*The Accountant*, January 3, 1885):

> ... [regarding] the absence from my book of exact rates of depreciation for different classes of plant, I am more on my ground, and I venture to assert that any positive statements of rates would be more likely to mislead than inform ... fixed rules are impossible, and examples, if offered for imitation, dangerous.

More recently, a strikingly similar view was expressed by the Chief Accountant of the Securities Exchange Commission, John C. Burton: "He was not happy with the old 18-man, part-time board. 'By writing precise rules,' he asserted, 'the board made it possible for people to observe the letter and avoid the spirit with the blessing—and often the assistance—of their auditors' " (*The New York Times*, June 25, 1972).

There were other arguments against regulation and they concerned the depreciation problem. For example, one writer said that legal requirements to charge depreciation before declaring dividends would be "injurious to companies and the public. ... It would stop all enterprise because it would be absolutely impossible for companies to pay dividends in the early years of their existence" (*The Accountant*, December 14, 1889). Similarly, Lord Justice Lindley, in the landmark 1889 decision in *Lee v. Neuchatel* (41 LR Ch. 1, 19) went so far as to argue that the legal requirement to charge depreciation regularly and periodically would "paralyze the trade of the country."

Still another argument against legally requiring depreciation, which the business historian might usefully consider, was made by "an eminent accountant in the north of England." He argued (*The Accountant*, November 29, 1884) that the provision for depreciation ("money retained out of profits"):

> enables managers and directors to undertake continual new work without consulting their shareholders. It is only another way of providing fresh capital or avoiding a call, which might be resisted by those interested if it came in that form; and further in cases where you have several classes of shares upon which the capital is not equally paid up, or where you have debenture holders as well as ordinary shareholders, the rights of the respective parties are prejudicially affected by what can only be styled the misappropriation of funds intended for a specific object.

There were differences of opinion among accountants over basic questions and they were vigorously debated. However, judicial and statutory authority did not play a significant role in resolving these differences (Brief, 1966). Rather, the profession attempted to establish the limits of its own responsibility and the aims were, according to Dicksee (1915, p. xiv), somewhat Utopian:[1]

> If it should be thought that the standard I have throughout advocated is somewhat Utopian in character, and unattainable in practice, I can only reply that I maintain that, to me, an incomplete investigation seems worse than useless, and I am convinced that it is only by voluntarily accepting, and even increasing the responsibilities of our position that we can hope to maintain and to increase the large measure of public confidence we at present enjoy.

Throughout the period, accountants fought to establish the profession as a permanent institution, but the battle still rages to determine whether "the honour [will be] appropriated by other and less capable hands."

> It is now likely that unless accountants and their corporate clients take the initiative in reducing the number of acceptable accounting practices, financial disclosure will become much more a matter of law. There seems to be increasing pressure to limit the diversity of accounting methods by establishing an arbitrary set of rules. . . . If the accounting profession does not do so, "its position of eminence may be lost to those who seize the larger opportunity"[2] (Chatfield, 1974, p. 280).

[1]The quote is taken from the preface to the first edition (1892) which was reprinted in subsequent editions.

[2]Chatfield is quoting from Mautz and Sharaf (1961, p. 200). Similar comments can be found elsewhere. For example, Hawkins (1963, p. 168) commented, "Once more, the possibility of further government intervention in industrial reporting matters is imminent, principally because of the accounting profession's inability to narrow the areas of difference in accounting principles and management's resistance to its critics' demands for improved corporate disclosure." The same idea is echoed by *Business Week* (April 22, 1972). "Before such sweeping moves are widely demanded, the Wheat proposals give the accounting profession another chance to demonstrate that workable accounting and auditing procedures can be set in the private sector, with the broad-based cooperation of accountants, financial executives, security analysts, and educators."

Although the business setting has changed, nineteenth century debate on disclosure and alternative methods has a modern tone and many of the issues before the profession in the present day are those which concerned its original members. How can disclosure be improved? How much disclosure is desirable? How can the range of accounting alternatives be reduced? What are the effects of regulation? Then, as now, accountants were searching for satisfactory answers to these questions. Nineteenth century debate on the audit certificate is also relevant to today's problems.

Scope of Audit and Audit Certificate

The pure laissez-faire attitude in the last century towards the scope of the audit was illustrated in the early legal case of *Turquand* v. *Marshall* which was decided in 1869 (20 LT 766):

> As to the publication of false balance sheets and including in them debts which were hopelessly bad, it was difficult to say where a debt was hopeless; and besides, if any shareholders were deceived into buying shares he might have his separate remedy, but each would have a different case, and the whole body could not sue.

The debtor in this case was the Confederacy! However, although the courts generally did not interfere in business affairs, accountants and other groups were more active in their advocacy of reform, and the audit and related problems quickly became a major issue which was actively discussed.

As early as 1883 there was an interesting controversy on the audit, sparked by a series of articles in a magazine called *Vanity Fair*. Significantly, *The Accountant* reprinted them in entirety, even though the comments were harshly critical of accounting practice.

Apparently, *Vanity Fair* thought that "auditors' certificates might be longer and better" and "legislation is needed" to achieve this objective. However, the editor of *The Accountant* argued that "In a simple matter such as an auditor's certificate we fail to see why any legal interference is called for. What the public and shareholders want is a readable assurance from the accountants, stating in plain English what they really have done" (October 27, 1883). With great sarcasm, the editor elaborated on this point (November 3, 1883):

> We would suggest that in future the auditors' certificates should, in accordance with the defense now made for them, run thus:—We having been allowed to audit not from month to month, but only once a year; having had too little time to make an exhaustive report, because the documents are required for the printer; knowing that shareholders are generally impatient to get through the business; being paid a fee out of all proportion to the work required to be done; and being aware that the voting power is in the absolute control of the Board—certify that, so far as we, under these disabilities, can ascertain and dare disclose the facts, it is all right. This would at any rate let shareholders know from the certificate, as we know from the general chorus of certifiers, what the true meaning and value of the certificate really amounts to. Our complaint was and is that at present they do not know this, but that they are led and

are meant to imagine that bladders are lanterns and auditors' certificates proofs of all excellences and complete solvency and security. . .

We are not to be drawn off the scent by any invitation to discuss the powers of auditors or the technicalities of auditing. That is not the question. The question is—What is worth, and what, therefore, the use of an auditorial certificate in its various forms as it is now commonly given? We say it is worth next to nothing. Our critics say, not that it is worth much, but that it is very hard to make it worth anything. Very well. Then we and our critics are agreed. The certificate *is* worth next to nothing, and this being so, it is a delusion and a snare.

Then, in response to a letter, the editor of *The Accountant* argued that to remedy the audit's deficiencies, a direct approach was called for: "Cease making those damnable faces which are called Auditors' Certificates." Rather than paraphrase, these remarks are quoted in entirety in order to give the flavor of the lively debate which took place during the profession's first decade of development:

There is however one correspondent of *The Accountant* who signs himself "Anti-Twaddle," and who deserves special remark. He is very rude, but not more rude than illogical and ungrammatical. He too sets forth the difficulties of the poor auditor, and so feelingly that he has evidently suffered from them. The auditor gets no power, no time, and no money to talk of; he is not responsible except for the verification of figures put before him; he is the slave of the directors, who do not like to look at the worst side of affairs, and he has to satisfy also the shareholders, for we believe that if they have sometimes a strong objection to knowing the truth, they have at least as often as strong an objection to having lies told to them. And it is quite clear that, if this venerable Aunty were herself set to audit accounts and to frame thereon an auditorial certificate, she would unhesitatingly avoid any difference of opinion with directors, would carefully abstain from looking at the worst side of affairs, would very generously indulge the shareholders' strong objection to knowing the truth, and would, in spite of the insufficient time, power, and money, frame and publish a certificate that would make everything pleasant for everybody, and above all for Aunty. This is exactly what we complain of.

And yet, in spite of this injurious disclosure of the way in which certificates are moulded from the dirty mud of facts by the Sculptor-Director, and invested with artistic merit by the Ghost-Auditor, Aunty wants to have herself fastened on all concerns by an Act of Parliament which shall supersede directors and everybody else, and make Aunty a first charge on the concern, just as though she were an official liquidator or trustee. And she proposes that *we* should get her Act passed for her! No; we cannot do this. On the contrary, we say—Amend your certificates and not your Statutes; tell the truth if you know it, and shame the Director. If you don't know and can't find out—why say that; but in any case, cease making those merely damnable faces which are now called Auditors' Certificates. (November 3, 1883)

Some leading accountants took a constructive view of this criticism. Thomas Welton, President of the Institute of Chartered Accountants in England and Wales in 1891–2, believed that *The Accountant's* remarks on the auditors' certificate "would do great good even if they did no more than induce shareholders to more closely scan the wording of these documents . . ." (October 27, 1883). But the basic complaint was that accountants lacked authority to impose exacting standards. For example, the problem of requiring firms to charge "adequate" depreciation was of great concern in those days and Pixley (1887, p. 127) complained that "It is in the earlier years of a company's existence the auditor has the greatest difficulty in inducing Directors to charge an amount sufficient to provide for the past depreciation of the period." A similar comment appears in the preface to the second edition of the first book on depreciation (Matheson, 1910, p. ix–x): "Auditors, and especially those who have to deal with joint stock or other concerns, where the remuneration of the management is made wholly or partly dependent upon declared profits, know in what varied forms resistance to an adequate charge against profits for Depreciation is presented."

This conflict between the accountant and management, and its effect on the accountant's responsibility to shareholders, was recognized in the first years of the profession's existence, and questions relating to the auditor's independence were connected to the proxy system which permitted persons in fiduciary positions to vote on matters affecting their own interest. Once again, *The Accountant* (October 27, 1883) identified a critical problem:

> The audit of Public Companies' accounts was designed to control and check the action of directors in their administration of the affairs of Public Companies: and yet, as a rule, the auditors who are chosen for this purpose owe their employment to the very directors whom they are presumed so to control and check in the interests of the shareholders. This is one of the evils arising out of the proxy system, which I trust we may some day see abolished, as being utterly pernicious and vicious in root and branch. It should be laid down as an invariable rule that directors, trustees, or other persons in fiduciary positions should never be allowed the direct or indirect use of proxies in voting, or in fact to vote personally, on any subject affecting the performance of the duties imposed upon them by the trusts under which they act, or on the passing of the accounts as presented by them to their proprietary or *cestui que* trust.

This problem of the auditor's autonomy remains a topic of current interest, and recent suggestions for reform (Hawes, 1974) echo *The Accountant's* earlier argument:

> At a time when auditors are subject to a staggering number of lawsuits, intense pressures from managements to adopt accounting treatment that will put the best face on the financial statements and the difficult task of codifying accounting principles, legislation is needed to make stockholder approval of the appointment of auditors mandatory.
>
> Such legislation would underscore the fact that the auditor's client is the stockholders and thus would have an important therapeutic effect on the corporation.

This historical review of the audit certificate and scope of audit has demonstrated that many modern problems are not new. From the first, accountants recognized the limitations of the audit certificate and they raised questions concerning the auditor's independence. Many recommended more effective regulation but some took a more straightforward approach: "Amend your certificates and not your statutes." In summarizing this section, one conclusion is inescapable. After nearly a century of debate,

> ... there is still no comprehensive, integrated statement of concepts on which accountants and statement readers can agree and rely. There is still no consensus as to the exact meaning of the standard audit opinion that financial statements present the results of operations "fairly" in accordance with generally accepted accounting principles. One result is that accounting methods have changed much more slowly than the accounting environment. And the profession has not solved its basic problems of disclosure, consistency and statement comparability (Chatfield, 1974, pp. 298–99).

The thesis of this paper is that accounting controversy persists because profit calculations involve "uncertainty about the future." The next section surveys the attitude toward the accountant's responsibility for estimates and forecasts.

ATTITUDE TOWARD ACCOUNTANT'S RESPONSIBILITY FOR ESTIMATES AND FORECASTS

In the discussion that follows it should be borne in mind that a formal framework for studying decision problems under uncertainty has become generally available only in the last decade or so. Therefore, nineteenth century accountants quite naturally made an effort to avoid uncertainty-related problems. Nevertheless, these early theorists did begin to discuss topics related to the subject, and their attitude towards them had a significant influence on the progress in accounting.

Historical Attitude Toward Uncertainty

One of the earliest references to the problem of uncertainty in accounting can be found in a series of articles on audits which appeared in several 1881 issues of *The Accountant*. Referring to balance sheet audits, the editor asserted (April 23, 1881) "that the real object to be aimed at is such a verification that will be practically sufficient." The auditor's task is then compared to a judge and jury who are often obliged to be content with "little more than a reasonable probability." Thus, at the end of a period "some matters outstanding . . . must be introduced by estimation . . . to make the apparent profit a real measure of what has been accomplished in the period under review." However, the auditor should not "indulge in forecasts or in expressions of feeling, but rather adhere as coldly and impassively as he can to facts—hard, dry realities."

This logical contradiction between the necessity to make estimates and the adherence to dry realities is not resolved, but the writer does suggest a "trend analysis" for specific problems like estimating "probable losses" such as "bad and doubtful debts." Since the facts "keep changing almost hourly," the auditor should study past trends and advocate reserves in good years to be used in years when losses exceed the average. However, when a loss is certain, "no rule can be laid down," but "broad principles" which "favour moderation in the distribution of dividends, and . . . ample reserves is [sic] desirable. Yet he should likewise remember the possibility of excess in the latter direction" which might induce shareholders "to part with their shares at an insufficient valuation."

The principle of conservatism and the auditor's responsibility for estimates is discussed again (June 4, 1881):

> Generally he [the shareholder] should be enabled to see in the balance sheet which of the assets are matters of opinion, and which are matters of fact. When this part of the subject is clear, little doubt can rest upon the estimate of profit or loss, which may be deemed correct or otherwise according to the spirit in which matters of opinion are apparently handled.
> Estimates are often proper things to make use of, where they relate to subsidiary matters, and enables the balance sheet to be speedily prepared, but all estimates should be slightly to the disadvantage of the company, rather than tending the other way.

In the first paper on the ethics of accountancy in 1888 (*The Accountant*, December 12, 1888), John Mather flatly opposed any idea of chance or uncertainty in accounting. However, once again, the views on this subject are not perfectly consistent:

> What is called the "glorious uncertainty of the Law"—illustrated not only in the varying interpretations of enactments, but often in the evidence of opposing experts in law suits—conveys an idea that rarely attaches to the figures, statements, or certificates of Chartered Accountants. And it is our hope and belief, that as we succeed in gradually raising the standard of the skill and the ethics of the profession, any such idea of chance or uncertainty will be still more foreign to its work in the future.

In other words, "There seems a general agreement that . . . the accountant may not prophecy 'unless he knows' . . . he must avoid the tempting region of fancy and stick to the prosaic facts." Stated differently, "in most cases an accountant is no better able than other people to forecast the business prospects of an undertaking which, however sound at the outset, may ultimately fail through mismanagement, change of fashion, invalidity of patents, or numberless unforeseen causes." Yet, according to Mather, the accountant, "in the opinion of many . . . is fully justified in dealing with those facts in their bearing upon the future. . . ." But how can the accountant do this if he must stick to the prosaic facts?

Further insight into the accountant's conflicting attitudes towards uncertainty is provided by Dickinson twenty-six years later. In concluding a discussion of the accountant's responsibility for earnings projections Dickinson (1914, pp. 226–27) said that:

> It should be clear, therefore, from the above considerations that any estimate of future earnings must necessarily depend upon so many contingencies that it would hardly seem desirable that it should be put forth without calling specific attention to the assumptions involved; and an

estimate with such qualification attached would hardly be of much service to the promoter and would not be incorporated in the prospectus.

However,

> *In as much as the community is being educated to consider that statements emanating from a public accountant deal only with facts*, it may be said in conclusion that in such a case as that supposed, the accountant's duty should end with the submission on request of a carefully prepared estimate, accompanied by all necessary qualifications, without, however, any certificate there to. . . . (italics added)

Even though Dickinson rejects the inclusion of estimates in the prospectus, his proposal that all estimates should be accompanied by the assumptions on which they are based reflects modern thinking on the subject. Of greater significance, however, is his remark concerning the effort *to educate* the community that financial statements deal only with facts. It suggests that a conscious attempt was made by the profession to convince the public that the accountant is responsible only for "facts," and it also helps to explain why so many generations have come to regard accounting as an essentially historical discipline.

At the same time, accountants understood the tenuous nature of their argument. Even Dickinson (p. 236) recognized that "Every balance sheet is a matter of opinion." But he failed to make any explicit connection between the problems which require the accountant to exercise his "opinion" and the conditions which give rise to these problems—namely, uncertainty about the future.

These references to the uncertainty problem are generally in terms of estimating balances in asset and liability accounts at the end of each period. This perspective is consistent with a balance sheet approach to income determination. However, there were also discussions about another class of estimation and forecasting problems in accounting and they concerned the relationship between reported profits and future profits.

The first of these provides an amusing illustration of the "interim reporting problem." In 1883 The Hotels and City Properties Share Trust, Limited issued a four-month report and estimated the year's results by doubling the figures for the interim period. *The Accountant* (October 27, 1883) published a scathing criticism of this report:

> Mr. Daniels has furnished the public with the result of working the Royal during the best four months of the year. But are we to understand that he pledges his professional reputation that *any* appreciable profit can be made during the remaining eight months, when Southend is little better than a howling wilderness, and when a stray Londoner at the Royal is looked upon with as much curiosity as if he were a friendly Zulu? During those dark and dreary months is there not an entire absence of excursionists, and as a rule are not the only occupants and best customers of that spacious bar which the prospectus says is a great source of profit, the neglected piermaster and the boatman?

In another reference to this general subject, Montgomery (1909, p. 324) seems to argue that the purpose of reporting the results of operations in past periods is to predict profits of future periods:

the certificate, therefore, should be a clear and unconditional certificate of accomplished facts, and not a mere estimate of possible—or even probable—future results, misnamed a "certificate." To the limited extent already mentioned it may be permissible, and even desirable, to modify the past results so that they may more usefully serve the purpose for which they are primarily intended—namely, provide a reliable index of future profits. But at the same time a certificate should relate not to the future, but to the past. . . .

Although Montgomery argues unequivocally that financial statements should reflect "accomplished facts," i.e., financial statements should be historical, he also points out that the primary purpose of reporting past results is to provide an index (estimate) of future profits. Clearly, the methods used to calculate past performance will influence this "index," but questions about this relationship were not raised.

Effect on Modern Accounting Thought

The early ideas on uncertainty and its relevance to accounting have not changed very much in the twentieth century. There are few extended discussions of the subject in modern texts and theoretical treatises and most references to the uncertainty problem are vague and ambiguous.

For example, van Pelt (1972, pp. 13–4) defines profitability as the "excess of revenues . . . over *known* costs . . ." (italics added), but also states that "estimates . . . will be required for the purpose of allocating costs." The *APB Accounting Principles* (1973, 1, p. 15) states that "Accountants have considered themselves primarily historians, not prophets. . . . However, *even* present accounting practices require estimates of the future" (italics added). How are estimates used in allocating costs? Which accounting practices require estimates of the future? What quantities must be estimated? What assumptions are the estimates based on? What estimating procedures are used? Questions such as these, and there are many others, have rarely been asked.

This historical review of the accountant's attitude towards uncertainty shows that the profession has always recognized that many of the numbers in financial statements are based on estimates of uncertain future events. At the same time, it also indicates that many accountants repeatedly stated that the accounts should reflect "prosaic facts" and "dry realities." This attitude toward uncertainty dominated thought; accountants, as well as the public, have been educated to believe that financial statements are essentially historical.

In the final section this attitude towards uncertainty is at least partly explained by the legal origin of the modern corporate concept of profit.

UNCERTAINTY AND THE CORPORATE CONCEPT OF PROFIT

It is uncertainty about the future that makes profit a return for risk bearing (Edwards and Bell, 1961, p. 9). It is also uncertainty about the future that provides the *logical* motivation for calculating the "profit of a period," and the common procedure in accounting of assuming certainty about the future completely obscures the information content of period earnings reports (Brief and Owen, 1970, p. 167). Thus, by assuming that the future is known with certainty (or by deemphasizing and minimizing the importance of uncertainty), accountants have eliminated, or at least have obscured, that which they set out to measure.

However, as a practical matter, the origin of the modern corporate concept of profit is in dividend law, not accounting, and the purpose of this legislation was to protect the rights of creditors and different classes of shareholders. This legal origin of the profit concept had an important influence on accounting.

Kehl (1941, p. 14) indicates that "During the 1600's charters began including dividend regulations among their provisions. The most common limitation required that dividends be paid from profits. Such was the restriction used in 1620 in the charter of James I to the New River Company." And "By 1700, there had already been adopted in England two statutory standards, one or the other of which still controls dividend distributions under present day statutes in a great many American states" (Kehl, p. 4).

This legislation governing the payment of dividends produced the "capital impairment rule" and the "profits tests" which were the first statutory references to the modern corporate concept of profit. Dividends cannot be paid out of capital and/or dividends must be paid out of the *profit of a period.*

Historically, railroads, utilities, and other quasi-public enterprise used a cash receipts-less-disbursements method of calculating profit. This method implied that the value of assets was "permanent." And although it became evident that this assumption was not valid, the cameralistic origin of the method seems to have blocked accounting reform for this class of enterprise.

The profit calculations of other firms are more difficult to assess. At the beginning of the nineteenth century the "inventory method" was employed. This method was a balance sheet (direct valuation) approach to profit determination. Eventually, this method was replaced by the modern accounting concept of profit that assumes a going concern and computes profit by "matching" revenues and expenses. All of these approaches have been sanctioned by the courts at various times (Brief, 1966).

Leake (1912, p. 2) correctly observed that "when commerce was carried on by individuals, each on his own account, in a vast number of small undertakings, and there was no regular income tax, it was a matter of small moment . . . whether the surplus of receipts . . . was economic profits." On the other hand, the coming of modern corporation and the development of capital markets interacted with dividend law to make the concept of a year's profit one of the most important ideas in economics and, as May (1936, II, p. 307) put it, "the central question of modern accounting." Yet, Hatfield's comment (1927, p. 241) about the profit concept is as valid today as it was nearly fifty years ago:

> It is a peculiar fact that while all business is carried on for the purpose of securing profits, while the distribution of profits is continually the subject of controversy in the courts, while the ascertainment of profits enters largely into the discussion of every economist, the term is still vaguely and loosely used and without definition by either economist, man of affairs, jurist, or accountant.

Thus, whereas dividend law conditioned businessmen, investors, and creditors to think in terms of the concept of "profit of a period," traditional accounting models that attempt to explain operationally the meaning of this concept in the context of the modern firm have been unsatisfactory. And as long as the term, "profit," is vaguely and loosely used and without definition, all areas of accounting responsibility that touch on questions concerning profit calculations must be a continuing source of controversy and dispute. This controversy will not subside until accountants become willing to acknowledge that in theory it is uncertainty about the future, not dividend law, that gives rise to the problem of determining the profit of a period.

CONCLUSION

Accounting thought in the nineteenth century is especially relevant to contemporary issues because the laissez-faire business environment produced a free and uninhibited exchange of views. The courts at this time were reluctant to interfere in business affairs and, unless fraud were an issue, business practices were determined by businessmen. Similarly, the statutes did not lay down specific rules governing accounting practices, and quasi-judicial administrative bodies such as the Securities Exchange Commission did not yet exist.

The last two decades of the nineteenth century were a "golden age" in accounting and most of the major issues connected with the subject of the accountant's responsibility were brought out in the period. Questions concerning full disclosure, alternative techniques, scope of audit and the meaning of the audit certificate were widely discussed in the first few years after the profession was formally established.

However, nineteenth century accountants did not "solve" most of the problems which they debated. One explanation for the perennial nature of controversy is the accountant's early attitude toward uncertainty. During the last century, the profession began to emphasize the historical nature of accounting calculations even though many theorists recognized that forecasts and estimates were inherent in most problems.

Thus one explanation for the persistence of accounting controversy is the failure to recognize that profit calculations involve uncertainty about the future. But given the legal origin of the profit concept, it is not surprising to find that accountants became more concerned with statutory and judicial references to profit than with the more abstruse questions associated with an uncertain future. What implications can be drawn from this historical study of the accountant's responsibility?

First, many modern proposals for reform can be traced directly to the nineteenth century. Indeed, the basic perspective of the accountant's responsibility has not changed very much, and recent suggestions for improving practice often repeat earlier ideas. Thus even though the economic environment was very different 100 years ago, the basic problems in accounting today closely resemble those which confronted the profession in the last century. Therefore, regulation and legislation do not seem to have produced many of the improvements in practice which were expected.

Second, there is recent evidence that the accounting profession's attitude toward uncertainty may be changing. The report of the Study Group on the Objectives of Financial Statements (1973) gives explicit attention to the problem of forecasting future cash flows. And the Forecasting Task Force of the MAS Development and Liaison Subcommittee of the AICPA (1974) considered questions concerning past profit as an "index" of future profit. This work could produce a radical change in the concept of profit.

If direct forecasts of cash flows and other information about the future are given in financial reports, the modern corporate concept of profit might become obsolete as a measure of either past performance or as an index of future performance. In the last analysis, a firm's performance depends on its cash flows, and if information about cash flows were provided by accountants, what purpose would be served by reporting profit figures that are based on conventional methods in accounting? And what purpose would be served by forecasting future profits, if direct estimates of future cash flows already were available? Questions like these will inevitably arise when more attention is devoted to the subject of uncertainty.[3]

Third, if the traditional opposition to forecasting and estimation overrides the current effort being made in some quarters to integrate forecasting and estimation problems within the mainstream of accounting theory, then the lesson of history will not have been learned. For most debate in accounting inevitably must lead to a discussion of uncertainty about the future. This is the one area of thought which nineteenth century accountants were unable to deal with, and twentieth century accountants have not yet faced the problem squarely.

REFERENCES

American Institute of Certified Public Accountants, Study Group on the Objectives of Financial Statements, *Objectives of Financial Statements* (1973).

American Institute of Certified Public Accountants, Forecasting Task Force of the MAS Development and Liaison Subcommittee, March 28, 1974 Exposure Draft, *Standards for Systems for the Preparation of Financial Forecasts* (1974).

APB Accounting Principles, Current Text as of June 30, 1973 (Commerce Clearing House, 1973).

Brief, R. P., "Nineteenth Century Accounting Error," *Journal of Accounting Research* (Spring 1965), pp. 167–77.

———, "The Origin and Evolution of Nineteenth Century Asset Accounting," *Business History Review* (Spring 1966), pp. 1–23.

———, "Depreciation Theory in Historical Perspective," *The Accountant* (December 26, 1970), pp. 737–39.

——— and Owen, J., "The Estimation Problem in Financial Accounting," *Journal of Accounting Research* (Autumn 1970), pp. 167–78.

Chatfield, M., *A History of Accounting Thought* (Dryden Press, 1974).

Dickinson, A. L., *Accounting Practice and Procedure* (Ronald Press, 1914).

Dicksee, L. R., *Auditing*, 10th ed., (Gee & Co., 1915).

Edwards, E. O. and Bell, P. W., *The Theory and Measurement of Business Income* (University of California Press, 1965).

Hatfield, H. R., *Modern Accounting—Its Principles and Some of Its Problems* (D. Appleton & Co., 1927).

Hawes, D. W., "Towards a More Muscular Audit," *New York Times*, April 14, 1974.

Hawkins, D. F., "The Development of Modern Financial Reporting Practices

[3]See, e.g., Thomas (1974).

Among American Manufacturing Corporations," *Business History Review* (Autumn 1963), pp. 135–168.

Kehl, D., *Corporate Dividends—Legal and Accounting Problems Pertaining to Corporate Distributions* (Ronald Press, 1941).

Leake, P. D., *Depreciation and Wasting Assets* (Henry Good & Son, 1912).

Matheson, E., *Depreciation of Factories*, 4th ed., (E. & F. Spon, 1910).

Mautz, R. K. and Sharaf, H. A., *The Philosophy of Auditing*, American Accounting Association Monograph Number Six (American Accounting Association, 1961).

May, G. O., *Twenty-Five Years of Accounting Responsibility 1911–1936*, B. S. Hunt, ed. (American Institute Publishing Co., 1936).

Montgomery, R. H. ed., *Dicksee's Auditing*, 2nd ed. (New York, 1909).

Pixley, F. W., *Auditors: Their Duties and Responsibilities*, 4th ed., (Henry Good & Son, 1887).

Thomas, A. L., *The Allocation Problem: Part II*, Studies in Accounting Research #9 (American Accounting Association, 1974).

van Pelt III, J. V., "The Future of Accepted Accounting Principles," A Digest of the 1971–72 Gold Medal Award Winning Article, *Management Accounting* (August 1972), pp. 11–14.

An "Events" Approach to Basic Accounting Theory

GEORGE H. SORTER

In 1966, after two years work, a committee of the American Accounting Association issued *A Statement of Basic Accounting Theory*.[1] Undoubtedly, the most startling recommendations were the sanctioning of current costs and the advocacy of two column (historical and current) reports. To this member of the committee, however, even more startling was that the near unanimous agreement on the recommendations was arrived at by following two very divergent paths originating from two very dissimilar basic concepts about accounting. This split is not confined to committee members but rather seems representative of a more widespread and pervasive difference in the world outside. The majority view of the committee and the predominant faction outside believes in what I here define as the "value" approach to accounting. The minority view, of which I am sometimes the only member, I describe as the "events" approach. This view although implied by some in the past[2] has never to my knowledge been explicitly stated but might have far-reaching implications. This paper seeks to describe and contrast the two schools, present arguments for and illustrate the consequences of an "events" approach to accounting theory; and examine the logic leading to the conclusions embodied in the *Statement of Basic Accounting Theory*. Hopefully, this will provide not only insights and help for the analysis and evaluation of the committee's monograph but perhaps also stimulate discussion and criticism of a new approach and suggest new avenues of research and experimentation to make accounting more responsive to present day conditions.

TWO VIEWS—VALUE AND EVENTS

The Value Theory

The "Value" school within the committee, or as they would probably prefer to be termed the "User need" school, assumed that users' needs are known and sufficiently well specified so that accounting theory can deductively arrive at and produce optimal input values for used and useful decision models. Most of

George H. Sorter, "An 'Events' Approach to Basic Accounting Theory," *The Accounting Review*, January 1969,, pp. 12–19. Reprinted by permission of *The Accounting Review*.

[1] American Accounting Association, *A Statement of Basic Accounting Theory*, A Report Prepared by the Committee on Basic Accounting Theory (American Accounting Association, 1966).

[2] This idea, like so many others had its origin primarily in the writings and thought of Professor William J. Vatter whom I hasten to absolve from any of its shortcomings.

the value theorists visualize accounting's purpose as producing optimum income and capital value or values.[3] This leads to the popular sport of proper matching of costs and revenue. The assumption is that "proper matching" associates costs and revenue to produce the right income figure or figures—the figure or figures optimal for users' decision models.

Several criticisms may be leveled at this value approach.

1. There are many and varied uses of accounting data and it is therefore impossible to specify input values that are optimal for the wide range of possible uses.
2. For each specified use different users utilize a wide range of different decision models, that they have so far been unable to describe, define, or specify. Further, neither economists nor accountants have been able to advance the theoretically correct decision models.
3. The value theory is unnecessarily restrictive. Thus, events such as leases or commitments have, until recently, tended to be excluded from the accounting universe, partially at least, because they did not affect income or net asset values.

   The orientation of accounting toward producing income and asset values which are nothing but simple attempts to adjust for the lag between cash outflows and cash inflows has impeded the development of more sophisticated lag models made possible by more sophisticated techniques.
4. The value theory is not useful in explaining many current developments in accounting. Income theory, for instance, does not provide a basis for the current sub-aggregates that are utilized in the income statement such as sales, cost of sales, etc. It has also not been helpful in explaining the advocacy of the Fund Statement or in helping the conglomerate and a host of other current problems.

The Events Theory

Proponents of the "Events" theory suggest that the purpose of accounting is to provide information about relevant economic events that might be useful in a variety of possible decision models. They see the function of accounting at one level removed in the decision-making process. Instead of producing input values for unknown and perhaps unknowable decision models directly, accounting provides information about relevant economic events that allows individual users to generate their own input values for their own individual decision models. In other words, given the state of the arts, less rather than more aggregation is appropriate and the user, rather than the accountant, must aggregate, and assign weights and values to the data consistent with his forecasts and utility functions. "Events" proponents suggest that the loss of information generated by aggregation and valuation by the accountant is greater than the associated benefit. While they would agree that the accountants' suggested weights and values deserve to be communicated, they would insist that these weights be communicated in disaggregated form so that users always had the non-weighted raw data available as well.

[3]Not all value theorists are income oriented. Chambers for example can be considered a "value" but certainly not an "income" theorist.

This viewpoint seems particularly appropriate today when little is known about how accounting data is used but may even be preferred when more knowledge about decision models becomes available. It is possible to visualize reasonable decision models that are consistent with an "events" approach rather than a "value" approach. An investor, for instance, attempting to forecast the value of a firm at some future point may utilize two methods: (1) He may base his estimate of future values on the trend, size, and variability of current income or other aggregated values. (2) Alternatively, he may wish to use current accounting data to predict specific future events and then base his estimate of future values on these predicted events. In other words, he may wish to predict income or he may wish to predict sales, cost of sales, taxes, etc. The first model is more consistent with a value approach, the second with an events approach.

The criticism must be met that the "events" approach relies just as heavily upon knowledge of users' models as does the "value" approach. The argument goes as follows. Decisions as to what events are relevant (surely not all events can be recorded) must be made and can only be made with users' needs in mind. Thus, the users' needs must still be known. This is correct. But it seems clear that less need be known about decision models to decide whether or not an event might be relevant for a model than to have to decide how the data fits a specific decision model and what specific weights should be assigned.[4] In the lease example, under an "events" approach, it is only necessary to decide that information about leases, commitments or orders are relevant to a host of decision models for such information to be included in accounting reports. It is unnecessary to justify how, if at all, this information should be weighted in an income valuation model.

To Aggregate or Not to Aggregate

As has been indicated, the real difference between the two schools lies in what level of aggregation and valuation is appropriate in accounting reports and who is to be the aggregator and evaluator. The question as to who is to aggregate or value is not unique to accounting. As Ijiri points out ". . . any aggregation generally involves loss of information in that the resulting total 'value' may be composed of many—possibly infinitely many—different *components*."[5] It is interesting to note that in two widely different areas there have recently been thrusts toward presenting less aggregated data. In modern statistics it is no longer considered good form to merely report confidence intervals. Instead the plea is for full presentation of the underlying data or distributions.[6] Only the user can decide what is or is not significant, given his loss function. In weather forecasts, we are no longer told that it will or will not rain or snow. Instead we are given probability estimates and must ourselves decide whether

---

[4] ". . . a goal which by itself may not be so capable of definition as to determine a single perfect solution may nevertheless be clear enough and important enough to rule out some solutions . . ." from: Guido Calabresi, "Fault, Accidents, and the Wonderful World of Blum and Kalven," *Yale Law Journal* (December 1965), p. 222.

[5] Yuji Ijiri. *The Foundations of Accounting Measurement* (Prentice-Hall, Inc., 1967), p. 120.

[6] See Howard Raiffa and Robert Schlaifer, *Applied Statistical Decision Theory* (Harvard University, Division of Research, Graduate School of Business, 1961), p. 68.

or not to carry umbrellas or to send out work crews. We are given the underlying raw data and must assign values consistent with our individual utility functions.

Accounting income has variously been thought of as a measure of how much can be spent and still be as well off as before, as a measure of managerial efficiency or as a basis for forecasting future values. But each of these depends on individual expectations, individual preference functions and individual decision models not on some never clearly defined concept of "proper matching of costs and revenues." Unfortunately this attempt to match, the assigning of weights to generate values, the attempt to aggregate into an income figure, destroys potentially useful information about important underlying events and increases possible measurement errors and biases. Every item on an income statement is the result of at least two processes—the underlying event and the accountants' allocation of the event to a particular time period. This allocation has the purpose of matching in order to derive a "true" income figure or figures. Lifo and Fifo for example are used in an attempt to produce better income figures. Both, however, destroy information about the consumption event. If either Lifo or Fifo is used consumption of two identical units bought at different prices will necessarily be described differently. A user interested in comparing consumption activity for two periods is unable to distinguish between variations caused by the measurement process, be it Lifo or Fifo, and real differences in the consumption levels.

Deferred taxes attempts to secure proper matching of costs and revenues and thereby destroys information about current tax payments. Conventional absorption costing in an attempt to secure proper matching destroys information about production inputs and outputs since cost of goods sold and inventory become dependent on both the level of production and of sales.

The loss of information due to aggregation also holds for the balance sheet. Necessarily, every balance sheet account is an aggregation of two or more types of events (the events recorded on the debit and credit sides of the account). Very often the events so aggregated vary greatly in type, measureability and variability and therefore destroy much information about specific events. For instance, if current costs or values are used, acquisition and consumption activities as well as environmental changes are combined and the reconstructibility of each specific event is impaired. Acquisitions and amortizations or acquisitions and dispositions are events differing widely in possible measurement error. By combining them in asset and liability accounts information about each is destroyed.

As already indicated, income and capital valuations are attempts to deal with lags between cash outflows and cash inflows. These appear to be unnecessarily crude and primitive given current advances in methodology and measurement technique. The presentation of less aggregated data suggested by the "events" approach might stimulate investigation of more complicated but more useful lag and forecast models that could vary for different industries, firms, time periods, or individuals.

SOME CONSEQUENCES OF AN EVENTS APPROACH

This is not the proper medium in which to describe some possible long-range consequences of the "events" approach. In a subsequent manuscript, I intend to speculate on the type of accounting reports appropriate to this approach.

Even under the existing accounting framework there are several implications of "events" theory which might help to explain this point of view.

The Balance Sheet

It is currently the fashion to say that the balance sheet or position statement has lost most, if not all, of its significance. But not for event theorists. We view the balance sheet not as a value statement nor as a statement of financial position but rather as an indirect communication of all accounting events that have occurred since the inception of the accounting unit. This indirect communication is provided by summing the effect of all events on the names used in describing these events and then recording the subsequent balances. Inventory, thus, does not report either value or costs but rather describes the acquisition and consumption activities that have occurred. This view has several advantages. It does not purport to report something that is not achieved (i.e., value) and it does facilitate the understanding and analysis of what is described. If the inventory figure, for instance, is visualized as a representation of the inventory, under value theory the accountant must somehow rationalize the particular costs or value figure that he uses. If historical cost is used, the validity of a representation of inventory that ignores value inevitably crops us. If value is used the argument centers about the justification of this rather than some other value. It is certainly difficult to justify either historical costs or any one representation of value. This difficulty does not create so grave a problem for the "event" theorist. Suppose original cost is used. Under an events notion this means simply that acquisition and consumption events, but not environmental changes, are recorded. Original costs need not be justified. One may certainly deplore the absence of information about environmental events (i.e., value changes) but one accepts information about the events that are described (i.e., acquisition and consumption) and uses them in whatever fashion is appropriate.

An "events" approach to the balance sheet could lead to operational rules about balance sheet construction and presentation. The following represents a possible rule. *A balance sheet should be so constructed as to maximize the reconstructability of the events being aggregated.* Various users may thus generate information about particular events they are interested in. One purpose of the balance sheet is to facilitate the preparation of Funds Statements and like reports that provide information about important events.

The Income Statement

For value theorists the purpose of an income statement quite simply is to report income value or values. Under an "events" approach the purpose of the income statement is to provide direct communication concerning the operating events or activities of the firm. Accounting utilizes two forms of communication: an indirect or effect communication of all events (the Balance Sheet) and direct, specific or event communication of certain critical events (Income Statement, Cash Statement, Production Statement, Funds Statement, etc.). The concern of event theorists is not primarily with the final income figure but rather with describing critical operating activities of a firm. The preferred title would be "Statement of Operating Events." Events theory can suggest an operational rule for income statements. For instance, *each event should be described in a manner facilitating the forecasting of that same event in a future time period given exog-*

enous changes. The deferred tax question would then be resolved by investigating which quantification more reliably forecasts future tax payments. Both Lifo and Fifo would be rejected because they impede the ability to forecast acquisitions and consumptions of inventory in the future.

The "events" school can justify the present organization of the income statement which reports several sub-aggregates such as sales, cost of sales, etc., because these are considered critical operating events. Perhaps this is one instance when an events orientation has already affected the accounting structure.

The Funds Statement

Value theorists, rigidly faithful to their doctrine, have the most difficulty in justifying this statement. They state rather feebly that ". . . the basic purpose of the Funds Statement is to account for the change in working capital during the period covered by the statement."[7] Such a concept certainly underrates the utility of this statement and leads to trivial discussions as to the proper definition of working capital. The "events" school thinks of this statement as "A Statement of Financial and Investment Events." The Working Capital account merely represents a useful technique to organize the events and prepare the statement. The important consideration is whether a financing or investment event is relevant and should be reported, not whether working capital is affected by a given event. This again demonstrates the flexibility of an "events" approach. Different financing or investment events may or may not be relevant for specific firms or at specific times. The content of the Funds Statement thus need not remain invariate for all times or for all firms.

"A STATEMENT OF BASIC ACCOUNTING THEORY" AND THE EVENTS THEORY

Most of the recommendations contained in *A Statement of Basic Accounting Theory* flow more logically from an "events" rather than from a "value" orientation. Why are standards or guidelines necessary at all if a "value" approach is adopted? If users' needs are in fact well specified then accounting should provide the values that make the decision models operate optimally. The only relevant standard then would be the ability of the data to perform in the model. There would be no need for values to be verifiable or free from bias if they work well in a specified model. If, however, users' needs are not well specified suggesting an "events" approach, then it is necessary to employ standards that limit the range and define the description of relevant events.

The need for two-column reporting under a "value" approach is not clear. Presumably, the need arises because different columns are useful for different users; that is, historical cost data is useful for the stewardship function and current cost data for the investment function. This rather inadequate rationale has led to the assumption that the historical costs column was only advocated as a stop-gap measure until current value could sweep the day. This was not the intent of the committee.

---

[7]Perry Mason, " 'Cash Flow' Analysis and The Funds Statement," *Accounting Research Study No. 2* (American Institute of Certified Public Accountants, 1961).

Multi-column reporting seems eminently compatible with an "events" view of accounting. The two column reports advocated by *ASOBAT* is a step in that direction. As the monograph states, "The historical information reflects market transactions, the current cost information reflects market transactions plus 'unrealized' market influences, and the difference shows the effect of unrealized environmental influences."[8] Since the historical cost column includes descriptions of events other than market transactions (i.e., depreciation, amortization, and other significant accruals) and because market transactions and environmental changes are not the only events that have relevance to the firm, the two columns advocated do not go far enough, but they represent a start.

Separate events should be reported in separate columns because (1) they vary in measurability, (2) they vary in controllability, and (3) they vary in importance from period to period. There is no question that market transactions and environmental changes, for instance, vary in measurability. Market transactions can be relatively satisfactorily described by single numbered quantifications (with relatively little measurement error). There is apt to be little variance around that single number. The same, however, cannot be said about environmental changes or forecasts where description by ranges or distributions could be more appropriate and where measurement errors could be material. As long as a single column is used there will be a tendency to continue to measure events by a single measurement process which is inappropriate for certain types of events and we shall continue to be faced with troubles in assessing measurement biases or errors.

These events also vary in controllability by the managers of a firm. Clearly, market transactions are more controllable than environmental changes but less controllable than conversions. If accounting reports are to be useful in evaluating management then a separation of events by controllability should help in fulfilling this objective.

Finally, the importance of the different classes of events may vary from period to period. An investor may predict a period of stability where certain environmental changes are expected to be minimal and in order to forecast adequately from accounting data he must then be able to separate the effect of environmental changes from market transactions. This he can do in multi-column reporting. As the importance of different types of events vary, users, according to their estimate of the future, can attach different weights to the different types of events.

At first blush, multi-column reporting seems a drastic departure from current practices—but is it really? Presently we use multi-row reporting. We break down the income statement into many sub-aggregates such as sales, cost of sales, S&A expenses, taxes, etc. We break down the balance sheet into many rows by classes of equities and assets. Very little research has been done as to what explains the current level of sub-aggregation and extreme proponents of the "value" school would have a hard time rationalizing the present format of the income statement. Presently the income statement is organized around a functional event structure, and the balance sheet around a functional effect structure. Multi-column reporting would add a "source of events" classification to both reports and instead of accounting reports consisting of a 7 by 1 matrix

---

[8]American Accounting Association. *op. cit.*, p. 31.

they would consist of a 7 by 5 matrix. This move from one matrix to another does not seem that revolutionary, and would be facilitated by an events approach.

CONCLUSION

Admittedly, the above represents only a rough and underdeveloped first approach toward a new orientation for accounting theory. Why, then, is it presented here and now? Only in the hope of encouraging the research activities suggested by this approach and also in the further hope that it might stimulate a reexamination of some essential if rarely expressed implicit tenets of present accounting thought. The areas of possible research opportunities indicated by an events approach are many. The following represent a few:

(1) Test whether line by line predictions of events, i.e., the prediction of sales, cost of sales, etc., are more efficient in explaining the future value of a firm than the use of more aggregated figures such as income.

(2) Investigate the present format of accounting reports to see how useful these formats could be, i.e., to what extent do the various subcategories of the income statement and balance sheet covary? To what extent do they provide additional information?

(3) Attempt to develop more sophisticated models to explain the lag between cash outflows and cash inflows, i.e., utilizing fund statements, production statements, and others in an attempt to predict cash flows.

(4) Investigate the information loss due to the aggregations presently used by accountants. How much information is lost by aggregating and combining events to produce one income figure or to produce the different balance sheet amounts? A subsequent extension of this would be an investigation of the information loss due to expressing all economic activities in dollar terms.

(5) Construct useful accounting reports based on an events approach.

Ultimately this paper will find its justification if what is presented here as the conclusion will serve as an introduction to the research activities and the reexamination advocated.

A Revolution in Accounting Thought?

M. C. WELLS

Although the decade of the 1960s has been described by Carl Nelson as a "golden age in the history of a priori research in accounting" [Nelson, 1973, p. 4], the works cited as examples of that kind of research also have been severely criticized.[1] Nelson states that, "impressive as the scholarship is, we are not significantly advanced from where we were in 1960" [Nelson, 1973, p. 15]. He also is reported as having "contended that the existing a priori studies are of doubtful value" [Dopuch and Revsine, 1973, p. 32]. In similar vein, Gonedes and Dopuch are critical because, they allege, the same works are theoretically deficient, and it is possible "to declare the superiority of just about any set of accounting procedures, depending on the particular a priori model adopted" [Gonedes and Dopuch, 1974, pp. 49–50].

It will be argued here that those criticisms are based on a misunderstanding of the role of so-called *a priori research* in the overthrow of outdated ideas and practices. Far from being unproductive, the works referred to were a necessary step in the revolution currently underway in accounting thought. Far from being of doubtful value, those works have helped to place us in a significantly different position from that of 1960. Whether the works were theoretically deficient is, to some extent, irrelevant in this context, and the circularity implied by Gonedes and Dopuch's second criticism is a normal and healthy characteristic of theoretical works of that kind.

SCIENTIFIC REVOLUTIONS

The notion of a revolution in accounting is taken from Kuhn's *The Structure of Scientific Revolutions* [1970].[2] His thesis is that science does not progress through accumulation. Rather, a series of tradition-shattering revolutions occur in which one "time-honored scientific theory is rejected in favour of another incompatible with it" [Kuhn, 1970, p. 6]. The new theory, or set of ideas, is unique in that it is not derived from the previously accepted dogma. It is "seldom or never just an increment to what is already known" [Kuhn, 1970, p. 7], and in the process of moving from the old set of ideas to the new, the community of scientists follows a number of identifiable steps:

M. C. Wells, "A Revolution in Accounting Thought?" *The Accounting Review*, July 1976, pp. 471–482. Reprinted by permission of *The Accounting Review*.

[1]The examples given were, "the writings of Chambers, Edwards and Bell, Sterling, and Ijiri" [Nelson, 1973, p. 3].

[2]Kuhn's exposition has been subject to widespread criticism. See for example Shapere [1964] and Lakatos and Musgrave [1974]. However, references in this paper are to the enlarged edition of Kuhn's monograph. The postscript to that edition contains Kuhn's reply to his critics.

1. Recognition of anomalies
2. A period of insecurity
3. Development of alternative sets of ideas
4. Identification of schools of thought
5. Domination of the new practices or ideas

The first step is a precursor to the whole process; it initiates the period of crisis which follows. During that period, scientists became increasingly dissatisfied with the existing theoretical framework, and a search for alternatives begins. Therefore, the second and third steps are mutually interactive. As dissatisfaction grows, the search for alternatives gains impetus; as alternatives are discerned and discussed, the dissatisfaction is heightened. Schools of thought emerge, and one set of ideas gradually gains ascendency over the alternatives.

Because these steps involve such fundamental changes in the outlook and practices of the community of scholars, Kuhn applies the political metaphor of revolution to the process. He argues that the change takes place only after a serious malfunction has occurred in the sense that "existing institutions [or practices] have ceased adequately to meet the problems posed by an environment that they have in part created" [Kuhn, 1970, p. 92]. Just as political revolutions "aim to change political institutions in ways that those institutions themselves prohibit" [Kuhn, 1970, p. 93], so do scientific revolutions change previously held concepts of the field of enquiry in a way which is incompatible with those concepts. Such a fundamental change cannot take place within the existing institutional or conceptual framework. The challenger is incompatible with the incumbent. "The parties to a revolutionary conflict must resort to the techniques of mass persuasion" [Kuhn, 1970, p. 93], and, "like the choice between competing political institutions, that between competing paradigms proves to be a choice between incompatible modes of community life" [Kuhn, 1970, p. 94].

The process, or revolution, is unlikely to be completed quickly. The assimilation of new ideas will not be complete until previously accepted theories have been reconstructed and previously held facts have been re-evaluated. This is "an intrinsically revolutionary process that is seldom completed by a single man and never overnight" [Kuhn, 1970, p. 7].

There is, of course, no necessary reason why the pattern of developments in science (and particularly the physical sciences from which Kuhn derives most of his examples) should be found also in accounting. Kuhn does consider the possibility of his thesis being applicable in other fields, despite some obvious differences [p. 208]. Nevertheless, just as scientific theories may both describe and prescribe physical phenomena, so may accounting theories describe and prescribe financial phenomena. Furthermore, if the pattern of events in accounting can be seen to be following the pattern of successful revolutions described by Kuhn, then we will be able to explain the reasons for and the importance of the "golden age of a priori research" referred to above. In doing that, we also will answer the criticisms made of the works which appeared during that golden age.

It should be emphasized that the analogy here is to accounting thought.[3] Given the political difficulties of initiating change in accounting practices, that

[3]Other attempts to apply Kuhn's thesis to financial accounting may be seen in Chambers [1966, pp. 373–376] and to cost accounting in Wells [forthcoming].

may well be an evolutionary rather than a revolutionary process. But it will not, I suspect, take place until the revolution described here is complete.

However, to apply the analogy to accounting thought, one initial condition must be satisfied: a community of scholars must be identified. This was emphasized by Kuhn in his postscript. He pointed out that "scientific communities can and should be isolated without prior recourse to paradigms" [Kuhn, 1970, p. 176]. Accordingly, I will specify the community to which this paper relates as comprising the members of academic and research organizations such as the American Accounting Association, the Association of University Teachers of Accounting of the United Kingdom, the Accounting Association of Australia and New Zealand, the Research Division of the AICPA and the Australian Accountancy Research Foundation.

The Accounting Disciplinary Matrix

The basic techniques used for keeping accounting records can be traced back more than 500 years, but the information conventionally stored within those records is largely a product of this century. Only within the last 75 years did the historical cost doctrine crystallize and come to dominate the literature and practices of accounting. More recently still, during the 1930s and the 1940s, attempts were made to formalize the framework underlying the rules for recording and reporting financial matters. The works of Gilman (1939), Sanders, Hatfield and Moore (1938), Paton and Littleton (1940)[4] and others[5] attempted to rationalize existing practices and to set the framework within which alternative ideas and procedures might be evaluated.

The framework of ideas which emerged during this period has characteristics of a paradigm. However, note that Kuhn used the term *paradigm* in a number of different ways. As this was a cause of considerable confusion and a matter he dealt with at length in the postscript appended to the 1970 edition of his essay, we will avoid the use of the term here. Instead, substitute terms introduced in the postscript will be used as far as possible. For the general set of ideas that binds together a community of scientists, Kuhn uses the term *disciplinary matrix* [p. 182]. There are several features which distinguish a disciplinary matrix (disciplinary because it refers to the common possession by the members of a particular discipline; matrix because it comprises ordered elements of various sorts, each requiring further specification) [Kuhn, 1970, p. 182]. There are: (1) symbolic generalizations—readily understood and undisputed symbolic representations common to the discipline [p. 182]; (2) shared commitments—beliefs which help determine what will be accepted as explanations or solutions [p. 184]; (3) values—the various qualities which members

---

[4]Paton and Littleton were also both members of the Executive Committee of the American Accounting Association which in 1936 produced *A Tentative Statement of Accounting Principles Underlying Corporate Financial Statements*. This was "one of the first major attempts to develop a framework which might be regarded as representing a structure of the fundamental principles of accounting" [Bedford and Ziegler, 1975, p. 438].

[5]In their review of the influence of Littleton on accounting thought and practices, Bedford and Ziegler [1975] also identify the late 1930s as "the era to which the roots of much contemporary accounting practice may be traced" [p. 437]. Coincidentally, it was not until 1940 that the U.S. Securities and Exchange Commission brought together all of its various rules on the form and content of financial statements in one document—Regulation S-X [Zeff, 1972, p. 151].

of the community expect in the work of their colleagues [pp. 184–186]; and (4) exemplars—the concrete problem—solutions which students entering the community encounter and which show by example how they are to go about seeking solutions [p. 187].

Following these descriptions, the disciplinary matrix of accountants which emerged during the 1940s may be described as follows: (1) The symbolic generalization included accepted notions and formulations such as the double entry equation, representations of income, current asset/fixed asset classifications and calculations of working capital, rate of return and debt/equity ratios. (2) The shared commitments included the so-called realization and matching principles, the notion of going concern and the cost basis of asset valuation. (3) The values included conservatism, consistency, materiality, etc.[6] (4) Finally, the exemplars were seen in the textbooks and expositions of the period. There was (and still is) a remarkable similarity in the contents of most texts—so much so that the content of academic courses and examinations had become almost completely predictable.

Once a student has absorbed the elements of a disciplinary matrix, he or she views all problem situations in the same way as other members of his or her specialist group. Writers and researchers have a common standard of practice, and problems tend to have common solutions, or shared examples [Kuhn, 1970, p. 187]. Thus, we have the commonality of training and outlook which helps to bind together a community of scholars.

However, the existence of a disciplinary matrix does not imply that a rigid, inviolable set of rules also exists. Rather, and because members of the community have been trained in problem-solutions (or as Kuhn expresses it "learning by finger exercises or by doing," p. 471), they do not need a full set of rules. Accounting was in this position prior to 1930. Writers took for granted, or simply explained, general principles.[7] Only after the criticisms of the 1920s and early 1930s were efforts made to formalize the framework of accounting ideas and were authoritative bodies set up for that purpose.[8] This development, too, is foreseen by Kuhn who suggests that only when accepted procedures come under attack, does consideration of the rules become important [p. 47].

However, the formalization of rules did not eliminate all of the contradictions and conflicts that had plagued accounting expositions in the past. Neither accounting writers nor practitioners apparently saw any conflict in certain departures from a strict application of the historical cost rule, such as the valuation of inventory at the lower of cost or market or the deduction of depreciation charges from the cost of fixed assets.[9] Even this is to be expected,

[6]Notice the similarity of symbolic generalizations, shared commitments and values to the conventions, doctrines and standards described by Gilman [1939], especially pp. 4, 41–43; 254; and 186, respectively.

[7]"There is, it is believed, a corpus of principles of accounting which are generally accepted. It is true that they are not 'written law', they have not been codified; they must be sought in accounts and financial statements," [Sanders, Hatfield and Moore, 1938, p.5]. For this reason, "the search for rules [is] both more difficult and less satisfying than the search for paradigms" [Kuhn, 1970, p. 43].

[8]For examples of this kind of reaction, see Zeff [1972, pp. 119–140].

[9]The first writer to pay particular attention to these conflicts, without resolving them, was Gilman [1939, pp. 128–130, 174, 235].

according to Kuhn. Because the rules are learned through their application in specific contexts, any diversity either is not apparent or may be explained away by the different facts of each case. Therefore, what the rules serve to do is to "limit both the nature of acceptable solutions and the steps by which they are obtained" [Kuhn, 1970, p. 38].

ANOMALIES AND PROFESSIONAL INSECURITY

> Discovery commences with the awareness of anomaly, i.e., with the recognition that nature has somehow violated the paradigm-induced expectations that govern normal science [or conventional practice] (Kuhn, 1970, pp. 52–53).

There have long been critics of conventional accounting practices and of solutions to problems proposed within the conventional framework [Brief, 1975; and Chatfield, 1974, pp. 273–276]. Outstanding examples in the period before the historical cost disciplinary matrix crystallized were Paton [1922], Sweeney [1936] and MacNeal [1939]. However, their criticisms appear to have had little impact on the subsequent ascendancy of the historical cost model. Recognition was not given in the literature of accounting to the great number of anomalies which defied resolution and which brought the accounting profession into public opprobrium until the 1960s and early 1970s. During this period, and since, the fundamental defects in the historical cost model repeatedly were identified and criticized by scholars, by businesspersons and in the courts.[10] The criticisms culminated in the almost simultaneous publication of Briloff's *Unaccountable Accounting* [1972] and Chambers' *Securities and Obscurities* [1973]. Leasco, Westec, Lockheed, Four Seasons, I.O.S., Rolls Royce, Reid Murray, Minsec and a host of other companies which were involved in cases which highlighted the "gap in GAAP" [Briloff, 1966, p. 484; 1972, pp. 31–33] became almost household names.

The reaction by theorists to the evidence thrust before them precisely follows that predicted by Kuhn; it corresponds to the period of *professional insecurity* [Kuhn, 1970, pp. 67–68] wherein the rules are subject to increasing scrutiny and occasional amendment. The disciplinary matrix is questioned, but not abandoned:

> . . . when confronted by anomaly [scientists] will devise numerous articulations and *ad hoc* modifications of their theory in order to eliminate any apparent conflict [Kuhn, 1970, p. 78].

[10]See, for example, the statement by the Inspectors of the Reid Murray Group of Companies, ". . . we believe that we are accustomed to the use of common sense, and common sense has compelled us to reject a number of accounting practices used in the group and, apparently regarded as acceptable by accountants," *Interim Report . . .* [1963, p. 107]. This case was commented upon by Stamp [1964]. This and similar comments by other inspectors provoked a Report by the General Council of the Australian Society of Accountants. See "Accounting Principles and Practices Discussed in Reports on Company Failures," *Members' Handbook*, Item 401 (January 1966). See also, Greer [1963]; "Unaccountable CPA.'s," [1966]; Louis [1968]; "Accounting—Profits Without Honor" [1970]; Raymon [1970]; Stamp and Marley [1970]; Birkett and Walker [1971]; Spacek [1969 and 1973]; de Jonquieres [1973]; and Bedford [1973].

During the 1960s and 1970s, the Accounting Principles Board in the United States and equivalent committees in other countries and innumerable authors proposed amendments to the rules to cope with the anomalies and criticisms.[11] Pronouncements, monographs and journal articles on problem areas such as purchase versus pooling, equity accounting, tax effect accounting and materiality followed. There were even attempts to increase the solidarity of the practicing profession. Carey wrote disparagingly of CPAs who gave evidence against their professional brethren [Briloff, 1972, p. 351], and the professional bodies issued statements requiring stricter conformance with official pronouncements [Zeff, 1972, pp. 76, 180–182, 294–295; 1973, pp. 22–23].

The ad hoc solutions which emerge during a period of crisis have a far-reaching consequence; they make it possible to contemplate rules which previously would have been unacceptable. That is, ". . . by proliferating versions of the [disciplinary matrix], crisis loosens the rules of normal puzzle-solving in ways that ultimately permit a new [disciplinary matrix] to emerge" [Kuhn, 1970, p. 80]. For example, the purchase versus pooling debate provoked discussion of asset values which were not original costs; equity accounting involved revaluing investments in associated companies; tax effect accounting extended the acceptance of nontransaction-based debits and credits. If accounting follows the revolutionary sequence of events, the acceptance of the techniques adopted in response to these problems will have hastened the ultimate acceptance of an alternative disciplinary matrix.

However, there is one class of anomaly which has proved to be intractable. The historical-cost based system fails to take account of changes in asset prices and changes in the purchasing power of the monetary unit. That failure has been a source of criticism, particularly during periods of inflation. It is anomalous in that, despite the going concern values in the financial statements, those statements no longer represent the state of affairs of the corporation. There have been numerous instances of the abuse of privilege by people in possession of current price data which have been denied to others [Chambers, 1973, Chapter 10]. Yet, accounting for the effects of inflation requires a substantial revision of the conventional thought in accounting. Partial solutions, such as equity accounting or, in the U.K. and Australia, occasional revaluations, are only partially successful.[12] The specific price and price-level problems are the sorts of anomalies which lead, finally, to the overthrow of the existing set of rules. Their "characteristic feature is their stubborn refusal to be assimilated to existing paradigms. This type along gives rise to new theories" [Kuhn, 1970, p. 97].

There is one further feature of the periods of crisis described by Kuhn for which we may find a parallel in accounting:

> It is, I think, particularly in periods of acknowledged crisis that scientists have turned to philosophical analysis as a device for unlocking the riddles of their field. . . . To the extent that normal . . . work can be conducted by using the paradigm as a model, rules and assumptions need not be made explicit. . . . But that is not to say that the search for assumptions (even

[11]See Zeff [1972, pp. 173–224] and the Australian Society of Accountants' Item 401, referred to above.

[12]For further examples, including the switches to and from accelerated depreciation and to and from LIFO inventory values, see Chambers [1973, pp. 93–103].

for non-existent ones) cannot be an effective way to weaken the grip of tradition upon the mind and to suggest the basis for a new one [Kuhn, 1970, p. 88].

Again, there has long been concern for the theoretical foundations of accounting practices [Chatfield, 1974, Chapter 16; Hendriksen, 1970, Chapter 2]. However, it is possible to discern two related developments like those referred to in the quotation above. The first is the search for assumptions. Of particular interest here are Littleton's *The Structure of Accounting Theory* [1953], Moonitz's *The Basic Postulates of Accounting* [1961], the American Accounting Association's *A Statement of Basic Accounting Theory* [1966], Ijiri's *The Foundations of Accounting Measurement* [1967] and various shorter contributions and comments.[13] These were, in varying degrees, attempts to define the underlying assumptions of accounting. Yet they did not lead to a widely recognized set of basic ideas. Rather, as Kuhn suggests, they served to highlight the defects of the disciplinary matrix and loosen the grip of tradition. Therefore, perhaps we should not be surprised to find that, despite the vast expenditure of time and money, the AICPA belatedly (in 1971) recognized a need for a statement of, and initiated a study of, the "objectives" of financial statements.[14] That the Trueblood Study fits the pattern of events is evident; the report includes discussion of both objectives and alternatives to generally accepted accounting principles. Those alternatives would have been rejected out of hand even 10 years previously.[15]

The other development which is particularly noticeable throughout this period is the concern with principles and theory construction generally. Commencing, perhaps, with Chambers' "Blueprint for a Theory of Accounting" [1955], notable contributions or comments by Mattessich [1957], Devine [1960], Chambers [1963], Vatter [1963] and Sterling [1970] followed. These philosophical discussions have served to increase the rigour of the discipline,[16] but hopefully, they also have helped to unlock the riddles of the field.

ALTERNATIVE PROPOSALS AND THEIR EVALUATION

One direct consequence of the philosophical discussions has been the emergence and refinement of alternatives to the disciplinary matrix of, e.g., asset values based on historical costs. There have been various attempts to derive logically consistent systems which overcome the defects of the historical cost system. Some of the authors proposing these systems which appeared during the golden age already have been identified—Edwards and Bell [1961] and Chambers [1966]; others include Sprouse and Moonitz [1962], Mattessich [1964] and Mathews [1965]. The works of these authors were debated throughout the 1960s, and that debate served to clarify and identify the alternatives. Without that identification, the next step of the revolutionary process could not proceed. It

[13]For a useful summary and list of references, see [Hendriksen, 1970, Chapter 4].

[14]Report of the Study Group on the Objectives of Financial Statements [the Trueblood Study] (1973). The study was commissioned in May 1971.

[15]See the alternatives listed [Trueblood Study, 1973, p. 41]. Notice also Sterling's observation of the change in attitudes [1970, p. vii].

[16]See Nelson [1973, p. 15] for a comment on the contribution of logic and other philosophical techniques to the accounting problem.

has proceeded, as shown by the published evaluations of the alternatives. The Trueblood Study report contained some discussion. More comprehensive evaluations have been undertaken by Chambers [1970], Macdonald [1974], McDonald [1972], Hanna [1974] and others, while the Price Waterhouse Study [Mueller, 1971] gives attention to the need for introducing consideration of the alternatives into regular teaching programmes.[17]

The fact that the evaluation process has taken place, and is continuing, is evidence of the importance of the so-called a priori works; hence, our disagreement with Nelson's comment that these works are of doubtful value. In the pattern of events described here, the works fulfill a critically important role; they are both a natural reaction to the recognition of anomalies and a vital step in the selection of a new disciplinary matrix. Furthermore, having those works to consider, and having the alternatives thus laid out, we are in a fundamentally different position from that of 1960. For while schools of thought embracing the various alternatives might now appear, that would not have been possible in 1960.

However, before discussing that possibility, there are some other characteristics of the evaluative stage which were described by Kuhn and which may be seen also in accounting. Kuhn drew attention to the similarities of the evaluative stage to the pre-paradigm period. It is the stage at which "frequent and deep debates over legitimate methods, problems and standards of solution" take place, although "these tend to define schools rather than to produce agreement" [Kuhn, 1970, p. 48].[18] In accounting, this stage has been marked by debates about the admissability of data relating to events external to the firm and data based on managers' intentions; on the presentation of cash flow statements, earnings per share calculations, etc.; the raisings of problems, such as the translation of holdings of foreign currencies, the reporting for diversified companies, long-term contracts and land development projects; the legitimacy of cost allocations; and reconsideration of the standards which the solutions must meet such as objectivity, independence and freedom from bias.

It is also because of the importance of these debates, and the evaluative process generally, that we contended that the alleged theoretical defects in the works published in the 1960s were, in a sense, irrelevant. This is not to suggest that "anything goes." On the contrary, tightly reasoned and empirically valid theoretical prescriptions have a greater chance of being adopted than do loosely constructed sets of ideas. However, theoretical defects will, presumably, be discovered during the evaluation process, and their existence may even add to the extent and heat of the debate, thus aiding this part of the revolutionary process.

Yet another characteristic of this step in the process identified by Kuhn and found in accounting is the diversity of activity is:

> In the absence of a paradigm or some candidate for a paradigm, all of the facts that could possibly pertain to the development of a given science are

[17]It is for the reason outlined here that Chambers was able to refer to Macdonald's book as a product of its time. See Chambers [1975]. The same comment might be made of May, Mueller and Williams [1975].

[18]Notice that Dopuch and Revsine saw a similar result emerge at the Conference on Accounting Research held at the University of Illinois in 1971: "As is true in the literature, many contributors were quite convinced that their approach was correct but were unable to persuade those who disagreed" [Dopuch and Revsine, 1973, p. 34].

likely to seem equally relevant. As a result early fact-gathering is a far more random activity than the one that subsequent scientific activity makes familiar [Kuhn, 1970, p. 15].

This perhaps, is the reason why so many proposals have emerged in recent years. They include suggestions for publication of multicolumn financial statements and forecasts; the development of human resource accounting; and, on a different level, the far-ranging research into share price movements and their information theory and cost benefit analyses to the provision of financial information.

SCHOOLS OF THOUGHT

It may be possible to identify schools of thought in respect of some or all of the matters of interest just referred to. However, one example will suffice—asset measurement alternatives. Four schools may be identified[19]:

1. Price-Level Adjusted (or Current Purchasing Power) Accounting
2. Replacement Cost Accounting
3. Deprival Value Accounting
4. Continuously Contemporary (or Net Realizable Value) Accounting.

Strong or widespread support for these schools is not yet discernible,[20] which is understandable. For, as Kuhn points out:

The man who embraces a new paradigm at an early stage must often do so in defiance of the evidence provided by problem solving. He must, that

---

[19]A fifth proposal—present value accounting—is not listed here. Although it has been argued cogently by Hansen [1966], it does not appear to have won support as in operational alternative. It has been discussed rather as an ideal against which alternatives might be evaluated. See, for example, Solomons [1961] and Lemke [1966].

[20]The following is an example of one attempt at identifying members of schools of thought in relation to generalized theories of accounting based on alternative asset measurement systems. Some people undoubtedly will want finer distinctions; some will object to being linked with others with whom they disagree in some respects; some will object to having been omitted. Nevertheless, at the risk of offending some or all of the people concerned, I would identify the following on the basis of their published work:

1. Price-Level-Adjusted:	Jones [1956]
	Mason [1971]
2. Replacement Cost:	Edwards & Bell [1961]
	Mathews [1965]
	Gynther [1966]
	Revsine [1973]
3. Deprival Value:	Baxter [1967]
	Wright [1970]
	Stamp [1971]
	Whittington [1974]
4. Continuously Contemporary	
(Net realizable value)	Chambers [1966]
	Sterling [1970]
	McKeown [1971]

For a slightly different version of these schools, see Sterling [1970, pp. 7–19].

is, have faith that the new paradigm will succeed with the many large problems that confront it, knowing only that the older paradigm has failed with a few. A decision of that kind can only be made on faith [Kuhn, 1970, p. 158].

Accounting researchers are not likely to rely on faith or make that decision lightly. But there are sufficient examples of dispute in the literature for us to identify some of the characteristics of "paradigm debates" [Kuhn, 1970, p. 110]. For example, "each group uses its own paradigm to argue in that paradigm's defense" [Kuhn, 1970, p. 94]. The Provisional Statement of Accounting Practice, No. 7, issued by the I.C.A. in England & Wales, refers to the need for a method which shows the "effect of changes in the purchasing power of money on accounts prepared on the basis of existing conventions" [para. 3] in arguing for Constant Purchasing Power Accounting; the Replacement Price School relies on the notion of "maintenance of productive capacity" which implies the need to replace assets in kind, in support of replacement cost accounting [Edwards and Bell, 1961, p. 99]; Wright [1971, pp. 60–61], refers to the possible loss which a firm might suffer if deprived of an asset when arguing for deprival value (or value to the owner) accounting; and Chambers [1966, p. 190] stresses the importance of adaptive behaviour when arguing for a measure of assets which is indicative of the firm's capacity to adapt.

These examples of apparent circularity are not intended as criticisms. Obviously, different systems of ideas can be evaluated only in the context to which those systems apply[21]; hence, the comment at the beginning of this paper that the charge of circularity by Gonedes and Dopuch is misplaced. The point is that arguments of this sort are a necessary and inevitable part of the process of trying to win support for the competing points of view [Kuhn, 1970, p. 94]. Like Nelson, Gonedes and Dopuch's error lies in their failure to identify the place of a priori research works in the transition to a new disciplinary matrix.

These debates have other characteristics. Adoption of a new disciplinary matrix will, normally, require a fundamental shift in the view which theorists have of the world. Thus, in accounting there have been changes: the view that the value of the monetary unit is stable has changed to acceptance of the view that it is variable; the view that the point of realization should be the point of recognition of gains is giving way to the view that other evidence of gains is admissible; and the view that only actual transactions give rise to objective data is giving way to a less restricted notion of objectivity.

Similarly, members of competing schools will have different views of the phenomena which are the subject of their discipline:

Practicing in different worlds, the two groups of scientists see different things when they look from the same point in the same direction. Again that is not to say that they can see anything they please. Both are looking at the world, and what they look at has not changed. But in some areas they see different things, and they see them in different relations one to the other. That is why a law cannot even be demonstrated to one group of scientists may occasionally seem intuitively obvious to another [Kuhn, 1970, p. 150].

[21]Sterling and Harrison [1974, p. 144] draw attention to the universality of this factor in their comments on the Gonedes and Dopuch paper.

Hence Gynther's view of firms is of ongoing nonadaptive organizations while Chambers sees organizations as being fluid and constantly adapting to environmental changes.[22] And, it seems, debate between them serves only to convince each of the validity of his own argument.

A NEW DISCIPLINARY MATRIX?

The analysis presented here suggests that financial accounting thought is undergoing a revolution. If that is so, then the criticisms of a priori research cited at the beginning of this paper are misplaced. The criticisms fail to recognize the importance of research which leads to the delineation of alternative sets of ideas. Those alternatives are candidates for a new disciplinary matrix; they are the basis of competing schools of thought.

If the analogy presented above is correct, i.e., if Kuhn's notion of a revolution can be applied to accounting, then it appears that accounting is emerging from a state of crisis [Kuhn, 1970, Chapter VIII]. Alternative sets of ideas have been proposed and debated, and schools of thought are beginning to emerge. Admittedly, the analysis does not enable us to identify neat periods of time which correspond with Kuhn's steps in the revolution. Yet, the characteristics of an accepted disciplinary matrix, the period of insecurity and the development of alternative sets of ideas appear to be well recognizable in accounting.

What will be the outcome? In accounting it is too soon to say. Researchers cannot be observed rushing to adopt any of the alternative sets of ideas. Continued debate, primarily amongst academics but increasingly involving the research organizations of the professional bodies is, however, serving to identify schools of thought. The next stage, according to Kuhn, will be "an increasing shift in allegiances" [p. 158] in favour of one of the alternatives. However, this is a process which takes time. After all, it involves the assimilation of a new theory, and that in turn involves a "reconstruction of prior theory and the reevaluation of prior fact"; i.e., "an intrinsically revolutionary process." But note, "it is seldom completed by a single man and never overnight" [Kuhn, 1970, p. 7].

REFERENCES

"Accounting: Profits Without Honor," *Time* (March 1970), p. 70.
American Accounting Association, "A Tentative Statement of Accounting Principles Affecting Corporate Reports," *The Accounting Review* (June 1936), pp. 87–91; reprinted as a Tentative Statement of Accounting Principles Underlying Corporate Financial Statements (1936).
Baxter, W. T., "Accounting Values: Sale Price Versus Replacement Cost," *Journal of Accounting Research* (Autumn 1967), pp. 208–214.
Bedford, Norton M., "The Need for an Evaluation of Accounting Research" in Dopuch and Revsine, eds., *Accounting Research 1960–1970: A Critical Evaluation*, Monograph 7 (Center for International Education and Research in Accounting, University of Illinois, 1973).

[22]Compare Gynther [1966, pp. 46–48] and Penman [1970, p. 338]: "Companies . . . just do not adapt": with Chambers [1966, p. 190].

————, and Richard Ziegler, "The Contributions of A. C. Littleton to Accounting Thought and Practice," *The Accounting Review* (July 1975), pp. 435–443.

Birkett, W. P. and R. G. Walker, "Response of the Australian Accounting Profession to Company Failures in the 1960's," *Abacus* (December 1971), pp. 97–136.

Brief, Richard P., "The Accountants' Responsibility in Historical Perspective," *The Accounting Review* April 1975), pp. 285–297.

Briloff, Abraham J., "Old Myths and New Realities in Accountancy," *The Accounting Review* (July 1966), pp. 485–495.

————, *Unaccountable Accounting* (Harper and Row, 1972).

Chambers, R. J., "Blueprint for a Theory of Accounting," *Accounting Research* (January 1955), pp. 17–25.

————, "Why Bother with Postulates?", *Journal of Accounting Research* (Spring 1963), pp. 3–15.

————, *Accounting, Evaluation and Economic Behavior* (Prentice-Hall, 1966).

————, "Methods of Accounting," Parts I–VI, *The Accountant* (February 1970), pp. 299–303; (March 1970), pp. 341–345; (March 1970), pp. 408–412; (April 1970), pp. 483–486; (April 1970), pp. 551–555; (April 1970), pp. 643–647.

————, *Securities and Obscurities: A Case for the Reform of the Law of Company Accounts* (Gower Press; 1973).

————, "Profit Measurement, Capital Maintenance and Service Potential: A Review Article," *Abacus* (June 1975), pp. 98–104.

Chatfield, Michael, *A History of Accounting Thought* (The Dryden Press, 1974).

de Jonquieres, Guy, "U.S. Firms Under Fire," *The Financial Times* (June 1973), p. 44.

Devine, Carl T., "Research Methodology and Accounting Theory Formation," *The Accounting Review* (July 1960), pp. 387–399.

Dopuch, Nicholas and Lawrence Revsine, eds., *Accounting Research 1960–1970: A Critical Evaluation*, Monograph 7 (Center for International Education and Research in Accounting, University of Illinois, 1973).

Edwards, Edgar O. and Philip W. Bell, *The Theory and Measurement of Business Income* (University of California Press, 1961).

Gilman, Stephen, *Accounting Concepts of Profit* (The Ronald Press, 1939; reprinted 1956).

Gonedes, Nicholas J. and Nicholas Dopuch, "Capital Market Equilibrium, Information Production and Selecting Accounting Techniques: Theoretical Framework and Review of Empirical Work," *Studies on Financial Accounting Objectives: 1974* (Supplement to Volume 12), *Journal of Accounting Research* (1974).

Greer, Howard C., "How to Succeed in Confusing People Without Really Trying," *The Journal of Accountancy* (March 1963), pp. 61–65.

Gynther, R. S., *Accounting for Price-Level Changes: Theory and Procedures* (Pergamon, 1966).

Hanna, John R., *Accounting Income Models: An Application and Evaluation* (The Society of Industrial Accounts of Canada, 1974).

Hansen, Palle, *The Accounting Concept of Profit* (North-Holland, 1966).

Hendriksen, Eldon S., *Accounting Theory* (Irwin, 1970).

Jones, Ralph Coughenour, *The Effects of Price Level Changes* (American Accounting Association, 1956).

Kuhn, Thomas S., *The Structure of Scientific Revolutions*, International Encyclopedia of Unified Science, 2nd enlarged edition (University of Chicago Press, 1970).

Lakatos, Imre and Alan Musgrave, eds., *Criticism and the Growth of Knowledge* (Cambridge University Press, 1974).

Lemke, Kenneth W., "Asset Valuation and Income Theory," *The Accounting Review* (January 1966), pp. 33–41.

Louis, Arthur M., "The Accountants are Changing the Rules," *Fortune* (June 1968), p. 177.

Macdonald, Graeme, *Profit Measurement: Alternatives to Historical Cost* (Accountancy Age, 1974).

MacNeal, Kenneth, *Truth in Accounting* (Ronald Press Co., 1939).

McDonald, Daniel L., *Comparative Accounting Theory* (Addison-Wesley, 1972).

McKeown, James C., "An Empirical Test of a Model Proposed by Chambers," *The Accounting Review* (January 1971), pp. 12–29.

Mason, Perry, *Price Level Changes and Financial Statements* (American Accounting Association, 1971).

Mattessich, Richard, "Toward a General and Axiomatic Foundation of Accountancy," *Accounting Research* (October 1957), pp. 328–356.

———, Richard, *Accounting and Analytical Methods* (Irwin, 1964).

Mathews, R. L., "Price-Level Accounting and Useless Information," *Journal of Accounting Research* (Spring 1965), pp. 133–155.

May, Robert G., Gerhard G. Mueller and Thomas H. Williams, *A New Introduction to Financial Accounting* (Prentice-Hall, 1975).

Mueller, Gerhard G., ed., *A New Introduction to Accounting* (The Price Waterhouse Foundation, July 1971).

Nelson, Carl L., "A Priori Research in Accounting" in Dopuch and Revsine, eds., *Accounting Research 1960–1970: A Critical Evaluation*, Monograph 7 (Center for International Education and Research in Accounting, University of Illinois, 1973).

Paton, W. A., *Accounting Theory–with Special Reference to the Corporate Enterprise* (Ronald Press Co., 1922; reprinted, Accounting Studies Press, 1962).

——— and A. C. Littleton, *An Introduction to Corporate Accounting Standards* (American Accounting Association, 1940, reprinted 1965).

Penman, Stephen H., "What Net Asset Value?—An Extension of a Familiar Debate," *The Accounting Review* (April 1970), pp. 333–346.

Raymon, R., "Is Conventional Accounting Obsolete?" *Accountancy* (June 1970), pp. 422–429.

Report of the Study Group on the Objectives of Financial Statements, *Objectives of Financial Statements* (American Institute of Certified Public Accountants, October 1973).

Revsine, Lawrence, *Replacement Cost Accounting* (Prentice-Hall, 1973).

Sanders, T. H., H. R. Hatfield, and U. Moore, *A Statement of Accounting Principles* (The American Institute of Accountants, 1938, reprinted 1959).

Shapere, Dudley, "The Structure of Scientific Revolutions," *Philosophical Review* (July 1964), pp. 383–394.

Solomons, David, "Economic and Accounting Concepts of Income," *The Accounting Review* (July 1961), pp. 374–383.

Spacek, Leonard, *A Search for Fairness* (Arthur Andersen & Co., 1969 and 1973).

Sprouse, Robert T. and Maurice Moonitz, *A Tentative Set of Broad Accounting Principles for Business Enterprises*, Accounting Research Study No. 3 (American Institute of Certified Public Accountants, 1962).

Stamp, Edward, "The Reid Murray Affair," *Accountancy* (August 1964), pp. 685–690.

———, "Income and Value Determination and Changing Price-Levels: An Essay Towards a Theory," *The Accountants' Magazine* (June 1971), pp. 277–292.

———, and Christopher Marley, *Accounting Principles and the City Code* (Butterworth, 1970).

Sterling, Robert R., "On Theory Construction and Verification," *The Accounting Review* (July 1970), pp. 444–457.

————, and William Harrison, "Discussion of Capital Market Equilibrium, Information Production, and Selecting Accounting Techniques: Theoretical Framework and Review of Empirical Work" in *Studies on Financial Objectives: 1974*, supplement to Vol. 12 of *Journal of Accounting Research*, pp. 142–157.

Sweeney, Henry W., *Stabilized Accounting* (Harper Bros., 1936; reprinted, Holt Rinehart & Winston, 1964).

"Unaccountable CPA's," *Forbes* (October 1966), p. 15.

Vatter, William J., "Postulates and Principles," *Journal of Accounting Research* (Autumn 1963), pp. 179–197.

Wells, M. C., *Accounting for Common Costs* (International Center for Education and Research in Accounting, University of Illinois, forthcoming).

Whittington, Geoffrey, "Asset Valuation, Income Measurement and Accounting Income," *Accounting and Business Research* (Spring 1974), pp. 96–101.

Wright, F. K., "A Theory of Financial Accounting," *Journal of Business Finance* (Autumn 1970), pp. 51–69.

————, "Value to the Owner: A Clarification," *Abacus* (June 1971), pp. 58–61.

Zeff, Stephen A., *Forging Accounting Principles in Five Countries* (Stipes Publishing Co., 1972).

————, *Forging Accounting Principles in Australia* (Australian Society of Accountants, March 1973).

Statement of Accounting Theory and Theory Acceptance: A Review Article

K. V. PEASNELL

The American Accounting Association's charge to the Committee on Concepts and Standards for External Financial Reports was, in the words of the Committee's chairman, Lawrence Revsine, 'to write a statement that would provide the same type of survey and distillation of current thinking on accounting theory as *A Statement of Basic Accounting Theory* (ASOBAT) provided in an earlier decade'.[1]

Committees of this sort can hardly be expected to break fresh ground; committees cannot efficiently conduct research, as SOATATA rightly points out (p. 49). A committee, particularly an academic committee, is bound to be dependent on the extant literature. As it is, we are told that during the two years it worked on the document the committee met but eight times as an entire group (p. ix); and this is hardly sufficient time to achieve breakthroughs of the consensus variety. Nor is novelty to be expected from documents of this sort, for much the same reason. And sure enough, the contents of SOATATA's sixty-one pages contains little on accounting theory that is new.

Nevertheless, the committee's report *is* an interesting contribution to the literature—not for what it says on accounting theory as such, but rather for its analysis of the reasons why the accounting community has been unable to make much progress in the development of a single universally accepted basic accounting theory. It is not that what the committee says on the matter is compellingly persuasive—to this reviewer it quite definitely is not. Rather it is the insights the committee afford us into the ways in which important groups of American accounting academics are thinking that is of interest. As the document's title indicates, this is a statement *about the process* of accounting theory *formulation* and theory *acceptance*, rather than a statement *of* accounting theory (as ASOBAT was).

This article provides an analysis and critique of the contents of SOATATA. Particular attention is paid to what the committee has to say on the prospects of developing theoretical frameworks capable of improving corporate disclosure

Thanks are due to the participants of the Staff Seminars of the Universities of Kent and Lancaster, where embryonic versions of this paper were first presented. The article also benefited greatly from a number of long discussions with Frank Clarke of the University of Sydney and I am indebted to him.

K. V. Peasnell, "Statement of Accounting Theory and Theory Acceptance: A Review Article," *Accounting and Business Research*, Summer 1978, pp. 217–225. Reprinted by permission of the author.

[1]Committee on Concepts and Standards for External Financial Reports, *Statement on Accounting Theory and Theory Acceptance* (American Accounting Association, 1977), p. ix; hereinafter referred to as the 'committee' and 'SOATATA'. Page numbers given without further reference in the main text are from SOATATA.

practices in the United States, and the lessons this offers to accountants in Britain and other countries concerning the situation there.

The review consists of three parts. In the first, a summary and critique is presented of the committee's 'Kuhnian view' of the reasons behind the current difficulties in achieving consensus in accounting. Next, a description and evaluation is provided of the document's survey of contemporary approaches to accounting theory development. The article concludes with a short section on the insights SOATATA provides us of the preoccupations of American academic accountants at this moment in history.

ACCOUNTING—A SCIENTIFIC REVIEW

An important feature of the committee's analysis is that it looks at developments in accounting thought from a 'philosophy of science' perspective: the current state of accounting theory is evaluated from the standpoint afforded by Kuhn's theory[2] of how progress occurs in science. Whether or not Kuhn's ideas provide the most illuminating 'meta-theory'[3] of how accounting theory development proceeds is a matter of some dispute. Let us therefore turn to the case that the committee puts forward for adopting this particular standpoint and the conclusions it causes the committee to reach. In order to do this, a brief overview of the chapters is called for.

A principal virtue of SOATATA is that the committee's views and the reasons for them are set out in a clear and easy to follow manner. This is obvious from the organisation of the chapters. Chapter One states the view of the committee that '. . . a single universally accepted basic accounting theory does not exist at this time. Instead, a multiplicity of theories has been—and continues to be— proposed' (p. I). It is argued there that this is due to '. . . the existence of basic differences in the way various theories view users [of financial accounting reports] and the preparer-user environments' (p. 3).

Chapter Two is descriptive in character, as its title, 'Alternative Theory Approaches', indicates; it is primarily a scene-setter for the following chapter, which is charged with substantiating and developing the thesis set out in Chapter One. Nevertheless, Chapter Two is the largest of the five chapters, taking up twenty-six pages in all, amounting to fifty per cent of the whole document (bibliography excluded). Here the committee identifies three basic theoretical approaches, which it labels the *classical*, the *decision-usefulness*, and the *information economics* approaches, respectively; it is (I will argue) from this choice of classification scheme that many of the (what the committee claim to be) 'fundamental and starkly visible' differences suggest themselves.

In Chapter Three, the committee provides examples from the literature of the 'steady stream of counterarguments and criticisms [which] appears to have prevented any of the [alternative theory] approaches from gaining a clear majority of accounting theory students as supporters' (p. 31). These are: (i) the problem of relating theories to practice; (ii) 'the irresolvability of . . . allocation-induced controversies' (p. 33); (iii) the potential suboptimality of normative

[2]T. S. Kuhn, *The Structure of Scientific Revolutions* (2nd edn., University of Chicago Press, 1970).

[3]I am indebted to Professor Maurice Moonitz for this useful term to describe SOATATA's attempt to develop a 'theory of accounting theory development'.

standards; (iv) difficulties in interpreting security price-behaviour research, and the fact that this approach cannot be employed to assess the desirability of unreported alternatives; (v) the need to take account of cost-benefit considerations, coupled with the present inability to do so; (vi) limitations of data expansion.

Chapters Two and Three attempt to show that there is no sign of the available theoretical approaches yielding a sufficient and compelling basis for specifying the content of external financial reports. The purpose of Chapter Four is to develop a plausible explanation for the lack of progress in achieving accounting theory consensus.

It is the committee's view that the '. . . prevailing expectation among accountants that those efforts [of researchers, academic committees, and professionally sponsored policy groups] would lead to some sort of unified theory . . .' (p. 41) is misplaced. The document '. . . suggest[s] that changes in the process of theorizing in accounting may be more revolutionary than evolutionary' (p. 42), and proceeds to analyse the current state of play from the perspective of Kuhn's general view of scientific revolutions.[4]

Viewed from this perspective, the current state of affairs, with its variety of approaches, and the seemingly unending recycling of arguments and counterarguments in the literature as to issues deemed to be significant, the appeals to different sets of empirical phenomena and to different tests or standards for resolving these issues, suggests to the committee the existence of several competing paradigms. The old matching-attaching paradigm is under attack. According to Kuhn, in science dissatisfaction with existing paradigms is accompanied by theorists being able to take no common body of knowledge for granted and hence feeling forced to build the field anew from its foundation; this seems to the committee to be 'what is happening in accounting at the present time' (p. 43).

In such a situation, the road to achieving a consensus is likely to be an extremely arduous one. 'The proponents of competing paradigms almost inevitably find their argumentative discourse to be fraught with communication failures. That is, those who employ different paradigms find it difficult to communicate with one another. Numerous examples can be observed in accounting debates' (p. 44). Like Kuhn, the committee is unable to identify the factors that would lead to the growing acceptance of one paradigm and the resultant 'theoretical closure' of accounting.

SOATATA concludes with a final chapter, Chapter Five, devoted to highlighting the main points made earlier: that near-term closure of theory is not likely and in any case cannot be dictated by 'authoritative' bodies (or committees); that the institutional policy-making framework must now be regarded as being part of the realm of accounting theory; that until consensus paradigm acceptance occurs, the utility of accounting theories in aiding policy decisions can only be partial.

The committee's thesis is that what is happening in accounting at the present time is an example of the 'paradigm wars' (to coin a phrase) which have taken place in the natural sciences (after a certain stage of development has been reached) and is best understood in those terms. However, the arguments

---

[4]Op. cit.

in support of this thesis are less than totally convincing, for two reasons. The first is that the variety of theory approaches described by the committee do not really constitute paradigms. This we shall turn to in the next section. A second, related, objection is that there seems to be good grounds for doubting the appropriateness to accounting of Kuhn's ideas on the nature and character of scientific revolutions; interesting though they undoubtedly are, it may be that Kuhn's ideas do not travel well.

Almost everywhere one looks in the social sciences, so it seems, one encounters approving references to Kuhn's theories on the revolutionary nature of scientific change. In this context, I dimly recall an article appearing a few years ago in the *Times Higher Educational Supplement*, the author of which was reporting on his experiences as a graduate social science student in the United States; one tip offered to those contemplating doing graduate work there was to invest in a copy of Kuhn's book: to cite Kuhn in essays (for a variety of courses) was a sure-fire way of getting better marks. Anyone, then, who doubts the universal applicability of Kuhn's ideas, and wishes to convince other academics (particularly American academics) that they should treat Kuhn's ideas with caution, has an uphill task ahead of him. And, to this extent, it has to be recognised that the committee's reliance on Kuhn's views on the historical development of scientific knowledge seems likely to commend widespread acceptance.

Not being a philosopher of science, I am badly equipped to comment on the validity of Kuhn's analysis of *science*. Moreover, any reasonably prudent reviewer cannot help but be mindful of the fact that the committee numbered Robert Sterling among its members; and it is a matter of public record[5] that Sterling favours a Kuhnian view of accounting development, as also it is that he has an earlier training in and considerable current knowledge of this area of philosophy. My own knowledge of the subject, on the other hand, extends little beyond the contents of Kuhn's book. What is more, I know little about science. But our concern is not with science as such; it is a question of the transmutation of ideas in the philosophy of science to accounting. On that there may perhaps be something I can say.

I cannot avoid being struck by what seem to me to be obvious inconsistencies between Kuhn's and the committee's reasoning. Kuhn seems to be so fundamental to SOATATA's case, that this is worthy of further analysis.

The first point that is worthy of comment is that it seems to me that Kuhn's theory of the nature of scientific revolutions is intended to apply only to the

---

[5]See, for example, R. R. Sterling, 'A Statement of Basic Accounting Theory: A Review Article, *Journal of Accounting Research*, Spring 1967, p. 100, footnote 5. Sterling was, to my knowledge, the earliest writer to refer to Kuhn's book—although my colleague Professor Edward Stamp has pointed out to me that R. J. Chambers mentions Kuhn in a footnote on page 374 in the 'Epilogue' of his book, *Accounting, Evaluation and Economic Behavior* (Prentice-Hall, 1966), albeit that the reference is to an earlier work of Kuhn's, viz. *The Copernican Revolution* (Harvard University Press, 1957).

It should be pointed out that what the committee means by paradigms is somewhat at variance to Professor Wells' meaning; see M. C. Wells, 'A Revolution in Accounting Thought?' *Accounting Review*, July 1976. The following criticisms are intended to apply only to SOATATA's usage of the term; I find Wells' usage much more satisfactory, with its emphasis on the thought processes of practitioners and teachers rather than academic researchers.

sciences, whereas the committee is of the opinion that it can be extended to cover accounting as well. The committee, to be sure, is 'sensitive to the potential validity of criticisms that analyses (such as Kuhn's) of scientific practices and methodologies probably were not intended to apply and, in fact, may not be applicable to such diverse areas of intellectual activity as physical sciences, social sciences, and accounting' (p. 41). This is understating things, to put it mildly, for Kuhn himself went to great lengths to *restrict* the scope of this theory to certain disciplines; he is uncertain, for example, where to place (in terms of historical development, that is) the various social sciences in his scheme of things. Is the committee seriously suggesting that accounting has developed to the point where it is fruitful to consider it a science, when there remains doubt (according to Kuhn) that some other social science disciplines, such as psychology, have yet reached this stage of development?

On this point, the committee seems to be confused. For on the one hand SOATATA argues that 'An expanding array of accounting theories and/or theoretical approaches suggests the existence of several competing paradigms' (p. 48); and reference to the notion of paradigm implies, if Kuhn's analysis is accepted, that accounting has reached a state of development where it warrants treating as a 'science'. However, the committee's description of what is happening in accounting at the present time, viz. where '[m]any theorists seem to feel the need to . . . build the field of accounting anew' (p. 43), seems to fit more closely with Kuhn's description of the pre-science stage of development.

Here it is worthwhile noting Kuhn's views on debates of the 'is our subject a science?' nature. Accounting has had its fair share of these debates in recent times. So have many of the social sciences. According to Kuhn:

> These debates have parallels in the pre-paradigm periods of fields that are today unhesitatingly labelled science. . . . Often great energy is invested, great passion aroused, and the outsider is at a loss to know why . . . . Probably questions like the following are really being asked: Why does my field fail to move ahead in the way that, say, physics does? What changes in technique or method or ideology would enable it to do so? These are not, however, questions that could respond to an agreement on definition. Furthermore, if precedent from the natural sciences serves, they will cease to be a source of concern not when a definition is found, but when the groups that now doubt their own status achieve consensus about their past and present accomplishment.[6,7]

The concern of the committee with accounting theory development and how its 'progress' can be speeded up seem to me to be more reminiscent of this pre-paradigmatic stage of development than with the paradigm conflicts of mature sciences.

As it is, the committee seems to be of the view that the present variety of accounting theory approaches is symptomatic of the paradigm conflicts of the

---

[6]Kuhn, op. cit., pp. 160–161.

[7]An interesting parallel to this kind of debate is that over 'Is internal auditing a profession?'. If the question has to be asked, then it isn't. See D. C. Burns and W. J. Haga, 'Much Ado About Professionalism: A Second Look at Accounting', *Accounting Review*, July 1977.

mature sciences. But the existence of a variety of conflicting approaches does not allow us to treat them as different paradigms. Kuhn is careful not to equate lack of unity of method with paradigm conflict, for this state of affairs was also typical of the pre-paradigm periods of the natural sciences. More important, he takes care to point out in the 'Postscript' to the 1970 edition of his book that the sciences develop in quite different ways than do other disciplines:

> This book, however, was intended also to make another sort of point, one that has been less clearly visible to many of its readers. Though scientific development may resemble that in other fields more closely than has often been supposed, it is also strikingly different. . . .
> Consider, for example, the reiterated emphasis, above, on the absence or, as I should now say, on the relative scarcity of competing schools in the developed sciences.[8]

The latter point in this quotation is especially important. For what Kuhn is saying here is that the hallmark of normal science is an *absence* of questioning of basics, not a marked tendency to ask such questions; a *paucity* of variety of fundamental approaches, rather than a *profusion* of them. The committee has done its job too well. It has convinced this reviewer that accounting is now characterised by a tendency to doubt existing methods, to start anew. If anything, though, this is surely a hallmark of an earlier stage of scientific development of the subject.

Further evidence could be called in support of the hypothesis that accounting is in a pre-scientific stage of development. For example, the committee itself notes (p. 41) that the vast bulk of accountants fall victim to the charge of never having committed themselves to the principle of falsifiability. Adherence to the falsifiability principle is put forward by Popper to be *the* most noteworthy feature of the natural sciences[9] and this, to my knowledge, has been almost universally accepted. What, then, can the committee have in mind when it states in the following breath: 'Nevertheless, we note striking similarities in the general objectives of science and accounting . . .' (p. 41)?

It seems to me that we can adopt one of (at least) two positions. We can accept that accounting is intended to be a scientific activity; in that case it would be helpful to decide if accounting (a) is in a pre-science, pre-paradigmatic stage of development or (b) is a fully developed science. Few, I think, would claim that the contemporary state of accounting warrants our treating it as a developed science; the committee has performed a useful task here in showing that there are too many competing viewpoints for anyone to be able to claim that accounting theory development is proceeding on 'normal' science lines.

Alternatively, we can treat accounting as a service activity. Unlike science, service activities are not ends in themselves; knowledge is acquired for pragmatic ends. This seems to be true of accounting.

It is, to my mind, a major mistake to treat accounting as a science. For to do so is only to run the risk of repeating the mistakes of the social sciences. Welfare economics, the 'policy' arm of economics, for example, has been con-

[8]Kuhn, op. cit., p. 209.

[9]K. R. Popper, *The Logic of Scientific Discovery* (2nd edn., Hutchinson & Co., 1968).

cerned with putting 'what ought to be' (social choice) on a scientific foundation; but to no avail.[10] Science is concerned with predicting and explaining the empirical world, the world that 'is'; and it is a basic philosophical proposition that 'ought' cannot be inferred from what 'is'.

Accounting is not a science, it is a service activity. Accounting therefore should be equated not with the sciences, but with fields like medicine, technology, and law, of which the principal *raison d'etre* is an external social need. Sure, service professions *make use* of scientific (i.e. empirical) knowledge—they often contribute to it—but their principal concern is with doing a particular job of work, fulfilling a social need.

The committee *almost* grasps this distinction when it notes:

> Other plausible views [than a philosophical perspective of the history of science] are possible. One example of an alternative view arises from an economic interpretation . . .
> From this economic perspective, disagreement ensues because we have heterogeneous opinions and tastes, and there is no neat, defensible method of putting our conflicting tastes and beliefs into a grand social function. Thus, the problem is by nature one of confrontation, and there is no generally accepted way of coming to agreement (p. 42).

However, the document goes on to say: 'So it is understandable that the current state of "theoretical" conflict in accounting exists and does not appear to be resolvable at the present time' (p. 42). This, unfortunately, completely misses the nature of the important distinction between science and technology, broadly construed.

For if the 'economic perspective' to which the committee refers, welfare economics, were to be applied to the theoretical disputes of *any* technology, then it is almost certain that *none* of those disputes would appear to be resolvable. If engineers, for example, were to subject all technical issues to this criterion of maximising social welfare, then no solutions would ensue because the requisite concept of social preference is just as missing in engineering as it is in accounting. Likewise with medicine and the law.

Service professions like medicine, technology, and law are generally content to go ahead and build their theories on less secure foundations. Doubtless medical, technological, and legal decisions are suboptimal by some global standard; indeed, they are frequently taken to task for this. Doctors, engineers and lawyers prefer to set themselves more operational goals, such as 'getting patients well', 'meeting detailed performance specifications at minimum out-of-pocket costs', 'consistency with basic legal principles, statutes and case precedents'. Why cannot accountants be judged by similar, operational, service-oriented criteria?

---

[10]Since this assumption [of Pigou's that rich and poor men have similar tastes] involved inter-personal comparisons of utility, it was argued by Robbins that it was a non-scientific, ethical assumption because inter-personal comparisons of utility could not be made scientifically. . . . [A]t that time Robbins' arguments gave rise to a great deal of dismay . . . Economists did not seem to want to admit boldly that no application of economic theory to any practical problem was possible without presupposing some ethical premises or other'. S. K. Nath, *A Reappraisal of Welfare Economics* (Routledge & Kegan Paul, 1969), pp. 94–95.

All this, it has to be admitted, is of secondary importance to the question of the current state of accounting theory: for *if* the committee is correct in its view that a single universally accepted basic theoretical foundation does not exist at this moment in history, *then* our view as to the 'nature' of accounting (science v. technology) is likely to be important in ascertaining suitable responses on the part of accounting researchers and policy-makers. But this presupposes that this *is* the current situation. To this issue we will turn in the next section.

Another way of looking at this is to ask ourselves the question: Do the variety of accounting theory approaches identified by the committee really constitute competing paradigms (or pre-paradigm 'schools of thought', for that matter)?

A paradigm, as I understand it, amounts to the frame of reference, or world-view, which the individual scientist brings to bear on his work. It is much more than a set of hypotheses or body of theory. It is the well from which the scientist draws his ideas, constructs his theories and devises his tests. It would seem, therefore, that there is little likelihood of an individual scientist accepting more than one *conflicting* (as contrasted with complementary) paradigm[11] at any one time. Thus, it would seem to be essential to the committee's view of things that there be little or no doubts as to which paradigm each major accounting theorist 'belongs'; nor indeed that there be serious doubts over the paradigm definitions. This the committee seeks to do in the second and third chapters of SOATATA.

SOATATA'S REVIEW OF ACCOUNTING THEORIES

Consider the committee's descriptions of what it calls the 'classical' and the 'decision-use' approaches and the distinction drawn between them.

To illustrate the classical approaches to theory development the committee selected thirteen major writers on accounting during the period 1922 to 1975 and classified them into either what they call the 'normative deductive' (also 'true income') school or the 'inductive' school of thought. Those identified as members of the normative deductive school—the likes of Canning, Paton, Sweeney, MacNeal, Alexander, Edwards and Bell, Sprouse and Moonitz—are deemed by the committee to be primarily interested in making accounting policy recommendations; inductive theorists such as Hatfield, Gilman, Littleton and Ijiri, especially Ijiri, on the other hand, attempt '. . . to rationalize . . . major elements of extant accounting practice' (p. 10).

The committee deems the key distinguishing characteristic of the decision-usefulness approach to be its '. . . explicit recognition of the usefulness objective' (p. 10). Again, two distinct strands or branches of thought are identified. 'In the first, decision *models* are stressed. Information relevant to a decision model or criterion is isolated and various accounting alternatives are compared to the data presumably necessary for implementing these decision models. In the

---

[11]In microeconomics, the behavioural and neoclassical theories of the firm can be viewed as complementary, rather than competing, paradigms in that they seem to serve quite different functions in economics, in the sense that an economist is not forced to choose between them; he can make use of one paradigm when dealing with one set of problems, and the other when he is concerned with different matters. See B. J. Loasby, 'Hypothesis and Paradigm in the Theory of the Firm', *Economic Journal*, December 1971.

second branch of the decision-usefulness approach, decision *makers* are the focus of attention. Their reactions to alternative accounting data are studied as a means of inductively deriving preferred reporting alternatives' (p. 10).

It should be noted that the distinction drawn between the classical and decision-use approaches is at odds with the distinction that has been made elsewhere in the literature between accounting works which are *a priori* and those which are empirical in nature.[12] For one complaint which has been levelled at those whom the committee refers to as 'normative-deductive theorists' is that their work relies entirely on logic; that is, their theories are not subject to any scientific test, there is no scientific 'confrontation' of theory with reality.[13] Viewed from this perspective, one way of categorising authors is as to whether or not they are willing to submit their theories to empirical test.

For example, normative-deductive theorists could be divided into one group consisting of those willing to test the 'predictions' (profit measurements) of their theory against 'true income' (presumably discounted present value) calculated *ex post*, and another group composed of those opposed to such a test. In which case, it would not be too fanciful to treat some decision-usefulness approaches, e.g. Revsine's, as being nothing more than alternative ways of defining true income under uncertainty. Revsine, being the chairman of this committee, might object to such an alternative classification scheme, but this is beside the point. What *is* the point is this: the committee's classification seems to border at times on the artificial.

Indeed, the choice of theorists for inclusion in and exclusion from the 'classical' camp borders on the curious. For a start, Chambers is left out of the normative-deductive group altogether—the place I feel confident that most would locate him. And his inclusion in the decision-usefulness group is not unequivocable. To be sure, it is granted that his 1955 '. . . "Blueprint" article might well have served as the starting point for a decision-usefulness theory of financial accounting' (p. 12); but the committee goes on to point out that '. . . in his subsequent works Chambers apparently rejected the idea of basing an accounting theory on the decision models of specific user groups' (p. 12), likening his approach to MacNeal's and Canning's. Why then is Chambers not included with them under the classical approaches?

One answer is that to do so would tend to blur the distinction between the classical and decision-usefulness approaches integral to the picture they paint of paradigm conflict. To do so would be to say, in effect, that it is possible to 'belong' to more than one paradigm at the same time; and this surely will not do.

[12]See, for example, the proceedings of the conference on accounting research held at the University of Illinois at Urbana-Champaign, April 1971, published in N. Dopuch and L. Revsine, eds., *Accounting Research* 1960–1970: *A Critical Evaluation* (Center for International Education and Research in Accounting, University of Illinois, 1973).

[13]'A far more damaging criticism is that all we have are hypotheses. The generation of hypotheses is useful, so the hypothesis-generator is far more productive than the man who merely retails what is provided by others or who serves as a carping critic. Nevertheless, we may ask whether too much energy has not been utilized to generate hypotheses and not enough to test hypotheses' (C. L. Nelson, '*A Priori* Research in Accounting', in Dopuch and Gonedes, ibid., p. 15). Incidentally, Nelson seems to take it for granted that all theorists would accept that decision-usefulness is the appropriate test criterion. But I am sure SOATATA is correct in implying that not *all* classical writers would do so; those who do the committee would place in the decision-usefulness camp.

Other examples are not hard to find. For instance, the committee does not hesitate in placing Edwards and Bell as members of the normative-deductive classical school—yet Revsine points out in his book that '[t]he contention that current operating profit can be extrapolated in order to generate useful predictions originates with Edwards and Bell'.[14] A good case can be made out therefore for treating Edwards and Bell as early members of the decision-usefulness school. A counter-case would be that the main concern of Edwards and Bell was with the provision of accounting information for the purpose of evaluating past decisions; but this stemmed from their view of the character of decision-making under uncertainty and so does not jeopardise the case for including them under the decision-use category.

Another example is R. Sterling's *Theory of the Measurement of Enterprise Income*[15] which is not listed under the classical approaches and gets (as far as I can tell) only a passing mention (on page 17) when 'predictive ability' is being discussed; and yet it is generally viewed as being one of the major *a priori* works of the past decade.[16] Is it because Sterling, too, defies easy categorisation?

While on this subject, it is interesting to note that all the thirteen major 'classical' writers discussed in Chapter Two of SOATATA are Americans. Leaving aside for the moment the parochialism suggested by this, the most important point is that it implies an almost complete lack of development on the classical front during the period following Sprouse and Moonitz's monograph in 1962[17] up to Ijiri's 1975 work[18] (the last writer cited); and yet this is the very period when the decision-usefulness and information economics approaches were receiving considerable attention in the theoretical literature, and even in the profession itself. The Trueblood Report,[19] after all, unequivocally comes down in favour of decision-usefulness being the ultimate criterion for determining the content of external reports. How, then, can the committee avoid drawing the one conclusion which its own logic points to, viz. that the 'classical paradigm' has been overthrown and is now of historical interest only?

As it is, this conclusion would not seem so compelling if other, more recent, studies had been included under the classical approaches. In particular, the hiatus in the literature between 1962 and 1975 could easily have been filled by non-American works; and it would have then become apparent that many of these recent writers do not fit neatly into the committee's boxes.

Wright, for example, is a normative-deductive theorist in the 'classical' mode, but in his influential 'Theory' article[20] he explicitly identifies the purpose of financial accounting as being to help investors in their share-trading decisions; similarly, his various attempts to provide a linear programming rationale

[14]L. Revsine, *Replacement Cost Accounting* (Prentice-Hall, 1973), p. 119.

[15]University Press of Kansas, 1970.

[16]See 'Editor's Preface' in Dopuch and Revsine, op. cit., p. iv.

[17]R. T. Sprouse and M. Moonitz, *A Tentative Set of Broad Accounting Principles for Business Enterprises* (American Institute of Certified Public Accountants, 1962).

[18]Y. Ijiri, *Theory of Accounting Measurement*, Studies in Accounting Research No. 10 (American Accounting Association, 1975).

[19]American Institute of Certified Public Accountants, Study Group on the Objectives of Financial Statements, *Objectives of Financial Statements*, 1973.

[20]F. K. Wright, 'A Theory of Financial Accounting', *Journal of Business Finance*, Autumn 1970.

to the Value to The Owner concept have a strong emphasis on decision-making, albeit in less precise terms[21] than later decision-use theorists have employed. Baxter,[22] too, goes to considerable pains to emphasise the decision-making orientation of his undoubtedly classical-looking theories. And Chambers is another very eminent writer who, as we have already noted, does not unequivocally fit into either the classical or decision-usefulness schools. No mention is made of recent professional and governmental developments elsewhere in the English-speaking world either; yet both *The Corporate Report*[23] and Sandilands,[24] for example, acknowledge the importance of decision-usefulness *and* rely on the normative-deductive classical literature without getting very bothered about the agonies of paradigm choice.

It is instructive to consider what SOATATA has in mind as the key distinguishing features of the classical and decision-usefulness approaches. As far as I can tell, the committee does not come out with a description of any *one* set of key unifying features of the classical approaches, so perhaps it is more helpful to state what it considers the current status of the decision model branch of the decision-usefulness approach to be (see pages 13 to 14 of the report);

1. Acknowledgement that the 'primary objective of accounting is to provide financial information about the economic affairs of an entity to interested parties for use in making decisions', including 'control' decisions.
2. To 'be useful in making decisions, financial information must possess several normative qualities', the primary one being 'relevance to the decision at hand'.
3. Selection of relevant attributes requires familiarity with user decision processes, and 'modelling' of these processes 'is often helpful to accounting theorists'.
4. The 'investment decision [to date, the only decision intensively analysed] models utilized by decision-usefulness theorists have been either simple present value models or two-parameter expected return and risk models'.
5. 'Investors' [postulated] desires to predict cash flows from the firm have led many decision-usefulness theorists to a [future] cash flow orientation'; whereas 'the impossibility of measuring a future event [has led others to] rule out the cash flow orientation', exit values being preferred instead.

I cannot help but feel that all this would have been quite acceptable to the likes of Alexander and Sir Ronald Edwards.

On the other hand, the committee is surely right to suggest that the decision-*maker* branch of the decision-usefulness approach is at odds with the classical approaches. The empirical domain has switched from accounting numbers to

[21]See, for example, F. K. Wright, 'Measuring Asset Services—A Linear Programming Approach', *Journal of Accounting Research*, Autumn 1968 and 'Dual Variables in Inventory Measurement', *Accounting Review*, January 1970.

[22]See, for example, W. T. Baxter, 'Depreciating Assets: The Forward-looking Approach to Value', *Abacus*, December 1970; or W. T. Baxter and N. H. Carrier, 'Depreciation, Replacement Price, and Cost of Capital', *Journal of Accounting Research*, Autumn 1971.

[23]Accounting Standards Steering Committee discussion paper, 1975.

[24]Report of the Inflation Accounting Committee, *Inflation Accounting*, Cmnd 6225 (HMSO, 1975).

the actions of individuals; it is the behaviour of decision-makers which is the object of inquiry. This might well indeed be too much for many classically-trained accountants to swallow. Similarly, the committee's distinction between the decision-usefulness and information economics approaches is undoubtedly a useful one.

The answer to all this is easy to find. The three accounting theory approaches identified by the committee represent the dominant interests of key researchers at different stages in the development of accounting thought: the 'inductive' variant of the classical approach arose out of the early need to create logical order out of the observable differences in accounting practices; the 'normative deductive' sprang from the desire to 'improve' on the prevailing state of the art; the 'decision-usefulness' approach, in turn, stemmed from difficulties encountered in trying to deduce what is the 'most useful' alternative; and finally 'information economics' has been employed largely because of the criticisms levelled at the decision-usefulness criterion of a useful-to-whom and cost-benefit variety. Each time, the objects of *direct* interest—or in the committee's words (p. 47), the 'empirical domain'—has shifted. First, it was the accounting practices; then it moved to users' decision outcomes; and now to economy-wide costs and benefits. Put differently, the scope of accounting theory has steadily widened.

Nevertheless, this widening of scope is not without its attendant costs. For all its weaknesses, the normative-deductive approach can (and does) generate policy recommendations which are defensible in its own terms; whereas the decision-usefulness approaches are weak in this area at present, but will (almost certainly) increasingly generate policy recommendations as theory is built up and evidence accumulates. Information economics, on the other hand, is so abstract in character that usable (to be distinguished, of course, from definitive) results are a long way off; its present theoretical value is its power '... in isolating general relationships and effects of alternative scenarios' (p. 25). Whether, though, information economics will ever be able to deliver anything beyond this remains a moot point.

I could go on, but enough has been said to indicate that SOATATA provides an interesting and stimulating review of the literature. It is almost inevitable that such surveys will provoke controversy; this is one of their functions. As it is, there are many criticisms that could be made of the committee's treatment of various issues. For example, in discussing Arrow's Paradox, the committee makes the somewhat naive statement that Arrow's imposition of the Pareto-optimality condition 'hardly seems surprising' (p. 37). Similarly, no mention was made of the important point that studies based on the API metric are critically dependent on the implied assumption that equilibrium share prices can be 'explained' (i.e. represented) by the Capital Asset Pricing Model.[25] But these are mere quibbles. The committee's review of the literature is an interesting one that will provide stimulating reading for all students of the subject.

[25]Basically, a nonzero API can be regarded as evidence against the Capital Asset Pricing Model (CAPM) rather than evidence of 'market reaction'. See J. A. Ohlson, 'On the Theory of Residual Analyses and Abnormal Performance Metrics', unpublished manuscript, School of Business, University of California at Berkeley, March 1977. Note as well that it has recently been demonstrated that the CAPM is untestable; see R. Roll, 'A Critique of the Asset Pricing Theory's Tests, Part I: On Past and Potential Testability of the Theory', *Journal of Financial Economics*, March 1977.

CONCLUDING COMMENTS

For non-Americans, SOATATA provides a useful source of data from which inferences can be drawn concerning the hopes and aspirations of American accounting academics, which in turn might aid in interpreting developments in their academic writings. (That the American accounting literature is of interest to non-Americans has been taken for granted throughout this article).

A striking feature of SOATATA is its concern with what it variously refers to as 'achieving accounting theory consensus' and 'theoretical closure'; these and similar phrases appear repeatedly throughout the document. This doubtless stems, at least in part, from the committee's charge, which was to prepare what might be called 'the child of ASOBAT'. But this is not the whole story, for the report does not attempt to identify the areas where there is common ground, as ASOBAT did. Thus, even the observation that '[t]here are a number of theorists who have become dissatisfied with the old matching-attaching approach' (p. 43), merely identifies a consensus of views on what it is that theorists are unhappy with, not on what they can accept. SOATATA catalogues areas where there is a *lack* of consensus. I have tried to show in the previous section that some of the differences identified by the committee are more apparent than real.

This leads one to wonder why the committees should look so hard for differences and inconsistencies in contemporary theory. The high-powered membership of the committee might, I suppose, be partly to blame: Demski, Revsine, Staubus and Sterling are well-known for their advocacy of particular approaches; whereas a committee composed of lesser lights, having given fewer published hostages to fortune, as it were, might have found it easier to identify areas of agreement. As it is, it is not really surprising that this particular committee could only agree to differ; consequently, Kuhn's theory of paradigm conflict was almost bound to appeal.

The committee's repeated use of the phrase 'theoretical closure' is of significance in another respect as well: it implies that one of the central objectives of accounting should be to provide a basis for settling disclosure disputes, i.e., in the committee's words, to 'provide a basis for determining the content of external financial reports and resolve accounting controversies' (p. 1). Viewed from this angle, failure to 'achieve consensus' is to admit defeat, or at least a state of disequilibrium.

One reason for this might be the considerable pressures—e.g. Senate investigations, hostile treatment from the press, and auditors being sued for astronomical sums—that are bearing down on the public accounting profession in the United States. Bearing this in mind, and the large sums being spent by the Financial Accounting Standards Board on research, it is not surprising that theorists should see their task as being that of developing a settled foundation on which the profession can erect an unequivocally acceptable superstructure capable of determining the content of corporate financial reports. In this environment, it is only natural that accounting theorists should turn to science for lessons on how progress towards this end might best be made; it is in the sciences that theory closure has been most frequently attained.

Whatever the reason, there is strong evidence of the attractiveness of a 'scientific solution' to accounting controversies, as witnessed by the frequently-expressed scorn for *a priori* research[26] and the swing (since the mid-1960s) to empiricism in the United States, whereas British and Australasian academics have continued to devote much of their intellectual resources to theorising.

The important message of SOATATA is that theoretical closure is not in sight; moreover, the committee points out that even in the sciences theoretical closure is fraught with difficulty. To this extent, SOATATA cautions against holding unreasonable expectations about what accounting theory can deliver. Theory closure is about the persuasiveness of arguments; and strictly speaking, persuasion is a matter of psychology, not scientific logic.[27]

Promise is held out, though, of a better future. The committee states: 'This limited theory role will not necessarily persist in the long run, nor is it unique to accounting' (p. 51). The old American optimism reasserts itself.

[26]Cf. note 13.

[27]Little argues convincingly that any persuasive statement needs to be regarded as a value judgment; see I. M. D. Little, A Critique of Welfare Economics (2nd edn., Oxford University Press, 1957). The same must hold, therefore, for the views expressed in both SOATATA and this review article.

On Theory Construction and Verification

ROBERT R. STERLING

I. INTRODUCTION

There are many disputes over the way in which theories are constructed. It seems that many theories come about by "intuitive flashes." There are "laws of nature" (observed regularities) which are discovered by induction. However seldom are the theories—which connect and explain these laws in a coherent and general way—discovered by induction. Thus, the process of theory construction is imperfectly understood. Clues for this lack of understanding are given by the language used to describe the process. For example, we characterize a great theoretician as a "genius," which implies that his intellect is beyond our understanding or that we could not have duplicated the process. The "intuitive flash" description implies a lack of understanding of the mental processes by which the discovery is made.

Even though we don't know how theories are constructed, we can note that a new theory usually arises as a result of "anomalies" in the old theory.[1] Scientific theories provide certain "expectations" or "predictions" about phenomena and when these expectations occur, they are said to "confirm" the theory.[2] When unexpected results occur, they are considered to be anomalies which eventually require a modification of the theory or the construction of a new theory. The purpose of the new theory or the modified theory is to make the unexpected expected, to convert the anomalous occurrence into an expected and explained occurrence.

Although the process of theory construction is imperfectly understood, it has been noted that the theories of empirical science have some common properties and that they share a structure. This paper will present a brief review of the nature of empirical theories for the purpose of providing a relief for some current and proposed theories of accounting.[3] Selected alternative interpretations of accounting theory will be examined and critiqued. An outline for a program for the construction of a theory of relevant measurements will then be suggested.

II. THE NATURE OF THEORIES

A "theory" is, first of all, a set of sentences. Theories are expressed in a language, and therefore the study of language is pertinent to the study of theories. Indeed, much of the philosophy of science is nothing but a study of language, although

This paper was prepared for submission to the American Accounting Association Committee on Theory Construction and Verification. The views expressed are those of the author and do not necessarily represent the views of the Committee or the Association.

Helpful comments from the members of the Ohio State University Accounting Colloquium and financial support from the Fourth National Bank of Wichita Foundation is gratefully acknowledged.

Robert R. Sterling, "On Theory Construction and Verification," Accounting Review, July 1970, pp. 444–457. Reprinted by permission of *The Accounting Review*.

it is a study of the language peculiar to the scientist. Morris,[4] Carnap[5] and others have distinguished three areas in the study of language: Syntactics, Semantics and Pragmatics.

Syntactics is the study of the relations of signs to signs. By themselves syntactical propositions have no empirical content. The disciplines of mathematics and logic are syntactical in that a mathematical or logical proposition says nothing whatsoever about the real world. Such propositions are often referred to as "analytic propositions" and are characterized by being logically true, as opposed to being empirically true. For example, "If all electrons have magnetic moments and particle x has no magnetic moment, then particle x is not an electron" is an analytic proposition. One does not need to know the meaning of "electron" or "magnetic moment" to see that this proposition is true. It is true by virtue of the form of the sentence and the agreed upon way in which the logical constants (if-then, and, not) are used. One could replace the descriptive terms with nonsense words without altering the truth value, e.g., "If all bzrs have wales and x has no wale, then x is not a bzr."[6] The proposition "$(a+b)^2 = a^2 + 2ab + b^2$" is analytic. It is true by virtue of the agreed upon rules of algebra which specify the way in which the signs of algebra may be arranged and manipulated.

Also, statements which are true by virtue of the meanings of their constituent terms are analytic, e.g., "a bachelor is an unmarried adult male" is true by virtue of the meanings of "bachelor," "unmarried," etc.[7] Note that analytic propositions require a prior commitment to a set of rules or definitions. "A bachelor is an unmarried adult male" is analytically true because of the prior linguistic commitment to define "bachelor" in a particular way. "Fifteen is one-half of thirty" is analytically true because of a prior commitment to the rules of arithmetic.

Semantics is the study of the relation of signs to objects or events. If signs are to have referents in the real world, it is necessary to have rules or under-

---

[1]Thomas S. Kuhn, *The Structure of Scientific Revolutions* (The University of Chicago Press, 1962), Ch. VI.

[2]Several different terms are used for this process. Rudolf Carnap, "Testability and Meaning," *Philosophy of Science*, Vol. 4, (1937), distinguishes between testable, verifiable and confirmable. I will use "verifiable" to refer to the intersubjective perception of observers concerning a proposition which specifies an individual occurrence. I will use "confirmable" to refer to a collection of propositions (a theory). It is the "verification" of the singular propositions which is taken to be the "confirmation" of the theory which contains those propositions.

[3]For a particularly lucid discussion of the nature of theories in accounting, see Thomas H. Williams and Charles H. Griffin, "On the Nature of Empirical Verification in Accounting," Working Paper 68–37, (The University of Texas, 1968).

[4]Charles Morris, *Foundations of the Theory of Signs* (University of Chicago, 1938).

[5]Rudolf Carnap, *Introduction to Semantics* (Harvard University Press, 1942).

[6]See Rudolf Carnap, *Philosophical Foundations of Physics* (Basic Books, Inc., 1966), Chs. 26–28 for a more complete discussion. The electron example appears on p. 266.

[7]Arthur Pap, *An Introduction to the Philosophy of Science* (The Free Press of Glencoe, 1962) distinguishes between "broadly analytic" and "strictly analytic" propositions. He argues that broadly analytic propositions like "a bachelor is an unmarried male" can be reduced to strictly analytic propositions with the help of appropriate definitions (p. 97). The distinction and the disagreement about the possibility of reduction is not pertinent to this study.

standings as to the linkage between a particular sign and a particular object or event. These are called "semantical rules," and it is these rules that give empirical meaning to the signs. It is possible, of course, to define a particular sign by showing how it relates to other signs, but it is impossible to define all signs in this way. More precisely, the definition of signs by reference to other signs can be done only on pain of circularity and lack of empirical meaning.[8]

It is generally agreed, especially in connection with metrical notions, that the semantical rules should be in the nature of *operational* definitions. The selection of a particular sign to refer to a particular object or event is quite arbitrary initially, but subsequent use of that sign requires careful specification of the operations by which we link the sign to the object or event.

Given the semantical rules for linking signs to objects or events and the syntactical rules for linking signs to signs, propositions with empirical content can be formed. In contrast to the analytic propositions discussed above, these "empirical propositions" are intended to say something about the real world and therefore their truth value is contingent upon observation.[9] For example, the proposition "John is a bachelor" is intended to say something about a thing in the real world, and "John" is the sign for that thing. The truth value of that proposition can be either true or false without contradiction.

Thus, the truth value of analytic and empirical propositions is discovered by different procedures. Analytic propositions are *proved* by the use of syntactical rules. They are either true (valid) or contradictory. Empirical propositions are *verified* by operations of observation. They are either true (conform with the observations) or false.

Pragmatics is the study of the relation of signs to the users of those signs. Different signs evoke different responses from a particular user even though those signs are intended to have the same referent. Different users may interpret the same sign in different ways.

This three-part division of the study of language provides the basis for a two-part division of the sciences. In general, sciences may be classified as empirical or nonempirical. Examples of the latter are logic and mathematics. These sciences are composed exclusively of analytic propositions and therefore do not depend upon empirical findings for their truth value. The empirical sciences have for their purpose the explanation and prediction of occurrences in the real world. The propositions of empirical science, therefore, are said to be true only if they correctly explain or predict some empirical phenomena.

Despite the empirical test for the assignment of truth value, the theories of empirical science are not composed entirely of propositions which can be verified by observations. Instead, a theory in empirical science is composed of a combination of analytic and empirical propositions. The syntactical or logical part of a theory can be abstracted and studied in isolation from the empirical part of that theory. This process is usually called the "axiomatization" or "formalization" of a theory and the result is called an "axiomatic" or "formal" system. Of course, the formal system per se is not an empirical theory. In order for the formal system to function as a theory of empirical science the semantical rules must be added.

These ideas are often illustrated by using geometry as an example. Geometry qua mathematics is a formal system. It says nothing about the real world and its theorems can be deductively derived from its axioms. It has a set of primitive terms—e.g., "point," "straight line"—which have no empirical meaning. By semantical rules these primitive terms are given empirical meaning, e.g., a point is taken to mean the intersection of cross-hairs or the tip of a surveyor's stake, a straight line is taken to mean a taut string or the path of light rays. In this way geometry becomes an empirical theory. It is now a theory of physics and as such it says some things about the real world. The outputs of geometry qua physics are intended to be empirical propositions and their truth value can be verified by observations. For example, the length of a hypotenuse can be calculated from the theory. The theory specifies the relevant empirical inputs (length of the two sides) and it specifies the way in which those inputs are manipulated. The output is the length of the hypotenuse and that output can be verified, within the limits of measurement error, by a separate empirical operation.

The last step, the verification of the output, is indispensable if the theory is intended to be empirical. It is not required that every proposition in an empirical theory be verifiable; there are many terms which operate within the formal system that are not subject to observation. (These are often called "theoretical terms" in contrast to "observational terms.") However, an empirical theory must have *some* propositions that are verifiable. The verification of these individual propositions is taken as a test of the theory. If the propositions are found to be true, then the theory is said to be "validated" or "confirmed."[10]

---

[8]"Definitions of terms by reference to other terms belonging to the same language system (for example, the language of physics) are *internal* definitions, and one might, by using this kind of definition alone, build a whole ingrown language whose terms referred to each other but to nothing else. Definitions which go outside the language system to something else—perception, for instance—are *external* definitions, and they are required if the whole system is to mean anything." Peter Caws, *The Philosophy of Science* (D. Van Nostrand Company, Inc., 1965), p. 46.

[9]There are several different names for the contrasting propositions. Since they are contingent upon observations, what I have called "empirical propositions" are called "contingent propositions" by some philosophers. Others contrast "a priori statements" with "empirical statements." Followers of Kant contrast "analytic" with "synthetic." Earlier writers were making the same distinction when they spoke of "necessary" and "accidental" truth. In this paper I will generally use the terms "analytic" and "empirical" to make the distinction.

[10]Carl Hempel, *Philosophy of Natural Science* (Prentice-Hall, Inc., 1966), p. 30, makes this point as follows:

But if a statement or set of statements is not testable at least in principle, in other words, if it has no test implications at all, then it cannot be significantly proposed or entertained as a scientific hypothesis or theory, for no conceivable empirical finding can then accord or conflict with it. In this case, it has no bearing whatever on empirical phenomena, or as we will also say, it lacks *empirical import*.

He then discussed an article entitled "Gravity and Love as Unifying Principles" and characterizes the view that physical bodies are attracted by love as a "pseudo-hypothesis" because:

No specific empirical findings of any kind are called for by this interpretation; no conceivable observational or experimental data can confirm or disconfirm it. In particular, therefore, it has no implications concerning gravitational phenomena; consequently, it cannot possibly explain those phenomena or render them "intelligible." To illustrate this further, let us suppose someone were to offer the alternative thesis that physical bodies gravitationally attract each other and tend to move toward each other from a natural tendency akin to hatred, from a natural inclination to collide with and destroy other physical objects. Would there by any conceivable way of adjudicating these conflicting views? Clearly not. Neither of them yields any testable implications; no empirical discrimination between them is possible. *Ibid.*, p. 31.

Hempel[11] presents all of this in a simple diagram:

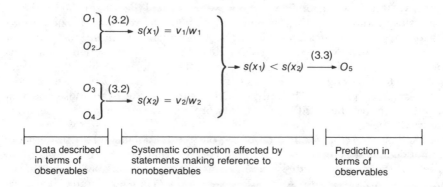

The arrow represents a deductive inference and the number above the arrow refers to a particular sentence by which the deduction is effected. These sentences are:

$$\text{"(3.2) Def. } s(x_i) = v(x_i)/w(x_i)\text{"}$$

which is the definition of the specific gravity of a body x_i where w_i and v_i refer to the weight and volume of that body; and

"(3.3) A solid body floats on a liquid if its specific gravity is less than that of the liquid,"

which refers to the expression $s(x_1) < s(x_2)$ in the diagram, i.e., (3.3) can be restated as "If $s(x_1) < s(x_2)$, then x_1 floats on x_2."

The particular values of weight and volume are obtained by "appropriate operational procedures," i.e., "in terms of the directly observable outcomes of specified measuring procedures," and the symbols O_1, O_2, O_3, O_4 are observation terms connecting O_1 to w_1, O_2 to v_1, etc. O_1 through O_4 are the observational inputs to the formal system. O_5 is the observational output. It is also necessary that the output be operationally defined so that it can be verified or falsified.

This diagram of an empirical theory, albeit an overly simple theory, is thought to capture the essentials of any empirical theory. Hempel intends it to be general and shows how more complex theories (Newtonian physics) can be cast in a similar schematic.[12] Margenau's "construct" and "percept" diagrams are almost identical. He says that theories "attain validity through empirical confirmation. This process represents a circuit, traceable in either sense, from perception (observation) via rules of correspondence to constructs and back along some other route to perception."[13]

[11]Carl Hempel, *Aspects of Scientific Explanation* (The Free Press, 1965), p. 181. Minor changes were made in the symbols for clarity and to correct a typographical error.

[12]*Ibid.*, p. 185.

[13]Henry Margenau, *The Nature of Physical Reality* (McGraw-Hill Book Company, Inc., 1950). The diagrams appear on pp. 85, 93 and 106. The quotation appears on p. 121.

In summary, a theory of empirical science may be divided into two parts: (1) A Formal System which is composed of abstract symbols and a set of syntactical rules for manipulating those symbols; and (2) An Interpretation of the formal system which connects certain symbols to observations via semantical rules. The propositions in the formal system are analytic in the sense that they are deduced from axioms or definitions. The propositions of the interpreted theory are intended to be empirical and they must be tested by observations. The semantical rules are concerned with two different kinds of observations: (1) Inputs and (2) Outputs. In order for a theory to be complete the kinds of observations to be made and the measurement rules must be specified. These are the empirical inputs to the formal system. Those inputs are then manipulated according to the syntactical rules. The outputs of the formal system are connected via semantical rules to observations. If the observations are as specified by the formal system, then that particular proposition is said to be verified.

This may be diagrammed as follows:

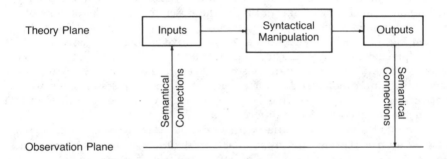

The formal system (on the Theory Plane) is concerned exclusively with the syntactical rules. The inputs and outputs are in the form of abstract symbols. The semantical rules provide specific values for the inputs in a particular case, i.e., numerals are inserted in place of the abstract symbols. These numerals are manipulated in the same way as the abstract symbols are manipulated, i.e., in accordance with the syntactical rules. Then the outputs are also specific numerals instead of symbols and they provide, via semantical rules, an expectation or prediction of an observable occurrence. If the occurrence is in fact observed then that particular case is said to be verified. If enough cases are verified the theory is said to be confirmed.

III. SOME ACCOUNTING INTERPRETATIONS

Theories are restricted to certain subjects or certain kinds of phenomena. Although generality is desirable, there is no general theory of the general scheme of things; instead each theory is limited to a particular subject matter. One of the difficulties encountered in accounting theory construction and verification is that different accounting theories are often theories about different subject matters. The problem is not so much that there are conflicting theories about the same subject matter as it is that the various theories are concerned with different subject matters. It is to be expected that different subject matters will produce different theories. Perhaps a review of some of these theories would be helpful.

An Anthropological Interpretation

Probably the most ancient and pervasive method of accounting theory construction is to observe accountants' actions and then rationalize those actions by subsuming them under generalized principles. The result is not a theory about accounting or a theory about the things to be accounted for; instead it is a theory about accountants. The "principles of accounting" then is a theory that says that under such and such conditions the accountant will act in such and such a way. The input is the condition and the output is the accountants' action.

This is quite similar to, say, the theory that "the essence of primitive religion is animism."[14] This theory allows anthropologists to predict that under certain conditions, primitive man will act in a certain way. The test of the theory is the observations of the actions of primitive man. In the same fashion, the test of an anthropological theory of accounting is the observations of the actions of accounting man. For example, if the accounting anthropologist has observed that accounting man normally records a "conservative" figure and generalizes this as the "principle of conservatism," then we can test this principle by observing whether or not accounting man does in fact record a conservative figure. If the accounting anthropologist sets forth the "principle of diversity," then we can test this principle by observing whether or not accounting man does in fact record similar occurrences in different ways. And so forth.

There are several difficulties with this kind of theorizing. First, it is not necessarily true that accounting man acts in the manner in which he ought to act. It is an error to conclude that because x is the case, then x ought to be the case. There is no way to arrive at the way accounting man ought to act from observing and generalizing how he in fact does act. Thus, this kind of theorizing may provide us with an explanation of why accountants act in a certain way and it may provide us with the ability to predict their actions, but it does not yield a judgment about the goodness of their actions. To judge the goodness of their actions requires other criteria. Second, the process does not permit change. By requiring the present generation of accountants to act in accordance with generally accepted principles of accounting—which principles were derived by observing the actions of the previous generation of accountants—change has been prohibited. If the requirement were strictly enforced, each generation would act just like the previous generation and this could be traced back to the first generation. Of course, changes have been made in accounting theory, but these changes are not explained or provided for by the anthropological interpretation. Third, subsequent to the first generation, the process is circular. We observe accountants' actions to discover what to teach, then we teach them how to act, then we observe accountants' actions to discover what to teach, etc. Fourth, and most importantly, is my value judgment that the theory of accounting ought to be concerned with accounting phenomena, not practicing accountants, in the same way that theories of physics are concerned with physical phenomena, not practicing physicists. The anthropological investigations

---

[14]Bronislaw Malinowski, *Magic, Science and Religion* (Doubleday & Company, Inc., 1948), p. 18.

provide useful information. It is important for us to know how practicing accountants act and to understand why they act that way. Comprehension of those actions is aided if they can be generalized under "principles of accounting." However, such knowledge does not provide a basis for a theory of accounting, as opposed to a theory of accountants' actions, and therefore the anthropological interpretation is not appropriate.

A Model-of-the-Firm Interpretation

The process of accounting may be cast in the form of the above schema as follows: There are observable occurrences (transactions, exchanges) which are inputs (entries) to the formal system. These are manipulated (partitioned or classified and summed) according to certain rules. The outputs (the financial statements or the balance of any particular account) are verified (audited). The formal system—the manipulation process—can be stated quite generally. Elsewhere[15] I have attempted to demonstrate that, given the inputs, the accounting outputs can be generated by an analytically defined process.

This interpretation indicates that the financial statements or the individual balances say something about the state of the firm. The accounting system under this interpretation is taken as a "model" of the firm in much the same way that a planetarium is a model of the sky. One can look at the financial statements and be able to determine the position of the firm in the same way that one can look at a planetarium and determine the position of a star. The individual propositions are verified every time the statements are audited and thus the theory has been confirmed many times.

The difficulty with this interpretation springs from the peculiar nature of the verification process in auditing. With minor exceptions, none of the outputs of an accounting system are *separately* verifiable. That is, there is no independent empirical operation which one can perform in order to verify the figures that were calculated from the inputs. Neither "net income" nor "total assets" are observable or separately measurable; instead they are summations of account balances. Account balances are not observable or separately measurable; instead they are summations of the entries.[16] The auditing process is not a verification of the outputs; instead it is, in essence, a *recalculation* of the outputs and an "examination" of the underlying business documents in order to check on the accuracy or verity of the inputs. Thus, the auditing process focuses on the inputs to the system and the way in which those inputs are manipulated. It does not verify the outputs of the system.

The inadequacy of this procedure to confirm a theory is immediately apparent. If one were to attempt to confirm a theory of astronomy, as exemplified

[15]Robert R. Sterling, "Elements of Pure Accounting Theory," *The Accounting Review*, Vol. XLII, No. 1, (January 1967).

[16]Contrast the verification of the quantity of inventory with the verification of the book value of that inventory. For quantities there is a well-defined formal system (perpetual inventory system) which specifies the relevant empirical inputs (receipts and issues) and the output provides an expectation or prediction of the quantity on hand. The physical count is a separate verification of that output.

For book values there is disagreement about the formal system (lifo or fifo) and disagreement about the relevant inputs (which costs are to be attached and which are to be expensed). The output provides no expectation and is not separately verifiable. It is the lack of verifiability of the output which prohibits resolution of the disagreement about the formal system and the inputs.

by a particular planetarium, then one might begin by checking on the accuracy of the observational inputs and one might also check for errors in computation. However, at some point the outputs of the system would be verified. One would look at the sky to see if the stars were in fact in the position indicated by the planetarium. In the absence of this last step, several absurdities could result. First, the set of equations could describe any situation whatsoever, e.g., a rectangular orbit. If one restricted the "verification" procedure to a check on the accuracy of the inputs and a recalculation, then one would certify that this planetarium presents fairly the position of the stars. The only way to discover that the orbit ought or ought not to be rectangular is to perform a separate operation and compare the results of that operation with the outputs of the system. If enough of these outputs were subjected to independent verification, the theory of rectangular orbits would be either confirmed or disconfirmed. Second, if there were two planetariums concerned with the same phenomena but with different sets of equations resulting in contradictory outputs, then the auditing procedure would require that both of them be certified as correct when at least one of them is necessarily wrong. Finally, the number of different sets of equations with different outputs is limitless.

The above example is similar to the problems currently faced in accounting. At the present time there are several different sets of equations for the allocation of cost. No matter how carefully one checks the accuracy of the inputs and the calculation, this process does not provide a method of confirming or disconfirming any of those sets of equations. As a consequence, any of those sets of equations are acceptable and the auditor has no way to choose among them. Two different sets of equations may be applied to the same inputs (in different firms) and the auditor will certify that the outputs of both present fairly when one must necessarily be wrong. Additional sets of equations can be added at will. For example, Thomas[17] has mentioned a sum-of-the-lunar-months method; Ijiri[18] has shown how the sum-of-the-year's-digits equation can be applied to inventory. The only reason that these suggestions appear to be odd is that they are unfamiliar. In the absence of the verification of the outputs of these equations, they are equally as good (or bad) a method of cost allocation as those equations presently in use.

Consider the depreciation equation. It says, in effect, a magnitude called "depreciation expense" is a function of time and the original cost. In some sense this is probably true; the market value of an asset normally declines over time. The difficulty is that the precise form of that function is open to question as is evidenced by the fact that there are several acceptable depreciation methods. Compare this situation to the problem of determining the function for a free falling body. The distance travelled by a free falling body is also a function of time, viz.,

$$d = 1/2 \, gt^2.$$

Suppose I argued that the above is wrong and that the correct function is

[17]Arthur L. Thomas, "The Amortization Problem: A Simplified Model and Some Unanswered Questions," *Journal of Accounting Research*, Vol. 3, No. 1, (Spring 1965), p. 110.

[18]Yuji Ijiri, "Logic and Sanctions in Accounting," unpublished paper presented at Accounting Colloquium I, (University of Kansas, April 1969).

$$d = 2\,gt/^{1/2}.$$

The only way to resolve the dispute is to observe the position of the body and the distance travelled and compare that observation to the calculated d's.[19] The same is true in regard to the depreciation equation.

Note, however, that current accounting practice *prohibits* separate verification. Auditors have substituted the word "examination" for "verification" because the latter is not "an accurate portrayal of the independent auditor's function."[20] Depreciation is an "allocation," not a "valuation," and that allocation is not "a measurement, expressed in monetary terms, of the physical deterioration within the year, or of the decline in monetary value within the year, or, indeed of anything that actually occurs within the year."[21] Therefore, independent observations of market prices or the physical state are not relevant to the examination of depreciation expense.[22]

[19]Another method of selection is to subsume the particular function under a more general theory. In this case, the former function "fits into" the general scheme of the Newtonian Laws of Motion and can be deduced therefrom. Thus, we could accept the former and reject the latter on that basis even if the distance travelled were not separately verifiable. However, in order to accept the theory into which this function fits, that theory would have to be confirmed by having some of its outputs verified. Otherwise, disputes about the theory are unresolvable. If the theory were well confirmed and this function could be deduced therefrom, we could claim that d was "indirectly verified." See James W. Cornman, "Indirectly Verifiable: Everything or Nothing," *Philosophical Studies*, Vol. XVIII, No. 4, (June 1967), and the literature he cites for a more complete discussion of indirect verification.

[20]*Auditing Standards and Procedures, No. 33* (American Institute of Certified Public Accountants, 1963), p. 94.

[21]*Accounting Research and Terminology Bulletins*, Final Edition, Terminology Bulletin 1 (American Institute of Certified Public Accountants, 1961), p. 24.

[22]The irrelevance of market prices to the examination of depreciation expense raises some questions about the original justification for the recording of that expense. If it were not for the prediction that the market price of the asset was going to decline from its purchase price to its salvage value, there would be no justification for recording an expense. If the salvage value were expected to be greater than or equal to the purchase price, then there would be no cost expiration to be allocated. Yet interim observations of prices are thought to be irrelevant to the allocation.

Of course it can be argued that the pattern of the cost allocation need not be the same as the pattern of price movements, but this raises the very question that has remained unresolvable: What should the pattern be? Moreover, in the absence of a verification, it is not certain that the expense should be a function of time. Making it a function of revenue would also result in a "rational" allocation. The usual objection to making depreciation a function of revenue is that it results in an undesirable smoothing of income. However, a function can be defined in which depreciation varies inversely with revenue. Such a function would result in less smoothing than the presently used straight-line method. That is, since income is the difference between revenue and expense, the smoothing of the expense results, cet. par., in the smoothing of the income. Thus, if smoothing is undesirable then the presently used depreciation method can be criticized on the same grounds that was used in the original justification given for instituting the present depreciation method.

In short, both the form that the depreciation equation should take and the kind of variables that should go into the depreciation equation are unresolvable issues in the context of current accounting theory because there is no separate verification of the output of that equation. If the objective of the depreciation equation were to describe or predict the path of some observable phenomena (such as price change or physical deterioration) then there would be some chance of deciding which equation is best. That objective seems reasonable in light of the fact that the very existence of the calculation depends upon the prediction of a price decline.

In summary, the outputs of present accounting theory are not separately verifiable. From the pronouncements in the literature, it appears that they are not intended to be a description of an empirical state and are not intended to be separately verifiable. Therefore, we must conclude that the model-of-the-firm interpretation is not an appropriate interpretation of present accounting theory.

A Psychological Interpretation

The model-of-the-firm interpretation can be broadened to include the receivers of the accounting reports. Under this interpretation the financial statements are not the final output of the theory; instead they are inputs to the receivers. The receiver's reactions to the financial statements are the observable outputs of the system. Thus, this interpretation is identical with the above model-of-the-firm interpretation except for the verification of the outputs. The inputs are the observable transactions or exchanges which are manipulated according to the syntactical rules of accounting. These rules produce financial statements (or other accounting figures) which are sent to the receivers. The receivers then react (or fail to react) and this is the observable output of the system. If the receivers react, it is taken as evidence that the financial statements are "useful" or that they contain "information."

Although usefulness has long been a tenet of accounting, it is only recently that the receivers' use or lack of use of the reports has been tested. There are some inconclusive results, but the tests that have been performed indicate that accounting reports are in fact used by the receivers. These results are important and continued research needs to be done in this area.[23] However, there are several lines of criticism that can be directed against this interpretation.

First, the subject matter of this interpretation is the reactions of people. This is the reason I call it a psychological interpretation. It follows the methodology of the stimulus-response school of psychology. The financial statements are the stimuli and the response is the receivers' decisions. The evidence has been gathered in respect to the effect of the frequency of the stimuli, the correlation of changes in the stimuli to changes in securities prices, the effects of different stimuli on investors and managers, the effect of the receipt of the stimuli upon price change and volume change, etc. This is quite similar to observing the effects of frequency, intensity, etc. of, say, electric shock upon people or laboratory animals. The resulting theory will also be quite similar. That is, it will be a theory which will explain or predict the reactions of people to stimuli. It is not clear that a theory of accounting should take on this character.

Second, if the response of receivers to accounting stimuli is to be taken as evidence that certain kinds of accounting practices are justified, then we must not overlook the possibility that those responses were conditioned. Accounting reports have been issued for a long time, and their issuance has been accompanied by a rather impressive ceremony performed by the managers and accountants who issue them. The receivers are likely to have gained the impression that they ought to react, and have noted that others react, and thereby have

---

[23]The importance of the results can be most vividly illustrated by considering the effects of the converse results. If it had been discovered that the receivers do not use accounting reports, the raison d'être of accounting would be open to question.

become conditioned to react. The fact that Pavlov's dog reacted to the sound of a bell does not provide justification for the existence of the bell.

Third, is the vital distinction between pragmatic informational content and semantic informational content. The study of pragmatics is concerned with the relation of signs to the users of signs. The study of semantics is concerned with the relation of signs to objects or events. If a person reacts to a sign, then that sign has pragmatic informational content. However, that reaction has nothing to do with the semantic informational content of that sign. People may react to a sign which we call a "lie." What we mean by the term "lie" is that it has negative semantic informational content, or, as we also say, it is "misinformation." The same is true with accounting reports. They are signs to which people react. However, the signs may or may not be connected to real world phenomena and the receivers may or may not be aware of the connection or lack of connection. The receivers may be interested in certain real world phenomena and may rightly or wrongly think that the signs allow them to discriminate that phenomena. Thus, the fact that receivers react to accounting reports does not necessarily mean that they ought to react.[24,25]

The final point of criticism can best be presented by an analogy. A physician will strike the knee of a patient and note the reaction. The physician does not conclude from this reaction that the patient has received information; instead the reaction is information to the physician. The physician then decides whether or not that reaction is pathological. The reaction is an observable input to the theory of medicine. It is my value judgment that the accounting profession ought to take a similar stance in regard to the reaction of the receivers. The fact that the receivers react is information to us and it is up to us to decide whether or not that reaction is pathological.

IV. A PROGRAM FOR CONSTRUCTING A THEORY OF RELEVANT MEASUREMENTS

In my view, accounting ought to be a measurement-communication process. Accountants ought to measure something and then communicate that measurement to the people who will make the decisions. Under this interpretation, the outputs of the accounting system are the inputs to decision theories. This interpretation focuses on decision *theories*, in contrast to the psychological interpretation which focuses on decision *makers*.

If there exists a well-defined decision theory, then that theory will specify what observations are to be made or what properties are to be measured. This provides a definition of relevance: All properties that are specified by a decision

---

[24]Beaver has carefully made this point in reporting his results. He says that his test is of the "investor *reaction* to earnings reports" and his "paper empirically examines the extent to which common stock investors *perceive* earnings to possess informational value." William H. Beaver, "The Information Content of Annual Earnings Announcements," *Empirical Research in Accounting: Selected Studies, 1968* (Institute of Professional Accounting, 1969) p. 67, italics supplied.

[25]In his discussion of pragmatics, S. S. Stevens, *Handbook of Experimental Psychology* (John Wiley & Sons, Inc., 1951) p. 4, reminds us of the reaction of Diderot to the mathematical signs presented by Euler. In an attempt to win a debate about the existence of God, Euler presented a symbolic expression which had nothing to do with the existence or nonexistence of God but which, nevertheless, routed Diderot.

theory are relevant to that theory. All properties that are not specified by a decision theory are irrelevant to that theory. Consider Hempel's example of specific gravity. The most obvious thing about this theory, so obvious that it remains tacit, is that somebody wants to know whether or not x_1 will float on x_2. The motivation for acquiring this knowledge in general form may have been idle curiosity. However, in any particular application of the theory, it is likely that the motivation is provided by a problematic situation. That is, someone must act; someone must decide between two or more courses of action and let us assume that the property of floating on is the basis for the decision. Therefore, this theory is applicable to that problematic situation. The theory clearly specifies that weight and volume are the relevant properties and that color, electrical resistance, and a host of other properties are irrelevant.

The reason for focusing on decision theories instead of decision makers is now apparent. Some or all of the decision makers may believe that the floating on property can be predicted by color or electrical resistance, i.e., their decision theories are wrong. If there were a large number of different decision makers with a large number of different erroneous decision theories, then it would be impossible to supply the data for all of them. More important is the fact that the erroneous decision theories are likely to produce erroneous decisions, i.e., decisions which do not produce the objectives desired by the decision makers. For these reasons, among others, I believe that accounting ought to supply the data specified by decision theories rather than the data desired by decision makers.[26]

[26]My critics sometimes attack this approach on grounds similar to the notion of consumer sovereignty. In their view, information is like any other good or service, and they argue that the accounting profession ought to give the decision maker the information he wants in the same way that any other producer ought to respond to the wants of consumers. The free play of market forces will then be the instrument that decides which information should be supplied. There is merit in this view but it depends upon some questionable assumptions.

First, the group that directly pays for the preparation of accounting reports, and influences their preparation, is only a part of the group of consumers. Investors receive the reports free of any direct payment. Thus, the value of the reports, in the sense of the price that people would be willing to pay for them, has not been tested in the open market. Second, the notion of consumer sovereignty depends upon the pristine will of the people. Joseph A. Schumpeter, *Capitalism, Socialism and Democracy* (Harper & Row, 1947), Ch. XXII, has pointed out that it makes little sense to justify one's actions on the basis of responding to the will of the people if that will has been manufactured. John K. Galbraith, *The Affluent Society* (Houghton Mifflin Company, 1958), Ch. XI, has made the same point more recently in what he calls the "dependence effect." Supra I made the same point by wondering whether or not the receivers have been conditioned to respond to accounting reports. Third, the efficacy of consumer sovereignty depends upon competition and free entry into the market so that alternatives can be provided. The provision of alternative kinds of accounting information is prohibited by requiring that it be in accord with generally accepted accounting principles. Entry into the accounting profession is limited by a licensing procedure. Of course, the consumer can choose different sources of information, e.g., he can choose between financial analysts and accountants, but this is like the consumer being able to choose between the local electric and gas companies (both of which are monopolies in many instances) for his source of power. It hardly meets the requirements of free competition which is so necessary to the defense of consumer sovereignty.

Finally is my value judgment that the notion is inapplicable in this instance. In my view, the accounting profession ought to devote some of its effort and resources to the education of the receivers. The profession ought to tell the receivers which decision theories

In one sense, under this interpretation, there is no separate theory of accounting. Every theory calls for measurements, and accounting is simply the measurement activity for certain kinds of theories. In the physical sciences the development of measurements is inextricably entwined with the construction of theories. After theory has been established and the measurement operations are well defined, then the measurement activity can be turned over to technicians. During the development stage, however, the very concepts that one seeks to measure are strongly influenced by the theory that one is trying to establish. Sometimes this is expressed by noting that the very act of measurement requires a commitment to a particular theory. Compare, for example, the measurements in relativistic time and space to the measurements "of the same phenomena" in absolute time and space. It is for this reason that I have previously argued that accountants qua metricians must become involved in the construction, refinement and elaboration of the decision theories.[27] Churchman has taken another tack. For similar reasons he has argued that operations researchers qua theoreticians must become involved with the development of measurements.[28] Whether it is the metricians who ought to become theoreticians or the theoreticians who ought to become metricians is not important. What is important is that theory construction and measurement development must be used. Part of our previous problems have been the result of conceiving of them as separable activities.

Theory without measurement is mere speculation. We noted above that one can construct a theory of love to replace the theory of gravity. Such theories can be constructed in any number. Measurement without theory is aimless wandering. Hempel's "hage" example makes this clear:

> Concepts with empirical import can be readily defined in any number, but most of them will be of no use for systematic purposes. Thus, we might define the hage of a person as the product of his height in millimeters and

are correct and then supply the data specified by those theories. Other professions have done this, e.g., the medical profession has gone to some lengths to convince the population that the germ theory of medicine is correct and that the demon theory of medicine is incorrect. In one sense this is a normative, as opposed to a positive, position. It results in an ought statement. The medical profession is saying, in effect, that the population ought to apply the germ theory. However, in another sense it is a positive position. The medical profession is not dictating the goal that the population ought to seek; instead it is informing them of the best method of achieving *any* health goal. If one seeks illness, then the germ theory is the most efficient method of achieving that goal in the same way that it is the most efficient method of achieving the goal of avoiding illness. The demon theory will not allow one to achieve either goal. Accounting can take a similar position. A theory that allows one to maximize profits can also be used to minimize profits, satisfice profits, earn a certain rate or amount, etc. On the other hand, an erroneous theory will not permit the achievement of any of those goals. For example, if one bases his decision upon sunk costs, then it is likely that he will not achieve his goal, regardless of whether that goal is to maximize or minimize. Thus, my normative position is that the accounting profession ought to assist in the achievement of efficient decisions and to let the decision makers choose their goals.

[27]Robert R. Sterling, *Theory of the Measurement of Enterprise Income* (The University Press of Kansas, 1970), p. 59.

[28]C. West Churchman, "A Systems Approach to Measurement in Business Firms," unpublished paper presented at Accounting Colloquium I, (University of Kansas, April 1969).

his age in years. This definition is operationally adequate and the term 'hage' thus introduced would have relatively high precision and uniformity of usage; but it lacks theoretical import, for we have no general laws connecting the hage of a person with other characteristics.[29]

This example is particularly pertinent to many accounting arguments. Regardless of many other *desirable* features—such as uniformity, precision, feasibility, objectivity, verifiability, freedom from bias, etc.—hage is a curiosity because it does not meet the *indispensable* requirement of being specified by some theory. The full disclosure of the method of calculation does not make the concept understandable or useful. That it is a fact or the truth does not make it meaningful. The same is true for the figures we generate in accounting. The theoretical import of accounting figures is the first question to be considered. Without a decision in regard to this question, the considerations of feasibility, objectivity, etc. are beside the point.

In short, theory construction and measurement development are inseparable. The theory specifies what is to be measured, how the measurements are to be manipulated and what measurable outcomes one can expect. This implies that the theory is constrained by what can be measured. It also implies that the measurements interact with the theory in that the predicted occurrences will be either verified or falsified by separate measurements. Some of the measurements may be considered anomalous and result in the modification or rejection of the theory. Thus, if accounting is to be a measurement-communication process, then the "theory of accounting" is only a part of the more general decision theories. Under this view it is the decision theories that need confirmation. Accounting figures are simply measurement inputs to the decision theories and we may want to verify those figures in the same way that we would verify any other measurement, but there is no separate theory of accounting to be confirmed.

The above is a long run proposal. If it were accepted, it would take years for it to be implemented. For the interim period I will briefly outline a short run program. First, decision theories that exist in the economics, operations research, etc. literature can be taken as givens. Instead of trying to construct our own decision theories we can search the literature for the extant decision theories. Thus, the "empirical research" that is required is a literature search. Second, the decision theories that are found in the literature can be classified and summarized in various ways. Perhaps the decision theories within a given class can be stated in a general form. It may be that some decision theories share a structure and the number of different theories can be reduced to manageable proportions by considering those with a common structure to be one theory. Third, an examination of the decision theories will reveal the relevant properties. There will be some properties that are specified by a number of theories. This may provide a basis for deciding which properties should be measured if we find that we cannot measure all of them.

This program is concerned with the discovery of the relevant properties. It appears that much of the previous accounting literature has not been concerned with that problem. Instead it has been concerned with *how* one measures and

---

[29]Carl G. Hempel, *Fundamentals of Concept Formation in Empirical Science* (The University of Chicago Press, 1967), p. 46.

what one measures has been taken as a given. My concern is with the discovery of what one ought to measure, i.e., what properties are relevant. *After* that has been established, then the question of how one goes about the measurement activity should be considered. Undoubtedly there will be a good many measurement problems, some of which may be unresolvable, but in regard to this interim program the measurement problems are of secondary concern.

Even the short run program is a formidable task. It is not, however, an insuperable task. Elsewhere[30] I have used this method in an analysis of the decisions regarding an oversimplified firm. Although the analysis was tedious, I was encouraged by the fact that it was possible to generalize the decision theories. If one were forced to examine each of the many decision theories and interpretations, the task might be well nigh impossible. The generalization of the decision theories allowed the task to be reduced to reasonable proportions. I was also encouraged by the findings. There were in fact some properties that were specified by all the decision theories, some properties that were specified by some of the decision theories, and some properties that were not specified by any of the decision theories. On this basis one can choose which properties to measure and communicate. Thus, a theory of accounting, in the sense of it being a theory of what to measure or account for, can be constructed from the specifications of the broader theories of economic decisions. The subject matter of accounting theory is, under this program, the broad theories of economic decisions. Thus, the observation plane of accounting is the theoretical plane of economics and related disciplines. The economic decision theories will have a separate set of confirmation procedures and problems.

The above is a cursory review of one possible method of constructing a theory of accounting. It is entirely programmatic and, like any other program, there will be many difficulties in its implementation.[31] I am not sure that these difficulties can be overcome, but I believe that this approach is more promising than the others that have been tried.

[30]Sterling, *Enterprise Income.*

[31]Beaver, Kennelly and Voss argue that the predictive ability of accounting figures is a more feasible approach because of the difficulty in determining the decision theories used and because the predictive ability approach requires a lower level of specificity regarding the decision theory. Their idea is appealing if one accepts the proposition that the decision theories are impossible to specify, and their discussion is most thorough and enlightening. However, I am not convinced that it is impossible to specify the decision theories. William H. Beaver, John W. Kennelly and William M. Voss, "Predictive Ability as a Criterion for the Evaluation of Accounting Data," *The Accounting Review*, Vol. XLIII, No. 4, (October 1968).

II-B/OBJECTIVES OF FINANCIAL STATEMENTS

Objectives of Financial Accounting: Review and Analysis

HECTOR R. ANTON

The standard-making role of the accounting profession in the United States has gone through various stages. However, the AICPA has not been able to obtain agreement on a *set* of accounting principles that is binding on the profession.[1] Nonetheless, the profession keeps trying. Three distinct efforts can be noted:

1. An inductive approach used by Sanders, Hatfield & Moore, *A Statement of Accounting Principles* (1938), furthered by Paul Grady's *Inventory of Generally Accepted Accounting Principles for Business Enterprises* (AICPA Accounting Research Study No. 7, 1965) and culminated in chapters 6 to 8 of APB Statement No. 4, "Basic Concepts and Accounting Principles Underlying Financial Statements of Business Enterprises" (1970).

2. A deductive approach generally espoused by the American Accounting Association in its earlier pronouncements and supported by some members of the AICPA. That approach was the base for Accounting Research Study Nos. 1 and 3,[2] but it was specifically rejected by the Accounting Principles Board in APB Statement No. 1 (1962). However, the deductive approach was used in chapters 3 to 5 of APB Statement No. 4 (1970).

3. An information-oriented approach that strives to satisfy information needs of readers of financial statements espoused by some academicians for over a decade and by the most recent pronouncement of the American Accounting Association.[3] It was also the approach used by the AICPA Study Group on the Objectives of Financial Statements (study group report).[4]

[1]For a fuller discussion of this point, see M. Moonitz, *Obtaining Agreement on Standards in the Accounting Profession* (Studies in Accounting Research No. 8, American Accounting Association, 1974), p. 12.

[2]M. Moonitz, *The Basic Postulates of Accounting*, Accounting Research Study No. 1 (New York: AICPA, 1961) and R. T. Sprouse and M. Moonitz, *A Tentative Set of Broad Accounting Principles for Business Enterprises*, Accounting Research Study No. 3 (New York: AICPA, 1962).

[3]American Accounting Association, *A Statement of Basic Accounting Theory* (1966); also see, for example: H. R. Anton, "Activity Analysis of the Firm" (1961) reprinted in

Although objectives for financial accounting and reporting have been implicit in the earlier approaches to standard-setting, the latter approach makes it mandatory to answer questions such as: Information for which user(s)? For what purposes? And at which time? In brief, the accounting and reporting system becomes dependent on desired information and expected (functional) behavior for its use.

The need for a comprehensive set of objectives and its inseparability from standard-setting was well recognized by the AICPA when it formed, concurrently, the Wheat committee and the Trueblood committee. The deliberations of the Wheat committee, of course, led to the establishment of the Financial Accounting Standards Board and those of the Trueblood committee led to the publication of *Objectives of Financial Statements* (study group report). Now the FASB is considering the study group report as a vital part of the Board's major continuing project on broad qualitative standards for financial reporting. The Board has issued an FASB discussion memorandum entitled "Conceptual Framework for Accounting and Reporting: Consideration of the Report of the Study Group on the Objectives of Financial Statements" (June 6, 1974), and has held public hearings on it. It remains to be seen whether the study group report or its approach will be accepted by the FASB or other standard-setting bodies.

The study group report is a comprehensive and complicated seminal document. For some it is not the kind of document that can be accepted or rejected; for others, it is a document that must be viewed in its entirety or not at all. The report appears to some to be a radical departure from accepted notions but appears to others merely to state matters that have been obvious all along.

The present article reviews and analyzes the objectives and qualitative characteristics proposed by the study group, proposes a hierarchical structure that gives cohesion to the set of objectives, and clearly identifies the relationships. The article also offers constructive criticism and recommendations for adoption of major segments of the report either explicitly for current use or as goals to be attained in the future. Other parts need rethinking or different exposition.

HIERARCHICAL STRUCTURE OF THE OBJECTIVES

The 12 Objectives are presented in the study group report as apparent equals.[5] Only as their order, wording, and relation to each other are analyzed does it become clear not only that they are not equal in nature and importance but

Contemporary Issues in Cost Accounting (H. R. Anton and P. A. Firmin, eds., 1966); R. Crandall, "Information Economics and Its Implications for Further Development of Accounting Theory," *Accounting Review*, July 1969; and J. T. Wheeler, "Accounting Theory and Research in Perspective," *Accounting Review*, January 1970.

[4]Report of the Study Group on the Objectives of Financial Statements, *Objectives of Financial Statements* (New York: AICPA, 1973).

[5]The study group report discusses 12 Objectives of Financial Statements and eight Qualitative Characteristics of Reporting. Both are unnumbered and otherwise undifferentiated in the study group report but for convenience they are numbered here in the order in which each appears in the report. Some of the Objectives are also divided into two or more parts and each part is given a subscript.

also that they form a definite structure or hierarchy.[6] The Objectives differ significantly from each other in aim or emphasis. Some are fundamental and some are only means of achieving other Objectives; some can stand essentially alone, and some depend heavily on other Objectives. The hierarchical structure gives cohesion to 10 of the Objectives, and the ability to see the structure is probably essential to interpret several Objectives and to see their relation to more basic or more general objectives.

The first 10 Objectives in the study group report form a structure with five levels, progressing from the more basic and general to the less fundamental and more specific:

I. One Objective (No. 1) that is the base underlying all the others.
II. Two Objectives (Nos. 2 and 3) that identify the primary users of financial statement information and their major use of that information.
III. Two Objectives (Nos. 4 and 5) that specify information about earning power and stewardship as the kinds of information needed for the use identified in No. 3.
IV. Five Objectives (Nos. 6, 7, 8, 9 and 10) that describe means for implementing No. 4.
V. Nine specific recommendations (6a, 7a, 7b, 7c, 8a, 8b, 9a, 9b, and 10a), each phrased with "should," pertaining to types of information, disclosure, classification, and the like, in financial statements.

The items in level V are not presented as separate Objectives in the study group report, but rather as parts and amplifications of Objectives Nos. 6 through 10. However, without exception, the nine items are not objectives but give directions about how things should be done.

Exhibit A shows the various Objectives, their position in the hierarchical structure and a recommendation relative to each. Exhibit B gives a diagrammatic depiction of the interrelationships between the Objectives.

OBJECTIVES OUTSIDE THE STRUCTURE

Two Objectives in the study group report do not fit into the proposed hierarchical structure, although they are not necessarily extraneous to the study group's task.
No. 11 "An objective of financial statements for governmental and not-for-profit organizations is to provide information useful for evaluating the effectiveness of the management of resources in achieving the organization's goals."
No. 11a "Performance measures should be quantified in terms of identified goals."

Objective No. 11 pertains to governmental and not-for-profit organizations, a subject that is largely separate from the rest of the report. For example, users of financial statements of those organizations are not ordinarily interested in

---

[6]The proceedings of the Robert M. Trueblood Memorial Conference at the University of Chicago, entitled *Studies on Financial Accounting Objectives: 1974*, include a paper by two members of the staff of the study group, George H. Sorter and Martin S. Gans, "Opportunities and Implications of the Report on Objectives of Financial Statements," that also offers a hierarchy of objectives.

either the earning potential of the organization or potential cash flows from it to themselves. Other objectives of financial statements of governmental and not-for-profit organizations probably should be specified and may well form a structure of objectives similar to but separate from those for business enterprises. The subject needs separate study.

No. 12 "An objective of financial statements is to report on those activities of the enterprise affecting society which can be determined and described or measured and which are important to the role of the enterprise in its social environment."

Objective No. 12 differs from the first 10 because it relates to the role of an enterprise in its social environment. The Objective and its discussion in the report are vague about users' identities and needs, purposes for the information, and implementation. In fact, the discussion mostly emphasizes problems. Financial statements may be a relatively poor way to communicate social costs and benefits. The subject needs study and attention, but it is not crucial to the proposed structure.

OBJECTIVES IN THE STRUCTURE

As shown in Exhibits A and B, the hierarchical structure is comprised of 10 Objectives and nine "recommendations" in five levels. Each level and each Objective merits description and analysis, some more than others.

BASIC OBJECTIVES

There is one basic Objective which underlies all the others:

No. 1 "The basic objective of financial statements is to provide information useful for making economic decisions."

The objective of producing information useful for investors' and creditors' decisions, though often stated in the literature, did not appear in AICPA pronouncements until APB Statement No. 4. Since the Objective focuses on information for decision making rather than on the traditional accounting purposes of stewardship reporting, it represents a fundamental change in attitude in setting financial accounting objectives.

IDENTIFYING OBJECTIVES

Two Objectives identify the primary users and use of information in financial statements. The second of the two identifies investors and creditors as the primary users and cash flows from the enterprise to them as their principal interest. The intent of the first of the two Objectives is less clear.

No. 2 "An objective of financial statements is to serve primarily those users who have limited authority, ability, or resources to obtain information and who rely on financial statements as their principal source of information about an enterprise's economic activity."

Although Objective No. 2 is positively stated, the Objective and the discussion that accompanies it in the study group report are much clearer about who is *not* encompassed in the Objective (managers, large-scale equity investors and creditors, and regulators) than about those whom the description is intended to fit.

EXHIBIT A
Hierarchical Structure for Objectives of Financial Accounting

Level		Objective No.[a]	Recommendation
I—Basic	1	Decision making	Adopt
II—Identifying: users and uses	2	Users with limited access	Needs further work
	3	Cash flows to users	Adopt
III—Specifying information needed	4	Enterprise earning power	Adopt
	5	Management's ability	Needs further work
IV—Implementing	6	Factual and interpretive information	Adopt (but needs further work)
	7	Statement of financial position	Adopt
	8	Statement of periodic earnings	Adopt
	9	Statement of financial activities	Adopt
	10	Predictions	Adopt (but needs further work)
V—Specific imperative recommendations	6a	Disclosure of assumptions	Needs further work
	7a	Incomplete earnings cycles	Needs further work
	7b	Current values	Needs further work
	7c	Segregation by uncertainty and timing	Needs further work
	8a	Completed earnings cycles	Needs further work
	8b	Changes in values	Needs further work
	9a	Cash consequences	Needs further work
	9b	Data requiring minimal judgment	Needs further work
	10a	Forecasts to enhance prediction	Adopt (if No. 10 is adopted)
Nonhierarchical	11	Governmental and not-for-profit organizations	Not part of main study
	12	Governmental and social environment	Not part of main study

[a]Numbers are assigned to Objectives in conformity with the FASB discussion memorandum, "Conceptual Framework of Accounting," June 6, 1974.

The study group clearly concluded that financial statements ought to be directed primarily to the needs of investors and creditors—all Objectives from Nos. 3 through 10 are concerned with those needs. However, it is not clear whether the study group intended to identify investors and creditors as the primary audience through the round-about language of Objective No. 2. Designating a primary audience for financial statements presumes a conflict of interest as to needs, a conflict that has not been established. An equally sound presumption is that most, if not all, users of financial statements share a common need to know of an enterprise's financial position, results of operations and other changes in financial position. If needs are common, to designate a primary user serves no particularly useful purpose. Unless a conflict of needs can be shown, a better approach is that used in APB Statement No. 4, which lists a number of potential user groups with direct or indirect interests in business enterprises and presumes a wide area of common interests and needs that justifies general purpose financial statements to meet the needs of many groups.

Alternatively, Objective No. 2 may be an indirect way of stating an objective about financial statements rather than about users of financial statements—namely, that an objective is to present a set of financial statements that standing alone contains relevant information for a fair presentation. That interpretation is supported by the study group's conclusion immediately before the statement of the Objective that "users who ordinarily rely on financial statements *alone* may be served most by developing accounting objectives" (report, p. 17, emphasis added). If the Objective is about financial statements rather than the identity of users, it should be reworded, with care to avoid the implication that financial statements provide all the information that users need to make rational economic decisions about investing or disinvesting in business enterprises. While it is obvious to many that financial statements cannot provide that much information, too many others have a clouded perception of what the statements can do—often with rather unfortunate results for both investor and accountant.

Financial statements should not be expected to stand completely alone. Accounting literature, including APB Statement No. 4, emphasizes that accounting information should be used in conjunction with other information about an enterprise, its industry, the state of the economy, etc. Financial statements are a good means of communicating certain kinds of information about business enterprises and a poor means of communicating other kinds. Thus, although the area of financial accounting and financial statements should be sufficiently general to permit continued development of accounting principles in response to changes in the legal and social setting of business and economic activity, specific limits should be recognized to prevent accounting from attempting to become all things to all people.[7] In sum, Objective No. 2 needs some rethinking, rewording and perhaps complete restatement to clarify its intended meaning.

No. 3 "An objective of financial statements is to provide information useful to investors and creditors for predicting, comparing, and evaluating potential cash flows to them in terms of amount, timing, and related uncertainty."

Objective No. 3 focuses on the needs of investors and creditors and identifies the basis of their interest in financial statements as cash flow from an enterprise to them. The Objective is critical to the whole structure of objectives because all the others, Nos. 4 through 10, reflect the same focus on investors and creditors and the same concern with cash flows to them.

The particular emphasis of Objective No. 3 stems directly from the study group's first assumptions about users' information needs and decision processes: "Users of financial statements seek to predict, compare, and evaluate the cash consequences of their economic decisions" (p. 13).

Many accountants will be disturbed because this crucial Objective is in terms of cash flow and fails to mention net income. Accountants have long had trouble keeping the relation between cash flow and net income in perspective, but earnings or net income have to be founded ultimately on flows of cash to and from the enterprise. The essence of the accrual basis is recognition of the

---

[7]The AICPA's accounting standards division has issued a discussion paper, "The Application of Generally Accepted Accounting Principles to Smaller and/or Closely Held Business," March 31, 1975.

equality of amount but difference in timing between earnings and cash. Accountants have long tried to walk the razor's edge between a criterion of "nearness to cash" and "accrual of revenue when it is earned." The latter, though sometimes abused in practice, is a more correct though a more abstract notion. At the level of Objective No. 3, accrual accounting points to an emphasis on cash flows to and from an enterprise. It requires another step, of course, from that point to an emphasis on cash flows from an enterprise to investors and creditors.

SPECIFYING OBJECTIVES

Two Objectives specify information about earning power of an enterprise and stewardship of enterprise resources as the kinds of information needed by investors and creditors to predict, compare, and evaluate the amount, timing, and uncertainty of cash flows from an enterprise to themselves.

No. 4 "An objective of financial statements is to provide users with information for predicting, comparing, and evaluating enterprise earning power."

Objective No. 4 translates Objective No. 3 (information about cash flows to investors and creditors) into an emphasis on earning power of the enterprise. It forms the basis for Objectives Nos. 6 through 10, which are all concerned with information for "predicting, comparing, and evaluating enterprise earning power." All six Objectives flow more or less directly from (1) the study group's second assumption about users' information needs and decision processes

"Information about the cash consequences of decisions made by the enterprise is useful for predicting, comparing, and evaluating cash flows to users. . . . ." (p. 14)

and (2) the study group's definition of earning power

". . . the enterprise's ability to be better off, to generate more cash, and to have earnings convertible into cash at some future date. . . .

"Enterprise earning power has as its essence the notion of ability to generate cash in the future. . . . earnings can only come from cash generated by operations; cash generating ability and earning power are equivalent" (p. 23).

The definition of earning power as the ability to bring in cash rather than as the ability to produce earnings continues the emphasis in Objective No. 3 on cash flows and is a shift in emphasis from traditional accounting ideas. But the difference is not as great as it might first appear. A major function of Objective No. 4 is to relate the emphasis in Objective No. 3 on cash flows to investors and creditors to more conventional accounting notions.

Even though the study group defined earning power in terms of cash flow to the enterprise rather than in terms of enterprise earnings, the group clearly indicated that information about periodic earnings is more useful than information about current cash flows to the enterprise for predicting those future cash flows that evidence its earning power (p. 22). The discussion of Objective No. 4 sets the stage for emphasis on measurement of periodic earnings and the income statement in later Objectives.

The discussion of Objective No. 4 in the report contains a good discussion of the relation between cash movements and periodic earnings and the effects of uncertainty on accounting measurements. In general, that discussion is superior to some of the Objectives that depend on it. One of the problems resulting from emphasizing the Objectives themselves is that important matters are often deemphasized or ignored altogether.

The study group's discussion of Objective No. 4 (and of No. 5 as well) is marred by an overemphasis, and a misplaced reliance, on a questionable "primary and continuing goal of every commercial enterprise," namely, "to increase its monetary wealth so that over time it can return the maximum amount of cash to its owners" (p. 21). First, the goal is asserted, not substantiated, although the proposition is by no means universally accepted. Second, the goal is not necessary to establish that investors and creditors are interested in cash flow from an enterprise and want accounting information to help them "predict, compare, and evaluate" those potential cash flows. The argument of whether the goal of an enterprise is, or should be, to maximize cash flow or some other amount or to optimize some alternative goal that involves constraints on maximum cash flow and maximum reported earnings, such as survival, growth or prestige, could and should have been avoided.

No. 5 "An objective of financial statements is to supply information useful in judging management's ability to utilize enterprise resources effectively in achieving the primary enterprise goal."

Objective No. 5 is apparently intended to make stewardship reporting an objective of financial statements. However, the stewardship contemplated by the study group is not the traditional fiduciary notion of safekeeping of assets by reasonable effort to prevent their loss. Rather, accountability of management is to encompass the results of management's decisions to use or not use assets, to convert or not convert, and to avert the unfavorable effects of inflation and deflation and social and technological change.

Objective No. 5 should be excluded from the Objectives of financial statements at this time. Perhaps the fiduciary notion of stewardship can be salvaged and converted into the broader concept described by the study group, but the Objective as stated has two flaws. First, the Objective sets a goal that cannot be met because accounting cannot measure "management's ability to use resources effectively in achieving the primary enterprise goal." Except for the most obvious management successes and failures (which are usually visible without accounting), the results reported by accounting are clouded by the interaction of management ability and a host of other factors that management cannot control and often cannot even be expected to anticipate. Moreover the data are not to be considered in light of managerial control, but rather in relation to another more basic objective—user decision making.

Second, the Objective as stated depends on the assumption that "the principal goal of a commercial enterprise is to maximize cash return to owners" (p. 25), a proposition that, as already noted, is neither substantiated in the report nor generally accepted. Moreover, it probably does not describe the behavior of most enterprises. The assumption of maximization of cash flow to owners is crucial to Objective No. 5 because it sets the standard against which management's stewardship is to be judged. Even if accounting could measure management against that standard, it would be misleading to owners if management did not or could not adopt that goal as a guiding star.

Since Objective No. 5 is not workable, it should not be adopted until the fiduciary notion of stewardship can be made compatible with the study group's concept of accountability of management or until ways can be developed to measure results against a workable standard.

IMPLEMENTING OBJECTIVES AND RECOMMENDATIONS

Five Objectives describe means of implementing Objective No. 4. Each of these implementing Objectives also contains imperative ("should") recommendations that are here separated from the Objective. That separation highlights the Objective and shows that the recommendations are at a different level in the structure of Objectives.

No. 6 "An objective of financial statements is to provide factual and interpretive information about transactions and other events which is useful for predicting, comparing, and evaluating enterprise earning power.

    6a "Basic underlying assumptions with respect to matters subject to interpretation, evaluation, prediction, or estimation should be disclosed."

    Objective No. 6 comes from the study group's third and last assumption about users' information needs and decision processes:

    "Financial statements are more useful if they include but distinguish information that is primarily factual, and therefore can be measured objectively, from information that is primarily interpretive" (p. 14).

    The distinction between factual, objective information and interpretive information also underlies several of the recommendations attached to Objectives Nos. 7 through 9.

    Unfortunately, neither Objective No. 6 nor its accompanying discussion specifically defines "other events." In accounting, that term has been applied to depreciation and other nontransactions that conventionally have been accounted for as transactions. The report implies that the term is meant to be broader, encompassing things such as changes in selling and replacement prices, appreciation or decline in values of securities, obsolescence of inventory or plant, possible effects of litigation, and changes in foreign exchange rates or general price levels. Disclosure of underlying assumptions (Recommendation 6a) must await further clarification of the nature of the "other events" and the distinction between factual and interpretive information. At present, disclosures would be required for all items with the possible exception of cash flows.

    The next three Objectives describe financial statements expected to be useful in meeting Objective No. 4. The report ties these Objectives on financial statements to No. 6 with four conclusions or recommendations that are not included in any Objective:

- "Financial statements should emphasize information about transactions and other events that significantly affect enterprise earning power or changes in it. Such information should be stated in terms of actual or prospective cash impact and should facilitate comparisons.
- "Financial statements should report both facts and interpretations about transactions and other events.
- "Financial statements should assist in the assessment of the uncertainties with respect to the amount and timing of prospective cash receipts and disbursements.
- "Financial statements should report on series of transactions and other events, including value changes, in terms of earnings cycles" (p. 34).

    Except for the names of the financial statements, Objectives Nos. 7 through 9 are worded exactly alike. The seven related recommendations involve some of the more controversial matters covered in the study group report.

No. 7 "An objective is to provide a statement of financial position useful for predicting, comparing, and evaluating enterprise earning power.

7a "This statement should provide information concerning enterprise transactions and other events that are part of incomplete earnings cycles.

7b "Current values should also be reported when they differ significantly from historical cost.

7c "Assets and liabilities should be grouped or segregated by the relative uncertainty of the amount and timing of prospective realization or liquidation."

No. 8 "An objective is to provide a statement of periodic earnings useful for predicting, comparing, and evaluating enterprise earning power.

8a "The net result of completed earnings cycles and enterprise activities resulting in recognizable progress toward completion of incomplete cycles should be reported.

8b "Changes in the values reflected in successive statements of financial position should also be reported, but separately, since they differ in terms of their certainty of realization."

No. 9 "An objective is to provide a statement of financial activities useful for predicting, comparing, and evaluating enterprise earning power.

9a "This statement should report mainly on factual aspects of enterprise transactions having or expected to have significant cash consequences.

9b "This statement should report data that require minimal judgment and interpretation by the preparer."

The Objectives themselves appear traditional, but the recommendations related to those Objectives contain a number of ideas that are unusual in authoritative accounting literature and presage some changes in financial statements. The recommendations would undoubtedly require changes in classification and probably changes in statement composition as well. Other changes may be inherent in the emphasis on the needs of financial statement users and the pervasive idea that financial statements are means of communicating information useful in making economic decisions, not ends in themselves.

In other ways, chapters 5 and 6, which discuss Objectives Nos. 6 through 9, are the most disappointing of the report. Several of the recommendations are controversial and the recommendations and their discussion often indicate compromise. Clear and relevant discussion of the issues would have highlighted other possible solutions and their characteristics. Apparently, the study group chose to play down internal differences, and as a result the discussion of several of the recommendations is either missing or woefully weak.

A number of bold and imaginative ideas framed by the group are inadequately explored in the report, for example

- A recommendation to classify assets and liabilities by uncertainty of amount and timing of cash flows rather than on the basis of liquidity.
- A recommendation to separate operations into complete and incomplete earnings cycles and to disclose separately the results of complete cycles and estimates of incomplete cycles.
- A recommendation to disclose current values and changes in values between statements of financial position.
- A recommendation (not included as part of an Objective) to disclose ranges of precision, reliability, and uncertainty.
- An observation about different characteristics of various financial statements—that statements of financial position and periodic earnings must

report on incomplete cycles and thus depend significantly on estimates and interpretations, while statements of financial activities report primarily on completed transactions and are essentially factual.

The study group apparently was divided on at least three of those ideas— (1) the usefulness of a cycle notion, (2) the place of current values in the Objectives and (3) the use of single valued estimates versus ranges. The report suffers from inadequate discussion of all those areas.

The report's ambivalence is most pronounced on the significance of current values in the Objectives scheme. Thus, although two recommendations (7b and 8b) specifically recommend disclosing current values and changes in current values, the study group does not indicate whether or not current values and changes in current values are to be specifically included in the statements. The discussions of cost and value, in general, and discounted cash flow, in particular, are poor in comparison with most of the rest of the report.

Several conclusions or comments pertaining to current values are also included without much evidence or discussion, for example, ". . . financial statements probably cannot present a single or unique measure of earning power or of the value of the enterprise . . ." (p. 31) and ". . . the objectives of financial statements cannot be best served by the exclusive use of a single valuation basis" (p. 41). The applicability of different bases cannot merely be asserted. There is no a priori reason to assume that different valuation bases are needed—on the contrary, a priori, a single valuation basis is a logically preferable measurement device—but different bases may become practical necessities if a relevant single basis should prove unworkable. The point is that to assert the need for different bases is to start from the wrong end—the first step is to ascertain what is relevant to the objectives and then to develop a measurement theory. After that is done, the need may be established for different bases or to substitute one basis that is measurable for a more correct basis that is not measurable.

The same ambivalence, minimal discussion, and tendency toward assertion that characterize the report's treatment of current values are also present in its treatment of complete and incomplete earnings cycles and the use of ranges. Both are substantially new ideas in financial accounting and both relate to providing information about the impact on financial statements of uncertainty, risk, variability, and similar factors, but neither is developed adequately in the report. Thus, although the report breaks new ground, implies some significant changes in financial statements, and contains several new and imaginative ideas that at least deserve to be explored fully and openly, the report also gives the impression that the study group desired to preserve as much of present accounting as possible.

Objective No. 10 deserves special attention not only because it is about forecasting but also because it is misplaced in the Objectives structure in the study group report.

No. 10 "An objective of financial statements is to provide information useful for the predictive process.

10a "Financial forecasts should be provided when they will enhance the reliability of users' predictions."

The wording of Objective No. 10 parallels that of Objectives Nos. 4 and 5, but otherwise it is more like Objectives Nos. 6 through 9. Since the emphasis in Objectives No. 4 and Nos. 6 through 9 is on the users' predictive process, no separate Objective should be necessary to state that "an objective ... is to provide information useful for the predictive process." Accordingly, the Objective should be considered to be an implementing Objective and reworded accordingly:

No. 10 "An objective is to provide a financial forecast useful for predicting, comparing, and evaluating enterprise earning power."

Publishing financial forecasts is still in an experimental stage; therefore, the subject needs intensive study before implementation of the Objective is feasible.

QUALITATIVE CHARACTERISTICS OF REPORTING

The study group report devoted one chapter to a discussion of eight characteristics that information in or related to financial statements should have to satisfy users' needs. The group of eight "qualitative characteristics of reporting" invites comparison with a similar group of seven "qualitative objectives" in APB Statement No. 4. Although the two lists differ in some respects, similarities predominate, as the following comparison shows:

Qualitative characteristics from study group's report	Qualitative objectives from APB Statement No. 4
1 Relevance and	0–1 Relevance
2 Materiality	(Included as basic features of
3 Form and substance ⎫	financial accounting)
4 Reliability	0–3 Verifiability
5 Freedom from bias	0–4 Neutrality
6 Comparability ⎫	
7 Consistency ⎰	0–6 Comparability
8 Understandability	0–2 Understandability
● (note only)	0–5 Timeliness
● —	0–7 Completeness

The study group and the APB generally agree on "relevance" and "understandability." For example, both sources describe understandability to a reasonably well-informed investor or creditor rather than either to a sophisticated analyst or to a more naive investor. And although "reliability" is a broader notion than "verifiability," both groups emphasize the impossibility of 100 percent accuracy because estimates and judgments are involved.

"Freedom from bias" and "neutrality" are somewhat further apart. The APB emphasizes common needs of users and the need to avoid spoiling the common data by biasing it toward the presumed needs of a particular user group. The study group notes that concern in passing but is more interested in bias introduced by conservatism and says that disclosing varying degrees of uncertainty as well as information about judgments and interpretations in the financial statements is a means of reducing bias.

Other differences show in the two lists. The study group is probably correct that "form and substance" and "materiality" are essential qualities of useful

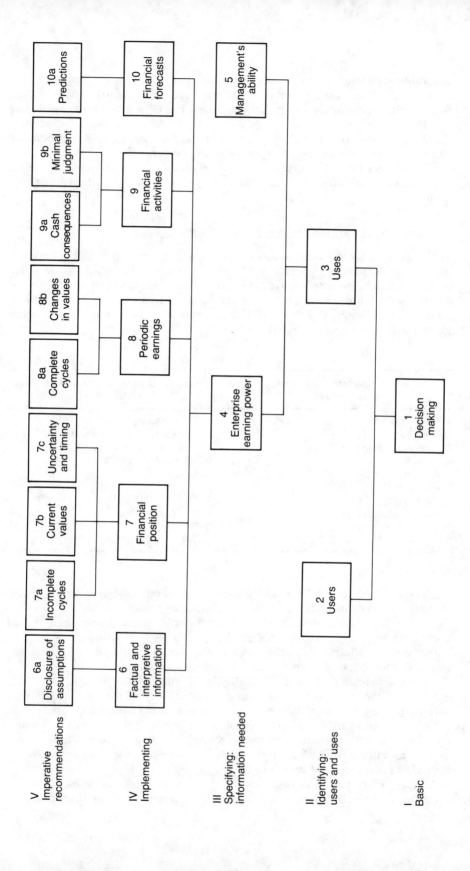

financial information, provided that the essentially negative nature of materiality is kept in perspective. That is, since accounting is concerned with significant information, accounting for insignificant information does not matter, and the benefit from accounting for items correctly should justify the effort. Materiality now commands much attention because of allegations that material information is being obscured, not from an overriding importance of the notion itself.

The APB includes "consistency" and regular reporting periods as factors in "comparability," a sounder view than the study group's classification of consistency as a separate, coequal characteristic. Consistency is a virtue for comparisons; inconsistency may be more useful for other purposes. The APB is also correct in including "timeliness" among its objectives. The study group's observation that users cannot await the entire life of an enterprise for information about its successes and failures is accurate but much too ambiguous.

SUMMARY AND CONCLUSIONS

Significant parts of the study group report are capable of present adoption, either explicitly to guide current practice or as goals to be attained in the future. That conclusion does not mean that any or all of the objectives that are ready for adoption cannot be improved or do not need further study or work. However, they could be improved and refined after adoption. Capable of present adoption are

- Basic Objective No. 1.
- Identifying Objective No. 3.
- Specifying Objective No. 4.
- Implementing Objectives Nos. 6, 7, 8, 9 and 10.
- Recommendation No. 10a (which should be adopted if Objective No. 10 is adopted).
- Qualitative characteristics—relevance, materiality, form and substance, reliability, freedom from bias, comparability, understandability and timeliness.

The wording of Objective No. 3 could be improved, and Objective No. 6 needs further work to clarify the meaning of "other events." Objective No. 10 is so hedged by its accompanying recommendation that adopting it now will do no harm, but both the Objective and the recommendation need much further study.

Other parts of the study group report should not be adopted now because they need significant additional study and work, they do not fit into the structure of Objectives in the report or they suffer from both those weaknesses. In that group are

- Identifying Objective No. 2.
- Specifying Objective No. 5.
- Unclassified Objective No. 11.
- Unclassified Objective No. 12.
- Recommendations Nos. 6a, 7a, 7b, 7c, 8a, 8b, 9a and 9b.
- Qualitative characteristic-consistency.

Objective No. 2 needs rethinking and rewriting before taking its place among the Objectives; at present, it is much too vague. Objective No. 5 should be completely reworked to remove its dependence on a questionable enterprise goal and to make it capable of implementation. Objectives Nos. 11 and 12 neither fit the hierarchical structure nor are capable of adoption without further major study. Conceivably, neither belongs as an objective of financial statements of business enterprises.

All of the recommendations about how to prepare financial statements to implement Objectives need further refinement before adoption. The recommendations, their implications and means of implementation need extensive study before accountants and others can respond to them as recommendations.

Finally, the basic attitude manifested by the study group report should be adopted now. Until gray areas in present accounting practice are covered by Objectives and Standards, doubts should be resolved by deferring to the needs of users of financial statements to the extent that those needs are known. That attitude on the part of those who prepare and audit financial statements alone would guarantee a significant contribution by the study group report.

FASB's Statements on Objectives and Elements of Financial Accounting: A Review

NICHOLAS DOPUCH AND SHYAM SUNDER

The Financial Accounting Standards Board (FASB) issued an exposure draft of the proposed statement on Objectives of Financial Reporting and Elements of Financial Statements of Business Enterprises on December 29, 1977. The first part of the Exposure Draft, dealing with the objectives of financial reporting, was issued in revised form a year later as the Statement of Financial Accounting Concepts No. 1 (SFAC 1)[FASB, 1978]. A final statement on the elements of financial statements has not yet been issued. In this paper we review the FASB's statement on objectives (as contained in SFAC 1) and on elements (as contained in the Exposure Draft). Though many of our comments could also be applied to other aspects of the project on the conceptual framework undertaken by the FASB, we shall limit our discussion to the two documents mentioned above.[1]

Few general criteria, other than internal consistency, have been proposed for evaluating conceptual frameworks. The approach taken in the reviews by Littleton [1962; 1963] of the Moonitz [1961] and the Sprouse and Moonitz [1962] monographs; by Ijiri [1971] of the APB *Statement No. 4* [AICPA, 1970]; by a subcommittee of the American Accounting Association (AAA) to respond to the FASB's Discussion Memorandum of the Conceptual Framework [AAA, 1977b]; by Sterling [1967] of the AAA's *A Statement of Basic Accounting Theory* [1966]; by Vatter [1963], Hanson [1940], and Kester [1940]; and by Deinzer [1964] of various statements sponsored by the AAA [1936; 1941; 1948; 1957; 1964a; 1964b] seem too diverse to provide common criteria for evaluating a conceptual framework. We decided, therefore, to use two criteria in our review: (1) To what extent do these statements differ from previous attempts of this nature; and, regardless of the answer to (1), (2) to what extent will these statements, if adopted, yield the benefits expected by the FASB? Since we arrive at pessimistic answers to both questions, we are led to consider two further questions: (a) What are the fundamental difficulties in developing a set of objectives of financial accounting, and (b) why do authoritative bodies persist in trying to develop a conceptual framework? The final section of the paper contains the summary and concluding remarks.

We have benefited from many helpful comments, in particular those by Professors Raymond J. Chambers, William W. Cooper, Sidney Davidson, Rashad Abdel-khalik, William R. Scott, Stephen A. Zeff, and the anonymous reviewers.

[1]These documents were preceded by two Discussion Memoranda [FASB 1974; 1976a]; the latter was accompanied by a statement of tentative conclusions on objectives of financial statements [FASB, 1976b].

COMPARISON WITH PREVIOUS ATTEMPTS
TO DEVELOP A FRAMEWORK

Objectives

The SFAC 1 is divided into two parts: Introduction and Background, followed by Objectives of Financial Reporting. The introductory section includes subsections on: (a) financial statements and financial reporting, (b) the environmental context of objectives, (c) the characteristics and limitations of information provided, (d) potential users and their interests, and (e) general-purpose external financial reporting. Financial statements are defined to be a subset of financial reporting, but no limits are provided on the number of elements of financial reporting that one may include in financial statements. The discussion of the environmental context of accounting bears a resemblance to the discussion by Moonitz [1961, Chapter 2] and by the Accounting Principles Board in Statement No. 4 (APBS 4) [AICPA, 1970, Chapter 3]. A discussion of the major characteristics of the U.S. economy in the statement of objectives would be justified if it were accompanied by a theory which linked the characteristics of various economies to alternative financial accounting systems. Since no such theory is provided, it is not clear how a vague description of the U.S. economy is useful for determining or understanding objectives.[2]

In the sections on potential users and general-purpose financial reporting it is stated that the specific objectives here refer to the general-purpose financial reports that serve the informational needs of external users who lack the authority to prescribe the financial information they want from an enterprise, a statement very similar to Objective No. 2 of the Trueblood Report [AICPA, 1973]. The FASB relies considerably on the Trueblood Report when it states that financial reporting "should provide information to help present and potential investors and creditors, and other users in assessing the amounts, timing, and uncertainty of prospective net cash receipts. . . . " [FASB, 1978, para. 37]. The need for information on cash flows leads to the need for information on "the economic resources of an enterprise, the claims to those resources (obligations of the enterprise to transfer resources to other entities and owners' equity), and the effects of transactions, events, and circumstances that change resources and claims to those resources" (para. 40). After more discussion, the Board arrives at the conclusion that the

> primary focus of financial reporting is information about an enterprise's performance provided by measures of earnings and its components. . . . Information about enterprise earnings and its components measured by accrual accounting generally provides a better indication of enterprise performance than information about current cash receipts and payments [FASB, 1978, para. 43–44].

This last statement is not an objective, but a means to an objective.

Although these paragraphs encompass many of the specific objectives of the Trueblood Report, the emphasis and order of presentation are different.

---

[2]For example, paragraph 13 refers to efficient allocations of resources within a market economy, but there are several definitions of allocation efficiency which might be employed. In the absence of an agreed-upon definition, inefficiencies cannot be identified.

Other departures from the Report are an omission of any reference to providing financial forecasts and to non-profit and social accounting (Objectives 10, 11, and 12, respectively, of the Trueblood Report).

In wording and substance, little is new or different in SFAC 1. Had the FASB pointed out the parts of the existing reports,[3] such as APBS 4 and the Trueblood Report, that it agreed with and emphasized its disagreements, its contribution would have been easier to discern. Without such aid, we are hard-pressed to discern the FASB's net contribution to these earlier efforts. Given that previous authoritative efforts to write objectives are generally considered inadequate in helping to resolve accounting issues, a basic test of the FASB's contribution is the extent to which SFAC 1 may succeed where others have failed. We shall apply such a test after discussing the elements of financial statements and characteristics of financial information as provided in the FASB's Exposure Draft [FASB, 1977].

Elements of Financial Statements

The second major section of the Exposure Draft [FASB, 1977], paragraphs 36 through 66, deals mainly with definitions of the main categories of accounts appearing in financial statements: assets, liabilities, owners' equity, revenues, expenses, gains, and losses. Supplementing these definitions are subsections containing discussions of the bases for definitions, the matching of efforts and accomplishments, and the need to provide financial statements which articulate with one another. The elements of financial statements are integrated—revenues and gains result in, or from, increases in assets, decreases in liabilities or combinations of the two; expenses and losses result in, or from, decreases in assets, increases in liabilities, *etc.*

A noteworthy feature of the FASB's definitions is their dependence on unspecified "accounting rules and conventions" [FASB, 1977, p. 19], again in the tradition of the definitions provided by two previous authoritative bodies, the American Institute of [Certified Public] Accountants' Committee on Terminology and Accounting Principles Board.[4] This qualification appears to be inconsistent with the claim that conceptual frameworks can lead to the selection of appropriate principles and rules of measurement and recognition. How can a

---

[3]Most and Winters [1977] analyzed the objectives promulgated by the Trueblood Study Group, APBS 4, several of the Big Eight firms, the AAA, the National Association of Accountants, *etc.* They found that of the ten main objectives issued by the Trueblood Study Group (Objectives 3 on cash flows, and 11 on non-profit accounting, were omitted), eight similar objectives could be found in APBS 4. Similarly, Objectives 1, 2, 4, 5, 6, 7, and 8 in the Trueblood Report had antecedents in from five to as many as eight other statements of objectives.

[4]For example, the Committee on Terminology defined assets in Accounting Terminology Bulletin No. 1 [AICPA, 1953] as follows:

"Something represented by a debit balance that is or would be properly carried forward upon a closing of books of account according to the *rules or principles of accounting* ... on the basis that it represents either a property right ... or is properly applicable to the future" (para. 26, emphasis added).

The APB in its Statement No. 4 defined assets as: "economic resources of an enterprise that are recognized and measured *in conformity with generally accepted accounting principles*. . . ." [AICPA, 1970, para. 132] (emphasis added).

conceptual framework guide choices from among alternative principles and rules if the elements of the framework are defined in these very same terms?

The dependence of the FASB's definitions on unspecified rules and conventions leaves little basis on which to evaluate them, since a specific evaluation of these definitions would be speculative as long as we do not know what conventions will be adopted by the FASB at the subsequent stages of its project.

A second feature of the FASB's definitions is that they provide only the necessary conditions for a resource or obligation to be included in the asset or liability categories, respectively, rather than both the necessary and sufficient conditions. For example, a resource other than cash needs to have three characteristics to qualify as an asset:

> (a) the resource must . . . contribute directly or indirectly to future cash inflows (or to obviating future cash outflows), (b) the enterprise must be able to obtain the benefit from it, and (c) the transaction or event giving rise to the enterprise's right to or interest in the benefit must already have occurred [FASB, 1977; para. 47].

Similarly, three characteristics are also necessary for an obligation to qualify as a liability:

> (a) the obligation must involve future sacrifice of resources—a future transfer (or a foregoing of a future receipt) of cash, goods, or services, (b) it must be an obligation of the enterprise, and (c) the transaction or event giving rise to the enterprise's obligation must already have occurred [FASB, 1977, para. 49].

Since these are only necessary characteristics, their presence does not imply that an obligation will qualify as a liability or that a resource will qualify as an asset. All of these conditions may be satisfied and an obligation still may not qualify as an asset or, alternatively, as a liability. In the absence of sufficient conditions, these definitions will be of limited use to accountants.

The definitions of revenues and expenses given by the FASB follow the traditional practice of defining these as increases and decreases in assets or decreases and increases in liabilities, respectively, provided that the changes in assets and liabilities relate to the earning activities of the enterprise (broadly defined). Gains and losses are defined as increases and decreases in net assets, *other* than revenues and expenses or investments and withdrawals by owners.

The definitions of revenue and expense in APB Statement No. 4 [AICPA, 1970] are similar to the above except that the definitions there do not explicitly distinguish between revenues and gains nor between expenses and losses. A distinction between revenues and gains is also made by Sprouse and Moonitz [1962, p. 50] and by Paton and Littleton [1940, p. 60]. But while a distinction between expense and loss is made by Sprouse and Moonitz, Paton and Littleton do not do so. Indeed, they do not even provide an explicit definition of expense, which is consistent with their emphasis on *cost* rather than on the asset-expense distinction. It is not until their discussion of income that Paton and Littleton stress a distinction between costs matched against revenues (expenses) and those deferred to future periods (assets) [1940, Ch. V.].

On the whole, the differences between the FASB and the APB definitions are small and seem unimportant. An explicit discussion of the main sources of disagreement would have been more fruitful than a "new" set of definitions. Circular as they are, the conflict on definitions seems to us to be only a proxy debate whose principal, to which we return later, is the debate about the accounting rules themselves.

Characteristics and Limitations of Financial Information

A part of the last major section of the Exposure Draft has been included in the introductory section of SFAC 1. There we find statements about: (a) the reliance of accounting on monetary transactions, (b) the emphasis of financial reports on individual enterprises and not on individual consumers or on society as a whole, (c) the role of estimation in accounting, (d) the fact that much of financial information reflects past events, (e) the coexistence of other sources of financial information, and (f) the costs of financial reporting.

The more well-known desirable "qualities" of accounting information, such as relevance, freedom from bias, comparability, consistency, understandability, verifiability, etc., are also referenced in the Exposure Draft, but are excluded from SFAC 1. The FASB acknowledges that trade-offs among these qualities are not easily accomplished in practice. The objectives and definitions of the elements of financial statements are expected to guide the Board in future phases of the conceptual framework project when these trade-off issues arise in more concrete form.

The characteristics and desirable "qualities" of accounting information discussed in the Exposure Draft are familiar to accountants and appear as "qualitative" objectives in APB Statement No. 4 and as components of accounting concepts or as postulates in other conceptual frameworks.

The above review of SFAC 1 and of certain parts of the Exposure Draft reveals little that is new on the objectives of financial reporting and definitions of the elements of financial statements. Lack of novelty, of course, does not imply worthlessness. It is quite possible that the FASB's effort may yet have the potential to yield some benefits. The FASB has suggested that the following benefits may manifest themselves as a result of achieving agreement on the conceptual framework [1976c, pp. 5–6]:

1. Guide the body responsible for establishing standards,
2. Provide a frame of reference for resolving accounting questions in the absence of a specific promulgated standard,
3. Determine bounds for judgment in preparing financial statements,
4. Increase financial statement users' understanding of and confidence in financial statements, and
5. Enhance comparability.

In reviewing this early part of the conceptual framework, it is probably fair to ask how reasonable it is to expect that the above-mentioned benefits will actually be realized. Of course, this evaluation may have to be changed when all the pieces of the conceptual project are in place. However, the evaluation of this part of the project, tentative as it is, should not await completion of the project.

In the following section we examine the degree to which the first two benefits stated by the FASB, *viz.*, guidance for establishing standards and resolution of accounting questions in the absence of standards, are likely to be attained on the basis of the given objectives and definitions. The effect of the project on users' understanding of, and confidence in, the financial statements is an empirical question and is beyond the scope of this review paper.[5] We are not sure what precisely is meant by (3), determination of the bounds of judgment in preparation of financial statements, and by (5), enhancement of comparability. Since the empirical or analytical contents of these benefits are not clear, it is difficult to evaluate, beyond purely subjective opinion, whether and to what extent these benefits will be derived from the FASB's objectives and definitions. We shall, therefore, confine ourselves to an evaluation of the first two benefits stated by the FASB.

RESOLUTION OF THREE ACCOUNTING ISSUES

As a means of evaluating the potential benefits the FASB's objectives and definitions may provide in resolving accounting issues, we selected three which have been debated for some time and which have received much attention from accountants and others. The issues are: (1) deferred credits, (2) treatment of costs of exploration in the oil and gas industry, and (3) reports on current values of assets and liabilities.

Deferred Credits

The FASB defines liabilities as "financial representations of obligations of a particular enterprise to transfer economic resources to other entities in the future as a result of a past transaction or event affecting the enterprise" [FASB, 1977, para. 49]. No specific reference to deferred credits appears in this section, although reference is made to liabilities arising from the collection of cash or other resources *before* providing goods or services, or from selling products subject to warranty. It is also stated that "legal enforceability of a claim is not a prerequisite to representing it as a liability" if future transfer is probable.

The APB, in Statement No. 4, is more direct:

> Liabilities—economic obligations of an enterprise that are recognized and measured in conformity with generally accepted accounting principles. Liabilities also include certain deferred credits *that are not obligations* but that are recognized and measured in conformity with generally accepted accounting principles [AICPA, 1970, Para. 132, emphasis added].

A footnote to the last sentence specifically singles out deferred taxes as an example of liabilities which are not obligations!

Neither Paton and Littleton [1940] nor Sprouse and Moonitz [1962] refer to deferred credits arising from differences between financial and tax reporting, with both concentrating on the obligations of enterprises to convey assets or to perform services in the future.[6]

---

[5]The FASB may wish to commission such a study now, so that a preconceptual framework measure of confidence and understandability can be taken before this opportunity is lost.

[6]The issue of deferred taxes did not appear in the accounting literature until about 1942. See AICPA [1942].

The FASB's definition of liabilities is so general that at this stage we cannot predict the Board's position on deferred taxes. However, those who favor the recognition of deferred taxes can adopt a somewhat broad interpretation of the FASB's definition of liabilities to justify the inclusion of deferred taxes as an element of financial statements, particularly at the individual asset level. In contrast, those who do not could take the FASB's statements literally and just as easily argue against the inclusion of deferred taxes. Hence, these broad definitions will not help resolve the issue.

Accounting for Oil and Gas Exploration Costs

Bitter controversy still surrounds the issue of how to account for petroleum exploration costs. The issue surfaced in the petroleum industry some two decades ago when the full-cost method was introduced. But the essence of the issue has an earlier precedent.

Hatfield [1927, Chap. 2] considers the problem of whether the acquisition costs of successful experiments should be limited to the costs of the successful experiments themselves or whether they should also include the costs of unsuccessful experiments. Hence, the full-cost versus successful-efforts debate is part of a more general issue of what constitutes the costs of assets when the acquisition process is risky.

The issue reflects a difference of opinion regarding the level of aggregation at which the historical acquisition cost principle is applied to record assets for subsequent amortization. But there is no reference in the Exposure Draft to alternative levels of aggregation for asset recognition and measurement. The only explicit statement bearing on this problem is that "[i]nformation about enterprise earnings and its components measured by accrual accounting generally provides a better indication of enterprise performance than information about current cash receipts and payments" [FASB, 1978, para. 44]. However, both full-cost and successful-efforts accounting are forms of accrual accounting, so that proponents of the former (*e.g.*, the Federal Trade Commission) have the same support for their position as do proponents of the latter (*e.g.*, the FASB). The fact that the framework supports two opposing principles of accounting is preliminary evidence that the framework is unlikely to be a useful guide in resolving this issue.

Selecting the Valuation Basis for Assets and Liabilities

Alternative theories of valuation and income were discussed in accounting texts published 50 years ago. For example, Hatfield [1927] states:

> Having accepted the principle that the original valuation of assets is normally their cost price, and having noticed the practical and theoretical difficulty in determining the exact cost price, there remains the more important question as to subsequent revaluations of assets. . . . Shall the accountant base revaluation on (1) the original cost . . . (2) on the estimated present cost of acquiring a similar asset . . . or (3) on what the asset might be expected to bring if thrown upon the market in the process of liquidation [p. 73]?

Similar discussions appear even earlier in Paton [1922], in Hatfield [1909], and in a much more detailed fashion in Canning [1929].

Liquidation values were generally ruled out in such discussions because they seemed inconsistent with the going-concern notion, and since discounted values had not yet achieved popularity then, the choice between alternative valuation bases was usually limited to historical or replacement costs.

With respect to these alternatives, it might be informative to quote some statements from Paton and Littleton [1940], who, some accountants believe, had no tolerance for valuation bases other than historical cost accounting. On pages 122–123, they state:

> With the passing of time, however, the value of the particular productive factor—as reflected in the current cost or market price of like units—is subject to change in either direction, and when a change occurs it becomes clear that the actual cost of the unit still in service or still attaching to operating activity is not fully acceptable as a measure of immediate economic significance.

Later, on page 123, they ask the question:

> [W]ould accounting meet more adequately the proper needs of the various parties concerned if, in the process of separating the charges to revenue from the unexpired balances, the estimated replacement costs or other evidence of current values were regularly substituted for recorded costs incurred? There seem to be no convincing reasons for an affirmative answer. Recorded costs are objectively determined data; estimated current values are largely matters of opinion and for some types of cost factors are conspicuously unreliable.

In the section on "Limitations of Estimated Replacement Cost," they comment: "In the first place continuous appraisals at the best are costly, and can be used only if the benefits to be derived clearly justify the additional cost incurred" (p. 132). They then suggest that in periods of price stability and situations involving complex enterprises, such benefits are unlikely to exceed the costs of implementation. Finally,

> The fair conclusion is that the cost standard of plant accounting holds up well, as compared with any alternative plan, when faced with typical business needs and conditions. . . . At the same time it would be going too far to hold that under no circumstances can any useful purpose be served by introducing into the accounts and reports, by appropriate methods, data designed to supplement the figures of actual cost [Paton and Littleton, p. 134].

The latter statement led them to recommend that alternative valuations be limited to supplementary schedules.

The above are practical, not theoretical, arguments and are probably representative of the views of many accountants who have expressed a reluctance to accept current costs in published financial statements. No conceptual framework, however logically conceived, can counter practical issues regarding the reliability of *estimates* of, say, replacement costs. The "true" replacement costs of assets are not observed until those assets are actually replaced (nor are "true" exit prices observed unless the assets are sold). So the issue is not whether current costs are useful "in making economic decisions"; rather, the issue is what criteria may be used to alternative estimates of unknown parameters. Unfortunately, neither SFAC 1 nor the Exposure Draft addresses this problem of estimation.

On the basis of the above analysis, we conclude that the results of the FASB's effort to write objectives and definitions are hardly different from previous attempts of this nature and, as such, are unlikely to help resolve major accounting issues or to set standards of financial reporting as the FASB had expected. Pessimistic as our conclusions are, they should not surprise those familiar with the standard-setting process during the past 30 years. The charge of the Trueblood Study Group was very similar to the first two benefits expected by the FASB:

> The main purpose of the [Trueblood] study is to refine the objectives of financial statements. Refined objectives should facilitate establishment of guidelines and criteria for improving accounting and financial reporting [AICPA, 1973, p. 67].

Both the supporters and the critics expressed doubts that this purpose of the study would be met. Bedford [1974, p. 16], while largely supporting the report, said, "I refer to the extremely difficult task of logically deriving accounting standards from objectives—not that I think it can be done but because I fear some will think it is appropriate." Miller [1974, p. 20], a critic of the report, stated, "The greatest shortcoming of the Trueblood Report is, it seems to me, that the accept/reject criteria are not sufficiently precise. I wish Professor Sorter and his associates had been less subtle." Sprouse stated, "I have no illusions about the use of such a document to prove that a particular accounting standard is 'right' " [1974, p. 28]. These doubts about the accomplishments of the Trueblood Report are very similar to our reservations about the fruits of the FASB's labors.

Since our conclusion about the potential value and effect of the FASB's objectives and definitions is pessimistic, we are led to inquire into the very nature of objectives of financial accounting and the fundamental difficulty of defining them in a social setting. The inability of different authoritative drafts of objectives produced in the last decade to achieve general acceptance on a conceptual framework is hardly due to the lack of diligence on the part of their authors; it may stem from addressing the wrong problem.

THE NATURE OF OBJECTIVES OF FINANCIAL ACCOUNTING

> An objective is something toward which effort is directed, an aim or end of action, a goal [FASB, 1974, p. 13].

Financial accounting is a social or multiperson activity. Members of society engage in financial accounting or in other activities when they are motivated by their individual goals and objectives. We shall assume that the meaning of the terms "goal" and "objective," as they apply to individuals or homogeneous groups of individuals, is self-evident for the purpose of the present discussion. Given a clear definition of the objectives that motivate each individual to engage in an aspect of a social activity, what meaning can we assign to the term "objective" when it is applied not to individuals or groups, but to the activity itself? In what sense can a social activity be said to have an objective?

We suggest three different interpretations of the meaning of the objectives of a social activity: functional objectives, common objectives, and dominant group objectives. In this section we shall first explain the meaning and implications of each interpretation and then examine the nature of the objectives of financial accounting in light of these interpretations.

Functional Objectives

The union of individual objectives could be referred to as the objective of the social activity in a *functional sense*. A functional explanation of social phenomena assumes that the consequences of a social arrangement or behavior are essential elements of the *causes* of that behavior (see Stinchcombe [1968], esp. pp. 80–100). Objectives that motivate individuals to engage in an activity on a continuing basis must also be the consequences of the activity; otherwise the individuals will not continue to engage in it. Thus, the functional explanation implies that the union of individual objectives can be identified without probing into the motivations of individuals by simply observing the set of consequences of the social activity. These consequences themselves therefore can be regarded as the objectives of the social activity. Since the consequences are observable phenomena, they can be objectively determined. However, the set of consequences may be so large that a complex and lengthy description may be the result. Nevertheless, a statement of consequences is one possible interpretation of the objective of a social activity.

Common Objectives

A second possibility is to define the intersection of individual objectives, *i.e.*, the subset of objectives common to all individuals, as the objective of the social activity. By definition, common objectives are equal to or fewer in number than the functional objectives. If all individuals are motivated by an identical set of objectives, common objectives are the same as the functional objectives; if each individual is motivated by different objectives, the intersection is null and there are no common objectives.

Dominant Group Objectives

A third possible interpretation of the objectives of a social activity is the objectives of an individual or subset of all individuals in the society who are able, through whatever mechanism, to impose their will on all others involved in the activity. In the presence of such a dominant group, the objectives of individuals not included in the group become irrelevant, since the dominant group objectives become the objectives of the social activity. Obviously, this interpretation cannot be used if the dominant group does not have the power to impose its will on the society.

Accounting as a Social Activity

Accounting is a social activity engaged in by (1) corporate managers who perform in activities that are recorded by the accounting system; (2) corporate accountants who gather the data and compile the reports; (3) auditors who scrutinize and attest to the fairness of the reports; (4) outside government and private agencies, investors, employees, customers, *etc.*, who read these reports; and (5) college and university personnel who train their students in accounting. Each group of individuals engaged in financial accounting possesses its own private motives or objectives leading to this involvement. In the light of the three possible interpretations of the objectives of a social activity discussed above, what meaning can we assign to the objectives of financial accounting?

Functional Interpretation of Accounting Objectives

Since all consequences of accounting are included in the functional interpretation of objectives, consider the following sample of objectives that would qualify under this interpretation:

1. Increase employment of accountants, auditors, and teachers of accounting;
2. Help companies market their securities to creditors and investors;
3. Help outsiders monitor the performance of management;
4. Maximize the wealth of the present owners of the company;
5. Minimize income tax burdens of companies;
6. Aid in controlling inflation;
7. Disclose the impact of enterprise operations on the quality of the environment;
8. Help management avoid hostile takeover attempts;
9. Systematically record, classify, and report data on the business transactions of the enterprise;
10. Aid in enforcing anti-trust laws.

Each of the objectives listed above could be viewed as legitimate by one or more sets of individuals involved in financial accounting. Note that a complete description of the consequences of financial accounting will include not only "facts" but what is regarded as "fiction" by specific individuals. For example, a manager may regard the avoidance of hostile takeover attempts as a valid objective of financial statements while a shareholder may believe that the effect of financial accounting practices on avoidance of hostile takeovers is non-existent. In order to be included in the set, it is sufficient that someone involved in financial accounting believe in that consequence or use it as a personal objective. Note also that this set includes contradictory objectives and consequences. For example, management may believe that one accounting method for inventory accounting will help market the firm's securities, whereas shareholders may believe that an alternative inventory method is more revealing of management's competence. Similarly, the objective of accountants to increase the demand for their services may be in conflict with the objective of corporate managers to maximize their own or the shareholders' wealth.

Although probably not intended as such, the objectives stated by the FASB may be viewed as functional objectives. For example, the first objective given by the FASB is:

> Financial reporting should provide information that is useful to present and potential investors and creditors and other users in making rational investment, credit, and similar decisions. The information should be comprehensible to those who have a reasonable understanding of business and

economic activities and are willing to study the information with reasonable diligence [FASB, 1978, para. 34].

If "should" is removed from each sentence, this objective is reduced to a mere statement of an empirically verified and a widely accepted consequence of financial accounting. Financial accounting does, indeed, provide information useful to investors and creditors, and it is comprehensible to those willing to study the reports with reasonable diligence. But, being purely descriptive, functional objectives themselves cannot serve as normative goals to guide policy making. Nevertheless, if they are reasonably complete, they can serve to improve the understanding of the role of financial accounting in society.

There is reason to believe that the FASB did not intend to offer its statement as one of functional objectives. First, the statement is far from complete, concentrating on a few facts and a few unverified theories about the consequences of financial accounting, without any effort to present, for example, the motivations behind the supply side of financial accounting services. And the normative tone of the statement precludes the possibility that the FASB has attempted to provide a statement of the union of individual objectives of all persons involved in financial accounting.

Common-Objectives Interpretation of Accounting Objectives

A second possible interpretation of the objectives of accounting is the subset of individual objectives which are common to all individuals involved in accounting. Cyert and Ijiri's [1974] model of heterogeneous interests can be modified to apply to the objectives. Cyert and Ijiri use a Venn diagram to illustrate their point. The elements of the sets considered by them are *pieces of information* which various interest groups—users, managers, and auditors—may be willing to use, provide, or attest, and the intersection of the three sets is the actual information provided by the financial statements. The choice problem posed by Cyert and Ijiri could be moved to a higher level of abstraction by considering the sets of *accounting principles* that each group would prefer to be used in the preparation of financial statements. A still higher level of abstraction would involve specific sets of objectives that each group would seek to fulfill through its involvement in financial accounting.

It is conceivable that the intersection of the three sets will become progressively smaller as we move to higher levels of abstraction from pieces of information to accounting principles to objectives, in which case the Venn diagrams at the three levels of abstraction might appear as in Figure 1.

We do not know whether the intersection of the sets grows larger or smaller as we move from items of information to principles to objectives and vice versa.[7] Generally, agreement on principles and objectives will be easier to obtain if such statements are sufficiently vague so as to allow room for various interest groups to adopt their own interpretations. But vagueness, while necessary to obtain initial agreement, will reduce the usefulness of a statement of objectives in setting accounting standards. The proposition is borne out by the statements of objectives we have seen thus far. The vagueness of statements of this nature

[7]The question is subject to debate; see, for example, the analysis of responses of various parties to the FASB's pronouncements by Coe and Sorter [1977–78] and Watts and Zimmerman [1978].

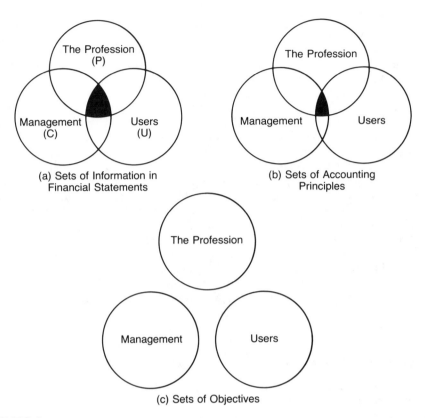

(a) Sets of Information in
Financial Statements

(b) Sets of Accounting
Principles

(c) Sets of Objectives

FIGURE 1
Accounting Information, Principles and Objectives Preferred by Various Parties

is consistent with the level of generality at which agreement is sought. It allows enough room for each interested party to maneuver to protect its own interest when actual accounting standards and rules are written.

Some empirical evidence is available on the non-overlapping nature of accounting objectives. In 1976, when the FASB carried out a survey to determine how many people involved in various aspects of financial accounting agreed with the Trueblood objectives, the Board was surprised to learn that only 37 percent of the respondents believed that providing information useful for making economic decisions was an objective of financial accounting:

> Let me point this up for you. In our first discussion memorandum on the conceptual framework of accounting, . . . we sought an expression of opinion from respondents on the following as a basic objective of financial statements; it is taken directly from the Trueblood Report:
>
>> The basic objective of financial statements is to provide information useful for making economic decisions.
>
> Could there be disagreement with a statement such as this? I am sure you will be astounded to learn that only 37 percent of our respondents were able to recommend the adoption of this objective. Twenty-two percent

recommended that it be rejected out of hand; and 10 percent insisted that it needed further study. It is difficult to believe that only 37 percent can agree that the basic objective of financial statements is to provide information useful for making economic decisions. I think this suggests the problem quite clearly [Armstrong, 1977, p. 77].

We are puzzled at the Board's puzzlement. Why should we believe all groups of interested parties would adopt the provision of information useful for making economic decisions as their motivation for being involved in the financial reporting process? For example, we should not be surprised if auditors, like everyone else, seek to maximize their own wealth through participation in the accounting process. If the provision of economically useful information implies greater exposure to the risk of being sued without corresponding benefits of higher compensation, they will not see the provision of economically useful information (however defined) as *their* objective of the financial accounting process. Similar arguments could be made about any other interested party who might have been surveyed by the FASB. The members of each group probably stated what they believed were their objectives for being involved in the process.

At present, we do not have data to determine which, if any, objectives are actually common to all participants in accounting. Consequently we cannot yet determine whether the common-objectives approach is a feasible interpretation of the objectives of accounting.

Dominant Group Interpretation of Accounting Objectives

Unlike the Trueblood Study Group, the FASB has not stated explicitly how it selected its subset of objectives from a much larger set of potential objectives. But from the objectives which the FASB did select, we can infer that it has followed the Trueblood Study Group in relying on the notion of user-primacy in financial accounting.[8] This notion represents the dominant-group approach to defining the objective of a social activity that we identified above.

Most of the discussion appearing in the literature on the objectives of financial accounting during the past ten years tends to rely on the notion of user-primacy. Beaver and Demski [1974], for example, concentrated their attention on the problems generated by the heterogeneity of tastes among the users of financial statements, on the assumption that this group would be the primary group whose interests would be reflected in the objectives of financial statements officially adopted by the authoritative agencies:

> There seems to be a consensus that the primary purpose of financial reporting is to provide information to financial statement users. Yet, the basic, fundamental role of objectives within this utilitarian, user-primacy framework remains obscure—largely we speculate because the problem of heterogeneous users has not been forcefully addressed. . . . A basic pur-

---

[8]"While mindful of the importance of the audit function, the Study Group has been primarily concerned with the nature of information and not its attestability" [AICPA, 1973, p. 10]. The Trueblood Study Group left the problem of attestation and the interests of the management to "implementation" and did not consider these interests worthy of consideration within the set of objectives of financial reporting.

pose of this summary and synthesis, then, is to offer a view of the nature and role of financial accounting objectives that explicitly rests on heterogeneous users [p. 170].

Cyert and Ijiri [1974] considered the heterogeneity of preferences for *information sets* among three diverse groups (assuming that the intragroup heterogeneity is unimportant) and analyzed the problem of determining accounting standards under the assumption that the user interest is primary. Referring to 1(a) of our Figure 1, they stated:

> This is a logical, if not a unique approach since in many user-corporate relationships the corporation is *accountable* to the users for its activities. If the users are in a position to demand information from the corporation based on a contractual or statutory relationship between them, it makes sense to define what Circle U is and then attempt to move Circle C toward it. Furthermore, in the interaction of the three groups, the profession's purpose is to help keep a smooth flow of information from the corporation to the users. Hence, Circle P is clearly subordinate to Circles C and U. Thus, it is perhaps the most practical way to state as objectives the need to move Circles C and P toward the goal of a newly defined Circle U [p. 32].

If the user group had the power to enforce its preferences at no cost to itself, the objectives of this group could be called the objectives of financial accounting. This would simplify the problem of setting objectives. Indeed, if the user group were homogeneous, the problem would be trivial. However, there is little evidence that the user group has the power to impose its preferences on financial accounting.

A considerable amount of confusion about the objectives of financial accounting has been generated by comparing them to the objectives of the firm. For example, Bedford [1974] notes, "The basic objective of financial statements is to provide information useful for making economic decisions.' This statement is as direct as the statement that 'the basic objective of private enterprise is to make a profit' *and it is equally operational*" [p. 15; emphasis is added]. Few would dispute that, as stated, the profit-maximizing objective of the firm is merely a shorthand way of stating the objectives of the *shareholders* of the firm under the assumption of homogeneous shareholder preferences; it does not represent the specific objectives of the managers, employees, creditors or of any other parties inside or outside the firm. Besides, profit is a net concept in the sense that it is the difference between revenues and expenses, and its use as an objective implies that additional revenue should not be generated beyond the point at which the additional cost exceeds it. Provision of information for decision making, unlike profit, is a gross concept and cannot provide guidelines as to how far the firm should go in providing information for economic decisions.

The analogy to the theory of the firm is more apparent than real. In that theory, if the objective is to maximize the owners' wealth, production-investment variables can be chosen in view of the cost and revenue functions which serve as the environmental variables. What is the FASB (or any other agency entrusted with the task of writing accounting standards) supposed to maximize or optimize? When the FASB recommends that the objective of financial statements is to provide information useful for making rational credit and investment decisions, should we understand that the provision of such information should be maximized without regard to the cost and other consequences of making such information available? What are the variables over which to optimize, and what is the trade-off among these variables? Unless these trade-offs are defined, a statement of objectives that will be useful in arriving at the most satisfying accounting standards cannot be said to have been laid down, nor can there be a way of determining if the recommended objectives have been achieved by a given accounting standard.

The extraordinary emphasis of the recent pronouncements regarding objectives of financial accounting on user primacy can probably be traced to inappropriate applications of single-person decision theory in a multi-person context. In single-person decision theory, the generation of information is regarded as a more-or-less mechanical process which remains unaffected by its ultimate uses. The person making the choice of an information system out of the available alternatives calculates the expected present value of the benefits to be derived from the use of information produced by each system and makes the choice on the basis of the excess of these benefits over the respective costs. The same underlying event-generating mechanism is assumed to be common to all information systems, and it remains unaffected by the choice of information system made. This model, developed by the physical scientists and engineers for the control of mechanical or inanimate systems, is inappropriate for social systems, where the object of control is not an unchanging chemical process but a human being with learning capabilities. In control systems where human beings stand at both the sending and receiving end of the information channel, the flow of information affects behavior at both ends. We cannot choose an information line on the assumption of a constant behavior pattern of the persons at the other end. Indeed, the two-way effect of the information makes the designation of one party as user and the other as sender somewhat ambiguous. A user-primacy notion in the selection of objectives of financial accounting which ignores how firm managers are likely to adjust their behavior to the new information system (and how this adjustment in management behavior will affect the interests of the so-called users) represents a very short-sighted view of the whole problem. As such, solutions derived from this simplified approach will not work. A similar argument could be offered regarding the exclusion of the auditors from the "primary" groups whose interests must be explicitly considered in any realistic set of objectives of financial accounting.

To summarize, we have examined three possible interpretations of objectives of social activities in general and financial accounting in particular. We have concluded that the union of individual objectives, being too diverse and contradictory, cannot serve to guide policy; intersection of individual objectives may be null; the dominant-group objectives, assuming user primacy, do not reflect the economic reality of the power of suppliers in the accounting marketplace and are, therefore, unworkable. Fundamental to an understanding of the nature of financial accounting as they are, these difficulties in interpreting the objectives of financial accounting have received little attention in the literature. This lack of attention stands in sharp contrast to the repeated efforts to prepare a statement of objectives and definitions and leads us to examine the possible reasons that may stand behind the efforts to prepare an authoritative statement of objectives and definitions.

WHY SEARCH FOR A CONCEPTUAL FRAMEWORK?

In the first section of the paper, we compared the SFAC 1 and the Exposure Draft to the previous attempts of this nature and found little substantive difference. In the second section, we examined whether the first two of the five benefits claimed by the FASB may reasonably be expected to flow from these statements and reached a negative conclusion. Then we probed the very meaning of the term "objectives" as applied to financial accounting and found that term too ill-defined. These conclusions led us to inquire into reasons why authoritative bodies have continued to search for objectives and a conceptual framework of accounting. We consider several of these.

The first reason could be that our negative conclusions in section two regarding the usefulness of these statements in resolving accounting issues and standard-setting problems are wrong. If so, it should be easy for someone to illustrate, possibly using issues other than the three we selected, that these objectives and definitions will indeed help resolve the accounting issues. We are not aware of any such illustrations.

A second reason for the search for conceptual frameworks could be provided in terms of the three potential benefits claimed by the FASB and not examined in this paper. It may turn out that the issuance of the conceptual framework increases the users' confidence in, and understanding of, financial statements. Someone may also give workable definitions of "bounds for judgment" and comparability and show that the issuance of conceptual frameworks may have desirable consequences in these respects. Again, neither the theoretical arguments nor the empirical evidence that bears on these issues is available.

Two further reasons are possible: One lies in the form in which accounting problems are brought to the authoritative bodies, while the second lies in the attempts of the accounting profession to keep the rule-making power in its own hands.

Repeated efforts of authoritative bodies to define the conceptual framework of accounting in general and the elements of financial statements in particular may arise from the genuine belief that a determination of precise definitions of certain terms will somehow help resolve accounting controversies.[9] Such belief is reinforced each time an accounting controversy surfaces and the proponents of alternative methods present their arguments in the established terminology of accounting so as to convince the policy makers that the weight of tradition, so highly prized in accounting, is on their side. Given a strong motivation to have an accounting standard accepted which is favorable to one's interests, it is not difficult to devise an argument as to why a given transaction should be recorded in a certain way under the currently accepted definitions of accounting terms.[10] Since the views of various parties are presented to the policy-making bodies not in the form of conflicting private interests, but in the form of conflicting interpretations of accounting definitions, it may appear that a clearer definition of each accounting term will solve the problem. A frank discussion of the private interests of various contending groups may be tactically disad-

---

[9]See Zeff [1978, pp. 57–58] for a typology of the arguments offered in accounting controversies.

[10]See Kitchen [1954] for a stimulating discussion of the problems of definition in accounting.

vantageous in open public discourse.[11] Hence, the overblown emphasis on authoritative definitions. However, definitions, no matter how carefully worded, cannot bear the burden of the struggle for economic advantage between various interest groups. Legal definitions survive in a similar environment only because their interpretations by the courts are backed by the power of the state to enforce them, a power not available to the FASB.

The conceptual framework-seeking behavior of the FASB and its predecessors can also be explained in terms of a self-interest perceived by the public accounting profession. The profession has long argued that its interests are best served if it can maintain control over prescription of accounting standards. This is revealed in its protests against any hint that the control of the profession over the standard-setting process may be weakened. Fear of governmental intervention has long been, and continues to be, the major reason for calls for action in the profession.[12] Consider, for example, the following:

> If the practitioners, after sufficient time has elapsed, have not come to some substantial agreement as to what are or should be considered accepted accounting principles and practices, we may well expect the Commission's [SEC's] staff accountants to prepare, and the Commission to publish what it shall demand in the way of such practices ... [Smith, 1935, p. 327].

Appropriate as it is today, note that the above statement appeared in an article published almost 45 years ago. Disagreements centering on diverse accounting standards continue to attract much of the criticism leveled at the accounting profession and are the source of the greatest threat to the profession's control over the standard-setting process. The presence of diverse accounting practices hurts the credibility of the standard-setting bodies in two ways. First, the existence of alternative accounting methods is taken as *prima facie* evidence that the accounting standard-setting body is not doing its work properly and is simply allowing firms to record transactions in an arbitrary fashion. Second, whenever the standard-setting body proscribes the use of all but one of the alternative accounting methods, the advocates of the methods were no longer permitted to criticize the agency for being arbitrary in not protecting their interests. No matter what it does, a body like the FASB can expect to find itself criticized by powerful interest groups. A good example is provided by the debate on accounting for oil and gas exploration costs. The FASB was instructed to develop a uniform accounting standard for the oil and gas industry or face the threat of having such a standard written by a government agency. When the FASB chose the successful-efforts over the full-cost method, it found, aligned

---

[11]Since everybody is assumed to be serving the interests of the information user, proponents of all accounting methods argue their case because it will benefit such user. Recall that in the heyday of the LIFO controversy, a major argument for LIFO was that it yields a better measure of income. Watts and Zimmerman [1979] have attempted to explain the existence of some normative theories in financial accounting, using a parallel argument.

[12]Of course, the auditors' fear of government intervention is asymmetric. Consistent with their self-interests, they do want the government to continue to require an audit of certain business firms to ensure demand for their services but want to keep the standard-setting process free of government control.

against it, a powerful industry group as well as some government departments and agencies. Being largely an offspring of the accounting profession, the FASB has (as did the APB) little defense against the criticism that it does not have legitimate authority to make decisions which affect wealth transfers among members of society.

Thus, a body like the FASB needs a conceptual framework simply to boost its public standing.[13] A conceptual framework provides the basis for arguing that: (1) the objective of its activities is to serve the users of the financial statements (it is easier to use the public-interest argument for the user group than for any other group), and (2) it selects among accounting alternatives on the basis of broadly accepted objectives and not because of pressures applied by various interest groups seeking a favorable ruling from the Board. The ability, intelligence, ethical character, and past services, *etc.*, of the members of the FASB are not sufficient to convince the parties adversely affected by its rulings that it makes social choices through an impartial consideration of conflicting interests in society. Rather, a conceptual framework is needed to provide the rationalization for its choices.

If a more representative body were to take over the function of setting accounting standards, perhaps there would be less of a need for a conceptual framework. Indeed, the demand to develop a conceptual framework may be inversely related to the power of enforcement which the standard-setting agency can command. For example, the Securities and Exchange Commission, which has the legal power to enforce its Accounting Series Releases, has not been hampered by the fact that it has not yet enunciated a conceptual framework of accounting.

CONCLUDING REMARKS

There is little evidence that official statements of objectives of financial accounting have had any direct effect on the determination of financial accounting standards. Whenever the APB or the FASB has had to consider a financial accounting standard, various interest groups presented arguments to support the methods that each perceived to be in its own best interests. The standards issued had to be compromises among the contending interests.[14] Whether the standard-setting process stays in the private sector or is transferred to some public agency, this feature is unlikely to change. What, then, will likely be the effect of the FASB's Conceptual Framework Project on the development of financial accounting standards in the future?

Our initial guess is that the objectives selected by the Board will be ignored in future rule-making activities, just as were those from previous authoritative attempts. Following the publication of these objectives, the Board will probably feel obliged to pay lip service to them in its future pronouncements, but these pronouncements will not be affected in any substantive way by what is contained in the present documents.

[13]A discussion of this public-interest argument appears in AAA[1977b].

[14]See, for example, Horngren [1973, p. 61], "My hypothesis is that the setting of accounting standards is as much a product of political action as of flawless logic or empirical findings."

It might have been a more fruitful exercise for the FASB to develop a set of objectives for itself and not for the entire social activity called financial reporting. A few examples of such objectives are provided for consideration:

First, the Board could explicitly recognize the nature of financial accounting as a social activity which affects a varied set of interests, both of those who actively participate and those who do not.[15] As the interests of each group are affected by the actions of the Board, it must expect to hear arguments in support of, and against, its decisions. The representations made by these parties could be viewed in the context of their own private interests. In the past, accountants in public practice (*i.e.*, auditors) have tended to be more vocal in their reactions to the Board's actions than have other parties. But perhaps accountants in public practice should have less direct influence on the rule-making process in the future. In its statement of objectives, the Board could define mechanisms for arriving at a compromise ruling after a hearing has been given to all affected groups in society. The Board's primary objective would simply be to arrive at a compromise ruling after considering various points of view on each issue.

A second objective for the FASB might be to limit the detail and specificity of its accounting standards. The pressure to write increasingly detailed and specific accounting standards is great and, in recent years, the resistance of the Board to such pressures seems to be weakening. In this connection, we might note that one of three conditions laid down by the Council of the Institute of Chartered Accountants in England and Wales for approving recommendations on accounting principles to its members was simply that the document be reasonably concise in form (see Zeff [1972, p. 11]).[16] Judging from the length and detail of some of its recent pronouncements (*e.g.*, those dealing with leases and oil and gas exploration costs), the FASB seems to have abandoned an attempt to keep its Statements of Financial Accounting Standards concise.

A third objective of the Board could be to abstain from issuing an accounting standard unless the pronouncement could command a substantial majority. The recent move to lower the minimum voting requirement for issuing an FASB recommendation to a simple majority of seven members will probably increase the frequency of FASB pronouncements which are widely opposed by large segments of interested parties and therefore undermine the basis of its support.

In short, the FASB could assume that various functions of financial statements are well established and known generally by those who produce, audit, and use accounting information. Its task would be essentially one of trying to appease conflicting interests in the presence of disagreements over accounting rules, measurements, disclosures, *etc.* But once this role were recognized, what would be the advantages and disadvantages of allowing a private board like the FASB to make compromise decisions? Is this not a function essentially similar to that performed by the courts, and, if so, are we now back to the proposal for an accounting court?[17]

[15]An explicit objective along these lines was also proposed in AAA [1977b, pp. 10–11].

[16]Of course, there is no government agency in the UK which serves an enforcement role like that of the SEC in this country. This factor may allow broader statements in the UK.

[17]First proposed by Littleton [1935].

These questions appear to offer fruitful areas of research, more so than trying to deduce *the* objectives of financial accounting. Perhaps we can achieve more progress by developing and testing theories regarding why a major part of the responsibility for standard setting continues to lie with a private agency, and why members of the profession and corporate managers continue to contribute time and money to the process of developing a conceptual framework. It is unlikely that a general fear of government regulation alone can account for the latter. And, finally, to conclude with Baxter [1962, p. 427]:

> Recommendations by authority on matters of accounting theory may in the short run seem unmixed blessings. In the end, however, they will probably do harm. They are likely to yield little fresh knowledge. . . . They are likely to weaken the education of accountants; the conversion of the subject into cut-and-dried rules, approved by authority and not to be lightly questioned, threatens to reduce its value as a subject of liberal education almost to *nil*. They are likely to narrow the scope for individual thought and judgment; and a group of men who resign their hard problems to others must eventually give up all claim to be a learned profession.

REFERENCES

American Accounting Association (1936), Executive Committee, "A Tentative Statement of Accounting Principles Affecting Corporate Reports," *The Accounting Review* (June 1936), pp. 187–91.
——, Executive Committee, "Accounting Principles Underlying Corporate Financial Statements," *The Accounting Review* (June 1941), pp. 133–39.
——, Executive Committee, "Accounting Concepts and Standards Underlying Corporate Financial Statements, 1948 Revision," *The Accounting Review* (October 1948), pp. 339–44.
——, Committee on Concepts and Standards Underlying Corporate Financial Statements, "Accounting and Reporting Standards for Corporate Financial Statements, 1957 Revision," *The Accounting Review* (October 1957), pp. 536–46.
——, Committee on Concepts and Standards—Long-Lived Assets, "Accounting for Land, Buildings and Equipment," Supplementary Statement No. 1, *The Accounting Review* (July 1964a), pp. 693–99.
——, Committee on Concepts and Standards—Inventory Measurement, "A Discussion of Various Approaches to Inventory Measurement," Supplementary Statement No. 2, *The Accounting Review* (July 1964b), pp. 700–14.
——, Committee to Prepare a Statement of Basic Accounting Theory, *A Statement of Basic Accounting Theory* (AAA, 1966).
——, Committee on Concepts and Standards for External Financial Reports, *Statement on Accounting Theory and Theory Acceptance* (AAA, 1977a).
——, Subcommittee on Conceptual Framework for Financial Accounting and Reporting, *Elements of Financial Statements and Their Measurement: Report to the Financial Accounting Standards Board* (AAA, June 1977b).
American Institute of [Certified Public] Accountants (1942), Committee on Accounting Procedure, *Unamortized Discount and Redemption Premium on Bonds Refunded (Supplement)*, Accounting Research Bulletin No. 18, (AICPA, 1942).
——, Committee on Accounting Terminology, *Accounting Terminology Bulletin*, No. 1 (AIA, 1953). Reprinted in FASB [1977b].

American Institute of Certified Public Accountants (1970), Accounting Principles Board, *Basic Concepts and Accounting Principles Underlying Financial Statements of Business Enterprises*, Statement No. 4 of the APB (AICPA, 1970).

———, Study Group on the Objectives of Financial Statements, *Objectives of Financial Statements* (AICPA, 1973).

Armstrong, M.S., "The Politics of Establishing Accounting Standards," *Journal of Accountancy* (February 1977), pp. 76–79.

Baxter, W. T., "Recommendations on Accounting Theory," in W. T. Baxter and S. Davidson, eds., *Studies in Accounting Theory* (Sweet & Maxwell, 1962), pp. 414–27.

Beaver, W. H. and J. S. Demski, "The Nature of Financial Accounting Objectives: A Survey and Synthesis," *Studies on Financial Accounting Objectives, 1974,* supplement to the *Journal of Accounting Research* (1974).

Bedford, N. M., "Discussion of Opportunities and Implications of the Report on Objectives of Financial Statements," *Studies on Financial Accounting Objectives, 1974,* Supplement to the *Journal of Accounting Research* 12 (1974), p. 15.

Canning, J. B., *The Economics of Accountancy* (The Ronald Press, 1929).

Coe, T. L. and G. H. Sorter, "The FASB Has Been Using an Implicit Conceptual Framework," *The Accounting Journal* (Winter 1977–78), pp. 152–69.

Cyert, R. M. and Y. Ijiri, "Problems of Implementing the Trueblood Objectives Report," *Studies on Financial Accounting Objectives: 1974,* Supplement to the *Journal of Accounting Research* 12 (1974).

Deinzer, H. T., *The American Accounting Association-Sponsored Statements of Standards for Corporate Financial Reports: A Perspective* (Accounting Department, University of Florida, 1964).

Financial Accounting Standards Board, FASB Discussion Memorandum, *Conceptual Framework for Accounting and Reporting: Consideration of the Report of the Study Group on the Objectives of Financial Statements* (FASB, 1974).

———, FASB Discussion Memorandum, *Conceptual Framework for Financial Accounting and Reporting: Elements of Financial Statements and Their Measurement* (FASB, 1976a).

———, *Tentative Conclusions on Objectives of Financial Statements of Business Enterprises* (FASB, 1976b).

———, *Scope and Implications of the Conceptual Framework Project* (FASB, 1976c).

———, *Objectives of Financial Reporting and Elements of Financial Statements of Business Enterprises*, Exposure Draft of Proposed Statement of Financial Accounting Concepts (FASB, 1977).

———, *Objectives of Financial Reporting by Business Enterprises*, Statement of Financial Accounting Concepts No. 1 (FASB, 1978).

Hanson, A. W., "Comments on 'An Introduction to Corporate Accounting Standards'," *Journal of Accountancy* (June 1940), pp. 440–42.

Hatfield, H. R., *Modern Accounting* (D. Appleton and Company, 1909).

———, *Accounting: Its Principles and Problems* (D. Appleton-Century Company, 1927).

Horngren, C. T., "The Marketing of Accounting Standards," *Journal of Accountancy* (October 1973), pp. 61–66.

Ijiri,Y., "Critique of the APB Fundamentals Statement," *Journal of Accountancy* (November 1971), pp. 43–50.

Kester, R. B., "Comments on 'An Introduction to Corporate Accounting Standards'," *Journal of Accountancy* (June 1940), pp. 442–45.

Kitchen, J., "Costing Terminology, *Accounting Research* (February 1954). Reprinted in W. T. Baxter and S. Davidson, eds., *Studies in Accounting Theory* (Sweet & Maxwell, 1962), pp. 399–413.

Littleton, A. C., "Auditor Independence," *Journal of Accountancy* (April 1935), pp. 283–91.

———, Review of Moonitz, *The Basic Postulates of Accounting, The Accounting Review* (July 1962), pp. 602–05.

———, Review of R. T. Sprouse and M. Moonitz, *A Tentative Set of Broad Accounting Principles for Business Enterprises, The Accounting Review* (January 1963), pp. 220–22.

Miller, H. E., "Discussion of Opportunities and Implications of the Report on Objectives of Financial Statements," *Studies on Financial Accounting Objectives: 1974*, supplement to *Journal of Accounting Research* 12 (1974).

Moonitz, M., *The Basic Postulates of Accounting*, Accounting Research Study No. 1 (AICPA, 1961).

Most, K. S. and A. L. Winters, "Focus on Standard Setting: From Trueblood to the FASB," *Journal of Accountancy* (February 1977), pp. 67–75.

Paton, W. A., *Accounting Theory* (The Ronald Press, 1922).

Paton, W. A. and A. C. Littleton, *An Introduction to Corporate Accounting Standards, Monograph No. 3 (AAA, 1940)*.

Smith, C. A., "Accounting Practice under the Securities and Exchange Commission," *The Accounting Review* (December 1935), pp. 325–332.

Sprouse, R. T., "Discussion of Opportunities and Implications of the Report on Objectives of Financial Statements," *Studies on Financial Accounting Objectives: 1974*, Supplement to the *Journal of Accounting Research* 12 (1974).

Sprouse, R. T. and M. Moonitz, *A Tentative Set of Broad Accounting Principles for Business Enterprises*, Accounting Research Study No. 3 (AICPA, 1962).

Sterling, R. R., "A Statement of Basic Accounting Theory: A Review Article," *Journal of Accounting Research* (Spring 1967), pp. 95–112.

Stinchcombe, A. L., *Constructing Social Theories* (Harcourt, Brace, and World, 1968).

Vatter, W. J., $\sum_{i=1}^{i=22} (M_3)_i$ —An Evaluation," The Accounting Review (July 1963), pp. 47–77.

Watts, R. L. and J. L. Zimmerman, "Towards a Positive Theory of Determination of Accounting Standards," *The Accounting Review 53* (January 1978), pp. 112–34.

———, "The Demand for and Supply of Accounting Theories: The Market for Excuses," *The Accounting Review* (April 1979), pp. 273–305.

Zeff, S. A., *Forging Accounting Principles in Five Countries* (Stipes Publishing Co., 1972).

———, "The Rise of 'Economic Consequences'," *Journal of Accountancy* (December 1978), pp. 56–63.

II-C/EVALUATION OF ACCOUNTING-POLICY DECISIONS

Predictive Ability as a Criterion for the Evaluation of Accounting Data

WILLIAM H. BEAVER, JOHN W. KENNELLY, AND WILLIAM M. VOSS

The evaluation of alternative accounting measurements is a problem of major concern to the accounting profession. With respect to this problem, Ijiri and Jaedicke have stated:

> Accounting is plagued by the existence of alternative measurement methods. For many years, accountants have been searching for criteria which can be used to choose the best measurement alternative.[1]

One criterion being employed by a growing body of empirical research is *predictive ability*. According to this criterion, alternative accounting measurements are evaluated in terms of their ability to predict events of interest to decision-makers. The measure with the greatest predictive power with respect to a given event is considered to be the "best" method for that particular purpose.

The criterion has already been applied in several different contexts. Brown has investigated the ability of models using alternative income measures (i.e., with and without tax deferral) to predict the market value of the firm. Green and Segall evaluated interim reports in terms of their usefulness in the prediction of future annual earnings. Horrigan has examined the predictive content of accounting data, in the form of financial ratios, with respect to bond rating changes and ratings on newly issued bonds. One of the authors has studied accounting measures as predictors of bankruptcy and bond default.[2]

William H. Beaver, John W. Kennelly, and William M. Voss, "Predictive Ability as a Criterion for the Evaluation of Accounting Data," *The Accounting Review*, October 1968, pp. 675–683. Reprinted with the permission of *The Accounting Review*.

[1]Yuji Ijiri and Robert K. Jaedicke, "Reliability and Objectivity of Accounting Measurements," *The Accounting Review*, (July 1966), p. 474.

[2]Philip Brown, "The Predictive Abilities of Alternative Income Concepts" (an unpublished manuscript presented to the Conference for Study of Security Prices, Graduate School of Business, University of Chicago, November 1966); David Green, Jr. and Joel Segall, "The Predictive Power of First-Quarter Earnings Reports: A Replication"; James Horrigan, "The Determination of Long-Term Credit Standing with Financial Ratios"; William H. Beaver, "Financial Ratios as Predictors of Failure," The last three papers appear in *Empirical Research in Accounting: Selected Studies, 1966* (Institute of Professional Accounting, Graduate School of Business, University of Chicago, 1967), pp. 21–36, 44–62, and 71–102, respectively.

Because the predictive ability criterion is currently being used and is likely to experience even greater use in the future, this paper examines its origin, its relationship to the facilitation of decision-making, and the potential difficulties associated with its implementation. In order to illustrate the issues under discussion, the paper will refer to a hypothetical research project. The project proposes to evaluate the merits of alternative methods of reporting financial leases in terms of the prediction of loan default.

Loan default was chosen as the dependent variable for two reasons. A large body of literature in financial statement analysis suggests loan default is an event of interest to decision-makers (e.g., bankers), and *a priori* arguments can be advanced that will relate accounting measurements to the prediction of loan default. A cash flow model of the firm, such as that developed by Walter, implies that the probability of loan default is a function of the ratio of total debt to total assets.[3] However the model does not specify how debt and assets are best operationally measured. The financial lease controversy provides two measurement alternatives—capitalization and noncapitalization.

A priori arguments have been advanced, supporting each alternative as the more meaningful.[4] Empirically testable implications can be drawn from these arguments if they are interpreted in the light of the cash flow model. If the capitalization of leases does provide a "more meaningful" measure of debt and assets, then a debt-asset ratio that includes the capitalized value of leases in its components ought to be a better predictor of loan default than a debt-asset ratio that ignores capitalization.

The empirical part of the hypothetical study would involve the collection of financial statement data for a sample of default and nondefault firms. The debt-asset ratio would be computed for each firm, under each of the two lease treatments. The object would be to see which debt-asset ratio was the better predictor. An index of predictive ability is provided by the dichotomous classification test, which classifies the firms as default or nondefault based solely on a knowledge of the debt-asset ratio. The classifications are compared to the actual default status of the firms to determine the percentage of incorrect predictions—the lower the error, the higher the predictive power. The lease assumption that resulted in a lower percentage error would tentatively be judged the better, the more meaningful, measurement alternative for the purpose of predicting loan default.[5]

---

[3]James E. Walter, "The Determination of Technical Solvency," *Journal of Business* (January 1957), pp. 30–43. Extension of the Walter model as applied to financial ratios appears in Beaver, *op. cit.* The lease study need not restrict itself to only the debt-asset ratio. Other ratios affected by capitalization could also be studied.

[4]Arguments for and against capitalization appear in John H. Myers, *Reporting of Leases in Financial Statements* (American Institute of Certified Public Accountants, 1962); and Donald C. Cook, "The Case Against Capitalizing Leases," *Harvard Business Review* (January-February 1963), pp. 145–155.

[5]The sample design described here parallels that used in the Beaver study. A more complete description of the classification test is discussed in that study (pp. 83ff.). Another index of predictive power is provided by an analysis of Bayesian likelihood ratios. In many respects, the likelihood ratio analysis is superior to the classification test. However, the classification test was used because it can be more briefly stated and more easily understood. Also both indices ranked accounting measures virtually the same in the Beaver study.

THE ORIGIN OF THE PREDICTIVE ABILITY CRITERION

Knowing the origin of the predictive ability criterion is important in understanding what is meant by predictive ability and why it is being used in evaluating accounting data. The criterion is well established in the social and natural sciences as a method for choosing among competing hypotheses.[6] It is our belief that alternative accounting measures have the properties of competing hypotheses and can be evaluated in a similar manner. Consider the following common features of competing hypotheses and alternative accounting measures:

(1) Both are abstractions, which disregard aspects of reality deemed to be irrelevant and retain only those few crucial elements that are essential for the purposes at hand. Because there are many ways to abstract from reality, an unlimited number of mutually exclusive alternatives can be generated. Hence there is a need for a set of criteria for choosing among them.

(2) Tests of logical propriety are one basis for evaluation. Conformity to these tests is a necessary but insufficient condition for selecting the "best." Two or more alternatives may pass the tests, and in that event it is futile to argue which is the "more logical." Ultimately, the choice must be made on the basis of which abstraction better captures the relevant aspects of reality. There is a need for an additional criterion that evaluates the alternatives in terms of the *purpose* for which they are being generated.

(3) A primary purpose is the prediction of events, and hence comparison of alternatives according to their relative predictive power is a meaningful basis for evaluation. Predictive power is defined as the ability to generate operational implications (i.e., predictions) and to have those predictions subsequently verified by empirical evidence. More precisely, a prediction is a statement about the probability distribution of the dependent variable (the event being predicted) conditional upon the value of the independent variable (the predictor). Typically, the prediction asserts there is an association between x and y such that the outcome of y is dependent upon the value of x [i.e., $P(y/x) = f(x)$].[7] But merely

[6]This section relies heavily upon the literature in scientific methodology, especially the following works: Morris R. Cohen and Ernest Nagel, *An Introduction to Logic and the Scientific Method* (Harcourt Brace, 1934); Ernest Nagel, *The Structure of Science* (Harcourt Brace, 1961); C. West Churchman, *Prediction and Optimal Decision* (Prentice-Hall, 1962); Abraham Kaplan, *The Conduct of Inquiry* (Chandler, 1964); and several articles appearing in Sherman Krupp's *The Structure of Economic Science* (Prentice-Hall, 1966). Additional bibliographic references appear in Carl Thomas Devine's "Research Methodology and Accounting Theory Formation," *The Accounting Review*, (July 1960), pp. 387–399.

[7]Occasionally, a hypothesis may specify an independent relationship among the variables [i.e., $P(y/x) = P(y)$]. For example, the random walk theory of security price movements asserts that the probability distribution of the price change in a given time period is independent of the price change in any previous period. See Eugene F. Fama, "The Behavior of Stock Market Prices," *Journal of Business*, (January 1965), pp. 34–105. In comparing competing predictors, the relative strength of association with the dependent variable becomes the relevant consideration. Strength of association can be measured in many ways, which will vary with the nature of the data and the inferences to be drawn from the data. In the lease study, the percentage error in classification was chosen as the index of association.

asserting the prediction does not make it "true." It must be verified by investigating the empirical correspondence between what the prediction asserts and what is in fact observed. Thus the determination of predictive ability is inherently an empirical question.

(4) The use of the predictive ability criterion presupposes that the alternatives under consideration have met the tests of logic and that each has a theory supporting it. The determination of predictive ability is not an indiscriminate search for that alternative which will maximize the R^2 (or any other index of predictive power). Theory provides an explanation why a given alternative is expected to be related to the dependent variable and permits the investigator to generalize from the findings of sample data to a new set of observations. Consequently, a complete evaluation involves both *a priori* and empirical considerations.

The lease study reflects each of the points listed above. Each measurement system (i.e., with and without capitalization) is an abstraction. One basis for choosing between them would be to subject the underlying *a priori* arguments to the tests of logical propriety, but in this case neither argument is inherently illogical. Hence it is impossible to resolve the controversy on solely *a priori* grounds. Note also it would be erroneous to prefer the capitalization of leases merely because noncapitalization abstracts from certain aspects of the lease event. To say one measurement system is more abstract than another is not an indictment of that system. The additional data provided by capitalizing leases may be irrelevant for the purposes at hand or may even be harmful in the sense of contributing only "noise" to the system. A choice can only be made by applying some purposive criterion. In the lease study, the purposive criterion chosen was predictive ability—in particular, the ability to predict loan default.

It is possible to generalize beyond the context of the lease controversy. Most, if not all, accounting controversies can be viewed as disputes over the relative merits of one measurement alternative versus another. The inadequacy of relying solely upon *a priori* arguments is generally recognized by the accounting profession. Several recent articles have drawn attention to this inadequacy and have called for more empirical research in accounting.[8] One factor that has impeded a movement in this direction is the inability to specify what the nature of the empirical research should be, although there is a consensus that the research ought to relate alternative measures to the purposes of accounting data. The predictive ability approach provides a method for drawing operational implications from the *a priori* arguments such that the measurement controversies become empirically testable according to a purposive criterion.

RELATIONSHIP TO THE FACILITATION OF DECISION-MAKING

A key issue in accepting this approach is the contention that predictive ability is a purposive criterion. This section will examine that contention in more detail and will relate predictive ability to what is generally regarded as the purpose of accounting data—the facilitation of decision-making.

---

[8]For example, R. J. Chambers, "Prospective Adventures in Accounting Ideas," *The Accounting Review*, (April 1967), p. 251.

The idea that accounting data ought to be evaluated in terms of their purposes or uses is one of the earliest and most prevalent thoughts in accounting. In 1922 Paton concluded:

> Accounting is a highly purposive field and any assumption, principle, or procedure is accordingly justified if it adequately serves the end in view.[9]

Recently the American Accounting Association's *A Statement of Basic Accounting Theory* stated:

> In establishing these standards the all-inclusive criterion is the usefulness of the information.[10]

In spite of the obvious appeal to the idea that accounting data ought to be useful, the utilitarian approach has lacked operationality. Chambers has noted:

> For, if accounting is utilitarian there must have been some concept or some theory of the tests which must be applied in distinguishing utilitarian from nonutilitarian procedures. . . . It is largely because the tests of "utilitarian-ness" . . . have not been made explicit that the body of accounting practices now employed contains so many divergent and inconsistent rules.[11]

One reason for the inability to specify tests of usefulness is the manner in which usefulness is interpreted. Almost without exception, the literature has related usefulness to the facilitation of decision-making. The primacy of decision-making has been stressed by both Paton and *A Statement of Basic Accounting Theory*:

> The purpose of accounting may be said to be that of compiling and interpreting the financial data . . . to provide a sound guide to action by management, investor, and other interested parties.[12]

> The committee defines accounting as the process of identifying, measuring, and communicating economic information to permit informed judgments and decisions by users of the information.[13]

However, the use of the decision-making criterion faces two problems. The first is to define the decision models (or processes) of potential users of accounting data. This problem has been noted by both Anton and Vatter.

> If we assume an operationalist view—that is, that information ought to be for decision-making purposes—the criteria [sic] is based upon an ex-

[9]William A. Paton, *Accounting Theory* (The Ronald Press, 1922), p. 472.

[10]American Accounting Association, *A Statement of Basic Accounting Theory* (American Accounting Association, 1966), p. 3.

[11]Raymond J. Chambers, "Why Bother with Postulates?" *Journal of Accounting Research*, (Spring 1963), p. 3.

[12]William A. Paton, *Essentials of Accounting* (The Macmillan Company, 1949), p. 2.

[13]American Accounting Association, *op.cit.*, p. 1.

tension of significance, i.e., for what is the information significant. . . . While this is a purposive criterion it also gives us the dilemma noted above as to who will be the decision-maker and the uncertainty of his context.[14]

Observation, analysis, and projection should be aimed at decision-making. This implies a view of the past and present that permits and facilitates decisions, without making them. How this fine line can be established depends upon what the decisions are, who makes them, and what data are relevant for those purposes. These questions still remain unanswered.[15]

Most business decisions currently are not made within the framework of a formally specified decision model. That is, in most decision-making situations, no model is available with which to evaluate alternative accounting measurements. Consider the lending decision faced by a loan officer in a bank. The specification of his decision model would require a knowledge of what the decision variables are, what weights are assigned to each decision variable, and what constraints, if any, are binding on the loan officer. It is unlikely that even the decision-maker would produce a formal model that would describe the process he went through in making lending decisions. Rules of thumb, such as "do not loan to any firm with a current ratio below 2," can be found, but it would be extremely difficult to determine the decision model implied by such rules. Specification of decision models, for the most part, is beyond the current state of knowledge. Although operations research and other quantitative techniques offer promise of greater specification in the future, it is not clear how soon, or to what extent, such specifications will be possible.[16]

The second problem is, even after the decision model is specified, it is not sufficient for determining which accounting measure produces the better decisions. Many, if not all, of the decision variables are capable of being measured in more than one way. For example, assume that a loan officer's objective function for the lending decision is a known function of promised return and probability of default on the loan. The lease controversy provides two operational measures for assessing the probability of loan default. The decision model can indicate whether different decisions are produced by using different definitions of the debt-asset ratio as a surrogate for the probability of default, but it cannot indicate which definition (i.e., with or without capitalization) will lead to the better decisions. Additional information is needed as to which ratio provides the better assessment of probability of default (i.e., which ratio is the better predictor of loan default).

At this point the relationship between predictive ability and decision-making becomes evident. Note the distinction between a prediction and a decision.

---

[14]Hector R. Anton, "Some Aspects of Measurement and Accounting," *Journal of Accounting Research*, (Spring 1964), p. 6.

[15]William J. Vatter, "Postulates and Principles," *Journal of Accounting Research*, (Autumn 1963), p. 197.

[16]The difficulties encountered in attempting to specify the decision processes of loan officers are well documented in several articles appearing in the text by Kalman J. Cohen and Frederick S. Hammer, *Analytical Methods in Banking* (Irwin, 1966). Of special interest is the article by Kalman J. Cohen, Thomas C. Gilmore, and Frank A. Singer, "Bank Procedures for Analyzing Business Loan Applications," pp. 219–249.

In the context of the bank's lending decision, a prediction states the probability of loan default if the bank loans to a firm with a set of financial ratios. The decision is whether or not the bank should grant the loan, which also involves additional decision variables such as the promised return. The illustration points out an important relationship between predictions and decisions. A prediction can be made without making a decision, but a decision cannot be made without, at least implicitly, making a prediction.

In a world where little is known about the decision models, evaluating alternative accounting measures in terms of their predictive ability is an appealing idea, because it requires a lower level of specificity regarding the decision model. To evaluate alternative lease treatments in terms of their ability to predict loan default, we assume only that the probability of loan default is a parameter of the decision process, even though we may know little about how the bank's loan officers use the assessments of probability of default in reaching their decisions. Hence the predictive ability of accounting data can be explored without waiting for the further specification of the decision models.[17]

Because prediction is an inherent part of the decision process, knowledge of the predictive ability of alternative measures is a prerequisite to the use of the decision-making criterion. At the same time, it permits tentative conclusions regarding alternative measurements, subject to subsequent confirmation when the decision models eventually become specified. The use of predictive ability as a purposive criterion is more than merely consistent with accounting's decision-making orientation. It can provide a body of research that will bring accounting closer to its goal of evaluation in terms of a decision-making criterion.

DIFFICULTIES OF IMPLEMENTATION

The purpose of this paper is to present the difficulties as well as the benefits of the predictive ability approach. However, none of the potential problems to be discussed are inherent to this approach. They are merely "facts of life" that are likely to be encountered in any meaningful attempt to evaluate alternative accounting measures.

(1) One difficulty of implementation will be the specification of what events constitute parameters of decision models and the specification of a theory that will link those events to the accounting measures in some sort of predictive relationship. The studies cited earlier suggest some of the events that could be predicted.[18] Also, portfolio theory appears to be a productive area for providing dependent variables, although as yet the relationships between the parameters of the portfolio models and the accounting data have not been explored.[19] However, a brief survey of the

[17]The relationship between predictions and the decision model is further discussed in the next section.

[18]See footnote 2 for the bibliographic references.

[19]Harry M. Markowitz, *Portfolio Selection: Efficient Diversification of Investments* (Wiley, 1959). William F. Sharpe, "Capital Asset Prices: A Theory of Market Equilibrium Under Conditions of Risk," *Journal of Finance* (September 1964), pp. 425–42.

disciplines from which the dependent variables and the predictive theory are likely to originate indicates that much remains to be accomplished. In large part then the evaluation of accounting data, using the predictive ability criterion, will occur in conjunction with development and testing of predictive relationships in related disciplines, such as economics and finance.

(2) The findings of a predictive ability study are conditional on how the predictive model is specified. The construction of the prediction model involves a specification of the functional form of the relationships (e.g., linearity) and also how the variables are operationally defined. In the financial lease study, the findings would be conditional upon the rates used to discount the lease payments and the particular set of financial ratios used in the study. If no difference in predictive ability is found between the two sets of ratios (capitalized, noncapitalized), the finding may be attributed to (a) the particular discount rates chosen were not the appropriate rates, (b) the ratio form is not a meaningful way to express relationships among financial statement items, (c) the particular ratios chosen were not the optimal ratios for the prediction of default, or (d) capitalization does not enhance predictive ability. Additional research regarding the possibility of (a), (b) and (c) must be explored before inference (d) can be drawn. The accounting measure and the prediction model are being jointly tested. Positive results constitute a joint confirmation, while negative results may be due to a flaw in either or both factors. In practice it may be difficult to isolate the source of the negative results.

Another problem arises when positive results are obtained (i.e., when a "significant" difference between alternative measures is observed). For example assume the debt-asset ratio computed under the capitalization assumption predicts better than the noncapitalized debt-asset ratio in a single ratio prediction model. If additional ratios were included in the prediction model, the noncapitalized form of the debt-asset ratio might contribute more to the predictive power of the multivariate model than the capitalized form. If different models suggest contrary conclusions regarding the relative predictive power of the two lease assumptions, additional research will be needed to explain the reason for the conflicting results. Even if consistent results are observed for all of the models tested, there is always the possibility of an untested model which possesses greater predictive power and yet suggests the opposite conclusion regarding the relative predictive power of the alternative measures under study.[20]

(3) A third difficulty occurs because accounting data are currently being used as decision variables. There are two possible reasons for observing an association between the accounting measures and the event being predicted. (a) There is a "true" causal relationship between the measures

---

[20]There are two other related qualifications regarding a predictive ability study. (1) The findings are conditional upon the population from which the sample is drawn. (2) The findings are conditional upon the alternative measures chosen for study. For example, a third unspecified and untested measure may be better than the two measures under consideration.

and the event. (b) Decision-makers perceive there to be a causal relationship, and this perception is sufficient to produce an observed relationship. In the lease study a relationship between financial ratios and loan default may be observed because there is a causal relationship such that a "poor" ratio increases the probability of default. However, a relationship may also be observed merely because bankers believe there is a causal relationship and use the ratios as decision variables. The bank may sever a line of credit because a firm fails to improve its ratios to a respectable level. The severing of the line of credit forces the firm into default. Similarly, the efficacy of capitalizing leases may be diminished or eliminated if loan officers do not incorporate the capitalization of leases into their credit analysis. Any observed relationship may be due to either (a) or (b) or both. It may be impossible to tell from the sample data the extent to which factor (b) is present.

If the objective is predictive ability, do we care what its source is? Yes, if source (b) is not expected to be permanent. Decision-makers' use of accounting data as decision variables may change over time. In fact, the findings of a predictive ability study may cause them to change, and this might change the predictive relationships observed in the future.

(4) The evaluation of relative predictive power may require an assumption about the loss function associated with the prediction errors, which in turn involves additional knowledge of other variables in the decision model. Without this knowledge it may be impossible to conclude which measure is the better predictor.[21]

For example, suppose the capitalized debt-asset ratio predicts the default status of a sample of default and nondefault firms with a lower number of total misclassifications. Can we conclude that capitalization is preferable? Not necessarily. Suppose the noncapitalized debt-asset ratio has more total misclassifications of both default and nondefault firms but fewer errors with respect to the classification of default firms. Since the loss of misclassifying a default firm is likely to be greater than the loss associated with misclassifying a nondefault firm, the latter measure may be the better predictor in terms of minimizing expected loss. More would have to be known about the loss function before one measure could be chosen over the other.

Moreover, even if the capitalized debt-asset ratio performed better with respect to both type errors, additional analysis is needed before capitalization of leases could be recommended, because capitalization involves a greater cost to collecting additional data and making the necessary computations. Capitalization might lead to better predictions, but are they sufficiently better to warrant the additional cost? The answer involves a cost-benefit analysis, which requires a knowledge of the loss function and hence the other decision variables.

---

[21]Every index of predictive ability involves some assumption regarding the loss function of the prediction errors and/or the distribution of prediction errors. If different indices suggest different measures are better, the inability to select which index is appropriate implies the inability to select which accounting measure is the better predictor, until the loss function can be specified.

The amount of additional knowledge of the decision model that will be required can only be assessed within the context of the empirical results of each predictive ability study. The margin of superiority of one measure over another may be so great that it is obviously the better predictor regardless of the form of loss function. In other situations, perhaps only the general form of the loss function (e.g., linear or quadratic, symmetric or asymmetric) need be specified. In instances where a greater knowledge of the loss function is needed than is available, the role of the predictive ability study may be to present the distribution of prediction errors for each measure and let the reader apply his own loss function in choosing among the measures. In any event the researcher must be constantly aware of this relationship to avoid drawing unwarranted inferences from the data.

(5) The findings of a predictive ability study are conditional upon the event being predicted. Even if a measure is a better predictor of one event (e.g., loan default), it is not necessarily a better predictor of other events. Additional research would be needed to investigate the predictive power of the measure for other purposes. If different measures are best for different predictive purposes, the problem of satisfying competing user needs arises.[22] If this problem exists, it would be difficult to resolve, although the use of multidimensional and special purpose statements offers a tentative solution.[23]

CONCLUDING REMARKS

Two implications emerge from the previous discussion: (1) The preference for an accounting measure may apply only within the context of a specific predictive purpose or prediction model. It may be impossible to generalize about the "best" measurement alternative across different contexts. (2) Even within a specific context, the conclusions must be considered as tentative.

The inability to generalize is a possibility, but not an inevitability. We have cited only *potential* difficulties, whose relevance can only be assessed empirically, not by *a priori* speculation. What is important is to know to what extent we can generalize across purposes, and the only hope of acquiring this knowledge is to conduct the predictive studies. If we discover that different measures are best for different purposes, it would be erroneous to believe that the predictive studies are any less important because of that discovery. The inability to generalize, if it does exist, is not a flaw of the predictive ability methodology. It merely reflects the state of the world or the state of accounting theory, but in neither case is it an indictment of the methodology that exposes that fact.

Even within a specific context, the preference for one measure over another is tentative. A measure that performed poorly may not be permanently rejected in the sense that the researcher may refine the measure (and its theory) or

---

[22]The decision-making criterion also faces the same potential problem. See comments made by both Devine and Moonitz. Carl Thomas Devine, *op. cit.*, p. 397. Maurice Moonitz, *The Postulates of Accounting* (American Institute of Certified Public Accountants, 1961), p. 4.

[23]For suggestions regarding multidimensional reporting see American Accounting Association, *op.cit.*

redesign the study in the hope that future research will demonstrate that the measure is really better. Also there is always the possibility of an unknown or untested measure that performs even better than the best measure tested. Theory construction in other disciplines is an evolutionary process, where the hypotheses are continuously being revised, redefined, or overturned in the light of new theory and new evidence. There is no reason to believe that accounting theory will be different.

Although it is important that a general awareness of these factors exists, neither the potential inability to generalize nor the tentative nature of the conclusions should be regarded as a deterrent to conducting the predictive studies. Extension of research efforts into the predictive ability of accounting data is necessary for the fulfillment of accounting's decision-making orientation and for the meaningful evaluation of alternative accounting measures.

The Politicization of Accounting

DAVID SOLOMONS

There was once a time, not so many years ago, when accounting could be thought of as an essentially nonpolitical subject. If it was not as far removed from politics as was mathematics or astronomy, it was at least no more political than psychology or surveying or computer technology or statistics. Even in areas of accounting such as taxation, which might be thought to be most relevant to questions of public policy, practitioners were generally content to confine themselves to technical issues without getting involved as accountants in the discussion of tax policy.

Today, to judge from current discussions of the standard-setting process, accounting can no longer be thought of as nonpolitical. The numbers that accountants report have, or at least are widely thought to have, a significant impact on economic behavior. Accounting rules therefore affect human behavior. Hence, the process by which they are made is said to be political. It is then only a short step to the assertion that such rules are properly to be made in the political arena, by counting heads and deciding accounting issues by some voting mechanism.

There are several articulate spokesmen for this point of view. Dale Gerboth writes that "a politicization of accounting rule-making [is] not only inevitable, but just. In a society committed to democratic legitimization of authority, only politically responsive institutions have the right to command others to obey their rules."[1] And, in another passage from the same article, Gerboth says, "When a decision-making process depends for its success on public confidence, the critical issues are not technical; they are political. . . . In the face of conflict between competing interests, rationality as well as prudence lies not in seeking final answers, but rather in compromise—essentially a political process."[2]

In the same vein, Charles Horngren writes that "the setting of accounting standards is as much a product of political action as of flawless logic or empirical findings. Why? Because the setting of standards is a social decision. Standards place restrictions on behavior; therefore, they must be accepted by the affected parties. Acceptance may be forced or voluntary or some of both. In a democratic

This article is adapted from a paper appearing in *Essays in Honor of William A. Paton—Pioneer Accounting Theorist*, edited by Stephen A. Zeff, Joel Demski and Nicholas Dopuch (Ann Arbor, Mich.: Division of Research, Graduate School of Business Administration, University of Michigan, 1978).

[1]Dale L. Gerboth, "Research, Intuition, and Politics in Accounting Inquiry," *Accounting Review*, July 1973, p. 481.

[2]Ibid, p. 479.

society, getting acceptance is an exceedingly complicated process that requires skillful marketing in a political arena."[3]

Robert May and Gary Sundem take a similar position: "In practice as well as in theory, the social welfare impact of accounting reports apparently is recognized. Therefore it is no surprise that the [Financial Accounting Standards Board] is a political body and, consequently, that the process of selecting an acceptable accounting alternative is a political process. If the social welfare impact of accounting policy decisions were ignored, the basis for the existence of a regulatory body would disappear. Therefore, the FASB must consider explicitly political (i.e., social welfare) aspects as well as accounting theory and research in its decisions."[4]

Other voices that call for an explicit recognition of the probable economic and social impact of a new accounting standard are not always easily distinguished from those asserting that political considerations should determine what the standard should be.[5] However, these two views should not be confused.

The structure committee of the Financial Accounting Foundation grappled with the question of the political nature of the standard-setting task in *The Structure of Establishing Financial Accounting Standards*. On the nature of the standard-setting process, it says: "The process of setting accounting standards can be described as democratic because like all rule-making bodies the Board's right to make rules depends ultimately on the consent of the ruled. But because standard setting requires some perspective it would not be appropriate to establish a standard based solely on a canvass of the constituents. Similarly, the process can be described as legislative because it must be deliberative and because all views must be heard. But the standard setters are expected to represent the entire constituency as a whole and not be representatives of a specific constituent group. The process can be described as political because there is an educational effort involved in getting a new standard accepted. But it is not political in the sense that an accommodation is required to get a statement issued."[6]

There is something here to please everyone. Yet the committee does finally come out on the side of the angels: "We have used the word constituency to indicate that the FASB is accountable to everyone who has an interest. We are not suggesting that the Board members are in place to represent them or that the standards must necessarily be based on a numerical consensus."[7]

That accounting influences human behavior, if only because it conveys information, is obvious enough, though research into the workings of "the efficient market" has cast doubt on some of the supposed results of accounting choices.

[3]Charles T. Horngren, "The Marketing of Accounting Standards," *Journal of Accountancy*, Oct. 73, p. 61.

[4]Robert G. May and Gary L. Sundem, "Research for Accounting Policy: An Overview," *Accounting Review*, October 1976, p. 750.

[5]John Buckley (in "FASB and Impact Analysis," *Management Accounting*, April 1976, p. 13) straddles this line most uncomfortably. His article has been thought to support politically slanted standards although he nowhere explicitly says that he does.

[6]Structure committee, *The Structure of Establishing Financial Accounting Standards* (Stamford, Conn.: FAF, April 1977), p. 19.

[7]Ibid.

There are, without question, political aspects of accounting. There are similarly political aspects of physics, which result in enormous expenditures on research into nuclear energy and weaponry. Geology, in its concern with the world's reserves of fossil fuels, obviously has political implications. Research into sickle cell anemia became a political question when the heavy incidence of this disease among black Americans came to light. There are very few areas of human knowledge which are devoid of political significance. But that does not mean that the processes by which knowledge is advanced or by which new applications are found for old knowledge are themselves political processes in the sense in which that term is usually understood. Political motives for asking a question may be entirely appropriate. A politically motivated answer may or may not be appropriate. It obviously depends on the nature of the question.

It may be useful to look more carefully at the part which politics should and should not play in accounting standard setting. The future of the FASB may depend on a better understanding of that issue. Indeed, the very credibility of accounting itself may be at stake.

ACCOUNTING AND NATIONAL GOALS

The most extreme expression, so far as I am aware, of the view that political considerations should enter into the formulation of accounting standards—not merely into the choice of accounting questions to be studied but also into the formulation of the standards themselves—is to be found in a lecture given in New York in November 1973 by Professor David Hawkins. He noted that Congress and the executive branch of the federal government were "becoming more and more aware of the behavioral aspects of corporate reporting and its macro economic implications. Increasingly, I believe, these policy makers will demand . . . that the decisions of those charged with determining what constitutes approved corporate reporting standards result in corporate reporting standards that will lead to individual economic behavior that is consistent with the nation's macro economic objectives. . . . This awareness on the part of economic planners brings accounting standards setting into the realm of political economics."[8]

Events since 1973 have not shown any diminution in this awareness. The question is whether this is to be regarded as a threat to the integrity of accounting or as an opportunity, perhaps even an obligation, on the part of accountants to cooperate with government in furthering its economic policy. Hawkins left us in no doubt where he stood in this matter: "The [FASB's] objectives must be responsive to many more considerations than accounting theory or our notions of economically useful data. . . . Corporate reporting standards should result in data that are useful for economic decisions *provided that the standard is consistent with the national macro economic objectives and the economic programs designed to reach these goals.*"[9] And, as if that were not enough,

[8]David M. Hawkins, "Financial Accounting, the Standards Board and Economic Development," one of the 1973–74 Emanuel Saxe Distinguished Lectures in Accounting, published by the Bernard M. Baruch College, City University of New York, April 1975, pp. 7–8.

[9]Ibid, pp. 17, 9–10.

he added that "because the [FASB] has the power to influence economic behavior it has an obligation to support the government's economic plans."[10]

In that last passage, the word "because" is noteworthy, implying as it does that the power to influence economic behavior always carries with it an obligation to support the government's plans. Even if the matter under discussion were, say, pricing policy or wage policy or some aspect of environmental protection, the assertion would be open to argument. In relation to accounting, where the end product is a system of measurement, the position which Hawkins urges on the FASB could, I believe, threaten the integrity of financial reporting and deprive it of whatever credibility it now has.

There is no question as to the sensitivity of some, indeed most, of the issues that have been or are now on the agenda of the FASB or its predecessors, and of course this sensitivity stems from the fact that standards dealing with those issues have influenced or will influence behavior. This can only mean that there is widespread skepticism about the "efficient market" hypothesis. The financial community is not indifferent to the accounting rules imposed on it by the FASB. It is not the purpose of this article to explore the nature of this concern.[11] It will be enough to recognize that the FASB's constituents think it matters whether leases are capitalized or not, whether foreign currency transactions are accounted for by one method or another, whether contingencies are provided for by charges against income or by allowing retained earnings to accumulate. These questions do not affect the amount of information that is disclosed but simply the way in which these economic phenomena are reported; yet this fact does not desensitize them. Perhaps investors *are* naive. Only on the basis of such an assumption (and on the assumption that no new information will be disclosed by a politically motivated standard) is the impact of politics on accounting standards worth discussing at all.

THE ECONOMIC IMPACT OF ACCOUNTING STANDARDS

Few if any accounting standards are without some economic impact. The requirement that U.S. companies write off purchased goodwill is said to give an advantage to foreign companies in bidding for American businesses because, not being subject to the same accounting requirement, they can afford to offer a higher price. FASB Statement no. 2, *Accounting for Research and Development Costs*, which requires that R&D be expensed as incurred, has been said to constitute a threat to technological progress, especially by smaller companies that may be contemplating seeking access to the capital market and will there-

---

[10]Ibid., p. 11.

[11]Yet one cannot ignore the troublesome paradox posed by the numerous empirical studies which have shown "that the capital market does distinguish between [accounting] changes that appear to be reporting changes of no economic importance and those that appear to have substantive economic implications." (Nicholas J. Gonedes and Nicholas Dopuch, "Capital Market Equilibrium, Information Production, and Selecting Accounting Techniques: Theoretical Framework and Review of Empirical Work," *Studies on Financial Accounting Objectives: 1974*, supplement to vol. 12 of the *Journal of Accounting Research*.) If the market can "see through" accounting changes that result from changes in standards, why do they generate so much heat?

fore want to show good profits before doing so.[12] FASB Statement no. 5, *Accounting for Contingencies*, by greatly restricting the circumstances in which an estimated loss from a loss contingency can be accrued by a charge to income, is said to have caused U.S. insurance companies to reinsure risks for which previously they would have relied on self-insurance.

One of the most sensitive standards has been that dealing with foreign currency translation (Statement no. 8, *Accounting for the Translation of Foreign Currency Transactions and Foreign Currency Financial Statements*). Under the so-called temporal method mandated by the board, monetary assets and liabilities of a foreign subsidiary of a U.S. corporation have to be translated, for consolidation purposes, as the rate of exchange current at the balance sheet date. Assets which, in accordance with generally accepted accounting principles, are carried at cost or cost less depreciation have to be translated at the rate current at the time they were acquired. Exchange gains and losses, realized and unrealized, have to be brought into the income statement. For companies that formerly used a current/noncurrent classification, the important changes lie in the treatment of inventories and of long-term debt. Inventories, as current assets, were formerly carried at the current rate and are now carried at the historical rate; long-term debt, as a noncurrent liability, was formerly carried at the historical rate and now, as a monetary item, is carried at the current rate. Moreover, unrealized translation gains, formerly kept out of the income statement, now have to be brought in. The result has been greatly to increase the volatility of the reported earnings of companies with important foreign operations. Criticism of Statement no. 8 has focused on this increased volatility rather than on whether the new rules result in a better or worse representation of financial performance.

Whatever one may think about the merits of FASB Statement no. 19, *Financial Accounting and Reporting by Oil and Gas Producing Companies*, there can be little doubt that the Securities and Exchange Commission would not have acted as it did at the end of August to overrule this standard if there had not been political pressure from certain oil and gas companies which felt that they would be injured by the mandatory use of the "successful efforts" method of costing. It will be some time before the full effect of this action on the standard-setting process can be seen in its true light.

Numerous other politically sensitive accounting issues could be cited, but none has received as much attention as accounting for inflation, for none has such widespread potential repercussions throughout the business world. Each method which has been proposed to replace or to modify traditional methods would affect different companies differently, making some look more prosperous than they are under present methods and others less prosperous. For example, current purchasing power adjustments to historical cost accounting (general price level accounting) tend to make utilities with heavy debt capital look better off; replacement cost accounting tends to make companies with a large investment in depreciable assets, such as steel companies, look relatively less profitable. A system using exit values (e.g., continuously contemporary accounting,

---

[12]This argument, when the treatment of R&D was still on the FASB's agenda, led Hawkins to say, in his 1973 Emanuel Saxe Lecture (p. 14), "I do not believe the Board can eliminate the alternative capitalization." Events proved him wrong.

or COCOA) would make firms using assets that are not readily salable look bad. Though the protracted arguments about the relative merits of these and other rival systems have not generally overtly recognized the vested interests that stand to gain or lose by the way the argument goes, the political implications of inflation accounting have probably had as much responsibility for the difficulty in reaching agreement on the direction in which to move as have the technical problems involved.

In some of these instances, notably those concerning contingency reserves and foreign currency translations, critics of the FASB are asserting that economic behavior, such as reinsurance or hedging, which would not have been rational under the old accounting rules becomes rational under the new ones. Such an assertion is difficult to defend because the new rules have not changed the underlying cash flows or the risks attached to them. Only if significance is attached exclusively to "the bottom line," rather than to the present value of the enterprise, can the change in behavior be defended.

MEASUREMENT AND POLITICS

The above examples will serve to illustrate some of the points of contact between accounting and politics. Many more could be cited. Indeed, because standards need to be set mainly in areas where there is controversy, it is highly probable that in every case someone will find the new treatment less favorable than the status quo and there is constantly a temptation for such people to rush off to their legislative representatives to get the government to interfere.[13] That sort of initiative represents the gravest threat on the horizon to the private control of standard setting.

If we are looking for ways to achieve political ends by tinkering with methods of measurement, there is plenty of scope outside the accounting field. Indeed, the danger has already been observed in other areas. For instance, the index of retail prices has a powerful effect on wage settlements in many industries. There is nothing absolute about a price index. The number obtained depends on the choice of base year, the items chosen for inclusion in the market basket and the weights attached to the items in constructing the index. A statistician who agreed with Hawkins about the responsibilities of those concerned with measurement could easily construct an index which would damp down price changes and could take credit for aiding in the fight against inflation.[14]

---

[13]The letter dated October 6, 1977, addressed to the FASB chairman-designate by Senator William Proxmire (D-Wisconsin) and four Wisconsin congressmen and reported in the FASB *Status Report* no. 55, "Persons Opposing the FASB Exposure Draft on Oil and Gas Accounting Apparently Seek Support in Congress for Retention of Alternatives," October 14, 1977, is a case in point.

[14]There is nothing farfetched about this. In *The Final Days* (New York: Avon Books, 1977, p. 177), Bob Woodward and Carl Bernstein state that "late in 1971, Nixon had summoned the White House personnel chief, Fred Malek, to his office to discuss a 'Jewish cabal' in the Bureau of Labor Statistics. The 'cabal,' Nixon said, was tilting economic figures to make his administration look bad." Another example came to my notice when I was in Singapore in 1976. There the administration was accused of keeping the price index down by changing the grade of rice included in the collection of food items going into the index.

I have suggested elsewhere[15] that one way of reducing the traffic accident rate would be for highway authorities to lower the average speed by arranging to have all speedometers consistently overstate speeds so that drivers would think they were driving faster than they actually were. Speedometers influence behavior. Why not influence it in a beneficient direction?

This last example will serve to lay bare the profound threat to accounting implicit in the propositions of Hawkins and of the others referred to above. If it ever became accepted that accounting might be used to achieve other than purely measurement ends, faith in it would be destroyed[16] just as faith in speedometers would be destroyed once it was realized that they were subject to falsification for the purpose of influencing driving habits.

Hawkins's view that "because the [FASB] has the power to influence economic behavior, it has an obligation to support the government's economic plans" is, I believe, not only destructive of accounting but it is also infeasible. Governments have a habit of changing their plans from year to year, and even from month to month. Are accounting standards to be changed with every change in the political climate? One has only to recall President Nixon's turn-about from a "no wage and price controls" stance to an espousal of rigorous controls in 1971–72—or President Ford's switch from proposals for tax increases to "whip inflation now" to an acceptance of tax cuts to stimulate employment in 1974—to see how futile it is to talk about supporting the government's economic plans or how impossible it would be for a standards board to keep up with the government.

THE IMPORTANCE OF NEUTRALITY

Simply because information has an effect on human behavior does not mean that it should not seek to be neutral as between different desired modes of behavior. Unless it is as neutral as the accountant can make it, it is difficult to see how it can be relied on to guide behavior. As Chambers observes, "If the form of accounting is permitted to change with changes in policy, any attempt to scrutinize and to evaluate specific policies will be thwarted."[17]

Neutrality in accounting implies representational accuracy. Curiously, it has been little discussed, though other terms related to it have received more attention. The American Accounting Association's 1977 committee on concepts and standards for external financial reports gets near the heart of the matter

[15]In my Price Waterhouse lecture at Stanford University in 1972 entitled "Financial Accounting Standards: Regulation or Self-Regulation?"

[16]Support for this view is to be found in Arthur R. Wyatt's article, "The Economic Impact of Financial Accounting Standards," *Arthur Andersen Chronicle*, September 1977, p. 49. Somewhat ironically in the circumstances, the same view has been espoused more recently by the chairman of the SEC. In his Statement of August 29 on accounting practices for oil and gas producers, setting aside FASB Statement no. 19, Harold M. Williams said: "If it becomes accepted or expected that accounting principles are determined or modified in order to secure purposes other than economic measurement—even such virtuous purposes as energy production—we assume a grave risk that confidence in the credibility of our financial information system will be undermined."

[17]Raymond J. Chambers, *Accounting, Evaluation and Economic Behavior* (Englewood Cliffs, N.J.: Prentice-Hall, Inc., 1966), p. 326.

when it says: "Users of financial information prefer that it have a high degree of reliability. Reliability is that quality which permits users of data to depend upon it with confidence as representative of what it purports to represent. But reliable information is not necessarily useful. It could, for example, be reliable but unrelated to the use at hand. Several relatively general terms are often used as synonyms for, or to cover parts of, the concept of reliability. Thus, verifiability, objectivity, lack of bias, neutrality, and accuracy all are related to reliability. Like relevance, reliability (above some minimal level) is a necessary but not a sufficient condition for usefulness of data."[18]

If the preceding sentence is true, these two qualities (relevance and reliability) together go far toward ensuring usefulness. Relevance comprehends subsidiary characteristics of information one might list, such as timeliness. And the essential element in the reliability of information (at least for our present purpose) is that it shall as accurately as possible represent what it purports to represent.[19] This implies neutrality.

Neutrality, in the sense in which the term is used here, does not imply that no one gets hurt. It is true, as the AAA 1977 committee on the social consequences of accounting information says, "Every policy choice represents a trade-off among differing individual preferences, and possibly among alternative consequences, regardless of whether the policy-makers see it that way or not. In this sense, accounting policy choices can never be neutral. There is someone who is granted his preference, and someone who is not."[20] The same thing could be said of the draft, when draft numbers were drawn by lot. Some people were chosen to serve while others escaped. It was still, by and large, neutral in the sense that all males of draft age were equally likely to be selected.

ACCOUNTING AS FINANCIAL CARTOGRAPHY

Information cannot be neutral—it cannot therefore be reliable—if it is selected or presented for the purpose of producing some chosen effect on human behavior. It is this quality of neutrality which makes a map reliable; and the essential nature of accounting, I believe, is cartographic. Accounting is financial mapmaking. The better the map, the more completely it represents the complex phenomena that are being mapped. We do not judge a map by the behavioral effects it produces. The distribution of natural wealth or rainfall shown on a map may lead to population shifts or changes in industrial location, which the government may like or dislike. That should be no concern of the cartographer.

[18]Committee on concepts and standards for external financial reports, *Statement on Accounting Theory and Theory Acceptance* (Sarasota, Fla.: American Accounting Association, 1977), p. 16.

[19]This is close to Yuji Ijiri's statement that "in general, a system is said to be reliable if it works the way it is supposed to" (*The Foundations of Accounting Measurement: A Mathematical, Economic, and Behavioral Inquiry* [Englewood Cliffs, N.J.: Prentice-Hall, Inc., 1967], p. 137). But his more formal definition of reliability is couched more in terms of the predictive value of information, an aspect of the matter with which I am not here concerned.

[20]Committee on the social consequences of accounting information, *Report of the Committee on the Social Consequences of Accounting Information* (Sarasota, Fla.: AAA, 1978), p. 24.

We judge his map by how well it represents the facts. People can then react to it as they will.

Cartographers represent different facts in different ways and match the scale of their maps to their purpose. Every map represents a selection of a small portion of available data, for no map could show physical, political, demographic, climatological, geological, vegetational and numerous other kinds of data and still be intelligible. The need to be selective in the data that one represents does not normally rob the map of its neutrality, although it could.

As with the geographic features that cartographers map, different financial facts need to be represented in different ways, and different facts are needed for different purposes. It is perfectly proper for measurements to be selected with particular political ends in mind or to be adapted to a political end if it is made clear to users of the measurement what is being done. For example, the government is entitled, for taxation purposes, to define taxable income in whatever way suits it. It would be quite another matter for it to tell accountants that they were to use this definition for all purposes to which an income number might be put.

SOME CONTRARY VIEWS

There have recently been some expressions of a different view of accounting from mine that deserve comment here. Sometimes the difference in the weight to be given to economic impact in standard setting is merely one of emphasis. Sometimes it is more fundamental in nature. Sometimes neutrality is dismissed on other grounds.

Probably no one argues that those who formulate accounting standards should do so with total unconcern for their economic consequences. Indeed, without some concern for such consequences, the selection of problem areas that call for standards could not be made. It was the economic consequences of not having a standard to deal with some particular problem which presumably directed attention in that direction in the first place. To require the FASB to report on the probable standard when an exposure draft is issued[21]—if it can be done, for the impact will often not be clear or unambiguous—is not at all objectionable, so long as the standard is designed to bring about a better representation of the facts of a situation, with whatever behavioral results flow from that, and not to promote some preselected economic objective or mode of behavior.

Some of those who would play down the value of neutrality in accounting standards do so because, they argue, the financial phenomena which accountants must report are not independent of the reporting methods selected. This view is expressed by the AAA 1977 committee on the social consequences of accounting information in the following passage from its report: "The view that measurement merely involves representing or describing stocks and flows is a static view. It assumes that the stocks and flows are history, fixed forever, no matter how you measure them. But what about tomorrow's stocks and flows? They are governed by the business decisions of enterprises—decisions which

---

[21]As recommended by Prem Prakash and Alfred Rappaport in "The Feedback Effects of Accounting," *Business Week*, January 12, 1976, p. 12.

might change depending upon how you choose to measure the stocks and flows. The traditional framework fails to take this interdependence of measurement and decisional behavior into consideration."[22]

It is true that, where human beings are the subjects of measurement, behavior and measurements are not independent of each other. But this does not make neutrality a less desirable quality of measurement in such cases. If one substitutes speedometers for accounting and driving behavior for stocks and flows in the AAA committee's statement above, one can see that as an argument against neutrality it is quite unconvincing. There is nothing static about the relationship between the speed of a vehicle and the reading on the speedometer, and there is unquestionably feedback. The behavior of the driver is reflected on the dial, and what is on the dial affects the behavior of the driver. Speedometers still should register speed accurately and neutrally. The decision about how to react to the reading must be left to the driver.

A different criterion for the selection of approved accounting methods is put forward by William Beaver and Roland Dukes in a discussion of interperiod tax allocation: "The method which produces earnings numbers having the highest association with security prices is the most consistent with the information that results in an efficient determination of security prices. Subject to [certain] qualifications . . . , it is the method that ought to be reported."[23] And, having found that "deferral earnings are most consistent with the information set used in setting security prices," they conclude that "if one accepts market efficiency, the results suggest that the [Accounting Principles Board] made the 'correct' policy decision . . . in the sense that it requires a method which is most consistent with the information impounded in an efficient determination of security prices."[24]

Beaver and Dukes themselves point out that any inferences to be drawn from their evidence are "conditional upon the prediction models used to test the accounting measures. . . . Any findings are the joint result of prediction models and accounting methods, and only appropriately specified joint statements are warranted."[25] In other words, the identification of the accounting method found to generate earnings numbers or cash flow numbers most closely associated with security prices depends on the way that "unexpected returns" are defined. The results of this analysis do not point unambiguously, therefore, toward a particular accounting method.

This could explain why, left to themselves, companies do not all choose the same accounting methods. They do not all use the same prediction models, and therefore the accounting method that has the most information content for one company is not the one with the most for another company. One moral that might be drawn from this is that we do not need accounting standards at all but, rather, that in an efficient market laissez-faire should prevail. A different

[22]Social consequences committee, p. 23.

[23]William H. Beaver and Roland E. Dukes, "Interperiod Tax Allocation, Earnings Expectations, and the Behavior of Security Prices," *Accounting Review*, April 1972, p. 321. They add, in a footnote, that "the criterion suggested above provides a simplified method for preference ordering of alternative measurement methods."

[24]Ibid., p. 331.

[25]Ibid., p. 332.

conclusion about the Beaver and Dukes study is reached by Gonedes and Dopuch when they say that "under the contemporary institutional setting, capital market efficiency—taken by itself—does not imply that the prices of firms' ownership shares can be used in assessing the desirability of alternative information-production decisions."[26] In any case, whichever way the efficient market points us, it does not point us toward politically motivated accounting standards.

LIMITATIONS OF THE ANALOGY WITH CARTOGRAPHY

There is a danger, with any analogy, of pushing it too far, and the analogy between accounting and cartography is no exception. Most maps represent external phenomena that have an independent existence of their own. The accountant is on safe ground only when he is doing the same thing—representing external phenomena such as cash flows, contractual rights, market values, etc. Of course, cartographers have sometimes amused themselves by drawing maps of fictitious countries, like Erewhon or Atlantis, an activity which, too, has had its accounting counterparts.

Whatever limitations representational accuracy may have in pointing us toward right accounting answers, it will at least sometimes enable us to detect a wrong answer. For instance, FASB Statement no. 2, which requires all R&D expenditures to be expensed as incurred, is bad cartography because to represent the value of the continuing benefits of past research expenditures as zero will usually not be in accord with the facts of the situation, however expedient the treatment may be. Off-balance-sheet financing requires that certain unattractive features of the landscape be left off the map, so that again the map is defective. The criterion by which rules are to be judged is not the effect which they may or may not have on business behavior. It is the accuracy with which they reflect the facts of the situation.

CONCLUSION

It is not at all palatable for accountants to be confronted by a choice between appearing to be indifferent to national objectives or endangering the integrity of their measurement techniques. But if the long-run well-being of our discipline is what matters, the right choice should be easy to make. It is our job—as accountants—to make the best maps we can. It is for others, or for accountants acting in some other capacity, to use those maps to steer the economy in the right direction. If the distinction between these two tasks is lost sight of, we shall greatly diminish our capacity to serve society, and in the long run everybody loses.

[26]Gonedes and Dopuch, p. 92.

The Rise of "Economic Consequences"

STEPHEN A. ZEFF

Since the 1960's, the American accounting profession has been aware of the increasing influence of "outside forces" in the standard-setting process. Two parallel developments have marked this trend. First, individuals and groups that had rarely shown any interest in the setting of accounting standards began to intervene actively and powerfully in the process. Second, these parties began to invoke arguments other than those which have traditionally been employed in accounting discussions. The term "economic consequences" has been used to describe these novel kinds of arguments.

By "economic consequences" is meant the impact of accounting reports on the decision-making behavior of business, government, unions, investors and creditors. It is argued that the resulting behavior of these individuals and groups could be detrimental to the interests of other affected parties. And, the argument goes, accounting standard setters must take into consideration these allegedly detrimental consequences when deciding on accounting questions. The recent debates involving foreign currency translation and the accounting for unsuccessful exploration activity in the petroleum industry have relied heavily on economic consequences arguments, and the Financial Accounting Standards Board and the Securities and Exchange Commission have become extremely sensitive to the issue.[1]

The economic consequences argument represents a veritable revolution in accounting thought. Until recently, accounting policy making was either assumed to be neutral in its effects or, if not neutral, it was not held out to the public as being responsible for those effects. Today, these assumptions are being severely questioned, and the subject of social and economic consequences "has become *the* central contemporary issue in accounting."[2] That the FASB has commissioned research papers on the economic consequences of selected standards and has held a conference devoted entirely to the subject[3] underscores the current importance of this issue.

This article is an abridged version of a paper presented on June 9, 1978, at the Stanford Lectures in Accounting, Graduate School of Business, Stanford University.

[1]Several articles have been written on "economic consequences." See, e.g., Alfred Rappaport, "Economic Impact of Accounting Standards—Implications for the FASB," *Journal of Accountancy*, May 77, pp. 89–98; Arthur R. Wyatt, "The Economic Impact of Financial Accounting Standards," *Journal of Accountancy*, Oct. 77, pp. 92–94; and Robert J. Swieringa, "Consequences of Financial Accounting Standards," *Accounting Forum*, May 1977, pp. 25–39.

[2]*Report of the Committee on the Social Consequences of Accounting Information* (Sarasota, Fla.: American Accounting Association, 1978), p. 4.

Accounting policy makers have been aware since at least the 1960s of the third-party intervention issue,[4] while the issue of economic consequences has surfaced only in the 1970s. Indeed, much of the history of the Accounting Principles Board during the 1960s was one of endeavoring to understand and cope with the third-party forces which were intervening in the standard-setting process. In the end, the inability of the APB to deal effectively with these forces led to its demise and the establishment in 1973 of the FASB.

The true preoccupations of the intervening third parties have not always been made clear. When trying to understand the third-party arguments, one must remember that before the 1970s the accounting model employed by the American Institute of CPAs committee on accounting procedure (CAP) and the APB was, formally at least, confined to technical accounting considerations (sometimes called "accounting principles" or "conceptual questions") such as the measurement of assets, liabilities and income and the "fair presentation" of financial position and operations. The policy makers' sole concern was with the communication of financial information to actual and potential investors, for, indeed, their charter had been "granted" by the SEC, which itself had been charged by Congress to assure "full and fair disclosure" in reports to investors. Third-party intervenors, therefore, would have had an obvious incentive to appeal to the accounting model used by policy makers rather than raise the specter of an economic consequences model preferred by the third parties.

When corporate management began intervening in the standard-setting process to an increasing degree, therefore, its true position was probably disguised. An examination of management arguments suggests the following range of tactical rhetoric. Arguments were couched in terms of

1. The traditional accounting model, where management was genuinely concerned about unbiased and "theoretically sound" accounting measurements.
2. The traditional accounting model, where management was really seeking to advance its self-interest in the economic consequences of the contents of published reports.
3. The economic consequences in which management was self-interested.

If one accepts Johnson's dictum that it requires a "lively imagination" to believe that management is genuinely concerned with fair presentation when choosing between accounting alternatives,[5] it could be concluded that the first

[3]*Conference on the Economic Consequences of Financial Accounting Standards* (Stamford, Conn.: FASB, 1978).

[4]In this article, I am chiefly concerned with third-party intervention in the standard setting for unregulated industries. Accounting policy makers in this country have been alive for several decades to the accounting implications of the rules and regulations of rate-making in the energy, transportation and communication industries. See, e.g., George O. May, *Financial Accounting: A Distillation of Experience* (New York: The Macmillan Company, 1943), chs. 7–8, and William A. Paton, "Accounting Policies of the Federal Power Commission—A Critique," *Journal of Accountancy*, June 44, pp. 432–60.

[5]Charles E. Johnson, "Management's Role in External Accounting Measurements," in Robert K. Jaedicke, Yuji Ijiri and Oswald Nielsen (editors), *Research in Accounting Measurement* ([n.p.], AAA, 1966), p. 91.

argument has seldom been employed in third-party interventions. In recent years, particularly since the early 1970s, management has become more candid in its dialogues with the FASB, insistently advancing the third argument and thus bringing economic consequences to the fore.

Two factors tend to explain why economic consequences did not become a substantive issue before the 1970s. First, management and other interested parties predominantly used the second argument cited above, encouraging the standard-setting bodies to confine themselves to the traditional accounting model. Second, the CAP and APB, with few exceptions, were determined to resolve, or appear to resolve, standard-setting controversies in the context of traditional accounting.

EARLY USES OF ECONOMIC CONSEQUENCES ARGUMENTS

Perhaps the first evidence of economic consequences reasoning in the pronouncements of American policy makers occurred as long ago as 1941. In Accounting Research Bulletin no. 11, *Corporate Accounting for Ordinary Stock Dividends*, the CAP, in accordance with "proper accounting and corporate policy," required that fair market value be used to record the issuance of stock dividends where such market value was substantially in excess of book value.[6]

Evidently, both the New York Stock Exchange and a majority of the CAP regarded periodic stock dividends as "objectionable,"[7] and the CAP acted to make it more difficult for corporations to sustain a series of such stock dividends out of their accumulated earnings. As far as this author is aware, the U.S. is still the only country in which an accounting pronouncement requires that stock dividends be capitalized at the fair market value of the issued shares,[8] and this position was originally adopted in this country, at least in part, in order to produce an impact on the stock dividend policies of corporations.

A second evidence of economic consequences' entering into the debates surrounding the establishment of accounting standards, this time involving management representations, occurred in 1947–48. It was the height of the postwar inflation, and several corporations had adopted replacement cost depreciation in their published financial statements.[9] Among the arguments employed in the debate involving the CAP were the possible implications for tax reform, the possible impact on wage bargaining and the need to counteract criticisms of profiteering by big business. Despite the pressures for accounting reform, the CAP reaffirmed its support of historical cost accounting for depreciation in ARB no. 33, *Depreciation and High Costs*, and in a letter issued in October 1948.

A clear use of the economic consequences argument occurred in 1958, when three subsidiaries of American Electric Power Company sued in the federal

[6]Accounting Research Bulletin no. 11, *Corporate Accounting for Ordinary Stock Dividends* (New York: American Institute of Accountants, 1941), pp. 102–03.

[7]George O. May, letter to J. S. Seidman, dated July 14, 1941 (deposited in the national office library of Price Waterhouse & Co. in New York), p. 1.

[8]Price Waterhouse International, *A Survey in 46 Countries: Accounting Principles and Reporting Practices* ([n.p.], PWI, 1975), table 145.

[9]*Depreciation Policy When Price Levels Change* (New York: Controllership Foundation, Inc., 1948), ch. 14.

courts to enjoin the AICPA from allowing the CAP to issue a letter saying that the deferred tax credit account, as employed in the then-recently issued ARB no. 44 (Revised), *Declining-Balance Depreciation*, should be classified as a liability.[10] The three public utility companies were concerned that the SEC, under authority granted by the Public Utility Holding Company Act, would not permit them to issue debt securities in view of the unfavorable debt-to-equity ratios which the proposed reclassification would produce. The case reached the U.S. Supreme Court, where certiorari was denied. In the end, the clarifying letter was issued. Nonetheless, the SEC accommodated the public utility companies by consenting to exclude the deferred tax credit from both liabilities and stockholders' equity for purposes of decisions taken under the Public Utility Holding Company Act.[11]

Shortly after the creation of the APB, the accounting treatment of the investment tax credit exploded on the scene. The three confrontations between the APB and the combined forces of industry and the administrations of Presidents Kennedy, Johnson and Nixon have already been amply discussed in the literature.[12] The government's argument was not that the accounting deferral of the investment tax credit was bad accounting but that it diluted the incentive effect of an instrument of fiscal policy.

In 1965, the subject of segmental reporting emerged from a hearing of the Senate Subcommittee on Antitrust and Monopoly on the economic effects of conglomerate mergers. The aim of the senatorial inquiry was not to promote better accounting practices for investor use but to provide the subcommittee and other government policy makers with accounting data that would facilitate their assessment of the economic efficacy of conglomerate mergers. Company managements naturally looked on such disclosures as potentially detrimental to their merger ambitions. Pressure applied by this powerful subcommittee eventually forced the hand of the SEC to call for product-line disclosures in published financial reports. The repercussions of this initiative, which had its origin in a Senate hearing room, are still being felt.[13]

In 1967–69, the APB responded to an anguished objection by the startled Investment Bankers Association of America (today known as the Securities Industry Association) to a provision, once thought to be innocuous, in APB Opinion no. 10, *Omnibus Opinion-1966*, which imputed a debt discount to convertible debt and debt issued with stock warrants. The IBA was concerned about the impact of the accounting procedure on the market for such securities. In Opinion

[10]*The AICPA Injunction Case—Re: ARB [No.] 44 (Revised)*, Cases in Public Accounting Practice [no. 1] (Chicago, Ill.: Arthur Andersen & Co., 1960).

[11]*SEC Administrative Policy Re: Balance-Sheet Treatment of Deferred Income-Tax Credits*, Cases in Public Accounting Practice [nos. 5 and 6] (Chicago, Ill.: Arthur Andersen & Co., 1961), pp. 35–59.

[12]See Maurice Moonitz, "Some Reflections on the Investment Credit Experience," *Journal of Accounting Research*, Spring 1966, pp. 47–61; John L. Carey, *The Rise of the Accounting Profession: To Responsibility and Authority 1937–1969* (New York: AICPA, 1970), pp. 98–104; and Stephen A. Zeff, *Forging Accounting Principles in Five Countries: A History and an Analysis of Trends* (Champaign, Ill.: Stipes Publishing Company, 1972), pp. 178–80, 201–2, 219–21 and 326–27.

[13]Charles W. Plum and Daniel W. Collins, "Business Segment Reporting," in James Don Edwards and Homer A. Black (editors), *The Modern Accountant's Handbook* (Homewood, Ill.: Dow Jones-Irwin, Inc., 1976), pp. 469–511.

no. 14, *Accounting for Convertible Debt and Debt Issued With Stock Purchase Warrants*, the APB rescinded its action in regard to convertible debt while retaining the rest.[14]

From 1968 through 1971, the banking industry opposed the inclusion of bad-debt provisions and losses on the sales of securities in the net income of commercial banks. Bankers believed that the new measure would reflect unfavorably on the performance of banks. Eventually, through a concerted effort by the APB, the SEC and the bank regulatory agencies, generally accepted accounting principles were made applicable to banks.[15]

From 1968 through 1970, the APB struggled with the accounting for business combinations. It was flanked on the one side by the Federal Trade Commission and the Department of Justice, which favored the elimination of pooling-of-interests accounting in order to produce a slowing effect on the merger movement and on the other by merger-minded corporations that were fervent supporters of pooling-of-interests accounting. The APB, appearing almost as a pawn in a game of political chess, disenchanted many of its supporters as it abandoned positions of principle in favor of an embarrassing series of pressure-induced compromises.[16]

In 1971, the APB held public hearings on accounting for marketable equity securities, leases and the exploration and drilling costs of companies in the petroleum industry. In all three areas powerful industry pressures thwarted the board from acting. The insurance industry was intensely concerned about the possible effects on its companies' stock prices of including the unrealized gains and losses on portfolio holdings in their income statements.[17] The leasing initiative was squelched after senators, representatives and even the secretary of transportation responded to a letter-writing campaign by making pointed inquiries of the SEC and APB. The letter writers raised the specter of injury that the board's proposed action would supposedly cause to consumers and to the viability of companies in several key industries.[18] The petroleum industry was unable to unite on a solution to the controversy over full costing versus successful efforts costing, as it was alleged that a general imposition of the latter would adversely affect the fortunes of the small, independent exploration companies.[19] Using its considerable political might, the industry succeeded in persuading the board to postpone consideration of the sensitive subject.[20]

[14]Zeff, pp. 202, 211.

[15]Carey, p. 134: Maurice Moonitz, *Obtaining Agreement on Standards in the Accounting Profession*, Studies in Accounting Research no. 8 (Sarasota, Fla.: AAA, 1974), pp. 38–39; Zeff, pp. 210–11.

[16]Robert Chatov, *Corporate Financial Reporting: Public or Private Control?* (New York: The Free Press, 1975), pp. 212–22; and Zeff, pp. 212–16.

[17]Charles T. Horngren, "The Marketing of Accounting Standards," *Journal of Accountancy*, Oct. 73, pp. 63–64.

[18]Leonard M. Savoie, "Accounting Attitudes," in Robert R. Sterling (editor), *Institutional Issues in Public Accounting* (Lawrence. Kan.: Scholars Book Co., 1974), p. 326.

[19]See the testimony and submissions in *APB Public Hearing on Accounting and Reporting Practices in the Petroleum Industry*, Cases in Public Accounting Practice [no.] 10 (Chicago, Ill.: Arthur Andersen & Co., 1972).

[20]Savoie, p. 326.

On each of the occasions enumerated above, outside parties intervened in the standard-setting process by an appeal to criteria that transcended the traditional questions of accounting measurement and fair presentation. They were concerned instead with the economic consequences of the accounting pronouncements.

"Economic consequences" have been invoked with even greater intensity in the short life of the FASB. Such questions as accounting for research and development costs, self-insurance and catastrophe reserves, development stage companies, foreign currency fluctuations, leases, the restructuring of troubled debt,[21] domestic inflation and relative price changes, and the exploration and drilling costs of companies in the petroleum industry have provoked widespread debate over their economic consequences.[22] The list is both extensive and impressive, and accounting academics are busily investigating the empirical validity of claims that these and other accounting standards may be linked with the specified economic consequences.

THE STANDARD-SETTING BODIES RESPOND

What have been the reactions of the standard-setting bodies to the intervention by outside parties and the claim that accounting standards should or should not be changed in order to avoid unhealthy economic or social consequences? In the 1940s and 1950s, the CAP enhanced its liaison with interested third parties through a wider circulation of exposure drafts and subcommittee reports. From 1958 to 1971, through appointments to key committees, joint discussions and symposiums, mass mailings of exposure drafts and formal public hearings, the Institute and the APB acted to bring interested organizations more

---

[21]At the FASB's public hearing, some bankers warned of the dire economic consequences of requiring banks to write down their receivables following restructurings. Walter Wriston, chairman of Citicorp, asserted that the restructuring of New York City's obligations might just not have occurred if the banks would have been required to write down the carrying value of their receivables. Walter B. Wriston, *Transcript of Public Hearing on FASB* discussion memorandum, *Accounting by Debtors and Creditors When Debt Is Restructured* (1977-vol. 1-part 2), pp. 69–70. Yet the FASB, in its lengthy "Basis for Conclusions" in Statement no. 15, *Accounting by Debtors and Creditors for Troubled Debt Restructurings* (in which the feared write-downs were not required), did not refer to bankers' claims about the economic consequences of requiring significant write-downs. Does that omission imply that the FASB paid no attention to those assertions? Did the FASB conduct any empirical research (as it did concerning the economic consequences claims raised in connection with Statement no. 7, *Accounting and Reporting by Development Stage Enterprises*) to determine whether there was adequate ground to sustain such claims?

[22]See, e.g., Joseph M. Burns, *Accounting Standards and International Finance: With Special Reference to Multinationals* (Washington, D.C.: American Enterprise Institute for Public Policy Research, 1976); Committee on the Social Consequences of Accounting Information, pp. 9–12; Rappaport, pp. 90, 92; FASB, *Conference on the Economic Consequences of Financial Accounting Standards;* U.S. Department of Energy, comments before the Securities and Exchange Commission, "Accounting Practices—Oil and Gas Producers—Financial Accounting Standards," unpublished memorandum, dated April 3, 1978. Evidence attesting to the attention given by the FASB to economic consequences issues may be found in the "Basis for Conclusions" sections of the applicable statements. In addition to companies and industry groups, government departments (such as the Department of Commerce, in Statement no. 7, and the Departments of Energy and Justice, in Statement no. 19, *Financial Accounting and Reporting by Oil and Gas Producing Companies*) were actively involved in the discussion of economic consequences.

closely into the standard-setting process. The hope was, one supposes, that these organizations would be satisfied that their views were given full consideration before the final issuance of opinions. These accommodations were, however, of a procedural sort, although it is possible that these outside views did have an impact on the substantive content of some of the resulting opinions. It would appear that the APB was at least somewhat influenced by economic consequences in its prolonged deliberations leading to the issuance of Opinions no. 16, *Business Combinations*, and no. 17, *Intangible Assets*.[23] During the public hearings in 1971 on marketable equity securities and the accounting practices of companies in the petroleum industry, management representatives on several occasions asserted economic consequences as relevant considerations. Yet members of the APB's subject-area committees neither asked for proof of these assertions nor, indeed, questioned their relevance to the setting of accounting standards.[24]

Since it was the APB's inability to cope with the pressures brought by outside organizations that hastened its demise, it is worth noting that the FASB included the Financial Executives Institute (FEI) among its co-sponsors. In my opinion, the incorporation of the FEI in the formal structure of the Financial Accounting Foundation (FAF, the FASB's parent) is one of the most significant advantages which the FASB possesses in relation to its predecessor.[25]

The procedural machinery established for the FASB is even more elaborate than that which existed in the final years of the APB. The object of these additional procedures has been to expand and intensify the interaction between the board and interested outside parties, notably companies, industry associations and government departments and agencies. A task force drawn from a broad spectrum of interested groups is appointed prior to the preparation of each discussion memorandum. The DM itself is much bulkier than the modest document the APB had issued before its public hearings; it contains a neutral discussion of the entire gamut of policy issues that bear on the resolution of the controversy before the board. A Financial Accounting Standards Advisory Council (FASAC), composed of representatives of a wide array of interested groups, was appointed to be a sounding board for the FASB. The board itself has been composed of members drawn from accounting practice, the universities, companies and government—again, so that it would be responsive, and would appear to be responsive, to the concerns of those "constituencies." In an effort to persuade skeptics of the merit of its recommendations, the board includes in its statements a lengthy explanation of the criteria, arguments and empirical considerations it used to fashion the recommended standards.

Following criticism from within the profession of the board's operations and procedures, the FAF conducted a study in 1977 of the entire FASB operation.

[23]Wyatt, p. 92–93.

[24]*Proceedings* of Hearing on Accounting for Equity Securities, Accounting Principles Board (New York: AICPA, 1971), section A—Transcript; and *APB Public Hearing on Accounting and Reporting Practices in the Petroleum Industry*.

[25]The inclusion of the FEI could arguably become the undoing of the FASB. If the FEI were to lose confidence in the board, it is possible that many of the companies which now contribute to the Financial Accounting Foundation might decline to continue doing so, provoking a financial crisis that could threaten the board's viability.

Among the FAF's many recommendations were proposals that the board expand its formal and informal contacts with interested groups and that it include an economic impact analysis in important exposure drafts. On this latter point, the FAF's structure committee concluded: "The Board need not be unduly influenced by the possibility of an economic impact, but it should consider both the possible costs and the expected benefits of a proposal."[26] In addition, the structure committee recommended actions that would strengthen the roles of the task forces and the FASAC.[27] In 1978, under pressure from Congress, the board began to conduct virtually all its formal meetings (including those of the FASAC) "in the sunshine."

The history of the APB and the FASB is one of a succession of procedural steps taken to bring the board's deliberations into closer proximity to the opinions and concerns of interested third parties. As in the case of the APB, it is possible that an effect of these more elaborate procedures has been a change in the substance of the FASB's conclusions and recommendations.

By the middle 1970's, however, it was decided that the FASB should add economic (and social) consequences to the substantive issues it normally addresses. The inclusion of "probable economic or social impact" among the other "qualities of useful information" in the board's conceptual framework DM,[28] the board's announcement of its interest in empirical studies of economic consequences[29] and the recommendation of the FAF structure committee that the board inform itself adequately on the "various impacts its pronouncements might have"[30] collectively confirm this new direction. The issue of economic consequences has, therefore, changed from one having only procedural implications for the standard-setting process to one which is not firmly a part of the standard setters' substantive policy framework.

ECONOMIC CONSEQUENCES AS A SUBSTANTIVE ISSUE

Economic consequences have finally become accepted as a valid substantive policy issue for a number of reasons:

• The tenor of the times. The decade of the 1970s is clearly one in which American society is holding its institutions responsible for the social, environmental and economic consequences of their actions, and the crystallized public opinion on this subject eventually became evident (and relevant) to those interested in the accounting standard-setting activity.

• The sheer intractability of the accounting problems being addressed. Since the mid-1960s, the APB and the FASB have been taking up difficult accounting

[26]Financial Accounting Foundation structure committee, *The Structure of Establishing Financial Accounting Standards* (Stamford, Conn.: FAF, 1977), p. 51.

[27]Ibid., pp. 23–25.

[28]Financial Accounting Standards Board discussion memorandum, *Conceptual Framework for Financial Accounting and Reporting: Elements of Financial Statements and Their Measurement* (Stamford, Conn.: FASB, 1976), par. 367.

[29]Financial Accounting Standards Board, *Status Report*, no. 45, February 7, 1977.

[30]Structure committee, p. 31.

questions on which industry positions have been well entrenched. To some degree, companies that are sensitive to the way their performances are evaluated through the medium of reported earnings have permitted their decision-making behavior to be influenced by their perceptions of how such behavior will be seen through the prism of accounting earnings. Still other such companies have tailored their accounting practices to reflect their economic performances in the best light—and the managers are evidently loathe to change their decision-making behavior in order to accommodate newly imposed accounting standards. This would also be a concern to managers who are being paid under incentive compensation plans.[31]

• The enormity of the impact. Several of the issues facing the APB and the FASB in recent years have portended such a high degree of impact on either the volatility or level of earnings and other key financial figures and ratios that the FASB can no longer discuss the proposed accounting treatments without encountering incessant arguments over the probable economic consequences. Particularly apt examples are accounting for foreign exchange fluctuations, domestic inflation and relative price changes and the exploration and drilling costs of companies in the petroleum industry.

• The growth in the information economics-social choice, behavioral, income smoothing and decision usefulness literature in accounting. Recent writings in the information economics-social choice literature have provided a broad analytical framework within which the problems or economic consequences may be conceptualized. Beginning with Stedry,[32] the literature on the behavioral implications of accounting numbers has grown significantly, drawing the attention of researchers and policy makers to the importance of considering the effects of accounting information. The literature on income smoothing has suggested the presence of a managerial motive for influencing the measurement of earnings trends. Finally, the decision usefulness literature, although it is confined to the direct users of accounting information, has served to lessen the inclination of accountants to argue over the inherent "truth" of different accounting incomes and, instead, to focus on the use of information by those who receive accounting reports.[33]

• The insufficiency of the procedural reforms adopted by the APB and the FASB. Despite the succession of procedural steps which both boards have taken to provide outside parties with a forum for expressing their views, the claims of economic consequences—and the resulting criticisms of the boards' pronouncements—have continued unabated. The conclusion has evidently been reached that procedural remedies alone will not meet the problem.

• The Moss and Metcalf investigations. By the middle of 1976, it was known that Congressman John E. Moss (D-Calif.) and the late Senator Lee Metcalf (D-Mont.) were conducting investigations of the performance of the accounting

[31]Alfred Rappaport, "Executive Incentives vs. Corporate Growth," *Harvard Business Review,* July–August 1978, pp. 81–88.

[32]Andrew C. Stedry, *Budget Control and Cost Behavior* (Englewood Cliffs, N.J.: Prentice-Hall, Inc., 1960).

[33]Committee on concepts and standards for external financial reports, *Statement on Accounting Theory and Theory Acceptance* (Sarasota, Fla.: AAA, 1977), pp. 5–29.

profession, including its standard-setting activities, and it could reasonably have been inferred that the responsiveness of the standard-setting bodies to the economic and social effects of their decisions would be an issue.

• The increasing importance to corporate managers of the earnings figure in capital-market transactions. Especially in the 1960s, when capital markets were intensely competitive and the merger movement was fast paced, the earnings figure came to be viewed as an important element of managerial strategy and tactics. This factor is of importance in today's markets, as the pace of merger activity has once again quickened.

• Accounting figures came to be viewed as an instrument of social control. The social control of American enterprise has been well known in the rate-regulated energy, transporation and communications fields, but in recent years the earnings figure has, to an increasing degree, been employed as a control device on a broader scale.[34] Examples are fiscal incentives (such as the investment tax credit and redefinitions of taxable income that diverge from accounting income) that have an influence on debates surrounding financial reporting,[35] the price-control mechanism of Phase II in 1972–73[36] and the data base contemplated by the Energy Policy and Conservation Act of 1975.

• The realization that outsiders could influence the outcome of accounting debates. Before the 1960s, accounting controversies were rarely reported in the financial press, and it was widely believed that accounting was a constant, if not a fixed parameter, in the management of business operations. With the publicity given to the accounting for the investment credit in 1962–63, to the fractious dialogue within the AICPA in 1963–64 over the authority of the APB and to other accounting disagreements involving the APB, managers and other outside parties have come to realize that accounting may be a variable after all—that the rules of accounting are not unyielding or even unbending.

• The growing use of the third argument, advanced earlier in the article, in accounting debates. Mostly for the reasons enumerated above, outside parties began to discard the pretense that their objections to proposed changes in accounting standards were solely, or even primarily, a function of differences over the proper interpretation of accounting principles. True reasons came out into the open, and accounting policy makers could no longer ignore their implications.

It is significant that economic consequences have become an important issue at a time when accounting and finance academics have been arguing that the U.S. capital markets are efficient with respect to publicly available infor-

---

[34]DR Scott, though writing in a different context, nonetheless was prophetic in his prediction that accounting would increasingly be used as a means of social control. DR Scott, *Cultural Significance of Accounts* (New York: Henry Holt and Co., 1931), esp. ch. 14.

[35]The "required tax conformity" issue of the early 1970s (see Zeff, pp. 218–19) is another instance.

[36]Robert F. Lanzillotti, Mary T. Hamilton and R. Blaine Roberts, *Phase II in Review; the Price Commission Experience* (Washington, D.C.: Brookings Institution, 1975), pp. 73–77; and C. Jackson Grayson, Jr., and Louis Neeb, *Confessions of a Price Controller* (Homewood, Ill.: Dow Jones-Irwin, Inc., 1974), pp. 71–76.

mation and, moreover, that the market cannot be "fooled" by the use of different accounting methods to reflect the same economic reality.[37]

THE DILEMMA FACING THE FASB

What are the implications of the economic consequences movement for the FASB? It has become clear that political agencies (such as government departments and congressional committees) expect accounting standard setters to take explicitly into consideration the possible adverse consequences of proposed accounting standards. This expectation appears to be strongest where the consequences are thought to be significant and widespread—and especially where they might impinge on economic and social policies being pursued by the government. In these instances, the FASB must show that it has studied the possible consequences but that the benefits from implementing the standards outweigh the possible adverse consequences. Where the claimed consequences have implications for economic or social policies of national importance, the FASB should not be surprised if a political resolution is imposed by outside forces.

To what degree should the FASB have regard for economic consequences? To say that any significant economic consequences should be studied by the board does not imply that accounting principles and fair presentation should be dismissed as the principal guiding factor in the board's determination. The FASB is respected as a body of accounting experts, and it should focus its attention where its expertise will be acknowledged. While some observers might opt for determining accounting standards only with regard to their consequences for economic and social welfare, the FASB would surely preside over its own demise if it were to adopt this course and make decisions primarily on other than accounting grounds.

The board is thus faced with a dilemma which requires a delicate balancing of accounting and nonaccounting variables. Although its decisions should rest—and be seen to rest—chiefly on accounting considerations, it must also study—and be seen to study—the possible adverse economic and social consequences of its proposed actions. In order to deal adequately with this latter function, the board may find it convenient to develop a staff of competent analysts from allied disciplines, notably economics.

Economic consequences bids fair to be the most challenging accounting issue of the 1970s. What is abundantly clear is that we have entered an era in which economic and social consequences may no longer be ignored as a substantive issue in the setting of accounting standards. The profession must respond to the changing tenor of the times while continuing to perform its essential role in the areas in which it possesses undoubted expertise.

---

[37]See, e.g., William H. Beaver, "What Should Be the FASB's Objectives?" *Journal of Accountancy*, Aug. 73, pp. 49–56.

III-D/IMPLICATIONS OF MARKET EFFICIENCY AND PORTFOLIO THEORY

What Should Be the FASB's Objectives?

WILLIAM H. BEAVER

Was the acrimony out of the investment tax credit much ado about nothing? Does it matter whether special gains and losses are reported in the ordinary income or in the extraordinary item section? When firms switch from accelerated to straight-line depreciation, what is the effect upon investors? Did the Accounting Principles Board allocate its resources in an appropriate manner? If its priorities needed reordering, where should the emphasis have been shifted? What objectives should be adopted for financial accounting standards?

To answer such questions, the Financial Accounting Standards Board plans to sponsor a sizable research program.[1] For this reason, now is an appropriate time to take stock of the current body of knowledge and assess its implications for the setting of financial accounting standards. This article summarizes the results of recent research that has explored several facets of the relationship between financial statement data and security prices. The findings have a direct bearing on the questions raised at the outset and suggest that our traditional views of the role of policy-making bodies, such as the APB, SEC and FASB, may have to be substantially altered.

Currently we have far too little evidence on important issues in accounting. However, given this paucity of knowledge, it would be unfortunate if we ignored the evidence that we do have. Aspects of this research have already had a considerable effect on the professional investment community. Yet there has been no awareness of this research in accounting at the practical level or in the setting of past standards, as reflected in the APB Opinions. If the hopes for success of the FASB are to be realized, it is imperative that we lead, not lag, in incorporating the current state of knowledge into the setting of standards. Regulating

The author wishes to acknowledge financial assistance provided by the Dean Witter Foundation. The conclusions expressed here are those of the author and do not necessarily reflect those of the foundation or any of its members.

William H. Beaver, "What Should be the FASB's Objectives?" *The Journal of Accoutancy*, August 1973, pp. 49–56. Copyright © 1980 by the American Institute of Certified Public Accountants, Inc.

[1]"Recommendations of the Study on Establishment of Accounting Principles," *Journal of Accountancy*, May 72, pp. 66–71.

financial accounting standards in ignorance of this evidence makes the prospects for success dim.

THE EVIDENCE

The behavior of security prices with respect to financial statement data is a widely discussed and hotly debated topic. The financial press is replete with articles of alleged effects of financial statement data on prices. In most cases, such allegations are not supported by any evidence. In a few cases, evidence of an anecdotal nature is offered. For example, the price of the stock of the ABC Company changed dramatically at approximately the same time the firm changed its method of depreciation to straight-line. Therefore, the cause was the change in accounting method. Such stories, while often entertaining, hardly constitute convincing evidence for several reasons. First, such an approach may select only those cases which are favorable to the hypothesis of the author while ignoring those instances that would refute it. For example, an examination of the price changes of only one firm or a few hand-picked firms that changed depreciation methods is insufficient. An examination must be made for all firms that changed depreciation methods or at least a large, randomly selected sample. Second, the analysis explains price changes after-the-fact on the basis of a single factor. There may be many factors that cause a price change. Usually, little or no care is taken to account for these other factors.

Unfortunately, until recently such evidence was the only type available. However, the issue is far too serious to be left to casual empiricism. Security prices are of obvious importance because of their impact upon the wealth, and hence the welfare, of investors. This importance is formally recognized in SEC legislation. Recent cases arising out of Section 10b-5 testify to the fact that accounting practices are evaluated in terms of their effect on security prices.[2] Moreover, it is inconceivable that the FASB could set optimal financial accounting standards without assessing the impact of their actions on security prices.

The prevailing opinion in the accounting profession is that the market reacts naïvely to financial statement information. This view is reinforced by the anecdotal data of the sort described earlier, and by the obvious fact that the market is populated with several million uninformed, naïve investors, whose knowledge or concern for the subtleties of accounting matters is nil. However, in spite of this obvious fact, the formal research in this area is remarkably consistent in finding that the market, at least as manifested in the way in which security prices react, is quite sophisticated in dealing with financial statement data. One rationale for the observed sophistication of security prices is that the professional investors "make the market" and competitive bidding among one another for securities effectively makes the prices behave in such a manner that they reflect a considerable amount of sophistication. In any event, regardless of what the actual causal mechanism may be, there is considerable evidence that se-

---

[2]For example, litigation is currently under way in the cases of *Memorex* and *Occidental Petroleum Corp.*, pursuant to SEC action under Section 10b-5. Brief summaries of issues appear in the June 25, 1971, and March 5, 1971, issues of *The Wall Street Journal*, respectively. In both cases, measures of damages being discussed are directly related to the effect of the firms' accounting practices on security prices.

curity prices do in fact behave in a sophisticated fashion. In the terminology of this literature, the securities market is said to be "efficient" with respect to financial statement data.[3]

A market is said to be efficient if security prices act as if they "fully reflect" publicly available information, including financial statement data. In other words, in an efficient market the investor is playing a "fair game" with respect to published information. Specifically, this means no investor can expect to use published information in such a way as to earn abnormal returns on his securities. Each investor can expect to earn a return on a security commensurate with its risk.[4] All securities of the same degree of riskiness will offer the same expected return, regardless of what accounting methods are used and no matter how much time is spent gleaning the secrets of the financial statements hidden in the footnotes. Hence, no amount of security analysis, based on published financial statement data, will lead to abnormal returns. There are obvious implications for the community of professional investors, among others. However, there are also equally dramatic implications for the accounting profession. For this reason, the evidence, which has examined several aspects of market efficiency with respect to financial statement data, is summarized below.[5]

One aspect of efficiency is the speed with which security prices react to public information when it is announced. Empirical evidence indicates that prices react quickly and in an unbiased fashion to a variety of events, including announcements of stock splits, stock dividends, secondary offerings and rights issues, as well as both annual and interim earnings announcements. This finding is exactly what one would expect in a market where the security prices at any point in time fully reflect the information released. Moreover, the studies of

---

[3]Three forms of efficiency have been delineated: (1) the weak form, which deals with efficiency with respect to the past sequence of security prices (e.g., the random-walk hypothesis), (2) the semistrong form, which concerns efficiency with respect to published information, and (3) the strong form, which involves all information including inside information. This article deals with efficiency in the semistrong form. There is also considerable evidence with respect to the weak form of efficiency, but it is beyond the scope of this article. For a summary of this literature, see W. Beaver, "Reporting Rules for Marketable Equity Securities," *Journal of Accountancy*, Oct. 71, pp. 57–61.

[4]A detailed discussion of security risk and how it relates to expected returns is beyond the scope of the article. However, there has been a substantial amount of research in the portfolio theory and capital asset pricing literature dealing with this relationship. Briefly, the literature suggests that expected return must be commensurate with the risk incurred, in that securities with greater risk must offer higher expected return. Of course, the actual return in a given period may differ from expected return. For a more complete discussion of this issue in a nontechnical manner, see C. Welles, "The Beta Revolution: Learning to Live With Risk," *The Institutional Investor*, September 1971, pp. 21–64; W. Sharpe, "Risk, Market Sensitivity and Diversification," *Financial Analysts Journal*, January-February 1972, pp. 74–79.

[5]A more detailed summary of the literature is provided in the article by Eugene Fama, "Efficient Capital Markets: A Review of Theory and Empirical Work," *Journal of Finance*, May 1970, pp. 383–417. The implications of this literature for accounting also have been discussed in the following articles: W. Beaver, "The Behavior of Security Prices and Its Implications for Accounting Research Methods," *The Accounting Review* (Supplement, 1972), pp. 407–37; R. Ball, "Changes in Accounting Techniques and Stock Prices" (unpublished paper, University of Chicago, 1972); and N. Gonedes, "Efficient Capital Markets and External Accounting," *The Accounting Review*, January 1972, pp. 11–21.

earnings announcements find security prices anticipate earnings for several months prior to the announcement.[6]

Another aspect is this: Does the market look behind accounting numbers or is it fooled by them? Does the market act only on reported accounting numbers or does it adjust for other information, such as the accounting method used to calculate those numbers? In other words, does the market use a broader information set than merely the reported accounting numbers? In this respect, there have been several studies of changes in accounting methods and the subsequent behavior of security prices.[7] All of these studies show essentially the same result. There is no increase in price by changing to an accounting method that reports higher earnings than would have been reported had no change been made. The market, as reflected in price behavior, is not so naïve as many people claim. Instead, it acts as if it looks beyond accounting numbers and takes into account the fact that earnings are being generated by a different method.

Further evidence compared the price-earnings ratios of firms that use accelerated methods of depreciation for both tax and reporting purposes (A/A group) with the price-earnings ratios of firms that use accelerated methods for tax purposes but straight-line for reporting purposes (A/S group).[8] The price-earnings ratio for the A/A group was larger than the price-earnings ratio for the A/S group. This finding is consistent with a market which recognizes that firms will report lower earnings under accelerated methods of depreciation than they would have under straight-line methods. Further analysis suggested that risk and growth could not explain the difference in the price-earnings ratios. In fact, the average riskiness and average growth rates were the same for both depreciation groups. However, when the earnings of the A/S group were converted to the earnings that would have been reported had they used an accelerated method for reporting, the price-earnings ratios of the two depreciation groups were essentially equal. In other words, when the firms were placed on a uniform accounting method, the price-earnings differences disappeared. Thus, the market appears to adjust for differences in depreciation methods among firms and, in effect, looks behind reported accounting data. Moreover, further testing found that changes in security prices more closely follow changes in certain nonre-

[6]The studies referred to here are E. Fama, L. Fisher, M. Jensen and R. Roll, "The Adjustment of Stock Prices to New Information," *International Economic Review*, February 1969, pp. 1–21; M. Scholes, "The Market for Securities: Substitution Versus Price Pressure and the Effects of Information on Share Prices," *Journal of Business*, April 1972, pp. 179–211; R. Ball and P. Brown, "An Empirical Evaluation of Accounting Income Numbers," *Journal of Accounting Research*, Autumn 1968, pp. 159–78; P. Brown and J. Kennelly, "The Informational Content of Quarterly Earnings: An Extension and Some Further Evidence," *Journal of Business*, July 1972, pp. 403–21; G. Benston, Published Corporate Accounting Data and Stock Prices," *Empirical Research in Accounting: Selected Studies, 1967, Journal of Accounting Research* (Supplement, 1967), pp. 1–54; and W. Beaver, "The Information Content of Annual Earnings Announcements," *Empirical Research in Accounting: Selected Studies, 1968, Journal of Accounting Research* (Supplement, 1968), pp. 67–92.

[7]The empirical studies referred to here include R. Kaplan and R. Roll, "Investor Evaluation of Accounting Information: Some Empirical Evidence," *Journal of Business*, April 1972, pp. 225–57; R. Ball, *op. cit.*; T. R. Archibald, "Stock Market Reaction to Depreciation Switchback," *The Accounting Review*, January 1972, pp. 22–30; and E. Comiskey, "Market Response to Changes in Depreciation Accounting," *The Accounting Review*, April 1971, pp. 279–85.

[8]W. Beaver and R. E. Dukes, "Interperiod Tax Allocation and Depreciation Methods: Some Empirical Results," *The Accounting Review* July 1973.

ported forms of earnings than they do changes in reported earnings. This finding is consistent with a market where a broad information set is used in assessing price changes in contrast to one where there is sole, unquestioning reliance upon reported earnings.

In sum then, the evidence, across a variety of contexts, supports the contention that the market is efficient with respect to published information.

IMPLICATIONS

This evidence, together with the evidence on the performance of mutual funds, has led to changes in the investment community.[9]

Many portfolio managers and their clients have moved away from a "beat-the-market," high-turnover philosophy to one where the emphasis is placed upon risk management and the minimization of operating costs. The Samsonite pension fund contract is but one recent example. Wells Fargo Bank has agreed to manage the Samsonite pension fund where the agreement stipulates the maintenance of a given level of risk within prespecified limits, a lid on the maximum amount of turnover that can occur and a restriction on the minimum number of securities comprising the fund.[10]

Given the practical impact that this research has had on the investment community, one might suspect that there are implications for the practice of accounting as well. In fact, there are several important implications for accounting in general and for the FASB in particular. However, there has been virtually no reaction on the part of the accounting profession. One reason is a general lack of awareness of this research, because its dissemination has essentially been restricted to academic journals. Another reason is that the anecdotal form of evidence discussed earlier continues to carry considerable weight among many members of the accounting profession. As a result, many readers may refuse to accept the evidence in support of market efficiency. But what if the mounting evidence in support of an efficient market finally becomes so overwhelming and compelling that it is accepted by all seven members of the FASB, all SEC Commissioners and staff, and all congressmen? What are the implications for the FASB? There are at least four major implications.

First. Many reporting issues are trivial and do not warrant an expenditure of FASB resources. The properties of such issues are twofold: (1) There is essentially no difference in cost to the firm of reporting either method. (2) There

[9]The empirical evidence finds that mutual fund returns fail to cover even research costs and brokerage commissions (let alone loading charges). After deducting these expenses, the net return to the mutual fund shareholder is below the return that could have been obtained from a simple strategy of buying and holding a portfolio of the same degree of riskiness. In fact, only after all such costs were added back in computing the return is the average mutual fund performance approximately equal to (but not greater than) the return from random portfolios of the same degree of riskiness. Moreover, these results not only apply to the average performance of all mutual funds but additional tests also indicate that no individual funds were able to produce superior returns consistently. For example, past performance by a fund appeared to be of no value in predicting superior performance in the future. See M. Jensen, "Risk, the Pricing of Capital Assets, and the Evaluation of Investment Portfolios," *Journal of Business*, April 1969, pp. 167–247. See also M. Zweig, "Darts, Anyone? As Market Pickers, Market Seers, the Pros Fall Short," *Barron's*, February 19, 1973, pp. 11–25.

[10]C. Welles, *op. cit.*

is essentially no cost to statement users in adjusting from one method to the other. In such cases, there is a simple solution. Report one method, with sufficient footnote disclosure to permit adjustment to the other, and let the market interpret implications of the data for security prices.

Unfortunately, too much of the resources of the APB and others has been devoted to issues that warrant this straightforward resolution. For example, the investment credit controversy belongs in this category, as do the issues regarding the definition of extraordinary items, interperiod tax allocation, earnings per share computations involving convertible securities, and accounting for marketable equity securities. By contrast, the FASB should shift its resources to those controversies where there is nontrivial additional cost to the firms or to investors in order to obtain certain types of information (for example, replacement cost accounting for depreciable assets). Whether such information should be a required part of reporting standards is a substantive issue.

Second. The role of financial statement data is essentially a preemptive one—that is, to prevent abnormal returns accruing to individuals by trading upon inside information. This purpose leads to the following disclosure policy: If there are no additional costs to disclosure to the firm, there is prima facie evidence that the item in question ought to be disclosed.

This relatively simple policy could greatly enhance the usefulness of financial statements. Many forms of information are currently being generated internally by the firm and could be reported with essentially no additional cost (e.g., the current market value of marketable equity securities). Such information, if not publicly reported, may constitute inside information. Merely because prices reflect publicly available information in no way implies that they also fully reflect inside information. One information cost that investors may be incurring currently is abnormal returns earned by those who have monopolistic access to inside information. Opponents of greater disclosure bear the burden of proof of showing that individuals can be prevented from earning excess returns with the undisclosed information or that the cost of disclosure exceeds the excess returns. Given the private incentives to trade on inside information, such a condition is very difficult to ensure.

Incidentally, efficient securities markets also have some important implications regarding the accountants' growing concern over legal liability. Accountants can be held legitimately responsible for insufficient disclosure. However, they should not be held responsible for using a "wrong" method (e.g., flow-through v. deferral) as long as they disclose the method that was used and sufficient data to permit adjustment to the nonreported method.

Third. The FASB must reconsider the nature of its traditional concern for the naïve investor. If the investor, no matter how naïve, is in effect facing a fair game, can he still get harmed? If so, how? The naïve investor can still get harmed, but not in the ways traditionally thought. For example, the potential harm is not likely to occur because firms use flow-through v. deferral for accounting for the investment credit. Rather, the harm is more likely to occur because firms are following policies of less than full disclosure and insiders are potentially earning monopoly returns from access to inside information. Harm is also likely to occur when investors assume speculative positions with excessive transactions costs, improper diversification and improper risk levels in the erroneous belief that they will be able to "beat the market" with published accounting information.

This implies that the FASB should actively discourage investors' beliefs that accounting data can be used to detect overvalued or undervalued securities. This also implies that the FASB must not attempt to reduce the complex events of multimillion dollar corporations to the level of understanding of the naïve, or, perhaps more appropriately labeled, ignorant investor. We must stop acting as if all—or even most—individual investors are literally involved in the process of interpreting the impact of accounting information upon the security prices of firms.

An argument often advanced against fuller disclosure is that the increased disclosure will befuddle and confuse the naïve investor. A specific manifestation of this argument is that earnings under market value rules are more volatile and hence may lead to more volatile security prices. For example, the insurance industry currently opposes the inclusion of such information on marketable securities in the income statement, even though market values are already reported on the balance sheet. Given that market values on the balance sheet are already part of public information, it is absurd to think that there is going to be any further effect on security prices because of the income statement disclosure. Yet considerable resources of the APB, the insurance industry and others have been wasted on an attempt to resolve this issue. In the more general case where there is no reporting of market values, the efficient market evidence implies that the market is not reacting naïvely to the currently reported numbers but, rather, is forming "unbiased" assessments of the market values and their effects on prices. Since the market is currently being forced to assess the effects of market values indirectly, they are probably estimating the values with error. Hence, if anything, reporting the actual numbers may eliminate the estimation errors which may be one source of volatility in security prices.

Moreover, one message comes through loud and clear from finance theory. The investor is concerned with assessing risk as well as expected return. In this context, one role of financial statement data is to aid the investor in assessing the risk of the security. By presenting less volatile numbers, we may be doing him a disservice by obscuring the underlying riskiness of his investment. Hence, it is impossible to argue that less volatile numbers per se are better than more volatile numbers. Taken together with the evidence in the efficient market, this suggests that the market can decide for itself how it wishes to interpret a given piece of information. The same sort of reasoning should be applied to the currently hot topic of reporting and attesting to forecasts. In an efficient market, a paternalistic attitude is unwarranted; furthermore, operationally, if it is used to rationalize lesser disclosure, it is much more likely to result in the protection of management than in the protection of investors, which is its ostensible purpose.

Fourth. Accountants must stop acting as if they are the only suppliers of information about the firm. Instead, the FASB should strive to minimize the total cost of providing information to investors. In an efficient market, security prices may be essentially the same under a variety of financial accounting standards, because, if an item is not reported in the financial statements, it may be provided by alternative sources. Under this view, which is consistent with the evidence cited earlier, the market uses a broad information set, and the accountant is one—and only one—supplier of information. One objective is to provide the information to investors by the most economical means. In order to accomplish this objective, several questions must be addressed: What are the alternative sources of information to financial statements? What are the costs of providing a given piece of information via the alternative source vis-à-vis the financial statements? Most importantly, do financial statement data have a comparative advantage in providing any portion of the total information used by the market, and, if so, what portion?

The nature of the costs has already been alluded to. One set of costs is the "cost" of abnormal returns' being earned by insiders because of monopolistic access to information. A second set of costs is excessive information costs. They can occur in two situations:

1. When the accountant fails to report an item that must be conveyed to the investing public through some other, more expensive source.
2. When the FASB requires firms to report an item that has a "value" less than its cost or items that could have been reported through other, less expensive sources of information. A third set of costs is incurred when investors erroneously believe that they can "beat the market" using published financial statement information. This set includes excessive transaction costs stemming from churning their accounts, improper diversification because of disproportionately large investment in "underpriced" securities and the selection of improper risk levels.[11]

NATURE OF FUTURE RESEARCH

One of the objectives the FASB must face is the establishment of a research program. Several areas should be explored:

1. Although the evidence in favor of market efficiency with respect to published information is considerable, the issue is by no means closed and further work on the particular types of accounting information items is needed.
2. Much more research is needed regarding market efficiency with respect to inside information. Such research will help to specify what the costs of nondisclosure are.
3. Evidence is needed on how individual investors, as opposed to the aggregate prices, react to information. Specifically, what is the process or mechanism by which information reaches individuals and is subsequently impounded in prices? What evidence is there of excessive transactions costs' being incurred by investors who act on information that

[11]The costs of holding erroneous beliefs regarding market efficiency extend beyond investors. For example, consider the recent decision by Chrysler to change inventory methods because of alleged inefficiencies in the capital markets (both debt and equity markets). Even though Chrysler had reported supplemental statements in its previous annual reports, this was judged to be inadequate to overcome the inability of the capital market to look behind the reported numbers. The initial effect of a switch in inventory methods for both book and tax purposes was an incremental tax bill of approximately $50 million spread over a 20-year period. The efficient market evidence suggests that such a decision was a serious misallocation of resources. In fact, if anything, Chrysler is in worse economic position now because it is paying higher tax bills. For a summary of facts, see "Chrysler Posts $7.6 Million Loss for the Year," *The Wall Street Journal*, February 10, 1971.

already has been impounded in prices? Research into volume activity, as opposed to price activity, may be particularly insightful here. What evidence is there that individuals incur improper selection of risk levels by taking speculative positions based on accounting data? There are currently research methods available in finance that can provide at least a partial answer to these questions. The application of behavioral science also offers promise here.

4. More research is needed regarding the association between certain specific financial statement items and security prices. For example, are there certain items that are now being reported which do not seem to be used by the market as reflected in security prices? Conversely, are there certain types of information which are not currently reported but, in spite of that fact, are reflected in security prices? In the former instance, such items are candidates for being considered for possible exclusion from currently reported items. With respect to the latter, such items are candidates for being considered part of currently reported items.

5. Further research is needed to examine to what extent financial statement data are helpful to individual investors assessing the risk of a security. In an efficient market, the usefulness of financial statement data to individual investors is not to find mispriced securities, since they are nonexistent. What then is the value, if any? The value lies in the ability of financial statement data to aid in risk prediction. Some recent findings in the area by Beaver, Kettler and Scholes are encouraging, but much more research is needed.[12]

ERRONEOUS INTERPRETATIONS

The implications of market efficiency for accounting are frequently misunderstood. There are at least two common misinterpretations.

The first belief is that, in an efficient market world, there are no reporting issues of substance because of the "all-knowing" efficient market. Taken to its extreme, this error takes the form of asserting that accounting data have no value and hence the certification process is of no value.[13] The efficient market in no way leads to such implications. It may very well be that the publishing of financial statements data is precisely what makes the market as efficient as

---

[12]W. Beaver, R. Kettler and M. Scholes, "The Association Between Market Determined and Accounting Determined Risk Measures," *The Accounting Review*, October 1970, pp. 654–82.

[13]In this regard it is imperative to distinguish between two important aspects of information: (1) The first is to aid the market in arriving at a given set of security prices. One aspect of this role is to provide a market where the investors are playing a fair game with respect to some given information set (e.g., accounting data). (2) The second is to aid individual investors, who face a given set of prices, to select the optimal portfolio. One aspect of this role is the use of financial statement data in risk prediction. It is entirely possible that future research will discover that financial statement data have no role to play at the individual investor level and that the sole role is a social one. In any event, the social level is of paramount concern to a policy-making body such as the FASB. The distinction is made particularly clear in E. Fama and A. Laffer, "Information and Capital Markets," *Journal of Business*, July 1971, pp. 289–98; and J. Hirshleifer, "The Private and Social Value of Information and the Reward to Inventive Activity," *American Economic Review*, September 1971, pp. 561–74; see also, W. Beaver, *op. cit.*, pp. 424–25.

it is. As I was careful to point out earlier, merely because the market is efficient with respect to published data does not imply that market prices are also efficient with respect to nonpublished information. Disclosure is a substantive issue.

A second erroneous implication is, simply find out what method is most highly associated with security prices and report that method in the financial statements. As it stands, it is incorrect for several reasons. One major reason is that such a simplified decision rule fails to consider the costs of providing information. For example, a nonreported method may be less associated with security prices than the reported method because the cost of obtaining the nonreported numbers via alternative sources is too high. Yet such information may be provided via financial statements at substantially lower costs. In another context, suppose the nonreported method showed the higher association with security prices; does it follow that the nonreported method should be reported? No, not necessarily. Perhaps the market is obtaining the information at lower cost via the alternative sources.[14]

Moreover, the choice among different accounting methods involves choosing among differing consequences, as reflected in the incidence of costs and security prices which affect individuals differently. Hence, some individuals may be better off under one method, while others may be better off under an alternative method. In this situation, how is the optimal method to be selected? The issue is one of social choice, which in general is an unresolvable problem because of the difficulty (impossibility) of making interpersonal welfare comparisons.[15]

There are certain specific issues (e.g., similar to those discussed in this article) which closely suggest a policy decision, if one is willing to accept the mild ethical assumption of Pareto-optimality.[16] However, such situations must meet a fairly specific set of conditions.

Regardless of the final resolution by the policymaker, it is still possible to specify the types of evidence that are relevant to choosing among alternatives. In simplest terms, although evidence cannot indicate what choice to make, it can provide information on the potential consequences of the various choices. Without a knowledge of consequences (e.g., as reflected in security prices), it is inconceivable that a policy-making body such as the FASB will be able to select optimal financial accounting standards. In spite of the importance of a knowledge of consequences, currently too little is known about price behavior and virtually nothing is known about the magnitude of the three types of costs outlined earlier.

CONCLUSION

Financial statement information is inherently a social commodity. However, it is clear that decisions regarding its generation and dissemination are of a much

[14]These issues are discussed at greater length in R. May and G. Sundem, "Cost of Information and Security Prices: Market Association Tests for Accounting Policy Decision," *The Accounting Review,* January 1973, pp. 80–94.

[15]K. Arrow, *Social Choice and Individual Values* (Yale University Press, 1968). The issue has been discussed in an accounting context in J. Demski, "Choice Among Financial Accounting Alternatives" (unpublished, Stanford University, 1972).

[16]The concept of Pareto-optimality states that a society prefers one alternative to another, if at least some people are better off and no one is worse off.

different nature than we have traditionally thought them to be. This change in the way we view the FASB is conditioned upon the assumption of market efficiency. While there is need for further future research in this area, there is sufficient credibility in the evidence to date that we should be prepared to face its implications:

1. Many reporting issues are capable of a simple disclosure solution and do not warrant an expenditure of FASB time and resources in attempting to resolve them.
2. The role of accounting data is to prevent superior returns' accruing from inside information and can be achieved by a policy of much fuller disclosure than is currently required.
3. Financial statements should not be reduced to the level of understanding of the naïve investor.
4. The FASB should strive for policies that will eliminate excessive costs of information.
5. The FASB should sponsor a full-scale research program in the areas indicated, so that it may have some evidence of the consequences of their choices among different sets of financial accounting standards.

Current Trends in Corporate Disclosure

WILLIAM H. BEAVER

It is self-evident that corporate disclosure requirements have substantially increased in the last five years—the Securities and Exchange Commission has issued more accounting series releases since 1972 than it had in the previous 26 years, and Financial Accounting Standards Board statements embody several additional disclosure provisions. It is also self-evident that the trend toward greater disclosure is likely to continue. The Moss and Metcalf subcommittee reports have commented on inadequacies in the current reporting practices and have called for an even more active role by the government. The financial analyst community has offered a number of suggestions for increased disclosure, as illustrated in the recent reports by Duff and Phelps and by the Financial Analysts Federation (FAF).[1]

What is not self-evident is the form of the increased disclosure. The purpose of this article is to examine the current trends in disclosure, the concepts underlying those trends, and their implications for accountants and management. In particular, the article will focus on four trends related to (1) the objectives of disclosure, (2) the nature of the disclosure process, (3) methods for evaluating the desirability of further disclosure and (4) the concept of materiality.

OBJECTIVES OF DISCLOSURE

The primary objective of corporate disclosure is informed decision making by users (who always include investors and sometimes others). Consider the recent statement of objectives adopted by the SEC Advisory Committee on Corporate Disclosure:[2] "To assure the public availability in an efficient and reasonable

I am indebted to my fellow members of the SEC Advisory Committee on Corporate Disclosure for the insightful discussions of disclosure issues during our meetings extending from February 1976 through September 1977. The opinions expressed are those of the author and not necessarily those of any other committee member. Financial support was provided by the Stanford Program in Professional Accounting. Major contributors are Arthur Andersen & Co.; Arthur Young & Company; Coopers & Lybrand; Ernst & Ernst; Peat, Marwick, Mitchell & Co.; and Price Waterhouse & Co.

[1] Senate Subcommittee on Reports, Accounting, and Management (Senator Lee Metcalf [D-Mont.], chairman), *The Accounting Establishment* (1976); Report of the Subcommittee on Oversight and Investigations, Committee on Interstate and Foreign Commerce (Representative John Moss [D-Calif.], chairman), *Federal Regulation and Regulatory Reform* (1976); Duff and Phelps, *A Management Guide to Better Financial Reporting* (a report prepared for Arthur Andersen & Co., 1976); and Corporate Information Committee, Financial Analysts Federation, *Response to the SEC's Advisory Committee on Corporate Disclosure*, reprinted in the *Financial Analysts Journal*, March and April 1977, p. 12.

[2] Report of the Advisory Committee on Corporate Disclosure to the Securities and Exchange Commission, (Washington, D.C.: Government Printing Office, 1976).

manner on a timely basis of reliable, firm-oriented information material to informed investment, and corporate suffrage decision making." This represents a primary emphasis upon the informational role of disclosure as opposed to its protective role.[3] The emphasis on the investor as the primary user is natural given the intent of the securities acts.

What is striking about this statement is its similarity to recent authoritative statements of the objectives of financial statements. The investor decision-making viewpoint has also been adopted by the AICPA objectives study group and by the FASB.[4]

An implication of this merging of objectives is that the already fuzzy distinction between disclosure and financial statement reporting becomes even less clear now that both are described as having essentially the same primary objective. Recent pronouncements by the FASB and the SEC confirm this. FASB Statement of Financial Accounting Standards no. 14 on segment reporting is considered by many to be essentially a disclosure standard, while the SEC's Accounting Series Release no. 190 on replacement costs deals with a central accounting issue of asset valuation and expense measurement. The inability to draw distinctions between disclosure and accounting standards has obvious implications for the current jurisdictional controversy concerning the FASB and the SEC.[5]

However, there is less than complete unanimity with respect to the objectives issue. Recently, former FASB Chairman Marshall Armstrong commented on substantial opposition to adopting an informational perspective with respect to the role of financial statements.[6] According to Armstrong, this is viewed as a shift away from the traditional perspective of stewardship and from a historical cost, past-events orientation to financial reporting. However, one of the most important aspects of the FASB's statement of objectives is the reformulation of the stewardship concept so that it becomes subsumed under the user, decision-making approach.[7] It is contended that stewardship should not be viewed in a narrow custodianship context but in a broader, performance evaluation role. According to this view, management's responsibility is more than merely safe-

---

[3]Excellent discussions of this dual role of disclosure appear in A. Anderson, "The Disclosure Process in Federal Securities Regulation: A Brief Review," *Hastings Law Review*, January 1974, pp. 311–54; The Wheat Report, "Disclosure to Investors: A Reappraisal of Administrative Policies Under the '33 and '34 Securities Acts" (New York: Bowne & Co., 1969).

[4]*Objectives of Financial Statements* (New York: AICPA, 1973); *Tentative Conclusions on Objectives of Financial Statements of Business Enterprises* (Stamford, Conn.: FASB, 1976).

[5]The jurisdictional boundaries have become further blurred now that the SEC is also regulating the contents of annual reports via rule 14a-3 of the 1934 act governing proxy solicitations.

[6]Marshall Armstrong, "The Politics of Establishing Accounting Standards," *Journal of Accountancy*, Feb. 77, p. 76.

[7]FASB, *Tentative Conclusions*, p. 59. Unfortunately, the stewardship notion has received little attention beyond intuitive discussions. However, there are two notable exceptions. Ijiri analyzes the concept of accountability. In particular, he draws out the potential differences in the reporting function under the stewardship, as opposed to the investor decision-making orientation. See Y. Ijiri, Study no. 10, *Theory of Accounting Measurement* (Sarasota, Fla.: American Accounting Association, 1975); also see R. Watts, "Corporate Financial Statements, A Product of the Market and Political Processes," *Australian Journal of Management*, April 1977.

keeping assets, but also includes the responsibility of earning a return on those assets.

A stewardship relationship arises when one party (management) assumes control over the resources of another party (investors) and has a responsibility to act in the best interests of that party. A reporting responsibility arises under stewardship in order to provide the intended beneficiaries with information upon which to base a performance evaluation of the steward. However, since the assets and financial claims of the company are not liquidated at each reporting date, this accountability function may well involve the disclosure of current value and future-oriented data in order to better assess the implications of current actions by management for the future of the company.

There are two major implications:

1. This reinterpretation sets the stage for the consideration of the inclusion of a broader set of disclosures in annual reports.
2. Stewardship can no longer be invoked as a defense against the intrusion of current value and future-oriented disclosures in financial reporting.

It is premature to conclude that such data are in fact desirable, nor has the FASB taken a position with respect to this issue. However, at least one public accounting firm believes that the FASB have made up their minds, in spite of the professed neutrality of the conceptual framework documents.[8]

Certainly the SEC has actively altered its long-standing discouragement and prohibition of current value and future-oriented data in SEC filings. ASR no. 190 on replacement costs and the releases on management forecasts (Release nos. 33-5581 and 33-5699) are two recent illustrations. Moreover, in an amicus curiae brief filed in the *Gerstle v. Gamble-Skogmo* litigation, the SEC took the position that failure to disclose such information may, in certain circumstances, constitute a violation of the securities acts.[9] This trend is being reinforced by recommendations of the analysts' community for more disclosure of future-oriented and interpretive data, as reflected in the Duff and Phelps and FAF reports cited earlier.[10]

THE NATURE OF THE DISCLOSURE PROCESS

The second major trend is a change in the way the disclosure process is viewed. In particular, there are two major aspects of the investment process that may influence future disclosure policy:

1. Investors, some perhaps with limited access and ability to interpret financial information, have the opportunity to avail themselves of the services of information intermediaries, such as analysts, to whom they can defer a portion or all of the information-gathering and processing function.

[8]Ernst & Ernst, "Conceptual Framework: Our Analysis and Response," (1977).

[9]Securities and Exchange Commission, (amicus curiae brief), *Gerstle, et al.* v. *Gamble-Skogmo, Inc.* (December 1968).

[10]See footnote 1.

2. Investors have the opportunity to invest simultaneously in a number of securities and hence to diversify out of some of the risks inherent in a single-security portfolio strategy.

THE PROFESSIONAL INVESTMENT COMMUNITY

The existence of financial and information intermediaries is undeniable. By recent estimates there are over 14,000 financial analysts. However, the precise role they play in the investment process is unclear. Management has incentives to provide information to analysts, and analysts have incentives to seek out and to disseminate such information. This informal information network appears to be enormous. It was reported that J. C. Penney logged in over 1,000 interviews with analysts in one year.[11] This does not appear to be unusual for a company of J.C. Penney's size. In fact, this informal information network may be the mechanism which permits security prices to promptly reflect a broad information set.[12] In other words, the competition among analysts for disclosures and for the interpretation of disclosures results in security prices that reflect a broad set of information. Statements of legislative intent at the time of the enactment of the securities acts indicate that at least some were relying upon the competition within the professional investment community to interpret the SEC filings and to effect an "efficiently" determined market price.[13]

PORTFOLIO THEORY

Recent developments in portfolio theory have stressed the importance of diversification in the reduction of much of the risk associated with holding a single security. It is unrealistic to believe that investors hold only one security (e.g., the one being described in a registration statement). In fact, investors have the opportunity to purchase well-diversified portfolios through financial intermediaries. The recent trend toward index funds is but one manifestation of the realization of the desirability of diversification.[14] If the investor holds a well-diversified portfolio, how, if at all, does this alter the way disclosure is viewed? It has been argued that diversification may substantially reduce the investor's

---

[11]Kenneth S. Axelson, "A Businessman's View of Disclosure," *Journal of Accountancy*, July 75, p. 42.

[12]The role of the analyst community is discussed in greater detail in William H. Beaver, "The Implications of Security Price Research for Disclosure Policy and the Analyst Community" (presented and to be published in the proceedings of the Duke Symposium on Financial Information Requirements for Security Analysis, December 1976).

[13]Consider the following statement by Justice Douglas, who at the time was teaching at Yale: "Even though an investor has neither the time, money, or intelligence to assimilate the mass of information in the registration statement, there will be those who can and who will do so, whenever there is a broad market. The judgment of those experts will be reflected in the market price." "Protecting the Investor," *Yale Review*, 1933, pp. 523–24.

The definition and implications of market price efficiency are discussed in W. Beaver, "What Should Be the FASB's Objectives?" *Journal of Accountancy*, Aug. 73, p. 49.

[14]A. Ehrbar, "Index Funds—An Idea Whose Time is Coming," *Fortune*, June 1976, p. 145.

demand for firm-specific information.[15] Portfolio theory tells us that the investor is concerned with assessing the attributes of risk and rewards (i.e., return) associated with a portfolio. The investor is concerned with firm-specific information only insofar as it is useful in assessing the portfolio attributes. While the investor may have considerable uncertainty about the risks and rewards associated with any one security, this uncertainty is considerably reduced at the portfolio level because of the effects of diversification. For example, while there may be considerable uncertainty as to the riskiness of any one security, typically the riskiness of the portfolio can be assessed with much greater confidence.[16] In other words, an overestimate of the risk of one security will tend to be offset by an underestimation of the risk of another security. The effects of diversification are potentially powerful and the benefits from incremental improvements in firm-specific information may be minimal.

In another context, suppose the investor is concerned that the security being purchased is mispriced, relative to the price at which it would sell if additional disclosures were available.[17] From the point of view of the additional disclosure, some of the securities will be overpriced but some will be underpriced. A diversified portfolio will likely contain some of each and their effects will tend to be offsetting. Hence, the net effects of additional disclosure may differ considerably from the effects analyzed on a security-by-security basis.

This is not to suggest that portfolio theory implies that additional disclosure is valueless, but only that it can alter the way in which disclosure issues are viewed. There are a number of obvious additional considerations.

● Many investors may choose to remain relatively undiversified, even though they have the opportunity to do so. These investors, for one reason or another, perceive that the disadvantages of diversification outweigh the advantages. Policymakers, such as the SEC, must then address the social choice question: To what extent should they impose disclosure requirements on companies in order to accommodate investors who have voluntarily chosen not to diversify? An implicit subsidy to undiversified investors is potentially involved here because all investors pay the costs of additional disclosure, while those who choose to remain undiversified may be the primary beneficiaries.

● Not all investors may have access to a given item (i.e., a problem of selective disclosure).

● Management may use nondisclosure to obtain greater compensation than would otherwise be the case.[18]

[15]Homer Kripke, "An Opportunity for Fundamental Thinking—the SEC's Advisory Committee on Corporate Disclosure," *New York Law Journal*, December 15, 1976.

[16]The rudiments of portfolio theory are discussed in FASB, op cit., pp. 65–78. Also see W. Sharpe, "Risk, Market Sensitivity, and Diversification," *Financial Analysts Journal*, January-February 1972, p. 74.

[17]A security is said to be overvalued (undervalued) if its price is above (below) what its price would be in light of the fuller disclosure.

[18]This aspect of disclosure has been discussed in some detail in S. Ross, "Disclosure Regulation in Financial Markets," *Key Issues in Financial Regulation*, (forthcoming).

• There may be effects on resource allocation that are ignored when the investor setting is narrowly viewed. However, both the SEC and the FASB have been reluctant to adopt a broader perspective implied by this latter consideration.

The role of institutional investors is obviously growing, and the importance of the lessons of portfolio theory is receiving increasing attention. However, the potential impact of portfolio theory on demand for firm-specific disclosures has not been fully appreciated or well thought out. Eventually, these implications will have to be faced and may considerably alter the context in which disclosure issues are viewed. At the present time, current trends in disclosure largely ignore the implications of portfolio theory, although there is a growing awareness of the role of the professional.

EARLIER PERSPECTIVE

By contrast, earlier views of the disclosure process had focused on the proverbial "average investor," unaided by intermediaries and with limited information and interpretive skills.[19] One prominent illustration of where this perspective affected disclosure policy was in the area of "soft" information (e.g., current value and forward-looking disclosures). The SEC had a long-standing policy prohibiting the inclusion of such data in filings. The rationale was that the average investor would not appreciate the "softness" or uncertainty surrounding such estimates and, hence, disclosure would be misleading.[20]

Apart from the fact that conventional financial statements accepted by the SEC at that time were also subject to substantial uncertainties of estimation, the potential "misleading" effect on the average investor is not a very compelling argument in the presence of a large, active professional community of analysts and in the face of the empirical evidence supporting market efficiency. As indicated earlier, the SEC is currently in the process of removing this incongruity in their regulations and, presumably, will continue to do so.

Emphasis upon the average investor is not only at odds with the way the investment process works but is even inconsistent with the basic nature of the SEC's mandated disclosure mechanism. Currently the disclosure mechanism consists of a series of highly technical documents that must be filed with the SEC and reside in their archives. There is little pretense that SEC filings are in fact disseminated to or read by most investors. Moreover, there is no pretense that, even if the filings were read, they would be understood by most investors. From the outset, the SEC has implicitly relied upon the existence of a professional community in order to justify its apparatus as an effective means of disclosure.

[19]An excellent discussion of the average prudent investor appears in Homer Kripke, "The Myth of the Informed Layman," *The Business Lawyer*, January 1973, p. 631. The demand for information in a portfolio setting is discussed in N. Hakansson, "Information Needs for Portfolio Choice," (presented and to be published in the proceedings of the Duke Symposium on Financial Information Requirements for Security Analysis, December 1976).

[20]Kripke, "The Myth of the Informed Layman"; R. Feintuch, "Soft Information; Liability Standards and Safe Harbours (Case Law)," (memorandum to M. Lipton, June 18, 1976). Provided to members of the Advisory Committee on Corporate Disclosure.

Future disclosure policy will likely give greater recognition to the professional as the prime target for mandated disclosures in SEC filings. One major implication for corporations is that fear of misleading the average investor will not excuse failure to disclose. Such a rationale probably has never been very successful anyway. However, now the rejection of such an argument will be based upon a framework which emphasizes disclosure to the professional. The evidence on market efficiency lends further support to this emphasis.

EVALUATING THE DESIRABILITY OF ADDITIONAL DISCLOSURE

A natural extension of acknowledging the existence of professional intermediaries is the use of this community as a source of ideas for further disclosure regulation. This brings us to the third trend in disclosure—viewing the financial analyst community as the major representative of investor demand for additional disclosure.

As indicated earlier, analysts typically have been active advocates of the "need" for additional disclosure of various sorts. This is hardly surprising. The analyst community is an industry whose product is information, analysis and interpretation. One major factor of production to this industry is disclosures by corporations. However, the costs of disclosures are borne in large part by the companies' shareholders (and perhaps indirectly by customers and employees), rather than by the analysts themselves. The analysts undoubtedly incur some cost in obtaining and processing the disclosures, but it is only a portion of the total cost of disclosure. Hence, corporate disclosures constitute a factor of production that will not be fully paid by the industry using that factor, and this constitutes a form of subsidy. Asking the analyst community about the potential desirability of increased disclosure may be tantamount to asking an industry if it wants a subsidy. We should not be too surprised when that industry responds in the affirmative.[21]

The question, however, could be rephrased. Suppose a tax were levied on the analyst community to reimburse companies for the costs of additional disclosures, how much would the analyst community be willing to pay in order to obtain the information? The purpose of this question is not to suggest that a tax should be levied, but rather to highlight the potential distortion in disclosure policy that may occur when desirability is assessed in a manner divorced from cost considerations. Nevertheless, to the extent that the SEC or the FASB continues to rely upon analysts' input, they are in a powerful position and their preferences will be an important barometer of future disclosure requirements.

MATERIALITY

The fourth major trend in corporate disclosure relates to the elusive concept of materiality. Given the forces operating toward more disclosure, what limits, if any, exist on the demand for additional disclosure? The securities acts provide little comfort in imposing a standard of "full and fair disclosure." It has been

[21]The above argument is a simplified interpretation of the analysts' incentives. There are potentially offsetting factors. For example, analysts may prefer to keep disclosures from being made public, so they can compete with each other to obtain that item in the informal information network. The net effect is unclear which underscores the earlier comment about how little is known about the analyst's role.

argued that full and fair disclosure, literally interpreted, is unattainable.[22] What limits, if any, are placed on that goal? The concept of materiality was intended to act in such a limiting manner.[23] The reasons for introducing such a limitation appear to be twofold: to avoid excessive preparation costs incurred by companies in producing, certifying and disseminating disclosures, and to avoid excessive processing costs by users (often referred to as "information overload").[24]

Alan Levenson, former director of the SEC's Division of Corporate Finance, has stated that the concept of materiality has not been successful in performing this limiting function.[25] Nor is this surprising, because definitions of materiality have developed independently of the fundamental reasons for having a materiality concept—the costs of preparation and processing.[26] Given the failure to formally incorporate cost considerations into materiality definitions, it is hardly surprising that the intended purpose has not been achieved. Furthermore, without an explicit incorporation of costs into the definition of materiality, there appears to be little basis for believing materiality will ever accomplish its limiting purpose.

By contrast, the SEC and the courts have introduced a legal fiction—the "average prudent investor." There are several difficulties in adopting this approach.

Investors, even average prudent ones, are likely to disagree among themselves as to the importance of any given item. For example, both expertise and other available information are likely to affect an investor's judgment. Yet the courts have uniformly denied the inherent subjective nature of the concept and instead have insisted that materiality is an objective test.[26] As a result, mate-

[22]Kripke, "An Opportunity for Fundamental Thinking."

[23]The intended limiting function of materiality is expressly stated in the SEC's definition of materiality. Rule 1.02(n) of Regulation S-X states, "The term, 'material' when used to qualify a requirement for the furnishing of information as to any subject, *limits* the information required to those matters about which an average prudent investor ought reasonably to be informed (emphasis added)." Similar statements appear in rule 405(1) of the 1933 act and rule 12b-2(j) of the 1934 act.

[24]Marshall Armstrong, "Disclosure: Considering Other Views," *Financial Executive*, May 1976, p. 36. The issue of "information overload" has not been well formulated. It is important to expressly recognize that the investor is not acting in an unaided fashion and to admit to the existence of the professional investment community. The issue is not one of overloading an individual acting in an isolated fashion, but rather the impact on an entire system which consists of several thousand analysts who typically specialize with respect to types of firms (i.e., an elaborate division of labor). Thus, the issue is not information overload per se but rather the cost of the system processing the additional disclosure. Among other factors, computer technology has greatly increased the data processing capacity of the analyst community.

[25]Statements made at the December meeting of the SEC Advisory Committee. See the minutes of that meeting.

[26]An excellent review of the evaluation of materiality from a legal viewpoint appears in a review by J. Hewitt, "Developing Concepts of Materiality and Disclosure," (San Diego, Calif.: Hewitt & Shaw, 1976). A broader review appears in the materiality discussion memorandum. See Financial Accounting Standards Board Discussion Memorandum, *Criteria for Determining Materiality* (Stamford, Conn.; FASB, 1975).

[27]Hewitt, "Developing Concepts of Materiality," p. 19. Most recently, see *TSC Industries* v. *Northway, Federal Securities Law Reporter* (1976), 95, 615.

riality becomes a basis for the SEC and the courts to substitute their judgment for that of investors.

Another difficulty is that emphasis upon the nonprofessional, the average prudent investor, is misdirected because it ignores the role played by the professional investment community in the disclosure process. In other words, there is a basic incongruity between relying upon the presence of a professional community to justify the current filings as an effective disclosure mechanism but essentially ignoring its existence when defining what constitutes a material item. It is not clear how soon or to what extent this incongruity will be removed. However, there are two aspects of disclosure that distinguish between the professional and the nonprofessional. These deal with the issues of differential disclosure and selective disclosure.

DIFFERENTIAL DISCLOSURE

The concept of differential disclosure suggests that two disclosure standards exist when making public disclosures through filings or annual reports.[28] One standard, which involves more detailed, more technical disclosures, is deemed appropriate for the professional, while shorter, less technical and more "understandable" disclosures are deemed appropriate for the nonprofessional. The practice of differential disclosure already exists with respect to periodic filings. The 10-K and 10-Q forms are viewed as documents to be consumed by the professional, while the annual report to shareholders is viewed as the document directed to the nonprofessional. For example, differential disclosure with respect to ASR no. 190 has been recently documented.[29] It has been suggested that this concept be extended to the 1933 act filings in the form of a bifurcated prospectus, although there has been opposition because of the potential liability problems.

The consequences of differential disclosure are unclear. For example, recent empirical research suggests that stock prices fully reflect publicly available information. If the more comprehensive disclosure in the SEC filings is effectively publicly available information, little or no effect on stock prices would be expected if the data were also provided in a simplified format. The defense for differential disclosure would presumably rest on effects on the investment process other than price effects. However, greater emphasis upon disclosure to the nonprofessional would appear to be counter to the current trend to recognize the central role of the professional in the disclosure process. As a result, differential disclosure does not appear to have a bright future.

In a related context, one court recently raised the issue of differential materiality standards for professionals and nonprofessionals. In *Feit* v. *Leasco*, the court held that, in filings prepared for registration purposes, items must be disclosed that are material under either of the two disclosure standards. Spe-

---

[28]The concept of differential disclosure is discussed in A. A. Sommer, Jr., "Differential Disclosure: To Each His Own," (The Second Emanuel Saxe Distinguished Accounting Lecture), Baruch College, (March 19, 1974); J. Burton, "Conflicts and Compromises in Financial Reporting," presented at Price Waterhouse Foundation-Stanford University *Lectures in Accounting* series, May 21, 1976; and *Feit* v. *Leasco*, 322 Federal Supplement (1971), 544–588.

[29]Arthur Andersen & Co., *Disclosure of Replacement Cost Data—Illustrations and Analysis*, May 1977.

cifically, immateriality to the average, prudent investor is not a valid defense for nondisclosure, if that item is material to the professional.[30] This is an important decision because it formally recognizes the role played by the professional investment community. It helps to remove the incongruity between viewing the SEC filings as a set of documents primarily intended for consumption by professionals and yet defining materiality of omissions from such filings in terms of the average prudent investor.

SELECTIVE DISCLOSURE

While differential disclosure addresses the issue of different disclosure standards for public disclosures, selective disclosure deals with the issue of disclosure to some but not all individuals. Kripke has characterized the issue of selective disclosure as one of the most important policy issues to be addressed by the SEC in the near future. In simplest terms, the selective disclosure issue concerns when and under what circumstances analysts or others may obtain information (not publicly available) and act on such information.

Currently, an answer to that question rests on the tenuous foundation of the "mosaic theory." As commonly stated, the mosaic theory asserts there are two types of information:

1. Information which, standing alone, has importance.
2. Information which, standing alone, has no importance but assumes importance when considered in light of the grand mosaic of other information about the company.

As stated, the mosaic theory is seriously deficient. No information is interpreted standing alone. The importance of any information is evaluated in light of other information available. Hence there is only one type of information. It is commonly acknowledged that it is virtually impossible to distinguish between the two. As a result, it is extremely difficult for management and analysts to predict how the SEC or the courts would interpret a transfer of information between them.

Alternatively, the mosaic theory can be characterized as a differential materiality standard. Under this interpretation, there are two levels of materiality. Specifically, an item may not be material to the average prudent investor, because of the investor's limited information and interpretive skills. Yet that same item may be material to a professional who possesses more information and greater interpretive skills. The implication of the mosaic theory is that such items can be obtained in the informal search process without fear of legal liability.

The purpose of positing the mosaic theory is to permit information to flow in the informal network. It is argued the stock prices will reflect a broader and more timely set of information than that contained in SEC filings or annual reports.[31] However, the idea is that some, but not "too much," information be

---

[30]As a point of fact, the court held that the item in question "surplus-surplus," was material under both standards. See *Feit* v. *Leasco*, op. cit.

[31]J. Lorie, "Public Policy for American Capital Markets," *Federal Securities Law Reporter* (1974), 79, 646.

permitted to flow via the informal network. The mosaic theory can be viewed as trying to accomplish this by positing a dual materiality standard. However, this concept rests on shaky grounds for a number of reasons.

It is an irrelevant measure of the value of the information being given. Materiality to the average prudent investor is not an indication of value. What is relevant is the value or materiality of that item to other professionals. As stated by Kripke, the mosaic theory assumes that "if a piece of the mosaic is of the kind that is addressed to the analyst only, there is no abuse of the market if he utilizes that information without having it generally disclosed to the public."[32] The validity of this assumption is open to question.

The importance of the role of the professionals in impounding information in security prices rests on the premise of competition among the professionals with respect to interpreting the implications of that item for the future cash flow and earning power of the company. If there is limited dissemination of the item, the competition in interpreting its implications cannot take place. It is one thing to have professionals compete with one another for the interpretations of a publicly disclosed item. It is quite another for one analyst (and the analyst's client) to have exclusive access to that item. In other words, the issue is not whether the average investor considers the item material but rather whether other analysts would consider the item material.

Second, it is at odds with the disclosure standards set down in *Feit* v. *Leasco*, which explicitly recognizes the value of a disclosure to the professional as an appropriate standard for materiality.

Third, it directly confronts one of the most primitive notions of disclosure regulation—the concept of "fair" disclosure, which is perceived to mean equal access to information. Although it is not immediately clear why fair disclosure necessarily implies equal access to information, the SEC has traditionally interpreted the term to mean precisely that. Recent actions of the SEC in the Bausch & Lomb litigation and their earlier efforts with respect to forecasts (i.e., Release no. 33-5581) are an expression of the SEC's concern over selective disclosure.[33]

The assumed innocuous nature of being able to grant or to obtain exclusive access to material information is not self-evident. In general, it would be thought that such information does have value since market prices would not necessarily reflect nonpublic information, even if they were efficient with respect to published information. The ability of analysts or their clients to earn abnormal returns can be viewed as one form of "cost" associated with making the market efficient. The issue is the extent to which such private search for information should be permitted or encouraged. Kripke, among others, argues that shutting down the informal information network may lead to a less efficient market.[34] The shutting down could occur by either imposing sanctions on the transmittal of such information (e.g., Bausch & Lomb) or by mandating its public disclosure.

[32]Kripke, "An Opportunity for Fundamental Thinking."

[33]"SEC v. Bausch & Lomb, Inc." *Federal Securities Law Reporter*, September 26, 1976, 90, 499–515.

[34]Kripke, "An Opportunity for Fundamental Thinking"; L. Bernstein, "In Defense of Fundamental Investment Analysis," *Financial Analysts Journal*, January-February 1975, p. 3.

Whether or not the SEC should do so is a difficult question which rests on many factors, including the potential reduction in the information reflected in security prices and the costs of attaining a given level of market efficiency via selective disclosure as opposed to other means. There are also resource allocation effects, such as potential impact on the demand for analysts' services.

For the reasons indicated, the life expectancy of the mosaic theory is short. It is a matter of time before the deficiencies of the concept are formally recognized. It is hoped that it will be replaced by a concept which gives consideration to the factors cited above.

THE MYTH OF INFORMATION NEEDS

The regulation of disclosure is essentially an economic issue, amenable to an analysis of the various consequences of disclosure. Instead, a legalistic approach pervades much of the current approach to disclosure. As a result, there is a danger that the promulgation of disclosure rules will inflict more damage on investors, the intended beneficiaries of the securities acts, than if there were no regulation at all.

The current viewpoint is epitomized by the concept of information "needs." According to this notion, it is virtually impossible for the investor to rationally function without certain information necessary to the investment decision. Similarly, it has been argued that investors have "inherent rights" with respect to corporate disclosures. The effect of this approach is to insulate disclosure policies from an analysis of their economic consequences.

On the other hand, information or disclosure can be viewed as an economic good, subject to the same sort of economic analysis as that applied to other goods, both private and public. For example, consider the analogy of food consumption. It was once estimated that an individual's "need" for food (in the sense of subsistence) could be met by a diet consisting of appropriate portions of flour, milk, cabbage, spinach and dried navy beans.[35] This is all we "need," yet it hardly describes typical food purchases. Moreover, consumers' food purchases are likely to depend upon income levels, personal tastes and the prices of various foods as well as other commodities. Quality differences are one dimension of this issue.

When this perspective is applied to disclosure regulation, several questions arise. Why is it "necessary" (i.e., desirable) to have the government mandate the amount and nature of information consumed by the investment community? This fundamental question is beyond the scope of the present article.[36] For the moment, take a mandated system as a given. What level of quality of disclosure does the SEC have a mandate to provide? Is it a bare subsistence level or some higher quality standard? If higher than a subsistence level, how is the quality to be determined? Apart from these normative questions, consider these descriptive ones. What level of quality is currently being mandated? Are investors

[35]G. Stigler, "The Cost of Subsistence," *Journal of Farm Economics*, 1945, p. 303.

[36]For a discussion of some of these issues, see G. Benston, "Evaluation of the Securities Exchange Act of 1934," *Financial Executive*, May 1974, p. 28; and A. A. Sommer, Jr., "The Other Side," *Financial Executive*, May 1974, p. 36. For example, corporate disclosure may induce externalities and possess aspects of a public good.

currently dining on a mandated menu of cabbage, spinach and dried navy beans or on caviar, champagne and truffles? What is the cost of the current system? Are the benefits consumed commensurate with the costs? Who is paying these costs? A common response is that corporations pay. However, a more complete answer is that shareholders of corporations (and perhaps others) pay the costs. Thus, the cost of the disclosure system is borne by the intended beneficiaries of that system. It cannot be automatically assumed that higher quality (even if of an undisputed nature) is necessarily better, given the price that must be paid. Shareholders wish to purchase other commodities besides corporate disclosure. Every additional disclosure which imposes additional costs on corporations leaves less available for distribution to shareholders and hence less available for their purchase of other desirable commodities. This article closes with a call for an additional trend—the infusion of an economic perspective to corporate disclosure decisions.

II-E / THE PROBLEM OF MATERIALITY

The Concept of Materiality

LEOPOLD A. BERNSTEIN

The current debate on the state of accounting theory and the practice which is a reflection of it, or the lack of it, is all too often conducted in terms of sweeping generalizations. In order to make further progress in accounting principles and their application, we must isolate from among the many problem areas revealed by practice those whose definition and resolution would make the greatest relative contribution to the furthering of better accounting. Recently concluded research clearly indicates that the concept of materiality is such a problem area.

TREATMENT OF EXTRAORDINARY GAINS AND LOSSES

The theory, as well as the treatment and presentation of extraordinary items of gain and loss were the subject of a research study recently completed by the author. One aspect of this research involved a comparison of a substantial segment of practice with the provisions of Chapter 8 of *Accounting Research Bulletin No. 43*, the accounting profession's principal pronouncement dealing with the treatment of extraordinary gains and losses. This Bulletin states, among other provisions, that there should be a general presumption that all items of profit and loss recognized during a period should be included in the determination of net income. The only possible exception represents items that are in the aggregate *material* in relation to the company's net income and clearly not identifiable with or result from usual or typical operations. Such items may be excluded from a determination of net income, and further, "they should be excluded when their inclusion would impair the significance of net income so that misleading inferences might be drawn therefrom."[1]

The following summary of findings of my research is pertinent to the present discussion:

(1) Out of 324 presentations of extraordinary items in the sample, 214 or 66% were excluded from the determination of net income. This does not

Leopold A. Bernstein, "The Concept of Materiality," *The Accounting Review*, January 1967, pp. 86–95. Reprinted with the permission of *The Accounting Review*.

[1]American Institute of Certified Public Accountants, *Accounting Research and Terminology Bulletins*, Final Edition, 1961; p. 63.

support the existence of a strong presumption for the inclusion of all items of income and loss in the determination of net income.

(2) In the main categories of extraordinary items, practice is so diffused that the size of an item in relation to net income appears hardly to have any important effect on whether an item is included in, or excluded from, the determination of net income. It can also be said that no percentage range emerges from our data as a border zone between what, under the Bulletin, should be considered as material and hence excludable from net income, or immaterial and hence includable therein. Thus, viewing practice as a whole, there emerges no pattern which would suggest that there are any agreed-upon criteria regarding the application of the concept of materiality. And yet, the concept of materiality is one of the most critical of all criteria enumerated in the Bulletin.

(3) Wherever enough examples were available to lend some validity to conclusions, the picture of practice at the level of the individual major accounting firm examined confirms what we have learned about practice as a whole, i.e., that, in most cases, it does not appear to be guided by any discernible standard of materiality.

(4) The study reveals that there is a definite bias towards showing extraordinary items with credit balances as special items in the income statements (65% of total credits) and debit items in retained earnings (77% of total debits.) Thus, it appears that in the absence of materiality guidelines, considerations other than those intended played a dominant role.

The lack of definition of materiality criteria can best be illustrated by the following examples taken from my study:

EXAMPLE 1: Archer Daniels Midland Co., in its 1964 annual report included in net income a profit on sale of depreciable assets of $1.1 million or 26% of net income. The item was not designated as extraordinary or non-recurring. This should be contrasted with the treatment by Lily-Tulip Corp. in its 1963 annual report of a net realized gain on disposition of fixed assets of $143 M. This item, representing 3% of net income, was credited directly to retained earnings.

EXAMPLE 2: Mueller Brass Co., in its 1964 annual report included in net income, without any special designation, prior years' investment credits of $184,000 representing 41% of net income. This should be contrasted with the treatment of such prior-year investment credits by Tecumseh Products Co., in the amount of $156,000, or about 1.3% of net income, which were credited to the retained earnings account in the company's 1964 annual report.

The concept of materiality has found its way into many aspects of disclosure. Thus, for example, we find it in *Accounting Research Bulletin No. 43*, Chapter 10, where it is applied to income tax allocation, in Chapter 11 where it is applied to treatment of renegotiation refunds, and in Chapter 15 where it is applied to the question of disclosure of unamortized discount. Materiality is, moreover, a central concept in Accounting Principles Board *Opinion No. 5* which deals with the accounting for leases. Finally, the Accounting Principles Board Opinion Exposure Draft entitled "Reporting the Results of Operations," dated September 9, 1966, which, if adopted, will make a significant contribution towards a resolution of the problem areas revealed in my aforementioned study, and towards the implementation of its principal recommendations, nevertheless retains the criteria of materiality as an element of major consideration.

THE MEANING OF "MATERIALITY"

What do we mean by the term "materiality?" The concept of materiality is part of the wisdom of life. Its basic meaning is that there is no need to be concerned with what is not important or with what does not matter. Man's work is burdensome enough without the need to pay attention to trivia.

In accounting, this concept of materiality assumes special significance. There are two basic reasons for this:

(1) Most users of accounting information do not comprehend it easily. Consequently, the introduction of redundancy into that information can make the task of absorption and analysis even more difficult. Furthermore, the presentation of significant data intermixed with insignificant data can also be misleading. Hence, to make the information not misleading, items which do not matter need no separate disclosure.

(2) The process of auditing aims to arrive at a satisfactory level of assurance regarding the fairness of presentation of financial statements at a point in time. Never is this assurance complete, nor is it economical or necessary to arrive at 100% assurance. Consequently, the limited time which the auditor can economically devote to obtaining this assurance must be spent on matters of importance and substance. This means that the auditor must always strive to avoid spending time on trivia or what we otherwise know as items which are not material. This is not always simple, since it sometimes takes a great deal of work to find out that an item is of no consequence.

The concept of materiality thus permeates the entire field of accounting and auditing. That people, and especially skilled professional people, should not spend their time on things that do not matter is common sense not requiring much elaboration. Nevertheless, the following statement is found in the introduction to the Accounting Research Bulletins:

> The committee contemplates that its opinions will have application only to items material and significant in the relative circumstances. It considers that items of little or no consequence may be dealt with as expediency may suggest. However, freedom to deal expediently with immaterial items should not extend to a group of items whose cumulative effect in any one financial statement may be material and significant.[2]

The Securities and Exchange Commission in its accounting regulations is also concerned with materiality. Their concern is that of a regulatory body trying to define the limits within which required information is to be furnished. Thus, they are concerned with the possibility that the reader of financial statements will be swamped with unimportant information which may be indiscriminately commingled with significant information. Moreover, they do not

[2]Ibid., p. 9.

want to burden the filing company and its accountant with a requirement to disclose information which is not material. The SEC's requirement is stated in *Regulation S-X:*

> The term "material" when used to qualify a requirement for the furnishing of information as to any subject, limits the information required to those matters as to which an average prudent investor ought reasonably to be informed before purchasing the security registered.[3]

The concept of materiality, when generally expressed, is simple to understand. However, when it is made a central concept in the *application* of accounting principles, a lack of specific definition converts it into a prime problem area. Nowhere is the impact of an application of the concept of materiality more important than in its effect on reported net income. This view is supported in the following statement taken from a recent Canadian study:

> An accounting error (or a total of accounting errors) is material if the distortion affects or should affect the decisions of an intelligent reader of the financial statements. Since the prime concern of most readers is the earning power of the enterprise, the most obvious type of error affecting the reader is one which distorts reported net profit. In this study, therefore, materiality will be considered as it relates to the total of known and unknown errors distorting the net profit figure.[4]

One of the outstanding weaknesses of the Bulletin on "Income and Earned Surplus" (Chapter 8 of ARB No. 43) was that the application of its most important provisions hinged in large measure on a determination of what is material and what is not. The proposed draft opinion of the Accounting Principles Board which is intended to supersede Chapter 8 of ARB No. 43 retains a most important role for the concept of materiality, particularly in the area of treatment of prior-year adjustments and the segregation of extraordinary items within the income statements.[5] No pronouncement can be stronger than the most weakly defined concept used in formulating it. Clearly, as in the case of other pronouncements, much hinges on an interpretation of what is material and what is not. In practice and even in theory there appears to be, however, no significant agreement on how to judge the materiality of an item.

LACK OF GUIDES

But what is material? The Accounting Research Bulletins offer no concrete guidance in this respect. The interpretation that is found in much of the literature on the subject is that this lack of guidance is due to the fact that the assessment of materiality is purely a matter of judgment.

[3]U.S. Securities and Exchange Commission, *Regulation S-X* Paragraph 1.02.

[4]The Canadian Institute of Chartered Accountants, *Materiality in Auditing*, Study Group on Audit Techniques, October 1965, p. 3.

[5]American Institute of Certified Public Accountants, *Exposure Draft of Opinion of Accounting Principles Board* on Reporting on Results of Operations, September 9, 1966.

From this association of materiality with professional judgment comes the next step—the elevation of this simple, common-sense concept to a position of cardinal importance in accounting practice.

A well-known writer on the subject of materiality has expressed this as follows:

> The concept of materiality is among the most important of the basic ideas by which an auditor is guided in reporting on his examination of financial statements and in the formulation and application of his audit procedures . . .[6]

The questions that immediately come to mind are these: Has the importance of materiality been overrated? Is this simple concept really of such great importance? Does it rank as a *basic* idea in accounting?

THE NEED FOR CRITERIA

The need for some guides on matters of materiality is well illustrated in a just published and eminently practical work which records the replies of the AICPA's Technical Services Department to member inquiries.[7] After receiving less than full satisfaction on a question involving materiality, the inquirer wrote, "If materiality is to be measured by net income, at which point does an item become or cease to become material? . . . Please understand that this letter . . . is intended to help us establish some guidelines for use in the future." In answer to follow-up inquiry the Technical Services Department of the AICPA closed the correspondence by saying in part that "it goes without saying, the question of 'materiality' is an elusive matter." In a similar response to a request for guidance on materiality questions, Carman G. Blough maintained that the Committee on Accounting Procedure did not consider it feasible to set down any general criteria on the subject.[8] As revealed by Carman Blough's reply, the alternatives available to an accountant faced with a decision on materiality are quite varied. First, an item must be considered in relation to not one, but a number of years of income. But presently this is an extremely flexible concept. There seems to be no reason why an average of five years is better than, say, eight years, or ten, or even fifteen. Surely the results can be substantially different depending on the number of years used. Actually, the income figure to be used should be representative of a recent (say five-year) earnings level if the current earnings figure differs markedly from such a representative level. It should be recognized also that to the decision-maker the most recent years are far more important than those of the more distant past.

Once the percentage relationship of an item to net income has been determined, further variation is possible. Some consider 10% as material enough to justify the exclusion of an item from income while others go as high as 20–25%.

---

[6]E. L. Hicks, "Some Comments on Materiality," *The Arthur Young Journal*, April, 1958.

[7]E. F. Ingalls, *Practical Accounting and Auditing Problems* (American Institute of Certified Public Accountants; 1966), Vol. I, pp. 289–293.

[8]"Some Suggested Criteria for Determining Materiality," *Journal of Accountancy*, April 1950, p. 353–4.

Moreover, Mr. Blough believes that the percentages could vary between one kind of item and another.

The above variations are only examples, for the suggested considerations extend to many more variables. Thus, one writer has suggested that consideration be given to the effect on the analytical measurements employed by security analysts when judging whether an item is material or not.[9] Here too, the focus on one type of relationship may yield results that differ from those which result from or focus on a different type of relationship.

THE IMPORTANCE OF JUDGMENT

All this suggests the existence of a serious dilemma. In a profession where objectivity is a consideration of cardinal importance, materiality seems to be its "Achilles' Heel." If materiality is really such an important concept, and it certainly does play a dominant role in a number of pronouncements, then how is the profession to attain any semblance of consistent or uniform treatment in this area? How are new entrants to the profession to be trained? What are they to be told about the judgment processes leading up to materiality decisions?

We are told that the determination of materiality is a matter of judgment. What kind of judgment? Professional judgment, of course, is the answer. And here it ends. We find no definition for the term "judgment" let alone a description of the process. Definition of these is completely lacking in the sparse literature on the subject.

In few areas of accounting practice is the term "judgment" invoked so categorically as in the area of materiality determination. We are told that we examine all the surrounding circumstances, and then, as if by inserting the information at one end of a black box, we get the results at the other end. This "black box" seems to be, moreover, a highly personal device, since the output can vary significantly on what are apparently the same or very similar sets of facts.

Judgment is, of course, a vital part of any professional's work. In accounting it plays an important role every step of the way. But that does not mean that it is a mysterious process, undefinable and inexplicable. We know that the processes that feed professional judgment are varied and complex, yet it does not follow that we cannot make some progress in their analysis and description.

Let us first see why the analysis and description of judgment processes are important and necessary. There are three main reasons:

(1) An undefined and all-embracing process described as "judgment" does not inspire the confidence of thinking men.
(2) The mere assertion that a vital professional process depends on "judgment" is of no help in educating and training entrants to the profession.
(3) Such an undefined approach is conducive to the kind of practice most likely to discredit the profession.

Let us examine these propositions more closely:

Judgment lies at the heart of any intelligent activity. It is, of course, not peculiar to accounting. In management, where it plays a vital role, it has, in

[9]D. Rappaport, "Materiality,"*The Journal of Accountancy*, April 1964.

recent years, come increasingly under study. Encouraging this study was the advent of the electronic computer which has displayed a remarkable capability for simulating our thought processes. Yet, in order to program a computer properly the thought and judgment process of managers had to be analyzed and understood. This led to an increasing dissatisfaction with the all-inclusive description of the manager's work as constituting "the exercise of judgment." This dissatisfaction was described by a leading student of decision theory in these words: "When we ask how executives make non-programmed decisions, we are told that they 'exercise judgment and that this judgment depends, in some undefined way, upon experience, insight and intuition.' "[10] This, Professor Simon maintains, is like describing a sedative as something that possesses a dormitive faculty.

We can thus see that the processes of judgment have come under increasing scrutiny and have resulted in computer applications and such specialized techniques as operations research, linear programming, Pert, and others comprising the modern spectrum of management science. Also, in the area of security analysis the judgment processes have come under more detailed and systematic study.

Nearer to the field under discussion, the auditor, in recognition of advances in related fields, has abandoned the complete reliance on a nondescript judgment process and has embraced statistical sampling techniques as well as ratio, change, and trend analyses—techniques which require a more thorough analysis and description of his work and which lend themselves to more objective evaluation.

It is clear that those most likely to subject accounting information to intelligent use, having embarked on a painstaking examination of their own judgment processes, are least likely to accept the description of some of the most vital processes leading up to the preparation of financial statements as representing the exercise of professional judgment when such judgment is neither defined nor explained and, moreover, when it can lead to substantial variations in conclusions having as a basis identical or similar facts.

One major reason for the interest in the judgment processes of managers is that the increasing complexity of managerial decision-making as well as the shortage of managerial talent have led to a study of judgment processes for training purposes. The same considerations apply to the accounting profession. It is not sufficient to say that a determination of materiality requires the exercise of professional judgment.

The profession's future progress requires that the criteria and processes of judgment in accounting matters be studied, analyzed, and described. While this may not be an easy task, it is an essential one. That does not mean that all judgment processes can be described, that there is a full substitute for experience, or that wisdom can be taught. However, it does mean that the processes leading up to professional conclusions should be described wherever possible.

Without some description of the processes of professional judgment, we cannot establish the essential norms which must guide and circumscribe it. Right now the undefined concept of professional judgment in accounting, and especially as it relates to materiality, can only result in a proliferation of loose

---

[10]Simon, H. A., *The New Science of Management Decision* (Harper & Brothers; 1960), p. 11.

standards and practices. Since, for example, the inclusion of an item in income or its exclusion therefrom does make a difference, the effect of loose practice is such that it may undermine confidence in the profession's work. That is especially so when, as in the area of the treatment and presentation of extraordinary items, practice as a whole shows a substantial lack of uniformity.

NEED FOR A REASONABLE DEGREE OF UNIFORMITY

But why is uniformity necessary? This question must be answered because the answer is by no means self-evident. Moreover, the need for more uniformity is an important reason why the processes of the accountant's judgment cannot be allowed to remain obscure. The debate around the uniformity-diversity dichotomy has been going on for many years among accountants. Unfortunately, often the positions which are under attack are characterized in too extreme a fashion. It is obvious that no accountant who believes in a free society would strive for dictation of his discipline by a book of rigid rules. No thoughtful and experienced accountant can believe that such a system can really work to the benefit of society. On the other hand, no serious believer in "diversity" can possibly mean by that, that judgment and practice can be cut off from any clearly defined central concepts and standards. Those who do believe that no constraints should be placed on professional judgments are not concerned with the profession's standing or future—they are merely convinced about the unquestionable quality of their own judgment and integrity.

But surely the substance of the entire debate lies in between these extreme positions. Greater uniformity is necessary for two major reasons:

(1) Because it facilitates comparability.
(2) Because it acts as a regulator of quality.

Comparison is a vital analytical tool. It is important because no decision involving the use of accounting information can be made in a vacuum or by the consideration of a single variable. Thus, investment decisions are made by comparing one investment with others, a decision to lend is made by contrasting one loan application with another, and so on. It is not relevant in this connection to say that there are many factors which make comparisons among companies difficult. The accountant must do his part in facilitating the comparison process as much as he can.

The dilemma posed by considerations of materiality in accounting is not a simple one. Given vague or nonexistent guides for the application of such an important concept, the result must be a wide variety of practice in an area where a reasonable degree of uniformity and comparability is essential. Without a common frame of reference, uniformity of practice is impossible. Adherence to a set of principles and the methods of their application will give the user a degree of assurance about the uniform application of minimum standards to the accountant's work.

FREEDOM AND DISCIPLINE

The professional accountant is naturally disinclined to accept constraints on the exercise of his judgment. He feels that having first-hand knowledge of all the circumstances of a case, he is in the best position to decide on what is material and what is not. That is of course true; but at the same time he may apply to this situation criteria which are different from those applied by his fellow professional or criteria which differ from those which the reader assumes to have been applied. The strong influences of management's viewpoint, as well as the absence of any clear standards, make this all the more likely.

The exercise of freedom of judgment is an important "value" in our society. It is first of all tied to the cherished concept of personal freedom. Moreover, in the sphere of economics, decentralization of decision making has great advantages in that it keeps down the magnitude of errors made and their effect on society.

The exercise of freedom by a professional man in arriving at a judgment in his field is an important consideration. If possible, it should not be abridged. Some would lead us to believe that this is the paramount "value" to be considered.[11] However, the public confidence in and understanding of the auditor's work, also, are matters of prime importance. In fact, without them auditing cannot serve as a profession. It is a "value" which justifies the profession's giving up of some of its freedom of action. A choice must therefore be made. Complete freedom of action and choice that are not governed by any defined criteria of materiality can be obtained only at the cost of a serious lack of uniformity in practice.

What is material and what is not cannot be left to the undefined realm of "judgment." Good judgment must receive guidance from clearly formulated standards and limits. The debate regarding which criteria are applied is useless if the resulting practice can produce a great diversity of results under similar conditions.

MATERIALITY GUIDELINES

It is therefore recommended that we establish definite standards which, given similar circumstances, will help accountants to arrive at meaningfully similar conclusions regarding questions of materiality. Such standards must be operative in areas where quantification is not possible. The establishment of such border zones has proved workable in the case of accounting policy regarding stock dividends. The SEC, in areas where a decision was made necessary by the need for clear directives, has also clearly designated the borderline of materiality.[12]

Such a suggested border zone is not meant to be a monument to rigidity, but rather an area of strong presumption from which an accountant could undertake a departure only for compelling reasons known to him and *disclosed* by him. There cannot be a presumption that circumstances are so complex that an accountant cannot disclose them. Communication of complex economic facts

[11]For example see, D. E. Browne, "Cost of Imposing Uniform Accounting Practices," *Financial Executive*, March 1966.

[12]For example, Rule 1.02 of Regulation S-X indicates that a significant subsidiary (for purposes of the regulations) is one whose assets exceed 15% of the consolidated assets or whose sales and revenues exceed 15% of the consolidated sales and revenues. (One can well imagine the practice which would result from leaving decisions in this area solely to "judgment.")

is a prime function of the accountant, and an area in which he can give full reign to the exercise of his judgment and skill.

A border zone has the advantage of meeting the arguments of those who will always point out that 10% is not so different from 10.1%. It brings the border or cut-off closer to the level of a concept and removes it from the numbers game. It still leaves plenty of room for the exercise of judgment.

A widely known and accepted border zone has other great advantages. It places the burden of proof on those who deviate from it. Moreover, it provides the profession and the users of financial statements with a known and explicitly stated norm. Professional accountants can use it as a guide and as an assurance of some degree of consistency of practice. Users of financial statements can rely on substantial adherence to it and can expect to be altered to any significant deviations from it.

What should the limits of such a border zone be? The modal area of practice revealed by the empirical study mentioned at the beginning of this article suggests a border zone of 10%–15% of net income after taxes as the point of distinction between what is material and what is not. As already indicated, by net income is meant a figure which is typical of recently experienced (five-year average) earning power. Such a border zone could be a starting point to progress and is probably one on which agreement within the accounting profession could be reached.

It must, however, be recognized that while the 10%–15% border zone may represent the thinking of many accountants, it does not necessarily coincide with that of many serious users of the income statement. In discussing materiality with regard to the treatment of "nonrecurrent items," Graham, Dodd, and Cottle state that "small items should be accepted as reported. For convenience we may define 'small' as affecting the net results by less than 10% in the aggregate."[13]

According to the 1957 Statement of the American Accounting Association, "an item should be regarded as material if there is reason to believe that knowledge of it would influence the decisions of an informed investor."[14] Many security analysts would probably consider items that affect net results by as little as 5% to be significant, and hence, material. The compound annual growth rate of earnings of a great many corporations is around 5%; hence, an influence on net earnings as great as the annual change due to growth factors must generally be deemed significant. The compound annual growth rate of all manufacturing corporations will vary greatly depending on the period selected. A recent study shows that during the postwar period, 1947–1964, it was at the rate of 2%.[15] Taking the longest period covered by the study, i.e., 1935–1964, we arrive at a 7% annual growth rate. This latter period starts at or near a major cyclical bottom and includes a major war. Another study of compound annual growth rates of earnings of 127 large and successful companies shows that for the years

[13]Graham, D., L. Dodd, and S. Cottle, *Security Analysis* (McGraw-Hill; 1962), p. 112.

[14]American Accounting Association Committee on Accounting Concepts and Standards, *Accounting and Reporting for Corporate Financial Statements and Preceding Statements and Supplements* (American Accounting Association, 1957), p. 8.

[15]Sidney Cottle, "Corporate Earnings: A Record of Contrast and Change," *Financial Analysts Journal*, November–December, 1965.

1947–1963 it was 6.9%.[16] Thus, a change considerably lower than 10%%15% can be deemed significant in many instances. While the experience of the individual company can be expected to vary from an average of the aggregates, we must, in setting the border zone between what is material and what is not, take the average experience into account.

The following examples of compound annual growth rates in earnings per share for the years 1953–1964 for some well-known and well-managed corporations point out the importance of a 5% change in earnings:

American Telephone & Telegraph Co.	4.8%
American Tobacco Co.	5.3%
General Motors Corp.	6.6%
Gulf Oil Corp.	6.4%
Sears Roebuck & Co.	7.3%

The border-zone of 10%–15% between what is presumed to be material and what is presumed not to be material is at best a broad guideline, but its establishment would at least be a starting point. There are many situations where items of a much smaller percentage impact on net income would require disclosure because of the intrinsic significance of the item itself. Cases involving conflicts of interest are examples of such instances.

Regulation S-X of the Securities and Exchange Commission provides an example of such low materiality criteria in the case of loans and advances to directors, officers, and principal holders of equity securities other than affiliates. In Rule 5-04 it is provided that an aggregate indebtedness to the filing corporation, by such parties of $20,000 or 1% of total assets, whichever is less, which is owed or was owed during the period covered by the profit and loss statements must, with certain exceptions, be shown in a separate schedule. It is quite obvious that the need to disclose such relatively small amounts is governed by considerations which stem from the significance of the transactions themselves.

When the accountant assesses materiality he looks backward in order to assess relationships, but he must also look forward in order to assess the probabilities of future and of cumulative effects. Thus, not everything is subject to quantification and some guiding qualitative judgment criteria affecting materiality decisions must be spelled out. Those should lower rather than lift the border-zone percentage range.

It is obvious that the problem of deciding on specific materiality criteria is very difficult and complex. This article suggests that a start must be made in the definition of the concept of materiality and in the establishment of more objective criteria of measurement. There may be another way of tackling this problem. It is to deemphasize the importance of "materiality" and by extending the degree of over-all disclosure in financial statements, make the impact of its application less critical. The accounting profession is, however, not moving away from according great importance to the concept of materiality. To the contrary, a recent Special Bulletin[17] issued by the Council of the American Institute of

[16]Edmund A. Mennis, "Perspective on 1965 Corporate Profits," *Financial Analysts Journal*, March–April, 1965.

[17]Special Bulletin, *Disclosure of Departures from Opinions of Accounting Principles Board*, October 1964.

Certified Public Accountants, which represents a milestone in efforts to strengthen the authority of pronouncements issued by the Accounting Principles Board, increases the importance of what is "material." Thus, the Special Bulletin states:

> 5. If an accounting principle that differs *materially* in its effect from one accepted in an Opinion of the Accounting Principles Board is applied in financial statements, the reporting member must decide whether the principle has substantial authoritative support and is applicable in the circumstances. . . .
> 6. Departures from Opinions of the Accounting Principles Board which have a *material* effect should be disclosed in reports. . . .
> (italics supplied)

No one should doubt the importance of the change that was instituted with the publication of the "Special Bulletin." Yet, most of its practical effect will depend on the leeway left in its interpretation. As in other important areas such leeway exists in large measure due to the undefined nature of the concept of "materiality."

The preceding discussion is made with full cognizance of the complexities facing the practicing accountant. This is not an attempt to underestimate the difficulty of defining and describing the accountant's judgment process. But a degree of definition is essential. Similarly essential is the setting of a border zone between what is material and what is not. Such a border zone will certainly not be perfect nor will it meet all situations equally well, but without it the concept of materiality cannot be useful to the profession or to the users of financial statements.

III/INCOME MEASUREMENT, ASSET VALUATION, AND CHANGING PRICES

This part is concerned with the nature of income and the problems involved in income measurement and asset valuation in a period of changing prices.

Section A, entitled "The Earnings Concept," provides a comparison of economic and accounting income concepts and an examination of the allocation problem in measuring accounting income. Solomons (1961) differentiates between economic and accounting income, and argues that accounting income is flawed as an indicator of the firm's success or failure due to its emphasis on realization, rather than value changes. Economic income, on the other hand, requires highly uncertain data. Solomons foresees a decline in the significance of the income statement, with a greater emphasis on funds statements.

Thomas (1975) is concerned with the thorny problem of allocating costs and revenues in income measurement. All such allocations are arbitrary, asserts Thomas, since they can neither be refuted nor verified. Because factors of production interact generating joint benefits, any attempt to allocate such benefits among the inputs is bound to be unsuccessful.

Section B includes two papers arguing for and against the constant-dollar or general price level (GPL) accounting model. Rosenfield (1975) presents one of the few cases for GPL accounting in the non-authoritative accounting literature and criticizes the FASB for failing to explain the relevance of this approach in its 1974 exposure draft on this subject. Stickney and Green (1974) argue against GPL accounting, and cite empirical studies casting doubt on the alleged usefulness and reliability of this approach in accounting for inflation. Users may be confused by GPL accounting, which need not provide a suitable measure of capital maintenance nor an appropriate reflection of management's hedging actions against inflation. Finally, Stickney and Green identify weaknesses in the available general price-level indices, which may make them unsuitable as general measures of inflation.

Section C focuses on current-cost valuation. Edwards (1975) discusses the general conceptual issues underlying current value accounting as well as practical issues in the use of this approach. The issues considered include: (1) whether accounting income should be partitioned into current operating income and holding gains, (2) whether GPL adjustments alone would be adequate to reflect the impact of inflation, and (3) whether current values should be reported in the balance sheet and the related gains in the income statement. Edwards is not convinced that exit values are a suitable approach for asset valuation and prefers replacement costs in most cases.

199

Revsine (1970) furnishes a comparative analysis of economic income and replacement-cost income, and concludes that under certain assumptions replacement cost income may be viewed as a surrogate of economic income with a view towards providing data to predict long-run cost-flow changes. Samuelson (1980) explores the arguments for and against reflecting holding gains in income due to changes in replacement costs and concludes that these changes should be capital adjustments. Samuelson argues that holding gains are adjustments to permanent capital, consistent with the concept of physical capital maintenance.

Section D, entitled "Exit Values" centers on the exit-value model, as defined in two papers by Sterling. Sterling (1972) evaluates different accounting valuation models and concludes that exit-value accounting is the best in terms of furnishing useful information for decision making. Since exit values "are necessary to define market alternatives, they express the investment required to hold assets and they are a component of a risk indicator." Sterling (1975) suggests the presentation of current value statements adjusted for price-level changes, on the grounds of relevance and interpretability. Sterling contends "*both* adjustments are necessary and that neither is a substitute for the other." He observes that exit valuation circumvents the problem of allocation inherent in historical costing and current replacement costing.

Section E provides comparative analyses of various methods of accounting for capital maintenance and inflation. Gynther (1970) reviews several different concepts of capital maintenance—proprietary (general purchasing power and consumer purchasing power) and entity (investment purchasing power and operating capacity of firm). He maintains that there is no compelling reason for the asset valuation methods to be consistent with the capital maintenance concepts. This possible separation of asset valuation rules from capital maintenance rules opens up an interesting array of possible combinations (for example, current-cost asset valuations combined with general purchasing power capital maintenance).

Chambers (1975) compares the constant-dollar, replacement cost, and exit-value models. Chambers asserts that neither general-price-level accounting nor current-value accounting is a complete method of accounting for inflation. A method of "continuously contemporary accounting" is advocated to take into account both changes in particular prices and changes in the general level of prices.

III-A / THE EARNINGS CONCEPT

Economic and Accounting Concepts of Income[1]

DAVID SOLOMONS

In recent years, discussion of the measurement of income has been largely colored and dominated by problems created by changes in the value of money. Serious as these problems are, they are really secondary ones, for they presuppose some basic agreement about the nature and measurement of income during a period of stable prices. Between accountants and economists, it need hardly be said, no such agreement exists. My purpose in this paper is first to examine these differences—a task which has been performed, with greater or less thoroughness, many times before—and then to consider the only attempt known to me to work out a concept of income which would, like the accountant's, be capable of practical use and yet would stay close to the fundamental definition of income with which we begin. The attempt at reconciliation to which I refer is Sidney Alexander's concept of variable income, put forward in his monograph, "*Income Measurement in a Dynamic Economy.*"[2] Alexander's suggestion deserves more discussion than it has received hitherto, whether we finally judge it to be a workable concept or not. It is for that reason that I shall have something to say about it here. My conclusion about the practical utility of the concept, as a matter of fact, will be adverse; and from that disappointing conclusion I am led on to the view that the time has come to develop other and more effective tools to do the jobs which periodic income so signally fails to do in the field of financial planning and control. As I shall suggest, there are signs that the central position which income occupies in accounting is already being usurped.

USEFULNESS OF THE INCOME CONCEPT

Any discussion of competing ideas of income ought, I think, to start with the question: "Do we really need an income concept, and if so, what for?" Only when we have asked and answered this question can we say whether there is

David Solomons, "Economic and Accounting Concepts of Income," *The Accounting Review*, July 1961, pp. 374–383. Reprinted with the permission of *The Accounting Review.*

[1]This paper was presented at the Northeast Regional Meeting of the American Accounting Association at the Massachusetts Institute of Technology on October 28–29, 1960.

[2]Published as the first of *Five Monographs on Business Income* by the Study Group on Business Income, 1950. Alexander's work in a slightly revised version, will shortly be republished in the 2nd edition of *Studies in Accounting*, to be edited by W. T. Baxter and Sidney Davidson.

anything we need to define, and whether one or more than one concept of income is necessary.

Let us consider income for taxation purposes first. It is really rather remarkable that income has become so universally accepted as a good measure of taxable capacity, for on closer inspection it seems to have grave defects. Command over capital resources would seem to be a much fairer guide to the subject's ability to pay taxes, and also to the demand made by the individual on various governmental services such as defense and law and order. Alternatively, as suggested by Mr. Kaldor, it might be more sensible to tax people according to what they spend rather than on what they earn. This is not a plea for the substitution of indirect for direct taxation, of course, but for the use of a computation of expenditure rather than of income as the basis of taxation. It is not necessary to go into this matter here. For my purpose, it is enough to note that our system of direct taxation could get along quite well, and, indeed, perhaps better, if we did not have a concept of income at all.

A second important purpose which the concept of income is said to serve is in the determination of corporate dividend policy. So long as dividends are paid out of income and not otherwise, it is asserted, the rights of creditors will not be prejudiced by the return of capital to stockholders. If this means, as it does in certain jurisdictions, that currently or recently earned net profits may be distributed without making good earlier losses of capital, it is clear that the rights of creditors are being very imperfectly protected. The payment of a legal dividend by no means implies, in such circumstances, that the stockholders' capital is intact. Moreover, a corporation may earn a profit and yet be too short of cash to be able to pay a dividend without endangering its short-term solvency. The existence of current net income, therefore, may tell directors nothing about the dividend policy they ought to follow. It makes much more sense for the law to require, as it sometimes does, either that stockholders' capital should be intact before a dividend is paid out of any excess, or to require some defined margin of assets over and above those necessary to pay creditors' claims, before allowing the payment of dividends to stockholders. Either type of restriction is more effective in protecting the rights of creditors than one based on an income concept, while at the same time being free of the difficulties of defining and measuring net income.

A third major need served, or said to be served by the concept of income, is as a guide to investment policy. Prospective investors seek to maximize their return on investment, and their search will be guided by the income earned on existing investments. This is related to another argument—that income provides the best measure we have of success in the management of business enterprise in a competitive economy. These are important needs, and they both point in the same direction. That investment is most attractive which offers us the greatest present value of future receipts per dollar invested, when discounted at the going rate of interest, and insofar as historical data can help us in the choice of investments, it will be data about the growth in present value of existing investments. Again, that manager is most successful who, during a given period, increases the present value of the enterprise entrusted to him proportionately the most. In both of these cases, it is growth in present value which alone appears to be significant; and since it seems to carry out the function generally attributed to income, growth in present value must be what we had better understand income to mean.

ECONOMIC INCOME

The concept of income to which we have been led corresponds of course, to Hicks's definition of income. For an individual, he defines income as the maximum amount a man can consume in a period and still be as well off at the end of the period as he was at the beginning. There is no doubt that when, as individual salary-earners and investors, we think of our personal income for a year, we commonly do not think of it in this way, but rather as a stream of prorated receipts, unaffected by any changes in the value of the tangible assets with which we started the year and certainly as having nothing to do with any change in our future prospects—in our "goodwill," in other words—which may take place during the year. But this does not lead me to conclude that "the income of a person or other entity is what he believes to be his income, . . ."[3] for we can be mistaken about the nature of income just as men were once mistaken about the nature of combustion when they attributed it to phlogiston. Rather, I would say "Income is as income does."

If we take Hicks's definition of income as applied even to an individual, it is easy to see, however we define our terms, income in Hicks's sense and income as the accountant measures it will only by accident ever be the same thing. As Hicks points out, the difficulty about his definition is in saying what we mean by "being as well off" at one date as at another. He offers us three different measures of well-off-ness, which, however, come together, if we abstract from changes in the value of money and from changes in the rate of interest, to give us a single measure of well-off-ness command over money capital. If we accept constancy of money capital as representing constancy of well-off-ness, then income in Hicks's sense becomes the amount by which the individual's net worth has increased during the period, due allowance being made for the value of what he has consumed or given away during that time.

To use Hicks's definition for the income of a business entity rather than for that of an individual, we need only modify it slightly; the income of the business, whether it is incorporated as a separate legal entity or not, is the amount by which its net worth has increased during the period, due allowance being made for any new capital contributed by its owners or for any distributions made by the business to its owners. This form of words would also serve to define accounting income, insofar as net accounting income is the figure which links the net worth of the business as shown by its balance sheet at the beginning of the accounting period with its net worth as shown by its balance sheet at the end of the period. The correspondence between the two ideas of increased net worth is, however, a purely verbal one: for Hicksian income demands that in evaluating net worth we capitalize expected future net receipts, while accounting income only requires that we evaluate net assets on the basis of their unexpired cost.

It is hardly open to question that you cannot really assess the well-off-ness of an enterprise by aggregating the costs, or the unexpired costs, of its assets and deducting its liabilities. Any differences between the current value of its tangible assets and their book value based on cost will be excluded; and any value which the enterprise may have over and above the value of its tangible assets will also be excluded. We may sum up the relationship between these

[3]"Scope and Method of Theory and Research in the Measurement of Income and Wealth," by Myron J. Gordon (*The Accounting Review*, Oct. 1960), p. 608.

two different concepts of increase in net-worth, economic income and accounting income, by starting with accounting income and arriving at economic income thus:

Accounting income
+ Unrealized changes in the value of tangible assets which took place during the period, over and above value changes recognized as depreciation of fixed assets and inventory mark-downs,
− Amounts realized this period in respect of value changes in tangible assets which took place in previous periods and were not recognized in those periods,
+ Changes in the value of intangible assets during the period, hereafter to be referred to as changes in the value of goodwill
= Economic income.

THE REALIZATION PRINCIPLE

Obviously the main difference between these two income concepts lies in the accountant's attachment to realization as the test of the emergence of income. The Study Group on Business Income, in its 1952 report, rather surprisingly suggested that "the realization postulate was not accepted prior to the First World War,"[4] and supported this with quotations from both American and British sources. It seems to me, on the contrary, that the trend has, for a long time now, been away from, rather than towards, placing emphasis on the importance of realization. For a long time the relationship of income to capital was likened to the relation of the fruit to the tree. Just as there was no difficulty in separating the crop from the tree, so there need be no difficulty in distinguishing income from the capital which produced it. It was in line with this thinking that, for the first thirty-six years after Peel had re-introduced the income tax in Britain in 1842, no relief was given by the British tax code for the using up of fixed assets in the course of carrying on a business. The introduction of income tax depreciation allowances in Britain in 1878, and their growth in importance there and here since then, constitute a movement away from the idea that you can evaluate the fruit without giving thought to the value of the tree—that realized profits can be measured in disregard of what have sometimes been called "mere value changes" in the assets of the business. Another earlier step away from the pure realization principle was the "cost or market-price" rule for valuing inventory. You will not find this in accounting literature before the mid-nineteenth century, for before that time consistent valuation at cost seems to have been the rule. The recognition of unrealized losses on inventory is a clear recognition of "mere value changes," if only in one direction, as being relevant to the determination of income. As final evidence of the same tendency, I suppose we might cite the development of cash accounting into accrual accounting as itself a de-emphasizing of the importance of realization. For what it is worth, we can perhaps say that over the years accounting income and economic income have moved a little closer together. Yet of course, when everything has been said, accounting income is still substantially realized income.

[4]*Changing Concepts of Business Income* (Macmillan, New York, 1952), p. 23.

The tableau set out above may make it easier for us to evaluate the two income concepts in terms of the two qualities which outweigh all others in importance, their usefulness and their practicality. It is because the results of this evaluation are what they are that it is natural to hanker after a compromise income concept which has a greater share of these qualities combined than either accounting or economic income has, taken by itself.

THE CASE FOR AND AGAINST ACCOUNTING INCOME AND ECONOMIC INCOME

Whether we use one concept of income or another, or indeed whether we use any concept of income at all, clearly should depend, as I have already said, on the purpose we want to serve and the income concept which will best serve it. In what follows I shall concentrate my attention on one aspect of this matter only, namely, the measurement of business income for the purpose of assessing entrepreneurial success or failure in the profit-making sector of the economy. From this point of view it must be said that accounting income is seriously defective. By focussing attention on the result of current realization of assets and ignoring all other value changes except such as are covered by the "cost or market" rule, and by depreciation, it can lead to some rather ridiculous results. One such result is that described by Kenneth MacNeal.[5] Two investors each have $1,000 to invest. One buys $1,000 worth of stock A, the other buys $1,000 worth of stock B. By the end of the year both stocks have doubled in price. The first investor sells out just before Dec. 31, and reinvests the $2,000 he gets from the sale in stock B. The second investor continues to hold his block of stock, which is also worth $2,000 at the end of the year. Thus both start equal, with $1,000 each in cash: they also finish equal, both holding equal quantities of stock B worth $2,000. It is impossible to say that one investor has been more successful than the other. Yet one of them shows an accounting profit of $1,000 as the result of his realization, while the other shows no accounting profit at all.

Another absurd result is cited by Sidney Alexander, that of the manager of a large corporation who is considering a deal which will increase his accounting profit by a million dollars but which will result in the destruction of the firm's goodwill by forcing it out of business. By looking only at changes in tangible equity (and only at a part of that), while ignoring changes in goodwill, accounting income provides us with a very unsatisfactory measure of managerial success. Another way of putting this is to say that if maximizing profit is ever a rational business goal, it is rational only if profit means economic profit, not accounting profit.

It may be said, and with truth, that the differences between accounting income and economic income are only short-run differences, i.e. if we take a sufficiently long period in the life of an enterprise the changes in the value of equity which distinctively enter into economic income will also be reflected in accounting income. Thus MacNeal's second investor will have his wise investment reflected in his profit when eventually he sells his stock in a later period, if by then it has not fallen in value. That over the whole life of an enterprise its

---

[5]In his article "What's Wrong with Accounting," *The Nation*, October 7–14, 1939, and reprinted in the 1950 edition of *Studies in Accounting*, ed. W. T. Baxter (London, Sweet & Maxwell, Ltd.).

total accounting income and economic income must be identical cannot be gainsaid. But this is poor consolation for short-run defects in our measure of income. *All* the problems of income measurement are the result of our desire to attribute income to arbitrarily determined short periods of time. Everything comes right in the end; but by then it is too late to matter.

Having cast some doubt on the effectiveness of accounting income as a gauge of managerial success, we have to recognize that it emerges satisfactorily from the other test, that of practicality. Insofar as objectivity is regarded as an indispensible quality of an income concept which is to have any claim to being practical, accounting income is practical enough. But this is of little moment if it does not measure what we want to measure. Objectivity without relevance is not much of a virtue. The question is whether we can retain some or all the objectivity of accounting income while answering the question which accounting income palpably fails to answer: How much better off has the accounting entity become during the period?

In passing, we might notice a contrary point view on the relevance of the two income concepts we are comparing in a statement by Professors Hill and Gordon.[6] Rejecting the idea that unrealized profits should be included in income, they argue that "information as to what management *expects to make* on the things it *has not sold* is no substitute for information as to what management *has made* on the things it *has sold.*" The answer to this is that neither is the second kind of information a substitute for the first, and it is only the second kind which accounting conventionally provides. Both kinds of information are necessary to assess managerial success. As I have already tried to show, to look at realized profits and losses only may be to ignore an important part of the total picture.

In advocating their particular brand of business income, economists have usually argued that the increase in net worth of the enterprise, which constitutes income, must be arrived at by valuing the whole enterprise at the beginning and the end of the period whose income we wish to measure. These valuations, they say, must be made by discounting, at each date, the expected stream of receipts less the expected stream of payments of the enterprise as far into the future as possible, to arrive at the present value of the net stream. Any amounts distributed by the enterprise to its proprietors during the period must, of course, be added back to give the increase in net worth which, in this view, is synonymous with income. Expressed in this way, the concept looks quite impractical, for it seems to demand a superhuman degree of foresight, not only about the broad sweep of events but also about the details of day-to-day transactions.

I do not think that too much should be made of this difficulty. We do not allow uncertainty about the future entirely to inhibit us from valuing property on the basis of expected net receipts, or at least on the best estimate we can make of them. Moreover, there are simplifying assumptions we could make which would render the valuation process more manageable. Nevertheless, the difficulties are still somewhat formidable.

A second difficulty about the concept of economic income is that in successive discounting of expected future receipts and payments, effect will have to be given not only to real foreseeable changes in the enterprise's future, but

[6]*Accounting: A Management Approach*, by T. M. Hill and Myron J. Gordon (2nd edition, 1960, Irwin), p. 143.

also to changes in human expectations about this future. Thus, suppose that at the beginning of the period a large receipt is foreseen as coming in in three years' time. At the end of the period (of, say, a year) the receipt is thought to be much less certain, and in any case probably smaller than was previously expected. The net worth of the enterprise will have apparently shrunk during the year, then, not because of a real change in the future but only because of a change in expectations about the future. Thus economic income will react both to real future changes and to changes in human expectations, and the effects of these two sets of factors will be inextricably combined.

THE CONCEPT OF VARIABLE INCOME

The concept of "variable income" attempts to eliminate the effect of a change in expectations from our measure of economic income. Alexander, it will be remembered, approaches the problem of measuring business income by considering first the income from a bond, indeed from quite a variety of bonds. He starts with a perpetual bond which pays no interest in the ordinary sense, but whose owner annually receives $10 if, on the toss of a coin, it comes down heads and nothing if it comes down tails. As a matter of fact this example is hardly more bizarre than the British premium savings bonds which have been in issue since 1956 and which, while securing the investor's capital, pay no interest in the ordinary sense but offer the chance, after a qualifying period of six months, of a prize in a monthly lottery. The amount of the prize fund is determined by calculating interest, at the rate prescribed from time to time, on the bonds eligible for the draw. In the case of Alexander's perpetual bond, he argues that, assuming a 5% rate of interest, the bond would maintain a steady value of $100, whatever the results of the tosses from year to year, for an even chance of receiving $10 or nothing is equivalent to an expectation of receiving $5 each year, giving a capital value, at 5%, of $100. As a matter of fact, according to the strength of the gambling instinct in the community in question, the bond might just as easily be worth more or less than $100; but so long as its value is accepted as being unaffected by the results of each toss, it does not matter just what that value is. And of course, since each toss is a separate event, the chances of success next time are unaffected by past results, so there is no reason why the value of the bond should be affected by the incidence of heads or tails. The income from the bond in any year is then equal to its owner's receipts from it, $10 or nothing according to the result of the toss.

We get closer to real life with Alexander's second bond, which is like the first but has a life limited to 20 years. This bond at the outset will have a capital value of $62.70, this being the present value, at 5%, of a 20 year annuity of $5 annually (the expectation of receipts from the bond). A year later, regardless of the outcome of the toss, it should be worth only $60.42, the present value of a 19 year annuity of $5, and each year as the bond's expectation of life diminishes, its value will continue to fall. In this case the bond-holder enjoys an income which is always less than his receipts by the amount of the diminution in the value of his security. The loss of capital value in the first year was $2.28, so that if the coin came down heads his receipts were $10 and his income was $7.72, while if the coin came down tails his receipts were zero and his income was— $2.28. This illustration leads us straight to Alexander's first definition of variable income, at least as it applies to income from securities, which is that variable income is equal to the net receipts from the security plus or minus any change in its value which was, *at the beginning of the period*, expected to take place during the period.

This it must be noted, is a first approximation to the definition of variable income for the full definition has to provide for the possibility that the net receipts of the period may themselves cause future expectations of receipts to be modified during the period, as where a particularly large distribution to owners of a security during the present period is made at the expense of distributions to be made in future periods. In such a case, variable income has to be defined as the net receipts from the security plus or minus any change in its value during the period which was expected at the beginning of the period, plus or minus the discounted present value of any consequential change in expected future receipts brought about by the level of current receipts. This modification of the definition to take account of consequential change in the value of the security will be seen to be of some significance when shortly we consider the determination of the variable income of a business enterprise.

Because changes in the value of a security which result from changes in expectations which occur during the period are excluded from the definition of variable income, this does not mean that they must be neglected altogether. What it does mean is that they are considered to be best kept separate from income, to be reported separately as unexpected gains. Here, another of Alexander's illustrations makes the point clear. Suppose, he says, the amount paid on the perpetual bond is suddenly raised from $10 or nothing on the toss of a coin to $12 or nothing. At a 5% rate of interest this announcement will raise the value of the bond from $100 to $120. There is an unexpected gain of $20, quite apart from any variable income there may be during that year.

This is perhaps a suitable point at which to compare the informativeness of the three income concepts we can choose from in this case. Accounting income would be reported as $10 for the year if the coin came down heads. The change in the terms of the bond would not be regarded as having any relevance to the determination of current income. Economic income would be reported as $30, the receipts for the period plus the increase in the value of the bond. Alexander's proposal is that we should report a variable income of $10 and an unexpected gain of $20. There seems to me to be no room for doubt that this last method of reporting is more informative than either of the others, if our purpose is to assess the success of the bondholder's investment policy for the year.

Incidentally, the relationship between economic income and variable income can be expressed symbolically quite simply, if we write V as the value of the asset whose income we are considering, R for the net receipts from it, use the subscripts 0 and 1 for the beginning and end of period 1, and the further subscripts a and e for actual magnitudes and expected magnitudes respectively. Then:

Economic income

$$= \text{Variable income} + \text{unexpected gain}$$
$$V_{1a} - V_{0a} + R_a$$
$$= (V_{1e} - V_{0a} + R_a) + (V_{1a} - V_{1e})$$

However, it has to be admitted that this formulation is incomplete insofar as it excludes from variable income and leaves in unexpected gain the consequential changes in V_{1a} which have already been referred to.

THE VARIABLE INCOME OF A BUSINESS ENTERPRISE

It is easy enough to separate the receipts of the owner of a security from the security itself. When we turn to a business enterprise, we cannot use the amounts distributed by the enterprise to its proprietors to help us in determining the income of the enterprise; and the net receipts of the enterprise will include the proceeds of converting non-cash assets into cash, which proceeds we obviously cannot reckon as income. What corresponds to R_a, in the case of an enterprise, is the change in net tangible assets during the period, all assets being valued at cost. This is equal to accounting net income before charging depreciation or providing for inventory mark-downs, and it is the first element in enterprise variable income.

The second element, $V_{1e} - V_{0a}$, is the change in the ex dividend value of the enterprise during the year which can be predicted with more or less certainty at the beginning of the year. This predictable change in value is, I suggest, what we ought to be measuring when we provide for depreciation, that is to say, it is depreciation based more on the expected loss of market value through use or obsolescence of assets rather than on allocations of historical cost.[7] Of course, in a world from which uncertainty had been banished, these two concepts of depreciation would amount to the same thing.

The third and last element in the variable income of a business enterprise, corresponding to the consequential change in the value of a security resulting from the year's distribution to proprietors, could be of major importance. We must include in variable income any change in the value of the enterprise which is the result of managerial activity during the year over and above the predictable change just discussed. Such change may take the form of a change in the value of tangible assets or a change in the value of goodwill. To qualify for inclusion in variable income these value changes must be brought about by the activity of the firm. If they are purely the result of factors extraneous to the firm, such as a change in the law or a change in the market rate of interest, then they are not part of variable income but are unexpected gains.

The distinction which has to be drawn here is between value changes which are merely the result of a change in expectations and value changes which are the result of managerial activity. If variable income is to measure the firm's success in adding to its well-off-ness, value changes of the latter type must be included in it. In his original formulation of the way in which the variable income of a corporation might be determined, Alexander did not draw a distinction between internally and externally generated changes in the value of goodwill, but suggested that any change in its value might be included in variable income. However, this seems to me to be inconsistent with his earlier definition. The principal difference between variable income and economic income, as I understand it, is that while economic income includes all changes in the value of net worth which have taken place during the period, variable income includes only those changes which inevitably result from the passage of time or are the result of the activities of the period. To implement this idea, we have to try to distinguish changes in the value of goodwill which are the result of managerial activity, those which reflect, that is to say, changes in

---

[7] I must repeat here that I am assuming away changes in the value of money. Insofar as these must be reckoned with, some form of stabilization would have to be built into the above scheme.

expectations brought about by the management and changes in the value of goodwill which cannot so be accounted for.

We have, then, these three constituents of variable business income:

1. The change in net tangible assets, valued at cost.
2. As a deduction, the expected loss of market value of assets through use or obsolescence.
3. Internally generated differences between the value of both tangible and intangible assets at the accounting date and their cost at date of acquisition (or their value at the previous accounting date), to the extent that these differences have not already been included in (2) above.

It is this third element, and especially the recognition of certain changes in the value of goodwill as constituting part of the firm's net income, which particularly distinguishes variable income from accounting income.

CAN WE MEASURE VARIABLE INCOME?

Variable income is a valuable idea, I think, in clarifying our thinking about what an income concept should give us and in recognizing the limitations of accounting income. But can we, in practice, hope to make the distinction between those value changes which are to be included in variable income and those which are to be included in unexpected gain?

Regretfully, I do not think that we can. We must remember that we have two problems, one of valuation and one of attribution, if we want to implement the idea of variable income for a business enterprise. Even if we are prepared to ignore any but quite substantial divergences between the depreciated cost and the current value of tangible assets, we should as a minimum have first to revalue goodwill at the end of each accounting period and then to apportion any change in its value between that part which was the result of managerial activity and that part which was the result of good or bad luck. One has only to state this difficulty to see that there can never be any simple solution to it. Even in very simple domestic situations we know that we can rarely separate the results of good luck and good judgment. In a complex business situation, how much less likely are we to be able to do so!

This difficulty, which would confront us even if our accounts were kept in monetary units of constant purchasing power, is exacerbated when we have to allow for price level changes. When an asset is bought for $1,000 and prices in general rise so that a year later the asset, though then partly worn out, is worth more on the market than when it was first bought, is this value change to be regarded as an "unexpected gain" or are we to attribute it to the good judgment of management in purchasing the asset in anticipation of a price rise? If the use of the variable income idea requires us to answer questions like this, I conclude that we simply cannot use it, except, perhaps in simple non-business situations.

CONCLUSION

Just as Hicks was led to the conclusion that income was not an effective tool of economic analysis, so it seems to me that we are led to the conclusion that periodic income is not an effective tool of financial planning or control. This conclusion seems to accord ill with the fact that income measurement has long been a central theme of accounting and the main preoccupation of the accounting profession. Yet this fact need not impress us. The practice of medicine once consisted largely of blood-letting. It may be that we are already witnessing a decline in the importance of income measurement. Certainly there is a livelier sense of the short-comings of ascertained profit figures than there once was, for most of the purposes for which such figures have traditionally been used. There is a rather striking confirmation of this in the preamble to Recommendation XV of the Institute of Chartered Accountants in England and Wales. This Recommendation is concerned with the price-level problem, and the passage I have in mind (paragraph 312) reads as follows:

> The Council cannot emphasize too strongly that the significance of accounts prepared on the basis of historical cost is subject to limitations, not the least of which is that the monetary unit in which the accounts are prepared is not a stable unit of measurement. In consequence the results shown by accounts prepared on the basis of historical cost are not a measure of increase or decrease in wealth in terms of purchasing power; nor do the results necessarily represent the amount which can prudently be regarded as available for distribution, having regard to the financial requirements of the business. Similarly the results shown by such accounts are not necessarily suitable for purposes such as price fixing, wage negotiations and taxation, unless in using them for these purposes due regard is paid to the amount of profit which has been retained in the business for its maintenance.

This seems pretty much to throw away the baby with the bath-water.

The fact is that, for several important purposes, periodic income, either historical or prospective, has already been or is being superseded. For decision-making purposes the idea of "contribution" has taken over from net income. In the field of taxation, we depart from income as the tax base every time we introduce special allowances for depletion, or provide for accelerated depreciation, or permit an anomalous treatment of capital gains. Even for reporting to stockholders, just as in the first half of this century we saw the income statement displace the balance sheet in importance, so we may now be de-emphasizing the income statement in favor of a statement of fund flows or cash flows. Each of us sees the future differently, no doubt. But my own guess is that, so far as the history of accounting is concerned, the next twenty-five years may subsequently be seen to have been the twilight of income measurement.

The FASB and the Allocation Fallacy

ARTHUR L. THOMAS

Off to an impressively active start, the Financial Accounting Standards Board has already wrestled with a broad range of accounting issues. Topics on its active agenda or on which it has issued Standards include

1. Accounting for leases.
2. Accounting for research and development costs.
3. Contingencies and future losses.
4. Gains and losses from extinguishment of debt.
5. Interest costs and capitalization.
6. Accounting for pensions.
7. Segment reporting.
8. Business combinations.
9. Interim financial statements.
10. Reporting by development stage entities.
11. Reporting in units of general purchasing power.
12. Translation of foreign currency transactions and financial statements.
13. The recommendations of the Trueblood Report.[1]

All these topics involve some kind of *allocation*, which is the assignment of a total to one or more locations or categories. A thesaurus gives "division," "partition," "slicing," "splitting" and "apportionment" as synonyms of "allocation." Accounting's allocations include assignment of a lease's costs to the individual years of its life, assignment of R&D costs to the single year of their expenditure and assignment of long term investment interest to successive annual revenues. All the FASB topics listed above fall into one of the following two classes of allocations, with items 7 through 9 falling into both:

1. The first nine topics require deciding when to recognize revenues, expenses, gains or losses—that is, deciding to what periods they should be assigned. For example, the FASB may eventually specify how to allocate pension costs to successive annual pension expenses.
2. The last seven topics involve ways of preparing financial statements composed mainly of allocated data. For example, this is implicit through-

I am grateful to Paul Rosenfield for his comments on an earlier draft of this article.

Arthur L. Thomas, "The FASB and the Allocation Fallacy," *The Journal of Accountancy*, November 1975, pp. 65–68. Copyright © 1975 by the American Institute of Certified Public Accountants, Inc.

[1]"Objectives of Financial Statements," Report of the Study Group on the Objectives of Financial Statements, Robert M. Trueblood, chairman (New York: AICPA, October 1973).

out the Trueblood Report and explicit in its position statement and income statement recommendations.

In fact, almost all of our revenue recognition and matching efforts require allocation.

THE ALLOCATION PROBLEM

The foregoing is background to a problem that we accountants acknowledge, but whose severity we usually misjudge. To use a term from formal logic, recent research indicates that, unfortunately, our allocations must almost always be *incorrigible*—that is to say, they can neither be refuted nor verified.[2] Incorrigibility will be a central concept in this discussion, and it is well to give a few examples even if doing so may initially seem to be a detour.

Let's suppose that someone claims that beings live among us who look and act exactly like humans, but who actually are aliens, seeded on this planet by flying saucers. We ask: do they come equipped with authentic looking birth certificates? Yes. Would tests of their internal structure, chromosomes or the like expose them? No. Could psychiatrists unmask them? No. The horrible thing is that they have such good counterfeit memories that even the aliens themselves don't know their real nature—you may be one yourself.

Such claims are incorrigible, for no experiment could prove either that such aliens exist or that they don't. Here are some other incorrigible claims:

- Charles Dickens may not have been a greater author than Shakespeare, but he was more of a person.
- Our bourbon is mellower.
- The official state flower of Unicornia is the marsh mallow.
- Even if the colonists had lost their war of independence, by now America would be independent of Britain.
- Since I've lost weight, I've become more spiritual.

Now, if our allocations are incorrigible, practicing accountants should be deeply concerned. We attest that financial statements present fairly the positions of companies and the results of their operations. But if both our revenue recognition and matching are founded upon allocations that we can neither refute nor verify, *we have no way of knowing whether these attestations are true.*

Are they incorrigible? I'll begin with matching and for brevity will disregard extraordinary items (and other nonoperating gains and losses), lower-of-cost-or-market writedowns and the like. Our matchings assign costs of a firm's nonmonetary inputs (inventories, labor, other services, depreciable assets, etc.) to the expenses of one or more accounting periods, temporarily reporting as assets costs assigned to future periods. We're all familiar with the theory behind these matching assignments: each input's purchase price should be allocated to successive periods in proportion to the contribution it makes to each period's revenues. Academics and most practitioners also know that an equivalent matching theory can be developed around contributions to net cash inflows.

[2]Arthur L. Thomas, Studies in Accounting Research No. 9, *The Allocation Problem: Part Two* (American Accounting Association, 1974), hereafter SAR 9.

The allocation problem has several dimensions, some of which are subtle. But one is easily described: to match costs with revenues, we must know what the contributions of the firm's individual inputs *are*. Unfortunately, as I'll illustrate below, there's no way that we can know this.

Seeing why this is so requires introducing a final concept, *interaction*. Inputs to a process interact whenever they generate an output different from the total of what they would yield separately. For instance, labor and equipment interact whenever people and machines working together produce more goods than the total of what people could make with their bare hands and machines could make untended. As this example suggests, interaction is extremely common. Almost all of a firm's inputs interact with each other—their failure to do so would ordinarily signal their uselessness.

Surprising as it may seem, it can be proved that whenever inputs interact, calculations of how much total revenue or cash flow has been contributed by any individual input are as meaningless as, say, calculations of the proportion of a worker's services due to any one internal organ: heart, liver or lungs. Thus, despite all textbooks and American Institute of CPAs or FASB releases to the contrary—despite what you've been trained to believe—our attempts to match costs with revenues must almost always fail. The next section tries to demonstrate this.

A SIMPLE EXAMPLE

A complete demonstration, meeting all possible counterarguments, is very lengthy.[3] But a simple example reveals the kernel of the matter. What follows is offered in the same spirit as Robert Sterling's recent illustration in these pages that only price-level-adjusted current-value financial statements are fully relevant and interpretable:

"A highly simplified case will be considered in this article. The advantages of simplified cases are that they are easily understood by both the reader and the author and they are more easily solved. If we cannot solve the simplified cases, then we can be fairly certain that we also cannot solve the complex cases. Thus, if a particular approach fails to provide a solution for simplified cases, then we can avoid wasting effort by trying that approach on complex cases."[4]

However, instead of Sterling's cash, securities, bread and milk trading economy, I'll describe a production process for bread alone and confine the discussion to strictly physical measures (to avoid complications introduced by monetary valuations).[5] If individual contributions are necessarily incorrigible even in the following example, it's hard to imagine how they could be otherwise in the vastly more complex processes by which business enterprises generate their products, services, revenues and cash flows.

A prospector manufactures sourdough bread by a three-stage process:

[3]See SAR 9, chapters 1–6, for the attempt.

[4]Robert R. Sterling, "Relevant Financial Reporting in an Age of Price Changes," *Journal of Accountancy*, February 75, p. 42.

[5]As a technical point, I've also simplified by discussing only incremental contributions of inputs. See SAR 9, especially pp. 32–40, 47–48 and 141–44, for the parallel problems that arise for their marginal contributions.

1. He makes leaven by mixing flour, sugar and water in a crock, then keeps it in a warm place for about a week (until it bubbles).
2. He makes bread by transferring all but a cup of leaven to a large pot, where he mixes it with soda and additional flour, sugar and water, kneads it slightly and then lets it rise. He digs a shallow pit, fills it with coals from his camp fire, covers the pot, places it in the pit, buries it in hot coals and keeps it there until the bread is baked.
3. He replenishes the leaven (for the next baking) by adding enough flour and water to restore the crock to its original level.

Water, airborne yeasts and wood are free goods here. We accountants would be concerned with the following inputs to this process: flour, sugar, soda, labor, the crock, the pot and a shovel. Finally, part of the flour and sugar leaven for one loaf becomes included in the leaven for the next. The output of each baking is one loaf of bread.

Although its manufacture is simple, the moment we try to calculate the contributions of any individual input to this output we face a dilemma. Each input (except, perhaps, the soda and the shovel) is essential. Therefore, we could plausibly assign all of the output to any individual input. For example, we could assign all of the output to the flour, reasoning that were flour withheld from the process there would be no bread. Yet we could equally well assign all of the output to the pot, since without it the loaf would have been incinerated.

Having assigned all output to any one input, we've implicitly assigned zero to each other input. But if either all or zero is appropriate for each input, any intermediate allocation will be equally appropriate—say, half the loaf to the flour and a sixth each to the pot, labor and the crock.

I'm unable to prove which of the infinitely many possible ways of allocating the loaf is correct. Therefore, I can't specify the individual contributions of the inputs; instead, all I'm entitled to say is that they generate the loaf jointly. Research shows that other writers on economics and accounting—even efficient-markets investigators—are equally unable to solve this problem. Perhaps the reader can. But until someone does, any contributions calculated for these inputs must be incorrigible:

1. One can't verify them, because any other calculation is just as good.
2. One can't refute them, because their calculation is just as good as any other.

Therefore, any attempts at matching based on these contributions (say, depreciation of the pot or calculation of a value for the ending leaven inventory) will also be incorrigible. But the sourdough process is so much simpler than the productive processes of business enterprises, that *matching must necessarily be incorrigible for them, too*—unless, again, the reader can show how complications ease the calculations. To generalize, when a company tries to match costs with revenues there's no way either to refute or to verify the results. Instead, all possible ways of matching will be just as good—or bad—as each other.

If it's any consolation, I don't like this conclusion either, and have spent years trying to disprove it. Nor should you accept it without further inquiry.

But I urge you at least to suspend disbelief in it (and in what follows) until you've read the detailed research, cited earlier, that backs it up.

And please notice that the difficulty here isn't one of being unable to allocate—there might be some way of getting around that problem. Instead, we're drowned in possible allocations, with no defensible way to choose among them. To be sure, since we must prepare reports, we eventually do pick one set of figures or another. Long before completing our training, we became accustomed to do this with few (if any) pangs. First, we narrow the possibilities by looking to generally accepted accounting principles and then select one of the survivors according to industry custom, apparent advantage to the company, apparent appropriateness of the method to the firm's circumstances or some other plausible rationale. But how can the incorrigible results be useful to decision makers?

Unless you (or someone) can suggest ways in which calculations that can neither be verified nor refuted assist decisions,[6] our allocations of the costs of depreciable assets, inventories, labor and other inputs are irrelevant to investor needs. Indeed, although it's painful to say this, they are mere rituals—solemn nonsense—and our beliefs in them are fallacies. This should trouble all of us, because practitioners spend much time conducting such rituals, and theorists much time elaborating on such fallacies.[7]

The Accounting Principles Board was well aware of this, but, underrating its severity, was satisfied to claim that exact measurements are seldom possible and that allocation often requires informed judgment.[8] With all due respect, acknowledging that few allocations are exact is like replying, "Few animals are ever completely healthy," in response to he statement, "Sir, your cow is dead."

Finally, since what's true of individual inputs also holds for groups of inputs, I'm forced to conclude that our revenue recognition practices are rituals, too. For revenue recognition allocates the firm's *lifetime* output to the groups of inputs that constitute its resources during the individual years of its life. Once again, the details of this appear in SAR 9.

THE FASB'S RESPONSIBILITY

What, then, of the FASB? We've seen it worry, or propose to worry, about which allocations are most appropriate for various accounting situations. The FASB should stop doing this. Instead, whenever possible, it should *eliminate* allocations. Such incorrigible figures don't do readers of our reports any real good, and they

1. Cost money.
2. Strain relations between auditors and clients (when they disagree about which incorrigible figures to report).
3. Cause many of the nonuniformity problems that plague us (since allocations are incorrigible, naturally GAAP conflict—there's no way to settle which rules are right).

[6]Assistance that goes beyond the unsatisfactory, short run utilities is described on pp. 8–9, 40–46, 65–70 and 163–74 of SAR 9.

[7]For examples of the latter, see SAR 9, pp. 94–110, 116–19 and 128–55.

[8]For examples, see APB Statement No. 4, pp. 11, 13–15, 21–22, 46–48 and 102.

4. Thereby confuse individual readers, thus violating what the Trueblood Report designates as the basic objective of financial statements.
5. Generally breed distrust in our profession.

When their elimination isn't possible, the FASB should keep allocations unsophisticated (if we must be incorrigible, at least let's be simple), choose allocation rules on expedient, political grounds (ceasing to worry about theory) and be candid about what it's doing. In particular, the FASB should actively

1. Try to convert conventional reporting practices to allocation-free ones. There are two main allocation-free alternatives to conventional accounting: current value reporting and the type of funds statement reporting that defines "funds" as net quick assets.[9] Certainly, Sterling is correct that merely adjusting allocated historical costs for changes in purchasing power serves little purpose: adjusted ritual remains ritual. The same is true of foreign currency translations.
2. Meanwhile, avoid launching any new incorrigible allocations in such areas as interim and segment reports, leases, contingencies, interest and pensions. And eliminate the more flagrantly incorrigible allocations that we now commit. A prime example of the latter (despite its being one of the APB's greatest political triumphs) is tax deferral: we take the difference between an incorrigible book allocation and an incorrigible tax allocation and allocate it, incorrigibly.

In conclusion, I would emphasize that none of these remarks is intended to disparage accounting practitioners. As SAR 9 points out (p. 157), practitioners have honestly believed that allocations are appropriate and have struggled to cope with them, while we academics saddled practitioners with a matching theory that requires such assignments, then failed to provide defensible ways for their calculation. But the hard fact remains that so long as we continue to certify that incorrigible allocations present fairly a firm's financial position and the results of its operations, we're making claims that we just can't back up. Professional responsibility urges that we, and the FASB, cease to tolerate this.

[9]See SAR 9, chapter 7.

III-B / CONSTANT-DOLLAR ACCOUNTING

GPP Accounting—
Relevance and Interpretability

PAUL ROSENFIELD

The proposal of the Financial Accounting Standards Board that enterprises be required to present information based on present generally accepted accounting principles in units of general purchasing power[1] has recently been criticized in two places in the same issue of the *Journal of Accountancy*,[2] on the grounds of lack of relevance and lack of interpretability. Both criticisms miss their mark. The principles prescribed in the FASB proposal (with a modification in the index specified, as explained below) result in improved information, and the proposal should be supported. The FASB, however, unnecessarily exposes its proposal to criticism by failing to indicate the relevance of the resulting information.

EVALUATING THE FASB PROPOSAL

The FASB proposal can be evaluated properly only by clearly understanding what it attempts to accomplish and what it does not attempt to accomplish. In turn, that understanding can be gained only by understanding the nature of general purchasing power restatement.

GENERAL PURCHASING POWER RESTATEMENT

The nature of general purchasing power restatement is to change the criterion of success or failure used in financial statements, and the purpose is to incorporate a more relevant criterion of success or failure.

[1]Financial Accounting Standards Board exposure draft, proposed Statement of Financial Accounting Standards, "Financial Reporting in Units of General Purchasing Power" (Stamford, Conn.: FASB, December 31, 1974).

[2]Robert R. Sterling, "Relevant Financial Reporting in an Age of Price Changes," *Journal of Accountancy*, February 75, p. 42, and John C. Burton, "Financial Reporting in an Age of Inflation," *Journal of Accountancy*, February 75, p. 68.

Standard Resource

The idea of a criterion of success or failure in financial statements can be explained by reference to a concept that can for convenience be called the "standard resource."

In financial statements, many types of resources, such as cash, receivables, inventories, property and intangibles, are all related to a single resource, money. That single resource may be called the standard resource.[3] Relating different types of resources to a standard resource is necessary to make comparisons of collections of those resources. For example, a collection of two lathes plus six cars cannot be compared with a collection of three lathes plus two cars unless the collections are related to a standard resource. Economic activities, such as purchases and sales, are also related to a standard resource.

Changing the Standard Resource

The use of money as the standard resource is so ingrained in accounting that the fact that it is only one of the standard resources that may be used is generally overlooked.

In times of price stability, using money as the standard resource is generally considered satisfactory. But during inflation, the general purchasing power of a unit of money declines, and when there is considerable inflation, people question whether money of declining value should be used to gauge economic activities.

Money is not prized for its own sake, but for its general purchasing power. Although general purchasing power is inherent in money, it is a resource[4] that is not identical with money. An enterprise may have an increase in the money it holds over a period during which the general purchasing power of the money it holds decreases because of inflation. Adopting general purchasing power as the standard resource avoids the problems caused by stating economic activity in terms of money whose value in terms of general purchasing power is declining.

[3] The concept of a standard resource in accounting is often discussed in terms of *units of measure*. Although that terminology is helpful for some purposes, it is at a level of abstraction that it not helpful for all purposes. The relevance of a standard resource, which exists in the world and is an object of desire, can be more easily examined than the relevance of a unit of measure. The single resource could also be given any number of other names, for example, "common resource." Contrary to Gynther's assumption in Reg S. Gynther, "Why Use General Purchasing Power?" *Accounting and Business Research*, Spring 1974, p. 146, the term "standard resource" does not refer to the relevance of any particular resource. Whether a particular resource is relevant for the purposes of the information in which it is used as the standard resource must be determined by reference to those purposes.

[4] General purchasing power has the characteristics required of a standard resource in accounting although it may not have all the characteristics that are usually associated with resources, such as existence independent of another type of resource. General purchasing power exists in the world; it is desired; it can be bought, held and sold, etc. Its relationship to money is similar to the relationship of horsepower to motors. Since different motors have different amounts of horsepower, accounting in terms of horsepower, which is really desired by owners of motors, may often be more useful than accounting in terms of motors. Similarly, accounting in terms of general purchasing power may often be more useful than accounting in terms of money.

General purchasing power restatement changes the standard resource in terms of which economic activity is stated from money to general purchasing power.

Criterion of Success or Failure

The selection of a standard resource for a set of financial statements establishes a criterion of success or failure used in those statements. If money is selected as the standard resource, a criterion of success or failure is whether over a period an enterprise has had an increase or a decrease in its holding, command over or prospects of obtaining money. More money means success (even if it is accompanied by less general purchasing power). Less money means failure.

In contrast, if general purchasing power is selected as the standard resource, more general purchasing power means success and less general purchasing power means failure, regardless of changes in terms of money.

IMPROVED INFORMATION

The selection of the criterion of success or failure is not the only problem area in financial accounting, of course. The standard resource that serves as the criterion of success or failure can be related to the different types of resources owned by the enterprise in several ways. The relationship[5] most widely emphasized is historical cost, that is, the number of units of the standard resource sacrificed to obtain the different resources held. Other relationships may be emphasized, for example, selling price (the number of units of the standard resource that can be obtained on sale of the different resources held) or replacement price (the number of units of the standard resource that would now have to be sacrificed to obtain resources similar to the resources held). Changing the relationship emphasized from historical cost to a more current relationship is current value accounting.

Selection of the standard resource and selection of the relationship are independent and complementary decisions.[6] Information in present financial

---

[5]The concept of relationships in accounting is often discussed in terms of *measurable attributes*. Although that terminology is helpful for some purposes, just as *unit of measure* is, it is at a level of abstraction that is not helpful for all purposes. A measurable attribute of an object sounds like an intrinsic part of the object and nothing else. However, all measurement involves comparison, that is, relating with things outside the thing measured. Discussing the relationships between an object and the external thing to which it is related avoids confusion that might arise by discussing measurable attributes. The term *measurable attributes* is misused, for example, in Sterling. The article does not define the concept and uses the term in senses as widely different as price-level adjusted income (footnote 2, page 43) and the number of goods that could be commanded in the market by resources held (page 46). The latter usage provides one answer to two independent questions: which standard resource to use (goods) and which relationship to emphasize (current selling price). The usage contributes to the difficulties of interpretation encountered in the article. The concepts used should facilitate separate consideration of those two questions rather than imply that only one question is involved.

[6]See Paul Rosenfield, "The Confusion Between General Price-Level Restatement and Current Value Accounting," *Journal of Accountancy*, Oct. 72, p. 63, for an elaboration of this point.

statements can be improved by adopting a more relevant criterion of success or failure, that is, by adopting general purchasing power restatement (the relevance of general purchasing power information is discussed in a subsequent section), although it could be further improved by emphasizing a more relevant relationship, that is, by adopting current value accounting. The type of improvement possible solely by adopting general purchasing power restatement can be seen by understanding the usefulness of present information.

Moderate Usefulness of Present Information

Present financial statements have two major defects in addition to incorporating arbitrary allocations[7] that limit their usefulness: (1) they use a criterion of success or failure, more or less money, that is less relevant to the users than another criterion that can be used, more or less general purchasing power, and (2) they emphasize a stale relationship, historical cost. Nevertheless, present financial statements have some usefulness that makes the users better off having them than having no information beyond dividends, interest, wages, etc., which are known in the absence of financial statements.

The useful information now presented is mainly found in the income statement. In general, the income statement for a year presents the cumulative money gain or loss on completed business transactions, that is, on those deals that have started with cash paid or payable some time in the past and ended[8] with cash received or receivable during the year. Knowing the history of how successful or unsuccessful were deals completed during each year in terms of money can give users some insight into the ability of the enterprise to pay dividends, interest, wages, etc., in the future. However, several things limit the usefulness of that income statement information:

1. The information is not as timely as possible. Information on the success or failure of deals while they are in process would be more helpful than information only when they are completed.
2. The trend of success or failure may be somewhat obscured. The enterprise does not experience success or failure only in the periods in which deals are completed. Reporting success or failure as the deals progress would help establish the past trends of successful or unsuccessful operations and perhaps help to forecast future trends.
3. Arbitrary allocations are used that do not represent real world events or conditions.
4. Gains and losses reported are in units of money whose general purchasing power changes.

Thus, present income statement information is only moderately useful.

---

[7]See, for example, Arthur L. Thomas, Studies in Accounting Research No. 3, *The Allocation Problem in Financial Accounting Theory* (American Accounting Association, 1969), Arthur L. Thomas, Studies in Accounting Research No. 9, *The Allocation Problem: Part Two* (American Accounting Association, 1974) and John H. Myers, "A Set of New Financial Statements," *Journal of Accountancy*, Feb. 71, p. 50.

[8]An expenditure for an asset that provides benefits for more than one period is treated as part of a series of deals, each of which ends in a different period. That treatment involves arbitrary allocations with their attendant problems.

In contrast, a large part of the information in present balance sheets is useless.[9] To be sure, the monetary assets and liabilities are presented at current amounts, but they are added to historical costs of nonmonetary assets. In themselves, those historical costs are no more than curiosities, which cannot be relied on for any current decisions concerning the assets, for example, whether to use them, sell them, rent them, replace them or discard them; whether to offer or accept them for security; how much to insure them for; and whether to invest in an enterprise that owns them.[10] And total assets and owners' equity, which are affected by irrelevant historical costs of nonmonetary assets, are also irrelevant. Important ratios based on the balance sheet are similarly tainted, for example, the current ratio, the debt to equity ratio and the rate of return. In contrast, the price–earnings ratio is not made useless by the amounts ascribed to nonmonetary assets, but that ratio is influenced by those amounts through their influence on the character of income reporting.

Although the balance sheet and the income statement interlock, the fault that makes much of the information in the balance sheet useless—the staleness of the amounts—only lessens the usefulness of the information in the income statement. The staleness affects the two statements differently. The balance sheet simply presents stale information with no relevance to the present. The information is simply too old to help. In contrast, the income statement presents cumulative results up to the present, which is helpful although it would be improved by being better related to periods. The information on results in the income statement is late, but it is better late than never.

Improving Moderately Useful Information

One of the deficiencies of present income statement information can be removed by adoption of the FASB proposal; a more relevant criterion of success or failure would be used. Gains and losses that are reported would not be simply gains and losses of money but would be gains and losses of general purchasing power, including presently unreported gains and losses of general purchasing power on holding monetary items during inflation or deflation. Those improvements are sufficient justification for adoption of the FASB proposal.

Clearly understanding the improvements that are possible by general purchasing power restatement to the moderately useful information now provided can help avoid being misled by misdirected criticism of the proposal. The criticism is often made that restating historical costs of assets held in balance sheets for changes in general purchasing power is no improvement. That criticism is true but irrelevant. Only a presently useful part of financial statement information can be improved by restatement, and the costs of assets held, reported in balance sheets, are not in the useful part.[11]

---

[9]"... the balance sheet ... is fundamentally a set of residuals left over from the determination of accounting income." Burton, p. 69.

[10]Historical costs may in some cases be found to approximate relevant current information.

[11]Although only the income statement is improved by restatement, systematic restatement of all financial statement items is the easiest way to restate the income statement correctly. Only the useful restated information need be presented.

CRITICISM ON THE GROUNDS OF
RELEVANCE AND INTERPRETABILITY

The two *Journal* articles that criticized the FASB proposal contain examples of the kind of criticism that can arise through misunderstanding of the nature of general purchasing power accounting and of what it is and is not designed to accomplish. The preceding analysis provides the means to determine the merits of that criticism.

Both articles criticize the proposal on the grounds of relevance; one also does so on the grounds of interpretability. Neither criticism is valid.

Burton's Criticism

The article by Burton implies that general purchasing power restatement is irrelevant to reflect the effects of rapidly changing specific prices. It cites the example of the threefold rise in the cost of crude oil in the first half of 1974 which is not reflected in present income statement information restated to reflect the 6 percent inflation for the period.[12]

That criticism specifies only what general purchasing power restatement does not do for income reporting, that it does not incorporate the effects of specific price changes to make the information more timely or to remove the difficulties in discerning trends of success or failure. (Elsewhere I have discussed the defects of the particular proposal made in Burton's article to reflect the effects of changing specific prices.[13]) General purchasing power restatement should be judged on what it is designed to do, not what it is not designed to do, and it is not designed to improve the reflection of the effects of changing specific prices on success or failure. It is designed to incorporate in the information already presented a more relevant criterion of success or failure considering the fact that the general purchasing power of money changes. And the article acknowledges the need for that improvement:

"If the value of the monetary unit is changing so rapidly that the combining of cash generation figures at different points within a year is misleading, an additional adjustment may be called for to equate cash at different points in time.[14]

Sterling's Criticism

The article by Sterling states explicitly that present financial statement information, both before and after general purchasing power restatement, is irrelevant and uninterpretable. It also states that present financial statement information adjusted for specific price changes is interpretable but irrelevant, and that only information adjusted for specific price changes and restated to units of general purchasing power is both relevant and interpretable.[15]

---

[12]Burton, p. 70.

[13]Paul Rosenfield, "Current Replacement Value Accounting—A Dead End," unpublished manuscript.

[14]Burton, p. 69.

[15]Sterling, p. 51.

If the criticisms in the article are valid, the FASB's proposal should be rejected. But the criticisms of present and restated financial statements are too sweeping and are not supported by the article's analysis.

The article illustrates its criticism by two cases, a complete exchange case and an incomplete exchange case. Both cases are simplified and do not involve allocation.

The article charges that unallocated historical costs ascribed to nonmonetary assets in the balance sheet in the incomplete exchange case are irrelevant and uninterpretable. But, although those amounts are irrelevant as discussed above, they are not uninterpretable. The article indicates that things are uninterpretable if we "don't understand their meaning or use." But a statement that an enterprise in the past paid a certain amount for an asset it now holds is understandable. The article does not work through the shorthand of the balance sheet. An item of inventory, at cost—$100—in a December 31, 1974 balance sheet is a complex item. It says something about December 31, 1974, that inventory was held at that date, and something about unspecified dates in the past, that on those dates sacrifices were made to obtain the inventory. Elsewhere, the article indicates that unallocated historical cost *is* understandable, when it is the unallocated historical cost of goods sold in the complete exchange case. The unallocated historical cost of goods held, presented in balance sheets, is no less interpretable than the same unallocated historical cost of the same goods when they are sold, presented in succeeding income statements.

The article concludes that *all* of present and restated financial information is irrelevant and uninterpretable simply because it finds that *balance sheet* amounts in the incomplete exchange case are irrelevant and uninterpretable. (There is no income statement in the article's incomplete exchange case.) That conclusion is not justified: even if the findings were correct, they could justifiably be extended only to present and restated balance sheets. They may not justifiably be extended to present and restated income statements, the useful part of present information.

The article makes a start on determining the relevance and interpretability of present and restated income statements. It examines income statements in the simplified complete exchange case and finds them relevant and interpretable. And as far as they go, those income statements resemble present and restated income statements—they present realized revenue less associated historical cost. Thus, all the evidence in the article is favorable to present and restated income statements.

Present and restated income statements do involve allocations not present in the simplified complete exchange case. Those allocations may hinder interpretability, and that problem requires the earnest attention of the accounting profession. But Sterling's article does not deal with the allocation problem, and nothing in his article justifies the conclusion that information in present and restated income statements is uninterpretable or irrelevant.

FASB POSITION

The FASB proposal does not deal with the relevance of the resulting information, and it would be less vulnerable to criticism if it did.

The FASB position is quite simple in outline. The general purchasing power of the dollar changes. The same dollar amounts in traditional financial statements can therefore represent different amounts of general purchasing power. Presenting information in units of general purchasing power avoids that problem. The same amounts in the restated information represent the same amount of general purchasing power. Revenue, gains, costs, etc., all represent amounts of general purchasing power rather than merely amounts of money whose general purchasing power changes.

Acceptance on Faith

The problem with the FASB position is that no reason is given as to why financial statement items should represent amounts of general purchasing power rather than amounts of money. We are in effect asked to accept it on faith. Mt. Everest, we are told, should be climbed because it is there. Apparently we should allow for inflation in the design of financial information because it is there. Only the converted accept propositions on faith, and not everyone is converted to that proposition.

The FASB position provides no means to choose between its proposal and alternative proposals concerning selection of the standard resource, except perhaps on the basis of who shouts the loudest. Competing proposals include:

1. *Proposal to adopt consumer and producer general purchasing power as the standard resource.* The FASB says the standard resource that incorporates changes in the general level of all prices, including prices of both consumer and producer goods and services, should be selected.[16]
2. *Proposal to adopt consumer general purchasing power as the standard resource.* The Institute of Chartered Accountants in England and Wales (jointly with other U.K. and Irish Institutes) says the standard resource that incorporates changes in the general level of prices of only consumer goods and services should be selected.[17]
3. *Proposal to adopt industrial purchasing power as the standard resource.* Some have proposed that each enterprise select the standard resource that incorporates changes in the prices of the goods and services the particular enterprise regularly buys.
4. *Proposal to stay with money as the standard resource.* Those who reject the use of general purchasing power restatement outright in essence are making a counterproposal to retain money as the standard resource rather than move to general or industrial purchasing power.

The type of shouting match that could develop is foreshadowed by the FASB. After asserting that general purchasing power is the concept to use, the FASB emphatically supports the use of the Gross National Product Deflator, an index of changes in both consumer and producer goods and services, by stating, "Because the GNP Deflator is more comprehensive than the Consumer Price Index, it is a better indicator of the *general* purchasing power of the U.S. dollar."[18]

---

[16]FASB, pp. 8, 9.

[17]Provisional Statement of Standard Accounting Practice No. 7, *Accounting for Changes in the Purchasing Power of Money* (The Institute of Chartered Accountants in England and Wales, London, May 1974), p. 11.

[18]FASB, p. 23. Emphasis in the original.

After asserting that consumer general purchasing power is the concept to use, a supporter could be equally emphatic and state, "Because the Consumer Price Index is confined to changes in prices of consumer goods and services, it is a better indicator of the *consumer* general purchasing power of the U.S. dollar." Supporters of the concept of enterprise general purchasing power and of the concept of money, respectively, could shout as loudly: "Because an index tailored for an enterprise is confined to changes in prices of the goods and services purchased by the enterprise, it is a better indicator of the *enterprise* general purchasing power of the U.S. dollar," and "Because ignoring changing in the general purchasing power of the U.S. dollar leaves the information in terms of numbers of dollars, the information is a better indicator of the *number* of U.S. dollars involved."

RELEVANCE OF GENERAL PURCHASING POWER INFORMATION

The two related issues—(a) whether financial statements should use general purchasing power as the standard resource and (b) which concept of general purchasing power should be used—can be more satisfactorily settled by reference to relevance than by shouting. The first issue, whether general purchasing power is or is not relevant to financial statements, is the more important, although both issues can be treated by the same analysis.

The Most Relevant Criterion of Success or Failure

A single set of financial statements should incorporate only one standard resource serving as a criterion of success or failure. General purpose financial statements should therefore incorporate the most relevant criterion of success or failure. In searching for the most relevant criterion, a decision is first required concerning to whom or to what the criterion should be relevant.

It is easy to lose sight of the fact that financial statements are intended to be a means to convey financial and economic information about the *operations* of an enterprise to the *users* of the financial statements. Operations and users are the starting points in searching for the relevant criterion of success or failure.

If the criterion of success or failure is sought by reference to the operations, the particular type of operations is the determining factor. One criterion of success in steelmaking is an increase in the quality of steel produced; one criterion of success in operating railways is an increase in the capacity to provide efficient rail service; and so forth.

Reports incorporating criteria of success or failure related to operations are helpful or even essential to managements in running enterprises. But that kind of report is not directly helpful as financial statements intended for the use of interested outside parties in making comparative investment decisions. All the information those parties use that is directly compared should have the same criterion of success or failure. Financial statements that make success equal to an increase in the quality of steel produced cannot be compared directly with other financial statements that make success equal to an increase in the ability to provide efficient rail service.

Not only should all financial statements to be used in a single comparison incorporate the same criterion of success or failure, but it should be the criterion held by the person doing the comparing. Telling someone that Company A has done and is likely to continue to do better than Company B in a certain respect is not helpful to that person if he does not care about success in that respect unless it portends success in terms in which he is interested. The criterion of success or failure in general purpose financial statements should be chosen in the light of the interests of the users of the statements.

A criterion by which to judge the success or failure of the operations of the *enterprise* should thus be sought in the interests of the *users*. The perspective of the users should control selection of the criterion, but it is the enterprise that is judged by the criterion and not the users or any aspect of the users.

In passing, it should be noted that reference to the *operations* for selection of the standard resource rules out general purchasing power. General purchasing power is the power to buy all goods and services (producer goods, consumer goods or both). But a particular enterprise buys and sells only a minute fraction of all the types of goods and services included in the concept of general purchasing power. The power to purchase the overwhelming majority of those goods and services has been and will be irrelevant to those operations. General purchasing power is therefore irrelevant to the operations of the enterprise. *Specific* goods and services are used in the operations, and their price changes may affect the operations. But changes in prices of specific goods and services are reflected in completed transactions under historical cost accounting, and incorporating specific price changes before they are reflected in completed transactions is current value accounting, not general purchasing power accounting. If users are ignored, using an index of changes in the general level of prices is indefensible.

The Interests of the Users

The interests of users need to be examined to determine the criterion of success or failure relevant to them. Users of financial statements may be persons acting on their own behalf or on the behalf of other persons or of enterprises. Persons acting on behalf of enterprises are acting ultimately on behalf of persons who have an interest in the enterprises.

Users, therefore, are acting on behalf of people. It is people's essential interests in the enterprises that should control the selection of the criterion of success or failure in the financial statements of the enterprises.

People can do two things with their resources. They can either use them for immediate consumption or they can save and hoard or invest them. Resources are not saved and hoarded or invested by people for the sake of saving and hoarding or investment. The purpose is to permit the people (or their donees or legatees) to consume in the future. Resources that are saved and hoarded or invested are meaningless to people except as they portend future consumption (except for the very few people who exult in the power provided by command over producer goods).

When people invest their resources, they exchange them for a variety of resources, including production resources and interests in enterprises that use production resources. But as investors, people are not essentially interested in production resources such as steelmaking capacity or railway equipment. They are interested in what their investments in production resources or in interests in enterprises that use production resources portend in terms of their basic interest—future consumption.

The standard resource serving as a criterion of success or failure used in financial statements should be selected on the basis of the basic interest of investors in consumption. The criterion should be an increase or decrease in the holding, command over, or prospects of obtaining consumption goods and services, and the standard resource should be consumer general purchasing power, rather than money. The standard resource requires the use of an index of changes in the general level of consumer prices only. That type of index should be required in establishing standards for inflation accounting.[19]

Modifying the FASB Proposal

The FASB proposal should be supported, but it should be modified to explain restatement in terms of a change to a criterion of success or failure that is more relevant to the users of the information than the criterion incorporated in traditional information. The FASB should determine the index that best reflects changes in the general level of prices of consumer goods and services only[20] and adopt that index in its proposal in order to incorporate that criterion of success or failure. The proposal would then not be vulnerable to criticism, for example, the irrelevant charge that individual enterprises are affected differently by changing prices. Incorporating those variously changing specific prices involves current value accounting, a process that is independent of, and complementary to, general purchasing power restatement.[21]

A GOOD STEP FORWARD

The FASB proposal to have financial information presented in units of general purchasing power has merit. Restatement results in a significant improvement in the moderately useful income statement information now presented. Furthermore, it represents the single most radical change that can be made in income reporting short of abandoning income reporting, by changing the very

[19]Arguments in support of that conclusion are also presented by The Institute of Chartered Accountants in England and Wales (jointly with other U.K. and Irish Institutes) and by a number of writers on general purchasing power accounting, including Henry W. Sweeney, the father of general purchasing power accounting in the U.S. (in his *Stabilized Accounting*, New York: Harper & Brothers Publishers, 1936, p. 4), Perry Mason (in his *Price-Level Changes and Financial Statements, Basic Concepts and Methods*, American Accounting Association, 1956, p. 12), Ralph C. Jones (in his *Price Level Changes and Financial Statements, Case Studies of Four Companies*, American Accounting Association, 1955, p. 3), Edgar O. Edwards and Philip W. Bell (in their *The Theory and Measurement of Business Income*, Berkeley, Calif.: University of California Press, 1965, p. 237), Raymond J. Chambers (in his *Accounting, Evaluation and Economic Behavior*, Englewood Cliffs, N.J.: Prentice-Hall, 1966, p. 229) and Robert R. Sterling (in his *Theory of the Measurement of Enterprise Income*, Lawrence, Kan.: The University Press of Kansas, 1970, pp. 337, 340, 341).

[20]Those who object that a consumer price index is not specific to particular consumers (for example, Reg Gynther, "Why Use General Purchasing Power?" *Accounting and Business Research*, Spring 1974, p. 146) are invited to consider whether using units of money, that is, using a constant zero inflation rate, is likely to be more or less specific to particular consumers than a consumer price index. Compare the following: ". . . the choice is between an imperfect general index and no index. In the absence of any index, the units are clearly not comparable." Sterling, *Theory of the Measurement of Enterprise Income*, p. 340.

[21]The FASB indicated it will deal with current value accounting separately (FASB, p. 22.)

nature of success or failure.[22] In contrast, current value accounting affects income reporting only by chopping it up differently into accounting periods, a less radical change but one that may be useful depending on the type of current value accounting. The proposal is a good step forward, and, contrary to expressed concerns,[23] it should encourage rather than discourage further steps to improve financial reporting, including steps toward current value accounting.

[22][Restatement] require[s] a businessman to abandon the underpinnings of all his financial calculations." Maurice Moonitz, "Price-Level Accounting and Scales of Measurement," *The Accounting Review*, July 1970, p. 472.

[23]See, for example, Burton, p. 70.

No Price Level Adjusted Statements, Please (Pleas)

CLYDE P. STICKNEY AND DAVID O. GREEN

Few question the problem: inflation (or deflation) does violence to the assumption of the period-to-period constancy of the monetary measuring unit, and the clamor for price-level adjusted accounting statements (PLAAS) as a solution is again increasingly audible.[1] It may be appropriate, therefore, to once again reconsider the alleged benefits of general price-level accounting. In this paper we summarize some of the rhetoric, evidence and conjecture; these are intentionally marshalled to rebut some of the asserted attributes of PLAAS. In particular, we question whether:

1. PLAAS present information useful for decision-making.
2. PLAAS indicate a firm's success in coping with inflation.
3. General price indexes are sufficiently reliable for use in accounting reports.

The rhetoric consists of selections from the voluminous literature on the topic; the evidence includes some results of empirical studies, while the conjecture consists of statements by individuals with extensive work in the area and our own speculations. Make no mistake, our use of the term rhetoric is intentionally pejorative, not because of our advocacy for historical cost, but because of our conviction that price-level adjustments are a poor answer to the accounting problems caused by inflation.

ARE PLAAS USEFUL INFORMATION FOR DECISION-MAKING?

Proponents of PLAAS, primarily accountants, have asserted that they provide information useful for decision-making, information which is not available

Clyde P. Stickney and David O. Green, "No Price Level Adjusted Statements, Please (Pleas)," *CPA Journal*, January 1974, pp. 25–31. Reprinted with permission of the *CPA Journal*. Copyright © 1974 New York State Society of CPAs.

[1]In their proposals submitted to the Accounting Objectives Study Group, sponsored by the American Institute of Certified Public Accountants, the following firms have taken a position favoring either partial or comprehensive restatement of conventional financial statements for changes in general purchasing power of the dollar:

(1) Arthur Andersen and Company, "Objectives of Financial Statements for Business Enterprises," 1972, p. 23;
(2) Arthur Young and Company, "The Objectives of Financial Statements: Responding to Investors' Needs," item 5;
(3) Ernst and Ernst, "Additional Views on Accounting Objectives," May, 1972, p. 21;
(4) Coopers and Lybrand, "The Objectives of Financial Accounting," 1973, p. 21.

The clamor is perhaps even louder on the other side of the Atlantic where the English Institute has recently circulated a discussion paper on PLAAS.

from conventional statements. For example, the Accounting Principles Board stated:

> General price-level financial statements should prove useful to investors, creditors, management, employees, government officials, and others who are concerned with the economic affairs of business enterprises.
>
> Current economic actions must take place in terms of current dollars, and restating items in terms of current dollars expresses them in the context of current action.[2]

Contrary Views and Circumstances

Evidence that seemingly rebuts the Board's guarded "should prove useful" assertion consists of the following:

> Estes requested financial analysts, bankers, and financial executives to rate PLAAS. He reports in 1968 that 32 per cent of those sampled felt PLAAS were "very useful," 38 per cent indicated they were "somewhat useful," and 30 per cent considered them "not useful."[3]
>
> Dyckman asked financial analysts to respond to a statement that PLAAS should be prepared and reported. His overall results reported in 1969 indicate that 23 per cent either mildly or strongly agreed, 20 per cent were neutral, and 57 per cent either mildly or strongly disagreed.[4]
>
> Garner surveyed members of four professional organizations making use of accounting reports. In response to a question regarding the need for general price-level adjusted data, only 36 of 160 persons surveyed during 1972 answered affirmatively (22.5 per cent).[5]
>
> Dyckman presented financial statements for two firms to three independent groups of financial analysts. The three groups received conventional statements, conventional statements with price-level adjusted statements as supplements, and PLAAS only. Firm 1 was made to appear superior in the conventional statements and Firm 2 in the adjusted statements. He hypothesized an increasing preference for Firm 2 as one moved from conventional to adjusted statements. He found the correlation between firm choice and reporting method to be .34. Dyckman indicated he would have been satisfied with a correlation of about .7 and hence concluded the relationship was not a "strong one."[6]
>
> At the Seaview Symposium held in 1968, analysts, bankers, and financial executives alike spoke out against PLAAS. To quote one analyst,

---

[2]Accounting Principles Board, *Financial Statements Restated for General Price-Level Changes*, Accounting Principles Board Statement No. 3 (New York: American Institute of Certified Public Accountants, 1969), para. .06 and .32.

[3]Ralph W. Estes, "An Assessment of the Usefulness of Current Cost and Price-Level Information by Financial Statement Users," *Journal of Accounting Research*, 6 (Autumn, 1968), p. 207.

[4]Thomas R. Dyckman, "Investment Analysis and General Price-Level Adjustments," *Studies in Accounting Research*, No. 1 (Evanston, Illinois: American Accounting Association, 1969). Percentages were derived from Table 5, page 16. Considering his relatively low usable response rate (33 per cent), care must be exercised when interpreting Dyckman's results.

[5]Don E. Garner, "The Need for Price-Level and Replacement Cost Data," *Journal of Accountancy*, CXXXIV (September, 1972), pp. 94–98.

[6]Dyckman, *op. cit.*, pp. 12–13.

"To me this is a typical academician's impractical theory and practitioner's morass."[7]

Not a single article linking PLAAS and investment analysis was found in a major United States financial periodical or journal (*Wall Street Journal, Financial Analysts Journal*) since the issuance of Statement No. 3.

The editions of *Accounting Trends and Techniques* for 1970, 1971, and 1972 indicate that "none of the survey companies presented financial statements adjusted to a common dollar basis."

Gap between Advocacy and Practice

One wonders why such a gap exists between those accountants who state "I believe there is a consensus in accounting circles that price-level information is a good thing" and statements users who increasingly argue against it and perhaps will ultimately ignore it altogether. Two explanations for this gap are suggested.

Users May Be Confused as to Meaning of Adjusted Statements

First, users might be confused as to the meaning of the adjusted statements. As one analyst put it, "I think the only problem analysts have with this [PLAAS] is when we get the answer, we have no idea what to do with it." A financial executive echoes, "I think, frankly, that any attempt at this stage to get to price-level accounting is going to be much more confusing than it will be desirable to anybody in the whole community that is going to use it."[8] Of Dyckman's subjects who received only conventional statements, 74 per cent selected Firm 1. Of the subjects who received only PLAAS, approximately one-third selected Firm 1, one-third selected Firm 2, and the remaining individuals could not make a decision. Also, analysts receiving only conventional statements were unable to make an investment decision in 22 per cent of the cases as compared to 32 per cent for those receiving only adjusted statements. These differences might be attributed to the creation of confusion.

If lack of understanding of PLAAS is the problem, an educational program could help. One wonders, though, whether confusion about PLAAS on the part of users or confusion about usefulness on the part of their advocates is the problem.

Conventional Statements Can Furnish Desired Information

A second explanation for the gap between demand for and supply of PLAAS is that users may be able to derive the desired information from conventional statements. A firm's pricing policy is, presumably, at least partially based on anticipated changes in the cost of factor inputs. Finance charges levied on receivables include an amount to offset the loss of purchasing power while the claim is outstanding. In many instances, then, conventionally calculated income already includes the effects of anticipated inflation. Unanticipated inflation should be reflected in excess or deficient returns relative to some standard for each firm.

[7]John C. Burton (ed.), *Corporate Financial Reporting: Conflicts and Challenges*, New York: American Institute of Certified Public Accountants, 1969), p. 56.

[8]These three quotations from *ibid.*, pp. 59, 56 and 58.

Further, even though unadjusted financial statements may not include all items reported in PLAAS (e.g., monetary gain on long-term liabilities during inflation), there may be such a close relationship between the unadjusted and adjusted values that a simple transformation is all that is required to estimate price-level adjusted effects. Several studies have used unadjusted and adjusted earnings and ratios to predict future earnings and ratios of return. These studies have generally found adjusted values to perform no or only slightly better as predictors than unadjusted values.[9]

In his analysis of the Institute-sponsored field study on PLAAS, Rosenfield states:

> Differences between net income on the general price-level basis and on the historical-dollar basis varied widely. One company showed no difference while all but one other company showed differences of almost every magnitude from 4% to 31%. Several companies showed considerable variation between years.
>
> ... the results nevertheless seem to support the view ... that presentation of supplementary general price-level financial statements would make available potentially useful information that otherwise is not disclosed.[10]

While absolute earnings did vary, a remarkably similar pattern emerges when one compares rates of return on stockholders' equity. We regressed adjusted on unadjusted rates of return using the data supplied by Rosenfield.[11] We obtained a coefficient of determination (R^2) of approximately 96 per cent, indicating a high degree of association between the two measures of rate of return. Similar results have been found by others.[12] The implication of this is that comprehensive restatement may not be necessary (even if useful) if the desired information can be obtained by merely transforming data from conventional statements.

DO PLAAS HELP READERS DETERMINE HOW WELL MANAGEMENT HAS COPED WITH INFLATION?

This section deals with the problem of (1) capital maintenance and (2) measuring managerial effectiveness in hedging against inflation.

[9]See, for example, John K. Simmons and Jack Gray, "An Investigation of Differing Accounting Frameworks on the Prediction of Net Income," *Accounting Review*, XLIV (October, 1969), 757–776; Richard A. Samuelson, "The Predictive Ability of Price-Level Adjusted Earnings: An Ex Post Valuation Approach to Accounting Measurement Validation," (Unpublished Ph.D. dissertation, UCLA, 1967); Patrick B. McKenzie, "The Relative Usefulness to Investors of Price-Level Adjusted Financial Statements: An Empirical Study," (Unpublished Ph.D. dissertation, Michigan State University, 1970).

[10]Paul Rosenfield, "Accounting for Inflation—A Field Test," *Journal of Accountancy* (June, 1969), 47 and 50.

[11]Credit is given to Ray Ball, University of Queensland, for pointing out this relationship to us.

[12]Russell J. Peterson, "Interindustry Estimation of General Price-Level Impact on Financial Information," *Accounting Review* XLVIII (January, 1973), 34–43. Also see Simmons and Gray, *op. cit.* Graph 1 on page 761 indicates a close relationship between unadjusted and adjusted net income for years one to 11 in their simulation.

Maintenance of Capital

The existence of inflation accompanied by the use of historic cost accounting results in the reporting of a nominal income which may exceed real or economic income. If dividends are declared on the basis of nominal income, the problem of the maintenance of real capital arises. It is said that PLAAS permit investors and managers to determine if dividend policy has resulted in the distribution of economic (real) capital.[13] This seems to be the stewardship problem case in real terms. An operational definition for such stewardship might be the ability of the firm to replace assets on a timely basis without the infusion of new equity (including debt). No one has demonstrated that the use of a general or comprehensive price index permits such a determination; intuitively, it seems impossible that it could, except by coincidence. A better proxy would seem to be a specific price index; even better, some measure of replacement cost.

Some idea of the possible divergence between general price-level change and real prices is shown in Table 1 where we compare (1) some actual prices of electric generating plant, (2) some estimates of such plant costs derived by others, and (3) the series of Gross National Product Implicit Price Deflator [GNPI]. The assets involved are those belonging to a more-or-less mature industry with a well-defined, easily measured output. We tried to develop a similar series for the less mature computer hardware industry where technological change is more rapid. Unfortunately, output is more difficult to measure since the generational changes influence several variables. Still, those knowledgeable allege that in comparing fourth generation to third generation computers, we now buy "twice the output for half the price," inflation notwithstanding.[14]

A different measure of real capital maintenance is required for the stockholder in a publicly traded firm. If the present stockholders are not the same constituents as the original stockholders, restating originally contributed capital is not meaningful for their measurement of capital maintenance. Furthermore, their measure of wealth can be directly obtained by observing market price quotations for their investments. Also, it seems highly unlikely that they need PLAAS to apprise them of the existence or extent of inflation.

Hedging Against Inflation

Management's actions as hedges against inflation could consist of any or all of the following.

> Early construction of a more capital-intensive plant in anticipation of increased labor costs.
> The purchase and holding of inventory in anticipation of increased acquisition costs.

[13]Staff of the Accounting Research Division, American Institute of Certified Public Accountants, *Reporting the Financial Effects of Price-Level Changes* (New York: American Institute of Certified Public Accountants, 1964), 15; Henry W. Sweeney, *Stabilized Accounting* (New York: Harper and Brothers, 1936), 184–185; Perry Mason, *Price-Level Changes and Financial Statements, Basic Concepts and Methods* (Evanston, Ill.: American Accounting Association, 1956), 13.

[14]As an indication of the effects of technological change on prices, University Computing Company wrote down its portfolio of technically obsolete, second and third generation computers held for lease by $26,000,000 to a net realizable value of $49,360,000 during 1972. *Wall Street Journal* (March 9, 1973) and 10-K Annual Report.

TABLE 1
Average Equipment Cost Per Kilowatt of New Utility Plant in the U.S.A. and a Price
Index for Conventional Steam Turbine Generators Compared with GNP Price Deflator

Year	Average Cost per Kilowatt Equipment Only[a]	Price Index[b]	GNP[c]
1970	$123.95	82.6	135.23
1965	102.73	82.6	110.86
1960	124.47	100.0	103.29
1955	135.45	82.5	90.86

[a]Source: *Steam-Electric Plant Construction Cost and Annual Production Expenses*, Various Supplements Federal Power Commission (Washington, D.C.: U.S. Government Printing Office, various years).

[b]A. J. Surrey, *World Market for Electric Power Equipment* (University of Sussex, England, 1971).

[c]*Economic Report of the President* (Washington, D.C.: U.S. Government Printing Office, 1973).

NOTE: Data for the full 20 years, 1951–70, available from the authors on request.

Levying charges on receivables to cover the loss in purchasing power from holding fixed sum claims.

Financing with debt rather than equity to take advantage of possible gains in purchasing power from owing a fixed sum of dollars.

How would the results of these actions be reflected in PLAAS? The first two involve nonmonetary assets. Depreciation expense and cost of goods sold would be restated upward for cumulative inflation since acquisition of the plant and inventory. Any economic advantage from early action is offset in the restated earnings report. As with financial statements based on historical costs, changes in the specific prices of nonmonetary assets are ignored in PLAAS. Since the acquisitions were made in anticipation of changes in the specific prices of these factor inputs (construction, labor and inventories), a statement reader is not provided with sufficient information to evaluate management's actions. PLAAS, though, compound the error by restating historical cost with an imperfect average, economy-wide, rate of inflation.

The last two examples involve monetary assets. One might expect PLAAS to fare better here since the effects of changes in the general purchasing power of the dollar on these claims are considered. Such need not be the case, however. Consider, for example, the upward restatement of interest revenue and expense for the full rate of inflation experienced during the period. Empirical studies have shown that a close relationship exists between interest rates and anticipated rates of inflation.[15] The underlying proposition holds that the nominal interest rate is equal to the real rate plus the anticipated rate of inflation. To the extent these interest rates reflect anticipated inflation, interest revenue and expense get an additional loading when restated for the portion of the change attributable to expected changes in the general price level.

[15]For a summary of these studies, see Richard Roll, "Interest Rates on Monetary Assets and Commodity Price Index Changes," *Journal of Finance*, XXVII (May, 1972), 251–277.

Consider also the strategy of financing with debt to take advantage of purchasing power or monetary gains and notice that this implies that borrowers are more clever than lenders. The reporting of a monetary gain for any rate of experienced inflation may be somewhat misleading because at least a portion of the reported gain is something purchased, like "Purchased Interest" when a bond is acquired between interest dates. Reporting the net monetary gain or loss and ignoring the effects of expected and unexpected inflation camouflages the firm's success or failure in anticipating inflation in its financing decisions.

Since it seems arrogant to assume borrowers are smarter than lenders, the accounting variable of interest should be the real gain or loss arising from the difference between actual and anticipated inflation. Unfortunately, this is a statistic that the PLAAS methodology does not and cannot provide.

HOW RELIABLE ARE THE GENERAL PRICE INDICES?

Either the Gross National Product Implicit Price Deflator (GNPI) or the Consumer Price Index (CPI) is recommended for use in preparing PLAAS. The former includes the latter plus several additional indices. Here we examine the alleged deficiencies in index construction. The purpose is to create uncertainty about the wisdom of employing what may be an unsuitable tool in an attempt to make accounting reports more meaningful.

The desirable approach would be to estimate the net effect on price indices of the deficiencies discussed and thereby the relative error in PLAAS, but available data are inadequate for making such comprehensive estimates. We examine several deficiencies and leave to others this more ambitious task. We focus on the following: (1) posted versus transaction prices, (2) market basket coverage, (3) fixed weights, and (4) quality changes.

Posted vs. Transaction Prices

For several items in the indices, it is standard procedure to collect quoted prices from sellers rather than actual transaction prices. In the CPI, for example, the physician's fees component is based on the usual fee for an office visit to a general practitioner or internist of a regular patient. The babysitting services component is based on the usual hourly rate with no allowance for actual fees charged during different days of the week, time of the day, or number of children.[16] The index for new one-family houses has been based on "normal" or quoted costs of material and labor inputs rather than the selling price of the house.[17] One might expect little difference between seller's posted prices and the prices of actual transactions, and perhaps this is the case for many items; but the results reported by Stigler and Kendahl tend to be unnerving.[18] The dustjacket of their book states that the conclusions will be required reading for

---

[16]U.S. Bureau of Labor Statistics, *The Consumer Price Index—Specification Manual* (Washington: Government Printing Office, as of March, 1972), Item 51-830-0.

[17]John C. Musgrave, "The Measurement of Price Changes in Construction," *Journal of the American Statistical Association,* 64 (September, 1969), 771–786.

[18]George J. Stigler and James K. Kendahl, *The Behavior of Industrial Prices,* National Bureau of Economic Research, No. 90, General Series, 1970.

economists, industrialists, and all connected with manufacturing in every kind of economy. We would specifically include accountants who will be well repaid for their efforts.

Market Basket Coverage

New products are continuously appearing as substitutes for those included in the market basket: for example: contact lenses for spectacles, color for black and white portable television sets, Toyota for other foreign and domestic lines of automobiles, and women's pants suits for dresses. At the present time, none of these substitutes is included in the coverage.

The issue is whether to maintain a *constant* market basket so that price changes can be more easily measured over time or to use a *current* market basket reflecting goods and services being purchased. The constant market basket suffers from soon being outdated and thus not reflecting current consumption. The current market basket, on the other hand, must cope with the problem of filtering price differentials between substitute goods attributable to quality differences and similar factors. In preparing the CPI, the approach of the BLS is between the two. Major groupings are retained (women's apparel, home furnishings), but individual items are updated roughly every two to three years. Probably the BLS waits too long. For example, until 1966, only white, all-cotton men's shirts were priced. Blends of synthetic fibers were added in that year. It was not until 1971 that long-pointed collars and colored stripes were added. As the Stigler committee concluded in its comprehensive study of federal price statistics: "No instance of the premature inclusion of an unsuccessful product is known to us."[19]

Fixed Weights

Aggregating individual price changes into an index requires a set of relative weights. Most presently compiled indices use what are termed Laspeyres' weights. These weights are based on expenditures for each of the items in the market basket as determined at the beginning of some period. The weights thereafter are not changed for extended periods of time. The present weights for the CPI are based on Consumer Expenditure Surveys conducted in the early 1960's. The "updating" problem, confronted in selecting items for pricing, is even more acute here since the weights remain constant for a longer period of time than does the market basket.

There are at least three factors that can cause those weights to be outdated. First, substitution may occur between major categories. Studies in Miami, Florida and Portland, Oregon indicate that consumer spending on food in these cities has decreased 15% since the early 1960's while spending on recreation has more than doubled. Yet the weights remained unchanged during this ten year period.

A second problem involved substitution among items in the market basket. For example, data for 1968 indicate a 3.3% increase in the consumption of pork

[19]Price Statistics Review Committee, *The Price Statistics of the Federal Government,* National Bureau of Economic Research, No. 73, General Series, 1961, p. 38.

in the U.S. and a 1.3% decrease in the consumption of poultry as the price of pork and poultry increased .02% and 3.1% respectively. During 1969 there was apparently substitution in the opposite direction. The consumption of pork decreased 2% and of poultry increased 4.5% as the price of pork and poultry increased 8.8% and 5.7%.

A third weighting problem involves what is often termed "trading down." This may take the form of buying a lower quality item than the one previously purchased as prices increase or buying a smaller amount of the same item. If this purchasing pattern differs from the one when the weights were derived, the index will not reflect this type of substitution. One study attempted to measure the effect of moving to a more economical market basket. Examining the cost of food for a hospital, Balintfy, Neter, and Wasserman[20] constructed two price indices. One index was of the fixed weight variety, using the percentage expenditures on various items during the initial month of their investigation as weights. Their second index, utilizing shifting weights, was based on the most economical composition which satisfied nutrient and other constraints (such as degree of repetition) imposed by the hospital. Not allowing for substitution, they observed an 8% rate of inflation. Including the effects of substitution to the more economical basket led to less than a 4% rate or an increase of less than half.

Quality Changes

Quality changes do occur and they must be dealt with in spite of their intractability. Quality changes falling within preset ranges specified by the BLS are ignored. The implication here is that attributes affecting quality have been satisfactorily identified and the ranges set sufficiently tight so that quality differences are assumed to be minimal.

When "notable" changes occur in a product (such as when new models of automobiles or refrigerators are introduced), an attempt is made to place a value on the change. Such valuation is based on cost data supplied by the manufacturer. There are at least three shortcomings of this approach. First, it is the demand price that is desired and not the manufacturer's cost data. If new quality items are not demanded, they do not affect consumption and should not therefore affect the price index. Second, problems arise in determining the attributes of a quality change to be costed. Consider, for example, the introduction of Teflon coated frying pans. Is the cost of the coating process the only relevant variable? Perhaps consideration should be given to the total cost of ownership, including cleaning costs, expected useful life, and nutritional content of foods prepared with the new cookware. Third, there does not appear to be any procedure for evaluating the cost data offered. As Triplett has noted:

> . . . there is no systematic procedure for evaluating the cost data. If conflicting information is at hand, there will probably be some editing of the cost figures before they are used . . .; otherwise, they are accepted at full value.[21]

---

[20]Joseph L. Balintfy, John Neter, and William Wasserman, "An Experimental Comparison Between Fixed Weight and Linear Programming Food Price Indexes," *Journal of the American Statistical Association*, 65 (March, 1970), 49–60.

Because of the confidential nature of manufacturer's cost data, empirical studies of the effect of these quality adjustments on price indices have not been made. One example of the use of manufacturers' cost data is in the case of automobiles. Only a slight increase in the new automobiles component of the CPI was reported over the entire decade of the 60's because most of the actual price change was attributed to quality improvements.

Summarizing the present system of handling quality changes, the Stigler committee studying government price indices writes:

> If a poll were taken of professional economists and statisticians, in all probability they would designate (and by a wide majority) the failure of the price indexes to take full account of quality changes as the most important defect in these indexes.[22]

Productivity Changes

A related aspect of the quality change problem is the treatment of productivity changes. For example, the price per ton of tinplate for beer cans rose from $208 to $248 between 1957 and 1966. However, because the number of cans produced from a ton of tinplate increased even more, the cost per 1000 beer cans decreased from $13 in 1957 to $10.66 in 1966.[23] In using quoted fees for physician services in the CPI, increases in their productivity are ignored. Studies have indicated that physicians have experienced a 6% annual increase in productivity over the period 1932 to 1964.[24] In addition, the cure or "product" of physicians' services has steadily improved over time due to better detection methods, more effective medicines, and greater specialization. The failure to take these productivity increases and related quality improvements into account perhaps partially accounts for the significant difference in the rate of increase in medical costs from 1946 to 1965 (which was 118%) and the overall CPI (60%). Another example of the neglect of productivity increases is in the pricing of construction. The index for new one-family houses, using quoted input costs, assumes a particular and constant mix of the contribution of each factor in weighting the price change. These weights, as discussed earlier, do not change often. Thus, an increase in the productivity of labor arising from new equipment or tools is not reflected in the index until the weights are updated.

SUMMATION

One of the writers confesses he was formerly an advocate of general price-level adjusted financial statements. In retrospect, the severity of the perceived effects of inflation on the stable monetary unit assumption overshadowed recognition of the need to adequately evaluate PLAAS as a solution to the problem. There

[21]Jack E. Triplett, "Quality Bias in Price Indexes and New Methods of Measurement," in *Price Indexes and Quality Change*, Zvi Griliches (ed.), (Cambridge, Mass.: Harvard University Press, 1971), p. 198.

[22]Price Statistics Review Committee, *op. cit.*, p. 35.

[23]Stigler and Kendahl, *op. cit.*, p. 32.

[24]Yoram Barzel, "Productivity and the Price of Medical Services," *Journal of Political Economy*, 77 (November–December, 1969), 1014–1027.

is a tendency to be seduced into the security of using historical costs and federal government prepared price indices for a problem which is far more pervasive. Firms take action in attempts to cope with changes in the general purchasing power of the dollar. As illustrated, in some cases, PLAAS camouflage any economic advantage gained from such actions. Also, a change in the general price level is only one variable to be considered by a firm in making decisions and evaluating performance. Probably more important is the change in prices of individual resources acquired and used. Finally, substantial uncertainty regarding the accuracy and reliability of the price indices seems warranted. The usual response that "all firms use the same indices and any misstatement across firms will be equal" must be discarded. Not only may the problem of inflation in relation to accounting reports be overemphasized, varying degrees of index accuracy through time do create differences across firms depending on the age and structure of assets and equities.

III-C / CURRENT COST VALUATIONS

The State of Current Value Accounting

EDGAR O. EDWARDS

The demonstrated and likely volatility of prices during this decade suggests a review of current value accounting is in order—where it stands today and what its future might be. The literature indicates a substantial acceptance of current value accounting in accounting theory, but an impressive lack of implementation in accounting practice. The promotion of practical application obviously needs executive direction; why else would a quality product remain on the shelf. Nevertheless, while current value accounting seems to have found a growing number of adherents to its principles, there are yet some major differences, many rough edges, and a few blind alleys exposed in the theoretical literature. I intend first to indicate the currency of the subject, then to bring out some of the conceptual issues involved in current value accounting, next, to discuss some of the valuation issues, and finally to identify some of the potential analytical uses of current value data.

THE CURRENCY OF THE MATTER

Economists are agreed that inflation is with us, that it lies ahead, and that it is international in character. To cite some figures (U. S. Department of Labor, 1974) which are undoubtedly familiar to everyone, the Consumer Price Index rose by 6.2% between 1972 and 1973 and by 10.7% between May 1973 and May 1974. The commodity element of that index, leaving services aside, rose by 7.4% and 12.0% respectively during those two periods. During the same two periods, on the other hand, the average spendable weekly earnings of those employed in manufacturing having three dependents rose by only 5.4% and 5.7% respectively, suggesting some latent pressure for further price increases as wage earners seek to recoup their losses. Additional inflationary pressures can be inferred from the comparable increases in the Wholesale Price Index of 13.8% between 1972 and 1973 and 16.4% from May 1973 to May 1974, increases which will almost certainly be soon reflected in the commodity portion of the Consumer Price Index.

What has been less widely discussed, both in the media and the professional literature, is the outlook for *differential* price changes, for changes in *relative*

This paper is a revision of one presented at the American Accounting Association Meeting in New Orleans, August 20, 1974. The views expressed are those of the author and are not necessarily shared by the Ford Foundation or the government of Kenya.

Edgar O. Edwards, "The State of Current Value Accounting," *The Accounting Review*, April 1975, pp. 235–245. Reprinted with the permission of *The Accounting Review*.

prices. I submit that over the next five years the principal economic and accounting challenge will come from substantial and pervasive shifts in relative prices. For example, between 1972 and 1973, while the Wholesale Price Index was rising by 13.8%, the farm products and processed foods and feeds portion of it rose by 30.0% and the industrial commodities portion by only 7.7%, a difference in rate of increase (which is a measure of dispersion) of 22.3 percentage points. The largest prior difference since 1950 occurred in 1953, and that difference was only 7.3 percentage points—against agriculture. Between May 1973 and May 1974, on the other hand, the farm portion of the Wholesale Price Index rose by only 7.7% while the industrial commodities portion rose by 20.1%.

But the dispersion within the Wholesale Price Index would of course be much larger than the figures for these major groups could suggest. Consider a few components of that index for the May 1973 to May 1974 period: refined petroleum products, up 79.5%; iron and steel, up 51.1%; coke, up 44.7%; coal, up 43.7%; all metals, up 28.1%; rubber and plastic products, up 19.9%; heating equipment, up 8.2%; drugs and pharmaceuticals, up 4.9%; *but* wool products, down 5.0%; eggs, down 8.1%; livestock, down 15.7%; live poultry, down 18.5%; and manufactured animal feeds, down 26.5%. Between the highest and the lowest of those I have cited, the difference in rate of price increase is 106 percentage points. Moreover this spread is still between *groups* of commodities and must underestimate the dispersion among individual commodity price movements. Finally, these data apply only to the United States; the dispersion of price changes internationally would be substantially greater.

One can see the economic pressures mounting. The heating equipment manufacturer, caught in a depressed housing market and a 51.1% rise in iron and steel prices, has only been able to increase his prices by 8.2%; the drug manufacturer who may be paying 79.5% more for his refined petroleum inputs is charging only 4.9% more for his product; and the steel maker who is getting 51.1% more this year than last must nevertheless pay 45% more for his coal and coke. There lies ahead of us a trying period of substantial economic adjustment as these shifting relative prices open up new and possibly international opportunities for some firms while they squeeze others out of international markets and possibly into bankruptcy. The question is whether or not accounting data should record these events as they occur and thereby flag the coming attractions, or only post the closing notices after the audience has gone.

CONCEPTUAL ISSUES

It is tempting in returning to a subject after a long absence, as I am doing, to take up again what seemed to be the most pressing issues in that earlier era (for those earlier views see Edwards, 1954 and 1961 and Edwards and Bell, 1961). But some—perhaps the most fundamental of those issues—while important to the understanding of current value accounting have retreated from the arena of active controversy, and a few seem to me to be largely of, if I may use the word, historical interest to accounting theoreticians. Other matters now take precedence over them in the theoretical literature.

The first of these issues is the argument that it is sufficient (as well as necessary) to record accounting costs in historical terms. In the midst of rapidly changing prices and values, it gives most of us little comfort to know that the historic cost of every asset now held by business firms throughout the world has not changed since its acquisition. The dictum, "Move ahead but keep your feet in one place," raises serious problems of equilibrium if the head gets too far to the fore. We all know what happens to accounting operating profits during periods of rising prices; they tend to be exaggerated or overstated because the costs charged against current sales are historic and usually lower than current costs. Moreover, the difference between the current and historic cost of inputs will normally be larger the more rapidly prices are rising for two reasons—first, given the time lag between purchase and sale of inputs, prices will rise more; second, inflationary circumstances may lengthen the time lag itself as larger inventories are carried as a buffer against delayed deliveries, the risk of running out, and as a means of making gains in anticipation of higher prices.

Thus, the heating equipment manufacturer whose selling prices have risen by 8.2% while one of his important inputs, iron and steel, has risen by 51.1% may yet show an operating profit by historic cost standards. Yet if prices level off and he can no longer cover current operating losses with holding gains, his competitive inefficiency or lack of opportunity may be revealed. One can argue, of course, that the astute manager or observer will not be misled by overstated operating profits, though certainly the observer and very probably the manager cannot make firm judgments about current costs in a complex firm unless they are actually *accounted for*. In any event, the argument does not justify—or explain—the overstatement. Even the use of the term "overstatement" suggests a standard other than historic cost, for profits are *not* overstated by that standard. The standard of comparison is current value accounting.

What seems to have been widely accepted is not, however, the whole set of current value concepts, but rather that one, a central one, which suggests that accounting operating profit should be split into two parts—current operating profit, determined by deducting the current cost of related inputs from sales, and holding gains realized through use, defined as the difference between the current and historic cost of the sale-related inputs. Note that no historic cost data are lost in this disclosure; new information has been provided.

The second issue about which controversy seems to me to have diminished is whether or not adjustments for the price level alone without accounting for individual price changes can do much for either the manager or the external analyst. All this adjustment can do is restate historic costs in terms of current or some base year's purchasing power. The real holding gains (or losses) which are realized when the price of a sale-related input has risen by more (or less) than the price level are still reported as an indistinguishable element of real accounting profit. The task of sorting out current operating profit and holding gains remains and can only be done by accounting for current values—how the prices of sale-related inputs have changed since acquisition—and then asking how much of these gains is real. Moreover, the operating profits of different firms or even of the same firm in different periods cannot be meaningfully compared to reveal genuine differences and trends unless this division, which only current value accounting makes possible, is first attended to. This principle, too, has won its share of adherents.

But these adjustments relate only to the income statement and indeed only to its operating profit section as customarily displayed. The position statement remains in historic cost terms, and improvements in position which result from price changes on unused assets and liabilities are not recorded either in the position or income statement. The issue of reporting current values in the position statement and related realizable gains or cost savings in the income statement seems still to be an issue commanding discussion (Davidson, 1966; Bell, 1971; Enthoven, 1973, Chapter 13).

Current value accounting rests on the principle that relevant, objective current events of the period should be reported on both statements. Current events are not only those related to the acquisition and disposition of assets and liabilities; they also relate to assets and liabilities carried *through* the period. In other words, the position of a firm is incompletely described if the only changes recorded are those marked by an exchange of assets and/or liabilities—the realization principle—while changes in value not marked by an exchange go unnoted. Of course it is a current event when a gain is realized through the disposition of an asset in the current period; but so too was the accrual of that gain a current event of the periods during which accrual took place. The event of the current period in this example is *not* the *gain*, but its *realization*; the portion of the gain which accrued in prior periods is a current event of *those* periods.

We are touching, of course, on the definition of income. But must we settle on one? There is no reason in my view why an income statement should not reveal both the accrual of income and its realization. Indeed, both are events of the current period and should be reported. It is only that the events are different and must be distinguished. The important issue in this instance is disclosure; labeling is a secondary matter.

The fourth conceptual issue to which I would draw attention concerns the role of subjective values in the accounting process. In some respects, this is also a valuation option. Since, however, I see a role for both subjective and objective values, their conceptual relationship strikes me as more important than the possible competition between them as a basis for accounting measurement. Subjective values depend entirely on future, or *ex ante*, events—expected quasi-rents, interest rates, asset and liability values, and time horizons—and are therefore basic to decision making. The essence of decision making is the choice among alternative progressions of future events contained within the decision-maker's set of expectations. That choice being made, never for all time, the chain of expected events associated with it represents the standard which will be tested as actual events unfold. That comparison of actual against expected events is essential to the evaluation of business decisions and of the effectiveness of the decision-making process itself.

Subjective values, depending as they do upon expectations about future events, cannot themselves be objectively measured. But those expectations from which they derive can be stated in objectively measurable and dated *dimensions* so that their accuracy can be tested against actual events as they transpire. It is the task of effective management to see that expected events are recorded in dated, objective dimensions; it is the task of accounting to record actual objective events as they occur. It follows that present values have no role to play in the measurement of actual events, except as they affect decisions and hence demand and supply in the marketplace and the prices established there.

The last conceptual issue I would mention is taxation—which elements of income should be subjected to income tax? First, it is important to draw a distinction between tax *payment* and contingent tax *liability*, along much the same lines as the distinction noted earlier between the *accrual* and *realization* of income. If a firm reports the accrual of income, it should also report the contingent tax liability on that income; otherwise its position statement will exaggerate the welfare of the firm. Second, if capital gains are to be taxed at different rates from other income—and I am not convinced that such a distinction is justified—those holding gains realized through use and product sale should be treated in precisely the same way as those realized through direct sale. Finally, taxes on income should be levied against real, not money, income, if equity considerations prevail over the anti-cyclical effects of taxing money income, as it seems to me they should. The problem here is one of relative equity; it is hard to justify taxing business firms on real income, if other entities, such as families and individuals, continue to be taxed on money income

ISSUES OF VALUATION

Let me turn now to valuation issues on which even more discussion seems to be focused today than on the conceptual issues mentioned above. To a degree, these, too, are conceptual in nature—I do not intend to discuss precise methods of measurement—but at a different level. Here we do not ask whether current values should be reported but rather which variation of current value should be employed? The issue, however, is not whether one is right and another wrong because the options commonly discussed all have roles to play either in the making of decisions or in their evaluation. Perhaps one day we will be able to account for several concepts simultaneously, but the question today is, If one concept of current value is to be most widely used, which should it be? The options are present or subjective value (already discussed), opportunity cost, and variations of replacement cost.

Opportunity cost can be either subjective or objective in nature. The opportunity cost of an asset is the value it would have in its best alternative use. But that alternative use could be a different pattern of employment of the asset *within* the firm. The value of the asset in that alternative pattern of use can be determined only be resorting to the present value of the quasi-rents expected to be earned in that use, a value which is just as subjective in nature as the present value of the asset in the pattern to which it is committed. If a present value is to be used at all for accounting purposes in these circumstances, it surely should be the highest.

If the alternative considered is to *dispose* of the asset on the open market, opportunity cost can for the most part be objectively measured as a potential current event. It is, therefore, in an accounting sense, a legitimate method of current cost valuation; it is, if I read them correctly, the method favored by both Chambers (1966) and Sterling (1970); it is an exit value, as opposed to an entry value, approach. The issue then is one of entry or exit values in determining current values. Phil Bell and I discussed this matter at some length in our book (1961) and concluded there that entry values were preferable as a normal method of valuation. We did so only after much soul searching and the detailed construction of the concept of realizable profit based on opportunity cost. Our arguments then against the strict application of exit values were essentially as follows:

1. Their use leads to anomalous revaluations on acquisition because of transport costs, installation and removal charges, and imperfect access to markets; immediately upon the purchase, delivery and installation

of a new machine or truck its net realizable value is normally substantially less than acquisition cost.

2. Their use implies a short run approach to business operations, posing, as they do, disposition and liquidation values for the position statement; a positive realizable profit only indicates that it is worth staying in business in the short run, not that it is worth replacing assets and inputs and staying in business over the longer term or as long as current price relationships continue.

3. Their use leads to the anticipation of operating profit before sale by valuing finished goods, and possibly nearly finished goods, in excess of the current costs incurred in their production.

I now think that this argument can be sharpened by drawing a clear distinction between exit prices derived from markets in which the firm is usually a buyer and those derived from markets in which the firm is usually a seller. A firm that values its assets at exit prices derived from markets in which the firm is normally a buyer reports *unusual* values—those which would obtain in a liquidation situation, at least so far as the assets being so valued are concerned. To employ such values when liquidation is not contemplated is surely misleading. Yet Argument (1)—incurring immediate losses upon acquisition—clearly assumes valuation by exit values in buyer markets for firms having no liquidation intentions. Indeed, Argument (2) is also premised on the assumption that most of the firm's assets would be valued as though they might be disposed of in unusual markets for the firm, though some, particularly finished products, might be valued as though sold through normal channels. Argument (3), on the other hand, clearly assumes exit prices in seller markets and therefore must be considered on different grounds.

I am not convinced of the merit of adopting, as a normal basis for asset valuation in the going concern, exit prices in buyer markets. These are *unusual* values suitable for *unusual* situations.[1] I would not object in principle to keeping track of such exit prices at all times and, as Solomons (1966) has suggested, substituting them for entry values when they are the lesser of the two *and* the firm has taken a definite decision not to replace the asset or even the functions it performs.[2] Indeed, such substitution is necessary if the recent write-downs of computer-leasing and calculator firms are to be justified in advance of actual disposal and if the real position of firms caught holding outmoded style goods is to be reflected in their accounts.

The point at issue, of course, is not *whether* to value by current entry or exit prices, but *when* to shift from entry to exit values. The extremes are (1) immediately upon acquisition of any asset or liability and (2) when accounts

[1]It should be noted that exit prices in buyer markets are important to decision making at the micro level, but being *unusual*, such values cannot be aggregated into anything meaningful for a nation as a whole, either as a component of national wealth or as a basis for valuing gross national product. Such values do not represent the normal flow of resources into product, but rather the unusual disposition of resources, a concept which is both undefined and unenlightening in aggregate form.

[2]Note, however, that Solomons would employ present value if that is less than replacement cost but greater than net realizable value, a recommendation I would oppose for reasons given earlier. Parker and Harcourt (1969, p. 18), on the other hand, adopt the Solomons view.

receivable are converted to cash, or when all services have been performed, whichever is later (Davidson, 1966). The realization principle normally rests on the sale event to signal the displacement of entry values by exit values. The valuation of all finished goods at exit values, a principle against which Argument (3) is directed, identifies an earlier stage—one which is close to sale for the manufacturing concern but at the point of acquisition of stocks in trade for the trading firm.

If the principle was adopted that all assets and liabilities of the going concern should be valued at current entry prices except for those that the firm normally sells, Arguments (1) and (2) above would be disposed of. Such a "usual market" criterion comes close to a rule of "replacement cost or net realizable value, whichever is higher," but it is not—as the example of a firm which is temporarily selling at a loss discloses.

We are left with Argument (3) about which I feel much less strongly, though pragmatic considerations may yet leave it some persuasiveness. There is no strong argument in principle against valuing assets which the firm normally sells at some version of selling prices. The question is only whether we seek to account for cost savings or unrealized gains. The problem is encountered in estimating selling prices. If these are determined by appraisal, given the location and accessibility of the goods in question, we assume again unusual disposal. If, on the other hand, prices are estimated by deducting still-to-be-incurred selling and delivery costs from expected selling prices (discounting both appropriately), we encounter subjective elements. These, I emphasize again, rightly belong in the list of expected events to be tested, and should not serve as the basis for valuing actual events, a position in accord with the American Accounting Association's Committee on Concepts and Standards—Inventory Measurement (1964, p. 708).

The issue of which entry values to use also merits discussion, particularly for long-lived assets. For most short-lived assets, replacement cost can be determined, and that therefore reflects the current entry value of the economy's resources being employed in the firm, which is, I think, what we want to approximate as closely as possible. For many longer-lived assets the cost of identical replacement can also be ascertained in regular markets. The problem arises when identical assets are no longer produced—and technological changes ensure that this will often be the case. I confess to being less than happy with the discussion Phil Bell and I offered on this matter (1961, Chapter 3) and also with those I have read since. The options, when the cost of identical replacement is not market determined, appear to be opportunity cost (an exit value), the cost of optimal replacement, or the cost of obvious replacement.

The argument for opportunity cost is that the asset is *not* going to be identically replaced, and that therefore it should be written down to its net realizable value and further depreciation should be determined on that basis. But if this is done, it is quite possible, as noted earlier, that subsequent reported operating profits of the firm will suggest that its outmoded assets are just as efficient as the new assets which will probably replace it. Moreover, the firm *does* intend to replace the *functions* or *services* of the asset in question.

Optimal replacement cost, on the other hand, can be determined only by making a comprehensive, hypothetical investment decision which will not in fact be made until some time in the future. (After all, if our firm decides to replace immediately, our problem evaporates.) Such a decision when it is made, may also involve the rearrangement of many related functions within the firm and the purchase and replacement of complementary equipment and facilities. The use of optimal replacement cost would not reflect all the value of the nation's economic resources now employed by the firm, but rather the value of a very different and hypothetical set. I don't believe its proponents are many.

The cost of obvious replacement probably comes close to what Parker and Harcourt (1969, p. 19) have called "the cost of currently acquiring the *services provided by the asset*," or what the American Accounting Association's Committee on Concepts and Standards—Long-Lived Assets (1964, p. 695) called "the purchase price of assets which provide equivalent service capacity." By obvious replacement I mean the clear means currently available for providing the identical physical services, *regardless of the operating costs which the hypothetical asset might entail.* A refrigerator may be replaced by another of the same cooling capacity and temperature range. Very probably this would not represent optimal replacement. There may also be problems of adjusting for size, temperature control, and asset life. Assuming these can be solved or do not exist, the cost of obvious replacement still has theoretical deficiencies.

A new machine, identical in physical performance, may make an old one obsolete in any of three ways: (1) by raising capital costs and lowering operating costs, (2) by lowering both capital and operating costs, or (3) by lowering capital costs and raising operating costs. By valuing the old machine according to the new one, current cost depreciation will be raised in the first case and reduced in the others. Assuming that operating charges will continue to be charged as actually incurred with the old machine, the operating profits now reported for the old machine as compared with a firm actually using the new one will be lower in the first two cases but higher in the third. In that case the firm employing the old machine has adopted the lower depreciation charges associated with the new machine but retained its own, lower, operating costs. The old machine will appear to be more efficient than the new one. This drawback may not be too serious in a practical sense if my guess is right that few new machines are in fact Type 3, but that is a matter for empirical research, not casual observation. In any event, the drawback is a serious conceptual deficiency.

I have not touched on matters of appraisal, price indices, and averaging formulas as means of approximating cost concepts in practice. Frankly, I regard them as marginal, if necessary, matters which will be satisfactorily resolved once the more important conceptual issues have been settled.

THE ANALYTICAL USES OF CURRENT VALUE ACCOUNTING

If the reluctance to employ current value accounting is rooted in the uncertainty which remains about the issues so far discussed, there is reason for optimism because the degree of uncertainty seems to be diminishing with research and the passage of time. It is also possible, however, that the analytical value of current value accounting data is not considered to be high enough to warrant the cost of producing it. Furthermore, several of the advantages of current value data can be realized only if current value accounting is widely practiced; interfirm comparisons are an obvious example. In any event, a brief review of the analytical potential of current value data seems in order. I suggest its discussion under three heads: the internal evaluation of business decisions, prediction, and the external evaluation of business performance.

I have already noted the essential role of current value data in providing information on actual current events as a means of identifying and analyzing variances from expected events. The accumulation of current value data is not in itself sufficient for this purpose; a statement of expected events is also required. Such statements can be found in budgets and standard costs, but the events identified in them may not always be dated or stated in dimensions which promote subsequent comparison with actual events. Furthermore, they normally relate to events which compose current operating profit, not holding gains. Statements of expected holding gains and losses are also of importance if business decisions are to be fully evaluated because decisions about operating profit and holding gains are related, not independent in nature. I was delighted, therefore, to see the article by Petri and Minch (1974) which provides a framework for the evaluation of decisions on holding gains.

The relationship between operating profit and holding gains is most clearly revealed in the case of inventories. In the absence of price changes, inventory levels are usually determined by purchase lags, delivery patterns, and the acceptable risk of running out. If prices of items in inventory are expected to rise, stockpiling is a natural business response both to make holding gains and to protect against anticipated delivery problems. If prices do not rise, current operating profit will nevertheless be reduced because of the cost of carrying excessive inventories; if they fall, current operating profit may rise, but the increase should be more than offset by holding losses. Without full statements of expected events, the precise causes of changing profit patterns cannot be pinpointed, nor the sources of error identified and the process of decision making improved. Financial decisions require similar analysis and evaluation.

Improving prediction depends upon the definition of better functional relationships between expectations about future events, "what will be," and past experience, "what has been," in which expectations are rooted. Such functions are the essence of econometric models. But if "what has been" is defined in strictly historic cost terms and reported operating profit represents an amalgam of current and differently dated historic costs, trends over time and comparisons among firms are distorted and the establishment of probable functional relationships is made exceedingly difficult.

Those who attempt to evaluate business performance from outside the firm normally do so largely to improve either private or public decisions. Those whose interests are largely private include present and prospective stockholders, creditors, customers, suppliers, and competitors, and the consultants and security analysts on whom they depend for information and advice. The makers of public policy and those who provide the analytical base for policy decisions are normally employed by governmental or multinational agencies. Private decision makers, on the other hand, are charged with representing wider public interests and promoting the general welfare. These two groups evaluate business performance with different purposes in mind. While their evaluations will have much in common, they also differ in important respects.

Those in the private group share an interest in *comparative evaluations*. The position and performance of a single firm as judged by an absolute standard are normally of considerably less importance to them than its position and performance relative to other firms whether in the same industry, in the same nation, or internationally. It is through comparative evaluations that external investors formulate their expectations about future events, choose their portfolios, and decide on new businesses or lines of activity—and by so doing, collectively influence security prices, interest rates, and the allocation of capital among firms, industries, and nations.

These external evaluations of business firms differ from the internal evaluation process discussed earlier in two important respects. In the first place, they do not involve direct comparisons of management expectations with objective accomplishments. Outsiders do not normally have access to management expectations. They seek to judge, therefore, not *internal* managerial efficiency, but rather *relative* managerial efficiency, by comparing performance among firms and over time.

In the second place, outsiders do not have access to managerial accounting data but must rely for their assessments on published financial reports and supplementary data as sources of current events. Making information available to external investors based on current rather than historic costs data is important as a means of improving external private decisions and hence the allocation of a nations's resources among its firms and industries.

Those who make public policy decisions, on the other hand, cannot normally assess business performance exclusively on the basis of reported business profits. In the first place, these may arise not only from the efficient production of quality products (which is normally in the public interest) but also from malpractices, monopolistic advantages, and situations of unusual scarcity. When such conditions come to light through the evaluation of business performance, various forms of regulation, antitrust actions, and excess-profit taxes may be employed to protect the public interest.

In the second place, business profits will not normally reflect those benefits which accrue to society from business operations in the form of unmarketable side effects of principal business activities, such as skills former employees take with them. Similarly, business profits will not naturally reflect certain social costs which society may have to bear as a result of business activity because they do not enter the accounts of the business firm; environmental effects are a widely discussed example. When the divergence between social and private costs becomes large, public policy will usually seek to establish systems of incentives and disincentives which will lead business firms to introduce into their private accounts those social costs and benefits which would otherwise accrue to society but not to the business community. Such incentive systems should induce business firms to modify their behavior in socially desirable directions.

Each firm or industry which is *socially* efficient should be able to cover the full current cost of its operation even though some of those costs may not usually reach the private accounts through existing mechanisms of the market, falling instead on others. To attempt such assessments requires the valuation of excluded social costs once they have been identified and allocated. There are two basic approaches to this problem—to measure social costs by the damages imposed on society by them or to measure such costs by the current value of the resources which would be required to prevent them from occurring. The point is that such social assessments, complex as they are, can be made more effectively if the operating profits, with which the analysis begins, are reported by business firms in current value terms.

I have not mentioned the advantages of current value data based on entry costs for aggregation into national accounts or for decomposition into input-output coefficients. Even leaving aside aggregate considerations, the many advantages of current value accounting seem to me impressive.

The end is in sight. There is only the matter of implementation to consider. Why has the "quality product" remained on the shelf? I have no illuminating answers, but one suggestion. Is an industry-wide experiment with current value accounting a feasible first step? Is there a trade association or an industry which might lend its cooperation? Would it be appropriate for the American Accounting Association to take the lead in initiating such an experiment?

REFERENCES

American Accounting Association, Committee on Concepts and Standards—Inventory Measurement, "A Discussion of Various Approaches to Inventory Measurement," *The Accounting Review* (July 1964).
——, Committee on Concepts and Standards—Long-Lived Assets, "Accounting for Land, Building, and Equipment," *The Accounting Review* (July 1964).
Bell, P.W., "On Current Replacement Costs and Business Income," in R. R. Sterling, ed., *Asset Valuation* (Scholars Book Co., 1971).
Chambers, R. I. *Accounting, Evaluation and Economic Behavior* (Prentice-Hall, 1966).
Davidson, S., "The Realization Concept," in M. Backer, ed., *Modern Accounting Theory* (Prentice-Hall, 1966).
Edwards, E. O., "Depreciation Policy under Changing Price Levels," *The Accounting Review* (April 1954).
——, "Depreciation and the Maintenance of Real Capital," in J. L. Meij, ed., *Depreciation and Replacement Policy* (North-Holland, 1961).
——and Bell, P. W., *The Theory and Measurement of Business Income* (University of California Press, 1961).
Enthoven, A. J. H., *Accountancy and Economic Development Policy* (North-Holland, 1973).
Parker, R. H. and Harcourt, G. C., eds., *Readings in the Concept and Measurement of Income* (Cambridge University Press, 1969).
Petri, E., and Minch, R., "Evaluation of Resource Acquisition Decisions by the Partitioning of Holding Activity," *The Accounting Review* (July 1974).
Solomons, D., "Economic and Accounting Concepts of Cost and Value," in M. Backer, ed., *Modern Accounting Theory* (Prentice-Hall, 1966).
Sterling, R. R., *Theory of the Measurement of Enterprise Income* (University Press of Kansas, 1970).
United States Department of Labor, *Monthly Labor Review* (July 1974).

On the Correspondence Between Replacement Cost Income and Economic Income

LAWRENCE REVSINE

Research is needed to establish the degree of correspondence between information generated by various measurement processes and the data needs of the users towards whom the resultant information is directed. Hopefully, knowledge about such linkages between detailed user decision processes and information required to satisfy the decision models will facilitate realization of a primary function of accounting—the provision of relevant information to decision-makers.

The accounting literature contains little decision-oriented research concerning the relevance of replacement cost income to a given, defined use. Nevertheless, it is possible to reconstruct from the literature a justification for the dissemination of replacement cost reports to investors.[1] This justification is based on the assumption that replacement cost income is a surrogate for economic income.[2,3] Economic income measurement embodies changes in the service potential of assets. Since the change in the service potential of assets is often regarded as an ideal income measure for investors,[4] the indirect approximation of this ideal by replacement cost income would explain its relevance to investors.

Beaver, Kennelly and Voss maintain that before we empirically test the predictive ability of a concept, the theory supporting such contentions must be developed.[5] However, the notion that replacement cost income represents an indirect measure of the results of economic income (hereafter referred to as the "indirect measurement hypothesis") has never been rigorously examined by its proponents. Therefore, in this paper we will develop an *a priori* model which will be used to assess the theoretical validity of the indirect measurement hypothesis.

The author is indebted to members of his doctoral committee at Northwestern University, particularly Professors John H. Myers (now of Indiana University), Thomas R. Prince, and Alfred Rappaport, for their counsel and guidance in the preparation of the dissertation upon which this study is based. Furthermore, the comments of Professor Nicholas Dopuch of the University of Chicago, and Professors Norton M. Bedford, James Wesley Deskins, James C. McKeown, and Frederick L. Neumann, colleagues at the University of Illinois, were particularly helpful. Financial assistance by the Ford Foundation, which supported the dissertation, is gratefully acknowledged.

Lawrence Revsine, "On the Correspondence Between Replacement Cost Income and Economic Income," *The Accounting Review*, July 1970, pp. 513–523. Reprinted with the permission of *The Accounting Review*.

THE INDIRECT MEASUREMENT HYPOTHESIS

References in the Literature

A brief examination of prior references to the indirect measurement hypothesis in the accounting literature accomplishes two objectives. First, it indicates that some accounting theorists have—at least implicitly—used the supposed relationship between replacement cost income and economic income as a rationale for replacement cost reporting. Second, these passing references should indicate that the basic nature of the assumed relationship between the two concepts remains to be explored.

Illustrative of the support given to the indirect measurement hypothesis in the literature is the statement by Zeff:

> But it can be argued that [Edwards and Bell's] "business profit" is not too bad an approximation of the current increment in the present value of future net receipts [economic income].[6]

Corbin advances a similar view:

> Given a satisfactory degree of competition, the prices of assets in the market place would then be based on estimates of their future income streams made by many independent individuals; market prices would serve as objective, indirect estimates of value. One could go to the stock exchanges to get present value estimates for stocks and bonds, to the commodities markets or dealers' catalogues for inventories and equipment, to the real estate markets for land and buildings, etc. In this manner the values of all assets and liabilities, *except Goodwill*, could be determined indirectly each period, in order to calculate net income as the increase in an enterprise's net [present] value during the period.[7]

Other authors have made similar explicit contentions that replacement cost income represents an indirect measure of economic income.[8] In addition, the indirect measurement hypothesis is implicit in certain other replacement cost income studies.[9]

However, none of these references contain a detailed examination of the conceptual foundation for the indirect measurement hypothesis. Nor is such an examination found in other studies which are highly critical of the indirect measurement hypothesis.[10] Therefore, in the next section we will explore the basic nature of the relationship between replacement cost income and economic income.

Theoretical Foundation

In this section, we will develop a model which provides the heretofore absent theoretical foundation for the indirect measurement hypothesis. We will see that in a perfectly competitive economy, the correspondence between replacement cost income and economic income is precise. Later, we will utilize the developed model to assess the validity of the indirect measurement hypothesis in an imperfect, but more realistic, competitive environment.

Before we develop this foundation for the indirect measurement hypothesis, we should isolate several characteristics of perfectly competitive economies which merit special emphasis. First, perfect competition implies the existence of perfect resource mobility. All firms are assumed able to adjust capital levels instantaneously in response to changed market conditions. Second, as a consequence of this resource mobility and other characteristics of a perfectly competitive economy,[11] the price of every asset at the beginning of the ith period (P_i) is equal to the discounted present value at the beginning of the ith period of the net cash flows expected to be generated by asset operations (V_i); i.e.,

$$(1) \qquad\qquad P_i = V_i$$

Finally, at any moment in time, all firms in a perfectly competitive economy have identical expectations regarding cash flows to be generated by owned assets.[12]

Economic income (as the term is used in this study) is measured as the change, over some period of time, in the value of a firm's assets. The total value of a firm's assets at any point in time can be determined by discounting, at some normal rate of return, the expected net cash flows from asset utilization. The total economic income figure which results from a comparison of beginning and ending period asset values can be fragmented into two components: (1) expected income, and (2) unexpected income.[13] The expected income (I_e) component of total economic income is the product of the normal rate of return (r) and the beginning of the period net present value of assets (V_i). Thus:

$$(2)[14] \qquad\qquad I_e = rV_i$$

The unexpected income component of economic income is equal to the sporadic increase in asset net present value which develops as a result of changes in expectations regarding the level of future net flows from operating assets.

We will now demonstrate that, theoretically, replacement cost income is virtually identical to economic income in a perfectly competitive economy. Most replacement cost income concepts promulgated contain two general components: (1) an operating profit segment, and (2) a price change segment. In the terminology of Edwards and Bell these components are called current operating profit and realizable cost savings, respectively. Current operating profit is generally measured as the difference between revenues for the period and the replacement cost of those assets consumed in generating revenues. If an *economic* depreciation concept is used to measure the expiration of long-lived assets (i.e., a concept which measures the periodic decline in the discounted earning power of an asset[15]) the resulting actual rate of return from operations for a single-asset firm is given by:

$$(3) \qquad\qquad r_a = \frac{C_i}{P_i}$$

In (3), r_a represents the actual operating rate of return, C_i is the current operating profit, and P_i, as before, denotes the market price of assets. Given a perfectly competitive environment, the following relationship should hold in equilibrium:

(4) $$r_a = r$$

Substituting V_i for P_i and r for r_a in equation (3) and rearranging gives:

(5) $$C_i = rV_i$$

A comparison of equations (5) and (2) indicate that:

(6) $$C_i = I_e$$

Thus, in a perfectly competitive economy, the current operating profit component of replacement cost income is equal to the expected income component of economic income.[16]

In similar fashion the second component of replacement cost income—realizable cost savings—is a direct counterpart to the second component of economic income—unexpected income. Realizable cost savings are equal to the change in the market price of assets held during the period. Unexpected income consists of the discounted value of the change in the amount of future flows expected from operating owned assets. In a perfectly competitive economy, such changes in cash flow expectations are directly translated into changes in asset market value [equation (1)]; therefore, the realizable cost savings component of replacement cost income is equal to the unexpected income component of economic income.[17]

Given that each component of replacement cost income is equal to its counterpart component of economic income, *total* replacement cost income must also equal *total* economic income. While our analysis assumed a perfectly competitive environment in which all firms have homogeneous expectations, this correspondence between the two income concepts can also be demonstrated to exist when there is divergence among firms' expectations.[18]

THE INDIRECT MEASUREMENT HYPOTHESIS IN IMPERFECTLY COMPETITIVE ECONOMIES

Removing the conditions of perfect competition introduces imperfect resource mobility into the economy. This restricted mobility, or friction, changes the equalities in (1) and (4) to mere approximations. Then, performing substitutions similar to those in the perfect competition illustration, (5) becomes:

(5') $$C_i \cong rV_i$$

Thus, under conditions of imperfect competition, current operating profit is merely an approximation of expected income.

An approximate correspondence can also be attributed to the cost savings and unexpected income components. Even in imperfectly competitive economies asset prices approximate the average net present value of asset revenue generating potential. Theoretically, changes in asset revenue generating potential precipitate appropriate changes in asset price. Proponents of the indirect measurement hypothesis apparently would contend that just as market price is related to asset net present value, so too the *change* in asset market price is related to the *change* in asset net present value. Therefore, realizable cost savings, measured as the change in the market price of held assets, approximate unexpected income for a period, measured as the change in the net present value of asset revenue generating potential.

The basis for the indirect measurement hypothesis in "realistic" economies should now be evident. There are two distinct correspondences underlying this supposed relationship between total replacement cost income and total economic income: (1) that the current operating profit component of replacement cost income is an indirect measure of the expected income component of economic income, and (2) that the realizable cost savings component of replacement cost income is an indirect measure of the unexpected income component of economic income.

However, there are *a priori* grounds for questioning the validity of the posited relationship between changes in asset prices and changes in service potential in realistic economies. Therefore, below, we will examine the reasonableness of this assumption of positive covariance between asset prices and asset flows. Furthermore, we will explore the impact of this covariance assumption (and its possible invalidity) on the relationship between *total* replacement cost income and *total* economic income.[19]

Market Prices and Cash Flow Potential

The relationship between replacement cost income and economic income rests, in part, on the assumption that changes in asset prices are in direct response to changes in the level of net cash flows expected to be generated by assets.

In an aggregate sense, this relationship between realizable cost savings and unexpected income is probably valid. Barring changes in the discount rate, etc., such a relationship between asset prices and asset cash flows must exist in the long-run for the economy as a whole. However, for any individual firm in the economy there is no *necessary* relationship between movements in asset prices and movements in cash flows. Actually, there are three possibilities regarding asset market price changes and changes in the service potential of assets to a firm. As an asset price changes:

A. Future cash flows resulting from asset operation could change in the same direction as the price change.
B. Future cash flows could remain constant.
C. Future cash flows could change in the opposite direction.

These three possibilities will be referred to as Type A, Type B, and Type C asset price changes respectively.[20]

If replacement cost income and economic income are indirectly related, there ought to be rather close correspondence between movements in each. This suggests that Type A price changes should predominate in order to validate the indirect measurement hypothesis.[21] However, if we can demonstrate that, theoretically, Type B and Type C price changes can be expected to occur with some frequency in realistic situations, and if we can further show that such price changes precipitate divergence between *total* replacement cost income and *total* economic income, then the essence of the indirect measurement hypothesis must be questioned.

This type of condition is illustrated in the following section.

An Illustrative Type C Price Change

Assume that the gamma industry manufactures a particular consumer good called a gamma. The industry is characterized by perfect competition and is initially earning an above normal rate of return at the beginning of 19x0.

Assume that the abnormal return induces capital movement into the gamma industry during 19x0 as new firms attempt to take advantage of inordinately high returns available therein. This movement will initially tend to raise asset prices to all firms in the gamma industry, including the established firms. Asset prices will rise because of the demand for fixed assets by entering firms; this demand is added to the replacement demand for productive equipment on the part of firms already producing gammas in the gamma industry. Unless perfect elasticity of supply in the capital goods industry is assumed, this increase in demand for gamma producing equipment will serve to raise the price of such equipment. However, the output of final goods, gamma, will not immediately increase since it is assumed that a certain lead time is necessary before the new firms entering the industry are able to utilize the new capacity for gamma production. Thus, in this initial stage, no change in the magnitude of established gamma firms' cash flows occurs, but asset prices are bid upward.

After the necessary lead-time passes, however, the gamma industry's new entrants begin production in 19x1. Utilization of this new capacity increases the supply of final output available. With demand constant (and not perfectly elastic), the increase in supply will tend to reduce the price obtained for each gamma unit sold; furthermore, the volume attained by new entrants is assumed to be garnered at the expense of established gamma industry firms. Each established firm, if we posit a constant demand for final output of the industry, will experience both a shrinking market and a decline in per unit gamma selling price. Furthermore, in an increasing cost industry, the increased output will trigger increases in the price of variable inputs used in production. The forces originally set into motion by the disparity in rates of return between the gamma industry and the remainder of the economy will eventually eliminate the disparity by: (1) raising the costs of factors of production, including fixed inputs, (2) lowering the average selling price of output, and (3) fragmenting the market into smaller individual shares.

The net effect of these events on the established firms in the industry will be: (1) a rise in the market price of capital assets used in production, and (2) a fall in expected future cash flows associated with operating the gamma producing equipment. Hence, a Type C price change (opposite movements in asset prices and future flows) is the likely result of this sequence of events. Thus, while it is apparently true that at the aggregate level changes in cash flow expectations translate directly into changes in asset prices, the possible existence of Type B and Type C price changes would indicate that this correspondence need not exist at the micro level. Furthermore, the quantification of this example in the Appendix demonstrates that this Type C price change precipitates opposite movements in *total* replacement cost income and *total* economic income.

It is not difficult to develop other examples of theoretical price movements of Type B or Type C. Since the conditions which give rise to these types of price changes (e.g., demand shifts in other industries, shifts in relative input prices, and technological changes[22]) appear to be representative of reasonable, real-world phenomena, the validity of the indirect measurement hypothesis must be viewed with some skepticism.

Empirical research is needed to determine the extent and frequency of such Type B and Type C price changes. Nevertheless, their possible existence, however infrequent, makes the relationship between replacement cost income and economic income uncertain and makes the indirect measurement hypothesis a potentially dangerous generalization.

SOME CONCLUDING COMMENTS

Summary

This study had as its primary purpose an examination of the relationship between replacement cost income and economic income. Our basic concern centered on the ability of replacement cost income to approximate the results' of economic income and thus provide statement users with information concerning changes in the cash flow potentialities confronting a firm.

Beaver, Kennelly and Voss have suggested that theoretical study must precede empirical analysis of the predictive ability of particular income concepts.[23] Since the presupposition of the indirect measurement hypothesis is that replacement cost income is a predictor of economic income, it seems appropriate to investigate the heretofore absent theoretical foundation for this contention.

In the final section of this paper, as a means of emphasizing the practical importance of the indirect measurement hypothesis, we will illustrate a conceivable inferential error which replacement cost reports might precipitate if Type B and Type C price changes are incorporated.

Consequences of Reliance on an Invalid Indirect Measurement Hypothesis

One rationalization for the dissemination of replacement cost reports to investors relies on the validity of the indirect measurement hypothesis. Investors are not primarily interested in the historical financial data provided to them in published financial statements, this argument goes. No rational investor purchases stock in a company because of its past profit performance; rather, it is the prospect of future profitability which induces investment.[24] Given this investor emphasis on the potentialities confronting the firm, indirect measurement hypothesis proponents have advocated the relevance of a replacement cost report to investors. They contend that since replacement cost income is supposedly an indirect measure of economic income, and since economic income incorporates the very potentialities of concern to investors, it follows that replacement cost reports should provide an indirect means of communicating potentialities to present and prospective investors.

However, a replacement cost report which contains Type B and/or Type C price changes could result in an investor making seriously misleading inferences regarding a company's prospects. For example, *if cash flow potentialities are indeed of paramount importance to the investor, the income concept reported to investors ideally should vary in the same direction and by the same magnitude that discounted cash flow expectations vary.* Thus, reported income should increase whenever the cash flow potential of the firm increases and should decrease whenever the cash flow potential decreases.[25] However, replacement cost income might not achieve this result whenever a Type B or Type C asset price change occurs. For example, in a Type C price change situation, replacement cost income theory necessitates the recognition of a realizable cost saving in response to a rise in asset price. This realizable cost saving will be recognized in the year of the price rise despite the fact that future flows accruing to the firm already owning an asset whose price has risen are expected to fall. Such a firm is clearly in a deteriorated long-run cash flow position relative to its position before the price rise. Yet it must show "income" as a consequence of the price change. Clearly, following the indirect measurement hypothesis, the term "income" should be reserved for those instances in which an augmentation of cash flow potential has occurred. Such is not necessarily the case using the replacement cost income framework, however. An investor relying on total reported replacement cost income for a period could be led to a conclusion in direct *opposition* to the potentialities actually confronting the firm whenever the impact of a Type B or Type C price change is sufficiently large to cause a disparity between reported replacement cost income and the direction of change in cash flow potential.[26]

The possibility that replacement cost reports might convey misleading information regarding cash flow potentialities has serious repercussions. Empirical research is certainly needed to support or refute our *a priori* analysis. If this research does in fact indicate possible serious divergence between replacement cost income and economic income, the conditions under which such divergence is possible must be isolated. Then, in preparing replacement cost reports for a firm subject to these divergence conditions, a caveat to the user regarding such divergences would be necessary.

Since investors and other statement users are concerned with firms' cash flow potentialities, it is imperative that accountants develop some external reporting techniques which will satisfy these needs for anticipatory information. Replacement cost reports might, in certain circumstances, provide this information. It is hoped that this paper, by providing some theoretical background for the indirect measurement hypothesis, has isolated certain relationships deserving of further research attention concerning the predictive ability of replacement cost reports.

APPENDIX

Presented in this Appendix is a quantification of the Type C price change illustration which was developed in the body of the paper. Our objective herein is twofold: 1) to illustrate in detail the effect of Type C price changes on the correspondence between the two income concepts, and 2) to demonstrate the potentially misleading inferences replacement cost reports might precipitate when Type C price changes are incorporated into the income determination process.

Using the basic facts presented in the gamma industry example above, let us assume that the industry in 19x0 is in temporary disequilibrium. Gamma producing equipment, which has a three year life, is expected to generate annual cash inflows of $110; given an economy wide normal rate of return of 5%, the equilibrium value of the asset would be:

YEAR	NET INFLOW	DISCOUNT FACTOR (AT 5%)	PRESENT VALUE
1st	$110	.9524	$104.76
2nd	$110	.9070	99.77
3rd	$110	.8638	95.02
Equilibrium Market Price			$299.55

The actual market price of the asset, given the temporary disequilibrium, ia $250.

Replacement cost income for 19x0 for an original firm in this industry which purchased a new gamma producing asset on January 1, 19x0 is:

ORIGINAL FIRM
REPLACEMENT COST INCOME
FOR THE YEAR ENDED DECEMBER 31, 19x0

Current Operating Profit:
  Net cash inflow $110.00
  Depreciation:
    Value of the asset at 1/1/x0 ....$299.55
    Value at 12/31/x0:
      19x1 flows ($110 × .9524) 104.76
      19x2 flows ($110 × .9070) 99.77
                                                              204.53
    Total Depreciation 95.02

  Total current operating profit 14.98

Cost Savings:
  Realizable Cost Savings 0.00
  Acquisition Income:[27]
    Value to the firm 299.55
    Cost 250.00
                                                                         49.55

  Total replacement cost income ....$ 64.53

Economic income for 19x0 is:

ORIGINAL FIRM
ECONOMIC INCOME
FOR THE YEAR ENDED DECEMBER 31, 19x0

Expected Income:
From operations ($299.55 × 5%) ....$ 14.98
On acquisition 49.55

Total expected income ....$ 64.53
Unexpected Income: 0.00

Total economic income ....$ 64.53

Since the inordinately high economic rents in this industry have persisted, new entrants are attracted during 19x1. Assume that the entering firms cannot begin production until 19x2; however, it becomes apparent that, as a consequence of their entry, net cash flows generated each year by the gamma producing equipment will fall to $95 starting in 19x2. (For simplicity, we assume that this change in expectations is perceived instantaneously on January 1, 19x1.) The equilibrium price per capital unit will become:

YEAR	NET INFLOW	DISCOUNT FACTOR (AT 5%)	PRESENT VALUE
1st	$95	.9524	$ 90.48
2nd	$95	.9070	86.17
3rd	$95	.8638	82.06
Equilibrium market price			$258.71

Let us compute 19x1 replacement cost income for the Original Firm whose statements for 19x0 were presented above.

ORIGINAL FIRM
REPLACEMENT COST INCOME
FOR THE YEAR ENDED DECEMBER 31, 19x1

Current Operating Profit:
Net cash inflow $110.00
Depreciation:
Value of the asset at 12/31/x0 ....$204.53
Value at 12/31/x1
19x2 flows ($95 × .9524) 90.48

Total Depreciation 114.05

Total Current Operating Profit .... (4.05)
Cost Savings:
Realizable Cost Savings ....6.21[28]

Total replacement cost income ....$ 2.16

Economic income for 19x1 would be:

ORIGINAL FIRM
ECONOMIC INCOME
FOR THE YEAR ENDED DECEMBER 31, 19x1

Expected income:
From operations ($204.53 × 5%) ....$ 10.23
Unexpected income:
Decline in 19x2 cash inflows ($15 × .9524) .... (14.29)

Total economic income .... $(4.06)

The two income concepts provide the reader with quite dissimilar measures of the Original Firm's performance during 19x1. The negative economic income figure indicates that the market position of the firm has deteriorated during 19x1, due to the decline in expected future flows. Replacement cost income measurements, on the other hand, result in income being reported for 19x1. Income arises only because the Type C price change is included. Were this item to be omitted from the replacement cost calculation then (except for rounding errors) the resultant income measure would be identical to economic income.

Given the "functional fixation" users may have concerning definitions,[29] and given the overriding importance of cash flow potential in investors' decision models, the tendency might exist to identify income—irrespective of the measurement mode by which it was developed—with changes in cash flow potential. This fixation mechanism could cause investors to consider positive reported replacement cost income to be a reflection of increased profit potential when, in fact, the profit generating potential of the firm has actually diminished.

FOOTNOTES

[1]The term investor as used in this paper refers to parties divorced from management who buy or sell, or contemplate buying or selling, ownership interest in an enterprise. The designation "investor" undoubtedly encompasses many distinct subclassifications. That is, the decision model (and thus perhaps the data needs) of the speculative investor conceivably differs from that of "widowed and orphaned" investors. Although we will not specify a particular type of investor in this paper, whenever the term appears, a need for a relatively long-term time horizon for data will be assumed.

[2]Proponents of this surrogate relationship argument implicitly suggest that historical cost income is not as accurate an approximation of economic income as is replacement cost income. Since this issue has been treated elsewhere in the literature [see Sidney S. Alexander (revised by David Solomons), "Income Measurement in a Dynamic Economy," *Studies in Accounting Theory*, ed. W. T. Baxter and S. Davidson (Richard D. Irwin, Inc., 1962), pp. 174–188, we need not dwell on it here.

The particular replacement cost income concept apparently implicit to these contentions of a surrogate relationship is essentially similar to the entry value concept of Edwards and Bell. [Edgar O. Edwards and Philip W. Bell, *The Theory and Measurement of Business Income*, (The University of California Press, 1961).] The specific economic income concept which this replacement cost concept supposedly approximates is measured as the difference between the beginning and end of the period net present value of future flows expected to be generated by owned assets.

In the remainder of this paper, whenever the term economic income is used, it should be understood to be a probabilistic expected value rather than a deterministic value. Furthermore, for ease of exposition, we will assume in the development which follows that no changes occur in prevailing interest rates; hence, changes in economic income can be attributed solely to underlying changes in the service potential of assets.

[3]An enumeration of the theorists who have posited this surrogate relationship is found in footnotes 6, 7, 8, and 9, *infra*.

[4]See, for example, John B. Canning, *The Economics of Accountancy* (Ronald Press Co., 1929), p. 184 ff.; The Committee on Accounting Concepts and Standards, "Accounting and Reporting Standards for Corporate Financial Statements 1957 Revision," *The Accounting Review*, XXXII (October 1957), p. 539; and Harold Bierman, Jr. and Sidney Davidson, "The Income Concept—Value Increment or Earnings Predictor," *The Accounting Review*, XLIV (April 1969), pp. 240–241.

[5]William H. Beaver, John W. Kennelly, and William M. Voss, "Predictive Ability as a Criterion for the Evaluation of Accounting Data," *The Accounting Review*, XLIII (October 1968), p. 677.

[6]Stephen A. Zeff, "Replacement Cost: Member of the Family, Welcome Guest, or Intruder?" *The Accounting Review*, XXXVII (October 1962), p. 623. However, in a later article [Stephen A. Zeff and W. David Maxwell, "Holding Gains on Fixed Assets—A Demurrer," *The Accounting Review*, XL (January 1965), p. 70], Professors Zeff and Maxwell seem to recant this earlier position.

[7]Donald A. Corbin, "The Revolution in Accounting," *The Accounting Review*, XXXVII (October 1962) p. 630.

[8]See, for example, Henry W. Sweeney, "Income," *The Accounting Review*, VIII (December, 1933), p. 325, and his earlier article, "Capital," *The Accounting Review*, VIII (September, 1933), pp. 189–191; and Joel Dean, "Measurement of Real Economic Earnings of a Machinery Manufacturer," *The Accounting Review*, XXIX (April 1954), p. 257.

[9]See, for example, Edwards and Bell, *Theory and Measurement*, p. 25; Norton M. Bedford, *Income Determination Theory: An Accounting Framework* (Addison-Wesley Publishing Company, Inc., 1965), p. 91; and George J. Staubus, "Current Cash Equivalent for Assets: A Dissent," *The Accounting Review*, XLII (October 1967), pp. 650–661. Professor Staubus explicitly refers to the asset valuation case. His comments extend to the income determination case by implication only.

[10]Robert L. Dickens and John O. Blackburn, "Holding Gains on Fixed Assets: An Element of Business Income?" *The Accounting Review*, XXXIX (April 1964), pp. 312–329; and Howard J. Snavely, "Current Cost for Long-Lived Assets: A Critical View," *The Accounting Review*, XLIV (April 1969), pp. 344–353.

[11]These other characteristics of a perfectly competitive economy are: (1) each buyer and seller is so small in relation to the market in which he operates that he cannot influence the price of what is sold therein, and (2) there are no artificial constraints placed on prices, supply, or demand. See, for example, Kalman J. Cohen and Richard M. Cyert, *Theory of the Firm: Resource Allocation in a Market Economy*, (Prentice-Hall, Inc., 1965), pp. 49–51.

[12]This is a derivative of the familiar perfect knowledge assumption. Since this general characteristic of perfect competition is frequently misunderstood, amplification is warranted. In this regard Cohen and Cyert state (*ibid.*, p. 50);

"This [perfect knowledge] assumption should be interpreted as meaning that all buyers and sellers in the market are aware of all current opportunities. . . . *We do not assume perfect ability to forecast the future, but only perfect knowledge of current opportunities.*" [*Emphasis supplied*]

[13]J. R. Hicks, *Value and Capital*, 2d ed. (Clarendon Press, 1946), pp. 171–188; Alexander (revised by Solomons), "Income Measurement," pp. 174–188; and Bedford, *Income Determination Theory*, pp. 25–27. If for simplicity we assume that all cash flows occur on the

last day of each period, these two components of economic income can be isolated symbolically in the following manner:

$$(Ye)_i = V_{i+1} - V_i$$

where $(Ye)_i$ represents the economic income for the ith period, V_i is the envisioned value of the firm's assets at the beginning of the ith period, and V_{i+1} is the envisioned value of the assets at the beginning of the $i+1$st period. Thus:

(a)
$$V_i = \sum_{j=i}^{n} \frac{F_j(i)}{(1+r)^{j+1-i}} + L_i$$

where $F_j(i)$ represents the expected net cash flow in the jth period as envisioned at the beginning of the ith period, r equals the normal rate of return, n represents the terminal date of the planning horizon, and L_i is the value of the liquid assets at the beginning of the ith period. Similarly:

(b)
$$V_{i+1} = \sum_{j=i+1}^{n} \frac{F_j(i) + \Delta F_j(i+1)}{(1+r)^{j-i}}$$
$$+ L_i(1+r) + R_i,$$

where $\Delta F_j(i+1)$ represents the change in the originally envisioned jth period cash flow now viewed from the beginning of the $i+1$st period, and R_i is the actually realized cash inflow of the ith period. Subtracting [a] from [b] and rearranging yields:

(c)
$$(Ye)_i = \underbrace{\sum_{j=i+1}^{n} \frac{F_j(i)}{(1+r)^{j-i}} - \sum_{j=i}^{n} \frac{F_j(i)}{(1+r)^{j+1-i}}}_{\text{expected income}} + \underbrace{L_i r + R_i + \sum_{j=i+1}^{n} \frac{\Delta F_j(i+1)}{(1+r)^{j-i}}}_{\text{unexpected income}}$$

This particular dichotomization of the income components is appropriate only if it is assumed that R_i, the actually realized inflow of the ith period, equals $F_i(i)$, the expected ith period inflow as envisioned at the beginning of the ith period. However, if R_i diverges from $F_i(i)$, then equation (c) must be altered slightly.

[14]From the preceding footnote we have, for expected income:

(c')
$$I_e = \sum_{j=i+1}^{n} \frac{F_j(i)}{(1+r)^{j-i}} - \sum_{j=1}^{n} \frac{F_j(i)}{(1+r)^{j+1-i}} + L_i r + R_i$$

which, after performing the indicated subtraction, yields:

(d')
$$I_e = \sum_{j=i+1}^{n} \frac{(1+r)F_j(i) - F_j(i)}{(1+r)^{j+1-i}} \quad \frac{F_i(i)}{(1+r)} + L_i r + R_i$$

Since $F_i(i)$ equals R_i in this *ex ante* income conceptualization, we can substitute $F_i(i)$ for R_i in equation [d'] and simplify:

$$I_e = \sum_{j=i+1}^{n} \frac{r F_j(i)}{(1+r)^{j+1-i}} - \frac{F_i(i)}{(1+r)} + L_i r + F_i(i)$$

$$I_e = \sum_{j=i}^{n} \frac{r F_j(i)}{(1+r)^{j+1-i}} + L_i r$$

$$I_e = r \left[\sum_{j=i}^{n} \frac{F_j(i)}{(1 + r)^{j+1-i}} + L_i \right]$$

$$I_e = rV_i$$

[15]See, for example, Eugene M. Lerner and Willard T. Carleton, *A Theory of Financial Analysis*, (Harcourt, Brace & World, Inc., 1966), pp. 50–51.

[16]Note that the conditions under which this relationship holds are rather limited. First, this relationship is valid only for economies in which all characteristics of perfect competition are satisfied and, because of equation (4), *only in equilibrium*. Second, equation (6) is valid only if the specific depreciation concept used in the replacement cost model is that of economic depreciation. However, Edwards and Bell (pp. 178–180) exclude economic depreciation from their model on both theoretical and practical grounds. Therefore, current operating profit as computed by Edwards and Bell need not equal expected income. Finally, a change in the composition or level of ending inventory of processed goods can destroy the equation (6) relationship. (See Edwards and Bell, pp. 105–108.) This is the case since the entry value replacement cost concept promulgated by Edwards and Bell specifically excludes value added by production.

[17]This correspondence between realizable cost savings and unexpected income is precise only if replacement cost depreciation is measured as the periodic decline in the earning power of an asset (economic depreciation). Only then will the difference between the book values of assets and ending market values correspond to the unexpected income component of economic income. If replacement cost depreciation is computed on a basis other than economic depreciation, realizable cost savings will vary from unexpected income by the amount of the divergence between economic depreciation and replacement cost depreciation as actually computed.

[18]For a development of the correspondence between replacement cost income and total economic income under conditions of divergent expectations, the interested reader is referred to a forthcoming article by the author.

[19]Heretofore, we have concentrated on the underlying correspondences between the subcomponents of each income concept. We did this in order to develop the theoretical foundation for the indirect measurement hypothesis in a comprehensible manner and to explain why this surrogate relationship has been extended to realistic economies by its proponents. When firms' expectations differ, however, we can demonstrate that these two underlying correspondences are not necessarily independent. (*Supra.*, footnote 18.) Since divergence of expectations is the norm in realistic economies, and since our concern centers on the *total* relationship between the two income concepts, in the remainder of the paper we shift our focus from the subcomponents to concentrate instead on the relationship between *total* replacement cost income and *total* economic income.

[20]It should be emphasized that for ease of exposition the general purchasing power of the monetary unit is assumed herein to be stable. Therefore, the influence on market prices of general inflation or deflation can be ignored.

[21]More specifically, not only must asset prices and cash flows move in the same direction, but also the magnitude of the price change must correspond to the magnitude of the change in the present value of expected cash flows.

[22]For a development of such examples see Lawrence Sherwin Revsine, "Replacement Cost Reports to Investors: A Relevance Analysis" (unpublished Ph.D. dissertation, Northwestern University, 1968), pp. 76–93.

[23]Beaver, Kennelly and Voss, "Evaluation of Accounting Data," (p. 677):

"The use of the predictive ability criterion presupposes that the alternatives under consideration have met the tests of logic and that each has a theory supporting it. . . . Theory provides an explanation why a given alternative is expected to be related to the dependent variable and permits the investigator to generalize from the findings of sample data to a new set of observations. Consequently, a complete evaluation involves both *a priori* and empirical considerations."

[24]See, for example, Robert T. Sprouse, "The Measurement of Financial Position and Income: Purpose and Procedure," *Research in Accounting Measurement*, ed. Robert K. Jaedicke, Yuji Ijiri and Oswald Nielsen (American Accounting Association, 1966), p. 106;

George J. Staubus, *A Theory of Accounting to Investors* (The University of California Press, 1961), p. 50; The Committee to Prepare a Statement of Basic Accounting Theory, *A Statement of Basic Accounting Theory* (American Accounting Association, 1966), p. 23; and William J. Vatter, *The Fund Theory of Accounting and Its Implications for Financial Reports* (The University of Chicago Press, 1947), p. 72.

[25]Cf., Committee on Accounting Procedure, *Accounting Research and Terminology Bulletins*, Final Edition (American Institute of Certified Public Accountants, 1961), pp. 87–88; and Bierman and Davidson, "The Income Concept," p. 241.

[26]A numeric illustration of this phenomenon is presented in the Appendix to this paper.

[27]The replacement cost income concept of Edwards and Bell takes no cognizance of "bargain" purchases until they are validated by a market price change. By introducing an "acquisition income" segment into the replacement cost income determination model, we are utilizing Bedford's approach. (*Income Determination Theory*, p. 176).

[28]The realizable cost saving of $6.21 is computed as follows:

Equilibrium value of expected flows as of 1/1/x1:
19x1 ($95 × .9524) ....$ 90.48
19x2 ($95 × .9070) 86.17

New market price for 1 yr. old asset $176.65
Less: Market price of 1 yr.
    old asset at 12/31/x0 .... 170.44

Realizable cost saving ....$ 6.21

The old market price of $170.44 is determined by solving for x where:

$$\frac{x}{\$204.53} = \frac{\$250}{\$299.55}$$

[29]Yuji Ijiri, Robert K. Jaedicke, and Kenneth E. Knight, "The Effects of Accounting Alternatives on Management Decisions," *Research in Accounting Measurement*, p. 194.

Should Replacement-Cost Changes Be Included in Income?

RICHARD A. SAMUELSON

In a replacement-cost accounting model, the non-monetary assets are period-ically adjusted to current cost at the balance sheet date. This adjustment is regarded by some as a "holding gain" includable in income, but by others as an adjustment of capital which is not part of income. During a period of rapid inflation, the classification of this adjustment could have a very significant effect on the reported income of a firm. Study groups in Australia, the United King-dom, and the United States which have considered the impact of inflation on accounts, have all recommended current value systems involving the wide use of replacement costs, but each has made a different recommendation regarding the treatment of replacement-cost adjustments.

The Institute of Chartered Accountants in Australia and the Australian Society of Accountants [1978] recommended in their exposure draft, "Current Cost Accounting," that replacement-cost adjustments be treated as direct ad-justments of owners' equity, with no effect on income for the period. The Infla-tion Accounting Committee (known as the Sandilands Committee) in the United Kingdom [Sandilands, 1975] took a somewhat ambiguous position, on the one hand including replacement-cost adjustments in a "Summary Statement of Total Gains and Losses" and on the other hand excluding them from the profit and loss account on the ground that they do not represent "operating profits." The Financial Accounting Standards Board in its exposure draft "Financial Reporting and Changing Prices" [1978] recommended supplementary reporting of replacement-cost adjustments as "holding gains." While not incorporating the holding gains in an overall measure of business income, the FASB argued that they should be viewed as income in the year of the price change.

In the academic literature, opinion has long been divided on the issue. Zeff [1962] provided an historical summary of the opposing views prior to Edwards and Bell. Edwards and Bell [1961, p. 93] argued that replacement-cost changes represented income. The American Accounting Association's Committee on Con-cepts and Standards [1964] and its Committee to Prepare a Statement of Basic Accounting Theory [1966] also supported the holding gains treatment. Sprouse and Moonitz [1962, p. 57–59] argued that changes in the replacement cost of inventories were holding gains but seemed to imply that changes in the re-placement cost of plant and equipment were capital adjustments. The prepon-derance of academic opinion since Edwards and Bell, however, has favored the holding gains treatment for all replacement-cost changes.

Justification for either the holding gains or capital adjustment treatment is often related to a particular definition of income. Proponents of the capital

Richard A. Samuelson, "Should Replacement-Cost Changes Be Included in Income?" *The Accounting Review*, April 1980, pp. 254–268. Reprinted with the permission of *The Accounting Review*.

adjustment treatment prescribe a definition of income based on the preservation of *physical capital* or "operating capability." In the Australian exposure draft [ICA Australia, 1978, p. 5], for example, the profit of an entity for a period is defined as "the total gain, arising during a period, which could be distributed in full whilst still maintaining capital, in the sense of the operating capability, at the level which existed at the beginning of the period." Since funds equivalent to the change in replacement cost are not available for distribution as dividends without impairing the entity's ability to replace the asset in the future, this definition implies that replacement-cost changes represent adjustments to capital.

Proponents of the holding gains treatment favor an income definition based on the preservation of *financial* capital, or the original amount of money invested in the assets of the entity. Profit, therefore, is considered to be the total gain, arising during a period, which could be distributed in full while still maintaining capital, in the sense of the original financial investment, at the level which existed at the beginning of the period. Under this definition, reinvestment in the same or similar assets is not a necessary condition for income recognition, but is viewed as a separate financial management decision unrelated to earnings measurement. Management could choose to invest available funds in some other form. There is no principle of financial management or of financial accounting which requires reinvestment of earnings in the same or similar assets.

Defining income in terms of the preservation of financial capital does not distinguish, however, between historical-cost income and replacement-cost income. While total income during the lifetime of an asset will be the same under historical-cost and replacement-cost accounting (if holding gains are included in income), the incomes reported in any one particular period are likely to be different. The difference relates to the timing of the recognition of the holding gain element of income. Under historical-cost accounting, the "holding gain" is effectively recognized in the period in which the asset is sold or otherwise consumed. Under replacement-cost accounting, holding gains are recognized in the period of price change. Replacement-cost holding gains can, therefore, occur independently of any transaction and do not necessarily coincide with any inflow of net assets to the entity. Since replacement-cost holding gains can occur independently of operating gains, they need to be defined independently, and since replacement-cost holding gains do not result in inflows of net assets they must be viewed as "gains" in some sense other than "amounts which could be *distributed*."

Two broad explanations have been given in the academic literature to justify the interpretation of replacement-cost adjustments as holding gains and losses. One view, associated with Edwards and Bell [1961, p. 93], is that holding gains represent "realizable cost savings." The entity is better off, according to this view, if replacement costs have increased from the time an asset was purchased, in the sense that it would now cost more to acquire the asset than it actually did when the firm acquired the asset in the past. The other explanation is that holding gains represent increases in the expected net receipts from either using or selling the asset in the future. The replacement-cost measure, according to this view, is a surrogate measure for the net realizable value or the discounted present value of expected receipts attainable from use of the asset in the future.

The purpose here is to analyze the validity of these two explanations for holding gains. It is assumed that replacement-cost financial statements would be used for general external financial reports aimed primarily at present stock-holders and potential investors, who are interested in knowing whether stock-holder wealth has increased or decreased during the period, and by how much. Other users such as creditors, employees, and taxing authorities may have sim-ilar information needs, and to the extent they do the analysis is appropriate for their use as well.[1] No judgment is made as to whether replacement-cost ac-counting is preferable to historical cost or to any other system of accounting. The holding gains issue is merely analyzed within the framework of a replace-ment-cost system. The major advantages of a replacement-cost system are usu-ally associated with the alleged usefulness of the current operating profit com-ponent, but it is not the intent here to evaluate those arguments. The analysis is, therefore, aimed at the limited question of how replacement-cost adjustments should be handled *if* a replacement-cost system were to be required for external financial reporting.

Before investigating the validity of the arguments supporting the holding gains treatment, the concepts of *benefit value, sacrifice value,* and *value differ-entials* will be examined, since these concepts are useful in gaining a better understanding of the issues at hand.

VALUE DIFFERENTIALS

Ijiri [1967, p. 34] has classified accounting values into two basic types: *sacrifice values* and *benefit values.* Sacrifice values, such as historical cost or replacement cost, represent the amount of disutility or sacrifice necessary to obtain economic goods and services. Benefit values, such as selling price, net realizable value, or discounted present value, represent the utility or benefits obtainable from consuming goods and services. This classification closely resembles the di-chotomy between the labor theory of value and the utility theory of value in economic theory. It is also essentially the same as the Edwards and Bell [1961, p. 75] dichotomy between entry prices and exit prices. Ijiri's terminology is used here because it is more desciptive of the underlying nature of the values and because Ijiri uses these terms in conjunction with the term "value differential."

Income measures are based on the difference between two accounting val-ues. They can be referred to, then, as *value differentials.* Historical cost income is based on a *benefit-sacrifice differential,* since it is measured by the difference between realized selling prices, which are benefit values, and historical costs, which are sacrifice values. "Continuously Contemporary Accounting" [Cham-bers, 1966] income is based on *benefit differentials* since, under this system of accounting, income is the difference between the net realizable value of net assets at the end and the beginning of the accounting period. Replacement-cost income is composed of two types of differentials where holding gains are in-cluded in income. Operating profit, the difference between realized selling prices and replacement costs, is a benefit-sacrifice differential, whereas the holding gain on assets held during the period is a *sacrifice differential,* since it is the difference between two replacement-costs.

---

[1]Taxing authorities, creditors, and other users may have information needs which vary considerably from those of present stockholders and potential investors. These in-formation needs can be satisfied by reporting data directly to the users rather than through the general financial reports made available to stockholders and investors.

The basic objective of economic activity is to maximize the difference between benefits and sacrifices. A benefit-sacrifice differential is regarded as income because it indicates that the basic objective has been accomplished. Benefit differentials also can be regarded as income, because they indicate improvement or progress toward the basic economic objective. A positive benefit differential means that the expected benefits obtainable from the resources of the enterprise have increased.

Sacrifice differentials, however, present a problem for interpretation. They are not based on a concept of benefits and hence do not necessarily imply any accomplishment of, or progress toward, an economic objective. They only imply that the sacrifice necessary to obtain the resources of the enterprise has changed. Since income involves the realization or the expectation of benefits, it is necessary to assume, if we are to interpret sacrifice differentials as income, that a change in sacrifice values is somehow a "benefit" to the firm. Otherwise, sacrifice differentials cannot be considered income.

The interpretation of a replacement-cost change as a benefit in the cost savings sense is referred to here as the "cost savings hypothesis." The interpretation that replacement-cost changes represent benefits since they are surrogate measures for changes in benefit values is referred to as the "surrogation hypothesis." These two hypotheses are now examined.

THE COST SAVINGS HYPOTHESIS

The cost savings point of view can be illustrated by a simple example. Assume that a particular item is purchased on January 1 for $100 and sold on February 15 for $175. At January 31, the replacement cost of the item was $120, and at February 15, $130. If replacement-cost changes are considered to be holding gains, then the firm would report a $20 ($120–$100) holding gain for January and a $10 ($130–$120) holding gain for February.

The replacement-cost change of $20 represents income for January according to this view, because the firm "saved" $20 by purchasing the item on January 1 instead of January 31. By the same reasoning, the firm "saved" an additional $10 by February 15, since the replacement cost was then $10 higher than at January 31. In total, the cost saving was $30 from buying this item on January 1 rather than the latest possible date, February 15.

Edwards and Bell attribute this cost savings to management's holding activities. They view management as engaging in two basic types of activities—holding activities, which are decisions relating to the quantity of assets to hold over time, and operating activities, which are decisions relating to the use of assets in the production and sale of goods and services. The change in the replacement cost of an asset held over time is a measure of how well management has performed its holding activities.

There is some question, however, whether holding gains interpreted in this way are useful as an indicator of management's performance of its holding activities. Drake and Dopuch [1965] point out that operating activities and holding activities are often inter-related and it is not feasible to evaluate them independently. If an asset is acquired to reduce future operating costs, then the benefits attributable to the asset are reflected in future operating profits, not in the changing replacement prices of the asset while holding it. It would not make sense to judge management's holding activities as unsuccessful if the replacement price were to fall but the operating profits were to increase sufficiently to justify the cost of the asset.

A limitation on the usefulness of the cost savings concept is that it is concerned with only one aspect of the decision to hold assets: *the timing of resource acquisitions*. Holding gains are based on a comparison of a cost actually incurred by the firm in acquiring an asset when it did, with the cost that would have been incurred if the asset had been purchased at some other time. While this comparison may be of some interest, it may not be the most important aspect of the decision to hold a particular quantity of assets. More often than not, management's holding activities can be judged more meaningfully from the level of operating profits than from the existence of holding gains or losses.

But let us assume for the moment that the *timing* of resource acquisitions is an important factor in judging management's performance and that a performance measure would be useful. Does the replacement-cost holding gain fairly measure management's success in timing its resource acquisitions? Probably not. The alternative decision (buying at the balance-sheet date or at the time the asset was used, whichever is later) would only by coincidence have been an optimal decision. In the numerical example discussed before, the $30 cost saving is based on the alternative of buying at February 15 instead of at January 1. A better alternative might have been to purchase on January 5 when the replacement cost of the item was, say, only $95. Compared to the alternative of buying at January 5, the decision to buy on January 1 was sub-optimal. Why not, then, attribute a $5 holding *loss* to management's holding activities instead of a $30 gain?

Given a set of alternative decisions, the relevant one for comparison with the decision actually made would be the one which, after the fact, would have been optimal. This would give some meaningful information on how management performed. As we have seen, however, the holding gain measure chooses an alternative which would only coincidentally be optimal. Not only is the comparative decision *sub-optimal*, but it is probably *infeasible* as well. By choosing the latest date at which the asset could be purchased, the cost savings measure implies that as an alternative to holding any assets at all, the firm could acquire all resources immediately before they are needed. This obviates the need to carry stocks of merchandise, or raw materials, or plant and equipment. Obviously, this assumption defies reality, and it results in a performance measure predicated upon an infeasible course of action.

If the cost savings concept is to be judged on its usefulness in evaluating management's holding activities, then it fails to be a very useful concept.

There is another, more fundamental weakness with the cost savings concept, however. Under the cost savings concept, income is viewed as an "opportunity gain" from taking one course of action versus another. The alternative course of action has been foregone, however, by the original course of action. Once the firm has acquired the asset, it has a "sunk cost" which cannot be avoided by any future course of action. The only alternatives remaining are to sell the asset or to continue using the asset in operations. These are the relevant opportunities on which to base a definition of income. Only these alternatives can result in cash inflows to the firm. Why base an income definition on an alternative course of action that no longer exists?

The basic problem here is that to view a cost savings as an economic benefit (and therefore income) the concept of "benefit" must be viewed differently than it normally is in defining income. All income definitions, of course, have some underlying concept of "economic benefits." The Hicksian definition [Hicks, 1939, p. 172], that a man's income is the "the maximum value which he can consume during a week, and still expect to be as well-off at the end of the week as he was at the beginning," implies that economic benefits are cash inflows. The "well-offness" which serves as the basis for Hicks' concept of income is the discounted present value of expected cash inflows. Cash inflows, either realized or expected, seem to be the usual interpretation of an economic benefit in defining the income of a firm.

In the cost savings concept of income, however, the benefits are neither *realized* cash flows nor *expected* cash flows, but *foregone* cash flows. The income attributable to the holding of an asset during a period of rising prices is the cash outflow foregone by purchasing the asset when the price was low instead of when the price was high. The amount of the gain is completely independent of any assumption that future cash inflows will be greater. In the previous example, the $30 holding gain exists whether or not the selling price of the item has changed. The firm may have continued to offer the item for sale at $175 from January 1 to February 15. A gain would still be reported merely on the basis of the change in replacement cost, even though no change in the expected cash inflows has occurred.

If foregone cash flows are to be included in income, then any further implications this might have for income measurement should be considered. The foregone cash flows due to the timing of resource acquisitions are only one of many foregone cash flows. What of the foregone cash flows from deciding to purchase asset X instead of asset Y, from borrowing money at time A instead of time B, from having a restrictive policy for extending credit instead of a lenient policy, and so forth? The fact is, the foregone cash flow from the timing of resource acquisition is only one of an infinite variety of opportunity gains and losses that might be included in income. There does not seem to be any apparent reason for selecting one type of opportunity gain or loss over another for inclusion in income. Is the timing of resource acquisitions such a critical aspect of management performance?

The following can, therefore, be concluded: (1) holding activities are often not independent from operating activities and should not be evaluated separately; (2) the holding gains measure is not a valid indicator of management's effectiveness in making holding decisions because of this interdependence and also because the holding measure is predicated upon an alternative course of action which may be either sub-optimal or infeasible; (3) cost savings are not benefits in the sense of cash inflows that have been either realized in the past or are expected to be realized in the future; and (4) cost savings represent foregone cash flows and there is no logical basis for selecting one type of foregone cash flow from an infinite number in the measurement of enterprise income.

THE SURROGATION HYPOTHESIS

An alternative explanation of holding gains is that the sacrifice differential represented by replacement-cost changes are surrogates for benefit differentials. This surrogation is viewed either as a correlation between changes in replacement cost and the discounted present value (or net realizable value) of an individual asset, or as a correlation between changes in replacement cost of an asset and the discounted present value of the entire entity.

Most often where surrogation is implied, the argument has been advanced in support of replacement costs for balance-sheet valuations. It is argued, for example, that under pure competition the equilibrium price of an asset is equal to its present value in marginal employment,[2] and that for a single resource firm the equilibrium market price is also equal to the per-unit or average present value of the capital assets employed by the firm.[3] While it is admitted that pure competition and long-run equilibrium rarely exist in the real world, it has been argued that there is a tendency toward them and that current replacement cost can be used as a reasonable approximation of discounted present value.[4]

The 1963 Committee on Concepts and Standards—Long Lived Assets also supported replacement costs as surrogate measures for discounted present value. The Committee [AAA, 1964, p. 694], for example, states that:

> ... service potential is the essential element in asset valuation. Where measurements of current service potential in terms of discounted cash flows can be supported by sufficient objective evidence, as in the case of most long-term receivables and payables, they are generally used. Whenever sufficient objective evidence is not available, or when cash flow estimates cannot be identified with specific assets, a practical approximate measurement of service potential may be attained by reference to the *current cost of securing the same or equivalent services.*

In the Committee's opinion, replacement cost is a second choice to discounted present value, but is used as a surrogate because it approximates discounted present value. The Committee then recommended the inclusion of replacement-cost changes in income since they represent changes in the service potential of the asset. That is, if replacement cost is greater than historical cost, the increase represents a holding gain, in the absence of price-level changes, since the current price of the asset reflects the currently expected cash flows from use of the asset, which are greater than the cash flows originally expected from the asset.

Revsine [1970] formalized the correlation between replacement-cost income (including holding gains and losses) and economic income (which is the increment in present value) under conditions of perfect competition and perfect resource mobility (*i.e.*, variable resources only).[5] Where these conditions exist,

---

[2]Sweeney [1933] is one of the earliest to make this point in support of replacement costs for balance-sheet valuations.

[3]Cook and Holzmann [1976].

[4]See Barton [1974] and Revsine [1976] for an exchange of views on this point. Bromwich [1975] analyzes the relationship between replacement costs and present values under varying assumptions of imperfect markets and concludes that replacement costs are not reliable surrogates for present value in many cases.

[5]Most investigations of the surrogation hypothesis (*e.g.*, Sweeney [1933], Barton [1974], Bromwich [1975], Cook and Holzmann [1976]) have analyzed the relationship between replacement cost and present value at a point in time (a balance-sheet approach) rather than the correlation between changes in replacement-cost and changes in present value between two points in time (an income-statement approach). For a firm already

he argued that replacement-cost income equals (or approximates) economic income. For the more important case, however, where the firm employs fixed resources which are not perfectly mobile, Revsine argued that the surrogation hypothesis is suspect during periods of long-run disequilibrium.

If resources are perfectly mobile, any change in existing market conditions can be accommodated by immediate expansion or retraction of capital in the industry. There is no gradual adjustment from one equilibrium state to another. Any change in expected cash flows may be immediately impounded in the prices of the variable resources. In the case of fixed, immobile resources, however, a change in market conditions may involve lead-times to adjust capital levels to the long-run profit-maximizing positions. Under these circumstances, the changes in expected cash flows to existing resources are not fully impounded in the replacement price of new resources; furthermore, the replacement-cost changes may not even be positively correlated with changes in the discounted present value of the entity.

Before illustrating these points as related to fixed resources, the validity of the surrogation hypothesis for individual assets held for sale in the normal course of business, such as marketable securities, finished goods inventory of a manufacturer, or merchandise inventory of a retailer, is considered. Marketable securities represent a special case in which replacement cost equals or approximates net realizable value. There is no argument here against including the holding gain in income, since the change in market price is equivalent to a change in the expected cash flows from disposing of the asset in the normal course of business. (In effect, the market value change is a benefit differential.)

For finished goods or merchandise inventory, however, there is a distinction between the replacement cost and the net realizable value of the asset, since the former will occur in entry markets and the latter will occur in exit markets. The surrogation hypothesis implies that changes in the replacement cost of the inventory are positively correlated with changes in net realizable value. While there is little reason to doubt that the firm will eventually increase its selling price if replacement costs have permanently increased, there is no assurance that the selling price of the individual asset being valued will increase. There may be a lag between cost and selling price changes which is longer than the expected holding period for the inventory. It would be premature to recognize a gain until it is known with greater certainty that the net realizable value of the individual asset being valued will also increase.

The surrogation hypothesis for fixed productive assets—*i.e.*, fixed assets which will be transformed in the production process into final products held for sale, such as intangibles, equipment, and plant will now be examined. Here the analysis is more complex since the cash flows will not be derived from direct sale of the assets in their present forms. Instead, the cash flows attributable to productive assets are represented by the cash flows realized from sale of products into which the productive assets will be transformed through the produc-

holding capital assets, the argument that replacement cost and present value may be correlated as of a point in time is not a valid argument for holding gains, since changes in replacement cost may not be correlated with changes in present value of the firm. Revsine [1970] directly analyzed the correlation between replacement cost income and economic income and cites others who either explicitly or implicitly adopted the surrogation hypothesis for income.

tion process. These cash flows cannot be attributed to specific productive assets, since they are produced jointly by all of the productive assets, so it is necessary to view the surrogation hypothesis as a correlation between the replacement cost of an individual asset and the discounted present value of the entire entity. (In a simplified case where only one type of fixed resource is used, it is possible to speak of the average present value of individual assets if it is further assumed that individual assets contribute equally to the production of the firm's output.)

To examine the surrogation hypothesis for fixed productive assets, assume that a firm is operating in a perfectly competitive industry—the alpha industry—and that both the firm and the industry are initially in long-run equilibrium.[6] Assume that the firm acquires alpha-producing equipment on December 31, $X0$ at $250 per unit, which is expected to yield annual cash flows of $91.80 per unit for three years, an internal rate of return of five percent per annum.

On January 1, $X1$, the very next day, an unexpected increase in the demand for alphas increases the expected cash flows to $110 per unit per year. This change in market conditions brings about a short-run equilibrium in which superior profits are available in the alpha industry and causes new capital movement into the industry. Assume, however, a necessary lead-time of three years for capital to shift into the industry. After three years, as a result of the entry of new firms and the expansion of facilities by existing firms, a new long-run equilibrium level of profits will be reached at an expected return of $95 per capital asset per year.

As of January 1, $X1$, the average discounted present value of the existing firm's assets is $299.55, the present value of an annuity of $110 for three years at five percent. The replacement cost of new alpha-producing assets would not rise to $299.55, however, since by the time new assets are employed in the industry the supply of alphas will increase and capital assets will yield only $95 per year. The price of new capital equipment will therefore be only $258.71, the present value of an annuity of $95 for three years at five percent.

The point at which the replacement prices of equipment actually rise to $258.71 may vary, depending upon the quickness of the market in reacting to the changed market conditions in the alpha industry. There may be a lag of several periods in order to allow the new expectation of superior profits to be verified by higher net receipts for existing firms in the alpha industry. For simplicity, assume, however, that the increased demand for alphas is diagnosed immediately on January 1, $X1$, new orders are placed for alpha-producing equipment, and the replacement price of alpha equipment becomes $258.71 as of January 1, $X1$. Under these conditions, replacement-cost income per unit of capital for the existing firm in the alpha industry would be as shown in Figure 1. (It is assumed that the firm uses "economic depreciation," so that the net value of the equipment is the discounted present value of the remaining cash flows implicit in the price of a new asset.)

In year $X1$, a replacement-cost holding gain of $8.71 would occur. Does this positive sacrifice differential imply a corresponding increase in benefit values? The position of the Committee on Concepts and Standards implies that the

---

[6]The example which follows is similar to Revsine's [1970, pp. 521–523] except that it is assumed here that the firm is initially in long-run equilibrium, whereas Revsine begins his analysis during a period of long-run disequilibrium. The analysis here is also extended to a second case not considered by Revsine.

EXHIBIT 1
Replacement-Cost Income for a Firm in the Alpha Industry under the Assumption that the Demand for Alphas Increases Unexpectedly on January 1, X1.

Year	Net Cash Receipts	Replacement Cost, Jan. 1	Replacement Cost, Dec. 31	Depreciation	Current Operating Profit	Holding Gain	Total Replacement-Cost Income
X0	—	—	$250.00	—	—	—	—
X1	$100.00	$258.71(1)	176.64	$ 82.07	$27.93	$8.71	$36.64
X2	110.00	176.64(2)	90.48	86.16	23.84	—	23.84
X3	110.00	90.48(3)	0.00	90.48	19.52	—	19.52
	$330.00			$258.71	$71.29	$8.71	$80.00

(1) $P_{\overline{3}|.05}$ $95.
(2) $P_{\overline{2}|.05}$ $95.
(3) $P_{\overline{1}|.05}$ $95.

replacement-cost change represents the increase in the discounted present value of expected net receipts to the firm (which are attributable to the capital assets). It does not, however. The present value of the incremental cash flows is $49.55 ($299.55 minus $250.00), which may be referred to as the *goodwill* of the firm. The Committee on Concepts and Standards' argument implies that the goodwill would be impounded in the replacement cost of new assets. But this confuses the market value of net assets held by existing firms (which command a premium because they can earn superior profits for a limited period of time) with the replacement cost of new assets. Competitive forces will eventually eliminate superior profits but not until capital levels can be adjusted and a new long-run equilibrium is reached. At that point, goodwill will be zero and the market value of existing capital assets will be equal to the replacement cost of new capital assets.[7]

Revsine recognized that replacement-cost holding gains would not *equal* changes in discounted present value, but he argued that they could be regarded as income if they signaled future changes in cash flows. He implied by this argument that replacement-cost changes could be viewed as income if they were *positively correlated* with changes in discounted present value, since a change in future cash flows meant that discounted present value would also change. In a case similar to the one just described, he argued that replacement-cost changes are negatively correlated with future cash flows since the $110 cash flow in period $X1$, the year of the holding gain, is to be followed by a decline in cash flows to $95 in period $X4$.

Revsine's criterion for the inclusion of holding gains in income is too stringent, however, to be acceptable. It implies that all reported gains should be lead-indicators of cash flows. The timing of cash collection is not a criterion for revenue recognition, however. Revenues collected in advance of service performance are deferred to later periods under accepted accounting practice, and their eventual recognition lags the inflow of cash. It might be argued that the $8.71 holding gain in the previous example is a lagged-indicator of cash flows from $91.80 in period $X0$ to $110.00 in period $X1$. It is also positively correlated with the market value of the firm's net assets which increased from $250.00 to $299.55.

[7]Edwards and Bell [1961, pp. 276–277] imply that management would foresee the impact of changing market conditions before the market would, and that subjective goodwill would eventually be validated by changes in market values. At one point [pp. 276–277] they seem to imply that the market validation would be in the form of replacement costs, but at another point they state [p. 71] that the market price they had in mind was net realizable value. In the analysis here, and also in Revsine's [1970], no distinction is made between management's evaluation of goodwill (subjective goodwill) and the market's evaluation of goodwill (market goodwill). The difference in perspective arises from Edwards and Bell's opinion that the primary objective of income measurement is the evaluation of management, rather than the more conventional view that the primary objective is to measure wealth or to provide an income measure which is useful in making projections about the future so that subjective estimates of wealth can be made. Under the more conventional approach, replacement-cost changes would represent income if they were validated by changes in cash flows. Under the Edwards and Bell approach, replacement-cost changes would be useful as validations of management's expectations, but Edwards and Bell did not justify their inclusion in income on these grounds. They are quite clear [p. 93] that holding gains represent income because they are *cost savings*, a concept already examined here.

Upon closer examination, however, it can be argued that this positive correlation between the replacement-cost change and cash flows (or market value of the firm) is merely incidental. The holding gain of $8.71 can be calculated as the present value of an annuity of $3.20 ($95.00 minus $91.80) for three periods at five percent. In other words, the holding gain represents the present value of the excess cash flows obtainable from an asset employed in the new long-run equilibrium compared to an asset employed under the old long-run equilibrium. It is not a measure of the increase in the discounted present value of the assets presently held by the firm, and it is difficult to attach any significance to the measure as a "gain."

If the example is changed slightly, the fallacy of interpreting the replacement-cost change as a surrogate for a benefit differential can be seen more clearly. Assume as before that the firm in the alpha industry acquires capital assets for $250.00 on December 31, $X0$, but that on January 1, $X1$ the demand for these capital assets increases because of an increased demand for their employment in another industry—the beta industry. Whereas previously the same capital assets were expected to earn annual cash flows of $91.80 in both the alpha and beta industries, an increase in demand for betas creates the opportunity to earn superior profits in that industry for three years. After three years, the supply of betas will be increased because of new entrants into the beta industry, and capital assets will earn a long-run equilibrium level of profits of $95 per year. In the meantime, capital will be shifted from the alpha industry, reducing the supply of alphas and increasing the price of alphas until the same return of $95 per capital asset is reached in a new long-run equilibrium for the alpha industry. If the same lead-time is assumed for exit from the industry as for entry to the industry, then the adjustment to a new long-run equilibrium in the alpha industry will not occur until $X4$. During years $X1$, $X2$, and $X3$ cash flows will remain at $91.80, since the demand for alphas has not changed and production levels remain the same until an exit of firms from the industry occurs in $X4$.

Replacement-cost income for years $X1$, $X2$, and $X3$ is reported in Figure 2 for this case. The holding gain of $8.71 for year $X1$ is unrelated to any changes in the expected cash flows for the alpha industry firm. Cash flows for the next three years are expected to remain the same, goodwill of the firm will be zero, and there will be zero correlation between the holding gain and the discounted present value of expected cash flows. Although cash flows are expected to increase in year $X4$ to $95, these are attainable only if the firm elects to acquire new capital assets at the end of year $X3$ for $258.71. At this price, the cash flows of $95 per year will yield the normal five percent return and the present value of that opportunity at year $X1$ is zero.

These examples illustrate several points about replacement-cost changes. First, if they relate to capital assets employable in other industries, they do not necessarily imply any corresponding change in the present value of cash flow expectations for a particular firm. There are many capital assets which fall into this category: general machinery, buildings, office equipment, *etc.* It would be misleading to interpret any increase in the replacement-cost of such assets as an improvement in the firm's position, since the factors affecting their prices are probably only marginally affected by market conditions in a given product industry.

EXHIBIT 2

Replacement-Cost Income for a Firm in the Alpha Industry under the Assumption that the Demand for Betas Increases Unexpectedly on January 1, X1.

Year	Net Cash Receipts	Replacement Cost, Jan. 1	Replacement Cost, Dec. 31	Depreciation	Current Operating Profit	Holding Gain	Total Replacement-Cost Income
X0	—	—	$250.00	—	—	—	—
X1	$ 91.80	$258.71(1)	176.64	$ 82.07	$ 9.73	$8.71	$18.44
X2	91.80	176.64(2)	90.48	86.16	5.64	—	5.64
X3	91.80	90.48(3)	0.00	90.48	1.32	—	1.32
	$275.40			$258.71	$16.69	$8.71	$25.40

(1) $P_{3|.05}$ $95.
(2) $P_{2|.05}$ $95.
(3) $P_{1|.05}$ $95.

Second, the immobility of fixed resources means that even for capital assets employable in a single industry (e.g., specialized machinery) the replacement price of new assets will probably not impound the entire, nor perhaps even the majority, of the expected cash flows induced from changes in market conditions within the industry. Evidence that replacement prices do not impound all expected cash flows may be indicated by the fact that under current generally accepted accounting principles, the purchase price of a going concern is allocated to individual assets on the basis of "fair value" (usually replacement cost for non-monetary assets), yet there is often goodwill, either positive or negative, after valuing all individual assets at fair values. While the existence of goodwill might indicate either measurement error or lack of competition in certain industries, it is probable that even in competitive industries goodwill exists because of continual changes in market conditions.

The argument that replacement costs approximate the average present values of assets in *long-run equilibrium* is therefore a very weak argument for accepting the surrogation hypothesis. Long-run equilibrium represents a direction toward which market conditions tend; it is not intended to be a description of the normal state of things. Without long-run equilibrium, changes in replacement cost are not reliable surrogates for changes in discounted present value.

THE CAPITAL ADJUSTMENT HYPOTHESIS

The analysis up to this point has rejected the interpretation of replacement-cost changes as "gains" includible in income. If they do not represent gains, then they must be interpreted as capital adjustments. Why?

The underlying support for the capital adjustment treatment comes from defining income as an amount that could be distributed while keeping intact the physical capital of the enterprise. This definition assumes that management intends to replace physical capital and that the owners view the firm as a going concern. Assuming replacement of assets and continuity of the firm is consistent with the choice of replacement costs for valuing the firm's assets. Replacement cost is relevant only where the firm intends to replace its assets. (If replacement is not intended, then some other basis of valuation would appear to be more relevant.) Given the intent to replace, income is consistently defined in terms of the maintenance of physical capital.

The capital adjustment treatment also has some appeal where accounting profit is viewed as a surrogate for "economic income." "Economic income" is based on the maintenance of capital in the sense of its cash-generating potential. Since directing measurement of cash-generating potential is impractical, alternative accounting concepts of capital may be substituted if they correlate well with "cash-generating potential."

Physical capital or "operating capability" may be viewed as reasonable surrogates for cash-generating potential. The level of future cash flows is related to the physical capacity of the firm's assets, or the quantity of output which the firm is capable of producing. Physical capital is not a perfect surrogate for cash-generating potential, obviously. Future cash flows also depend upon the value of future output. It is quite possible that a lower level of physical capital could sustain the same level of cash flows if the value of the output were to rise sufficiently in future periods. Nevertheless, there is probably a fairly high correlation between the expected cash flows of future periods, and the firm's operating capability at the present time.[8]

The capital adjustment treatment has recently been criticized for failing to account for certain economic impacts which changing replacement prices are alleged to have on the firm.

Prakash and Sunder [1979, p. 13] point out that where relative prices have changed in the economy there are "redistributive effects" upon economic agents, including business firms. The capital adjustment treatment, according to Prakash and Sunder, ignores these effects by eliminating replacement price changes from income. Using a benefit-sacrifice value analysis, it would be argued that "redistributive effects" can only be measured by changes in benefit values. The previous analysis of the surrogation hypothesis has shown that a change in the replacement cost of an asset does not necessarily benefit the owner of that asset. To the extent that redistributive effects do produce an impact upon particular firms, their benefits would be recognized by higher revenues, either through sale of the asset whose replacement cost has increased or through use of the asset in producing output whose exchange value has increased.

In its exposure draft on "Financial Reporting and Changing Prices," the FASB [1978, p. 35] makes a similar charge that the maintenance of physical capital definition of income fails to indicate the change in "purchasing power" which has accrued to the owners of the firm when replacement prices change. Again, their analysis is not made within a benefit-sacrifice value framework, and they therefore imply that all price changes reflect changes in purchasing power. It is argued here that the owners' purchasing power increases only when benefit values change. Furthermore, even *realized* "holding gains" do not represent increased purchasing power if the purchasing power is viewed in terms of the same assets presently held by the firm. By defining income in terms of increments to "general purchasing power," the FASB has adopted an income definition consistent with one accounting model (constant-dollar historical-cost) and applied it to another accounting model (replacement-cost) which it does not fit.

The FASB is also critical of the capital adjustment treatment for denying "the possibility that earnings can be increased by the wise timing of purchases of assets for use by the enterprise" [FASB, 1978, p. 35]. This criticism appears to adopt a cost savings notion of holding gains which has been previously analyzed and rejected here. The FASB criticism is also misleading if it implies that firms which consistently are able to purchase resources at lower prices compared to some other firm would not have this reflected in income. Replacement costs should be measured in terms of the conditions normally prevailing when purchases are made. The more efficient firm would therefore show lower replacement costs (compared to the less efficient firm) for the same resources.[9]

---

[8]Even if it could be proven that financial capital is more highly correlated with future cash flows than physical capital, this would not imply that replacement-cost adjustments represent income. Since replacement-cost changes can occur independently of operating profits, they must be justified as income independently. The discovery that financial capital is highly correlated with cash-generating potential may imply, however, that historical-cost income is preferable to replacement-cost income.

[9]The FASB may have recognized that careful measurement of replacement costs would reflect the benefits of the wise timing of asset purchases when it states that "the concept [of physical productive capacity of capital] can be adapted to avoid that anomaly [*i.e.*, no

CONCLUSION

Some proponents of the holding gains treatment for replacement-cost changes do not distinguish between benefit values and sacrifice values and therefore find no problem in viewing replacement-cost changes as "gains." Sacrifice values (including replacement costs) are fundamentally different than benefit values, however, and income can emerge only where benefits exceed sacrifices. If sacrifice differentials (such as replacement-cost changes) are viewed as income, then they must be interpreted as changes in "benefits." Two explanations—the "cost savings hypothesis" and the "surrogation hypothesis"—have been advanced to support the treatment of replacement-cost changes as "gains." The conclusion here, however, is that neither explanation is satisfactory.

Alternatively, replacement-cost changes can be interpreted as adjustments to the permanent capital of the firm. This interpretation is consistent with a definition of income based on the preservation of physical capital. Preservation of physical capital is, furthermore, consistent with the choice of replacement cost to value the firm's assets in the first place. Since replacement-cost changes can be meaningfully interpreted as capital adjustments whereas they cannot be meaningfully interpreted as "gains," they should be treated as capital adjustments within the context of a replacement-cost accounting model.

REFERENCES

American Accounting Association, Committee on Concepts and Standards— Long Lived Assets, "Accounting for Land, Buildings, and Equipment—Supplementary Statement No. 1," *The Accounting Review* (July 1964), pp. 693–699.

American Accounting Association, Committee to Prepare a Statement of Basic Accounting Theory, *A Statement of Basic Accounting Theory* (AAA, 1966).

Barton, A. D., "Expectations and Achievements in Income Theory," *The Accounting Review* (October 1974), pp. 664–681.

Bromwich, M., "Asset Valuation With Imperfect Markets," *Accounting and Business Research* (Autumn 1975), pp. 242–253.

Chambers, R. J., *Accounting, Evaluation and Economic Behavior* (Prentice-Hall, 1966).

Cook, J. S., and O. J. Holzmann, "Current Cost and Present Value in Income Theory," *The Accounting Review*, (October 1976), pp. 778–787.

Drake, D. F., and N. Dopuch, "On the Case for Dichotomizing Income," *Journal of Accounting Research* (Autumn 1965), pp. 192–205.

Edwards, E. O., and P. W. Bell, *The Theory and Measurement of Business Income* (University of California Press, 1961).

Financial Accounting Standards Board, "Proposed Statement of Financial Accounting Standards: Financial Reporting and Changing Prices," Exposure Draft dated December 28, 1978 (FASB, Stamford, Connecticut).

Hicks, J. R., *Value and Capital* (Oxford, Clarendon Press, 1939).

impact on earnings of the timing of purchases] but only at the cost of an increase in complexity" [FASB, 1978, p. 35]. If "complexity" refers to the difficulty in measuring replacement costs accurately, then the Board appears to be attacking the logic of the concept on the grounds that measurement techniques would be too complex. This criticism is hardly fair to the concept. The cost of increased complexities in measurement should be weighed against the potential benefits from more accurate measurements (such as reflecting efficient buying practices in income).

Ijiri, Y., *The Foundations of Accounting Measurement* (Prentice-Hall, 1967).

Institute of Chartered Accountants in Australia and Australian Society of Accountants, Explanatory Statement, "The Basis of Current Cost Accounting" (Issued October 1976; Amended August 1978).

Prakash, P., and Sunder, S., "The Case Against Separation of Current Operating Profit and Holding Gain," *The Accounting Review* (January 1979), pp. 1–22.

Revsine, L., "On the Correspondence Between Replacement-Cost Income and Economic Income," *The Accounting Review* (July 1970), pp. 513–523.

Revsine, L., "Surrogates in Income Theory: A Comment," *The Accounting Review* (January 1976), pp. 156–159.

Sandilands, F. E. P. (Chairman), Inflation Accounting Committee, *Inflation Accounting* (London, Her Majesty's Stationery Office, 1975).

Sprouse, R. T. and M. Moonitz, "A Tentative Set of Broad Accounting Principles for Business Enterprises," *Accounting Research Study No. 3* (American Institute of Certified Public Accountants, 1962).

Sweeney, H., "Capital," *The Accounting Review* (September 1933), pp. 185–199.

Zeff, S. A., "Replacement Cost: Member of the Family, Welcome Guest, or Intruder?," *The Accounting Review* (October 1962), pp. 611–625.

III-D/EXIT VALUES

Decision Oriented Financial Accounting

ROBERT R. STERLING

I. INTRODUCTION

The purpose of this paper is to consider the various measures (valuation methods) of wealth and income that have been proposed in the recent literature. A prerequisite to the consideration of that issue is the development of criteria by which the various measures are to be judged. I will review some of the major conflicts that have arisen about the criteria, state my reasons for selecting an overriding criterion and then attempt to show how that criterion can be applied.

II. CONFLICTING OBJECTIVES

There are conflicting viewpoints about the objective of accounting reports. This conflict is rather difficult to detect. One must look closely for it. Almost all the literature on accounting states that accounting reports must be 'useful' or that accounting is a 'utilitarian art'. It seems that we all agree that the objective of accounting is to provide useful information. However, we discover conflicts when we examine the remainder of the 'basic concepts' of accounting. Consider the requirement that accounting data be objective and verifiable. It is possible for a measure to be useful even though it is not objective and verifiable. Thus, a conflict arises: Should we accountants provide useful data even if it is not objective, or should we provide objective data even if it is not useful?

There are many other conflicts. The particular terms that are used depend upon the author that one is reading. In regard to income, many authors begin their discussion with a remark about the need for providing useful information, but then they switch their attention to the realisation convention. It is possible that realised income is not the most useful measure of income. Thus, there is a conflict between realisation and usefulness. Other authors speak of the need to be conservative, and since it is possible for the most useful measure to be liberal, there is a conflict between conservatism and usefulness. Other authors note that a particular measure would violate the going concern assumption and reject the measure on those grounds without regard to the usefulness of that measure. And so forth for most of the other concepts of accounting. Each one of them may be set off against the notion of usefulness and be seen to be in conflict with it at some point.

Given the conflicts, we must decide which of the concepts is to be the overriding criterion. If we simply pay lip service to the notion of usefulness by allowing it to be constrained by all of these other concepts, then we are in fact

Robert R. Sterling, "Decision Oriented Financial Accounting," *Accounting and Business Research*, Summer 1972, pp. 198–208. Reprinted by permission of the author and *Accounting and Business Research*.

denying the criterion of usefulness. Of course, if we can have our measures meet all of these requirements, then we are in the happy position of having no conflicts. The unfortunate fact is that they often are conflicting and we must decide which is the overriding criterion.

I think the overriding criterion should be usefulness. The other concepts are important but they are secondary. If, in order to make a decision, someone needs a measure of a particular property, then a rough guess at the magnitude of that property is useful. Of course, a precise, objective measure of that property is *more* useful, but the converse does not hold. If one does not need to know the magnitude of a particular property, then a measure of that property is useless no matter how precise and objective it may be.

Thus, I view accounting as a measurement-communication activity with the objective of providing useful information. Once we have discovered which properties are useful, then we must devise methods of measuring those properties. Hopefully, we can devise measurement methods which fulfil the requirements of objectivity, verifiability, etc. However, these requirements are secondary. They are desirable, but usefulness is indispensable. Therefore, providing useful information must be the primary objective of accounting.

III. CONFLICTING DEFINITIONS OF USEFULNESS

Problems arise whenever we attempt to define the concept of usefulness. Like other hortatory concepts (e.g. truth, justice, fairness) everyone is in favour of usefulness in the abstract. All of us agree with Spacek's postulate of fairness. Who could speak out in favour of being unfair? The difficulty is in defining fairness. In the same way, the difficulty with 'usefulness' is in making its meaning precise enough to be applicable to a concrete situation. In an attempt to be more precise, I have in previous works[1] replaced 'usefulness' with 'relevance'.

The dictionary defines 'relevant' as 'bearing upon or relating to the matter in hand'. This is what I mean by 'relevant information', except that I substitute 'decision model' for 'matter in hand'. In the same way that one cannot determine what is relevant to the matter in hand without being aware of the matter in hand, I cannot determine what is relevant information without being aware of the decision model. One of the characteristics of a well defined decision model is that it will specify the measurement (or estimation) of certain properties. This allows my definition of relevance to be simple and straight-forward:

> If a property is specified by a decision model, then a measure of that property is relevant (to that decision model). If a property is not specified by a decision model, then a measure of that property is irrelevant (to that decision model).

One conflict that has arisen is concerned with that definition. Several people have argued that we should focus on decision *makers* instead of decision *models*. They say that if decision makers want to know the measure of a particular property, then that property is relevant or useful. Some of them have run tests

[1]Robert R. Sterling, *Theory of the Measurement of Enterprise Income* (The University Press of Kansas, 1970), pp. 50, 132, 354, *et passim* and 'On Theory Construction and Verification', *The Accounting Review*, July 1970, p. 454.

designed to determine whether or not people (decision makers) use certain kinds of accounting data. When they found a certain kind of data being *used*, they concluded that this data was *useful*. They argue that we should supply the decision makers with the kind of data that they want and that this is the end of the question of relevance.

At first glance this view is rather appealing. In the same way that we give the voter and consumer a free choice, so the argument goes, we should give the decision maker a free choice. Thus, the argument is stated in terms of democracy or consumer sovereignty, and it is difficult for anyone to be against democracy. At the risk of making you think that I am a dictator, let me briefly outline my reasons for being opposed to this view.

(1) In the present system, the decision maker can either use the accounting reports that we give him or make his decision in the absence of that information. His choice is to use or not use our data. There is no third alternative.[2] If we were to adopt my suggestions for changing the kind of data to be included in accounting reports, the decision maker would have the same choice. Therefore, the adoption of my suggestions would be equally as 'democratic' as the present system. The only difference would be in the kind of data being reported.

(2) Decision makers are a diverse lot. They make their decisions on a wide variety of different bases. We have all heard about people who trade the market on the basis of astrological signs or arthritic pain. 'Technical analysts' on Wall Street trade the market on the basis of the 'flags', 'heads and shoulders' and 'double bottoms' they see in their charts. Given this diversity, it is an economic, if not a physical, impossibility for us to supply *all* the information that *all* decision makers want. Therefore, we must select and in the process of selection, we will fail to satisfy the wants of some decision makers. What we are arguing about then is the *basis* for selection.[3]

(3) The basis for selection that I prefer is to supply information for rational decision models. The modifier 'rational' is defined to mean those decision models that are most likely to allow decision makers to achieve their goals. Since I don't believe that astrology allows people to achieve their stated goals, I am not interested in supplying them with an astrology report even though they use that kind of information in trading the market. For the same reason, I am not interested in supplying de-

[2]This is the basis for a technical criticism of the tests that have been run to see if decision makers use accounting data. Most experiments require a 'control' of some kind. The tests would have more force if the decision makers were offered a choice between using accounting data and using some kind of control data. To put it another way, suppose we ran a test in which decision makers could choose either (1) zero information or (2) x information. I suspect that the decision makers would choose x information. A more powerful test would be to offer them the choice between x and y information.

[3]Section II was, in effect, an argument about the basis for selection. That is, it was an argument against excluding data on grounds of objectivity, realisation, etc. Thus, accountants are *now* being selective in the kind of data that they report. Indeed, they must be selective since no information system can report everything. The pertinent grounds for argument then must be the basis for selection and it is impertinent—the commission of the fallacy of alleging a non-existent difference—to argue on the grounds that one information system is selective (dictatorial) and another is not.

cision makers with some of the kinds of data now being included in accounting reports even though they use that data.

The above is only a rough sketch of the conflict. I have gone into some other aspects of the problem elsewhere.[4] Although there are a good many scattered remarks in opposition to this view, insofar as I know, there is only one article devoted exclusively to the problem.[5] As I have said before,[6] I believe that the proponents of the decision maker view have overlooked the distinction between pragmatic and semantic information. Pragmatic information is defined by the receivers' reaction to the report. For example, if I yelled 'Fire' and all of you ran to the exits, my report would be said to contain pragmatic informational content. Semantic informational content is concerned with the connection of reports to objects and events. For example, if there were a fire, my report would be said to contain semantic informational content. If there were no fire, it is semantic misinformation, or in plain English, a lie. Note that the two kinds of information are separable and that one kind does not imply anything about the other. Of course, we accountants know this from harsh experience. Everybody agrees that decision makers used the McKesson-Robbins financial statements and therefore there was pragmatic informational content. The problem was the absence of the inventory and therefore the presence of semantic misinformation.

Although many of my critics agree in principle with the decision model approach, they throw up their hands in despair at the prospect of trying to apply it. There are a great many different kinds of decision models, e.g. EOQ, PERT, Linear Programming, Capital Budgeting, etc. Such decision models are applicable to only certain kinds of decisions, e.g. inventory ordering, scheduling, allocations, investments, etc. In addition, there are a great many choice criteria that are used in reaching decisions, e.g. minimax, maximin, Hurwicz, least regret, etc. Thus, we have a great variety of decision models applicable to a variety of decision situations with a variety of proposed criteria. It appears to be impossible to set up a general information system or to design a set of general purpose financial statements which would meet the requirements of all these models. An even more difficult problem arises whenever we encounter decision situations for which there is no well defined decision model.[7]

The trick is to generalise—to try to capture the elements that are common to all decisions. Although such a generalisation, like all other generalisations, leaves out many important details, it allows us to get a handle on the problem. Let me attempt such a generalisation. All decision models require information about:

1. Alternatives $= A = \{a_1, a_2, \ldots, a_n\}$
2. Consequences $= C = \{c_1, c_2, \ldots, c_n\}$
3. Preferences $= P = a$ function for ordering consequences.

[4] Sterling, *Enterprise Income*, pp. 54–61.

[5] A. Rashad Abdel-khalik, 'User Preference Ordering Value: A Model', *The Accounting Review*, July 1971, pp. 457–71.

[6] Sterling, 'Theory Construction', p. 453.

[7] See Robert R. Sterling, 'A Statement of Basic Accounting Theory; A Review Article', *Journal of Accounting Research*, Spring 1967, p. 107.

Alternatives (or possible courses of action) must be presently feasible. There is no point in choosing a course of action that is not feasible. One may plan what he will do if and when an alternative becomes feasible or he may ruminate about past alternatives, but the choice is always restricted to the alternatives that are feasible at the time of the decision—the present. The alternatives must be competing in the sense that the selection of one obviates the selection of the other, and hopefully, the list would completely specify all alternatives. If alternatives are not competing, then no decision is required. One need not choose between x and y if one can select both x and y. If the list is not complete, then one may not know about the existence of a preferred alternative. Thus, a decision maker is faced with a set of alternatives, the elements of which are mutually exclusive and exhaustive. The decision maker may contemplate a broad range of possible courses of action but he must select from 'alternatives'—those courses of action that are available to the decision makers at the moment of choice.

Consequences (or outcomes or payoffs) of the alternatives lie in the future. They must be predicted. The consequences may be stated in terms of certain uncontrollable events, and then probabilities assigned to the uncontrollable events. For example, one can predict that if a_i is selected the consequence will be c_i^1 if event x_1 occurs, c_i^2 if event x_2 occurs, etc. By assigning probabilities to events, $x_1, x_2, \ldots$ and aggregating $c^1, c_i^2, \ldots$ one can speak of 'the' consequence, c_i, associated with a_i.

Preferences are personal. Even though different decision makers are faced with the same alternatives and they predict the same consequences, they may make different decisions. This may come about from different assignments of probabilities or different choice criteria of different utility functions or simply the inexplicable choice of the decision maker. I include such things under the category of 'preferences' and in the present state of the art they are 'matters of taste' that are personal to the decision maker. Given the one to one correspondence of alternatives and consequences, the preference for a given consequence uniquely determines the alternative to be selected.

A summary of the decision process is shown in Figure 1.

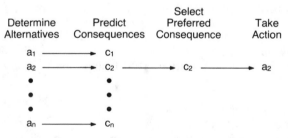

FIGURE 1
The Decision Process

Decision models are abstractions which are separate and apart from decision makers. For example, the EOQ model is an idea which can be thought about separately from the persons who hold or use that idea. It is the decision *model* that requires information about alternatives, consequences and preferences. The decision maker can be thought of as a supplier of information to the decision model. Consider Figure 2.

The accounting system is also a supplier of information, but it is not necessary for it to supply all of the information required by the model. In non-feedback situations, such as providing financial statements to investors, it is impossible for the accounting system to provide information about the preferences of the decision makers. Since the decision makers already know their preferences, the point may seem to be unimportant. However, there are many accountants who have become bogged down in their efforts to design an information system because they were unable to specify the decision maker's utility function or because there were several different decision makers with different utility functions. If we view the decision maker as the supplier of this kind of information to the decision model, then this problem is by-passed, if not solved. The accounting system could then concentrate on supplying information which would aid in defining alternatives and predicting consequences.

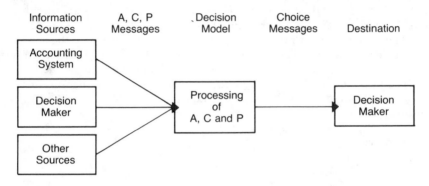

FIGURE 2
Information System

In summary, an accounting system should be designed to provide relevant information to rational decision models. The accounting system cannot supply all the information desired by all decision makers and therefore, we must decide to exclude some kinds of information and to include other kinds. Restricting the decision models to rational ones permits the exclusion of a raft of data based upon the whims of decision makers. It permits us to concentrate on those models that have been demonstrated to be effective in achieving the decision makers' goals. Information specified by decision models may be classified as alternatives, consequences and preferences. Excluding information about preferences, on the grounds that the decision makers already possess this information, permits us to concentrate on supplying information concerning the definition of feasible alternatives and the prediction of consequences.

IV. CONFLICTING VALUATION METHODS

Although we sometimes attempt to separate the question of how to value assets from the question of how to measure income, the two are, in fact, inextricably entwined. This is indicated by the fact that we often say that our financial statements 'articulate'. It is even clearer whenever we consider the basic accounting equation.

(1) $$A = L + P$$

Almost every elementary accounting textbook has a problem which is concerned with the determination of income by utilising this equation. They assign a time index (t_i) and state the proprietorship as a residual.

(2) $$A(t_i) - L(t_i) = P(t_i)$$

Then the income (neglecting investment and disinvestment) for the period t_i to t_{i+1} is given by (3).

(3) $$P(t_{i+1}) - P(t_i) = Y$$

It is obvious that if the assets take on different values, then the income for the period will take on different values. For example, a switch from straight-line to accelerated depreciation or from FIFO to LIFO will affect both the reported asset values and the reported income. The same is true if we state the assets at their historical cost as opposed to, say, current market value. Thus, when one talks about different methods of valuation, and the conflicts between them, then one is also at the same time talking about conflicts in income measurement.

There are four major valuation methods that have been proposed in the literature:

(1) historical cost (HC),
(2) replacement cost (RC),
(3) exit values (EV), and
(4) discounted cash flows (DCF).

Some people have argued that price-level adjusted historical costs should be listed as a fifth valuation method. However, one could adjust each of the above methods for changes in price-levels and thereby add a total of four more methods. I am in favour of price-level adjustments, but I think that the selection of a valuation method is a separate problem. We must first select the valuation method(s) and *then* we can consider the necessary adjustment for price-level changes. Therefore, I will neglect the problems of price-level adjustments in this paper and concentrate on specific price changes.

The incomes that result from applying these valuation methods have been called

(1) realised income,
(2) business income
(3) realisable income, and
(4) economic income.

All of these names are somewhat inaccurate. Some economists would say that 'realisable income' is 'economic income' and therefore, they would object to the names that we have used. 'Historical cost' is somewhat inaccurate in that there are many assets on the balance sheet that are not valued at cost, e.g. cash and accounts receivable. 'Realised income' is somewhat inaccurate as, for example, when the percentage of completion method of revenue realisation is used. In addition, these methods sometimes borrow from one another. For example, HC sometimes uses DCF in accounting for bonds or notes. In the same way, some of the authors who propose, say, EV will occasionally revert to either RC or HC. Thus, none of the methods are pure. Finally, there are different procedures within each of the methods. Just as income may be calculated by using either LIFO or FIFO, and both of them referred to as 'realised income', there are different procedures within the other methods. I will not attempt to discuss all of these exceptions and differences; instead, I will concentrate on describing the major differences among the methods.

All four valuation methods use a price of some kind as the basis for valuing, but each method endorses a different price. The endorsed prices differ by their temporal location and by the market in which they are found. Both HC and RC use the prices found in the purchasing market. They differ only in the temporal location of those prices. A past (time of purchase) price is used in HC while a present (time of statement preparation) price is used in RC. Thus, except for the temporal location of the prices, RC is identical to HC. EV, by contrast, focuses on the present (time of statement preparation) prices in the selling market. EV is similar, but not identical, to the 'net realisable values' used in HC in applying the lower of cost or market rule to inventories.

DCF uses both purchase and selling prices, but it focuses on the future—the prices that will be in effect at the time of future exchanges. DCF is similar to the 'present value method' of accounting for bonds used in HC. In DCF the cash receipts from the future sale of the products and the cash expenditures for the future purchase of the factors of production are predicted and then discounted to get 'present value' or 'present worth'. Hereafter, I will substitute 'discounted value' for 'present worth' to avoid confusion.

These differences are summarised in the following matrix.

Time / Market	Past (Purchase)	Present (Statement Preparation)	Future (Exchange)
Purchasing	HC	RC	DCF
Selling		EV	DCF

The differences in income may also be described in general terms. The revenues (asset inflows from sales) would be the same for all four methods, but the amount charged to expense would differ considerably. We all know how the allocations are made in HC. RC uses the same allocation techniques, but it costs out the quantities at their current purchase prices. The argument is that we should match current costs with current revenues and thus the line of reasoning is the same as that of many LIFO proponents. However, unlike LIFO, RC also uses current purchase prices on the balance sheet which results in including 'holding gains' (also called 'cost savings') in income. EV looks to the market to determine the expenses. Initially, the expense is the difference between the purchase price and the exit value at the date of statement preparation. Subsequently, it is the difference in the exit values at two statement preparation dates. Both HC and RC are *allocations* (amortisations) of a purchase price on the basis of use or sale or passage of time. EV attempts to avoid the allocation problem by going to the market to determine how much the asset could be sold for. The decrease (increase) in the amount it could be sold for is the amount of the cost (gain) of using or holding that asset.

DCF recognises a gain at purchase equal to the difference between the discounted value of the products produced by the acquired asset and the face value of the cash sacrificed. The amount of the subsequent income is simply the interest earned (the interest rate times the discounted value) in exactly the same way that interest income is the yield rate times the discounted value of bonds receivable in HC. Adjustments are required in DCF whenever events are different from those predicted. These adjustments present problems similar to those encountered in HC when, say, the actual life of an asset is different from its predicted life.

There are many arguments in favour of and in opposition to all of these valuation methods. However, the proponents of the various schools rely most heavily on the usefulness or relevance criterion. Each school claims that its particular valuation method would be more useful than the others. For this reason, and also because I believe that usefulness should be the overriding criterion, I will ignore the other criteria and try to select the appropriate valuation method by applying the criterion of relevance.

V. APPLICATION OF RELEVANCE CRITERION TO MARKET DECISIONS

Although there are a good many decisions that do not involve a market exchange, in a market economy such as ours probably a majority of decisions are concerned with whether or not to make an exchange in the market. The market operates with prices, and since the conflicting valuation methods differ mainly in their endorsement of certain prices, a general consideration of prices and market decisions is pertinent to the conflict.

Market Alternatives

The market alternatives that are available to any person or any firm depend upon two factors:

(1) The funds that are currently available to invest in the contemplated project.
(2) The magnitude of the investment required to engage in the contemplated project.

Specifically, the funds available for a given project must be greater than or equal to the investment required for that project. Otherwise, that project is not a feasible market alternative.

Although this point is obvious, I wanted to make it explicit in order to demonstrate that 'profitability' is *not* the first nor the sole criterion for selecting projects. There are many projects which I think would be very profitable, but I cannot undertake them because my available funds are less than the required investment. For example, I would like to purchase General Motors, but since my available funds are less than the purchase price this is not a feasible alternative for me.

Market Consequences

The market consequences of undertaking a given project are the future cash flows that result from that project. There may be non-market consequences which the decision maker should consider (e.g. one may be sent to jail for engaging in an illegal project or one may get satisfaction from beating the competition), but I will concentrate on the market consequences. Since these cash flows lie in the future, they must be predicted.

Preferences

The decision maker is faced with an array of future cash flow magnitudes. He must select one of those magnitudes by applying his personal preference function. He may do this by converting the money magnitudes to utility magnitudes, assigning subjective probabilities to the flows under varying conditions, and utilising one of the various choice criteria. Such information is to be supplied to the decision model by the decision maker because it is a matter of personal preference.

In addition, the discount rate should be supplied by the decision maker because each decision maker is likely to have different needs for liquidity and different views on the time value of money. That is, people are likely to have different 'reservation rates' and these rates are likely to be different from the cost of capital rate of the firm. For this reason, I will distinguish 'future cash flows' (FCF) and 'discounted cash flows' (DCF) henceforth.

After appropriate adjustment for risk, I would select the project with the largest cash flows. That is, I am a maximiser. However, that is a personal preference and there may be some who have different preferences. The above discussion does *not* depend upon the assumption of profit or wealth maximisation for its validity. If one wants to minimise he can be a more efficient minimiser by following this general outline for decisions.[8]

The main point about preferences is that, as before, they are to be supplied to the decision model by the decision maker. Therefore, in the following discussion I will concentrate on supplying information about alternatives and consequences.

Price Interpretation

The market alternatives and consequences have been defined and the preferences have been left to the decision makers. It is now necessary to give these alternatives and consequences a price interpretation. Recall that the market

---

[8]This point should be underscored because several people have criticised my previous works for assuming profit maximisation or postulating an economic man. In the above classification scheme, the goal of the decision maker is included in the category of preferences. A maximiser's preferences will cause him to select a consequence different from the one selected by a minimiser. A satisficer will cease searching for additional alternatives whenever he has found a satisfactory consequence. Regardless of the goal, an accounting system which provided information about alternatives and consequences would aid all the decision maker in achieving that goal. Of course, decision models are not usually designed to minimise, but that is simply an indication that few people are minimisers and that most minimisation problems are trivial. For example, a linear programming model could be used to search for the lowest profit-highest cost solution by simply altering the objective function, but a minimiser could more easily achieve his goal by considering the consequences of selling his product at a negative price or by burning his plant.

alternatives depend upon the available funds and the required investment. In turn, the available funds depend upon:

(1) The present selling prices of all assets held, including the 'selling price' of cash.
(2) The ability to borrow.
(3) The ability to raise equity capital.

I will consider (2) and (3) *infra*. In regard to (1), note that the present selling prices are the only prices relevant to defining the available funds. Past prices are irrelevant, because they are no longer obtainable and future prices will be relevant to defining future alternatives, but they are irrelevant to defining the current alternatives. Purchase prices are obviously irrelevant if one is trying to determine how much cash he can get if he sells.

The required investment is given by:

(1) The present purchase price of assets *not* held.
(2) The present selling prices of assets held.

Obviously, if one is contemplating the purchase of an asset, then the present purchase price of that asset is relevant to the determination of whether or not the alternative is feasible. The investment required for maintaining the status quo, however, is given by the selling prices of the assets held. Since the individual or firm already holds the assets necessary to maintain the status quo, then there is no need to contemplate their purchase. Instead, the (implicit) required investment is the amount of cash that one could get if one sold those assets. That is, the decision not to disinvest is structurally identical to the decision to invest, and therefore, the required investment for continuing the status quo is the amount of cash that was not received by not disinvesting.

The future cash flows require a prediction of the future selling prices of the outputs of the project as well as the quantities that will be sold. The future selling prices of the inputs are also relevant. That is, the salvage values of productive assets at the termination or abandonment of a project are future cash inflows and are, therefore, relevant. If a project requires future replacement of productive assets or the purchase of the factors of production, then the future purchasing prices of the inputs are also relevant.

The decision requires the comparison of the future cash flows of each project. Other things equal, the decision maker can make his selection by scanning the array of future cash flows and applying his preference function. However, in this case other things are seldom equal. Usually, the required investments are not of equal magnitude. If the projects have unequal required investments, it is not possible to make a rational decision by considering only their future cash flows. One project may have large cash flows but an even larger required investment. A common method of overcoming this difficulty is to calculate the rate of return on the required investment and then compare the rates of return. Note that this method is a comparison of the required investment to the future cash flows, i.e. rate of return is the time adjusted quotient of the future cash flows and required investment. In general, whenever required investments are not equal one needs to compare the required investment to the future cash flows.

The above is simply a generalisation of the capital budgeting model, absent an explicit consideration of discounting. The capital budgeting model specifies the prediction of future cash inflows and outflows, and then the time adjusted net flows of the various projects are compared to one another or to the required investment. Since the capital budgeting model is usually applied to new projects, we tend to forget that it is also applicable to existing projects. Sometimes our predictions are wrong and sometimes we change our predictions after initiating a project. For this reason, existing projects should be re-evaluated periodically. In this re-evaluation, the decision model specifies a comparison of the *updated* prediction of cash flows to the *present* required investment. That required investment is given by the selling prices of assets held. Obviously, if one wishes to maximise, he should discontinue a project and sell the assets if the future cash flows are less than the sum of the selling prices. Just as in the case of a new project, a maximiser should not commit the required investment if it is greater than the predicted cash flows. In the case of an existing project, the required investment is the sum of the present selling prices of the assets.

In summary, a rational market decision model specifies the following prices:

(1) The present selling prices of all assets held because
   (a) when compared to (2), they define the feasible market alternatives, and
   (b) they completely define the investment required to maintain the status quo.
(2) The present purchase prices of all assets not held because
   (a) when compared to (1), they define the feasible market alternatives, and
   (b) they completely define the investment required for new projects.
(3) The future purchase and selling prices associated with a given alternative because when compared to the required investment [(1b) or (2b)], they permit a rational decision.

Creditor and Investor Market Decision Models

The above analysis is general. In addition to managerial decision models it is also applicable to creditor and investor decision models. Each creditor and investor must determine the feasible alternatives by comparing the available funds to the required investments. The available funds are defined, as before, by the selling prices of the assets held (by the creditor-investor) and the ability to borrow or raise equity capital. That is, investors borrow and creditors issue equity shares, and therefore, the funds available to them are determined in exactly the same way as outlined above. The required investment for new projects is the amount of the loan application or the present purchase price of the stock. For existing projects, the required investment is the present selling price of the debt or equity instrument.

The creditor-investor decision model also calls for a comparison of the required investment to the future cash flows. In this case, the future 'selling prices' of the 'output' is the interest or dividends. The 'salvage value' is the maturity or liquidation value of the instrument. Since the project may be abandoned or aborted prior to the maturation of the debt or liquidation of the firm, the salvage value may be a future selling price of the instrument.

In short, the investor-creditor decision model specifies exactly the same prices as those given above. However, these prices refer to assets held *by the creditor-investor* and to the various prices *of the debt-equity instrument.* Strictly speaking, this is *all* that the creditor-investor needs to know. That is, after an investor has narrowed the stocks down to those that are feasible alternatives, the only thing he needs to know is their purchase prices and their future selling prices (including dividends) *in the stock market.* He can then compare and make his choice(s).

If the creditor-investor can predict these future prices without regard to the operations of the individual or firm to whom he is lending-investing, then we need go no further with this analysis. Many investors do not look beyond the securities market when they make such predictions. They act as if the price fluctuations in the stock market were completely independent of the economic fluctuations of the firms that issue the stock. If this is true, then the stock market is simply a lottery with no underlying economic meaning, and we accountants should quit wasting our time and paper by issuing financial statements. Instead, we should draw the income numbers out of a hat and thereby determine who has won and lost. However, I, personally, am not interested in the stock market qua lottery. I believe that stock prices (as well as dividends, interest and ability to repay loans) do in fact depend upon the economic conditions of the firms. Moreover, I believe that stock prices *ought* to depend upon the economic conditions of the firms and that if we accountants supplied better information about the firms, the stock prices would conform more closely to those conditions. In short, I believe that a well designed investor-creditor decision model should specify information about the states and operations of the firms. I am not trying to dictate to investors. If they want to trade the market by 'reading the tape', then that is their business. If they can be successful on that basis, then more power to them. However, I believe that information about the firms should be available to investors, whether they use it or not. For all these reasons, I will concentrate upon the information specified by a rational creditor-investor decision model and assume that other information about the market will be supplied from non-accounting sources.

Future cash flows of the firm. The ability of a firm to service a debt, pay dividends or simply to survive depend upon its future cash flows. Thus, the future cash flows of a debt-equity instrument depend upon the future cash flows of the firm. It follows that the future cash flows of the firm are relevant to the creditor-investor.[9] The creditor-investor may make his own predictions of the flows or be supplied those predictions by someone else. The predictor may assign probabilities to the completion of the project and the abandonment of the project and predict the cash flows under both conditions. Many other refinements of this kind could be listed. The only point that I want to make is that the future cash flows of the firm are relevant to the investor-creditor, because the future flows of debt-equity instruments depend upon them.

I would urge that the prediction of the future cash flows used by the creditor-investor be independent of the prediction made by the management. This is not

[9]Again, there are many other factors that are relevant, such as the 'character' of debtors and the 'resilience' and 'ingenuity' of management. However, I will focus on the more immediate market factors.

to impugn the honesty of managements, but rather to note that managements are likely to be optimistic about their own projects. If they were not, they would not have proposed them. Thus, an independent prediction is called for. This means that, as a minimum, the creditor-investor needs to know *which* projects are planned by management. Then, the creditor-investor (or his agent) can independently assess the probability of success and independently predict the future purchase and selling prices of the project, as well as applying his personal discount rate.

Selling prices of firm assets. Whenever someone lends, invests or purchases, he is acquiring some value that exists now as well as some values that are predicted to exist in the near and distant future. The presently existing values can vary from zero to 100 per cent of the purchase price. For example, if I 'purchase' a ten dollar bill with two fives, then the presently existing value of the ten is 100 per cent of the purchase price. Moreover, the ten will not increase in value in the future. On the other hand, if I grubstake a miner in return for a share of his find, then the presently existing value is zero—*all* of the value that I have purchased lies in the future. That future value may be much greater than $10, or it may be zero. Obviously, grubstaking a miner is much riskier than purchasing a ten dollar bill. This risk relationship of the presently existing value to the purchase price is true in general. The smaller the presently existing value in relation to the purchase price, other things equal, the higher the risk.

This means that the present selling prices of the assets held (and the selling prices that will exist immediately after purchase) are relevant to the decision. Perhaps the point in regard to an investor can be made clear by considering mutual funds. Suppose you have the option to purchase one share of either the L or the N fund for $100. Now the managers of both funds would promise you the moon if the SEC would let them get by with it. Therefore, you ought to make an independent prediction of the future 'performance' of both funds. Suppose you predict that the selling prices x years from now will be $140 and $120 for the shares of the L and N funds, respectively. Without further analysis, you can make your selection. If you are a maximiser, you will select the L fund. However, let me add two facts and then see if you agree that these facts should be specified by a well-designed decision model.

The L fund is a load fund and the amount of the load is $90. The N fund is a no-load fund. That is, the per share exit value[10] is $10 for the L fund and $100 for the N fund. Therefore, the value of the assets held by L must increase by 1,300 per cent to reach the predicted price while the increase required by N is only 20 per cent. Almost all of the value of L lies in the future while most of the value of N exists presently. Other things equal, L is a much riskier investment.

As many people have correctly pointed out, one should go ahead and buy a load fund if one thinks that it will out-perform a no-load fund by more than the amount of the load. However, the amount of the load is relevant to a well-designed decision model. This amount is determinable if the present selling prices of the assets held are disclosed.

---

[10]The sum of the present selling prices of the assets held by the fund less the liabilities divided by the number of shares outstanding.

There is also a 'load' or 'premium' on the price of the stock of industrial firms. The price of some stock is several hundred times its per share exit value. In such cases the purchased value lies almost wholly in the future. Other things equal, the greater the portion of the value that lies in the future the higher the risk. That is, if the firm does not perform in accordance with expectations the price of the stock is likely to drop drastically. By contrast, some stocks sell at a 'discount'—the price of the stock is less than its per share exit value. Closed-end funds, for example, often sell at a discount. The future price and dividends of discounted stock still depend upon the future cash flows of the firm, but, other things equal, it is much less risky. The value presently exists and therefore even if the firm liquidated immediately the investor would not lose. Indeed, he would profit.

Therefore, I conclude that the magnitude of the discount or premium is relevant to a well-designed decision model. That accountants know this is evidenced by their lower of cost or market rule. Although formally applicable only to inventories, it is also applied to a great many other assets. For example, I know of a case where the auditors insisted upon writing the value of land down to 'fair market value', even though they knew that this write-down would be likely to result in the liquidation of the firm. The land had been purchased at a price which reflected the expectation of mineral deposits which had failed to materialise. The auditors evidently thought that the 'fair market value' (exit value?) of this land was relevant to investors and creditors.

The problem is that this is a one-way rule. I know of another case where the stock of a retail chain is selling at about $10 per share. Based on its poor earnings, this is a reasonable price. That is, if it continues in the future as in the past, its future cash flows will be meagre and its reported income even less. However, this firm owns the land upon which its stores are built and the per share exit value of the land alone is conservatively estimated to be $40 per share. This land is carried on the balance sheet at its ancient historical cost of about 20¢ per share. I believe that the exit value of that land is equally as relevant in this case as in the above case.[11] If the *Gerstle* v. *Gamble* case[12] is taken as evidence, it appears that the SEC also believes that exit values are relevant to investors.

Although these cases are extreme, they illustrate the fact that the price of stock ought to depend upon the presently existing exit values of the firm as well as depending upon the future cash flows of the firm.

I have spoken only of investors above because creditors have long recognised the relevance of the selling prices of assets. They are usually willing to loan only at a discount. That is, if a particular asset is pledged, they are willing to loan only a fraction of that asset's selling price. If they are general creditors, they are willing to loan only a fraction of the conservative (lower of cost or market) value of the total assets. Of course, creditors also look to the future cash flows of firms, if for no other reason than that they would prefer to avoid the expense of foreclosure. However, the selling prices are also relevant to them and they explicitly recognise the risk relationship when they speak of the

---

[11] The only reason why I don't buy all the stock and liquidate the firm is that I lack the required investment of $10.00 per share for over two million shares.

[12] *Gerstle* v *Gamble-Skogmo*, 298 Federal Supplement 66 (1969).

amount of the discount or the amount of the net worth as providing a 'cushion of safety'.

VI. IMPLICATIONS FOR WEALTH AND INCOME MEASUREMENT

If the above analysis is correct and complete, then the implications are fairly straightforward. We noticed that

(a) Present selling prices (EV) of assets held by the firm,
(b) Present purchase prices (RC) of assets not held, and
(c) Future cash flows (FCF) of the firm are relevant to well-designed market decision models of managers, investors and creditors.

Conspicuous by their absence from this list are past purchase prices (HC). I do not find them specified by any market decision model, and therefore, I conclude that they are irrelevant. This is a conclusion that I have held for many years and one that I have spoken about and written about many times. On one occasion, I challenged all readers to demonstrate just one case where historical costs were relevant to economic decisions.[13] It has now been five years since that challenge was made, and no one has published a direct reply. Since then, several people have argued for historical cost on the grounds of objectivity, feasibility, etc. This is the reason why I said in Section II that there were conflicting views on the objectives of accounting. Other people have argued for historical costs because managers, creditors and investors do, in fact, use the financial statements that we give them. However, the fact that they use HC does not indicate that they would use HC if other information were supplied or that they ought to use them, in the sense that other information may be more likely to allow them to achieve their goals. This is the reason why I discussed the conflict between decision makers and decision models in Section III. If we really mean it when we say that accounting data should be useful or relevant, then we should demonstrate the relevance of HC or the superiority of HC to other valuation methods, and if we cannot do that, then we should abandon HC as a valuation method.

I exclude present purchase prices (RC) for a different reason. Present purchase prices of the assets *not* held are relevant to market decisions models. The source of information about these prices is the market itself, and they are already being supplied to management by the purchasing department. Financial statements report on assets held, and since present purchase prices are not relevant to assets held, they should not be used as a basis for the valuation of assets on financial statements.[14]

---

[13]Sterling, *ASOBAT Review*, p. 111.

[14]Future purchase prices of planned replacements and additions are also relevant since they are a component of FCF. Many people argue that income should be calculated on the basis of RC because it is a good predictor of FCF. This may or may not be true. It is an empirical question that cannot be settled here. It is important to note, however, that the claim of this argument is not that RC are relevant per se but rather that RC are good predictors of FCF. Note that this is my interpretation of the argument. It is usually stated that RC income is superior to other income concepts because it is a better predictor of future *RC income*. Using this reasoning, one could argue that straight-line depreciation is the superior depreciation concept because it is a perfect predictor of future straight-

Every decision requires a prediction of the future consequences of various alternatives. For this reason, if I thought it were possible, I would urge that accountants report future cash flows. Knowledge of the future is always the most valuable kind of information. The reason it is so valuable is that it is so scarce. We have no way of knowing what the future holds, and there are many conflicting views about it. The existence of these conflicting views of the future partially makes the market operate. Except for specialisation and liquidity requirements, there would be no market if buyers held the same view of the future as sellers. This is most obvious in the commodity markets, where there is a long for every short. The speculators hold diametrically opposed views of the future—the long (buyer) expects a price increase and the short (seller) expects a price decrease. One of them must be wrong. The same thing happens in varying degrees in other markets. Thus, differing predictions of the future are an inherent part of the operation of a market.

It is this difficulty which causes me to reject the notion that accountants ought to report FCF. First, we cannot report FCF, we can only report predictions of FCF. If we were perfect predictors, we would destroy the market, i.e. prices would be set equal to the discounted value of the future cash flows and, except for liquidity requirements and specialisation, no exchange would occur. For example, if we all had access to future issues of the *Wall Street Journal*, the price of every stock would be bid so as to equal the discounted value of the known future prices and dividends.[15]

Of course, we really needn't worry about destroying the market because it is not very likely that we will be perfect predictors. That is, accountants are, in the present state of the art, about as prone to err in predicting FCF as are decision makers. Thus, we have the choice of (1) not predicting or (2) presenting erroneous predictions. Erroneous predictions are not relevant to decision models. Indeed, they are likely to be harmful and, given the attitude of the courts about accountants' legal liability, this harm is likely to redound to accountants. For these reasons, I don't think that accountants should at this time report their predictions of FCF.[16] Since DCF is simply FCF discounted by a rate

line depreciation. Obviously, this is not what the RC proponents mean. I think they mean that business income is the superior concept because it is a good predictor of a relevant property (FCF), not that it is superior because it is a good predictor of itself.

[15]*Supra* I said that the reason that knowledge of the future is so valuable is that it is so scarce. Note that in this case, it would not be valuable because it is not scarce. That is, the price of exclusive access to future issues of the *Wall Street Journal* would be extremely high. However, when everyone has equal access, the price would probably be about the same as the price of today's issue.

[16]This leaves the predictions of FCF up to the decision makers. This presents no problem insofar as managements are concerned. A major part of managements' function is to try to peer into the future in order to select the preferred consequence. The problem is that the managements' decisions, based upon *their* predictions, affect the well being of the creditor-investor. Unless the creditor-investor is willing to rely solely upon the managements' predictions, he must make independent predictions. In order for the creditor-investor to make an independent prediction, he must know, at least in broad outline, the managements' plans. The budget is the most likely source of information about managerial plans. The creditor-investor can peruse this budget and then make (or have his agent make) a prediction of the future cash flows that will result. Therefore, I would urge that we include a partially audited management budget in our reports because it provides the basis for an independent prediction of the future cash flows.

and since different rates are appropriate for different decision makers, it follows *a fortiori* that DCF is not an acceptable method of measuring income and wealth.

We noted that selling prices (EV) were relevant to all three market decision models. They are necessary to define market alternatives, they express the investment required to hold assets and they are a component of a risk indicator. For all of these reasons, I conclude that the items on the balance sheet should be valued at their present selling prices. Since income is defined as the difference between wealth (net worth) at two points in time, it follows that the income statement would be an explanation of the changes in the exit values on two successive balance sheets.

Thus, I am not opposed to expanding the accounting function so that it includes information about expected futures. On the contrary, I think that we should provide all the relevant information that we can. However, I don't think that erroneous predictions are relevant. (This includes those erroneous predictions which are disguised as 'past' cost allocations in HC. Recall those costs capitalised because of the 'future benefits' expected from the Edsel, Cleopatra, TFX, supersonic transports, etc.) If we get to the point where our ability to predict is better than that of the decision makers, then I will argue that we ought to report our predictions. In the meantime, I think the best we can do is to supply information to decision makers which will aid them in making their predictions.

Relevant Financial Reporting in an Age of Price Changes

ROBERT R. STERLING

This article has the modest goal of clarifying the concept of price level adjustments. Since price level adjustments have been debated for a great many years, it may seem that the concept has previously been made quite clear. Perhaps so, but my reading of the recent literature, especially the testimony presented to the Financial Accounting Standards Board, persuades me that concept clarification is needed rather desperately. To put it negatively, I fear that if we take action on price levels—establish a standard—prior to further classification of the concept, we may make things worse instead of better.

A highly simplified case will be considered in this article. The advantages of simplified cases are that they are easily understood by both the reader and the author and they are more easily solved. If we cannot solve the simplified cases, then we can be fairly certain that we also cannot solve the complex cases. Thus, if a particular approach fails to provide a solution for simplified cases, then we can avoid wasting effort by trying that approach on complex cases. The main disadvantage of simplified cases is that even if we can solve them, there is no guarantee that the obtained solution can be extended to realistic cases. But the problem with realistic cases is that they are too complex to be easily understood or solved. I chose the simplified case in this article in the hope that the concept, once clarified, can be extended to more complex cases.[1]

THE NECESSITY OF CHOOSING ATTRIBUTES AND THE CRITERIA FOR CHOOSING

A measurement requires that one consciously decide which attribute is to be measured. Consider a physical object. It is impossible to measure that object; instead, one must decide which attribute (e.g., length, weight, hardness, color, density, carbon half-life, etc.) of that object is to be measured. The same is true

I am grateful for the support of Arthur Young & Company in the preparation of this article. The conclusions, however, are mine and do not necessarily reflect the views of Arthur Young & Company.

Robert R. Sterling, "Relevant Financial Reporting in an Age of Price Changes," *The Journal of Accountancy*, February 1975, pp. 42–51. Copyright © 1975 by the American Institute of Certified Public Accountants, Inc.

[1]The choice of a simplified case reflects my general feeling that we accountants often err by immediately tackling the complex cases. I think that one of the reasons we can't get more solutions (or more agreement) is that we try to run before learning to crawl. Compare the procedure in the sciences where they first study highly simple cases. As Nelson Goodman *Fact, Fiction, and Forecast* (New York: Bobbs-Merrill, 1965), p. xii, puts it:

for accounting measurements: we must decide which attribute is to be measured.[2]

The decision as to which attribute ought to be measured cannot be made on the basis of one's being "wrong" and the other's being "right." In regard to measuring a physical object, for example, one cannot say that it is wrong to measure the attribute of, say, length and right to measure the attribute of, say, weight. For some purposes, length is the relevant attribute and, for other purposes, weight is relevant. The same is true in accounting. We cannot say that unadjusted figures are wrong and adjusted figures are right. Instead, we must provide interpretations of the attributes that are being measured and then decide which one we ought to measure. The decision as to which attribute we ought to measure must be based on the relevance of the attributes, not on one's being wrong and the other's being right.

The interpretation of an attribute is related, but not identical, to its relevance. A thorough discussion of interpretation and relevance requires distinctions that cannot be drawn here. The reader interested in pursuing these notions should see May Brodbeck, especially the discussion of the significance of concepts,[3] or Carl G. Hempel, especially the discussion of the theoretical import of concepts.[4] For the purpose of this article, the following brief discussion will suffice.

Interpretation

When an attribute involves an arithmetical calculation, the "empirical interpretation" of that attribute requires that it be placed in an "if . . . then . . ." statement. For example, the attribute "area" is defined as the product of the length and width of a plane, i.e., $A = LW$. To repeat the definition of that attribute is not an empirical interpretation. Instead, an empirical interpretation would require a statement such as "if this space were to be covered with tiles of this size, then it would require x tiles" This "if . . . then . . ." statement provides the listener with an understanding of the meaning of "area" as well as demonstrating one of the uses of the concept.

". . . science has to isolate a few simple aspects of the world. . . . This, admittedly, is over-simplification. But conscious and cautious over-simplification, far from being an intellectual sin, is a prerequisite for investigation. We can hardly study at once all the ways in which everything is related to everything else."

By contrast, in accounting we seem to think that simplification is an intellectual sin. I think we would make more progress more rapidly if we took the roundabout route of examining simple cases before going on to the complex cases.

[2]Unfortunately, a single accounting term is often used to describe different attributes. It is clear, for example, that the income figure derived by using Fifo is different from the one derived by using Lifo, yet we refer to both as "income." Similarly, "price-level adjusted income" and "unadjusted income" are measures of different attributes despite the fact that both are called "income." The point is that it does not help to simply state that the attribute sought is "income" because that single term is used to refer to different attributes. Precise distinction of these attributes requires the use of different names—jargon—in this article.

[3]May Brodbeck, ed., *Readings in the Philosophy of the Social Sciences* (New York: Macmillan, 1968), pp. 6–9.

[4]Carl G. Hempel, *Fundamentals of Concept Formation in Empirical Science* (Chicago: University of Chicago Press, 1952), p. 46.

A counter example will show that the repetition of the definition does not aid in understanding the meaning of an attribute. I hereby define the attribute "ster" as the quotient of the length and width of a plane, i.e., $S = L/W$. If you were to ask me the meaning of that attribute, you would be justly disappointed if I simply repeated that it is the quotient of the length and width of a plane. Since "ster" cannot be inserted in an "if . . . then . . ." statement, it is not empirically interpretable and, therefore, it should be regarded with suspicion. We don't have any idea of the meaning or use of "ster" because we haven't been able to interpret it. We should be highly suspicious of attributes if we don't understand their meaning or use. We therefore arrive at Criterion 1: *Attributes must be interpretable.*

Relevance

Everyone agrees that accounting information should be useful. As with other abstractions (e.g., truth, justice, fairness), however, we run into difficulty when we try to apply the concept. In an attempt to be more precise, to make the concept more concrete, in previous works I have replaced the term "usefulness" with the term "relevance."[5] I define relevance as follows:

"If a decision model specifies an attribute as an input or as a calculation, then that attribute is relevant to that decision model."

The negation, of course, is that if the attribute is not specified by the model, then that attribute is not relevant to that model.

Consider, for example, the decision about which object one should select as a life raft. One needs to know which, if any, of the available objects will float on water. The decision model specifies two attributes (weight and volume) as inputs and one attribute (density, the quotient of weight and volume) as a calculation. Then it specifies that one compare the density of the object to the density of water. Indeed, the interpretation of the calculated attribute of density is "if object x is less dense than fluid y, then x will float on y." Thus, three attributes—weight, volume and density—are relevant to the model. All other attributes are irrelevant.[6]

As the example makes clear, relevance is concerned with what ought to be measured. If someone were to measure the area of the object, it would not be

[5]For example, see Robert R. Sterling, "Decision Oriented Financial Accounting," *Accounting and Business Research*, Summer 1973.

[6]Note the distinction between relevant to the decision *model* and relevant to the decision *maker*. Some decision makers may think that, say, area (instead of volume) is relevant to the decision. Others may think that color is relevant. Still others may think that a third attribute is relevant. Given a large number of decision makers, it would be impossible to supply measures of all of the attributes that all of them think are relevant. Moreover, all attributes other than weight, volume and density are of no help to the decision maker, despite the beliefs to the contrary.

The analogy fits accounting. We service a large number of decision makers (e.g., investors and potential investors), many of whom have demonstrably erroneous ideas about which attributes are relevant to their decisions. For example, despite the fact that the efficient market research has demonstrated that "technical analysis" (price charting) is of no use in trading the market, many investors and financial analysts still use it. Others use other attributes. It is impossible for us to supply measures of *all* the attributes that *all* investors think are relevant. Worse, such attributes are of no help in making the decision despite the fact that decision makers use them and think they are relevant. Hence, we must define relevance in relation to decision models, not decision makers.

wrong—it would simply be irrelevant to the decision. The area attribute meets the interpretability criterion, but it does not meet the relevance criterion. Applying this to accounting means that the selection of the attributes that we ought to measure and report requires that we examine the decision models and determine which attributes are specified by those models. Therefore we arrive at Criterion 2: *Attributes must be relevant.*

COMPLETE EXCHANGE CASE

Description of the Case

Consider the highly simplified problem of accounting for a trader on the New York Stock Exchange. The only activities of this simplified firm are the purchase and sale of securities in a near perfect market. To further simplify, assume that there are zero transaction (e.g., commission) costs and that all exchanges are for cash. There are no liabilities, which means that the total assets figure is equal to that of total owner's equity. In addition, assume that at the time of statement preparation all of the inventory has been sold so that the only asset on hand is cash.[7] Hence, there is only one asset—cash—to account for.

To simplify even further, assume that the only good that the trader consumes is bread, so that the Consumer Price Index is just the ratio of the prices of bread at two dates. Thus, there are only two real (nonmonetary) goods in this economy: securities (measured in shares) are the only producers' goods, and bread (measured in loaves) is the only consumers' good.

The facts of the case are that at January 1 the firm had $1,000 in cash. At the same date it purchased 100 shares for $10 per share. At February 1 the price has increased to $15 per share, and the entire inventory is sold. During the same period the price of bread increased from $.50 to $.60 per loaf, resulting in a Consumer Price Index of 1.2 (= $.60/$.50).

Measuring NOD

Exhibit 1, next page, shows the standard (unadjusted) financials for this firm. The interpretation is straightforward. The attribute being measured is number of dollars (NOD). The balance sheets report the stocks of NOD at two dates, and the income statement reports the increment in NOD during the period.

Many people assert that unadjusted financials, such as those in Exhibit 1, are "wrong." Accompanying this assertion are a variety of comments about "changing purchasing power," "changing value of the dollar," etc. Although many different terms are used to make the criticism, they all refer to the ability of dollars to command goods and services. It is true that the financials in Exhibit 1 do not measure command over goods (COG). However, it is equally true that those financials accurately measure NOD. Thus, the criticism cannot possibly

---

[7]This is what I mean by a "complete exchange." See Robert R. Sterling, *Theory of the Measurement of Enterprise Income* (Lawrence: University Press of Kansas, 1970), pp. 27–28, for further discussion. For a discussion of the related notion of "complete cycles," see *Objectives of Financial Statements*, a report of the Accounting Objectives Study Group, Robert M. Trueblood, chairman (New York: AICPA, 1973).

EXHIBIT 1
Measuring Number of Dollars

Complete exchange case

	Comparative Balance Sheets	
	January 1	February 1
Cash	$1,000	$1,500
Invested capital	$1,000	$1,000
Retained earnings	-0-	500
Total owner's equity	$1,000	$1,500

	Income Statement Month of January
Revenues	$1,500
Cost of securities sold	1,000
Net income	$ 50

be that the financials are "wrong," because they are quite correct. I believe that the critics intend to say that the financials do not measure the relevant attribute—the COG attribute.

I don't mean to quibble over words. However, I do want to be clear as to the source of the difficulty. If the objective is to measure NOD, then auditors must certify the financials in Exhibit 1. However, if we decide that the objective is to measure COG, then it is easy to demonstrate that those financials do not meet that objective. This is an important distinction. It shifts the basis of the argument from wrong vs. right to what we ought to measure and report. Consideration of what we ought to measure requires that we focus on the appropriate criterion—relevance.

It is axiomatic that money per se is not desirable. Rather, it is the ability of money to command real goods that is desired. Witness Confederate money. Measuring the stocks of or increments in Confederate money is irrelevant—no one is interested in the results of such measurements—precisely because that money has no ability to command goods. As the extreme case of Confederate money makes clear, measurements of NOD are not specified by decision models; hence, NOD is irrelevant. Instead, decision models specify the measurement of COG; thus, Proposition 1: *COG is the relevant attribute.*

Measuring COG

As the name makes clear, the command over goods (COG) attribute is a measure of the number of goods that could be commanded in the market. Since the goods that could be commanded are physical objects, COG is a physical measure. The measurement is accomplished by multiplying the monetary units by a price index. The purpose of such price level adjustments is to permit the adjusted monetary units to be interpreted as physical units. Economics and statistics textbooks state this point explicitly. Wallace C. Peterson, for example, writes, "If we adjust by the above price index, the result will be a measure of *physical output. . . ."*[8] To put it another way, if price level adjustments are done properly, then the resulting figures can be interpreted as a measure of physical units.

Recall that there is only one consumer good in this simple case and therefore the Consumer Price Index is the ratio of the prices of that good at the two dates. The price of bread was $.50 and $.60 at January 1 and February 1, respectively. Hence, the Consumer Price Index is 1.2 (= $.60/$.50). In order to convert the NOD attribute in Exhibit 1 to the COG attribute, we need only multiply each of the January 1 figures by 1.2. The result is shown in Exhibit 2, this page.

The point to be stressed is not the procedure, however, but rather the ability to interpret those figures. We can divide all of the figures in Exhibit 2 by the $.60 per loaf price of bread at February 1 and obtain the following interpretation:

- If all of the assets of the firm had been used to purchase bread at January 1, then 2,000 loaves (= $1,200/$.60) could have been purchased.
- If all of the assets of the firm had been used to purchase bread at February 1, then 2,500 loaves (= $1,500/$.60) could have been purchased.
- Hence, the increment (income) in COG is 500 loaves (= $300/$.60).

The figures can be interpreted; therefore, they meet the interpretability criterion. Indeed, in this simple case we could prepare financials in physical units as shown in Exhibit 3, next page. One can check the accuracy of these financials by using the unadjusted January 1 figures and dividing by the price per loaf at January 1. For example, the unadjusted cash on hand at January 1 was $1,000 and the price per loaf was $.50. Therefore, the firm could have

EXHIBIT 2
Measuring Command Over Goods in Price Level Adjusted Dollars

Complete exchange case

	Comparative Balance Sheets	
	Jan. 1	Feb. 1
Cash (January 1 = $1,000 × 1.2)	1,200	$1,500
Invested capital ($1,000 × 1.2)	$1,200	$1,200
Retained earnings	-0-	300
Total owner's equity	$1,200	$1,500
	Income Statement Month of January	
Revenues	$1,500	
Cost of securities sold ($1,000 × 1.2)	1,200	
Net income	$ 300	

[8]Wallace C. Peterson, *Income, Employment, and Economic Growth* (New York: W. W. Norton & Co., 1962), p. 68.

EXHIBIT 3
Measuring Command Over Goods in Physical Units

Complete exchange case

	Comparative Balance Sheets	
	January 1	February 1
Cash	2,000 loaves	2,500 loaves
Invested capital	2,000 loaves	2,000 loaves
Retained income	0 loaves	500 loaves
Total owner's equity	2,000 loaves	2,500 loaves

	Income Statement Month of January
Revenues	2,500 loaves
Cost of securities sold	2,000 loaves
Net income	500 loaves

commanded 2,000 loaves (= $1,000/$.50) at January 1. In addition, note that all of the ratios of the figures in Exhibit 3 are the same as those in Exhibit 2. For example, Exhibit 2 shows a $300 net income on sales of $1,500, a return on sales of 20 percent. Exhibit 3 shows a 500 loaf net income on sales of 2,500 loaves, a return of 20 percent.

Market basket interpretation. Interpretation of price level adjusted figures is usually more difficult because the price index is made up of a collection ("market basket") of goods. However, the concept is identical to the one-good index used in this simple case. To illustrate, consider a two-good, equally weighted index composed of bread and milk.

Assume prices of $.50 per loaf and $1 per gallon at January 1 and $.60 per loaf and $1.20 per gallon at February 1. Thus, the index is the same: ($.60 + $1.20/($.50 + $1) = 1.2.

The January 1 cash figure of $1,000 would be adjusted to the same $1,200 (= $1,000 × 1.2). The interpretation, however, requires the use of both goods with equal budget allocations. One-half of the adjusted $1,200 divided by $.60 per loaf and by $1.20 per gallon yields 1,000 loaves (= $600/$.60) and 500 gallons (= $600/$1.20). Thus the interpretation is:

- If all of the assets of the firm had been used to purchase bread and milk with equal budget allocations at January 1, then the firm would have been able to buy 1,000 loaves of bread and 500 gallons of milk.

With a two-good index the preparation of financials in physical units would be cumbersome. The addition of more goods to the index would make it even more cumbersome. However, the concept is the same. The price level adjustment converts a monetary measure into a physical measure. It allows one to interpret the figures as the number of physical units that could have been bought.

INCOMPLETE EXCHANGE CASE

Description of Case

The difference between the "incomplete exchange" and the "complete exchange" cases is that, in the former, some noncash assets are held; hence, some securities have been bought but, since they have not yet been sold, the exchange (or cycle from cash to cash) is said to be "incomplete." Assume that on January 1 the firm purchased 70 shares at $10 per share, leaving a cash balance of $300. No other transactions occur. The price of the securities has increased, as before, to $15 per share. Also, as before, the price of bread has increased from $.50 to $.60, resulting in a Consumer Price Index of 1.2.

Although this case is highly simplified, its consideration is complicated because there are four different proposed methods of accounting for it:

1 Historical cost.
2 Price level adjusted historical cost.
3 Current value.
4 Price level adjusted current value.

EXHIBIT 4
Unadjusted Historical Cost

Incomplete exchange case

| | Comparative Balance Sheets | |
	January 1	February 1
Cash	$300	$300
Securities	700	700
Total assets	$1,000	$1,000
Invested capital	$1,000	$1,000
Retained earnings	-0-	-0-
Total owner's equity	$1,000	$1,000

	Income Statement Month of January
Revenues	$ -0-
Cost of securities sold	-0-
Net income	$ -0-

Historical cost. The familiar historical cost financials are presented in Exhibit 4, this page. Despite the increase in the prices of both bread and securities, the February 1 figures are exactly the same as those at January 1. It seems to me that these financials do not meet the criteria.

First, I am unable to interpret the figures. I don't know how to place them in an "if . . . then . . ." statement. Thus, I don't think they meet the interpretability criterion. However, my inability to interpret them may be due to a deficiency in my thinking rather than a deficiency in the figures. Therefore, instead of concluding that they are not interpretable, I will challenge the readers to provide an interpretation.

Second, I have not been able to find decision models that specify the figures. Thus, I don't think they meet the relevance (or usefulness) criterion. Again, however, since I may have overlooked the decision models that specify these figures, I will challenge the readers to demonstrate their relevance rather than concluding that they are irrelevant.

Third, the figures clearly do not measure the COG attribute. There is no way to interpret them—prepare financials in physical units such as Exhibit 3— as measures of the ability to command goods.

Price level adjusted historical cost. A number of people have suggested— e.g., see Accounting Research Study No. 6[9]—that historical cost financials be adjusted by the following procedure:

1. Multiply the January 1 cash balance by the price index and take the difference between the adjusted January 1 balance and the unadjusted February 1 balance as a loss.
2. Multiply the January 1 securities cost by the price index and carry that adjusted figure forward to the February 1 balance sheet.

Financials adjusted by this procedure are shown in Exhibit 5, next page. The cash figures can be interpreted as follows:

- If the firm had used its cash at January 1 to purchase bread, then it could have purchased 600 loaves. (Adjusted cash of $360 divided by February 1 price per loaf of $.60 equals 600 loaves. Alternatively, the unadjusted cash of $300 divided by the January 1 price per loaf of $.50 equals 600 loaves.)
- If the firm had used its cash at February 1 to purchase bread, then it could have purchased 500 loaves (= $300/$.60).
- Hence, the loss from holding cash is $60 (= $360 − 300), which is equivalent to 100 loaves (= $60/$.60 and = 600 − 500).

Thus, the cash figures are (1) interpretable and (2) measurements of the relevant COG attribute. This is a major improvement over the unadjusted historical cost financials.

The problem lies with the figure for securities at February 1. First, I cannot find a true interpretation of the figure. I am not able to place it in an "if . . . then . . ." statement. Perhaps the figure is interpretable. Perhaps it is just that I don't know how to do it. For that reason, I will again challenge the readers to provide an interpretation rather than concluding that it is not interpretable.

Although I am not certain of the proper interpretation, I am certain that the figure cannot be interpreted as either NOD or COG:[10]

[9]Accounting Research Study No. 6 *Reporting the Financial Effects of Price Level Changes* (New York: AICPA, 1963), p. 11.

[10]It is possible to interpret the figures as a measure of both NOD and COG by making the contrary to fact assumption of proportional price changes.

EXHIBIT 5
Price Level Adjusted Historical Cost

Incomplete exchange case

	Comparative Balance Sheets	
	Jan. 1	Feb. 1
Cash (January 1 = $300 × 1.2)	$360	$300
Securities ($700 × 1.2)	840	840
Total assets	$1,200	$1,140
Invested capital ($1,000 × 1.2)	$1,200	$1,200
Retained earnings (deficit)	-0-	(60)
Total owner's equity	$1,200	$1,140

	Income Statement Month of January
Revenues	$ -0-
Cost of securities sold	-0-
	-0-
Loss in COG from holding cash ($360-$300)	60
Net income (loss)	$(60)

- If the securities were sold (or replaced) at February 1, then the NOD received (or required) would *not* be $840.

Thus, NOD cannot be the proper interpretation.

If the securities were sold (or replaced) at February 1 and *if price changes were proportional*, then the NOD received (or required) would be $840, which is equivalent to COG of 1,400 loaves (= $840/$.60).

The statement is false. Price changes were not proportional in the case under consideration. More importantly, they are not proportional in the real world. In fact, many changes are in opposite directions. For example, last year refined petroleum products went up 79.5 percent while animal feeds went down 26.5 percent, both of which are components of the Wholesale Price Index which went up 16.4 percent. Clearly then, we cannot assume proportional price changes any more than we can assume a stable measuring unit.

When writing *Enterprise Income* (p. 347), it occurred to me that since price level adjusted historical costs were interpretable if all price changes were proportional, perhaps the proponents had implicitly assumed proportional price changes. I rejected the idea, however, because the assumption was contrary to fact. That the proponents were implicitly assuming proportional price changes now seems more plausible because several authors mention what would be the case if it were true. For example, in "Problems of Implementing the Trueblood Objectives Report," *Empirical Research in Accounting: Selected Studies* (Chicago: Institute of Professional Accounting, 1974). Richard M. Cyert and Yuji Ijiri correctly claim that "[price level adjusted historical costs] are exactly the same as current values if all prices move up or down in the same proportion." The problem is that price changes have not been proportional in the past and they are not likely to be proportional in the future.

- If the securities were sold at February 1 and the cash proceeds used to purchase bread, then the number of loaves that could be purchased (i.e., the COG) is *not* 1,400 (= $840/$.60).

Thus, COG cannot be the proper interpretation. This makes it difficult to interpret the total assets figure. As demonstrated earlier, the cash figures can be interpreted as COG and it seems clear that the intent of ARS No. 6, among others, is to measure COG. So, the cash figure is a COG measure, and the securities figure is not a COG measure. Since the total assets figure is the sum of a measure of COG and a measure of not-COG, what is its interpretation? For the reasons given above, I again challenge the readers to provide an interpretation.

Second, I do not know of any decision model that specifies the securities or the total assets figure; therefore, I will tentatively (until the readers demonstrate otherwise) conclude that these figures are irrelevant. I can firmly conclude that they are irrelevant in regard to Proposition 1 since they do not measure COG.

In summary, price level adjusted historical costs do not fully meet the criteria. The cash figures are interpretable and are measures of the relevant COG attribute. However, the securities and total asset figures are not interpretable (by me), are not specified by any decision model that I know of and are not measures of COG.

Current value. The current value financials are shown in Exhibit 6, next page. Recall that 70 shares were purchased at January 1 for $10 per share. Hence, the current value of securities at January 1 was $700 as shown. At February 1 the price has increased to $15 per share for 70 shares or $1,050 current value.

The figures can be interpreted as measures of NOD:

- If the securities were sold at February 1, then $1,050 would be received.

The total assets figure can be interpreted similarly:

- If all of the assets of the firm were converted into cash at February 1, then the firm would hold $1,350.

That is, there is no difficulty in adding the $300 on hand to the number of dollars that could be acquired if the securities were sold. The sum is a straightforward interpretation of the number of dollars that would be held if the securities were sold.[11] The income statement shows the increment in NOD due to the $5 per share price increase for 70 shares. If desired, this increment could be labeled "unrealized" since the securities haven't been sold.

---

[11]Technically, there is a difference between this figure and the NOD figure in the complete exchange case. Perhaps they should be distinguished by calling the above figure COD (command over dollars) instead of NOD. However, since the difference is slight and since I have already tried the readers' patience by introducing new jargon, I didn't make the distinction. Interested readers should consult Raymond J. Chambers (*Accounting, Evaluation, and Economic Behavior* (Englewood Cliffs, N.J.: Prentice-Hall, 1966) for a description of current cash equivalents (CCE) which is, as I read it, identical to COD. Chambers also provides for a price level adjustment of CCE.

The figures for individual and total assets can also be interpreted as measures of COG. For example:

- If the firm had used all of its assets at February 1 to purchase bread, then it could have purchased 2,250 loaves (= $1,350/$.60).

This is a major improvement over the price level adjusted historical cost financials.

The problem lies with the income figure. The $350 NOD increment (net income) does not reflect the increment in COG. COG at January 1 was 2,000 loaves (= $1,000/$.50) and, at February 1, it was 2,250 loaves (= $1,350/$.60), an increment of 250 loaves. Division of the $350 NOD increment by the January 1 price per load of $.50 yields 700 loaves. Division by the February 1 price per loaf of $.60 yields 583$\frac{1}{3}$ loaves. Since neither division yields the actual 250 loaf increment, the current value income statement does not measure the COG increment.

EXHIBIT 6
Current Value

Incomplete exchange case

| | Comparative Balance Sheets | |
	January 1	February 1
Cash	$ 300	$ 300
Securities	700	1,050
Total assets	$1,000	$1,350
Invested capital	$1,000	$1,000
Retained earnings	-0-	350
Total owner's equity	$1,000	$1,350

	Income Statement Month of January
Revenues	$ -0-
Cost of securities sold	$ -0-
	-0-
Gain on price increase of securities	350
Net income	$350

In summary, current values do not fully meet the criteria. All of the figures are interpretable as measures of NOD, but only the assets figures are interpretable as measures of COG. The income figure can only be interpreted as NOD. Since COG is the relevant attribute, current value income does not meet the relevance criterion.

Price level adjusted current values. In order to "price level adjust" the current value financials in Exhibit 6, we need only multiply each of the January 1 figures

EXHIBIT 7
Price Level Adjusted Current Value (Measuring Command Over Goods in Price Level Adjusted Dollars)

Incomplete exchange case

	Comparative Balance Sheets	
	Jan. 1	Feb. 1
Cash (January 1 = $300 × 1.2)	$ 360	$ 300
Securities (January 1 = $700 × 1.2)	840	1050
Total assets	$1,200	$1,350
Invested capital ($1,000 × 1.2)	$1,200	$1,200
Retained earnings	-0-	150
Total owner's equity	$1,200	$1,350

	Income Statement Month of January
Revenues	$ -0-
Cost of securities sold	$ -0-
	-0-
Gain from holding securities ($1,050-$840)	210
Loss from holding cash ($360-$300)	(60)
Net income	$150

by the Consumer Price Index of 1.2.[12] The adjusted financials are shown in Exhibit 7, this page.

All of the individual figures as well as the sums and differences in Exhibit 7 can be interpreted:

- If all of the assets of the firm had been used to purchase bread at January 1, then 2,000 loaves (= $1,200/$.60) could have been purchased.
- If all of the assets of the firm had been used to purchase bread at February 1, then 2,250 loaves (= $1,350/$.60) could have been purchased.
- Hence, the increment (income) in COG is 250 loaves (= $150/$.60), which is the net of a gain of 350 loaves (= $210/$.60) from holding securities and a loss of 100 loaves (= $60/$.60) from holding cash.

The complete interpretation is given in Exhibit 8, next page. As before, note that the ratios of all the figures in Exhibit 8 are the same as those in Exhibit 7. For example, the increase in total assets is 12.5 percent in both exhibits.

The figures can be interpreted. Moreover, they are interpreted as measures of the relevant COG attribute. Therefore, price level adjusted current values meet both criteria.

---

[12]This is "inflating" the past financials. It is possible to "deflate" the current financials without destroying the interpretability. The reasons for preferring to adjust the past financials is given in Sterling, *Enterprise Income*, p. 339. For the same reasons, I prefer the "roll-forward" procedure.

EXHIBIT 8

Interpretation of Price Level Adjusted Values Measuring Command Over Goods in Physical Units)

Incomplete exchange case

	Comparative Balance Sheets	
	January 1	February 1
Cash	600 loaves	500 loaves
Securities	1,400	1,750
Total assets	2,000 loaves	2,250 loaves
Invested capital	2,000 loaves	2,000 loaves
Retained earnings	-0-	250
Total owner's equity	2,000 loaves	2,250 loaves

	Income Statement Month of January
Revenues	-0- loaves
Cost	-0-
	-0-
Gain from holding securities	350
Loss from holding cash	(100)
Net income	$250 loaves

SUMMARY AND CONCLUSION

The modest objective of this article was to clarify the concept of price level adjustments. The first clarification was concerned with what we ought to be arguing about. We should not be arguing that one set of figures is right and another is wrong; instead we should be arguing about which attribute we ought to measure and report. Selection of the attribute that ought to be measured requires precise criteria, rigorously applied. I agree fully with the Trueblood Committee that the primary objective (or criterion) of accounting is usefulness. The substitution of "interpretability" and "relevance" for "usefulness" was an attempt to make that criterion more precise and more concrete, not a disagreement.

The criterion of interpretability is that a given attribute be capable of being placed in a true "if . . . then . . ." statement. The failure of an attribute to meet that criterion should cause us to be skeptical of that attribute. The criterion of relevance is that an attribute be specified by a decision model. This must be what is meant by "usefulness," since if an attribute is not specified by any decision model, then I can't imagine how it could be useful.

These criteria were utilized in the examination of the simple problem of accounting for a trader on the New York Stock Exchange under the two cases of a complete and an incomplete exchange. The examination of the first case—complete exchange—revealed that although the NOD attribute is interpretable, it is irrelevant. COG is the relevant attribute. The conclusion that COG is the relevant attribute permitted a more precise application of the relevance criterion in examining the incomplete exchange case, i.e., determination of whether or not the attribute could be interpreted as COG.

When accounting for an incomplete exchange, there are four competing methods. Each of these methods was subjected to the criteria. Some methods partially meet the criteria but only one method—price level adjusted current values—fully meet them. The results are summarized in Exhibit 9, this page. Since the cells that contain "no" may be due to a deficiency in my examination rather than a deficiency in the figures, the readers were challenged to demonstrate their interpretability and relevance. Until such a demonstration is provided, I will maintain that only price level adjusted current value financials fully meet both criteria.

It follows that the appropriate procedure is to (1) adjust the present statement to current values and (2) adjust the previous statement by a price index. It is important to recognize that *both* adjustments are necessary and that neither is a substitute for the other. Confusion on this point is widespread. For example, a business executive recently announced that his firm had converted to current value accounting when, in fact, the firm had done nothing but make price level adjustments to historical costs. In addition, several CPAs seem to be saying that current value accounting is a substitute for price level adjustments. Also, although I am not entirely clear on the Securities and Exchange Commission's position on this issue, it seems that it is leaning toward current replacement costs as a substitute for price level adjustments. Finally, the phrasing of the FASB's questions seemed to indicate that it thought of current values and price level adjustments as competing methods, only *one* of which should be selected.

I hope that the consideration of this simple case demonstrates that both are required.

EXHIBIT 9

Method \ Criteria	Interpretable	Relevant
Historical cost	No	No
Price level adjusted historical cost	No	No
Current value	Yes	No
Price level adjusted current value	Yes	Yes

ECLECTIC APPROACHES TO CHANGING PRICES

Capital Maintenance, Price Changes, and Profit Determination

REGINALD S. GYNTHER

Over the years the matters of accounting for price changes, valuing assets, calculating depreciation charges, determining profit, and maintaining capital seem to have become entwined in the literature in a way that is confusing for most concerned. It is not suggested that these matters are not inter-related, but it is believed that the effects of price changes on capital maintenance can be isolated in a way that lessens this confusion.

The endeavors of this paper are: (a) to set out the effects that the various perceptions of capital maintenance have on accounting for the effects of price changes, (b) to argue that accounting for the effects of price changes is more directly concerned with capital maintenance—and not with periodic asset valuations and *short*-term profit determinations, (c) to argue that (therefore) accounting for price changes is more directly concerned with *long*-term profit— *and that this long-term profit is related to the lives of assets*, and (d) to suggest that teachings, discussions and debates on accounting for the effects of price changes on the one hand, and on short-term profit determination and asset valuation on the other, will be more fruitful if they are dealt with as separate components in an overall problem area.

PERCEPTIONS AND CAPITAL MAINTENANCE

The matters of perceptions, attitudes, frames of reference, values, reference groups, environment, culture, and personality systems overlap and are inextricably inter-related. Each individual in this complex society is influenced by the many groups of which he is a member. Geographic, religious, educational,

Some of my original thinking in this area was triggered by Jean St.G. Kerr's paper, "Three Concepts of Business Income," *Australian Accountant*, April 1956—and since reproduced in *An Income Approach to Accounting Theory* ed. by Sidney Davidson *et al.* (Prentice-Hall, Inc., 1964). This paper endeavors to develop further some thoughts expressed by me in a section of the "28th Research Lecture Endowed by the Australian Society of Accountants in the University of Melbourne" in October, 1967 (Society Bulletin No. 5, October 1968) and then expanded somewhat within a paper presented to the "18th Victoria University of Wellington Advanced Accounting Seminar" in August 1969. An earlier version of this paper was presented at Ohio State University and at the Wharton School of Finance and Commerce, University of Pennsylvania, in January 1970.

Reg. S. Gynther, "Capital Maintenance, Price Changes, and Profit Determination," *The Accounting Review*, October 1970, pp. 712–730. Reprinted with the permission of *The Accounting Review*.

peer, and socio-economic group memberships all provide a person with group norms—and hence his attitudes. Many of these attitudes relate to both work situations and to our industrialized society.[1] It is not suggested that each individual will take over and internalize all the values of the social groups in which he moves, but they will have some lasting effect on him if he becomes psychologically involved. In some cases, too, the attitudes of people have been developed, not by actual membership within a reference group, but by the fact that they aspire to membership within a group, and so adopt its viewpoints.

In a previous paper[2] this writer claimed that these are the reasons for the different perceptions that people have of firms, that these different perceptions tend to fall into either of two main viewpoint groups (i.e., proprietary viewpoint and entity viewpoint—with some variations in each), and that these different viewpoints give rise to the different capital maintenance concepts that underlie the various different proposals made for accounting for the effects of changing prices.

Those who hold the *proprietary* viewpoint perceive the firm as being owned by a sole proprietor, a set of partners, or a number of shareholders. The firm's assets are seen as being the property of these proprietors, and the liabilities incurred by the firm are *their* liabilities. The proprietors are the center of interest, and a main object of accounting is to account for their interests in the records of the firm. Profits are perceived to be the property of the proprietors at the time they are earned, whether they are distributed or not. (Σ Assets $- \Sigma$ Liabilities = Net Worth of Proprietors.)

On the other hand, those who hold the entity viewpoint perceive the firm as being something separate and distinct from those who contributed capital (of various classes). They see the assets and liabilities as being those of the firm itself, and not those of the proprietors. Profits as earned by the firm are seen to become the property of the firm; they accrue to the shareholders only if and when a dividend is declared. The entity is the center of interest, and a main object of accounting is to account for its interests; in this way it can better serve shareholders and other members of society, who, incidentally, maintain their own accounting records as separate entities. (Σ Assets = Σ Equities; and here, "Equities" include "the entity's equity in itself."[3])

Capital Maintenance Concepts

It is now contended that the proprietary and entity viewpoints (and their psychological and sociological origins) underlie the following capital maintenance concepts which are basic to different proposals for accounting for the effects of changing prices:

[1]D. Katz, "The Functional Approach to the Study of Attitudes," in T. W. Costello, and S. S. Zalkin, *Psychology in Administration* (Prentice-Hall, Inc., 1963, p. 261.

[2]Reg S. Gynther, "Accounting Concepts and Behavioral Hypothesis" *The Accounting Review* (April 1967), pp. 271–290.

[3]G. R. Husband, "The Entity Concept in Accounting," *The Accounting Review* (October 1954), p. 554.

Proprietary Viewpoint Capital Maintenance Concepts

1. General Purchasing Power.
2. Consumer Purchasing Power.

(Note: These focus on maintaining the general or consumer purchasing power of funds contributed by *equity holders.*)

Entity Viewpoint Capital Maintenance Concepts

3. Investment Purchasing Power.
4. Operating Capacity of the Firm.

(Note: Although these are concerned with specific purchasing power of *all* long-term funds contributed, the real focus here is on maintaining the *firm's assets*. That is, the emphasis is on the other side of the balance sheet from that of the proprietary viewpoint capital maintenance concepts.)

It is not meant to imply that people deliberately endeavor to maintain a certain exact amount of capital, but each of us uses (whether we realize it or not) a certain capital concept to measure long-term profit (or loss). That is, our particular capital maintenance concept underlies the determination of the amount of long-term profit that we believe could be distributed without impairing the capital that must be maintained.[4]

Many people, with both proprietary and entity viewpoints, still adhere to a *money* capital maintenance concept, and this could be because most external financial statements are still prepared in this way. This merely requires the maintenance of the quantity of money units invested in an entity, irrespective of movements in their purchasing powers. Anything in excess of the contributed dollars is recorded as "profit." As we are only concerned with concepts relating to proposals *to* account for the effects of price changes, we will not discuss the money capital idea any further here.

1. *The General Purchasing Power Capital Maintenance Concept* is the first of the two proprietary viewpoint concepts to be discussed. Those with this capital maintenance concept do not recognize profit until they have maintained capital (and as we will see, this is some version of shareholders, funds) which has been adjusted (through the use of a Capital Maintenance Adjustment Account or similar) to reflect movements in a *general* purchasing power index.[5] They want to maintain the purchasing power of this capital in accordance with the movements in the prices of all goods and services in the economy; a Gross National Product Implicit Price Deflator index is often advocated for this purpose.

[4]When J. R. Hicks, in his *Value and Capital* (Clarendon Press, 1946) used his notion of "well-offness" as the rule against which to measure income, he realized that the different concepts of "well-offness" would produce different income figures.

[5]For example, the Staff of the Accounting Research Division of the A.I.C.P.A., *Reporting the Financial Effects of Price-Level Changes* (Accounting Research Study No. 6) (American Institute of Certified Public Accountants, 1963); and L. A. Wilk, *Accounting for Inflation* (Sweet & Maxwell Limited, 1960).

It is a proprietary viewpoint concept of capital maintenance for two main reasons. Firstly, the general price index used is based on *all* goods and services, including *consumer* goods. Entity viewpoint people are merely interested in movements in prices which relate to the assets of entities, and in most cases these are mainly certain investment (capital) goods.[6] To use a general index in *all* cases would not provide the capital maintenance they desire. The maintenance of purchasing power in general is considered by entity people to be not relevant for each firm.

Secondly, when there is a movement in the general index, the adjustment entries made by general purchasing power capital maintenance concept people are usually based on the total of *common* shareholder funds, and not on the total of *all* funds invested in the entity.[7] This results in holding gains being recorded (assuming rising prices) in respect of balances of long-term liabilities and preferred capital stock. On the other hand, entity viewpoint people aim at maintaining some form of specific purchasing power of *all* long-term funds (irrespective of their source) because this is needed to support the total *assets* of the entity. To entity people, it would be just as inconceivable to create gains on holding long-term liability items during price rises as it would be to calculate such gains on common share capital. They would argue that such "gains" are not distributable without a contraction of the entity's activities—and therefore cannot be gains *to the firm*.

As stated previously, proprietary viewpoint people see a main objective of accounting to be the accounting for their interests in the records of the firm, while entity viewpoint people perceive a need to account for the interests of the entity in their endeavors to serve shareholders and others.

Before leaving this general purchasing power capital maintenance concept, it should be mentioned that some people advocate the use of a general index to restate *all* accounting balances in accordance with movements in the general value of money itself. Their idea is to produce data in current prices, but to adhere to the cost principle by merely restating historical costs.[8] Whether they mean to or not, these people are advocating a proprietary viewpoint of capital maintenance because the gains and losses on monetary items have always included those calculated on long-term liabilities in all such methods seen by this writer.

2. *The Consumer Purchasing Power Capital Maintenance Concept* is the other of the two proprietary viewpoint concepts to be discussed. It, too, has many adherents among the "reformers."[9] Under this concept, profit is not recognized

---

[6]A general index could be said to be made up from the price movements in both consumer and investment goods and services.

[7]For example, L. A. Wilk *(ibid.)* at p. 80 says, "Capital maintenance reserve will therefore be restricted to maintaining the purchasing power of ordinary capital." However, some proprietary people include preferred stockholders in the proprietary group. For example, see A. N. Lorig, "Some Basic Concepts of Accounting and Their Implications," *The Accounting Review* (July 1964), pp. 563–573.

[8]For example, see *Statement of the Accounting Principles Board No. 3* (American Institute of Certified Public Accountants, 1969), p. 3 and elsewhere.

[9]Notable examples are R. J. Chambers in *Accounting, Evaluation and Economic Behavior* (Prentice-Hall, Inc., 1966); E. O. Edwards and P. W. Bell in *The Theory and Mea-*

until shareholders' funds (here, too, usually *common* shareholders) have been restated to reflect movements in the *consumer* price index, and the idea is to maintain the purchasing power of these capital funds in accordance with price movements of *consumer* goods (and not *all* goods as in the previous concept). This is a proprietary viewpoint concept for reasons similar to those listed under the general purchasing power concept. It, too, concentrates on shareholders' funds and not on the assets of the entity.

3. *The Investment Purchasing Power of the Firm Capital Maintenance Concept* is the first of the two entity viewpoint capital maintenance concepts. It is an entity concept because the firm and all its assets are the center of interest— and not the shareholders and shareholders' funds. The focus of attention shifts to the asset side of the balance sheet.

Under this concept, profit (i.e., the amount that could be distributed[10]) is not recognized until the *investment* purchasing power of the firm has been maintained, and the concept requires *all* long-term capital to be restated (through a Capital Maintenance Adjustment Account or similar) by an index which represents this "investment purchasing power." Three main and different kinds of gradations of investment purchasing power could have supporters:[11]

(a) *General* investment purchasing power, which would require the use of an overall index for *all* the investment goods (e.g. capital items etc.) which any company might purchase. (i.e., an index of *all* goods and services other than consumer goods.)[12]

(b) *Industry* investment purchasing power, which would require the use of one index for each industry to reflect movements in the prices of all the investment goods that firms in a *particular industry* are likely to purchase.

(c) Investment purchasing power relating to the activities of *each firm*. This would require the use of one index for each firm, and each index would be based on the particular investment goods that *each firm* is likely to purchase.

In each case the emphasis is on maintaining all the long-term capital of firms in accordance with price movements of investment goods, as distinct from maintaining the purchasing power of common shareholder funds (only) with the aid of an index largely influenced by price movements of consumer goods.

The entity viewpoint people, who would use one of these investment purchasing power indexes for capital maintenance purposes when accounting for

---

surement of Business Income University of California Press, 1961); and the Research Foundation of The Institute of Chartered Accountants in England and Wales in *Accounting for Stewardship in a Period of Inflation* (1968).

[10]To entity viewpoint people, "profit" is that which remains after distributing dividends. However, in an endeavor to avoid confusion, the word "profit" is used in a consistent manner throughout the paper, and in the way it is commonly used (i.e., as that which *could* be distributed without impairing capital—if sufficient cash were available).

[11]Eldon S. Hendriksen, *Accounting Theory* (Richard D. Irwin, Inc., 1965), pp. 179–180.

[12]It is often possible to construct such an index series from the national income and expenditure figures for a nation; i.e. by dividing investment totals in current prices by similar figures expressed in constant prices.

the effects of price changes, would *not* calculate holding gains on long-term liability or preferred stock balances. Not only would this be contrary to their entity viewpoint, but it would also be "internally inconsistent" to use such an index for such a purpose. When shareholders and others perceive such gains, they are in some form of *consumer* power.

4. *The Operating Capacity of the Firm Capital Maintenance Concept* is the other of the two entity viewpoint capital maintenance concepts to be discussed. As in the previous concept, the firm itself and its assets are the center of interest. Under the operating capacity concept, profit is not recognized for each firm until its specific operating capacity has been maintained. The concept requires *all* long-term capital to be restated (e.g., through a Capital Maintenance Adjustment Account) and this is done in accordance with market buying price changes relating to individual assets held. Total net assets = operating capacity, and the price changes for individual assets have to be accounted for separately because they change in different ways. (To the extent that individual price changes might not be available, specific price indexes are used.)

However, different kinds of operating capacity have their supporters; three of these are:

(a) Operating capacity identical to that which existed during the period concerned. This involves taking into account, for capital maintenance purposes, changes in the current market prices (to buy or to reconstruct) of assets *actually possessed* throughout their lifetime.[13]

(b) Operating capacity based on the latest equipment and other assets (i.e., incorporating any technological improvements) needed to produce the *same volume* of identical output of goods and services—i.e. the same as that now produced by the existing assets.[14] For capital maintenance purposes this involves taking into account the current market buying prices of this latest equipment. (To the extent that the entity already possesses the latest equipment, this view of operating capacity is identical to that in "(a)" above.)

(c) Operating capacity based on the latest equipment, etc., needed to produce the same *value* of identical goods and services. This involves taking into account the current market buying prices of any such latest equipment, and it takes care of any reduction in the current unit selling price of goods and services produced with the technologically improved equipment.[15] (Here too, this view of operating capacity is identical to that in "(a)" above if the entity already possesses the latest equipment.)

---

[13]An objective of this method is to produce the results (in current prices) from operating the entity in each short period, for the way it actually existed in its industry, with the assets it did have, in the geographic locations it occupied, etc. This information is relevant to management and shareholders, and would be needed for any decision making relating to change. For detailed procedures see R. S. Gynther, *Accounting for Price-Level Changes: Theory and Procedures* (Pergamon Press Ltd., 1966).

[14]For example, see R. L. Mathews, "Price-Level Changes and Useless Information," *Journal of Accounting Research* (Spring 1965), pp. 133–155; and F. K. Wright, "Depreciation and Obsolescence in Current-Value Accounting," *Journal of Accounting Research* (Autumn 1965), pp. 167–181.

Before proceeding, it should be made clear that the use of an operating capacity concept of capital maintenance need not imply an intention to replace assets in their existing or improved form. The aim of each version of operating capacity capital maintenance is to account for the entity in the way it actually existed during the accounting period concerned. During the lifetime of each asset, capital is maintained (and *lifetime* profit for each asset is determined) in a way that (all else being equal) would permit the assets to be replaced *if* replacement is subsequently desired by management.

If asset combinations are altered, added to, or reduced *during* any accounting period, the accounting is based on the two or more different operating capacities that existed during that period, e.g., on asset combination X for 3 months and on asset combination Y for 9 months. (In such cases monthly financial reports are more relevant for decision making than the combined one for the year.) There is no real difference here from the situation that exists under other concepts of capital maintenance; there, too, the capital to be maintained can be altered within an accounting period by the decisions of directors, e.g., by decisions to alter the size or composition of shareholders, funds.

ACCOUNTING FOR PRICE CHANGES AND CAPITAL MAINTENANCE

In this section it will be argued that accounting for the effects of price changes is more directly concerned with capital maintenance—and not with periodic net asset valuations and *short*-term profit determinations.

In the previous section, capital maintenance concepts based on general indexes, consumer price indexes, investment indexes, and individual current market buying prices were described. The fact that some people advocate revaluing assets in accordance with movements in the same indexes and prices that they see as being relevant for capital maintenance purposes has caused some of the confusion that this paper is endeavoring to "unravel."

Assets can be valued in *several different ways* (depending on the underlying asset concepts), and there are several different ways in which a person with a *general* purchasing power concept of capital maintenance (for example) could value assets. Four of these methods are now examined briefly, and it will be noticed that a general index forms the base for only *one* of them:

1. Historical costs adjusted for changes in the general price level.
2. Historical costs adjusted for changes in current market buying prices.
3. Net present values.
4. Net realizable values.

The point is that although these different asset valuation methods result in different periodic asset valuations and short-term profit determinations, the

---

[15]See Irving H. Siegel's paper presented to the 37th Session of the International Statistical Institute in London in September, 1969 (probably not yet published). Here he suggests building this idea into the production of specific price indexes for capital equipment items.

same general purchasing power concept of capital is maintained. (This will be demonstrated in Example 1.)

1. When historical costs of assets are merely adjusted for changes in the *general* price level, the underlying asset concept is the same as that which underlies pure historical cost. It is one which is related to assets being debit balances, or deferred charges, or revenue charges in suspense. The focus is on the unexpired costs, and not on the asset item itself or its value. There is now a growing move to adjust historical cost balances in this way in order that the balance sheet might show the unexpired costs expressed in current general-value-of-money terms. That is, there are some people who want to use the same general index for both net asset valuation (hence depreciation and cost of revenue charges) *and* capital maintenance purposes.[16]

2. With the second asset valuation method—historical costs adjusted for changes in *current market buying prices*—the underlying asset concept is one of service potentials. Asset valuation is based on the current input costs of the (remaining) service potentials that the asset "contains." When this net asset method is used in conjunction with a general purchasing power concept of capital maintenance, the effects of any differences between movements in specific current input prices for non-monetary assets on the one hand, and in the general index on the other, are treated as holding gains and losses.[17]

3. The net present value asset valuation method has an underlying asset concept relating to future economic benefits. The value of each asset is the present value of the net cash flows the asset is expected to generate in the future. It is a direct method of valuation, and depreciation charges are calculated by working in a reverse direction from that of conventional methods. Depreciation is the difference between the latest net present value and that calculated at the beginning of the period in question (but as adjusted by any movements in the index relevant to the particular capital maintenance concept held). There are many problems associated with applying this net present value asset valuation method in practice, but to many people it is an ideal at which to aim.[18]

4. With net realizable values, the underlying concept of assets is one of severable means legally possessed. The value of each asset is what it will bring in the resale market place. One strongly argued reason for such an approach to asset valuation is to provide on a regular basis the "current cash equivalents" of assets (and presumably of the company itself) for the purposes of decisions regarding possible adaptations.[19] This, too, is a direct valuation method, and depreciation charges are calculated by

[16]For example, see the *Statement of the Accounting Principles Board, No. 3, op. cit.*

[17]For example, see Committee to Prepare a Statement of Basic Accounting Theory, *A Statement of Basic Accounting Theory* (American Accounting Association, 1966), Appendix B. See also Appendix 1 to this paper.

[18]For example, see Eldon S. Hendriksen, *Accounting Theory* (Richard D. Irwin, 1965), pp. 202–203.

[19]See R. J. Chambers, *op. cit.*

working back from the latest valuation. Depreciation is the difference between the latest net realizable value of the asset and the one that applied at the beginning of the period (but adjusted by any movements in the index relevant to the particular capital maintenance concept held).

These four different asset valuation methods are now applied to the same basic data, in conjunction with a *general* purchasing power concept of capital maintenance.

Example 1: An asset X with a 3-year life is purchased for $3,000. It earns net annual revenues of $2,000 (billed and received at the end of each year), all profits are paid out as dividends, and cash accumulations from the depreciation charges are not reinvested in other assets (in order to concentrate on the main issue here). The general index increases by 5% in year 2 and by 10% in year 3 (i.e. an increase of 15.5% over the 3 years); and the current market buying price of an identical new asset increased to $3,300 in year 2 and to $3,600 in year 3. For depreciation purposes the straight line method is used for both of the historical cost adjusted asset valuation methods (no salvage value), a discount rate of 20% is used in conjunction with the net present value method, and the net realizable values of the asset were $1,800 at the end of year 1, $800 at the end of year 2, and zero at the end of year 3.

Appendix I contains the relevant journal entries, profit statements and balance sheets. *Even though the following different periodic net asset valuations and short-term profit determinations occurred, the same general purchasing power of contributed capital was maintained in each case at $3,150 (105% of $3,000) at the end of year 2, and at $3,465 (115.5% of $3,000) at the end of year 3.* (Compare the different relative figures *across* the table):

Item	Asset Valuation Method			
	Historical Costs Adjusted by General Index	Historical Costs Adjusted by Current Market Buying Prices	Net Present Values	Net Realizable Values
Periodic Net Values of Asset X:	$	$	$	$
End Year 1	2,000	2,000	3,055	1,800
End Year 2	1,050	1,100	1,666	800
End Year 3	Nil	Nil	Nil	Nil
Periodic Cash Balances:				
End Year 1	1,000	1,000	−55	1,200
End Year 2	2,100	2,050	1,484	2,350
End Year 3	3,465	3,465	3,465	3,465
Short-term Net Profits:				
For Year 1	1,000	1,000	2,055	800
For Year 2	900	950	461	850
For Year 3	635	585	19	885

The profit figures below would have been different again if it had been assumed that interest had been earned on the cash balances, but this does not affect the point being made here.

It can also be demonstrated that the use of different depreciation methods does not affect the argument that accounting for the effects of price changes is more directly concerned with capital maintenance—and not with periodic net asset valuations, and this is done in the example which follows.

Example 2: Assume the same data as in Example 1, but with the sum-of-the-digits depreciation method being used (in lieu of the straight line method) in conjunction with the historical costs adjusted by a general index asset valuation method for Asset *X*. The entries, profit statements and balance sheets in Appendix II reveal the following further *different* periodic asset valuations and short-term profit determinations (but the *same* capital maintenance effects), and they can be compared with the "straight-line figures" in column one above:

	$
Periodic Net Values of Asset *X*:	
End Year 1	1,500
End Year 2	525
End Year 3	Nil
Periodic Cash Balances:	$
End Year 1	1,500
End Year 2	2,625
End Year 3	3,465
Short-term Net Profits:	$
For Year 1	500
For Year 2	875
For Year 3	1,160

We could now proceed to give similar illustrations based on the other three capital maintenance concepts discussed in this paper (i.e., those based on consumer purchasing power, investment purchasing power and operating capacity of the firm), but exactly the same sort of results would be obtained. If a *consumer* purchasing power capital maintenance concept had been held (for example), and if the consumer price index had increased by 20% over these three years, capital would have been maintained at $3,600 (and not $3,465) at the end of year 3—and there would have been further sets of different periodic net asset and short-term net profit figures for each of the different asset valuation methods.

However, it should be mentioned that it is most unlikely that the asset valuation method of "historical costs adjusted for changes in the *general* price level" would be used in conjunction with any of these three other capital maintenance concepts. If consumer purchasing power and investment purchasing power capital maintenance people see assets as deferred charges or as revenue charges in suspense, and therefore merely wish to restate unexpired historical costs of assets, it is more likely that they would want to do so using changes in *consumer* price indexes and *investment* price indexes (respectively). Further, operating capacity capital maintenance concept people are more likely to be interested in only current market buying price, net present value, and net realizable value asset valuation methods—and in that order.

A chart showing the main possible combinations of asset valuation methods and capital maintenance concepts is presented on page 328.[20]

It is because current market buying prices, net present values and current market selling prices can be used in conjunction with several different capital maintenance concepts[21] that it is claimed in this paper that accounting for the effects of price changes is more *directly* concerned with capital maintenance (than with periodic net asset valuations, etc.). *If* the above chart consisted of only the diagonal combinations it would be different. Current market buying prices, net present values and current market selling prices of specific assets can quite easily remain unaltered, for example, when there *are* changes in the general, consumer price, and investment indexes.

Before leaving this section, it should be demonstrated how accounting for the effects of price changes is more directly concerned with capital maintenance (than with periodic net asset valuations and short-term profit determinations) when different *revenue recognition methods* are employed for inventories.[22]

Example 3: Companies A and B are identical, and their sole assets are inventories they have produced at a cost of $70,000. Company A recognizes revenues of $100,000 on production in year 1, while Company B recognizes revenues on sale. All prices rise by 10% early in year 2. The inventories are sold for $110,000 later in year 2.

Appendix III contains the relevant journal entries, profit statements and balance sheets, and from these it can be seen that, although the following different short-term profit determinations and inventory valuations occurred, the capital was maintained in each case at $77,000 ($70,000 plus 10%):

ITEM	COMPANY A	COMPANY B
Net Profit:	$	$
Year 1	30,000	Nil
Year 2	Nil	33,000
Inventory Value:		
Year 1	100,000	70,000

ACCOUNTING FOR PRICE CHANGES AND LONG-TERM PROFIT

In the previous section it was argued that accounting for the effects of price changes is more directly concerned with capital maintenance than with *short-term* profit determinations. It will now be argued (as an extension of this) that accounting for the effects of price changes is more directly concerned with *long-term profit—and* that this long-term profit is related to the lives of assets.

[20]This chart is something similar to ones produced by this writer on p. 13 of *Society Bulletin No. 5* (Australian Society of Accountants, 1968), and by K. Shwayder, in his "Capital Maintenance Rule and the Net Asset Valuation Rule," *The Accounting Review* (April 1969), p. 308.

[21]With resultant holding gains and losses in some cases.

[22]Keith Shwayder, *op. cit.*, pp. 304–316, has demonstrated this capital maintenance matter when different asset *value* methods are used for inventories.

Some Possible Combinations of Net Asset Valuation Methods and Capital Maintenance Concepts[a]

CAPITAL MAINTENANCE CONCEPTS	Net Asset Valuation Methods						
	HISTORICAL COSTS	HISTORICAL COSTS × GENERAL INDEX	HISTORICAL COSTS × CONSUMER PRICE INDEX	HISTORICAL COSTS × INVESTMENT INDEX	CURRENT MARKET BUYING PRICES	NET PRESENT VALUES (OF EXISTING ASSETS)	CURRENT MARKET SELLING PRICES (OR N.R.V's. OR C.C.E's.)
Money Capital	X				X	X	X
General Purchasing Power		X			X	X	X
Consumer Purchasing Power			X		X	X	X
Investment Purchasing Power				X	X	X	X
Operating Capacity					X	X	X

[a]Please see Appendix IV to this paper for a current chart showing combinations of asset valuation methods and capital maintenance concepts, as well as a corresponding set of references.

From the results of Example 1 and Example 2 we now find that it *cannot* be claimed that we will always arrive at the same total *company* "lifetime" profit no matter what asset valuation method we use in conjunction with the one capital maintenance concept.[23] It is shown in the table on page 330 that when the total profits from the four different asset valuation methods (which were used in conjunction with the general purchasing power capital maintenance concept) are expressed in end of year 3 general purchasing power they are *different*.[24]

However, if we separate out from these profits those that were contributed by Asset X over its lifetime (i.e., if we eliminate the gains and losses from the cash balances), we find that the totals of these *are* identical in end-of-year 3 general purchasing power (see table on page 331), irrespective of the *different* asset valuation or depreciation methods employed in conjunction with the *same* capital maintenance concept.[25]

Further, if we compare the profits recorded by Companies A and B over the lifetime of the inventories, we find that they are identical too:

Company	Annual Profits from Inventories in End Year Prices		Adjusting Factor (from Price Movements)	Annual Profits from Inventories in End of Year 2 Prices	
A	Year 1	$ 30,000	1.1		$ 33,000
	Year 2	Nil	1.0		Nil
				Total	33,000
B	Year 1	Nil	1.1		Nil
	Year 2	33,000	1.0		33,000
				Total	33,000

It can be claimed, therefore, that when accounting for the effects of changing prices, the lifetime profit of *each asset* (whether a long-lived fixed asset or short-lived inventory) is affected by the particular capital maintenance concept employed, but not by the different asset valuation, depreciation, and revenue recognition methods that might be used.[26] The fact that the lives of various assets overlap in practice merely makes this more difficult to see.

[23]In the way Keith Shwayder appears to do. (*Ibid.*)

[24]They would be the same *if* the cash had been loaned at interest rates of 5% in year 2 and 10% in year 3; but this, of course, is only one of many possibilities—including that of investing in stocks and bonds with fluctuating market prices, etc.

[25]It is the presence of *different* amounts of monetary items (and hence the different amounts of holding gains and losses thereon) that result in different *company* lifetime profits.

[26]It is important to keep this in mind when dealing with the operating capacity of the firm capital maintenance concept because the price movements relating to each asset can be different.

Asset Valuation Method	Annual Profit in End of Year Prices		Adjusting Factor (from General Index Movements)	Annual Profits in End of Yr. 3 Prices	
		$			$
Historical costs adjusted by general index (straight-line depreciation)	Year 1	1,000	1.155		1,155
	Year 2	900	1.1		900
	Year 3	635	1.0		635
				Total	2,780
Historical costs adjusted by current market buying prices	Year 1	1,000	1.155		1,155
	Year 2	950	1.1		1,045
	Year 3	585	1.0		585
				Total	2,785
Net present values	Year 1	2,055	1.155		2,373
	Year 2	461	1.1		507
	Year 3	19	1.0		19
				Total	2,899
Net realizable values	Year 1	800	1.155		924
	Year 2	850	1.1		935
	Year 3	885	1.0		885
				Total	2,744
Historical costs adjusted by general index (sum-of-digits depreciation)	Year 1	500	1.155		578
	Year 2	875	1.1		962
	Year 3	1,160	1.0		1,160
				Total	2,700

CONCLUSION

It is believed that this paper has established:

(a) that accounting for the effects of price changes is more directly concerned with capital maintenance than with periodic asset valuations and *short*-term profit determinations, and

(b) that, when accounting for price changes, the *lifetime* profit of *each asset* is affected by the particular capital maintenance concept employed, but not by the different asset valuation, depreciation, and revenue recognition methods that might be used.

It seems highly desirable, therefore, that in discussions, debates and teachings we separate out and treat as separate components of an overall problem:

(1) the matter of accounting for price changes—with its roots in the various capital maintenance concepts,

(2) the various asset concepts and the valuation methods that tend to arise out of them, and the related profit determination ideas.

If this is done we will be able to better identify the different viewpoints within each of these different components, to engage in discussions of a more enlightened nature and, perhaps, achieve more agreement at a faster pace.

Asset Valuation Method	Annual Profit from Asset X in End of Year Prices*		Adjusting Factor (from General Index Movements)	Annual Profits from Asset X in End of Year 3 Prices	
		$			$
Historical costs	Year 1	1,000	1.155		1,155
adjusted by general	Year 2	950	1.1		1,045
index (straight-line	Year 3	845	1.0		845
depreciation)				Total	3,045
Historical costs	Year 1	1,000	1.155		1,155
adjusted by current	Year 2	1,000	1.1		1,100
market buying prices	Year 3	790	1.0		790
				Total	3,045
Net present values	Year 1	2,055	1.155		2,373
	Year 2	458	1.1		504
	Year 3	168	1.0		168
				Total	3,045
Net realizable values	Year 1	800	1.155		924
	Year 2	910	1.1		1,001
	Year 3	1,120	1.0		1,120
				Total	3,045
Historical costs	Year 1	500	1.155		577.50
adjusted by general	Year 2	950	1.1		1,045
index (sum-of-the-digits	Year 3	1,422.50	1.0		1,422.50
depreciation)					3,045

(*See Appendix I for these "Annual Profits from Asset X," i.e. Annual Net Revenues less Depreciation in each case and plus holding gains or losses on Asset X in the case of historical costs adjusted by current market buying prices.)

Further, in view of the leading role that capital maintenance concepts play in this matter of accounting for changing prices, it is important that the implications of their behavioral origins be understood. This, too, will better equip us to appreciate the underpinnings of the various proposals made in this important area.

APPENDIX I

DETAILED WORKINGS OF EXAMPLE 1

General Purchasing Power Concept of Capital Maintenance

1. *In conjunction with historical costs adjusted for changes in the general price level* (with straight-line depreciation)

Year 1:

Profit Statement for Year 1

Net revenues	$2,000
Less Depreciation	1,000
= *Net Profit* (and Dividend)	$1,000

Balance Sheet at End of Year 1

Asset X $3,000			Contributed capital	3,000
Less Accumulated depn 1,000	$2,000			
Cash	1,000			
	$3,000			$3,000

Year 2:

Relevant journal entries for year 2 to account for the increase of 5% in the general index—and the resultant depreciation charge:

(a) Asset X .... Dr.   150
    Loss on cash held during price rise .... Dr.   50
      Accumulated depreciation .... Cr.   50
      Capital maintenance adjustment .... Cr.   150
    (5 % on Year 1 balance sheet items)
(b) Depreciation .... Dr. 1,050
      Accumulated depreciation .... Cr. 1,050
    (Depn. for year 2, one-third of $3,150)

Profit Statement for Year 2

Net revenues		2,000
Less Depreciation	1,050	
Loss on cash held during price rise	50	1,100
=*Net Profit* (and Dividend)		$ 900

Balance Sheet at End of Year 2

Asset X $3,150			Contributed capital	3,000
Less Accumulated depn. 2,100	$1,050		Capital maintenance	150
			adjustment	
Cash	2,100*			
	$3,150			$3,150

(*After paying dividends out of cash from revenues.)

Year 3:

Relevant journal entries for year 3 to account for increase of 10% in the general index—and the resultant depreciation charge:

(a) Asset X .... Dr.   315
    Loss on cash held during price rise .... Dr.   210
      Accumulated depreciation .... Cr.   210
      Capital maintenance adjustment .... Cr.   315
    (10% on year 2 balance sheet items)
(b) Depreciation .... Dr. 1,155
      Accumulated depreciation .... Cr. 1,155
    (Depn. for year 3, one-third of $3,465)

Profit Statement for Year 3

Net revenues		$2,000
Less Depreciation	$1,155	
Loss on cash held during price rise	210	1,365
=*Net Profit* (and Dividend)		$ 635

Balance Sheet at End of Year 3

Asset X	$3,465		Contributed capital	$3,000
Less Accumulated depn.	3,465	Nil	Capital maintenance adjustment	465
Cash		3,465*		
		$3,465		$3,465

(*After paying dividends out of cash from revenues.)

2. *In conjunction with historical costs adjusted for changes in current market buying prices*

Year 1:

Profit Statement for Year 1

Net revenues	$2,000
Less Depreciation	1,000
= *Net Profit* (and Dividend)	$1,000

Balance Sheet at End of Year 1

Asset X	$3,000		Contributed capital	$3,000
Less Accumulated depn. ...	1,000	$2,000		
Cash		1,000		
		$3,000		$3,000

Year 2:

Relevant journal entries for Year 2 to account for the increase of 5% in the general index and the increase of $300 ($3,000 to $3,300) in the current market buying price of an identical new asset—and the resultant depreciation charge:

(a) Asset X .... Dr.   300   ($3,000 to $3,300)
    Loss on cash held during
    price rise .... Dr.   50   (5% of $1,000)
      Accumulated depn. .... Cr.   100   ($1,000 to $1,100)
      Capital maintenance adjustment .... Cr.   150   (5% of $3,000)
      Holding gain on non-monetary asset .... Cr.   100   ($2,200–$2,100)
(b) Depreciation .... Dr. 1,100
      Accumulated depreciation .... Cr. 1,100
    (Depn. for year 2, one-third of $3,300)

Profit Statement for Year 2

Net revenues		$2,000
Less Depreciation	$1,100	
Loss on cash held during price rise	50	1,150
		$ 850
Plus Holding gain on non-monetary asset		100
= *Net Profit* (and Dividend)		$ 950

Balance Sheet at End of Year 2

Asset X $3,300		Contributed capital		$3,000
Less Accumulated depn. 2,200	$1,100	Capital maintenance adjustment		150
Cash	2,050*			
	$3,150			$3,150

(*Revenues to date minus dividends.)

Year 3:

Relevant journal entries for year 3 to account for the increase of 10% in the general index and the increase of $300 ($3,300 to $3,600) in the current market buying price of an identical new asset—and the resultant depreciation charge:

(a) Asset X .... Dr. 300   ($3,300 to $3,000)

    Loss on cash held during price rise .... Dr. 205   (10% of $2,050)

    Holding loss on non-monetary asset .... Dr. 10   ($1,210–$1,200)

        Accumulated depreciation .... Cr. 200   ($2,200 to $2,400)

        Capital maintenance adjustment .... Cr. 315   (10% of $3,150)

(b) Depreciation .... Dr. 1,200

        Accumulated depreciation .... Cr. 1,200

    (Depn. for year 3, one-third of $3,600)

Profit Statement for Year 3

Net revenues		$2,000
Less Depreciation	$1,200	
Loss on cash held during price rise	205	
Holding loss on non-monetary asset	10	1,415
= *Net Profit* (and Dividend)		$ 585

Balance Sheet at End of Year 3

Asset *X*	$3,600		Contributed capital		$3,000
Less Accumulated depn. ...	3,600	Nil	Capital maintenance		
			adjustment		465
Cash		3,465*			
		$3,465			$3,465

(*Revenues to date minus dividends.)

3. *In conjunction with net present values*

The net present value of the asset at the beginning of year 1 (@ 20%) was:

$$\$2,000 \times .8333 = \$1,666$$
$$\$2,000 \times .6944 = \ \ 1,389$$
$$\$2,000 \times .5789 = \ \ 1,158$$
$$\overline{\$4,213}$$

Year 1:

Profit Statement for Year 1

Net revenues	$2,000	
Plus Appreciation at purchase	1,213	($4,213–$3,000)
	$3,213	
Less Depreciation	1,158	($4,213–$3,055)
= *Net Profit* (and Dividend)	$2,055	

Balance Sheet at End of Year 1

Asset *X* $4,213			Contributed capital	$3,000
Less Accumulated depn. ..	1,158	3,055	Amount borrowed to	
			pay dividend	55
		$3,055		$3,055

Year 2:

Relevant journal entries for year 2 to account for the 5% increase in the general index—and the resultant depreciation charge:

(a) Asset *X*	Dr.	211		
Accumulated depreciation			Cr.	58
Gain on cash owing during price rise			Cr.	3
Capital maintenance adjustment			Cr.	150
(5% on year 1 balance sheet items)				
(b) Depreciation	Dr. 1,542			
Accumulated depreciation			Cr. 1,542	
(Depn. for year 2, $3, 208–$1,666)				

Profit Statement for Year 2

Net revenues	$2,000
Less Depreciation	1,542
	$ 458
Plus Gain on cash owing during price rise	3
= *Net Profit* (and Dividend)	$ 461

Balance Sheet at End of Year 2

Asset X	.....$4,424		Contributed capital		$3,000
Less Accumulated depn. ...	2,758	$1,666	Capital maintenance		
Cash		1,484*	adjustment		150
		$3,150			$3,150

(*Revenues to date minus dividends.)

Year 3:

Relevant journal entries for year 3 to account for the 10% increase in the general index—and the resultant depreciation charge:

(a) Asset X	Dr.	442	
Loss on cash held during price rise	Dr.	149	
Accumulated depreciation		Cr.	276
Capital maintenance adjustment		Cr.	315
(10% on year 2 balance sheet items)			
(b) Depreciation	Dr. 1,832		
Accumulated depreciation		Cr. 1,832	
(Depn. for year 3)			

Profit Statement for Year 3

Net revenues		$2,000
Less Depreciation	$1,832	
Loss on cash held during price rise	149	1,981
= *Net Profit* (and Dividend)		$ 19

Balance Sheet at End of Year 3

Asset X	.....$4,866		Contributed capital		$3,000
Less Accumulated depn. ...	4,866	Nil	Capital maintenance		
			adjustment		465
Cash		3,465*			$3,465
		$3,465			

(*Revenues to date minus dividends.)

4. *In conjunction with net realizable values*

Year 1:

Profit Statement for Year 1

Net revenues	$2,000	($,3000–NRV
Less Depreciation	1,200	of $1,800)
= *Net Profit* (and Dividend)	$ 800	

Balance Sheet at End of Year 1

Asset X	.....$3,000		Contributed capital	$3,000
Less Accumulated depn. ...	1,200	$1,800		
Cash		. 1,200		
		$3,000		$3,000

Year 2:

Relevant journal entries for year 2 to account for the 5% increase in the general index—and the resultant depreciation charge:

(a) Asset *X* .... Dr. 150
    Loss on cash held during price rise .... Dr. 60
       Accumulated depreciation .... Cr. 60
       Capital maintenance adjustment .... Cr. 150
    (5% on year 1 balance sheet items)
(b) Depreciation .... Dr. 1,090
       Accumulated depreciation .... Cr. 1,090
    (Depn. for year 2 $1,800 − NRV of $800)

Profit Statement for Year 2

Net revenues $2,000
Less Depreciation $1,090
    Loss on cash held during price rise 60   1,150
    = *Net Profit* (and Dividend) .... $ 850

Balance Sheet at End of Year 2

Asset *X* ....$3,150   Contributed capital $3,000
Less Accumulated depn. ... 2,350 $ 800 Capital maintenance
                                adjustment 150
Cash 2,350*
                           $3,150 $3,150

(*Revenues to date minus dividends.)

Year 3:

Relevant journal entries for year 3 to account for the 10% increase in the general index—and the resultant depreciation charges:

(a) Asset *X* .... Dr. 315
    Loss on cash held during price rise .... Dr. 235
       Accumulated depreciation .... Cr. 235
       Capital maintenance adjustment .... Cr. 315
    (10% on year 2 balance sheet items)
(b) Depreciation .... Dr. 880
       Accumulated depreciation .... Cr. 880
    (Depn. for year 3)

Profit Statement for Year 3

Net Revenues $2,000
Less Depreciation 880
    Loss on cash held during price rise 235   1,115
    = *Net Profit* (and Dividend) .... $ 885

Balance Sheet at End of Year 3

Asset X	$3,465		Contributed capital	$3,000
Less Accumulated depn. ...	3,465	Nil	Capital maintenance adjustment	465
Cash	3,465*			
	$3,465			$3,465

(*Revenues to date minus dividends.)

APPENDIX II

DETAILED WORKINGS OF EXAMPLE 2

General Purchasing Power Concept of Capital Maintenance

In conjunction with Historical Costs adjusted for changes in the General Price Level (with sum-of-the-digits depreciation)

Year 1:

Profit Statement for Year 1

Net Revenues	$2,000
Less Depreciation	1,500
= Net Profit (and Dividend)	$ 500

Balance Sheet at End of Year 1

Asset X	$3,000		Contributed capital	$3,000
Less Accumulated depn. ...	1,500	$1,500		
Cash		1,500		
		$3,000		$3,000

Year 2:

Relevant journal entries for year 2 to account for the increase of 5% in the general index—and the resultant depreciation charge:

(a) Asset X ..... Dr. 150
Loss on cash held during price rise ..... Dr. 75
    Accumulated depreciation ..... Cr. 75
    Capital maintenance adjustment ..... Cr. 150
(5% on year 1 balance sheet items)
(b) Depreciation ..... Dr. 1,050
    Accumulated depreciation ..... Cr. 1,050
(Depn. for year 2, two-sixths of $3,150)

Profit Statement for Year 2

Net Revenues		$2,000
Less Depreciation	$1,050	
Loss on cash held during price rise	75	1,125
= *Net Profit* (and Dividend)		$ 875

Balance Sheet at End of Year 2

Asset X $3,150			Contributed capital	$3,000
Less Accumulated depn. ... 2,625	$ 525		Capital maintenance adjustment	150
Cash	2,625*			
	$3,150			$3,150

(*Revenues to date minus dividends.)

Year 3:

Relevant journal entries for Year 3 to account for increase of 10% in the general index—and the resultant depreciation charge:

(a)	Asset X .... Dr. 315		
	Loss on cash held during price rise .... Dr. 262.50		
	Accumulated depreciation		Cr. 262.50
	Capital maintenance adjustment		Cr. 315
	(10% on year 2 balance sheet items)		
(b)	Depreciation .... Dr. 577.50		
	Accumulated depreciation		Cr. 577.50
	(Depn. for year 3, one-sixth of $3,465)		

Profit Statement for Year 3

Net Revenues		$2,000
Less Depreciation	$577.50	
Loss on cash held during price rise	262.50	840
= *Net Profit* (and Dividend)		$1,160

Balance Sheet at End of Year 3

Asset X $3,465			Contributed capital	$3,000
Less Accumulated depn. ... 3,465	Nil		Capital maintenance adjustment	465
Cash	3,465*			
	$3,465			$3,465

(*Revenues to date minus dividends.)

APPENDIX III

DETAILED WORKINGS OF EXAMPLE 3

1. Company A. (Recognizes revenues on *production* of inventories)

Year 1:

Profit Statement for Year 1

Revenues	$100,000
Less Cost of revenues	70,000
= *Net Profit*	$ 30,000

Balance Sheet at End of Year 1

Inventories (@ sales value)	$100,000	Contributed capital	$ 70,000
		Retained earnings	30,000
	$100,000		$100,000

Year 2:

Relevant journal entry for Year 2 to account for the increase of 10% in all prices:

Inventories ....Dr. 10,000	
Capital maintenance adjustment	Cr. 7,000
Retained earnings	Cr. 3,000
(10% of Year 1 balance sheet items)	

Profit Statement for Year 2

Revenues	Nil
Less Cost of revenues	Nil
= *Net Profit*	Nil

Balance Sheet at End of Year 2

Cash (from sale of inventories)	$110,000	Contributed capital	$ 70,000
		Capital maintenance adjustment	7,000
		Retained earnings	33,000
	$110,000		$110,000

2. *Company B.* (Recognizes revenues on *sale* of inventories)

Year 1:

Profit Statement for Year 1

Revenues	Nil
Less Cost of revenues	Nil
= *Net Profit*	Nil

Balance Sheet at End of Year 1

Inventories (@ cost)	70,000	Contributed capital	70,000
	$70,000		$70,000

Year 2:

Relevant journal entry for Year 2 to account for the increase of 10% in all prices:

Inventories .... Dr. 7,000
    Capital maintenance adjustment .... Cr. 7,000
    (10% of Year 1 balance sheet items)

Profit Statement for Year 2

Revenues	$110,000
Less Cost of revenues	77,000
= *Net Profit*	$ 33,000

Balance Sheet at End of Year 2

Cash (from sale of inventories)	$110,000	Contributed capital	70,000
		Capital maintenance adjustment	7,000
		Retained earnings	33,000
	$110,000		$110,000

APPENDIX IV

Financial Accounting Models
Chart Showing Combinations of Assets Valuation Methods and Capital Adjustment Methods on Which Various Models are Based
By Reg. S. Gynther, May, 1980

Capital Adjustment (or Maintenance) Methods \ Asset Valuation Methods	1. Historical Costs	2. Historical Costs × GDP Deflator Index	3. Historical Costs × Consumer or Retail Price Index	4. Net Realizable Values (NRVs)	5. Both Current Costs & NRVs for "Deprival Values" (or Surrogates Thereof)	6. Both Current Costs & NRVs as Surrogates for DPVs
A. Money capital	"Pure" historical-cost accounting Ijiri (a) Paton & Littleton (b)					
B. General Purchasing power of shareholders' (only) funds (a proprietary concept)		First Australian "preliminary exposure draft" (c)		Branford (d)	Mitchell (e)	
C. Consumer purchasing power of shareholders' (only) funds (a proprietary concept)			FAS 33 (USA) general inflation alternative (f)	Chambers (g) Sterling (h)	Baxter (i)	FAS 33 (USA) Current cost alternative (j) Staubus (o)

		"Richardson report" (New Zealand) (k) SSAP 16 (UK) (See comments under "l")	Gynther (n)
D. *Specific* purchasing power of *shareholders'* (only) funds (i.e. operating capability of shareholders' funds.) (A proprietary concept)			
E. *Specific* purchasing power of *all* capital funds—i.e. based on movements in current costs of relevant assets. (i.e. operating capability of *all* capital funds) (an entity concept)		PAS 1.1 and 1.2 (Australia) (m)	

Note:
This chart first appeared in this approximate form in Reg. S. Gynther, "Accounting for Changing Prices: Some Recent Thinking, Recommendations and Practice". *The Chartered Accountant in Australia*, December, 1971, pp. 12–23. An earlier version appeared in Reg S. Gynther, *Accounting for Price Changes-Theory and Practice* (Society Bulletin No. 5) Australian Society of Accountants, Melbourne, 1968 and in "Capital Maintenance, Price Changes, and Profit Determination", *Accounting Review*, October, 1970, pp. 712–730. The chart has been amended several times since in order to incorporate new publications.

References:
(a) Yuji Ijiri, *The Foundations of Accounting Measurement*, Prentice-Hall Inc., Englewood Cliffs, New Jersey, 1967.
(b) W. A. Paton & A. C. Littleton, *An Introduction to Corporate Accounting Standards*, American Accounting Assn., 13th printing, 1967.
(c) The Institute of Chartered Accountants in Australia and the Australian Society of Accountants, "A Method of Accounting for Changes in the Purchasing Power of Money" (A [First] "Preliminary Exposure Draft"), December 1974 (since superseded).
(d) B. L. Branford, "Current Monetary Measures in Accounting", *Accounting Bulletin*, Queensland Division of the Australian Society of Accountants, Brisbane, November, 1968.
(e) G. B. Mitchell, "Current Value Accounting", *Chartered Accountant in Australia*, December, 1975, pp. 4–9, and 46.
(f) Financial Accounting Standards Board, "Financial Reporting and Changing Prices." (Statement of Financial Accounting Standards No. 33), September, 1979. (See paras. 39 to 50).
(g) Raymond J. Chambers, *Accounting Evaluation and Economic Behaviour*,

(h) Robert R. Sterling, *Theory of the Measurement of Enterprise Income*, The University Press of Kansas, Lawrence, Kansas, 1970.
(i) Wm. T. Baxter, *Accounting Values and Inflation*, McGraw-Hill (U.K.) Ltd., 1975.
(j) Financial Accounting Standards Board, "Financial Reporting and Changing Prices" (Statement of Financial Accounting Standards No. 33), September, 1979. (See paras. 51 to 65, and para. 120).
(k) "Report of the Committee of Inquiry into Inflation Accounting", Government Printer, Wellington, New Zealand, 1976.
(l) Accounting Standards Committee, "SSAP 16: Current Cost Accounting", March, 1980. This model only attempts to recognise *realised* gains on holding loan capital. but it does this in accordance with the capital adjustment method indicated in the chart.
(m) The Institute of Chartered Accountants and the Australian Society of Accountants, "Statement of Provisional Accounting Standards" titled "Current Cost Accounting" (PAS 1.1) and its "Explanatory Statement" titled "The Basis of Current Cost Accounting" (PAS 1.2), August, 1978, "The Recognition of Gains and Losses on Holding Monetary Items in the Context of Current Cost Accounting" (Revised Exposure Draft) August, 1979, *and* "Omnibus Exposure Draft", March, 1980. All of those make up one "package".
(n) R. S. Gynther, *Accounting for Price Level Changes: Theory and Procedures*, Pergamon Press Ltd., Oxford, 1966; "Some Problems Associated with the Implementation of Current Value Accounting", *Chartered Accountant in Australia*, July, 1976, and other recent writings.
(o) George J. Staubus, *Making Accounting Decisions*, Scholars Book Co., Houston, 1977.

Accounting for Inflation

R. J. CHAMBERS

Conventional (historical cost based) accounting is almost universally recognized to be defective under inflationary conditions. Experience under these conditions has prompted the search for a dependable alternative.

There have been under consideration two major alternatives or supplements to conventional accounting: (1) current purchasing power (C.P.P.) accounting, and (2) replacement price accounting (R.P.A.) of which current cost accounting is a variety.

The first method deals with ways of taking account of some of the effects of changes in the purchasing power of money, but disregards the effects of changes in the prices of particular assets. The second proposes the use of the replacement prices of assets in financial statements, but disregards the general effects of changes in the purchasing power of money. As both types of change occur concurrently during inflationary periods, both of the above methods are partial or incomplete, and therefore potentially misleading.

This Exposure Draft deals with a method of accounting—continuously contemporary accounting—which takes into account both changes in particular prices and changes in the general level of prices. It is thus more comprehensive than the two methods previously mentioned. And the financial statements it yields are up-to-date, more realistic and more readily comprehensible.

PART I—ACCOUNTING GENERALLY

1. The discussion and conclusions to be presented will have reference to business firms generally.

Any method of business accounting should be expected to be serviceable in substantially the same ways, no matter what the form of ownership of the business to which accounts relate. However, the most extensive array of uses of accounting information is exemplified by the relationships between companies and their shareholders, creditors and others. For this reason much of the discussion will relate to companies and company accounting. But, because the principles or rules which emerge are equally pertinent to companies and other types of business ownership, the general term "business firm" or simply "firm" will be commonly used. Also the terms "net profit" and "net income" will be used interchangeably, as synonyms.

344 R. J. Chambers, "Accounting for Inflation," Exposure Draft, University of Sydney, Australia, September 1975. Reprinted by permission of the author.

2. Financial statements are expected to represent fairly and in up-to-date terms the financial characteristics of firms.

The products of the accounting process are dated balance sheets and income (profit and loss) statements. These are expected, by the laws relating to companies, to give a true and fair view of the financial positions and of the results of companies as at the dates and for the periods to which they relate. They are put to use by a variety of parties; by actual and potential investors and creditors; by investment advisers and underwriters and trustees for creditors; by tribunals concerned with wages and prices; and by governmental authorities for fiscal and other regulatory purposes. The decisions and actions of all of these parties are taken in the light of what they know, at the time, of the past results and present financial positions of companies (or of firms generally). Unless the financial statements of companies correspond fairly well with their actual positions and results, actions based upon them may affect adversely, and quite unexpectedly, the interests of companies or of other parties related to them.

3. The survival and growth of firms depends on their command of money and money's worth.

The actions of all the above mentioned parties are directly related to money receipts and payments of a company—receipts by way of sales income, loans or credits, subsidies or bounties, and the proceeds of new share issues; payments by way of purchases, wages, taxes, interest, and loan repayments. The capacity of a company to grow or to change its operations, on a small or large scale, as new opportunities arise and present operations become less attractive, depends on its command of money or money's worth. In the ordinary course of events, companies are expected to pay their debts to others when they fall due. In some circumstances they may find it worth while, or be forced, to repay debts before they fall due. Generally, then, the ability to meet debts owed is a condition of survival. For all these reasons, it is a matter of importance that the managers of companies, and that other parties having financial interests in companies, shall know from time to time the money and money's worth at the command of companies and their outstanding financial obligations.

4. Financial position is a dated relationship between assets and equities.

The money and money's worth at the command of a company at a point of time is given by the sum of its holdings of cash and receivables and the market (resale) prices of its other (non-monetary) assets. The resale price of an asset at a given date is its money equivalent at that date. Possession of the asset is financially equal to possession of the sum of money representing its resale price. It is therefore possible to add amounts of cash and receivables and the money equivalents of other assets to obtain a financially significant aggregate. The total amount of liabilities to short and long term creditors represents money claims against the aggregate money's worth of assets. The difference between total assets and total liabilities is a genuine money amount, since the amounts of total assets and total liabilities are genuine money amounts. This difference represents the residual interest of shareholders or owners in the total assets, or the total investment at risk in the business of the company. It also represents the amount of net assets, or assets financed otherwise than by credit.

5. The amount of income is deduced from changes in dated financial positions.

A balance sheet in which assets are represented at their money equivalents gives to all users of it an up-to-date indication of the total wealth of a company at a point of time and total claims against or interests in that wealth. Given two such balance sheets, in the absence of inflation, the increment in the amount of net assets represents the retained profit of the intervening period (provided there has been no new share issue). The sum of retained profit and the dividends paid in the period is the net profit or net income of the period. Net income may be calculated by setting out the several classes of gain or loss of a company in a period. But the amount so obtained is necessarily equal to the difference between the opening and closing money amounts of net assets. It is a genuine increment in money's worth, since the net assets figures are genuine money amounts (para. 4).

6. Financial positions and results are aggregative; their elements must satisfy the rules of addition and relation.

Total wealth, total liabilities, the amount of net assets, the calculation of net profits, all entail addition and subtraction. Other calculations made by investors and creditors, such as rates of return and debt to equity ratios, are relations between aggregates. All particular elements of financial statements must therefore be capable of proper addition and relation. The money amounts and money equivalents referred to in the two previous paragraphs satisfy this condition. By contrast, no logical or financial significance can be assigned to the sum of an amount of money and the purchase price, past, present or future (including replacement price) of any good. No such sum can properly be related to any debt outstanding, or to any plan to purchase goods or services, or to pay taxes and dividends.

7. Financial positions and results are both the consequences of past actions and the cases of future actions.

The financial position of a firm is a consequence of past (historical) events up to the date for which it is ascertained. No future event or expectation of a future event has any bearing on it. But given an ascertained financial position (and other information and expectations), choices may be made among the courses of action available to the firm. If at a given date the liquidity of a firm is strained, action to restore its liquidity is necessary. If at a given date a firm is heavily in debt, liquidity cannot readily be restored by further borrowing. If the results of the immediately past period are unsatisfactory in any sense, action must be taken to improve the result in the following period. All deliberate actions having financial consequences must be considered in the light of the aggregative financial characteristics of the firm at the time of choice. And all estimations of the probable financial consequences of future actions must be based on the position of the firm at the time of choice of future courses of action. Financial position as described is the one common element in all calculations relating to choices of future actions.

8. The money equivalents of assets, the purchase prices (replacement prices) of assets and the user-values of assets are used in conjunction; none is a substitute for the other.

If a prospective course of action entails the "replacement" of an asset, it is necessary to know the money equivalent of the present asset and the purchase price of the new asset. If a prospective action entails the purchase of additional assets, their purchase prices must be known. Whether or not any such course is financially "feasible" can only be ascertained by comparison of those purchase prices with the money equivalents of present assets, or some selection of present assets. Which is to be preferred of the feasible courses of action is indicated, inter alia, by comparisons of the expected net proceeds of the alternative projects or investments in assets. Expected net proceeds, or present (discounted) values, are user-values. They are personal estimates based on expectations of the future; they are therefore subjective. They represent the expected outcomes of specific possible future actions. They cannot therefore be used in balance sheets as indicative of the financial feasibility of *any* course of action, even of those courses to which they relate. In short, the money equivalents of assets, the purchase prices of goods not presently held, and user-values of assets or projects are used when considering specific possible courses of action. But each is used for its own purpose and in its own way. None is a substitute for the other. None of them may properly be added together. Only the money equivalent of assets are properly useable for the representation of financial position at a given date.

PART II—THE EFFECTS OF INFLATION

9. Changes in the structure and in the general level of prices occur concurrently but not equally.

In an inflationary period two things occur which affect the positions and results of companies. The prices of particular goods change relatively to one another. There is a change in the *structure* of prices. Such changes may occur at any time as the wants of consumers change, technology changes or the policies and outputs of companies change (collectively, supply and demand conditions). There is also a change in the general *level* of prices. "Inflation" is descriptive of a rise in the general level of prices, or of its counterpart, a fall in the general purchasing power of money. When inflation occurs all prices do not rise to the same extent or at the same time. Some may fall as rises in others force business firms and consumers to change their spending habits. Inflation may thus cause changes in the structure of prices, to the benefit of some firms and to the detriment of others. The beneficial or detrimental effects may arise from changes in the money equivalents of assets held, or from changes in the profit margins obtainable for goods and services sold.

10. The effects on a firm of changes in the structure and level of prices can only be ascertained in the aggregate.

When changes in the structure of prices and changes in the general level of prices occur in the same period, it is not possible to say that any particular price change is caused by inflation, or by the shift in the relation between the supply and demand conditions, or partly by the one and partly by the other. All that is known is that prices and the level of prices are different from those of an earlier date. Nevertheless, it is possible to calculate the aggregate effects of changes in prices and the general level of prices on the positions and results of firms. Because changes in particular prices and changes in the general level of prices influence one another, the effects of both should be brought into account. One cannot be considered as isolated from the other. Whatever the outcome, it cannot be said whether any part of the result is due solely to managerial judgements or solely to accidental or unforeseeable factors. Managers may be expected to use their best judgements at all times. Only the results in aggregate will indicate with what effect firms have been able to meet the conditions through which they have passed.

11. The conventinal money unit, in terms of which financial positions are represented, is equally serviceable for that purpose in inflation.

Financial position has been described as the dated relationship between amounts of assets and equities (para. 4). The dating of a financial statement represents both (a) that the money unit used in it has reference to that date and (b) that the number of money units appearing beside any item is the appropriate money equivalent of that item at that date. To suppose otherwise would be anachronistic, and confusing. The money unit is by its nature the unit of general purchasing power and debt-paying power at any specified date whatever, and the unit in which the money equivalents (resale prices) of assets are expressed. That the same nominal money unit may have a different general purchasing power at some other date is of no consequence when determining a dated financial position.

12. The increment in the nominal amount of net assets during a year is not serviceable as indicating net income in an inflationary period.

Calculation of net income in the manner described in para 5 brings into account the effects of all changes in the money equivalents of assets, in the absence of inflation. If particular assets have risen or fallen in price during a year, for whatever reason, these changes in the structure of prices will be captured by taking the resale prices of assets at the opening and closing dates of the year. Since, in the absence of inflation, there is no change in the general purchasing power of money, the net income so calculated will represent a genuine increment in the general purchasing power or debt-paying power of the net assets of a firm. Part of it will be the resultant of trading costs and revenues, and part the resultant of rises and falls in the money equivalents of assets since the beginning of the period or since (the subsequent) date of purchase. The rises and falls during the year in the money equivalents of assets held at the end of a year may be described as *price variation adjustments*. But if the purchasing power of the money unit has changed during the year, the difference between the opening and closing amounts of net assets will not represent a genuine increment in general purchasing or debt-paying power.

13. Provision must be made for the loss of purchasing power in an inflationary period of the amount of net assets (or capital employed) at the beginning of the accounting period.

Money holdings and claims to fixed amounts of money may be described as monetary assets. Their money equivalents at any date may be discovered directly. All other assets are non-monetary assets. Their money equivalents at any date must be discovered by reference to market resale prices at or near that date. Monetary assets held during an inflationary period lose general purchasing power. Likewise every dollar representing the money equivalent of non-monetary assets at the beginning of a period loses general purchasing power. And likewise every dollar owed during an inflationary period loses general purchasing power; borrowings thus constitute a "hedge" against losses in the purchasing power of money. By subtraction, the amount at risk of loss in general purchasing power during inflation is the amount of net assets (total assets less liabilities) at the beginning of the accounting period. The amount of the loss thus sustained must be made good out of other surpluses before it can be said that a surplus in the nature of net income has arisen. This amount may be described as a *capital maintenance adjustment*, since its object is to secure that, in calculating net income, provision is made for the maintenance of the general purchasing power of the opening amount of net assets (or capital employed).

It may be noted that, across a whole community, the aggregate amount of price variation adjustments might be expected to correspond with the aggregate amount of capital maintenance adjustments, since the general price index is indicative of the average of changes in specific prices. But particular firms are affected differentially by changes in prices and in the price level. Rises in the prices of particular goods do not correspond with or offset falls in the general purchasing power of money. That is why the aggregates of both should be taken separately in the accounts of firms.

14. Net income is the algebraic sum of trading surpluses, price variation adjustments and the capital maintenance adjustment.

The amount of the capital maintenance adjustment is the opening amount of net assets multiplied by the proportionate change in the general level of prices. Thus, if a firm begins a period with net assets of $1,000 and an index of changes in the general level of prices rises from 130 to 143 in the period, the amount of the capital maintenance adjustment is $1,000 × 13/130, or $100. A general price index is used because the amount of net assets is a genuine dated money sum, irrespective of the composition of assets, and because the firm is considered to be free to lay out any part of its assets or the increment in its assets in any way it pleases. The index to be used would be chosen on the basis of competent statistical advice. From the two preceding paragraphs, net income will be the algebraic sum of trading surpluses, price variation adjustments and the capital maintenance adjustment. The amount charged as capital maintenance adjustment will be credited to a capital maintenance reserve. If any part of this reserve were appropriated as a dividend, it would impair the general purchasing power of the opening amount of net assets. (See also para 34).

PART III—GENERAL PRINCIPLES OF CONTINUOUSLY CONTEMPORARY ACCOUNTING

15. The method of accounting described is called continuously contemporary accounting (CoCoA).[1]

Asset valuations are brought up-to-date, at least at the end of each accounting period, by reference to independent sources of information. Those valuations are in terms of the purchasing power unit at the time. That the balance sheet is a dated statement implies that the amounts stated in it relate to that date and that the dollars in which those amounts are expressed are dollars of dated purchasing power (see para 11). CoCoA satisfies this requirement. Shareholders' equity amounts are augmented by the capital maintenance adjustment periodically and the balance of net income is a sum also expressed in dollars of the same dated purchasing power as other items in the balance sheet. All reported balances of a given date are therefore contemporary with that date. There are no prices of different dates nor purchasing power units of different dates in the balance sheet of any date. Hence the description "continuously contemporary accounting".

16. Accounts may be brought up to date periodically or more frequently.

The price changes affecting a firm may be occasional or frequent, and individually large or small. As up-to-date information on a firm's assets and liabilities is the only dependable basis for managerial action, the accounts may be continually adjusted for changes in the prices of assets. In principle this is the most desirable mode of accounting. But for external reporting it is sufficient to bring the account balances to their money equivalents at the end of each reporting period. Accounts could be kept just as they are presently kept during the accounting period. But at the end of the period all account balances are adjusted to their current money equivalents. The variations of money equivalents from book balances are summarized and charged or credited, as price variation adjustments, in the income account. And of course the capital maintenance adjustment is computed and charged. The method may be called "continuously contemporary" because, in principle, accounts can be kept continuously up-to-date, even though in practice adjustments may be made less frequently than price changes occur. Under either process the results will be exactly the same.

---

[1]The text of the original publication (1975) used "CCA" with reference to continuously contemporary accounting, an abbreviation used by the author since 1967. That abbreviation has since been widely used with reference to "current cost accounting." To avoid confusion, in this reprint "CoCoA" is used as an abbreviation for continuously contemporary accounting. Some minor changes have also been made in the prefatory note and the introductory material of Appendix B.

17. CoCoA conforms with the established principle of periodical, independent verification of account balances (the objectivity principle).

To verify the physical existence of, and legal title to, assets at balance date is a well established principle. Independent checking of cash balances and receivables balances has long been regarded as a necessary safeguard against misrepresentation. But the same process of verification is not applied, under traditional historical cost accounting, to the money amounts assigned to other assets. The mere checking of physical existence and legal title is inconsistent with the fact that financial statements relate to the *financial* characteristics of firms, not to physical or purely legal characteristics. The financial characteristics of assets should be independently verified, no less than other characteristics. CoCoA applies this principle uniformly to all assets.

18. CoCoA conforms with the well-established accrual principle.

The accrual principle entails accounting for changes in the financial characteristics of a firm independently of the conversion of assets and obligations to cash. Revenue is brought into account when customers are billed; earlier, that is, than cash is received from customers. Depreciation is brought into account periodically; that is, long before the diminution in value of an asset is discovered on its resale. Applications of the principle pervade current practice. Yet there are also numerous cases in traditional practice where the principle is not applied. Changes in the prices of assets are not accrued usually, unless they are downward changes. And quite generally the effects of advantageous changes are not accrued but the effects of disadvantageous changes are accrued; thus depreciation is charged, but appreciation is not brought into account. These inconsistencies cannot yield realistic and up-to-date statements of financial position and results. CoCoA avoids inconsistency by applying the accrual principle uniformly to all assets and liabilities, and hence also to shareholders' equity.

19. CoCoA conforms with the well-established going concern principle.

The going concern principle entails that the financial position as represented in a balance sheet shall be indicative of the position of a firm as a going concern. The significant financial characteristics of a going concern are its ability to pay its debts when due, to pay for its supplies of goods and labour service, to change the composition of its assets, liabilities and operations if the present composition hinders its survival or growth, and the ability to earn a rate of profit consistent with the risks of the business. The ability of a firm to pay its debts, to pay for its necessary inputs, to borrow on the security of its assets, and to change the composition of its assets and operations, is indicated only if assets are shown at their money equivalents, since all the matters mentioned entail receipts and payments of money. The ability of a firm to earn an adequate rate of profit may be judged only if the profit earned is a genuine increment in purchasing power and the amount of net assets (or shareholders' equity) to which it is related is a genuine money sum. The use of market (resale) prices in CoCoA has nothing to do with liquidation of a business; it is simply the only way to find the present money equivalents of non-monetary assets from time to time.

20. CoCoA satisfies the requirements of stewardship accounts.

As financial statements indicate in general terms the disposition of assets and increments in assets from time to time they are regarded as the basis upon which the performance of a company and its management may be judged. Such judgements must be supposed to be made periodically in respect of the year recently past; their formal expression lies in the resolutions of annual general meetings. It is necessary, therefore, to know the amount of the assets available for use and disposition by the management at the beginning of each year, if a satisfactory account is to be given of the use, disposition and increase of assets in that year. If the amounts of assets from time to time were stated on any basis other than their money equivalents, there would be no firm and satisfactory basis for determining the use and disposition of assets. Since all uses and dispositions in a period entail movements of money or money equivalents, financial statements based on the money equivalents of assets provide information on which periodical performance may fairly be judged.

21. CoCoA adheres closely to the principle of periodical accounting.

Financial statements generally purport to represent dated positions and the results of defined periods. But the effects of events in one period are frequently allowed to influence what is reported of another. This occurs whenever some future event or outcome is anticipated (as in the usual calculation of depreciation charges), or whenever some actual effect on results or position is "deferred" for recognition in a later period. CoCoA makes no such concessions, on the ground that reports which do not represent the effects of events in a defined period cannot properly be interpreted, singly or in series, by reference to the dated context of business events and circumstances. It may be objected that to base accounts on a dated selling price could be misleading if the price were anomalous. But exactly the same can be said of dated purchase prices which are used in other forms of accounting. In any case the anomaly might be expected to be explained rather than concealed.

PART IV—THE DETERMINATION OF MONEY EQUIVALENTS

22. Any asset for which there is not a present resale price cannot be considered to have a present financial significance.

A company may have assets for which there is no present resale price. They may have a high user-value (see para 8), but they cannot be considered to have financial significance in the sense of purchasing or debt-paying power or as security for loans. Investors, creditors, suppliers and others would be misinformed of the financial capacity for action by balance sheets in which money amounts were assigned to assets having no current money equivalents. The assets to which this rule applies include some work in progress, and specialized plant and equipment for which there is no market in the ordinary course of business. The same rule applies to expenditures on exploratory or developmental work which has yielded no vendible product or asset. The notion of conservatism in traditional accounting would tend to have the same effect as the treatment suggested. But that notion is vague and loosely applied, whereas the principle here stated is definite and it yields information which is relevant to the judgements and decisions of parties financially interested in companies. If it is desired, on any ground, to indicate that a company has assets, or has incurred costs and outlays, having no present money equivalent, parenthetical or footnote information may be given.

23. The determination of the money equivalents of assets at a stated date is necessarily approximate.

Prices may vary from place to place for the same goods on any given day. What is required is a fair approximation to the current money equivalent of each asset. This may require the exercise of judgement, but abuse of judgement is constrained by the necessity of approximating a definite characteristic of the asset and by the prices discovered at or about the balance date. In any case, no form of accounting escapes the use of dated prices; even historical cost accounting uses dated prices which may or may not have been the only prices, or representative prices, at dates of purchase. Any attempt to distort results and positions by the choice of prices which are not fair approximations to money equivalents is constrained by the independent inspection and judgement of auditors. It is also constrained by the fact that the whole of the asset balances of one year determine the amounts of the price variation adjustments, and hence the income, of the following year. There are no alternative permissible rules by resort to which this constraint may be avoided.

24. Resale prices are accessible to most firms for most assets.

All proposals considered in anticipation of purchases and the settlement of debts include at some point sums of money which are presently available, or which could shortly become available by the sale of assets (inventory or other assets), or which could be borrowed on the security of assets. In the latter two cases some approximation to the money equivalent or resale price of non-monetary assets is required. Changes in the prices of goods and services used and in the markets for a firm's products may at any time force its management to reconsider the costs of its present mode of operations. And if it is assumed that one of the functions of management is the pursuit of efficiency or economies, the possibility of changes in its operations and assets will be under examination from time to time. It follows that some person or persons will be acquainted with the approximate market prices of the assets the firm presently holds, and with changes in those prices from time to time. It is possible for any firm to draw on its purchasing officers, salesmen, engineers and project evaluation officers for information on the prices of assets; and to have recourse to prices published in trade journals and the general press as well as direct inquiry. A great deal of information of this kind is readily available without recourse to specialist valuers. But valuations by specialists on an asset resale basis may also be obtained, where necessary of themselves, or as a check on the information available otherwise.

25. Receivables: The amount to be reported will be the amount deemed, on the evidence available, to be recoverable from debtors in the ordinary course of business.

Generally this will be the face value or book value of debtors' accounts, for that is the amount of the claims against debtors at balance date. There is no need to speculate about the possibility that some debtors may take advantage of discounts offered for prompt settlement. Whether they do so or not, the consequence will lie in the following period and will be then reported. Where there is evidence that the full amount of a debt will not be recovered, the amount of the debt may be reduced or written off according to the evidence then available. The amount of receivables yielded by these rules will be the best approximation to the money equivalent of receivables in the light of the information then available, without speculative allowances for what may subsequently occur.

26. Inventories will be valued consistently on the basis of their present market selling prices in the parcels or quantities in which they are customarily sold by the firm.

In the ordinary course of events, raw materials will have a somewhat lower money equivalent than their recent purchase prices, since the user is not a trader in those materials. Work in progress inventories may have a substantially lower money equivalent than their costs, for such work in progress may not be salable in its then state and condition. Finished goods inventories will generally have higher money equivalents (current selling prices) than their costs.

To report inventories at market resale prices is not novel. Nor is it novel that work in progress may appear at a low or zero value; for the traditional rule, "lower of cost and market", should produce the same result. By comparison with the recorded costs, the higher money equivalents of finished goods will to some extent "offset" the lower money equivalents of raw materials and work in progress. But whether the resulting aggregate differs much or little from a cost-based aggregate is less important than the fact that a uniform rule—market price—is used throughout, and that the aggregate has a definite, dated money significance which "cost" and the "lower of cost and market" do not have.

27. Plant and equipment will be valued at market resale prices, in the units or combinations in which, in the ordinary course of business, they are bought, sold, or put out of use.

The object of the traditional method of accounting for plant is to record its cost and to provide out of periodical revenues sufficient to reduce that cost to its market resale price, or scrap value, by the time it is put out of service. The method of CoCoA has exactly the same object; but it is attained by direct reference to market prices year by year, rather than by relying on an arithmetical formula and disregarding the actual changes, up or down, in market prices from time to time. Market resale prices may be estimated from information obtained by the methods mentioned in para 24. The prices sought are not prices obtainable on liquidation or under duress. They are to be the best approximations to the money equivalents of assets in the ordinary course of business. To determine the best approximation entails skill and judgement; but judgement is to be applied to the information obtainable on prices, not to construct imaginative valuations. Checks on the possibility of manipulation are (i) that auditors must be satisfied that the assigned market values are based on current price information, (ii) that excessive understatement reduces the profit of the year and the asset backing of shares and debt at the end of the year, and (iii) that excessive overstatement reduces the profit of a subsequent year and improperly boosts the asset backing of shares and debt. The use of market resale prices may entail heavy charges, due to the sharp drop from cost to money equivalent of some plant, in the early years of use. Some assets may have virtually no resale price, but high user-value. Such occurrences necessarily reduce the adaptive capacity of firms, their command of money and money's worth. The reduction is made explicit in the amounts by charges against revenues, or against other shareholders' equity accounts if the amounts are extraordinary. (See also para 22 above).

28. Land and buildings will be valued at market resale prices, or approximations based on official valuations, prices of similar property and expert valuations.

The same considerations apply to land and buildings as to plant and equipment. Local government valuations (for taxing or rating purposes) provide evidence additional to that from other sources. No single valuation or price need necessarily be taken as a proper approximation to money equivalent; but the chosen valuation must be justifiable in the circumstances. The checks mentioned in para 27 tend to limit arbitrary or unusual valuations.

29. Investments in the shares of other companies will be valued at net market prices where the shares are publicly traded; otherwise at the proportionate interest in the net assets of the investee company.

Holdings of listed shares are readily priced by reference to stock exchange quotations (i.e. "buyer"). Allowance may be made for commissions payable on sale, to obtain the net money equivalent of the investment. There is no readily available and dependable price for non-listed shares. An alternative is required which yields the best approximation to the money equivalent of the investment. If CoCoA is used uniformly, the proportionate interest in the net assets of the investee will provide an approximation; for the accounts of the investee will represent assets at money equivalents. Strictly the amount so calculated will not be the same as a share price; but it is a better approximation than the original cost, or a valuation related to user-value (e.g. based on capitalized prospective earnings).

30. Liabilities will be represented by the amounts owed and payable to creditors in the ordinary course of business.

No amount shall be shown as a liability unless it represents an amount owed to and legally recoverable by a creditor. Whether the due date is near or distant is immaterial. Long-dated obligations may become due and payable if any circumstance threatens the security of creditors.

PART V—OWNERS' EQUITY ACCOUNTS

31. All transactions of a period will be recorded at their actual effective prices, and so charged or credited in the income (profit and loss) account.

All transactions have determinate effects on balances of cash or receivables and payables. The general purchasing power of the cash receipts and payments during an inflationary period will change from time to time. But the aggregate effect of changes in the purchasing power of the money unit is brought into account by way of the capital maintenance adjustment at the end of the accounting period. By showing the actual amounts of receipts and payments, all such amounts are traceable, and identical with their counterparts elsewhere in the accounts.

32. Price variation accounts will be credited with all increases in the book values of assets, and debited with all decreases, during the period.

The book balances of accounts, other than monetary item accounts, may be adjusted for changes in asset prices during the year. The valuation of all assets at the end of the year at their resale prices gives effect to all variations in prices which have not previously been brought into account. The amounts by which the book values of assets are increased (decreased) during the year to correspond with market resale prices will be debited (credited) to the asset accounts and credited (debited) to the price variation accounts. There may be price variation accounts for as many separate asset classes as is deemed necessary. Under CoCoA, the depreciation account, representing a fall in the market resale price of an asset or class of assets, is a price variation account. The price variation accounts are closed by transfer of their balances to the income account.

33. The capital maintenance adjustment will be calculated by applying to the opening amount of net assets the proportionate change in the index of changes in the general level of prices.

The net amount of price variations will tend to be (but will not necessarily be) positive during inflation. But these are gross increments, and the resulting asset balances are in units of year-end purchasing power. The full effect of the change in the purchasing power of money on the results of the year is given by the calculation of the capital maintenance adjustment. The calculation is a mathematically proper calculation, since under CoCoA the opening amount of net assets is a genuine, dated money sum to which a change in the index may legitimately be applied. The capital maintenance adjustment is debited in the income account (in inflationary years).

34. The amount of the capital maintenance adjustment will be credited proportionately to the opening balance of undistributed profits and to other opening balances of owners' equity accounts.

The amount of net assets at the beginning of a year is equal to the sum of the balances of the owners' equity accounts. The object of crediting the amount of the capital maintenance adjustment to owners' equity accounts is to restate the aggregate of the opening balances in units of purchasing power at the end of the year. Part of the capital maintenance adjustment may therefore be credited directly to the retained profits account, a part equal to the opening balance of retained profits multiplied by the proportionate change in the index of changes in the general level of prices. The remainder of the adjustment will be the appropriate amount to credit to a capital maintenance reserve. Where the amount subscribed by shareholders is required to be shown in balance sheets, this money amount may be carried indefinitely in the accounts. Following the above rules, the sum of the amount described and the balance of the capital maintenance reserve at the end of any year will be the purchasing power equivalent at that time of all sums deemed to have been subscribed by shareholders.

35. Where there are outstanding issues of preference shares, these shall be treated as equivalent to outstanding debt, for the purpose of calculating the capital maintenance adjustment.

Preference shares are, like debts, redeemable at fixed, contractual money amounts. Therefore, like debts, they provide a hedge against the effects of changes in the general purchasing power of money. The amount of outstanding preference shares will therefore be deducted (together with all other liabilities) from total assets to obtain the amount of net assets to be used in the calculation of the capital maintenance adjustment.

36. Net income of a year will be the algebraic sum of transaction surpluses (para 31), price variation adjustments (para 32), and the capital maintenance adjustment (para 33).

The balance of the income account after incorporating the consequences of transactions and the price variation and capital maintenance adjustments will be the net income in units of year-end purchasing power. The whole of it may be paid out without impairing the purchasing power of the opening amount of net assets. Or if it or any part of it is transferred to a retained profits account, the whole of the balance of that account could be paid out (as dividends) without impairing the purchasing power of the amounts subscribed or deemed to have been subscribed by ordinary shareholders.

PART VI—SOME FEATURES OF THE SYSTEM

37. All original entries relate to the amounts of transactions; all adjustments are based on information from sources external to the firm.

These features ensure that all amounts represent actually experienced or accrued effects on a firm's position and results. Doubts about the magnitudes of accrued effects are resolved by recourse to external information, not to internal formulae. There are no arbitrary apportionments, no questionable assumptions about future events or uniformities, and no arbitrary demarcations between outcomes which are and which are not controllable, in some sense, by firms and their managements. The accounts and financial statements may be audited, therefore, with reference to independent sources of information; and the representations they make will be pertinent to the financial relations of the firm with the rest of the world.

38. CoCoA applies a single valuation rule throughout, avoiding the addition of different kinds of magnitudes in balance sheets.

There are no optional rules for asset valuation, as there are in all other systems. There is no possibility, therefore, that the significance of aggregates will be distorted by the addition of magnitudes of different kinds. Although the transactions figures and price variation adjustments are magnitudes expressed in money units of different purchasing powers, the combined effect of them and the capital maintenance adjustment is a net income in units of the same purchasing power as other items in a closing balance sheet.

39. CoCoA entails uniform valuation rules for all companies, making possible comparison of the financial features of companies.

Under accounting systems which allow optional valuation rules, the financial significance of the resulting figures is always open to doubt, and strictly to direct comparison of financial magnitudes, rates and ratios is possible. Financial statements based on market resale prices, on the other hand, yield technically proper and practically significant indications of the composition of assets, of current ratios, debt to equity ratios, and rates of return—all of which may be directly compared with corresponding features of other companies and with corresponding features of the same company in prior years.

40. Some of the figures yielded by CoCoA may seem unusual by contrast with traditional accounting; they should be considered, not separately, but as parts of the whole system.

To value finished goods inventory at market price, when higher than cost, may seem unusual; and to value raw materials and work in progress at current market price, when lower than cost, may also seem unusual. It may appear that to calculate net income on such a footing is to "anticipate profits". But in the first place, the use of one valuation rule yields a comprehensible aggregate. Second, the "unusual" effects are to some extent offsetting. And third, the overriding charge for the capital maintenance adjustment is built-in protection against the overstatement of periodical net income. The same reasoning applies to the bringing to account of changes in the market prices of other non-monetary assets.

41. No right or advantage which arises only on disposal of the company as a whole is brought into the accounts.

CoCoA is strictly concerned with a company as a going concern. No value is assigned to such things as developmental costs, goodwill and specialized plant having no resale value, which are realizable only on liquidation or disposal of part or whole of the company. Insofar as any amount has been paid out in respect of these items, it constitutes a sunk cost, and is not available as such for any financial purpose in the ordinary course of business. Such amounts may be charged against shareholders' equity directly, or treated in the manner of the "double account" system, above the balance sheet proper. This treatment is in accordance with the practice of financial analysis, and avoids the impression that the company has assets which are convertible to cash in the ordinary course of business. The mixing of subjective user-values with objective financial values has led, in many cases, to serious misdirection of investors and other financial supporters (see also para 8).

42. The information given by CoCoA is consistent with that demanded by lenders and analysts of business affairs, and with the sense of the legislation relating to financial disclosure.

Lenders on the security of property are concerned with the up-to-date market values of assets; they alone constitute effective cover for debt. Press discussion of company affairs has drawn attention repeatedly to the differences between "accounting values" and market values—both when specific prices have been rising and when they have been falling. The statutory requirements relating to financial disclosure have increasingly stipulated the publication (by footnote or otherwise) of market values, or have indicated that realizable value is important information to users of financial statements. Examples are the disclosure of the market values of listed securities, general provisions relating to the valuation of current assets, provisions relating to the valuation of property charged as security by borrowing companies, and the U.K. provision requiring directors to comment on differences between market values and book values of interests in property. CoCoA does systematically what all these practices, in piecemeal fashion, imply.

43. The financial statements yielded by CoCoA constitute, in series, a continuous history of the financial affairs of a company.

Because the method of CoCoA embraces the consequences of actual transactions and of external changes which affect the wealth and results of companies, the statements for any period and at any date are all-inclusive. Taken in series, they represent a continuous record of shifts in wealth, solvency, gearing or leverage and achieved results. They are historical, avoiding the defects of dated speculation about the future; they are fully historical, avoiding the defects of partial representation of what has occurred up to any date or between any two dates.

PART VII—SUMMARY

44. The rules of continuously contemporary accounting are:

(a) All assets should be stated at the best approximation to their money equivalents, in their then state and condition, at the date of the balance sheet.

(b) All transactions shall be accounted for in the amounts at which they occurred.

(c) All variations from the costs or book values of assets, which are not already brought into account by the sale of assets in the period, shall be brought into the income account at the end of the period as price variation adjustments.

(d) There shall be charged against total revenues, in calculating net income, the amount of a capital maintenance adjustment, so that the amount of net income is a surplus by reference to the maintenance of the general purchasing power of the opening amount of net assets.

(e) Net income is the algebraic sum of the outcomes of transactions, price variation adjustments and the capital maintenance adjustment.

APPENDIX A

Illustration of Method of Continuously Contemporary Accounting

The simplified example which follows traces the recording of transactions, the making of closing adjustments and the derivation of the final statements. All transactions are recorded at their cost throughout the year. The closing price adjustments convert closing book balances to their ascertained money equivalents, represented in the final two columns of the Work Sheet. The workings are shown fully in the Work Sheet. The transactions and adjustments are alphabetically keyed, in the following description and in the Work Sheet, so that the counterparts of all entries may be traced. The figures in the columns headed "Balances" are the money equivalents at the respective dates.

The paragraph numbers in the right hand column of the table of data are the paragraphs in the text of this Draft where the accounting treatment is described.

Transactions of the Year		$	Para.
A	Credit sales	410	31
B	Receivables collected	390	31
C	Raw materials purchased (on credit)	160	31
D	Suppliers on credit paid	140	31
E	Wages and other costs (to Work in progress)	90	31
F	Raw materials to Work in Progress	145	
G	Work in progress to Finished Goods	225	
H	Cost of finished goods to Income Account	270	
J	Administrative and other cash costs	60	31
K	Interest paid	4	31
L	Taxes paid	20	31
M	Dividends paid	14	31
N	Dividends received	2	31
P	Plant purchased	25	31

Year-end Adjustments	$	Para.
Price variation adjustments (differences between book values and ascertained money equivalents at year-end)		
Q —raw materials	10	32
R —work in progress	15	32
S —finished goods	−55	32
T —plant and buildings	20	32
U —land	−6	32
V —shares	3	32
W Provision for taxes	30	30
X Provision for dividends	26	30
Capital maintenance adjustment (assuming the general price index rose by 10 per cent in the year). Apply this to the opening balance.		
Y —undistributed profits (71 × 10/100)	7	34
Z —capital maintenance reserve (150 × 10/100)	15	34
AA Net profit transferred to Undistributed profits	39	36

WORK SHEET FOR YEAR ENDED 31 DECEMBER 19x4

	Balances 31 Dec. 19x3		Transactions and Adjustments		Balances 31 Dec. 19x4	
Assets	Dr	Cr	Dr	Cr	Dr	Cr
Cash	20		390(B)	140(D)		
			2(N)	90(E)		
				60(J)		
				4(K)		
				20(L)		
				14(M)		
				25(P)	59	
Trade debtors (receivables)	40		410(A)	390(B)	60	
Inventories—raw materials	25		160(C)	145(F)		
				10(Q)	30	
—work in progress	30		145(F)	225(G)		
			90(E)	15(R)	25	
—finished goods	80		225(G)	270(H)		
			55(S)		90	
Investments in listed shares	15			3(V)	12	
Plant and buildings	80		25(P)	20(T)	85	
Land	40		6(U)		46	
Equities						
Trade creditors (payables)		30	140(D)	160(C)	50	
Provision for taxes		20	20(L)	30(W)	30	
Provision for dividends		14	14(M)	26(X)	26	
Long-term creditors (10% p.a.)		25			25	
Preferred shareholders (10% p.a.)		20			20	

Ordinary shareholders						
—paid in		120				120
—capital maintenance reserve		30		15(Z)		45
—undistributed		71	26(X)	7(Y)		91
profits				39(AA)		

Income (profit and loss) items

Sales				410(A)		
Finished goods sold—book value			270(H)			
Price variation adjustments						
—raw materials			10(Q)			
—work in progress			15(R)			
—finished goods				55(S)		
—plant and buildings			20(T)			
—land				6(U)		
—shares			3(V)			
Administrative and other cash costs			60(J)			
Interest paid			4(K)			
Dividends received				2(N)		
Provision for taxes			30(W)			
Capital maintenance adjustment						
—undistributed profits			7(Y)			
—capital maintenance reserve			15(Z)			
Net profit			39(AA)			
Totals	330	330	2,181	2,181	407	407

INCOME [PROFIT AND LOSS] ACCOUNT
FOR THE YEAR ENDED 31 DECEMBER 19x4

Sales		410
Dividends received		2
		412
Finished goods sold (book value)		270
Inventory price variation adjustments (net)		(30)
Depreciation, plant and buildings		20
Price variation adjustment, land		(6)
Price variation adjustment, shares		3
Administrative costs		60
Interest paid		4
Capital maintenance adjustment		
—undistributed profits	7	
—capital maintenance reserve	15	343
Profit before tax		69
Provision for taxes		30
Net income		39

BALANCE SHEETS AT 31 DECEMBER

	19x3	19x4
Assets		
Cash	20	59
Trade debtors	40	60
Inventories	135	145
Investments in listed shares	15	12
Plant and buildings	80	85
Land	40	46
	330	407
Equities		
Trade creditors	30	50
Provision for taxes	20	30
Provision for dividends	14	26
Long term creditors (10%)	25	25
Preferred shareholders (10% p.a.)	20	20
Ordinary shareholders		
—paid in	120	120
—capital maintenance reserve	30	45
—undistributed profits	71	91
	330	407

Note: All assets are shown at the best available approximations to their money equivalents at the respective balance dates.

APPENDIX B

Comparative Evaluation of Price Level Adjusted Historical Cost Accounting [C.P.P.] Replacement Price Accounting [R.P.A.] and Continuously Contemporary Accounting [CoCoA]

If a choice is to be made from the above alternatives to historical cost accounting, it must be based on the respective capacities of the systems to provide information which is unambiguous and significant for the purposes of investors, creditors, managers and others. There are many particular calculations and comparisons which these parties, and others concerned with the regulation and assistance of business, may make. The three systems may therefore be ranked according to their capacities to give reliable, significant and readily understandable figures. That system should be considered as the best which satisfies these tests.

The following assessment indicates whether or not each system satisfies the "test" points. For the purpose of making the assessment the three systems have been analyzed in detail. The analyses are lengthy; they may be found in Chambers, *Price Variation and Inflation Accounting* (1980). For present purposes the three systems are described in terms of their salient features. The descriptions are brief and do not cope with the many variations of each "system-type" that occur in the literature. However, they are sufficient to identify the general elements of each of the types of system.

Current purchasing power accounting (C.P.P.) The general basis of asset valuation is, for monetary assets their face values, for non-monetary assets, original cost "indexed" by changes in an index of the general level of prices. Discretionary variations from the rule for non-monetary assets are permissible. Periodical charges against gross revenues in respect of non-monetary assets are based on the "indexed" cost figures. Gains or losses of purchasing power in respect of monetary items are brought into account in income calculation.

Continuously contemporary accounting (CoCoA). The general basis of asset valuation is the money's worth, or money equivalents, of assets, which in the case of non-monetary assets means the best approximation to their resale prices at balance date. Charges against (or credits to) gross revenues are based on changes in the money equivalents of assets. Gains or losses of purchasing power are brought into account in respect of the whole of the opening amount for the year of net assets (or net owners' equity) by use of a readily calculated capital maintenance adjustment.

There are possible tests beside those listed below. There is, for example, the cost of doing the accounting. As C.P.P. and R.P.A. require numerous calculations to be made additional to the processing of original entries, and CoCoA requires only one additional calculation, the last is the least costly. There is the cost of getting the closing balance sheet valuations. Under C.P.P. (taking the historical cost accounts and supplementary C.P.P. accounts together), there are costs of getting several valuations and choosing between alternative valuation rules. Under R.P.A., there are the costs of getting replacement prices and choosing between alternative valuation rules. Under CoCoA, there are the costs of getting values according to only one valuation rule; and, as para 24 of the main text indicates, most of the valuations required are generally accessible. It could also be shown that CoCoA is superior in respect of most of the general "principles" of accounting; consistency of method, application of the accrual principle, representation of the facts of a company as a going concern, periodical matching of revenues and costs, and so on.

However, as financial statements are expected to be serviceable to their users, all the tests which follow relate to the usefulness of the products of the three systems.

EVALUATION

	CPP	RPA	CoCoA
1. Are assets shown at their money (or purchasing power) equivalents at each balance date?	No	No	Yes
2. Does net income, as calculated, represent a genuine increment in purchasing power up to balance date?	No	No	Yes
3. Can particular figures in balance sheets properly be added and related?	No	No	Yes

Monetary items are, in all systems, represented by money equivalents. It is logically improper and practically misleading to add to these figures any others which are not money equivalents. Hence the answer to (3). From (1), (2) and (3) flow the following consequences:

	CPP	RPA	CoCoA
4. Does the balance sheet yield a proper current ratio?	No	No	Yes
5. Does the balance sheet yield a proper debt to equity ratio?	No	No	Yes
6. Do the statements yield a proper rate of return?	No	No	Yes
7. Does the aggregate of asset values fairly represent gross wealth?	No	No	Yes

To make certain judgements or decisions it is necessary to compare the positions and results of different companies as at a given time and of the same company in successive years. Comparisons of the first kind are invalid unless all companies use the same valuation rules; comparisons of the second kind are invalid unless a given company uses the same rules from year to year and those rules embrace all types of change in financial position and results. Therefore:

	CPP	RPA	CoCoA
8. Is the rate of return technically comparable with the rate of return on other types of investment?	No	No	Yes
9. Are the aggregates and ratios yielded comparable from year to year and fair indicators of trends?	No	No	Yes
10. Are the main ratios comparable as between firms?	No	No	Yes

The information in financial statements is used by managers and by outsiders in a variety of settings. The particulars and aggregates must be understandable by and useful to those parties.

	CPP	RPA	CoCoA
11. Are the figures free of ambiguity and equally interpretable by and useful to managers and others?	No	No	Yes
12. Do particular asset figures represent amounts of money accessible for alternative use?	No	No	Yes
13. Are the figures a firm basis from which to calculate prospective results and positions?	No	No	Yes
14. Does the net asset figure suggest a minimum acceptable takeover bid?	No	No	Yes
15. Are the statements fair and serviceable for negotiations and other relations with public and other bodies?	No	No	Yes
16. Are the statements complete as statements of results and position, needing no supplementary information or statements?	No	No	Yes

	CPP	RPA	CoCoA
17. Are the statements a fair basis for periodical "stewardship" evaluation?	No	No	Yes
18. Do the statements give a true and fair view of financial results and position?	No	No	Yes
19. Are the amounts representing assets and liabilities verifiable independently of the company's internal calculations?	No	No	Yes

No specific reference has been made above to inflation or its effects, except by references to purchasing power (1), (2), and to supplementary statements (16). There are several specific tests, however, which should be satisfied.

	CPP	RPA	CoCoA
20. Are retrospective corrections or adjustments to previously reported figures avoided?	No	No	Yes
21. Are any adjustments made in respect of changes in the prices of particular assets?	No	Yes	Yes
22. Are any adjustments made in respect of changes in the purchasing power of money?	Yes	Yes	Yes
23. Are adjustments made for the gain or loss of purchasing power during each period in respect of all assets and liabilities?	No	No	Yes
24. Is the method of accounting a method of accounting for inflation?	No	No	Yes

Two further points might be made. Although C.P.P. accounting makes reference to current purchasing power, a C.P.P. balance sheet does *not* represent assets by amounts which are in fact their current purchasing power (or money) equivalents. The point is covered in (1) above; but it may escape notice because of the description of the system.

Secondly, although replacement price accounting purports to provide for the replacement of assets by charges against gross revenues, the figures it yields do *not* indicate whether or not a firm could in fact replace those assets; a replacement price valuation does not represent purchasing power at the command of the firm, yet purchasing power is the only means of buying a "replacement" asset.

These inconsistencies with their apparent or avowed aims score against the two systems mentioned.

The practical superiority of CoCoA is demonstrated.

IV/EXPANSION IN THE CONTENTS OF ACCOUNTING REPORTS

This part considers three distinct types of expansion. The first section deals with forecast reporting, which suggests that accounting reports be expanded to include the projected results of future operations. The second section examines proposals to include human asset values in the calculations of income and financial position. The third section deals with social reporting, which is based upon a redefinition and broadening of the concept of the reporting entity, to encompass "externalities" or the social costs and benefits of a firm's actions, which are not reflected in conventionally measured revenues and expenses.

Section A includes two articles on forecast reporting. Carmichael (1973) outlines the recent British experience in the preparation and dissemination of forecast reports as accounting documents, and provides an assessment of the practical issues in implementing a forecast reporting system. Gonedes, Dopuch, and Penman (1976) deal with two fundamental questions: Do forecast disclosures convey relevant information to the financial markets? How do forecast disclosure rules affect the allocation of resources? The article furnishes a summary of the current debate concerning forecast disclosures and a framework for the evaluation of accounting disclosure rules in general.

In section B, entitled "Human Asset Accounting," Lev and Schwartz (1971) argue that human capital is on a par with nonhuman forms of earning assets, and attempt to provide a practical measurement procedure as a first step toward incorporating human resources in financial statements. The article outlines ways in which human resource information might be used to improve investor decisions, and explores a variety of related conceptual issues. Flamholtz (1972) attempts to specify the nature and determinants of a person's value to an organization, drawing on behavioral as well as psychological variables. This theory of the value of people to organizations is intended to lead to methods of providing useful monetary and nonmonetary measurements of human resource value.

Section C contains two papers on the topic of social reporting. Ramanathan (1976) notes that traditional performance criteria may be in conflict with social priorities, and provides an approach to incorporating social impacts into the firm's formal performance measurement system. Ramanathan accepts the notion of a "social contract," which implies a set of performance dimensions can be developed. A definition of socially responsible performance may then lead to methods of performance measurement and evaluation. Thomas (1976) questions

367

whether the accountant as traditionally educated has any role to play in improving the relevance and reliability of data needed for social planning, beyond his more conventional role in helping to improve the clerical accuracy of the data.

IV-A/FORECAST REPORTING

Reporting on Forecasts: A U.K. Perspective

D. R. CARMICHAEL

Should an independent accountant report on a company's published earnings forecast? In the United Kingdom (U.K.) accountants do publicly report on profit forecasts. The purpose of this article is to examine the U.K. practice and assess its import for U.S. accountants.

Investors and their financial advisers are showing increasing interest in corporate earnings forecasts. Some limited information is disclosed by companies in published reports and interviews, but practice is constrained by the general position of the Securities and Exchange Comission on the inappropriateness of forecasts in prospectuses. Financial analysts frequently attempt to make their own forecasts for companies and these are available to some, but not all, investors. Consequently, suggestions are frequently heard that public companies should present projected financial statements in their published reports.

CENTRAL ISSUES

Disclosure of company forecasts for the use of outsiders, such as investors, lenders and governmental agencies, involves several critical questions which may conveniently be divided into three categories—publication, presentation and attestation.

Publication

The most fundamental question is—should companies publish forecasts? This question involves complex considerations such as the need of investors and other outsiders for the information, the potential dangers of market manipulation by irresponsible issuers, possible competitive damage to issuers from disclosure of corporate plans, the capability of users to understand the inherent limitations on the accuracy of forecasts, the internal capabilities of companies to prepare forecasts for publication and finally, and of major importance, the reliability potential of published forecasts.

Presentation

Subsidiary to the fundamental issue of publication are a number of questions related to the details of the content and process of disclosure. Should publication of forecasts be permissive or mandatory? How far into the future

D. R. Carmichael, "Reporting on Forecasts: A U.K. Perspective," *The Journal of Accountancy*, January 1973, pp. 36–47. Copyright © 1973 by the American Institute of Certified Public Accountants, Inc.

should the forecasts extend? Should the information be in condensed format or as detailed as historical financial statements? How frequently should forecasts be issued or updated? Should the information be presented as single figure estimates or as ranges?

Attestation

If forecasts are published, having them attested to by an objective and competent outsider would seem desirable. Whether this function should be assumed by the public accounting profession is another issue. Pertinent questions include fundamental yet complex matters, such as the propriety of the association of the name of a public accounting firm with forecasts, and other more detailed matters, such as what aspects of a forecast an accountant may appropriately obligate himself to report on.

SOURCE OF INFORMATION

This article explores the feasibility and desirability of attestation of published company forecasts by independent accountants based on in-depth interviews with chartered accountants in England. The public accounting profession in the U.K. has taken a professional position on public reporting on forecasts and their experience presents a useful background for consideration by public accountants in the U.S. The English experience is relevant for questions concerning attestation if significant differences in environment, particularly the legal climate, are kept in mind. It also offers an interesting perspective on questions of presentation. The greatest problems concerning the transferability of the English experience to this country arise in connection with the fundamental issue of publication and, consequently, that issue is not considered. However, if company forecasts were widely published in the U.S., the public accounting profession would need answers to the questions of attestation and presentation. Consequently, first-hand knowledge of the English experience was sought.

The Institute of Chartered Accountants in England and Wales co-operated in arranging interviews with (1) accountants regarded as generally knowledgeable on the subject of reporting on forecasts, (2) members of the technical staff of the Institute itself, (3) several members of the Takeover Panel Executive and (4) a number of merchant bankers. Approximately 30 chartered accountants from ten firms of varying size were interviewed. The firms included the "Big Four" of England (a designation analogous to the "Big Eight" in this country), four firms at the next level of size and two smaller firms. Accountants were interviewed in groups at a firm and the interviews were augmented by informal discussions with a larger number of accountants at many firms. The views attributed to the accountants are based on the general attitudes which prevailed rather than a numeric tabulation by number of accountants.

HISTORICAL BACKGROUND OF U.K. EXPERIENCE

In the U.K. forecasts are published in both prospectuses and in circulars issued in takeovers and mergers. Forecasts must be published in a prospectus when the company is quoted or is seeking quotation on the London Stock Exchange. Although forecasts are considered desirable in a takeover and are naturally permitted, they are not required. Perhaps the most frequent misstatement by U.S. accountants concerning U.K. practice is that "in England forecasts are required in takeovers and mergers." In fact, the majority of circulars published in connection with bids and mergers during the period May 1, 1969, to September 30, 1970, did not include forecasts.

Prospectuses

In a U.K. prospectus the "profits and prospects" section normally contains a forecast of profits before tax, estimated taxes on the forecasted profit, projected dividend payment dates and amounts, and the dividend yield and price earnings ratio calculated by reference to the offer price. The information normally relates to the expected profitability of the current year and may sometimes be issued only one or two months before year end.

Attestation of the profit forecast in a prospectus is indirect; the accountant is not required to report on the forecast. However, the accountant is required to consent to the publication of his report on the prior year financial statements "in the context in which they are presented." Traditionally, all parties involved would expect the accountant to withhold his consent if he was dissatisfied with the forecast. In addition, the merchant bank handling the issue normally requests the accountant to report the current trading, future prospects and working capital position of the client company in a "comfort letter." The comfort letter is private between the professional adviser writing it and the addressee and, consequently, sets forth in detail the information and assumptions that form the basis of the profit forecasts and explains the work the accountants performed in reviewing the company's preparation of the forecast. The conclusions, if any, are frequently couched in the form of negative assurance.

Traditionally, forecasts in a prospectus are conservative. Many accountants interviewed commented that a company is expected to exceed its forecast by at least 10 per cent and that a company which does not meet its forecast may be "damned forever in the market."

Bids and Mergers

In the U.K. a considerable amount of activity takes place in the area of takeover bids and mergers. An unwelcome bid is fought with financial rather than legal tactics and one important tactic is the inclusion of a statement by the directors about future prospects and profits in the documents sent to shareholders by both the offerer and offeree.

Merger and takeover activity is generally overseen by the City Working Party, a voluntary association of financial organizations created in the late 1950's to cope with increasing problems in the field. The "City Code on Takeovers and Mergers" was prepared by the City Working Party and issued in March 1968 as a code of practice for takeovers and mergers. A revised City Code was issued in April 1969. The Code is administered by the panel on takeovers and mergers (the Panel) and a full-time secretariat (the Panel Executive). From time to time the Panel issues "practice notes" as supplements to the Code. Space does not permit a detailed account of the history of the Panel and the Code.

The most significant aspect of the Code to public accountants is a requirement that if a forecast appears in a takeover document, an independent accountant must report on the forecast. Rule 16 (previously Rule 15) states in part that:

> When profit forecasts appear in any document addressed to shareholders in connection with an offer, the assumptions, including the commercial assumptions, upon which the Directors have based their profit forecasts, must be stated in the document.
>
> The accounting bases and calculations for the forecasts must be examined and reported on by the auditors or consultant accountants. Any financial adviser mentioned in the document must also report on the forecasts. The accountants' report and, if there is an adviser, his report, must be contained in such document and be accompanied by a statement that the accountants and, where relevant, the adviser, have given and not withdrawn their consent to publication.

Prior to issuance of the revised Code, accountants had no public reporting responsibility for forecasts appearing in takeover documents. However, accountants frequently reported to merchant bankers on these forecasts in comfort letters as was the practice for prospectuses.

This private reporting was inadequate for takeovers because of the differing pressures on directors in the bid situation. While prospectus forecasts are traditionally conservative, in fighting off an unwelcome takeover bid the directors are under considerable pressure to project the best possible results of future operations and no attempt may be made to build in a "cushion."

The financial press and others severely criticized some missed forecasts and, as a part of the reforms instituted in response to this criticism, accountants were asked to report on forecasts for bids and mergers as a means of controlling overly optimistic forecasts. Interviews with accountants, merchant bankers and members of the Panel Executive confirmed that the public reporting requirement had generally had the desired effect.

ATTESTATION

The views of chartered accountants were sought on many questions pertinent to the issue of whether the public accounting profession in this country should accept the responsibility of attesting to published forecasts.

Association

If the name of a public accounting firm is associated with a forecast, the forecast may be given an undue aura of credibility by many members of the financial community who do not fully appreciate the uncertainties inherent in forecasts and the nature of the accountant's role in their preparation.

The U.K. accountants uniformly admitted that they were at first quite reluctant to report publicly on forecasts in takeover documents even though they had had a fair amount of experience in reporting privately on prospectuses. In fact, the first technical release on reporting on forecasts by the English Institute—S-11 issued in July 1968—specified that the accountants' report would be submitted in writing to the directors and the Panel, but would not be published in the takeover document. However, S-11 was superseded by S-15, "Accountants' Reports on Profit Forecasts," in July 1969. The new English Institute release recognizes that the takeover document should contain the accountants' report. If no grounds for qualification exist, the English Institute suggests the following form of report:

To the directors of X Limited:
We have reviewed the accounting bases and calculations for the profit forecast (for which the directors are solely responsible) of X Limited for the period _____ set out on pages _____ of this circular. The forecasts include results shown by unaudited interim accounts for the period _____ . In our opinion, the forecasts, so far as the accounting bases and calculations are concerned, have been properly compiled on the footing of the assumptions made by the board set out on page _____ of this circular and are presented on a basis consistent with the accounting practices normally adopted by the company.

Thus, the English Institute acknowledges that, within specified limits, accountants may appropriately assume responsibility for an objective review of the accounting bases and calculations for profit forecasts and can form an opinion on whether the forecasts have been properly compiled from the underlying assumptions and data and are presented on a basis consistent with the accounting principles used in historical financial statements.

After approximately three years of experience of public reporting under the present requirement, the accountants interviewed seemed "comfortable" with the public reporting responsibility. The requirement to report publicly was initially accepted with reluctance at the insistence of the Panel. However, when asked if they would report publicly if it was not for the Panel, an overwhelming number of accountants said yes, they would report publicly. Many pointed out that they had been reporting privately on profit forecasts for some time and they felt that public reporting was not that different. Some mentioned that some public reports had been issued before the Panel came into existence. One accountant expressed the view that reporting responsibility normally follows this progression:

(1) accountants review matters as part of their concern with being associated with a document;
(2) they then report privately on these matters; and
(3) finally the reporting becomes public.

The influence of the Panel on the U.K. experience was explored to determine whether this voluntary self-disciplining system had a sufficient impact on practice to reduce the transferability of its experience to the U.S.A. None of the chartered accountants believed they derived protection from the Panel. Most mentioned that the existence of the public reporting requirement gave them needed "muscle" in restraining overly optimistic forecasts since mere association with the document in which the forecast appeared was not always sufficient.

The main benefit they felt they derived from the Panel was the availability of panel members for informal consultation so that questions concerning presentation and similar matters could be resolved prior to publication of a takeover document. One question that does arise is the definition of a profit forecast. If directors make a statement about the prospects of the company, that projection even if not quantified may be deemed a forecast and, hence, an accountant's report may be required if the company subsequently becomes involved in a takeover bid. Informal consultation with the Panel may indicate that a narrative description of company prospects is a forecast and identifies the potential need for an accountant's report.

When the profit forecast is in narrative form the standard wording suggested by the English Institute is not applicable. However, the general guidelines of the English Institute's statement apply to accountants' reports on all forecasts. S-15 is not limited to reports on forecasts in takeover documents although takeover documents are the only instance in which they are required.

To test the willingness of accountants to report publicly on a forecast they were asked if they would allow their reports on a forecast in a prospectus to be published in that document. Less than a third of the accountants said they would have any hesitation about reporting publicly on a forecast in a prospectus in the manner they now report in a takeover document. Some mentioned that a few accountants' reports had already appeared in prospectuses. While most of the accountants indicated they would not volunteer to report publicly, if they were requested to by the directors or the merchant banker, they would.

Some accountants in the U.S. have expressed the view that a report confined to the mechanical aspects of forecast preparation, that is, a report confined to the accounting bases and calculations and consistency with the stated assumptions, was of little real worth and would amount to lending unwarranted credibility to forecasts.

U.K. accountants believed, overwhelmingly, that a report of this type combined with an implicit concern with assumptions served a valuable function. The reporting requirement provides for an essentially objective view. In general, U.K. accountants were thoroughly convinced of the value of forecasts and accountants' reports thereon to investors. They expressed some dismay over the U.S. practice of informal and unequal dissemination of information about forecasts through press releases and management comments to analysts.

Obligation

If the propriety of the association of a public accountant with a forecast is accepted, the next critical question is the reporting obligation the accountant should assume. Should the accountant report on the reasonableness of the assumptions and estimates underlying the forecast?

S-15 contains the following statement concerning the accountant's concern with assumptions:

> *The assumptions on which the forecasts are based.* If a circular includes profit forecasts, . . . the Code requires the assumptions, including the commercial assumptions, upon which the directors have based their profit forecasts to be stated. It is the responsibility of the accountants to report on the accounting bases and calculations for profit forecasts. In discharging their responsibility they must satisfy themselves that forecasts are consistent with the given assumptions, economic, commercial, marketing, and financial, which underlie them.

Thus, the official position of the English Institute on the reporting obligation assumed by accountants is highly circumscribed. No responsibility is taken for the validity or reasonableness of assumptions.

However, the attitude of almost all of the accountants on their responsibility for assumptions is reflected in the following excerpt from an accounting firm program:

The firm is not prepared to associate its name with a forecast *unless* we are satisfied not only that the accounting bases and calculations are appropriate, but also that there appear to be reasonable grounds for the assumptions on which the forecast is based.

In general, an understanding exists that accountants would not publicly report on a forecast without qualification unless they were satisfied that the assumptions were reasonable.

Uniformly, the accountants cited Practice Note No. 6 of the City Code which states in part:

Although the accountants have no responsibility for the assumptions, they will as a result of their review be in a position to advise the company on what assumptions should be listed in the circular and the way in which they should be described. The financial advisers and accountants obviously have substantial influence on the information in a given circular about assumptions. Neither should allow an assumption to be published which appears to them to be unrealistic (or one to be omitted which appears to them to be important) without commenting on it in their reports.

The accountants were all aware of this requirement and some have issued qualified reports based upon the unreasonableness of an assumption. Several accountants stressed that the need to be alert for the omission of an important assumption was equally as important as noting an unrealistic assumption.

Thus while the written report of accountants does not indicate any acceptance of responsibility for assumptions, accountants (1) believe they have some responsibility, (2) do a substantial amount of work on the assumptions, and (3) will qualify their report if they believe the assumptions are incomplete or unreasonable. Normally, a dispute between the directors and the accountants on the reasonableness of the assumptions will be resolved by not publishing the forecast. However, if the directors have already made a statement that is subsequently defined as a forecast, the accountant's report must also be published. For example, the Panel construed the following statement by the chairman of Enots Limited in his address to shareholders circulated with the annual report for the period ended July 31, 1971, as a profit forecast:

While we see no basis for great optimism in the present trading period, current sales have now leveled out and we feel that the effects of recent government action will probably lead to sales rising in the second half of our financial year. In the past month we have moved our commercial offices onto the same site as our factory at Lichfield which in itself should effect economies due to shorter lines of communication and leaves us free to sell our Aston office block. We therefore predict a rise in turnover for the current year as a whole and, with our organization now geared to the present situation, profits should be in step with turnover.

When the company became involved in a takeover bid the profit forecast was reported on by the accountants as follows:

We refer to the paragraph headed "Profit Forecast" in appendix II on page 11 of the offer document dated 22nd November 1971 to be sent to shareholders of Enots Limited in which there is reproduced an extract from the chairman's address to shareholders, accompanying the accounts of the company for the financial period to 31st July 1971.

We understand that the Panel on Takeovers and Mergers construes this extract as a profit forecast. In view of this construction of the chairman's words we have examined PA Management Consultants Limited's Report dated October 1971 and the internal accounting documents of the company and we have also had regard to the penultimate paragraph on page two in the chairman's letter to shareholders, regarding the relationship of profits to turnover.

In our opinion if the company's forecast of sales substantiated by PA Management Consultants Limited is achieved, there will be an increase in profit. However, comparatively minor variations in turnover can produce disproportionate effects on the profits and, so early in the financial period, some doubts must remain as to whether the sales estimates on which the forecast is based can be achieved and as to the consequences of any short-fall.

The accountants interviewed overwhelmingly agreed that the report is only an instrument of attestation. The critical factor is association of an accounting firm's name with a forecast and the exact wording of the report is of lesser significance.

The private reports to merchant bankers on forecasts sometimes contain assertions about the assumptions. The method of reporting varies as follows:

- Assumptions reasonable or not unreasonable.
- Assurance on due care of preparation.
- Negative assurance on assumptions.
- No overall conclusion on assumptions.

Since their public reports do not disclose the extent of responsibility the accountants say they feel concerning the assumptions, they were asked to report publicly, in some manner, on assumptions. The responses were about evenly divided:

- "Yes, should,"
- "Inevitable, a matter of time,"
- "Reluctant, but would" and
- "No, should never."

The type of responsibility that many accountants believed they could assume for assumptions was dependent upon whether management had prepared the assumptions with due care and consideration.

The extent of reporting responsibility is closely related to the type of evidence available to support the forecasts and the methods of acquiring that evidence that an accountant is capable of employing.

Evidence

The accountants interviewed furnished the programs and checklists which they use in examining forecasts. These programs place heavy reliance on the forecasting system and the past forecasting success of the company. Critical stress is placed on the forecasting methods of the company in a manner somewhat similar to reliance on an internal control system, with one important exception. The accountants determine the reliance which may be placed on the forecasting system, but not as a basis for the extent of other work. It is difficult and sometimes impossible, they believe, to compensate for a poor or nonexistent forecasting system. In addition, a knowledge of the industry and the company is also stressed. A composite of U.K. accounting firm programs is appended to illustrate the nature of the work performed (see page 384).

Although these programs bear similarities to many procedures followed in audit engagements, the public accounting firm programs and the statement of the English Institute emphasize that forecasts cannot be "audited." Paragraphs 4 and 5 of S-15 read, in part, as follows:

> It is emphasized that profit forecasts necessarily depend on subjective judgments and are, to a greater or lesser extent, according to the nature of the business, subject to numerous and substantial inherent uncertainties, which increase markedly the further forward in time the forecasts stretch.

> In consequence profit forecasts ... are not capable of confirmation and verification by reporting accountants in the same way as financial statements which present the final results of completed accounting periods and there is no question of their being "audited," even though the reporting accountants may also be the company's auditors.

Consequently, the work performed in reporting on a forecast should not be equated with an audit of historical financial statements. If this caveat is kept in mind, however, the work performed on a forecast may usefully be described as taking an "audit approach." An audit is a *critical investigation;* it is error oriented. In auditing historical financial statements, the auditor does not reconstruct the accounting process which initially produced the statements. He searches for things that could go wrong in the process of statement preparation and focuses his investigation on these areas. A similar approach is applied to a forecast. The accountant searches for those things which would invalidate the forecast. The following questions from one program illustrate the approach:

1. To what extent does the forecast depend on the success of new and untried products or markets?
2. Are any previously successful products now vulnerable from obsolescence or new competition?

Another important aspect of *evidence* on forecasts involves an accountant's competence to evaluate a forecast, particularly the use of management advisory services (MAS) skills. U.K. accountants were queried on the importance of MAS skills, such as market research, in their review of forecasts. Their responses on the need to use MAS skills were evenly divided among the following:

- "Never use,"
- "Might use in special circumstances" and
- "Use on certain limited aspects."

In general, they believed use of MAS skills would be of value if the forecast incorporated a substantial change in operations. For example, if a substantial increase in production was contemplated, engineering skills might be needed to determine whether the company was physically capable of the planned levels of production. However, the critical skills which the accountants felt necessary were good business judgment and the ability to marshal vast quantities of data and the related skills of measuring, comparing and evaluating financial information. All accountants regarded the value of MAS skills with a "healthy skepticism." They did not feel that assumptions could be expertised since no one can predict the future with assurance.

U.K. accountants were also asked if they believed the accountant reporting on a forecast would have to be the company's auditor—that is, is an audit base essential? All responded negatively. It is the knowledge acquired in an audit and not the audit itself which is important. The needed base of knowledge can be acquired in other ways.

Since their programs place heavy reliance on a company's past forecasting ability, they were also asked if they would report on a forecast of a new venture, one without a history of operations and forecast preparation. All accountants expressed great reluctance to be associated with forecasts of this type. Responses ranged from "no, never" to "possibly in limited circumstances." In the U.K. new ventures do not "go public" or frequently become involved in takeovers.

Objectivity

Another significant point which should be considered if accountants report on forecasts is the pressure on objectivity that would result if an accountant reported on a forecast then served as the company's auditor on historical financial statements for the same period as the forecast.

U.K. accountants admitted that certain obvious pressures existed to have actual results come near to a forecast. However, they overwhelmingly believed that the pressure exerted by management had not been undue or pronounced. They believed that the pressures exerted did not differ significantly from a management's natural desire to achieve acceptable operating results when forecasts are not published.

If accountants became involved in forecast preparation, to the point that the forecasts are in effect made by the accountant, pressures on objectivity would exist. U.K. accountants believed this potential pressure was countered by the requirement for management's acceptance of the forecast and the assumptions on which it is based as their own responsibility.

The accountants expressed a unanimous and extremely strong view that management must accept a forecast as its own. S-15, paragraph 8, provides in part that:

> . . . the directors assume full responsibility for the forecasts under review (as required by the Code) and that they will signify such responsibility by formal adoption by the board and by inclusion of their statement of overall responsibility (required to be made under Rule 13 of the Code) of a specific reference to profit forecasts.

This acceptance of responsibility is viewed as far more than a formality. U.K. accountants would not be associated with a forecast unless management fully accepted the forecasts and assumptions as its own in substance and spirit as well as in form.

This belief is strongly held even though the accountants do get involved in the development of assumptions. Normally management "roughs out" the assumptions at the beginning of an engagement to report on a forecast. The accountants refine these assumptions and frequently write the assumptions which appear in the circular. Sometimes the involvement of the accountants is even more extensive and may include—for forecasts in a prospectus which allow ample planning—establishment of the forecasting system.

Nevertheless, U.K. accountants believe that, because only management is in a position to assure that plans are executed and that operations achieve the planned level, only management can make the forecast. Only through the efforts of management will a forecast be achieved and only those responsible for operations can truly be responsible for the forecast.

Therefore, when the accountant has had extensive involvement in assumption development it is essential that he sit down with management, discuss the forecast and assure that management has accepted the forecast as its own. Another safeguard of objectivity frequently employed is the use of different supervisory personnel on the forecast review and audit to ensure a "fresh viewpoint."

Liability

The most striking difference between the U.K. and the U.S. investment communities is the different degree of legal liability and the attitude toward it. U.K. accountants showed a remarkable lack of apprehension about liability that might arise in reporting on forecasts. In general, a lesser propensity to litigate exists in the U.K. Several factors that play an important role in the U.S. legal scene do not have U.K. counterparts. British attorneys cannot accept contingent fee engagements. Class actions and derivative suits are not possible. Nothing comparable to the burden of proof placed on the defendant by the Securities Act of 1933 plagues U.K. practitioners. Finally, third-party allegations against accountants come under the list of things which are "just not done" in the City.

The City has been able to rely largely on informal sanctions. Although these sanctions are informal they nevertheless appear to be effective. One who fails to adhere to the recognized norms may be ostracized by the investment community.

In the U.S. the policy of using formal sanctions is firmly rooted. Thus, any attempt to transfer the experience and resultant attitudes of U.K. accountants to the U.S. should recognize the environmental differences. For example, Section 11(a) of the Securities Act of 1933 provides the following liability for "experts," including accountants, who sign the registration statement:

> In case any part of the registration statement, when such part became effective, contained an untrue statement of a material fact or omitted to state a material fact required to be stated therein or necessary to make the statements therein not misleading, any person acquiring such security ... may ... sue ... every accountant ... who has with his consent been named as having ... certified any part of the registration statement ... with respect to the statement in such registration statement ... which purports to have been ... certified by him.

The applicability of this provision to forecasts is unclear and raises many questions. Given the nature of a forecast, a difference between forecasted and actual results, no matter how material, should not be prima facie evidence of misrepresentation.

Under Section 11(b) (3) of the Act an expert has a defense to liability if he can sustain the burden of proof that:

> ... as regards any part of the registration statement purporting to be made upon his authority as an expert ... he had, after reasonable investigation, reasonable ground to believe and did believe, at the time such part of the registration statement became effective, that the statements therein were true and that there was no omission to state a material fact required to be stated therein or necessary to make the statements therein not misleading. . . .

It seems unlikely that an accountant, or any other expert, could assume an expert's responsibility for a forecast in a registration statement as long as the responsibility is coupled with the present criterion for misrepresentation.

PRESENTATION

The chartered accountants also expressed their views on several of the issues involved in the presentation of forecasts.

Forward Period

U.K. accountants expressed great reluctance to be associated with forecasts extending too far forward in time. S-15 provides in paragraph 7, in part, that:

> ... reporting accountants should not normally undertake to review and report to directors on profit forecasts for more than the current accounting period, and, provided a sufficiently significant part of the current year has elapsed, the next following accounting year.

The typical view of "a sufficiently significant part of the current year" is six months and the maximum forward period is, therefore, 18 months.

Uniformly, the accountants viewed this period as maximum because of extreme doubt about the possible validity of forecasts extending beyond this period. A shorter period is common when uncertainty is high. Sometimes the forecasts extend only a few months into the future. Merchant bankers and accountants will insist on a short period if they believe forecast validity is low.

Frequently accountants review a longer period of time, but these projections are not made public and are viewed more as company plans and not projections. In some rare cases, a few accountants indicated a projection covering a longer period may be unusually relevant to investors' decisions and might be disclosed and reported on.

Range or Point Estimates

Somewhat related to the general issue of potential accuracy of forecasts is the desirability of presenting forecasts in a range. Most accountants were either unenthusiastic or opposed to this form of presentation. While they recognized the desirability of the objective—communicating the probabilistic nature of a forecast—they did not believe that the range presentation was an adequate means of achieving the goal.

Some mentioned that investors would probably use the median figure anyway. Others suggested that ranges might become so wide as to make the forecast useless. The most informed view was that the critical aspect of forecast uncertainty was not the range but the probabilities associated with the projections. Thus, a probability profile and not a range is necessary and forecasting methods are not sophisticated enough to develop meaningful probability profiles.

Condensed or Detailed Data

In addition to the underlying assumptions, the published circular for a takeover or merger proposal normally includes only a profit forecast including a single profit figure sometimes supplemented by turnover (sales) and pretax profit. Lines-of-business information may be given, but infrequently. Generally, the financial information is highly condensed and may include only the forecasted profit or sometimes may be limited to a narrative on future prospects.

The limited nature of the information normally disclosed is partially attributable to a characteristic British preference for brevity of financial information. However, several other reasons for the condensed nature of the information exist. An important consideration in the U.K. option for brevity is a judgment concerning the need of investors for more detailed information. For example, the private report to merchant bankers in connection with a prospectus normally contains a great deal more information about the future prospects of a company than is disclosed in the published document. Merchant bankers can use this information since it has a direct impact on their decisions. They can request the directors to obtain additional financing and even request changes in aspects of operations. In addition, some of the information is highly confidential and its disclosure would be detrimental to the company.

Of critical importance is the need to emphasize the distinction between a historical statement and a projection. If forecasted information can be compared line by line with historical information, an undesirable implication of comparable exactitude may result.

Consequently, the U.K. practice of presenting forecasted information in more condensed form than historical information has much to recommend it.

Mandatory or Permissive Disclosure

Many facets of U.K. practice support a conclusion that disclosure of forecasts should not be mandatory for all companies. Forecasts are not required in takeover bid documents and frequently a forecast is not included because the accountants have concluded that the company cannot prepare a sufficiently valid forecast. U.K. accountants would not be associated with a forecast on a new company without a past history of operations and forecast preparation. Although a forecast is required in a U.K. prospectus, only established companies issue prospectuses and the accountant and the merchant banker can exert control over the length of the forecasted period. If necessary to achieve the essential validity, this period can be shortened to a few months. Perhaps the only sort of mandatory disclosure requirement that would be feasible is that a company should publish a forecast or explain why one was not published.

CONCLUDING REMARKS

The many differences between the U.K. and U.S. investment communities preclude making a judgment on the desirability of permitting companies to publish forecasts based solely on an analysis of the English experience. However, if U.S. companies do publish forecasts, U.S. accountants may be able to provide a useful and important service by attesting to these forecasts. But before attestation would be feasible, a number of critical matters would need clarification. Two of the most important are communication with report users and liability.

Communication

The U.K. accountants interviewed were sent a preliminary copy of this report. In commenting on the report, one chartered accountant included a piece of advice which had been offered repeatedly by several accountants in the course of the interviews. The following is an excerpt from his letter:

> I would repeat my strong advice that your Institute should mount a publicity campaign, if you get involved in profit forecasting, on the inherent inaccuracy of forecasts. I regard this as essential, particularly in the U.S. environment, to avoid misunderstanding and subsequent recrimination by third parties such as investment analysts, lawyers and others.

In the U.K. investors and others have had a fair amount of experience in using profit forecasts in financial decision-making. Nevertheless, many U.K. accountants felt that the general understanding of the inherent inaccuracies of profit forecasts was inadequate. Presenting forecasts in ranges rather than as point estimates is one way of communicating the probabilistic nature of forecasts. While U.K. accountants were quite sympathetic to this objective, they did not believe range presentation was an adequate means of communicating the inherent inaccuracy of a forecast.

If publication of forecasts is permitted, some sort of publicity campaign on the nature of forecasts would seem essential.

Liability

Because of the nature of forecasts and the nature of the attest function with respect thereto that an accountant can reasonably be expected to perform, a clear understanding of the legal responsibilities for a forecast would be essential. The type of responsibility that exists for historical financial statements under the Securities Acts could not be imposed with respect to forecasted data.

One possible solution would be for the SEC to establish a panel similar to the Panel in the U.K. to fulfill the important function of informal consultation and to determine whether a missed forecast could be the subject of litigation. In the U.K. the Panel reviews the conduct of all proposed takeover or merger proposals and investigates all forecasts not achieved. A profit forecast is regarded as achieved if the result is within approximately 10 per cent (plus or minus) of the forecast. In the period between October 1, 1970, and September 30, 1971, the Panel reviewed 331 takeover or merger proposals. Of the 331 proposals, 185 contained forecasts. In their report on the year ended March 31, 1972 the Panel indicated that they had been able to consider 173 out of the 185 forecasts. Only

35 of these forecasts were deemed failures and "of the 35 failures, satisfactory explanations were not forthcoming in only two cases."

With these odds, if failure to explain satisfactorily a failed forecast were regarded as prima facie evidence of misrepresentation, few U.S. accountants would be willing to be associated with forecasts. However, it would be a mistake to equate lack of satisfactory explanation with misrepresentation and perhaps this matter would require specific coverage in law or regulation.

Reporting

If the problems of communication, liability and other critical problems are satisfactorily resolved, U.S. accountants might perform an attest function for company forecasts and report in a manner somewhat analogous to the U.K. accountants' report. The report recommended by the English Institute does not specifically cover responsibility for assumptions. Whether this approach would be appropriate in the U.S. is a matter for consideration. Another possible form of report is as follows:

> We have studied the projected statement of operations of the XYZ Company for the year ended December 31, 1972. Our study was conducted in accordance with applicable standards published by the AICPA. We performed such tests and procedures with respect to the compilation of the forecast from the stated assumptions as we considered necessary in the circumstances. However, assumptions as to future events must remain the sole responsibility of management. Our procedures with respect thereto were generally limited to those which accountants might reasonably employ and were chosen in order to appraise the care and consideration given to the selection of assumptions by management.
>
> On the basis of our study, we believe that the projected statement of operations gives effect to the assumptions described on the basis of accounting principles regularly employed by the company. We believe that management has chosen the assumptions with due care and consideration. We express no opinion as to whether the projected statement may approximate actual future results.

Since projections are dependent on the consummation of events that have not yet taken place and that cannot be known with any degree of certainty, positive assurance may be inappropriate. However, a third type of report expressing negative assurance might be appropriate. The concluding paragraph of this type of report might be worded as follows:

> On the basis of our study, we believe that the accompanying projected statement properly gives effect to the assumptions described in Exhibit A, using generally accepted accounting principles as described in Exhibit B. Further, nothing came to our attention as a result of our study that caused us to believe that such assumptions, which have been selected by management, do not constitute reasonable bases for the preparation of the estimates in the statement. Since the statements (or projections) are predicated on the occurrence of future events which are subject to changes in economic and other circumstances, we express no opinion on the likelihood of their achievement.

The AICPA's committee on auditing procedure is presently considering a Statement on Auditing Procedure on reporting on forecasts. Whether any of the above reports will be adopted is problematical.

APPENDIX
COMPOSITE PROGRAM PROFIT AND WORKING CAPITAL FORECASTS

I. PRELIMINARY REVIEW
    A. Nature of business. Establish the general nature of the company's activities, its main products, markets, customers, suppliers, divisions, locations, labor force and trend of results.
    B. Relative risk. Consider whether any matters, prima facie, might create difficulties.
        1. Business activities which are difficult to forecast.
        2. Unreliable costing and accounting methods.
        3. Inadequate forecasting methods.
    C. Overall materiality. Identify any aspects of the business which are of particular importance to the ultimate achievement of the forecast.
        1. An activity which is large in relation to the business as a whole.
        2. Major limiting factor. Isolate the most important limiting factor governing the level of profits forecast by the company, such as sales potential, production capacity or availability of financing.
        3. Unusual operating conditions affecting the business to a material extent.

II. ACCOUNTING PRINCIPLES
    A. Obtain a statement of the accounting principles and methods adopted by the company.
    B. Consider whether any accounting principles:
        1. Have not been applied consistently during the years under review.
        2. Are not normally acceptable.
        3. Differ from those used by other parties in any takeover or merger.
    C. Ensure that the published documents disclose the effect of any change in principle during the periods under review.

III. ACCOUNTING SYSTEM
    A. Obtain copies of:
        1. A manual of accounting procedures or a description of methods used in preparing the company's financial and management accounts.
        2. A reconciliation of the last published audited accounts with the management accounts for the same period.
        3. The supporting working papers.
    B. Review the methods used to determine the principal items of income and expense, assets and liabilities to establish whether:
        1. The methods can be relied upon to produce accurate accounts.
        2. There are inconsistencies in the methods used to prepare financial and management accounts which might affect their comparability.
    C. Particular attention should be paid to the practices adopted for the following items:

1. Costing of inventory.
2. Provision for inventory obsolescence.
3. Recognition of revenues for long-term contracts.
4. Treatment of intercompany profits.
5. Capitalization of research and development costs.
6. Depreciation of fixed assets.
7. Provision for bad debts.
8. Recognition of revenues or other income, particularly goods on consignment and sale or return.
9. Cost of pension plan, including past service cost.
10. Computation of cost of sales.
11. Treatment and disclosure of extraordinary items.

IV. FORECASTING SYSTEM
   A. Method of preparation:
      1. Obtain from the company statements of:
         (a) Procedures used when preparing forecasts for management purposes. (Documentation by the company of the preparation of the forecasts is of particular importance. The company should maintain records of the arithmetical construction of forecasts, the reasoning adopted and the assumptions made.)
         (b) If different, the procedures used in preparing the forecasts under review. (If forecasting is a normal company procedure and not an *ad hoc* exercise, the established basis of preparation can be examined and relied upon.)
      2. Determine that the forecast represents management's best estimates of the results it reasonably expects to be achieved as distinct from targets which management has set as desirable.
      3. Ascertain the persons responsible for preparing the forecasts.
         (a) Is each functional section (sales, cost of production, etc.) prepared by or under the guidance of the executive in charge of the department?
         (b) Are all senior executives involved and is there adequate consultation for co-ordination?
      4. Determine that the established procedures are followed in practice.
      5. Consider the adequacy of the procedures followed and their appropriateness for the business.
   B. Reliability of previous forecasts:
      1. Compare the budgets, management accounts and financial accounts for the last two financial years.
      2. Investigate material variances between the budgeted and actual results.
      3. Consider the company's practices in revising and updating forecasts.

V. EXAMINATION OF PROFITS FORECAST
   A. Obtain from the company:
      1. The forecasts in the form in which they are to be published.
      2. The assumptions on which they are based.
      3. The supporting detailed forecasts and assumptions.
      4. Published interim statements, if available, for the completed part of the period under review.

B. Evaluate the assumptions to determine the sources of information and the anticipated changes including the support for those changes and whether based on internal or external sources. In particular, the following should be considered:
1. Volume of sales.
2. Price level of sales.
3. Productive capacity.
4. Levels of cost.
5. Availability of working capital.
6. Any special features peculiar to the business.
C. Compare the forecast with any earlier forecast for the same period and obtain explanations for any material changes.
D. Compare the results shown by the most recent management accounts with the budget for the same period.
E. If the forecast results differed materially in the past from the actual results achieved, inquire whether any alterations have been made to the forecasting procedures which should help to reduce future differences.
F. Consider the higher relative risk associated with the following circumstances.
1. Businesses where sales levels or profit margins are especially difficult to predict.
2. New or unproven products or processes.
3. Dependence on a few large outlets or sources of supply.
4. Long-term contracts at fixed prices.
5. Long-term credit arrangements.
6. Reorganization or disposition plans.
G. Discuss the forecasts and assumptions with the senior executives of each major subsidiary or division to establish that all relevant factors have been considered and that the views of all managers have been coordinated.
H. Obtain letters of representation from the senior executives confirming their opinion that the forecasts are properly compiled and are attainable.

VI. EXAMINATION OF CASH FLOW FORECAST
A. Obtain from the company:
1. A cash flow statement for a period not less than that covered by the profit forecast.
   (a) The review should extend beyond the period reported on to assure that payments due soon after the end of the period are covered.
   (b) The statement should be prepared on a monthly or quarterly basis so that seasonal fluctuations are shown.
2. A forecast balance sheet at the end of the review period and at any interim periods if available.
B. Compare the present cash flow forecast with any earlier forecast for the same period and obtain explanations for any material changes.
C. Compare on a test basis the actual receipts and payments for the last three years with the budgeted cash flow statements for the same period.

D. Review the detailed forecasts prepared by subsidiaries or divisions to determine that:
1. The assumptions used for the cash flow forecast are the same as those used for the profit forecast.
2. The changes in level of inventories (including work in progress), debtors and creditors appear reasonable for the budgeted level of activity.
3. Planned capital expenditures and other major disbursements and receipts are included in the correct period.
4. The forecast balance sheet reconciles with the forecast level of profit.
E. Obtain written confirmation from bankers and other loan creditors for the overdraft and loan facilities assumed to be available during the period of the forecast. If material, obtain advice from the company's financial advisers as to the likely course of interest rates during the period of review.

VII. CONSOLIDATION OF FORECASTS
A. Check that the forecasts of subsidiaries or divisions which have been the subject of detailed examination have been correctly included in the consolidated forecast.
B. Test the arithmetical accuracy of the consolidation working papers.
C. Determine that the forecast has been properly adjusted for inter-group or -divisional transactions, unrealized profits and, if applicable, minority interests.
D. Review the consolidated forecast and assumptions in conjunction with the assumptions on which the subsidiary forecasts are based to establish that:
1. The assumptions on a consolidated basis are consistent with the detailed assumptions.
2. The consolidated forecast appears reasonable on the basis of the overall assumptions.

VIII. APPROVAL BY BOARD
Ensure that the profits and cash flow forecasts together with the assumptions on which they are based are formally approved by the board.

NOTE: The composite program does not contain those steps typically performed to clarify the firm's responsibility for forecasts, formalize the engagement arrangements, and those proofing and approval steps normally taken in connection with any published financial document.

Disclosure Rules, Information-Production, and Capital Market Equilibrium: The Case of Forecast Disclosure Rules

NICHOLAS J. GONEDES, NICHOLAS DOPUCH, AND
STEPHEN H. PENMAN*

1. INTRODUCTION

This paper deals primarily with forecast disclosure rules, a topic that has attracted the attention of both the Securities and Exchange Commission and the accounting profession. We consider two fundamental and related aspects of such a rule: (1) the extent to which the type of information to be disclosed conveys information pertinent to valuing firms; and (2) the extent to which a rule requiring public forecast disclosure is consistent with Pareto optimal allocations of resources. We deal with the first by presenting empirical evidence on the information content of income forecasts, and the second by discussing various theoretical issues that seem to have been ignored in debates on forecast (and other) disclosure rules. Our analysis of both aspects applies to disclosure rules enacted by any kind of regulatory body, such as the Financial Accounting Standards Board (FASB) or the Securities and Exchange Commission (SEC). We often refer to the SEC's proposals and rulings, however, simply because it has issued specific rules and proposals dealing with forecast disclosure. Finally, our analysis deals only with external accounting and, in particular, with accounting numbers transmitted to capital market agents.

The remainder of this paper is organized as follows. In Section 2, we identify issues and briefly describe the available literature on forecast disclosure. Section 3 discusses the consistency of forecast disclosure rules with Pareto optimal allocations of resources. Our empirical analysis of the information content of income forecasts appears in Section 4. A summary of the paper is provided in Section 5.

2. IDENTIFICATION OF ISSUES AND REMARKS ON AVAILABLE LITERATURE

Much has been written recently concerning the publication of management's forecasts of earnings. Some attribute this concern to the shift in the

*The comments and criticisms of William Beaver, Joel Demski, Eugene Fama, George Foster, Robert Hamilton, Shyam Sunder, and Robert Magee are gratefully acknowledged.

Nicholas J. Gonedes, Nicholas Dopuch, and Stephen H. Penman, "Disclosure Rules, Information-Production, and Capital Market Equilibrium: The Case of Forecast Disclosure Rules, *Journal of Accountancy*, Spring 1976, Sections 1–3, pp. 89–106. Reprinted with the permission of *Journal of Accountancy*.

SEC'S position regarding the inclusion of projections in documents submitted to it. In February 1973, the SEC proposed a departure from its longstanding prohibition of the inclusion of "projections" and "forecasts" in filings with that agency.[1] It announced its intention to adopt rules whereby a corporation that discloses a forecast to an outsider would have to make a public filing of that forecast with the SEC. In April 1975, the SEC announced its proposed rules for implementing its plan to integrate projections into the SEC disclosure system.[2] In April 1976, the SEC altered its position in response to negative reactions to its 1975 proposals. Its new position calls for voluntary filing of forecasts with the SEC (see the *Wall Street Journal,* April 10, 1976, p. 10).

Of course, the question about whether forecasts or other budgetary data should be included in public financial reports has been debated for a much longer period. Cooper, Dopuch, and Keller [1968] attribute the first public discussion of the relevance of budgetary data to S. A. Rice, who advocated such disclosures in a speech delivered in 1947. Since then, a rather lengthy bibliography has developed on the advantages and disadvantages of disclosing various types of budgetary data.[3] Then, too, the revised version of the English City Code on Take-Overs and Mergers (1972) has given further impetus to the debate. The Code requires that any profit forecasts included in documents addressed to shareholders in connection with take-over offers must be supported by statements of the assumptions underlying the forecasts and an auditor's statement covering the accounting bases and calculations. The requirement of the auditor's participation in the process has raised the interest of accountants in this country, to say the least.

The basic issues raised in the debate on forecast disclosure rules—such as those in the City Code or the SEC 1975 proposal—can be summarized by two fundamental questions. First, to what extent do the required forecast disclosures convey information pertinent to establishing firms' equilibrium values? We label this the "information content" issue. Second, to what extent are the disclosure rules consistent with optimal allocations of resources? In asking the second question, we view disclosure rules as a form of institutional arrangement for information-production and dissemination. We label the second issue the "resource allocation" issue. Of course, these two issues are related. If one is confident that forecasts of, say, income convey no information pertinent to valuing firms, then the entire debate over forecast disclosure is of little interest, insofar as external accounting is concerned.[4] A necessary condition for public disclosure of forecasts to be consistent with Pareto optimality is that the forecasts convey information pertinent to resource allocation. In our discussion of the resource allocation issue—in both this section and Section 3—the existence of information content is assumed.

[1] Securities and Exchange Commission [1973]. A discussion of this release, the SEC's motivation for issuing it, and some of the SEC's plans on forecast disclosure are provided by Burton [1974].

[2] Securities and Exchange Commission [1975].

[3] Some examples are: Burton [1974], Bevis [1962], Birnberg and Dopuch [1963], Nielson [1962], Wilkinson and Doney [1965], and Davidson [1969].

[4] Unless, of course, a forecast disclosure rule is viewed as only a tool for redistributing wealth by altering institutional arrangements, rather than an institutional arrangement for producing information pertinent to allocations of real resources.

2.1 The Resource Allocation Issue

The resource allocation issue encompasses a variety of factors dealing with social "costs" and "benefits." Among the costs to be considered are the costs of complying with and enforcing forecast disclosure rules. Those costs include the direct marginal costs of preparing forecasts and documents monitoring subordinates' behavior so as to comply with forecast disclosure rules. In this regard, note that a rule requiring public disclosure of forecasts disclosed to some individual may induce the production of forecasts that would not otherwise be produced. This may occur if a "silent" management is viewed as attempting to hide information with unfavorable implications. Note also that the task of monitoring (auditing) the behavior of subordinates who provide forecasts (or components thereof) involves a variety of novel difficulties because a forecast is not an observable factor (as is, e.g., a unit of inventory). Nor is a forecast's existence or nature exogenous to the forecaster. That is, there is no "true" or "actual" forecast with which a reported forecast may be compared, after or at the time the forecast is reported. Some of the resulting implications for subordinates' incentives are discussed by Gonedes and Ijiri [1974]. In many respects, the problems that arise here are similar to those encountered in trying to get honest revelations of preferences for "public goods" (see, e.g., Samuelson [1954; 1955].)

Other costs include those induced by whatever liability provisions are adopted in conjunction with the disclosure rules and any costs induced by alterations of nonmanagement agents' incentives to produce forecasts.[5] The latter kind of cost may arise if a forecast disclosure law requires managements to produce forecasts that were previously provided by more efficient producers. The other producers may have no incentive to produce in this situation, unless they can produce forecasts on behalf of managements. Of course, the effect of the disclosure law on incentives may be the opposite. If, for example, the liability provisions associated with the forecast disclosure rules induce managements to avoid disclosing forecasts to any outsider, then outside producers may be motivated to produce forecasts that they would not otherwise produce. If they are the less efficient producers, then the disclosure rule will have induced avoidable information-production costs.

The benefits of a forecast disclosure law are, of course, also pertinent to the resource allocation issue. Is it the case, for example, that a forecast disclosure law will eliminate opportunities to exploit "inside information," and will that elimination lead to a more efficient allocation of resources? The SEC seems to have answered this question in the affirmative.[6] Whether that answer can be justified is considered in Section 3. The extent to which a forecast disclosure law reduces either unnecessary duplication of efforts in producing forecasts or transactions costs is another factor bearing on the social benefits of such a law.

For the most part, only two aspects of the resource allocation issue are considered in the available literature, that is, (1) the type and consequences of whatever liability provisions might be adopted along with a forecast disclosure rule and (2) the "inside information" issue. Presumably, the liability provisions

[5]In this regard, the marginal costs imposed upon a particular firm are affected by the direct liability of the firm and any increases in the costs of auditing services traceable to auditors' direct liability.

[6]See, e.g., Burton [1974].

associated with forecast disclosure rules will be consistent with Section 11 of the Securities Act of 1933 and Rule 10b-5 of the Securities Exchange Act of 1934. Section 11 imposes civil liabilities for false registration statements. Rule 10b-5 imposes civil liability for misstatements or omissions made in connection with the sale of any security. Apparently, the generality of these liability assignments is what is troubling some managements and auditors since the specific ways in which exposure to damage suits can be avoided is unclear. Taken by itself, the generality of Section 11 and Rule 10b-5 need not represent a deficiency of those provisions. Under some circumstances, very specific rules can induce inefficiencies in resource allocation just as can overly general rules.[7] In any event, the most that can be inferred from the few relevant court cases on this issue is that managements and auditors probably will not be held liable for damages ascribed to forecasting errors if the forecasts were developed with "reasonable care."[8]

The "inside information" issue seems to be one of the primary reasons for at least the SEC's interest in forecast disclosure rules. For example, in the SEC's February 1973 Release (see n. 1 above) it is stated that, "The Commission recognizes that projections are currently widespread in the securities markets. . . . The Commission is concerned however that all investors do not have equal access to this material information" (p. 2). Whether the SEC has really identified a problem, and whether that problem, if it exists, warrants the imposition of a disclosure rule are issues discussed in Section 3. Suffice it to note here that the nature of the market for information is a critical factor in dealing with these issues. To date, the debate over forecast disclosure does not seem to be based upon any explicit characterization of that market.

2.2 The Information Content Issue

The "information content" issue has been examined at both the a priori and empirical levels. The specifics of the a priori arguments about information content vary, depending upon the types of forecast (or budgetary) data under examination. The crux of the various arguments seems, however, to be the same. It is essentially argued that managements' forecasts convey information not conveyed by nonmanagement forecasts because managements' forecasts reflect managements' expertise and, more important, managements' planned actions— actions about which outsiders are alleged to have little information. This argument is, at least, a twofold one. First, it is asserted that the managers of a firm, because of their decision-making positions, have access to information for which no reasonable substitutes are available to outsiders. Second, it is asserted that these managers will be motivated to use (or at least disclose) that information in the formulation and presentation of forecasts. These two assertions imply that managements' forecasts have information content. Evidently, most writers on this subject view the first assertion as being correct and the second as being a logical consequence of the first. But that is not obvious to us. For example, whether the second assertion (conditional on the first) is or is not

---

[7]See, e.g., Ehrlich and Posner [1974].

[8]See, e.g., Herwitz [1974]. Herwitz's discussion deals with managements' liability. But we have little reason to believe that the liability assigned to auditors will be more extensive than that assigned to management.

correct depends upon managements' incentives and feasible information-production decisions, and not only the latter—which is all that the first assertion deals with. Most writers also seem to assume that forecasts having information content is sufficient to justify a forecast disclosure rule. That is certainly not obvious, as will be clear from the discussion in Section 3.

The available empirical work on information content deals with earnings forecasts voluntarily made available by firms.[9] The bulk of this work examines the prediction performance or "accuracy" of earnings forecasts. The implicit assumption here is that greater accuracy, however measured, corresponds to greater information content. Some studies assess accuracy in an absolute sense. The studies by McDonald [1973] and Daily [1971] are examples. It has been argued, however, that this approach is overly narrow. For example, Davidson [1973, p.8] opines that, "the important consideration is not the accuracy of managements' forecasts themselves but rather the accuracy of users' predictions with and without the availability of published forecasts. . . ." That opinion seems to underlie the works which compare the accuracy of managements' forecasts to the accuracy of forecasts from benchmark (e.g., "naive" mechanical) models. The work by Copeland and Marioni [1972] is an example of the latter kind of work.

All of the studies dealing with forecast accuracy suffer from some kind of statistical or interpretive deficiency. For example, they often do not allow for the possibility that the accuracy of forecasts for firms in one industry may differ from the accuracy of forecasts for firms in another industry because of substantive economic phenomena, rather than managements' forecasting ability. The earnings numbers of some industries may simply be more erratic than those of other industries. Thus, in order to make inferences about accuracy using data for firms from different industries, some kind of adjustment for interindustry differences may be appropriate.

The works that use benchmark models exhibit other deficiencies. For example, it is not always clear that the benchmark models' performance is an appropriate standard for assessing the accuracy of managements' forecasts. In the Copeland and Marioni paper, the data on managements' forecasts of annual income included forecasts released after a significant portion of the forecast period had already elapsed. At least six months of the forecast year had elapsed for about 25 percent of the forecasts. In contrast, their mechanically produced benchmark forecasts use only the previous years' data or, at best, the first-quarter earnings of the forecast year. Given these timing differences, it is not clear that their benchmark models' prediction performance is an appropriate standard for assessing the accuracy of managements' forecasts.

There is a more fundamental deficiency in these prediction performance studies and the a priori arguments on information content. Specifically, they are not based upon any explicit theoretical structure that connects their frameworks to resource allocation decisions made under uncertainty. In order to

[9]The restriction to only earnings forecasts can be ascribed to the availability of data on such forecasts. Sufficient data on forecasts of other random variables are not readily available. Of course, the use of forecasts voluntarily provided by firms may induce a bias in these studies' empirical results. This will occur if there are systematic differences between the forecasts voluntarily made available and those that would have been available under a rule requiring forecast disclosure.

determine whether forecasts convey information pertinent to valuing a firm, one needs a theoretical model that identifies the determinants of firms' values, conditional on the way in which resource allocation decisions are made. The familiar two-parameter asset-pricing framework is an example of such a model. Without a theoretical foundation connecting earnings forecasts to resource allocation decisions, it is not clear that much can be said about the information content of managements' forecasts.[10] The issues involved here are essentially the same as those discussed by Gonedes and Dopuch [1974, sect. 9].

The recent papers by Foster [1973] Patell [1975], and Nichols and Tsay [1975] are among those that attempt to deal with the information content issue by exploiting a theoretical framework for resource allocation under uncertainty. Our own empirical work—discussed in Section 4—represents another step in that direction, using different and more extensive data and a more refined testing approach.

2.3 Summary

Summing up, we argued that the basic issues raised in the debate over forecast disclosure rules are captured by two fundamental questions: (1) to what extent do required forecast disclosures convey information pertinent to establishing firms' equilibrium values? And (2) to what extent are disclosure rules consistent with optimal allocations of resources? In our judgment, the second question seems to be either completely ignored or inadequately handled by available works on forecast disclosure rules. The a priori arguments dealing with the first question seem to suffer from various theoretical deficiencies. The available empirical work is not so extensive and/or theoretically well founded that the first question can be viewed as having been settled.

The remainder of this paper deals with both the resource allocation and information content issues. The resource allocation issue is considered first.

3. DISCLOSURE LAWS AND INFORMATION-PRODUCTION

3.1 Introduction

The objective of this section is to discuss the extent to which a rule requiring forecast disclosure is consistent with Pareto optimal allocations of resources. As indicated earlier, we view a disclosure rule as a type of institutional arrangement for information-production. Our discussion applies to disclosure rules enacted by any kind of regulatory body, such as the FASB or the SEC.

Some of the issues discussed below pertain to disclosure rules in general. Others are specific to forecast disclosure rules. Our discussion provides no unambiguous resolution of these theoretical issues. It does clearly indicate, however, that many widely accepted conclusions and justifications have, as yet, little theoretical support.

We cannot pursue our ultimate interest until we say more about the market setting for information-production. Throughout, we deal with a world of pro-

---

[10]This does not imply that the statistical properties of managements' forecasts are of no interest in their own right or that evidence on such properties is irrelevant to all aspects of the information content issue.

duction and exchange. We assume that the market for inputs (e.g., labor and capital) used by information-producers and the capital market are "perfect markets." The framework and results provided by Gonedes [1975] are used as a starting point. Some key technical aspects of his framework and results are summarized in Section 3.2. Various relaxations and modifications will be considered in our discussion of disclosure laws in general (Section 3.3) and required forecast disclosures in particular (Section 3.4). The remainder of this section deals with some general aspects of the setting used in Gonedes' work and Sections 3.3 and 3.4.

At the outset, we assume that each firm's managers attempt to maximize the current market value of the shares held by its current stockholders. This is the so-called market value rule. Under appropriate conditions, this rule is consistent with the current shareholders' assumed objective of expected utility maximization. A detailed discussion of sufficient conditions is provided by Fama and Miller [1972, pp. 176–81, 299–301].[11]

The mechanism through which resource allocation is affected by produced information can be loosely described as follows.[12] Capital market agents must assess the distribution functions of returns on firms' shares (or firms' market values) in order to make optimal portfolio decisions. In the framework reviewed in Section 3.2, newly produced information permits the use of distributions conditional upon completely reliable signals on the exact distributions of returns. Thus, produced information affects the distributions used by investors in making optimal portfolio decisions and, consequently, it affects the equilibrium prices of firms' ownership shares. So, given firms' adherence to the market value rule, this information affects firms' production-investment decisions or the allocation of real resources. In short, information produced for investors' use on personal account affects firm's production-investment decisions via the information's effects on the prices of firms' shares. Details on this process are discussed in Gonedes [1975].

One of the basic problems in considering the market for the results of information-production is that, unlike "private" goods, one person's use of produced information does not reduce the "amount" or affect the attributes of produced information that is available for other users. Suppose, for example, that rates of return on assets can be characterized by the familiar two-parameter model. This model implies that the equilibrium expected rate of return on an asset is linearly related to that asset's relative risk, which is conditional upon the portfolio held by an agent in equilibrium. Next, suppose that one provides a completely reliable signal pertaining to the true value of an assets' relative risk. That signal can be used by that person in assessing the equilibrium ex-

---

[11]The extent to which Pareto optimality is attained when production-investment decisions are made according to the market value rule and the capital market is perfect is discussed by Fama [1972], Jensen and Long [1972], Stiglitz [1972], and Merton and Subrahmanyam [1974], among others. Our assumption about value maximization is really stronger than what we need. The important points made below could also have been derived by invoking the unanimity conditions given by Ekern and Wilson [1974]. But use of the value maximization assumption results in a less complicated discussion.

[12]See Gonedes [1975] for additional details. For reasons given below, we deal only with information having implications for allocations of real resources.

pected return on the asset. But the same signal can be used by any other agent who wishes to assess the equilibrium expected return on the asset. And the first person's use or nonuse of the signal does not affect the information content of the signal insofar as any other agent's assessments of equilibrium expected returns are concerned. In short, produced information is a "public good."

Information's being a public good does not imply, however, that the market mechanism cannot be used for information-production. It does imply that special care is needed in specifying the kind of market setting that can be used. Two plausible specifications are discussed by Gonedes and Dopuch [1974, sect. 5]. One is based upon the game-theoretic perspective used by Gonedes [1975]. The other involves a setting discussed by Demsetz [1970] regarding the private production of public goods. Using either specification, one gets a setting for information-production that leads to a competitive pricing mechanism for the results of information-production. The equilibrium induced by this mechanism will consist of a Pareto optimal set of information-production decisions. Much of the discussion in Sections 3.3 and 3.4 is expressed in terms of such a competitive pricing mechanism. Our exposition is couched in terms of the game-theoretic approach used by Gonedes [1975]. Some important assumptions and results of that approach are summarized in Section 3.2.

3.2 Equilibrium in the Market for Information

Under the market-game-theory scheme, it is assumed that there is costless and unrestricted bargaining among participants in the process of producing and disseminating information. No participant is forced to produce or purchase information. Any number of participants may enter into a contract for information at mutually acceptable terms. Produced information resulting from any such contract is made available only to those who entered into the contract. In short, under this scheme, the production and dissemination of information is handled via the contracting and recontracting of groups or "coalitions." The available technology for information-production is assumed to be equally available to all agents. The major tool used to characterize this process is the *core* of a market game. An outcome is said to be in the core if that outcome is consistent with individual rationality, group rationality, and Pareto optimality. An outcome is consistent with group rationality if no subgroup can improve its payoffs, relative to those dictated by the outcome, by not cooperating with others and entering into a contract involving only the members of that subgroup. When information-production is the issue at hand, the "outcomes" or "payoffs" are the net gains from information-production (see Gonedes [1975]). Outcomes in the core are such that no agent can do better by using the resources under his control.

Gonedes [1975] shows that, under specified conditions, applying the game-theoretical approach to the problem of information-production leads to the following conclusions (among others): *(i)* a *core* for the problem of information-production does exist. Since this result assumes unrestricted competition amongst coalitions, and since outcomes in the core are equilibria, this implies that a competitive equilibrium exists for information-production. *(ii)* The net gains of consumer-investors and information-producers converge to a competitive allocation in the classical sense. *(iii)* Each competitive equilibrium is a Pareto optimal state.

The limiting result given in *(ii)* is obtained when the number of agents of all types becomes arbitrarily large. (See Gonedes [1975, pp. V.11–V.12].) This result states that, in the limit, the net gain of any agent converges to his marginal contribution to the results of information-production. This, in turn, implies the existence of competitive prices (in the limit) for each equilibrium outcome of the information-production process. These prices fulfill the same roles as competitive prices in more conventional analyses of resource allocation in a competitive situation. Given the public good attribute of information, the equilibrium price paid by one agent need not be the same as that paid by another agent.

Gonedes' formal results pertain to the implications of information for optimal allocations of real resources via firms' production-investment decisions. The implications of information for trading profits, resulting from private access to new information, were not given much attention. His framework does, however, have implications for the latter kind of information, which was recently examined by Fama and Laffer [1971] and Hirshleifer [1971]. When his framework is applied to information used for trading purposes, as discussed in the Fama/Laffer and Hirshleifer papers, no information for trading is produced if doing so requires the use of real resources (see Gonedes [1975, sect. II and n. 4]). This does not imply, however, that there will be no wealth transfers, since side payments may be needed to prevent the use of real resources for information-production that merely induces wealth transfers. We rely upon this result in the following sections, which deal only with external accounting (i.e., the production of information for use by capital market agents). Thus, our remarks pertain directly to information having implications for the allocation of real resources.

3.3 General Remarks on Disclosure Laws

Given our objectives, the pertinent aspect of disclosure laws is that firms are required to produce information about themselves. The accounting data that firms are now required to report are examples of this type of information. The forecasts that firms may be required to report, and which they are being encouraged to report, constitute another example. In this section, we consider issues more directly related to required forecast disclosure.

The objective of this section is not to justify disclosure laws or replacements for such laws. We simply consider some arguments that can be advanced in support of disclosure laws and some arguments pointing to limitations of such laws.

Given our assumption on each firm's objective, the decisions made by firms are made on behalf of those who hold shares in that firm. Thus, under our assumption, the effect of a disclosure law is to impose a decision to produce specified types of information on a predefined coalition, that is, the current shareholders of the firm. In effect, decisions made by (or imposed upon) firms are equivalent to decisions made by (or imposed upon) a coalition of that firm's current shareholders. If the legally imposed information-production decisions involve the use of information-production opportunities that are available to any possible coalition, then those decisions were feasible decisions for the coalitions. Therefore, in the absence of additional assumptions, there appears to be no economic motivation for disclosure laws. Indeed, since the legally imposed information-production decisions are feasible, but not necessarily optimal, disclosure laws may induce a suboptimal allocation of resources to the production of information.

In the above situation, disclosure laws may induce a suboptimal allocation of resources for at least two reasons. First, they may lead to the production of information that would not be produced by coalitions operating on personal account. Second, they may not lead to production by the most efficient producer. Suppose that the information-production opportunities available to firms are available to coalitions operating on personal account. In this case, alternative arrangements for producing information may be more efficient than production by firms in accordance with disclosure laws. But contemporary disclosure laws require that certain kinds of information be produced about firms and that those firms do the producing. Alternative arrangements for production of the information required by disclosure laws may not be prohibited. However, the disclosure laws may remove incentives for the adoption of such alternatives.

There are, of course, a variety of arguments that can be used to justify disclosure laws. Each involves a violation of one or more of the assumptions used in the framework outined in Section 3.2. We shall consider two basic arguments. The first argument is that the optimal allocation of resources to information-production will not be attained because of difficulties in enforcing the rule of excluding nonpurchasers. This is the so-called free-rider problem. The second argument is that optimality will not be attained because of discriminatory terms of trade in the production of information, due to differential costs of or opportunities for information-production. Such discrimination can lead to the problems of, for example, "adverse selection," of the kind discussed by Akerloff [1970], and "signaling" behavior, of the kind discussed by Spence [1974].

One justification for disclosure laws turns on the extent to which coalitions operating on personal account can exclude nonpurchasers. Exclusion of nonpurchasers played an important role in Gonedes' [1975] game-theoretic treatment of information-production. In general, if each agent feels that he will have rights to receive and use produced information whether he does or does not pay for those rights, then his optimal strategy is to pay nothing for those rights. This perspective assumes, of course, that each agent considers the actions of other agents to be given. This situation corresponds to the concept of a noncooperative equilibrium. For the case of public good, this leads, in general, to a non-Pareto optimal equilibrium unless cooperative strategies are adopted. That depends, in turn, on the extent to which an appropriate system of property rights is established and enforced. The general issues involved here were adequately summarized by Cheung [1970, p. 67]:

> The transfer of property rights among individual owners through contracting in the marketplace requires that the rights be exclusive. An exclusive property right grants its owner a *limited* authority to make decisions on resource use so as to derive income therefrom. To define this limit requires measurment and enforcement. Any property is multidimensional, and exclusivity is frequently a matter of degree. But without some enforced or policed exclusivity to a right of action, the right to contract so as to exchange is absent.
> The absence of exclusivity in property may be due to the absence of recognition by legal institutions of that exclusivity, or to the costs of de-

lineating and policing the limit of the right being prohibitively high. The general issue is thus whether contractual arrangements and exclusive rights exist so that gains and costs of actions are weighed in the market; if not, whether alternative legal arrangements or government regulations are economically desirable.

Clearly, one can view disclosure laws as one set of alternative legal arrangements designed to achieve what the market mechanism cannot achieve because of the prevailing system of property rights and feasible (acceptable?) changes thereof. It is certainly not obvious, however, that much attention has been given to changing the prevailing system of property rights so that the market mechanism can adequately deal with the allocation of resources to information-production (see Gonedes and Dopuch [1974, sec. 10]). Indeed, insofar as the accounting literature is concerned, all that is typically available on alternative institutional arrangements is a somewhat emotional objection to governmental influence on accounting.[13]

A second way of justifying disclosure laws turns on viewing them as if they are the results of agents' colluding via regulatory bodies, rather than on personal account. One might then argue that such forms of collusion minimize the collusion costs associated with information-production. The literature on collective choice provides some motivation for this viewpoint (see, e.g., Breton [1974], Niskanen [1971], and Buchanan and Tullock [1962]). It also suggests, however, that the results of regulatory bodies' actions may not be consistent with the choice criteria that would otherwise guide agents' colluding on personal account. Hence, the extent to which regulatory bodies' actions are best viewed as decisions collectively adopted by agents rather than decisions imposed upon at least some agents is not resolved by either available theory or evidence. Presumably, resolution of this issue turns, in part, on the extent to which there are discriminatory costs of collusion via regulatory bodies.

Another way of justifying disclosure laws is to argue that there are discriminatory terms of trade in the market for information, due to differential costs of or opportunities for information-production. One kind of discriminatory setting is one in which a firm is a "monopolist" in the market for information about itself.

Suppose that some of the information-production decisions available to a firm are not available to coalitions operating on personal account. This implies that the firm has a monopoly position with respect to producing some information about itself. Consider the implications of this when each firm does seek to maximize the value of its current shareholders' wealth.

If a firm does adhere to the market value rule and if it is a monopolist in the market for information about itself, then it may be motivated to prevent disclosure of produced information that has negative implications for the price of its shares. If so, then the firm's "optimal" production-investment decisions

---

[13]That governmental influence "involves politics" is usually one ingredient of this objection. See, e.g., Armstrong [1975, p. 30]. The political nature of, for example, the FASB's and the AICPA's internal workings is usually ignored or simply not recognized. In short, there are no obvious basic theoretical differences between a governmental and a nongovernmental regulatory body. Thus, there is little theoretical support for the claim that "There is no visible alternative to keeping the function of setting accounting standards in private hands to the greatest extent possible" (Horngren [1973, p. 66]).

(with respect to outputs other than information) must be defined in terms of less than all *available* information, because capital market agents do not have access to all the information produced by the firm. Consequently, the firm cannot select the production-investment decisions that are, in fact, optimal if it adheres to the market value rule. Correspondingly, capital market agents cannot select portfolios that are, in fact, optimal relative to all available information. In effect, the disclosed information in this setting is "distorted" relative to the produced information that is available.

A similar problem can arise when there are conflicts between the interests and/or expectations of a firm's management and its security-holders or when different groups of security-holders have conflicting interests and/or expectations. If the firm, or one of the groups, has some monopoly power over the production of information about the firm, then the firm, or one of the groups, may prevent or delay the disclosure of information if it implies that management, or some group, is being favored by the firm's decisions at the expense of some other group. Relative to the produced information that is available, the disclosed information would be distorted in this situation.

The situations involving distortion would not arise if all agents faced the same costs of and opportunities for information-production. When they do arise, one can argue that disclosure laws represent a way of resolving issues of discriminatory costs or opportunities so as to attain Pareto optimality. But this result is certainly not automatic. In order to achieve the desired effect, such laws would have to establish a mechanism for: (1) making optimal (or at least "better") information-production decisions to be imposed on firms, and (2) efficiently disseminating the produced information. These tasks do not appear to be trivial ones. Moreover, it is not clear that disclosure laws are the only institutional arrangements that can be used in this situation.

For example, under an appropriately structured system of property rights, one expects the problem of potentially distorted disclosed information to provide incentives for the existence of various "authentication" institutions. These institutions would sell information of the authenticity of disclosed information. To some extent, Consumers Union—which publishes *Consumer Reports*—is an example of such an institution. One might also argue that "auditing" activities fulfill this role. Of course, any kind of authentication institution faces the problem of establishing the authenticity of the information that it produces. Depending upon the market setting, that may lead to the kinds of "signaling" and "filtering" problems discussed by Spence [1974].

Other alternatives to disclosure laws are guarantees, warranties, and other forms of insurance that protect, for a fee, a capital market agent against losses from distorted information, which can be viewed as being analogous to a defective product. The issues that arise here are, at a fundamental level, similar to those arising in the area of "products liability" (see, e.g., McKean [1970], Oi [1973], and Brown [1974]).

The above discussion indicates some of the ways of justifying disclosure laws. It also points to some issues that should, it appears, be considered before disclosure laws are chosen as institutional arrangements for the production of the kind of information considered in this paper. The purpose of the discussion is not to support one set of institutional arrangements over another. It is to point out some options that are rarely, if ever, considered in the literature on disclosure laws.

Since the above discussion applies to disclosure laws in general, it applies to the proposed disclosure laws dealing specifically with managements' forecasts. In view of our discussion, there are at least two issues to be considered in evaluating the arguments advanced in favor of those proposals. First, do those arguments identify situations in which disclosure laws can be justified? Second, do those arguments uniquely identify disclosure laws as the appropriate form of institutional arrangement? We deal with these questions in the next section.

3.4 Required Disclosure of Managements' Forecasts

In this section, we consider some specific arguments that can be or have been advanced in favor of the required disclosure of forecasts. Most, if not all, of the arguments advanced in the existing literature can be viewed as special versions of those considered here. The reason for considering these arguments is to determine (1) whether they actually identify situations wherein disclosure laws may facilitate attainment of Pareto optimal results and, if they do, (2) whether the details of the arguments identify disclosure laws as the appropriate form of institutional arrangement.[14]

One of the most frequently given justifications for a rule requiring the public disclosure of forecasts involves issues of alleged discrimination. For example, John C. Burton (Chief Accountant of the SEC) stated that one of the main reasons for the SEC's current position on forecast disclosure is the

> ... increasing evidence of discriminatory disclosure of forecast data by corporate management. At the same time as many companies announced their projections publicly, a number of others communicated their expectations to a select few. Favored analysts might be advised of current budget data either directly or by letting them know that their estimates were "in the ballpark." Through a variety of such devices, many corporations sought to be sure that "market" estimates of their earnings were not far off the mark while still not taking any public position on the projected results. While the overwhelming majority of such efforts were done in good faith, the end result was lack of knowledge as to what forecasts were those of management as opposed to those of analysts working independently. In

---

[14]Of course, one might argue that these resource allocation issues are not the main factors considered by those who regulate disclosure, such as the SEC and the FASB. One might argue, instead, that "equity" and "egalitarianism" are the main factors. That the latter are important factors in, say, the SEC's and FASB's thinking is undeniable. Yet, based upon our reading of the analyses and explanations provided by these bodies' representatives, it seems that "egalitarianism" and "equity" are viewed as means for attaining efficient resource allocation, not as ends in themselves. For example, in a recent discussion of insider trading rules, which contains references to ethical issues and egalitarianism, A. A. Sommer (Commissioner of the SEC) notes the importance of capital market efficiency to resource allocation, and he states that, "Such a market is the ideal for which we strive" (Sommer [1975, p. 12]). In his discussion of the "accounting environment," John C. Burton (Chief Accountant at the SEC) concludes that, "In the final analysis [the SEC's] goal is congruent with that of the [utility] industry: an efficient capital market in which resources will be attracted to meet the needs of society" (Burton [1973, p. 46]). The SEC's endorsement of the "differential disclosure" concept provides some additional support for our interpretations (see Sommer [1974]). This concept was "officially" recognized in the SEC's October 4, 1973 "Notice of Proposed Amendments to Regulation S-X Providing for Disclosure of Significant Accounting Policies" (see Securities and Exchange Commission [1973]).

a few cases there was evidence of selective disclosure to institutional investors interested in the stock and unfair use of such insider information (Burton [1974, p. 86]).

Taken as it stands, this argument does not provide much justification for any intervention with the market mechanism. The fact that there is discriminatory disclosure does not imply a "failure" of the market mechanism. This is most easily seen by applying Burton's argument to some private good. Suppose that the market for that good is perfectly competitive. Then there will necessarily be discrimination in the sense that only those agents who pay the going price for the good will acquire the right to use that good. All other agents are excluded from using the good. In a sense, this is discrimination. It is not clear, however, that one should want to eliminate it, assuming that the allocation of resources defined by a competitive equilibrium is acceptable (and attainable).

The same reasoning can be applied to information-production, even though produced information is a public good (see Section 3.1). Indeed, given the arguments of Sections 3.1 and 3.2, there are only two basic theoretical differences involved in extending that reasoning to produced information. First, one will not be dealing with bids for private control over identifiable resources. Instead, the bidding will be for rights to receive and use produced information. In a sense, the prices represent entry fees which, once paid, entitle the payer(s) to enter the group of persons allowed to receive and use the information. Second, unlike the case of private goods, the existence of different equilibrium prices for different individuals is consistent with a competitive equilibrium and Pareto optimality when one is dealing with produced information, or any other "public good" (see, e.g., Samuelson [1954; 1955] and Demsetz [1970]).

In short, our argument is that the discrimination troubling the SEC may be the result of a well-functioning market for information. Is this a reasonable argument? If one adopts the perspective outlined in Section 3.2, then it does seem reasonable, even though the situation observed by the SEC involves various kinds of collusion. The framework summarized in Section 3.2 implies that collusion is to be expected when dealing with information-production, because of the public good attribute of information having implications for resource allocation.[15] For example, one can argue that institutional investors and managements are in a position to effect mutually advantageous arrangements for information-production, management producing information on its own firm and the institutional investors producing information on other (perhaps competing) firms and macroeconomic phenomena. If so, then there are incentives for the formation of coalitions of the kind described in Section 3.2.[16]

Of course, if the kinds of "imperfections" described in Section 3.3 obtain, then the situation observed by the SEC may not be consistent with attaining Pareto optimality. For example, one can argue that the costs and opportunities

[15]The same result can be attained via the Theory of Clubs advanced by Buchanan [1965]. See Ng [1973; 1974] for additional analyses of that approach.

[16]This possibility raises other important issues. Who gains from managements' "sales" of information to other agents, assuming such sales take place? Do the gains, if any, go to managements or to firms' current shareholders? If there are economic rents, how are they dissipated, if at all? Dealing with these issues involves aspects of the market for corporate control and the market for information, among other things.

for information-production are not the same for all agents. Specifically, one can argue that the information-production costs and opportunities facing a coalition involving managements are not the same as, and are superior to, those facing other coalitions. This seems to be one aspect of the SEC's position. However, even if this kind of "monopolistic" position does prevail, it is not clear that it should be eliminated by a disclosure law. The situation here may be similar to those covered by patent and copyright laws, namely: without the (perhaps temporary) monopolistic position, the kinds of information produced may be different and any difference may induce undesirable effects on resource allocation (see, e.g., Bowman [1973] and Scherer [1970, chap. 16]). Moreover, as was indicated in Section 3.3, there are other institutional arrangements that can be used to deal with "imperfections" in the market for information.

Another argument that can be advanced in support of forecast disclosure involves a possible reduction in the extent to which efforts are duplicated. Suppose that agents external to the firm allocate resources to the kinds of information-production activities leading to forecasts. The "duplication" argument would essentially state that it is more efficient to have one entity, and in particular management, produce and distribute forecasts than to have many agents produce forecasts on the same terms of trade. This argument, as reasonable as it seems, is based upon several critical implicit assumptions, two of which are considered below.

In order to assert that there really is wasteful and completely avoidable duplication, it must be that the forecasts being produced are perfect substitutes, so that all agents could use any of the forecasts (including managements' forecasts) just as they would their own. Loosely speaking, the information content of one forecast in this situation is the same as that of any other forecast. This appears to be a very strong assumption, especially if the forecasts are based upon different models. A priori, it would seem that the forecasts produced by different models represent competing or rival products. This may be the case when, for example, the "quality" of managements' forecasts is not viewed as being the same as that of other forecasts. Such a viewpoint might be motivated by the incentives and opportunities that managements might have for issuing "distorted" forecasts (see Section 3.3). If different forecasts are viewed as competing products, then each may provide an important contribution, in terms of information content. In general, dealing with this issue involves some heady issues of model comparisons (see, e.g., Geisel [1970], Roberts [1965], and Gonedes [1972]). These technical issues are not reviewed here. The main point that we wish to emphasize is that different forecasts may not be perfect substitutes and, thus, the "duplication" argument seems less forceful than it did at first glance.[17]

Suppose that there is completely or partially avoidable duplication. What does this imply about the structure of the market for information? Clearly, if there is such duplication, then there are opportunities for the formation of coalitions on terms that are advantageous to at least one member of each coalition and not detrimental to any member. Thus, asserting the existence of avoidable duplication seems equivalent to asserting the existence of barriers to

---

[17]Perhaps a fruitful approach is formally to treat forecasts as providing multidimensional services. Some relevant frameworks are discussed in Lancaster [1971] and Becker [1965].

the formation of coalitions or prohibitive costs. There may be some truth to such an assertion. It is well to note, however, that there are many existing arrangements that are inconsistent with it. For example, there are many institutions (e.g., Data Resources, Inc., Wharton Econometrics, and Chase Econometrics) that provide—for a subscription (or "entry") fee—the results of forecasting and other information-production activities to their subscribers (or members of their "club"). Such institutions can be viewed as coalitions that arose in order to eliminate avoidable duplication associated with information-production activities. Moreover, a variety of changes in the prevailing system of property rights can be made to facilitate the development of such institutions.

Another argument frequently given in support of required forecast disclosure states that such forecasts are types of inside information and that the present way of disclosing them induces unfair uses of such inside information. This argument is really a special case of the first (i.e., the "discrimination") argument, because it involves differential opportunities for information-production.

3.5 Summary

Summing up, this section considered several arguments that can be or have been given in support of required forecast disclosure. Each argument alleges some kind of "market failure" (conventionally defined) in the market for information. Whether the alleged forms of "market failure" really exist is, of course, an empirical issue, about which there is little reliable empirical evidence. Our discussion indicates that, on theoretical grounds, the arguments considered here are not sufficient for concluding that there are market failures. Moreover, even if one does believe that market failures exist, those arguments are not so specific that they identify forecast disclosure laws as appropriate remedies. In short, the general conclusions of Section 3.3 regarding disclosure laws apply here as well. "Market failures," if they exist, can be overcome by a variety of institutional arrangements. Disclosure laws represent just one possible means of dealing with such situations. We have, as yet, no basis for stating either that they are the best or the worst means.

REFERENCES

Akerloff, G. A. "The Market for 'Lemons': Quality Uncertainty and the Market Mechanism." *Quarterly Journal of Economics* (August 1970): 488–500.

Anderson, T. W. *An Introduction to Multivariate Statistical Analysis.* New York: John Wiley & Sons, 1958.

Armstrong, Marshall S. "FASB Prospects." *Arthur Young Journal* (Spring 1975): 28–31.

Ball, R. J., and P. Brown. "An Empirical Evaluation of Accounting Income Numbers." *Journal of Accounting Research* (Autumn 1968): 159–77.

Basu, S. "Investment Performance of Common Stocks in Relation to Their Price-Earnings Ratios: A Test of the Efficient Market Hypothesis." Manuscript, McMaster University, December 1974.

Becker, G. S. "A Theory of the Allocation of Time." *Economic Journal* (September 1965): 493–517.

Bevis, H. W. "The CPA's Attest Function in Modern Society." *Journal of Accountancy* (February 1962): 28–35.

Birnberg, J., and N. Dopuch. "A Conceptual Approach to the Framework for Disclosure." *Journal of Accountancy* (February 1963): 56–63.

Black, F., M. Jensen, and M. Scholes. "The Capital Asset Pricing Model: Some Empirical Results." In *Studies in the Theory of Capital Markets*, edited by M. Jensen. New York: Praeger, 1972.

Bowman, W. S., Jr. *Patent and Antitrust Law.* Chicago: University of Chicago Press, 1973.

Breton, A. *The Economic Theory of Representative Government.* Chicago: Aldine Publishing Co., 1974.

Brown, J. P. "Product Liability: The Case of an Asset with a Random Life." *American Economic Review* (March 1974): 149–61.

Brown, P., and R. J. Ball. "Some Preliminary Findings on the Association Between the Earnings of a Firm, Its Industry and the Economy." *Empirical Research in Accounting: Selected Studies 1967.* Supplement to Vol. 5, *Journal of Accounting Research*, pp. 55–77.

Buchanan, J. M. "An Economic Theory of Clubs." *Economica* (February 1965): 1–14.

Buchanan, J. M., and G. Tullock. *The Calculus of Consent.* Ann Arbor: University of Michigan Press, 1962.

Burton, J. C. "Some General and Specific Thoughts on the Accounting Environment." *Journal of Accountancy* (October 1973): 40–46.

———. "Forecasts: A Changing View from the Securities and Exchange Commission." In *Public Reporting of Corporate Financial Forecasts*, edited by P. Prakash and A. Rappaport. New York: Commerce Clearing House, 1974.

Cheever, J. K. "Investor Actions and Forecasted Earnings in an Efficient Market." Ph.D. dissertation, University of Southern California, 1975.

Cheung, S. N. S. "The Structure of a Contract and the Theory of a Non-Exclusive Resource." *Journal of Law and Economics* (April 1970): 49–70.

Cooper, W. W., N. Dopuch, and T. Keller. "Budgetary Disclosures and Other Suggestions for Improving Accounting Reports." *The Accounting Review* (October 1968): 640–48.

Copeland, R., and R. J. Marioni. "Executives' Forecasts of Earnings per Share versus Forecasts of Naive Models." *Journal of Business* (October 1972): 497–512.

Daily, R. A. "The Feasibility of Reporting Forecasted Information." *The Accounting Review* (October 1971): 686–92.

Davidson, S. "Accounting and Financial Reporting in the Seventies." *Journal of Accountancy* (December 1969): 29–37.

———. "The Study Group on Objectives of Financial Statements: A Progress Report." Stanford Lectures in Accounting, Graduate School of Business, Stanford University, 1973.

Demsetz, H. "The Private Production of Public Goods." *Journal of Law and Economics* (October 1970): 293–306.

Ehrlich, I., and R. Posner. "Economic Analysis of Legal Rulemaking." *Journal of Legal Studies* (January 1974): 257–86.

Ekern, S., and R. Wilson. "On the Theory of the Firm in an Economy with Incomplete Markets." *Bell Journal of Economics and Management Science* (Spring 1974): 171–80.

Fama, E. F. "Perfect Competition and Optimal Production Decisions under Uncertainty." *Bell Journal of Economics and Management Science* (Autumn 1972): 509–30.

———, and A. B. Laffer. "Information and Capital Markets." *Journal of Business* (July 1971): 289–98.

———, and J. MacBeth. "Risk, Return and Equilibrium: Empirical Tests." *Journal of Political Economy* (May/June 1973): 607–36.

————, and M. H. Miller. *The Theory of Finance*. New York: Holt, Rinehart & Winston, 1972.

Foster, G. "Stock Market Reaction to Estimates of Earnings per Share by Company Officials." *Journal of Accounting Research* (Spring 1973): 25–37.

Geisel, M. S. "Comparing and Choosing Among Parametric Statistical Models: A Bayesian Application with Macroeconomic Implications." Ph.D. dissertation, University of Chicago, 1970.

Gonedes, N. J. "Discussion of: Analysis of the Usefulness of Accounting Data for the Portfolio Decision: A Decision-Theory Approach." *Empirical Research in Accounting: Selected Studies 1972*. Supplement to Vol. 10, *Journal of Accounting Research*, pp. 85–101.

————. "Properties of Accounting Numbers: Models and Tests." *Journal of Accounting Research* (Autumn 1973a): 212–37.

————. "Evidence on the Information Content of Accounting Numbers: Accounting-Based and Market-Based Estimates of Systematic Risk." *Journal of Financial and Quantitative Analysis* (June 1973b): 407–44.

————. "Capital Market Equilibrium and Annual Accounting Numbers: Empirical Evidence." *Journal of Accounting Research* (Spring 1974a): 26–62.

————, "Risk, Information, and the Effects of Special Accounting Items on Capital Market Equilibrium." *Journal of Accounting Research* (Autumn 1975): 220–56.

————. "Information-Production and Capital Market Equilibrium." *Journal of Finance* (June 1975): 841–64.

————, and N. Dopuch. "Capital Market Equilibrium, Information-Production and Selecting Accounting Techniques: Theoretical Framework and Review of Empirical Work." *Studies on Financial Accounting Objectives* 1974. Supplement to Vol. 12. *Journal of Accounting Research*, pp. 48–169.

————, and Y. Ijiri "Improving Subjective Probability Assessments for Planning and Control in Team-Like Organizations." *Journal of Accounting Research* (Autumn 1974): 251–69.

Gray, W. S. "The Role of Forecast Information in Investment Decisions." In *Public Reporting of Corporate Financial Forecasts*, edited by P. Prakash and A. Rappaport. New York: Commerce Clearing House, 1974.

Herwitz, D. R. "The Risk of Liability for Forecasting." In *Objectives of Financial Statements: Selected Papers*, edited by J. J. Cramer, Jr. and G. H. Sorter. Vol. 2. New York: American Institute of Certified Public Accountants, 1974.

Hirshleifer, J. "The Private and Social Value of Information and the Reward to Inventive Activity." *American Economic Review* (September 1971): 561–74.

Horngren, C. T. "The Marketing of Accounting Standards." *Journal of Accountancy* (October 1973): 61–66.

Jensen, M. C. "Capital Markets: Theory and Evidence." *Bell Journal of Economics and Management Science* (Autumn 1972): 357–98.

————, and J. B. Long, Jr. "Corporate Investment under Uncertainty and Pareto Optimality in the Capital Markets." *Bell Journal of Economics and Management Science* (Spring 1972): 151–74.

Lancaster, K. *Consumer Demand*. New York: Columbia University Press, 1971.

Latané, H. A., and D. L. Tuttle. "An Analysis of Common Stock Price Ratios." *Southern Economic Journal* (January 1967): 345–47.

————, D. L. Tuttle, and C. P. Jones. "E/P Ratios versus Changes in Earnings in Forecasting Future Price Changes." *Financial Analysts Journal* (January/February 1969): 2–3.

————, O. M. Joy, and C. P. Jones. "Quarterly Data, Sort-Rank Routines, and Security Evaluation." *Journal of Business* (October 1970): 427–38.

Magee, R. P. "Industry-Wide Commonalities in Earnings." *Journal of Accounting Research* (Autumn 1974): 270–87.

McDonald, C. L. "An Empirical Examination of the Reliability of Published Predictions of Future Earnings." *The Accounting Review* (July 1973): 502–10.

McKean, R. N. "Products Liability: Implications of Some Changing Property Rights." *Quarterly Journal of Economics* (November 1970): 611–26.

Merton, R. C., and M. G. Subrahmanyam. "The Optimality of a Competitive Stock Market." *Bell Journal of Economics and Management Science* (Spring 1974): 145–70.

Morrison, D. F. *Multivariate Statistical Methods.* New York: McGraw-Hill, 1967.

Ng, Y. K. "The Economic Theory of Clubs: Optimal Tax/Subsidy." *Economica* (August 1974): 308–21.

———. "The Economic Theory of Clubs: Pareto Optimality Conditions." *Economica* (August 1973): 291–98.

Nichols, D. R., and J. Tsay. "Security Price Reactions and Executive Earnings Forecasts." Manuscript, University of Texas at Arlington, 1975.

Niederhoffer, V., and P. J. Regan. "Earnings Changes, Analysts' Forecasts, and Stock Prices." *Financial Analysts Journal* (May/June 1972): 65–71.

Nielson, O. "New Challenges in Accounting." *The Accounting Review* (October 1962): 584–85.

Niskanen, W. A., Jr. *Bureaucracy and Representative Government.* Chicago: Aldine-Atherton, 1971.

Oi, W. Y. "The Economics of Product Safety." *Bell Journal of Economics and Management Science* (Spring 1973): 3–28.

Patell, J. M. "Corporate Earnings Forecasts: Empirical Tests and a Consumption-Investment Model." Manuscript, Carnegie-Mellon University, 1975.

Prakash, P., and A. Rappaport, eds. *Public Reporting of Corporate Financial Forecasts.* New York: Commerce Clearing House, 1974.

Roberts, H. V. "Probabilistic Prediction." *Journal of the American Statistical Association* (March 1965): 50–62.

Samuelson, P. A. "Diagrammatic Exposition of a Theory of Public Expenditure." *Review of Economics and Statistics* (November 1955): 350–56.

———. "The Pure Theory of Public Expenditure." *Review of Economics and Statistics* (November 1954): 387–89.

Scherer, F. M. *Industrial Market Structure and Economic Performance.* New York: Rand McNally, 1970.

Securities and Exchange Commission. "Statement by the Commission on the Disclosure of Projections of Future Economic Performance." Release No. 5362 (Securities Act of 1933), Release No. 9984 (Securities Exchange Act of 1934). Washington, D. C., February 2, 1973.

———. Release No. 5427 (Securities Act of 1933), Release No. 10420 (Securities Exchange Act of 1934), Release No. 18110 (Public Utility Holding Company Act of 1935), Release No. 8023 (Investment Company Act of 1940). Washington, D.C., October 4, 1973.

———. Release No. 5581 (Securities Act of 1933), Release No. 11374 (Securities Exchange Act of 1934). Washington, D. C., April 28, 1975.

Sommer, A. A., Jr. "Differential Disclosure: To Each His Own." *Journal of Accountancy* (August 1974): 55–58.

———. "Another Look at Insider Trading." Paper presented at the Southwestern Legal Foundation Symposium on Securities Regulation, Dallas, Texas, April 17, 1975.

Spence, A. M. *Market Signaling: Informational Transfer Hiring and Related Screening Processes.* Cambridge, Mass.: Harvard University Press, 1974.

Stiglitz, J. "On the Optimality of the Stock Market Allocation of Investment." *Quarterly Journal of Economics* (February 1972): 25–60.

Wilkinson, J. R., and E. D. Doney. "Extending Audit and Reporting Boundaries." *The Accounting Review* (October 1965): 753–56.

IV-B/HUMAN ASSET ACCOUNTING

On the Use of the Economic Concept of Human Capital in Financial Statements

BARUCH LEV AND ABA SCHWARTZ

> "The most valuable of all capital is that invested in human beings."
> Alfred Marshall, *Principles of Economics*.

INTRODUCTION

The dichotomy in accounting between human and nonhuman capital is fundamental; the latter is recognized as an asset and therefore is recorded in the books and reported in the financial statements, whereas the former is totally ignored by accountants. Most economists, on the other hand, have a different view on this issue. Milton Friedman, for example, states:

> From the broadest and most general point of view, total wealth includes all sources of "income" of consumable services. One such source is the productive capacity of human beings, and accordingly this is one form in which wealth can be held. [8, p. 4]

The definition of wealth as a source of income inevitably leads to the recognition of human capital as one of several forms of holding wealth, such as money, securities, and physical (nonhuman) capital. This attitude toward human capital has a broad range of applications in economics. For example, the value of human capital appears in some demand functions for money (of business enterprises as well as households) as an argument along with other forms of nonhuman wealth [8, pp. 9, 13], human capital is recognized as an important factor in explaining and predicting economic growth [2], etc. Human capital is thus treated in modern economic theory on a par with other forms of earning assets.

On the other hand, the different attitude of accountants toward human capital was succinctly expressed as follows:

> A favorite cliché for the president's letter in corporate reports is "our employees are our most important—our most valuable—asset." Turning

The authors are deeply indebted to Professor Sidney Davidson, Dean of the Graduate School of Business, University of Chicago, for helpful comments.

Baruch Lev and Aba Schwartz, "On the Use of the Economic Concept of Human Capital in Financial Statements," *The Accounting Review*, January 1971, pp. 103–112. Reprinted with the permission of *The Accounting Review*.

from the president's letter and looking to the remainder of the report, one might ask, "where is this human asset on these statements which serve as reports of the firm's resources and earnings? What is the value of this most important or most valuable asset? Is it increasing, decreasing, or remaining unchanged?" [4, p. 217]

The objective of this article is to provide a practical measurement procedure by which some of the questions raised in the preceding quotation can be answered. Specifically, the possibility of using the economic concept and measurement of human capital in financial statements is explored. It is shown that the suggested method provides decision makers with information about organizational matters hitherto not reported by accountants. The order of discussion is as follows: Section II provides a discussion of the concept of human capital and its measurement. Section III extends this concept to the firm's level. Section IV elaborates on implications for decision makers from human capital reporting. Section V discusses some conceptual accounting problems involved in incorporating human capital values in the financial statements. Finally, Section VI provides some concluding remarks. The Appendix presents a hypothetical example demonstrating the measurement of a firm's human capital.

THE CONCEPT OF HUMAN CAPITAL

Irving Fisher, one of the originators of human capital theory, notes:

Capital in the sense of capital value is simply future income discounted, in other words, capitalized. . . . But the basic problem of time valuation which nature sets us is that of translating the future into the present, that is, the problem of ascertaining the capital value of future income. *The value of capital must be computed from the value of its estimated future net income, not vice versa.* [7, pp. 12–14, emphasis supplied.]

Capital is thus defined as a source of income stream and its worth is the present value of future income discounted by a rate specific to the owner of the source (or to the potential buyer).

Fisher's definition does not distinguish between human capital, which is a source of income embodied in a person (in the form of his brute force and his natural and acquired skills), and nonhuman capital. There is, however, an important distinction: the ownership of human capital is nontransferable (in a nonslave society) while nonhuman capital can be traded in the market. In a world of certainty this distinction is of no consequence for the determination of capital values since certainty implies a perfect knowledge of future income streams associated with the source and of future discount rates. Given this knowledge, the present value (i.e., worth) of human as well as nonhuman capital can be uniquely determined. In a world of uncertainty, however, future income streams and discount rates are not perfectly known and consequently the present value of the source cannot be uniquely (objectively) determined. Nevertheless, in the case of nonhuman capital we can still infer its value from observed market prices which reflect the present value of future earnings to the traders. Such a derivation of value from market prices cannot be made in the case of human capital since it is not traded. Thus, in a world of uncertainty an important distinction exists between human and nonhuman capital.

The difficulty in determining the value of human capital under uncertainty is responsible for the initial lack of systematic treatment of the subject in economics. However, during the last two decades economists have become aware of the grave consequences of this omission, as Gary Becker notes:

> Recent years have witnessed intensive concern with and research on investment in human capital, much of it contributed or stimulated by T. W. Schultz. The main motivating factor has probably been a realization that the growth of physical capital, at least as conventionally measured, explained a relatively small part of the growth of income in most countries. The search for better explanation has led to improved measures of physical and to an interest in less tangible entities, such as technological change and human capital. [2, p. 1.]

Consequently, a theory of human capital measurement has been developed and its impact on macroeconomic problems investigated [2, 3, 9, 11, 12, 14, 15, 16, 17, 18]. An extension of this approach to the firm's level, as advanced in this paper, seems natural.

The Earnings Profile

An earnings profile is a graphic or mathematical presentation of the income stream generated by a person (i.e., by his human capital), see Fig. 1. A typical earnings profile first increases with age, reflecting the capability of human beings to learn (on the job or elsewhere) and thus increase their productivity. As the person ages, productivity declines because of technological obsolescence and health deterioration, a fact expressed by a decrease in the annual earnings. Since the profile reflects only earnings from employment and not from capital assets it terminates at retirement or on death if that occurs earlier.

Measurement of Human Capital

The value of human capital embodied in a person of age π is the present value of his remaining future earnings from employment. This value for a discrete income stream is:

(1)
$$V_\pi = \sum_{t=\pi}^{T} \frac{I(t)}{(1+r)^{t-\pi}}$$

where:

V_π = the human capital value of a person π years old.
$I(t)$ = the person's annual earnings up to retirement. This series is graphically represented by the earnings profile.
r = a discount rate specific to the person.
T = retirement age.

Strictly speaking, expression (1) is an *ex post* computation of human capital value at any age of the person, since only after retirement is the series $I(t)$ known. This is of little use in our case where we need the *ex ante* values of human capital. Hence, the observed values of $I(t)$ in (1) should be replaced by

FIGURE 1
Earnings Profiles of U.S. Males, 1949
SOURCE: U.S. CENSUS OF POPULATION (1950), SER. P-E, NO. 5-B: EDUCATION, TABLES 12, 13

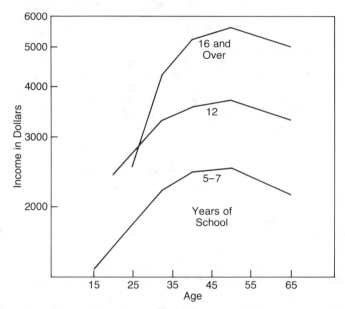

estimates $I^*(t)$ of future annual earnings. The best source of information for these estimates is current data on earnings distribution classified by age, education, skill, etc. Consider, for example, the problem of estimating the future earnings series of an industrial engineer, 25 years of age. We have current data (from the census and other sources) on average earnings of industrial engineers 25 years of age, 26 years of age, and so on up to retirement. We can, therefore, estimate next year's earnings of our 25 year old engineer on the basis of current earnings of an equivalent engineer 26 years of age, the estimate of earnings two years hence will be based on current average earnings of 27 year old engineers, and so on. Generally, the observed *across persons* earnings profile $I°(t)$ can be transformed to *over-time* earnings profile, providing the required estimates of future earnings $I^*(t)$:

$$(2) \qquad I^*(t) = f[I°(t)], \qquad t = r, \dots, T.$$

The function f in (2) is a transformation of current to future earnings reflecting expectations of future technological changes, changes in demand for the specific skills of the person, government intervention, and most important—the person's subjective evaluation of his capabilities relative to others in the professional group. Since information on such future events is difficult to obtain, it is customary in human capital studies to assume that the function f is the identity transformation, i.e.,

$$(3) \qquad I^*(t) = I°(t), \qquad t = \pi, \dots, T$$

Thus, the prediction of next year's earnings of the 25 year old engineer will be equal to (not just based on) current earnings of a 26 year old equivalent engineer.[1] The estimated human capital value of a person π years old is thus:

$$
(4) \qquad V_\pi^* = \sum_{t=\pi}^{T} \frac{I^*(t)}{(1+r)^{t-\pi}}
$$

where $I^*(t)$ is determined by (3).

Expression (4) ignores the possibility of death occurring prior to retirement age. This can be incorporated into the model by the use of mortality tables which provide the death probabilities. Specifically, the probability of a person dying at age t is presented by the long-run mortality rates of persons with the same characteristics (race, sex, education, etc.). When this probability is $P_T(t)$, the *expected value* of the person's human capital is:[2]

$$
(5) \qquad E(V_\pi^*) = \sum_{t=\pi}^{T} P_T(t+1) \sum_{i=\pi}^{t} \frac{I_i^*}{(1+r)^{t-\pi}}
$$

Statistical Sources

Since our main purpose is to advance a *practical* application of human capital concepts in accounting we briefly discuss some sources of data.

Practically all empirical studies concerned with human capital measurements in the U.S. are based on the 1960 census data published by the Bureau of the Census [19]. This census provides cross-sectional data on earnings classified by age, race, sex, education, geographic area of employment, etc., and most useful for our application—by profession or skill. Average earnings profiles of professional groups of employees (e.g., unskilled employees in the meat packing industry) can be determined from these data. The earnings profiles can be refined by keeping constant several personal characteristics. For example, if an average earnings profile for electrical engineers is too crude (i.e., the group of electrical engineers in the U.S. is too heterogeneous), the earnings profile of white, male electrical engineers, employed in the automobile industry, can be determined, thereby making the group for which an earnings profile is determined more homogeneous.[3]

Of special importance for practical use is a condensed version of the 1960 census available on magnetic tape. This is a 0.1 percent random sample of the total U.S. population included in the census. Since a complete census is taken every 10 years, current data will soon be available.

Mortality tables, needed for formula (5), are available for every country and region. Such tables are extensively used by life insurance companies in determining their premium scale and reserves.

[1]In cases where price level changes are significant, an adjustment for these changes can be made. Specifically, $I^*(t)$ will equal $I°(t)$ adjusted for expected price level changes.

[2]$P_r(t)$ is the conditional probability of a person of age π dying in year t.

[3]For the practical construction of such refined profiles, see [9].

HUMAN CAPITAL VALUE ASSOCIATED WITH THE FIRM

We have discussed thus far the conceptual and practical problems involved in measuring the capital value of a person or a homogeneous group of persons. The determination of the total value of a firm's labor force is a straightforward extension. The firm's labor force will be divided into homogeneous groups of employees such as unskilled employees, semi-skilled, skilled, engineers of different kinds, salesmen, managerial staff, etc. Average earnings profiles, based on census data, will be constructed for each group and the present value of human capital calculated. The sum of present values over the various employee groups will provide the total human capital value associated with the firm. A simple hypothetical example of such a computation is provided in the Appendix.

The firm's value of human capital thus measured is based on average earnings data of homogeneous groups of employees in the U.S. A given firm, however, may employ persons of higher or lower quality than the average and accordingly pay different wages and salaries than those indicated by the census-based data. If the firm employs a large number of employees of different kinds it will be possible to determine earnings profiles based on the firm's own wage scale. Specifically, cross-sectional data on wages currently paid to groups of employees will be substituted for the census data to determine the earnings profiles. We can thus compute for a firm's labor force a *general* value of human capital and a *specific* value, the former based on overall census data and the latter on the specific wage scale of the firm. It should be emphasized again that the specific value of human capital can be computed only if the firm's labor force is large, i.e., when there is an ample amount of cross-sectional data to form the earnings profiles. The appropriate discount rate for determining the firm's human capital value seems to be the cost of capital. This is the rate used in capital budgeting decisions and also the opportunity cost of the firm's resources.

IMPLICATIONS OF HUMAN CAPITAL REPORTING

Disclosure of human capital values by business enterprises will provide financial statement users with valuable information. The relevance of this information lies in the fact that it concerns organizational changes in the firm's labor force hitherto not reported by accountants. Following are some inferences for decision makers (investors as well as management) that could be drawn from reported values of human capital.

(a) The determination of human capital values suggests a new set of financial ratios. For example:

The ratio of human to nonhuman capital indicates the degree of labor intensiveness in the firm. The extent of labor intensity is believed to have widespread implications for the firm's operations. For example, economists, especially in the area of industrial organization, investigate the effect of labor (or capital) intensity of inter- and intra-industry variations in rates of return. The relative degrees of labor and capital intensity within countries are believed to affect world trade.[4] Lacking direct measures for labor intensity, economists use

[4]This is the well-known Heckscher-Ohlin factor proportions theory which asserts that each country exports that commodity which is most intensive in the country's abundant factor.

indirect ones such as value added per employee, or sales per employee. Such measures are crude since they treat all employees as equal; a highly skilled engineer and a janitor are given the same weight in the measure. The suggested ratio of human to nonhuman capital assigns different weights to different employees according to their earning power. Labor intensity thus measured reflects the quality as well as the quantity of the labor force.

The firm's total value of human capital can be disaggregated according to sub-groups of the labor force (see example in the Appendix). Several ratios are suggested by such a disaggregation; for example, the ratio of the value of scientific staff to the total value of human capital. This ratio indicates the extent of "skill (scientific) intensity" in the firm. Skill intensive industries are those with a relatively large scientific and research staff, e.g., chemical products, electronics, pharmaceuticals, etc. The effect of skill intensity on rate of return and growth is a currently debated issue. Here again researchers use extremely crude measures to detect the effect of skill intensity such as R & D expenses, number of college graduates as a percentage of the total number of employees, etc. Such measures are not sensitive to variations within the scientific employee group, whereas the suggested measure reflects such variations.

(b) Reported human capital values will provide information about changes in the structure of the labor force. For example, differences over time in the values of a firm's human capital may result from changes in the age distribution (i.e., "vintage") of employees. Recall that human capital values are determined by capitalizing earnings over the expected useful life (to the enterprise) of employees. Therefore, a change in the age distribution of the labor force would obviously affect the firm's human capital values. Suppose, for example, that no change has taken place in the structure of the labor force during 1969 (i.e., no employees were hired or laid off). In this case, the value of the firm's human capital at the end of 1969 would be smaller than that of the previous year (assuming, of course, no changes in the earnings profiles). The firm's time series of human capital value thus contains information about changes in the structure of the labor force. The phenomenon of an "aging firm" often discussed in organization theory, will be indicated by such a time series when other factors (e.g., number of employees) are held constant. It has been suggested that the aging of the firm's labor force affects its rate of growth and relative share in the industry vis-à-vis the "younger" and more aggressive firms. Such hypotheses can be tested by using the reported values of human capital.

(c) The difference between the general and specific values of human capital (discussed in the preceding section) is another source of valuable information for management and the analyst. The specific value of human capital is based on the firm's actual wage scale while the general value is based on industry-wide wage averages. The difference between the two therefore indicates the level of the firm's wage scale relative to the industry average. Specifically, if the industry-wide wage averages are taken as a standard, this difference indicates to what extent the firm's wage scale is above, on a par with, or below the standard. Such information, which is not currently communicated to users, may explain the observed phenomenon of firms which consistently pay higher wages than the industry averages. It is sometimes argued that such firms employ the professional elite and hence experience a higher rate of return or growth than their competitors. Others are skeptical about such a hiring policy claiming that when wages are equal to employees' marginal productivity[5] then no extra returns can result from employing superior employees. Reporting the general and specific values of human capital will thus enable users to investigate the effects of specific wage and hiring policies.

Management might try to increase profits in the short run by hiring low quality employees. Such a policy can produce damaging effects which will be realized only in the long run. However, if human capital values are reported they will *currently* reflect the change in hiring policy and thereby deter management.

CONCEPTUAL ISSUES IN REPORTING HUMAN CAPITAL VALUES

The problem of reporting human capital values in financial statements has two distinct aspects: (a) the measurement of the value of the firm's work force which is the subject of this article, and (b) measurement and amortization of the firm's *investment* in human resources. The few articles concerning human capital reporting in financial statements [4, 5, 6, 13] deal exclusively with the second aspect.[6]

> It is often assumed that the objective of human resource accounting is to determine the net worth, or dollar value of an individual employee to a firm. This is not the case. Rather, we are trying to develop concepts and techniques for measuring a firm's investment in its human organization, the rate at which those investments are being consumed, and which investments are more productive than others. This is not the same as measuring the value of individuals, and surely raises *fewer objections*. [13, p. 46, emphasis supplied]

What are the objections that can be raised against the incorporation of human capital values in accounting reports?

(a) It can be argued that human capital (excluding a slave society) cannot be purchased or owned by the firm and therefore would not be recognized as an asset in accounting. This is obviously true with respect to individual employees who can usually resign at will;[7] however, it is not so obvious with respect to the firm's *labor force* as a whole. As long as employees can be replaced it does not matter for our purpose whether the labor force always contains the same persons or is a rapidly changing group. The labor force as a whole is constantly associated with the firm and it can be constructively regarded as being "owned" by it.

Moreover, in modern economies where firms are usually purchased as going concerns (e.g., merger), payment is often made for intangible assets such as a

---

[5]This will be the case when the firm's production function is homogeneous to the first degree.

[6]Most of the research on the subject has been conducted by R. Lee Brummet, Willard Graham Professor of Business Administration at the University of North Carolina, and William J. Pyle of the Institute for Social Research at the University of Michigan. Preliminary results of this research are reflected in the 1969 financial reports of R. G. Barry Corporation which was the first to report investment in human resources. For a description of this case, see [13].

[7]This statement ignores long-term employment contracts whose importance in the U.S. is declining.

stable and high quality labor force.[8] For example, it is customary in the insurance industry to determine the value of the sales force at the time of acquisition or sale. This is usually done by forecasting the firm's future earnings, determining its present value, and then allocating a portion of the present value to the human resources. A firm's human capital can thus be purchased and in a sense "owned" by it.

(b) It can be argued that the labor force is not an asset since it does not have a "service potential" extending beyond the current period. Specifically, employees are paid for rendering *current* services, and no asset is formed by these payments. If this were true then no firm would invest in (as opposed to maintain) human capital. However, the prevalence of programs such as orientation courses for new employees, executive programs, employees' training programs, facilities for improving employees' morale, etc., is evidence to the contrary. Such expenditures are made with the expectation of future returns, i.e., they increase the service potential embodied in human capital and this creates an asset.

The problem of reporting human capital values is closely related to the issue of long-term leases and other executory contracts. In both cases the firm rents the services of capital (human in the former, physical in the latter) owned by others. Those who favor the presentation of leased assets on the balance sheet would similarly endorse the reporting of human capital.

> Accounting at present recognizes most market transactions involving goods, services or money as one of the elements of the transaction. Present accounting also generally ignores, except in special circumstances, transactions involving an exchange of a promise for a promise. Leases, purchase commitments, executive and other labor contracts are generally denied recognition until the services or goods specified in the contract are either used, delivered, or paid for. Many of these contracts meet the standards of verifiability, freedom from bias, and quantifiability at least as well as other reported events. [1, p. 32]

In accordance with the suggested presentation of long-term leases, human capital values may be presented on the assets side of the balance sheet and the present value of the firm's liability to pay wages and salaries on the liabilities side. The two values are equal by definition: Changes in the values of human capital from period to period would not be recognized as income but would merely be matched by changes in the liability.

(c) Some accountants might accept the notion of human capital being an asset yet object to reporting it on the grounds that it cannot be "objectively" measured. We feel, however, that the preceding sections demonstrated that the degree of objectivity in human capital measurements, which are usually based on census data, is not lower than that of many conventional valuations in accounting. For example, depreciation charges are often estimated from industry-wide equipment mortality data,[9] the determination of reserves by life insurance

[8]All payments for intangible assets are aggregated by accountants in the goodwill resulting from acquisition.

[9]See in this context a recent suggestion for using the life expectancy of physical assets for estimating depreciation [10].

companies is based on general mortality tables, pension liabilities and product guarantees are also statistically estimated.

The above arguments suggest that human capital values may be an integral part of financial statements. This conclusion is consistent with the recommendations of the AAA committee in *A Statement of Basic Accounting Theory:*

> External users may wish to know degrees of employee morale, customer satisfaction, product quality, and reputation of a given entity. If quantification of these were possible, a substantial amount of additional relevant information could be provided the external users. The accountant must constantly be alert to the possible applications of new measurement methods to develop additional quantifiable information for external users. [1, p. 29]

CONCLUDING REMARKS

The value of the human capital associated with a business enterprise is not reflected in its financial reports. While some initial strides have been made toward measuring and amortizing the investment in human resources, the determination of human capital values is still an unsolved (and untouched) problem. The economic theory of human capital provides the basis for a practical solution to this problem.

The major limitation in the concept and measurement procedures advanced above is that the firm's value of human capital is not necessarily equal to the portion of the firm's income contributed by the labor force. Specifically, labor is one of several inputs in the production process; its value, therefore, should be determined on the basis of that portion of total income contributed by it. Such a determination of value accords with the well-known accounting concept of "service potential." However, in real life, input factors are interdependent and there is probably no practical way of dividing the total contribution among them. Consequently, accounting values of physical assets are determined by their market prices and not by their relative contribution to the firm. Therefore it seems reasonable that values of human capital may also be similarly determined. In the absence of market prices for human capital, the best approximation to its value is the measurement procedure based on census or firm earnings data.

APPENDIX

The computation of the firm's value of human capital is demonstrated in the following hypothetical example. Table 1 shows the decomposition of employees in the firm by age groups and degrees of skill. Table 2 shows average annual earnings for each age and skill group. These data can be obtained from the census or from the firm's own current wages. The data in Tables 1 and 2 are sufficient for calculating the present values of future earnings for each group of employees, i.e., the values of human capital. These values (assuming a capitalization rate of 10 per cent) are presented in Table 3. For example, the total human capital value of the 700 unskilled employees in the age group 25–34 is $35,822,500.[10] The total human capital associated with the firm is $69,184,080.

The degree of skill intensity in the firm is measured by the ratio of professionals to total human capital value:

$$\frac{11,058,790}{69,184,080} = 0.16.$$

TABLE 1
Distribution of Employees by Age and Skill

Age	Unskilled	Semi-skilled	Skilled	Professionals	Total
25–34	700	—	10	40	750
35–44	300	40	10	30	380
45–54	—	10	20	20	50
55–64	—	—	—	10	10
Total	1,000	50	40	100	1,190

TABLE 2
Average Annual Earnings (Dollars) Classified by Age and Skill

Age	Unskilled	Semi-skilled	Skilled	Professionals
25–34	5,000	6,000	7,500	10,000
35–44	5,500	7,000	8,000	12,000
45–54	6,000	7,500	9,000	13,000
55–64	5,500	7,000	9,000	15,000

TABLE 3
Total Values of Human Capital (Dollars) By Age and Skill (Capitalization Rate = 10 Percent)

Age	Unskilled	Semi-skilled	Skilled	Professionals	Total
25–34	35,822,500	—	764,310	4,281,760	40,868,570
35–44	15,908,400	2,686,880	786,990	3,546,990	22,929,260
45–54	—	626,670	1,529,540	2,308,440	4,464,650
55–64	—	—	—	921,600	921,600
Total	51,730,900	3,313,550	3,080,840	11,058,790	69,184,080

[10]This value is obtained by the following calculation. Assume, for simplicity, that all the 700 employees are 25 years old. The future earnings stream (based on Table 2) for each employee is:

$5,000 a year for the next 10 years,
$5,500 a year for years 11 to 20,
$6,000 a year for years 21 to 30, and
$5,500 a year for years 31 to 40.

The present value of this series of 40 numbers multiplied by 700 (the number of employees in the group) is equal to $35,822,500. This discount rate is 10 percent. All other values in Table 3 were similarly calculated.

REFERENCES

[1] AAA, *A Statement of Basic Accounting Theory* (American Accounting Association, 1966).

[2] G. S. Becker, *Human Capital* (Columbia University Press, National Bureau of Economic Research No. 80, 1964).

[3] M. J. Bowman, and R. G. Meyers, "Schooling, Experience, and Gains and Losses in Human Capital Through Migration," *Journal of the American Statistical Association*, LXII (September 1967) pp. 875–98.

[4] R. L. Brummet, E. G. Flamholtz, and W. C. Pyle, "Human Resource Measurement—A Challenge for Accountants," *The Accounting Review*, XLIII (April 1968), pp. 217–30.

[5] ———, ———, and ———, (Editors), *Human Resource Accounting: Development and Implementation in Industry* (Ann Arbor, Michigan: Foundation for Research on Human Behavior, 1969).

[6] J. Douthat, "Accounting for Personnel Training and Development Costs," *Training and Development Journal*, XXIV (June 1970), pp. 2–6.

[7] I. Fisher, *The Theory of Interest* (A.M. Kelley, Reprint of Economic Classics, 1961).

[8] M. Friedman, "The Quantity Theory of Money—A Restatement," in *Studies in the Quantity Theory of Money* (The University of Chicago Press, 1956).

[9] G. Hanoch, "Personal Earning and Investment in Schooling," unpublished Ph.D. dissertation, University of Chicago, 1965.

[10] Y. Ijiri, and R. S. Kaplan, "Probabilistic Depreciation and Its Implications for Group Depreciation," *The Accounting Review*, XLIV (October 1969), pp. 743–56.

[11] J. Mincer, "Investment in Human Capital and Personal Income Distributions," *The Journal of Political Economy*, LXVI (August 1958), pp. 281–302.

[12] ———, "On-the-Job Training: Costs, Returns, and Some Implications," *The Journal of Political Economy*, LXX (October 1962), pp. 50–79.

[13] W. Pyle, "Accounting for Your People," *Innovation*, X (1970), pp. 46–55.

[14] A. Schwartz, "Migration and Earnings in the U.S.," unpublished Ph.D. dissertation, University of Chicago, 1968.

[15] T. W. Schultz, "Investment in Human Capital," *American Economic Review*, LI (March 1961), pp. 1–17.

[16] ———, "Reflections on Investment in Men," *The Journal of Political Economy*, Supplement, LXX (October 1962), pp. 1–8.

[17] ———, *The Economic Value of Education* (Columbia University Press, 1963).

[18] L. Sjaasted, "The Costs and Returns of Human Migration," *The Journal of Political Economy*, LXX (October 1962), pp. 80–93.

[19] U.S. Bureau of the Census, *U.S. Census of the Population: 1960.* Vol. I. Characteristics of the Population, Parts 1–50. (Washington, D.C.: U.S. Government Printing Office, 1963). See especially, Subject Reports: Education Attainment, Final Report PC(2)5B. (U.S. Government Printing Office, 1963).

Toward a Theory of Human Resource Value in Formal Organizations

ERIC FLAMHOLTZ

This paper deals with the problem of measuring the value of people as organizational resources. This problem is important to management, investors and accountants as well as to others for two basic reasons.

First, there is evidence that the present failure to measure and report the value of human resources to management can conceal suboptimal decision-making in organizations. Specifically, the failure to measure the economic value of people may cause managers to ignore the effects of their decisions upon the value of human resources. The problem is a tendency for management to base decisions only on variables which can be quantified. Thus, so-called intangibles such as human resources tend to be ignored. Consequently, a decision or policy that *seems* beneficial may actually harm an organization by unintentionally depleting human resources. For example, decisions to undertake cost-control programs are typically based upon expected cost savings without consideration of the effects of such programs upon employee attitudes, motivation and satisfaction. Yet these programs may cause deterioration in employee motivation and satisfaction which is equivalent to a liquidation of human asset value. Thus, decision makers considering such programs should take into account the expected opportunity cost of lost human resources as well as the expected benefits of cost-savings.

Second, measurements of human resource value are also anticipated to be useful in several aspects of manpower planning and control. For example, they are expected to be useful in manpower acquisition, development, allocation, replacement and compensation decisions. They are also expected to be useful in evaluating the effectiveness of management's maintenance and utilization of human assets.[1]

An earlier version of this paper was selected for "Honorable Mention" in the 1971 Call for Papers of The Academy of Management and presented at the Annual Meeting at Atlanta, Georgia in August, 1971. Research for this paper was supported, in part, by a grant from the Accounting-Information Systems Research Program of the Graduate School of Management at the University of California, Los Angeles. I am grateful to Gordon Shillinglaw for many helpful comments on a previous version of this paper.

Eric Flamholtz, "Toward a Theory of Human Resource Value in Formal Organizations," *The Accounting Review*, October 1972, pp. 666–678. Reprinted with the permission of *The Accounting Review*.

[1]For further discussion of the importance of measures of human resource value, see Rensis Likert, *The Human Organization: Its Management and Value* (McGraw-Hill Book Co., 1967); James Hekimian and Curtis Jones, "Put People on Your Balance Sheet," *Harvard Business Review* (Jan.–Feb. 1967), pp. 105–13; and Eric Flamholtz, "Should Your Organization Attempt to Value Its Human Resources?" *California Management Review* (Winter 1971), pp. 40–45.

THE ACCOUNTANT'S ROLE

Given their managerial importance, the accountant's role as an information-supplier is to develop the required methods of quantifying human resource value. It may be necessary for the accounting information system to provide not only monetary measurements of human resource value but also non-monetary measurements.

PRIOR RESEARCH

Recently, some theoretical and empirical research has been focused upon the problem of developing monetary measures of human resource value.[2] However, no attempt has been made to understand or explain the nature and determinants of a person's value to a formal organization. In other words, there has been no attempt to develop a theory of human resource value.

NEED FOR THEORY OF HUMAN RESOURCE VALUE

A theory of the value of people to organizations is an essential prerequisite for the problem of developing methods of measuring of human resource value. First, the theory would, by definition, identify the variables which determine a person's value to an organization. This means that it would suggest the specific variables which need to be considered in developing valid and reliable monetary measures of human value. Second, by identifying the variables comprising a person's value, the theory would facilitate the development of nonmonetary surrogate measures of human value. In other words, since it identifies the determinants of the value of people, measures of these determinants might be used as nonmonetary indicators of human resource value, which would serve as a proxy for monetary measures of human value.

THE STUDY'S OBJECTIVES

This paper attempts to formulate a model of the nature and determinants of a person's value to an organization. The model represents a first step toward the development of a theory of human resource value.

The model is shown schematically in Figure 1. It draws upon a variety of behavioral (social and psychological) as well as economic variables.

This model attempts to synthesize or integrate these variables in order to explain the nature and determinants of an individual's economic worth to an organization. Its main purposes are: (1) to identify a set of variables which purport to explain a person's value to a firm, and (2) to discuss the variables' interrelationships. Since the model is quite complex, it may be helpful for the reader to refer to this schematic model in order to visualize the relations among the variables.

---

[2]For discussions of human resource valuation, see for example Baruch Lev and Aba Schwartz, "On the Use of the Economic Concept of Human Capital in Financial Statements," *The Accounting Review* (January 1971), pp. 103–18; and Eric Flamholtz, "A Model for Human Resource Valuation: A Stochastic Process with Service Rewards," *The Accounting Review* (April 1971), pp. 253–67.

FIGURE 1
Model of the Determinants of an Individual's Value to a Formal Organization

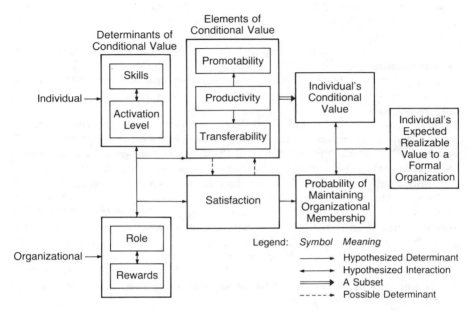

THE CONCEPT OF HUMAN RESOURCE VALUE

All economic theories of value are based explicitly or implicitly upon the premise that the attribute determining whether and to what extent an "object" possesses value is the perceived ability to render future economic "utility," "benefits," or "services." Thus, Von Mises once wrote that "whoever wants to construct an elementary theory of value and price must first think of utility."[3] Similarly, Fisher said that:

> . . . no one will dispute that the buyer of any article of capital will value it for its expected services to him, and that "at the margin" of his purchases, the price he will pay is the equivalent to him of these expected services, or, in other words, is their "present worth," their "discounted value," or "capitalized value."[4]

If an object is not capable of rendering future economic services, it has no value. In these terms, an object's value is typically constitutively defined as the present worth of the services it is anticipated to render in the future.[5] Thus, a "resource" may be defined as an object that possesses expected future services; objects which do not possess expected future benefits can not, by definition, be "resources."

[3]Von Mises, *Human Action* (Yale University Press, 1963), p. 121.

[4]Irving Fisher, *The Nature of Capital and Income* (MacMillan and Company, Ltd., 1927), p. 189.

[5]This notion of value is attributable to Fisher. See *Ibid.*, pp. 188, 202.

The concept of "human value" is derived from general economic value theory. Like all resources, people possess value because they are capable of rendering future services. In principle, then, the value of people, like that of other resources, can be defined as the present worth of their expected future services.

From a macroeconomic viewpoint, the services people can potentially provide constitute a form of capital. [6] Similarly, from the viewpoint of a specified firm or other organization, the expected services of employees are a form of asset.[7] In either case, people are resources because they possess expected future service potential.

The concept of an individual's value to an organization is derived from the generic concept of human value. Thus, an individual's value to an organization can be defined as the present worth of the set of future service he is expected to provide during the period he is anticipated to remain in the organization.

Unlike other resources, however, human beings are not owned by organizations, and hence they are relatively free either to supply or to withhold their services. From an organization's viewpoint, this means that the probability of realizing an individual's services is typically less than certainty. This also suggests that there is a dual aspect to an individual's value: (1) the amount the organization could potentially realize from a person's services if he maintains organizational membership during the period of his productive service life and (2) the amount actually expected to be derived, taking into account the person's likelihood of turnover.

DETERMINANTS OF AN INDIVIDUAL'S VALUE

An individual's value to an organization is thus multidimensional. It is comprised of two interacting variables: (1) the individual's "conditional value" and (2) the probability that the individual will maintain membership in the organization. An individual's "conditional value" is the present worth of the potential services that could be rendered to the organization, if the individual maintained organizational membership throughout his expected service life. The probability that the individual will maintain membership in the organization is the complement of the probability of turnover or exit. It determines the extent to which the organization will realize the individual's potential services or conditioned value. The product of these two variables is thus the individual's "expected realizable value"—the present worth of services actually expected to be derived during the individual's anticipated tenure in the organization, as shown in Figure 2.

Conditional Value

An individual's conditional value is a multidimensional variable, and is comprised of three factors: productivity, transferability and promotability.

[6]Theodore Schultz, "Investments in Human Capital," *American Economic Review* (March 1961), pp. 1–17.

[7]Although relatively few writers have considered the question of whether people are a form of asset, Chambers has argued that human beings are not "assets" in the traditional accounting sense. See Raymond J. Chambers, *Accounting, Evaluation, and Economic Behavior* (Prentice-Hall, Inc., 1966), p. 104.

FIGURE 2
Variables Interacting to Produce an Individual's Expected Realizable Value

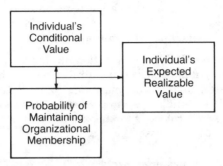

"Productivity" refers to the set of services an individual is expected to provide while occupying his present position. A synonym for productivity is performance. "Transferability" is the set of services an individual is expected to provide if and when he transfers to other positions at the same position level in a different promotion channel. "Promotability" represents the set of services the individual is expected to provide if and when he occupies higher level positions in his present or different promotion channels. Productivity, transferability and promotability are, in other words, subsets of the set of "services" which the person is expected to render, and which are the elements of conditional value, as shown in Figure 3.

The hypothesized relations among the elements of conditional value are also indicated in Figure 3. In this model, productivity is the central or causal variable. It is hypothesized to influence both promotability and transferability. Productivity influences promotability—or, more accurately, *perceived* promotability—because it affects an individual's eligibility for promotion. In other words, since promotion practices in formal organizations are at least in part a function of past performance or prior services rendered, an individual's promotability is affected by evaluations of his past and expected productivity. Similarly, transferability is influenced by productivity, which may affect the likelihood that the organization will consider the individual for a possible trans-

FIGURE 3
Elements of Conditional Value and Their Interrelationships

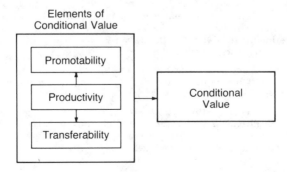

fer. In some cases, transfer may also indicate promotion eligibility. For example, the rotation of "high potential" MBAs through various jobs, functional areas, and geographical locations may indicate grooming for future promotion.

Determinants of Elements of Conditional Value

The elements of an individual's conditional value are the product of certain attributes of the individual and certain dimensions of the organization. The major "individual determinants" of conditional value are the individual's skills and activation level. The major "organizational determinants" of conditional value are the individual's role and the nature of organizational rewards. Each of these variables will be discussed below.

Individual Determinants of Conditional Value: Skills and Activational Level.— The individual's "skills" represent his currently developed potential to provide services to an organization. Drawing upon Floyd Mann, we are primarily concerned with a trilogy of technical, administrative and human interaction skills.[8] These general skills are relatively stable and enduring. However, they can be changed by various forms of training. In principle, the set of skills a person possesses sets limits on the nature and magnitude of the services he can render to an organization. At a more elementary level, such skills are the product of cognitive abilities and personality traits.

The individual's "activation level" is another determinant of his conditional value. The term "activation level" can be defined ". . . as the extent of release of the stored energy of the organism through metabolic activity in the tissues."[9] In other words, it is the neuropsychological counterpart of the notion of "motivation." The level of activation is a major variable influencing human behavior. An individual's activation level is not constant and may vary as a result of changes in physiological and psychological determinants.

It is hypothesized that an individual's skills and activation level (motivation) interact to determine the person's potential for rendering services to an organization.[10] Although an individual's skills set a theoretical limit upon the services that can be rendered, in practice his activation level is very probably also a crucial determinant of the potential services to be realized by an organization.[11] Thus, while an engineer may be limited in his ability to solve technical problems by his intelligence, and a manager may be limited in his ability to cope with interpersonal problems by his personality, individuals can also compensate to a great extent for a lack of specific skills by increasing their activation

[8]Floyd C. Mann, "Toward an Understanding of the Leadership Role in Formal Organization," in R. Dubin, G. C. Homans, F. C. Mann, and D. C. Miller, *Leadership and Productivity* (Chandler Publishing Co., 1965), as cited in D. Bowers and S. Seashore, "Predicting Organizational Effectiveness with a Four-Factor Theory of Leadership," *Administrative Science Quarterly* (September 1966), p. 245.

[9]Elizabeth Duffy, *Activation and Behavior* (John Wiley & Sons, 1962), as cited in William E. Scott, Jr., "Activation Theory and Task Design," *Organization Behavior and Human Performance* (Sept. 1966), p. 11.

[10]Some of the evidence for this hypothesis has been reviewed by Lawler and Vroom. See E. E. Lawler, "Ability as a Moderator of the Relationship between Job Attitudes and Job Performance," *Personnel Psychology* (Summer 1966), pp. 153–64, and V. H. Vroom, *Work and Motivation* (John Wiley & Sons, 1964).

level. On the contrary, even an individual possessing a high degree of technical, administrative, and interpersonal skill may provide less service to an organization than warranted by his potential because of a relatively low activation level. The relationships between skills and activation level in producing productivity is quite complex. The hypothesized relations among these determinants and conditional value is shown in Figure 4.

Organizational Determinants of Conditional Value: Role and Rewards.—The individual determinants of conditional value also interact with certain organizational determinants. Although an individual may possess a set of skills and the motivation to apply them, the organizational role he occupies influences the extent to which he is offered the opportunity to render his potential services. In this context a "role" refers to the set of behaviors expected from all persons occupying a specified position in an organization. For example, a person with a high degree of administrative skill may occupy the role of engineer, or the individual with great skill in solving mathematical problems may occupy the role of salesman. In either case, the individuals' conditional value to the organization is determined, in part, by the interaction between his skill and his organizational role. In other words, the individual is included in his role on only a partial or segmented basis. This occurrence is very probably quite typical in organizations, for, as Katz and Kahn observe: "Unlike the inclusion of a given organ in the body in the biological system, not all of the individual is included in his organizational membership. The organization neither requires nor wants the whole person."[12]

To clarify the nature of the interaction between the individual and his organizational role as a determinant of a person's conditional value, their relationship is shown schematically in Figures 5, 6, and 7. Figure 5 shows two subsets, P and R with P representing a person and R a role. From the diagram it can be seen that $P \cap R = E$, where E denotes the empty set. That is, there is no overlap or intersection between the person and his role. The skills available are

FIGURE 4
Relation of Individual Determinants to Conditional Value

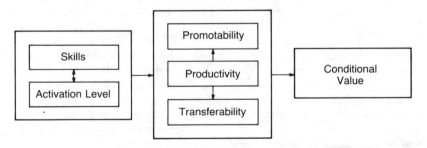

[11]See E. A. Fleishman, "A Relationship Between Incentive Motivation and Ability Level in Psychomotor Performance," *Journal of Experimental Psychology*, 1958, 56, No. 1, pp. 78–81.

[12]Daniel Katz and Robert L. Kahn, *The Social Psychology of Organizations* (John Wiley and Sons, 1966), p. 50.

FIGURE 5   FIGURE 6

$P \cap R = E$ $P \cap R \neq E$

simply not required by the role to which the person has been allocated. In Figure 6, the situation can be expressed as $P \cap R \neq E$; the intersection of the person and the role is not empty. The individual is partially included in the role.

When the individual is totally included in his role—that is, when the set of behavior required by the role exactly match those exhibited by the individual—then $P = R$. Figure 7 diagrams this situation.

FIGURE 7

$P = R$

The relation between the individual and the role is not merely a question of fit or matching. Both the role and the individual interact with one another. Considered abstractly, there is a set of role requirements, which refer to the formal or prescribed behaviors expected from all occupants of a specified role, position or office. For example, the role of manager generally connotes certain universal expectations, and in a particular organization these expectations are made even more precise by systemic values, traditions and norms. However, the perceptions of the role incumbent also affect the role. The set of attributes of the role perceived by the incumbent may or may not correspond closely to the role's formal requirements. For example, a newly promoted manager may "bring with him" a set of activities which were typically associated with his previous position.

The role and the individual also interact in other ways. Role prescriptions, as mechanisms specifying the tasks and jobs which people are to perform, are important influences upon an individual's activation level. Scott has reviewed several neuropsychological studies on the determinants of activation, and has noted their implications for a better understanding of the relation between the structure of tasks and the degree of activation of an individual. He cites studies which give some evidence that there are several aspects of a task's structure which may be determinants of activation level, including such variables as stimulus variation, intensity, complexity, uncertainty and meaningfulness.[13]

[13]Scott, pp. 3–30. For a discussion of the mechanisms through which the dimensions of tasks interact with the characteristics of individuals to influence role performance, see J. Richard Hackman, "Nature of the Task As a Determiner of Job Behavior," *Personnel Psychology* (Winter 1969), pp. 435–44.

Another organizational determinant of an individual's conditional value is the "rewards" which people expect to derive from different aspects of their membership in an organization. As Katz has pointed out, "it is important to distinguish between rewards which are administered in relation to individual effort and performance and the system rewards which accrue to people by virtue of their membership in the system."[14] "Instrumental individual rewards"—rewards which are administered in relation to individual effort—are intended to motivate optimal role performance. "Instrumental system rewards"—rewards which accrue by virtue of membership in the system—are more effective for holding members within the organization, but they will not necessarily lead to higher productivity.

In terms of the proposed model, it is hypothesized that instrumental individual rewards influence the individual's conditional value by affecting the degree of activation. The rewards associated with behaviors required by an individual's role influence the extent to which there is a fit between the person and the role. That is, the extent to which task-performance will be instrumental in satisfying an individual's needs will determine the likelihood that he will fulfill role requirements. This is the essence of the so-called "path-goal hypothesis" presented by Georgopoulos, Mahoney and Jones.[15] Thus, it is hypothesized that the more likely it is that the behaviors required by a given role will lead to rewards perceived to be instrumental in satisfying an individual's needs, then the greater the inclusion of the person in the role, and, therefore, the greater the individual's conditional value to an organization. The hypothesized relations among the variables which determine an individual's conditional value are shown schematically in Figure 8.

FIGURE 8
Relations Among Variables Determining an Individual's Conditional Value

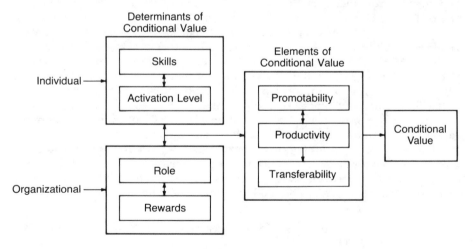

[14]Daniel Katz, "The Motivational Basis of Organizational Behavior," *Behavioral Science* (April 1964), p. 137.

[15]B. S. Georgopoulos, G. M. Mahoney and H. W. Jones, "A Path-goal Approach to Productivity," *Journal of Applied Psychology*, 1957, Vol. 41, pp. 345–53.

Probability of Maintaining Organizational Membership

Since people can leave an organization, it is necessary to consider not only the determinants of conditional value but also the determinants of the probability that an individual will maintain membership in an organizational system. Research on causes of turnover have suggested that there is an inverse relationship between need satisfaction and the likelihood of exiting. For example, Ross and Zander found that ". . . the degree of satisfaction of certain personal needs supplied by an individual's place of employment has a significant direct relationship to his continuing to work for that company." They concluded that ". . . workers whose personal needs are satisfied on the job are more likely to remain in the organization."[16] Similarly, in reviewing the findings of research on the relation between job satisfaction and turnover, Fournet, Distefano and Pryer concluded that the findings consistently show turnover negatively related to job satisfaction.[17] Thus, there seems to be evidence to support the generality of the relation between these variables, as depicted in Figure 9.

To the extent that satisfaction with organizational membership is related to the perceived opportunity to satisfy individual needs, then it is hypothesized that satisfaction is the product of the interaction between the individual and organizational determinants of an individual's value. This means, in other words, that satisfaction is presumed to be caused by the same *process* that produces an individual's conditional value—the interaction between and among the individual's skills, activation level, role, and the organizational reward structure. These hypothesized relations are shown schematically in Figure 10.

It should be noted that "satisfaction" is a global construct. Thus the variable "satisfaction" is really a composite of several separate variables such as satisfaction with pay, satisfaction with working conditions and satisfaction with supervision.

In addition to the relation between satisfaction and the probability of remaining in the organization, there is also a possible relation between satisfaction and one of the elements of an individual's conditional value, i.e., productivity. Research findings have generally tested the hypothesized relation between productivity (performance) and satisfaction from the viewpoint that the latter is determinant of the former. Unfortunately, in reviewing and analyzing the results of such studies, Brayfield and Crockett argued that ". . . we expect the relation between satisfaction and job performance to be one of concomitant variation rather than cause and effect." In addition, they concluded that ". . . satisfaction with one's position in a network of relationships need not imply strong motivation to outstanding performance within that system. . . ."[18]

Although many researchers expected to find a positive relationship between satisfaction and productivity, some have found a negative relationship. Obviously the relationship between these variables is quite complex, and it is likely that there are other variables which moderate their effect upon each other. Accord-

[16]Ian C. Ross and Alvin Zander, "Need Satisfactions and Employee Turnover," *Personnel Psychology* (Autumn 1957), pp. 327–38.

[17]G. P. Fournet, M. K. Distefano and M. W. Pryer, "Job Satisfaction: Issues and Problems," *Personnel Psychology* (Summer 1966), p. 176.

[18]A. H. Brayfield and W. H. Crockett, "Employee Attitudes and Employee Performance," *Psychological Bulletin* (Sept. 1955), pp. 416, 421.

FIGURE 9
Determinants of the Probability of Maintaining Organizational Membership

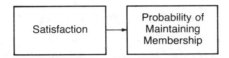

ingly, there is presently insufficient evidence to fully support a hypothesis on the nature of the relation between these variables.[19] It may be just as likely that satisfaction is caused by productivity as it is that productivity is determined by satisfaction.[20]

The Model as a Whole

The model of the nature and determinants of an individual's value developed in this paper was shown schematically in Figure 1. Taken as a whole, it rep-

FIGURE 10
Relations Among Variables Determining an Individual's Satisfaction

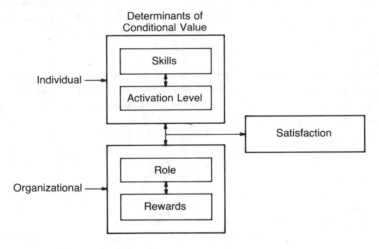

[19]This argument is supported by the conclusion of Schwab and Cummings, who reviewed the various theories of the relation between performance and satisfaction. They stated that: "We are frankly pessimistic about the value of additional satisfaction-performance theorizing at this time. The theoretically inclined might do better to work on a theory of satisfaction *or* a theory of performance. Such concepts are clearly complex enough to justify their own theories." See Donald P. Schwab and Larry L. Cummings, "Theories of Performance and Satisfaction: A Review," *Industrial Relations* (October 1970), p. 420.

[20]Indeed, Porter and Lawler have developed a model of the relationship between managerial attitudes and performance in which there is circularity in the relationship between performance and satisfaction. See Lyman W. Porter and Edward E. Lawler, III, *Managerial Attitudes and Performance* (Homewood, Illinois: Richard D. Irwin, Inc., 1968), especially Chapters 2 and 8.

resents a framework for understanding the factors comprising and influencing an individual's value to an organization.

IMPLICATIONS OF THE MODEL FOR ACCOUNTING

According to the Committee to Prepare a Statement of Basic Accounting Theory, the objectives of accounting are to provide information for the following purposes: (1) Making decisions concerning the use of limited resources, including the identification of crucial decision areas, and determination of objectives and goals; (2) effectively directing and controlling an organization's human and material resources; (3) maintaining and reporting on the custodianship of resources; and (4) facilitating social functions and controls.[21] The model developed in this paper can help accounting achieve all of these objectives.

Decision Making

This theory will increase the effectiveness of decision-making concerning resource utilization because it will assist accountants in developing methods of measuring human resource value. As noted previously, measurements of human resource value are required to facilitate decisions involving a mix of human and other resources so that managers will not overlook the effects of such decisions upon the value of human assets. In addition, measurements of human resource value are required to facilitate a variety of manpower management decisions, including human resource acquisition, development, allocation, compensation and replacement.

The theory will help to develop such measurements in two ways. First, the model's constructs indicate the kinds of variables which must be considered in developing a monetary measure of an individual's worth to an organization. For example, the model suggests that the ultimate measure of a person's worth is his expected realizable value. It also suggests that the penultimate measure of a person's worth is his conditional value. The differential, if any, between these two measures represents the opportunity cost of the anticipated probability of turnover. Thus, it represents the amount a firm ought to be willing to spend to reduce the probability of turnover to zero.

Another example of the model's implications for the measurement of human value is suggested by the kinds of variables it includes. To illustrate, suppose we were to ask managers or accountants or organizational psychologists: "What factors determine the value of people to an organization?" One might reasonably expect a sample of respondents to mention such things as a person's skills, personality traits and intelligence. These variables are all individual determinants—attributes associated with the individual per se. However, it is doubtful that many people would mention the organizational determinants of a person's value such as the role a person occupies. It is even possible that satisfaction might not be mentioned as a determinant of the person's value.

There is a rather deceptively simple explanation for the probable failure to cite organizational determinants. For a variety of reasons, we tend to assess the

[21]American Accounting Association, Committee to Prepare a Statement of Basic Accounting Theory. *A Statement of Basic Accounting Theory* (American Accounting Association, 1966), p. 4.

value of human resources by using a different framework than for other resources. With respect to material resources, we are aware that it is a fallacy to value the agent rather than the services provided by the agent. Not so for people. Here it is common practice to value the agent rather than its services. Thus, the model contributes an important insight: a person's value to an organization is not merely a function of personal attributes; rather, it is the product of a set of interacting human and organizational determinants.

The second major way in which the model will help develop measures of human resource value is by identifying the variables which might be used as nonmonetary measurements of a person's value. In other words, the variables simultaneously provide a theoretical foundation for developing monetary representations of the value of people; they also constitute a set of possible quantitative but nonmonetary accounting measurements. This recommendation is consistent with the Committee to Prepare a Statement of Basic Accounting Theory's conclusion that "while the measurement process currently focuses on economic dollar-valued data and relates the performance of the organization to either profitability or to the extent of budgeted expenditure, accounting in the future can well consider several aspects of a transaction or event simultaneously."[22] Thus, this model may be used by accountants to determine user information needs with respect to the value of human resources, and the future accounting information system may well include measures of these determinants of human resource value, where each variable possesses its own unit of measurement.

Effective Management of Resources

According to the Committee, the second objective of providing accounting information is to facilitate the effective management of an organization's human and material resources. The proposed theory can play an important role in helping achieve this objective. Specifically, the proposed theory provides the basis for a new paradigm for the management of human resources.

At present, the management of human resources in organizations is less effective than it might be because it lacks a unifying framework to guide it. Managers have neither a valid criterion to guide decisions affecting people nor a methodology for assessing the anticipated or actual consequences of such decisions. Clearly the criteria of productivity and satisfaction which frequently underlie strategies of human resource management have not been entirely helpful in coping with the problems of managing people. Similarly, since it is exceedingly difficult to measure productivity and satisfaction, or to assess the tradeoffs a manager should rationally be willing to make to increase one by decreasing the other, it is not frequently possible to predict the economic consequences of alternative actions with respect to people.

The notion of "human resource value" seems to provide one possible solution to these problems. It can serve as the *raison d'être* of human resource management: it can simultaneously provide the goal and the criterion for the management of human resources. More specifically, the aim of human resource management can be viewed as the need to contribute to the value of the organization as a whole by optimizing the value of its human assets; the effec-

[22]*Ibid.*, p. 65.

tiveness criterion can be the measured change in the value of the organization's human resources.

If the aim of human resource management is seen as the optimization of human resource value, then task design, selection, role assignment, development, performance appraisal and compensation are not merely a set of service functions to be performed; rather, they are a set of available strategies that can be adopted to change the value of human assets, and, in turn, the value of the organization as a whole.

Thus, the theory provides the basis for a new paradigm because it establishes an ultimate criterion of effective human resource management. Accounting can help to operationalize this paradigm by providing measurements of management's effectiveness in utilizing human resources, as described above.

Reporting on Custodianship of Resources

One aspect of the present failure of organizations to account for human resources is the resulting lack of information about the extent to which a firm's human resources are being appreciated, maintained, or depleted. One measure of human resource liquidation is, of course, turnover. However, there are other, more subtle ways for a firm's human resources to be depleted without management being aware of it. For example, the model clearly shows that a decrease in employee satisfaction is actually equivalent to depletion of an organization's human resources. We know that turnover is inversely related to satisfaction, and that, therefore, an increase in a person's dissatisfaction with an organization is likely to increase the probability that he will exit. This, of course, means that there has been a decrease in the probability that the organization will actually realize an individual's expected future service potential. This is equivalent to a decrease in the person's expected realizable value, which, as previously noted, is the measure of an individual's ultimate worth to a firm.

Accountants should report changes in such variables as employee satisfaction and motivation to management. The expected effects of such observed changes upon personnel turnover and the opportunity cost of unrealized human resource value should also be reported. This information will enable management to evaluate the extent to which the organization has effectively maintained stewardship over human resources. It will also provide an indicator of the need to take corrective action prior to the time that decreases in satisfaction are translated into increased turnover or decreases in motivation are translated into decreased productivity.

Facilitation of Social Controls

The proposed theory also has possible implications for accounting's role in facilitating social functions and social controls over organizations. For example, many firms are currently engaged in hiring and developing the so-called "hard core unemployed." One measure of a firm's social contribution in this case might be the observed increase in the value of the underdeveloped human resources. This information might be reported in the president's letter of a corporate annual report.

Another illustration of the social aspect of this theory concerns the current trend toward a greater concern with the "quality of life." As a product of a changing social ethos, we can anticipate a greater emphasis upon the satisfactions people derive from their work. It is possible that organizations of the future may be required to account for the satisfaction of employees as an end in itself. Government may, for instance, decide to assess a tax upon so-called Theory X organizations, or provide investment credit incentives to organizations to motivate them to undertake organizational change programs in order to increase opportunities for employee satisfaction.

CONCLUDING COMMENTS

The model presented in this paper is intended as a first step toward a theory of human resource value in formal organizations. This theory seems to have relevance to accounting's objectives of measuring and reporting information for decision-making, management of human resources, custodianship of human resources and social controls over the utilization of people. Thus, the model can potentially help enlarge the scope of accounting in accordance with the recommendations in *A Statement of Basic Accounting Theory*.

There are, of course, some limitations involved in the model. First, the model's scope is restricted to the nature and determinants of an individual's value to an organization. Thus it should not be inferred that the model purports to explain the value of groups of people in formal organizations. Similarly, it should not be inferred that the model purports to fully explain the nature of an individual's value. Future research may find that other variables should be included or that present variables are unnecessary. Similarly, the validity of the hypothesized relations among the variables needs to be assessed. These are empirical questions.[23]

The model treats an individual's value as an independent or marginal phenomenon. The validity of this treatment depends upon several variables including the nature of the organization and the degree of interdependence of organizational roles. Accordingly, this model does not fully take into account the dynamic aspects of organizational phenomena. For example, an individual's promotability may be determined not only by his own skills, activation level and expected service potential but also by the promotability of others.

These limitations suggest the need for further research on this complex problem. In the meantime, it is hoped that the model provides a useful preliminary framework for analyzing and understanding the nature and determinants of a person's value to an organization, and that it makes a contribution toward the development of a very necessary theory of the value of an organization's human resources.

[23]For some preliminary results on these issues, see Eric Flamholtz, "Assessing the Validity of a Theory of Human Resource Value: A Field Study," *Empirical Research in Accounting: Selected Studies 1972* (forthcoming).

IV-C / SOCIAL REPORTING

Toward A Theory of Corporate Social Accounting

KAVASSERI V. RAMANATHAN

A contemporary problem of concern to all technology-rich industrialized societies is that of continuing to provide a high level of motivation for private enterprise while ensuring that its aggregate impact upon society is consistent with social goals and aspirations. This is an exceedingly complex problem for several reasons. Traditional performance criteria for private enterprise have emphasized results which may be in conflict with societal priorities. There are many divergent views as to the most desired social goals and aspirations. The qualitative dimensions of social goal formulation and evaluation add further to the complexity. Yet, the problem is of such significance that there is a pressing need to explore its many dimensions and find ways of formulating solutions.

The nature of the problem can be related further to performance as it is typically viewed from a management perspective. A corporate management's attention, decisions and actions are focused more on those components of the firm's performance which are included in the firm's formal measurement system. To the extent that a firm's social impacts are not subjected to formal measurement process, these aspects are not likely to enter into the firm's planning decisions or performance evaluation.

The traditional view of corporate performance is idealized in the quest to maximize profits. It also is widely acclaimed that a firm's only social responsibility in a free market system is to maximize its profits, for in so doing, it is presumed to maximize its contribution to society. Under this notion, the profits of a firm which operates within the society's legal framework would provide the all-inclusive criterion for evaluating its social performance. However, the economic depression phenomenon of arriving at full equilibrium with substantial unemployment; the relentless disparities in income and employment opportunities among different social groups; and the serious erosion in the quality of environment caused by productive activities have led to sharp criticisms of the use of profits as an all-inclusive criterion of corporate social performance.[1]

A comprehensive analysis of the social impact of private enterprise suffers, at the present time, from a general absence of reliable data on aggregate social costs and benefits of business and on how these are shared among various social

Kavasseri V. Ramanathan, "Toward A Theory of Corporate Social Accounting, "*The Accounting Review*, July 1976, pp. 516–528. Reprinted with the permission of *The Accounting Review*.

[1]The literature on this debate is voluminous. Sethi [1974] contains discussions on most of the pertinent issues.

groups. However, some progress has been reached in recent years toward gathering and reporting data on corporate social performance, both as a result of internal initiatives of progressive corporations and in response to external influences. Thus, Beresford's [1973] annual survey reports that 298 of the Fortune 500 industrial firms disclosed some type of social performance data in their 1973 annual reports. The majority of these disclosures were in the environmental control category. Other broad categories used in the Beresford survey were minority employment, responsibility to employees, community activities and product improvement. Disclosure practices varied considerably as regard to scope, format, use of quantitative and financial measures and the significance of items disclosed. The trend appears to be toward greater disclosure. Apparently, this follows from firms' increasing concern with their social responsibility and their attempts to institute some form of social audit [Ackerman, 1973; Dierkes and Bauer, 1973].

There have been several other attempts to gather data on corporate social performance from firms on an ad hoc or routine basis by private research groups such as the Council of Economic Priorities [American Accounting Association, 1975; pp. 57–63]. Further, several statutory agencies, such as the Federal Trade Commission, Environmental Protection Agency, Occupational Safety and Hazards Agency and the Office of Equal Employment Opportunity, are requiring data from firms in specific aspects of social concern. Recently, the Securities and Exchange Commission has proposed increased disclosure of corporate environmental policy, plans and performance.

The challenges involved in accounting for corporate social performance has engaged the particular attention of the major accounting institutions in the United States. The Study Group on Objectives of Financial Statements [1973, pp. 53–55 and 66] proposed as an objective of financial statements the reporting on those activities of the firm which have major social impacts. An American Institute of Public Accountants' committee is studying the problems of developing measurement systems for corporate social accounting. The National Association of Accountants' Committee on Accounting for Corporate Social Performance published its report in the February 1974 issue of *Management Accounting*. Several American Accounting Association Committees have been concerned with the broad area of social accounting [1971, 1972, 1973, 1974, 1975, 1976]. The Association also has sponsored a major research study on social cost measurement problems.

Despite such widespread and growing concern and support for accounting for corporate social performance, progress has been slow and sporadic. "Apparently, no corporation has yet designed or implemented anything approaching a systematic information system for its socially relevant actions" [American Accounting Association, 1975, p. 64]. Historically, the theory and practice of accounting has evolved in four interrelated areas—a framework of objectives, valuation concepts, measurement methodology and reporting standards. There is no reason to believe that evolution in social accounting will not follow the same course. This paper will concentrate on developing a theoretical framework consisting of a proposed set of social accounting objectives and concepts in the belief that an acceptable framework of objectives is fundamental to the development of social accounting theory in the areas of valuation, measurement methods and reporting standards.

BASIC PREMISES

Although there is considerable debate about which corporate actions constitute socially responsible corporate behavior, there appears to be a general acceptance of two assumptions.

1. The solutions to many of the current social problems require the active and willing involvement of private business organizations; and
2. To the extent that measured corporate profits are an inadequate guide to policy, a broader scheme of corporate performance measurement is necessary.

The absence of a broader scheme of corporate social performance measurement is partly due to the recency of the public's concern over corporate social impact. But in a large measure it also is due to the failure to arrive at an operational definition of the role of a corporation in its broader social context [Preston, 1975; Bell, 1971, Ch. 6]. The elements of such a definition and the philosophical justification for a broader scheme of corporate social performance measurement is to be found in the notion of a social contract whereby a firm agrees to perform certain socially desirable functions in return for certain rewards. This notion of a social contract, which is of fundamental importance to this paper, is explained well by Shocker and Sethi [1974, p. 67]:

> Any social institution—and business is no exception—operates in society via a social contract, expressed or implied, whereby its survival and growth are based on:
> (1) the delivery of some socially desirable ends to society in general, and
> (2) the distribution of economic, social, or political benefits to groups from which it derives its power.
> In a dynamic society, neither the sources of institutional power nor the needs for its services are permanent. Therefore, an institution must constantly meet the twin tests of legitimacy and relevance by demonstrating that society requires its services and that the groups benefiting from its rewards have society's approval.

Social Performance Criteria—the Macro Context

The development of a set of social performance criteria is essential for bringing the notion of social contract from the level of ideas to the realm of operationality and to provide answers to the following types of questions:

1. What are the performance dimensions implied by the social contract?
2. What is socially responsible performance?
3. How is it to be measured and evaluated in the aggregate social context?

The task of developing social performance criteria, particularly at the macro-level, is unlikely to be the exclusive province of any one group of specialists or of any one discipline. There is ample evidence to suggest that such criteria will result from the combined efforts of philosophers, historians, sociologists, psychologists, political scientists, measurement theorists and others [See footnote 4].

Social Performance Criteria—the Micro Context

Once such macro-level dimensions and criteria for social performance measurement become generally available and accepted, the unique tasks of the accountant are (1) to develop corresponding micro-level criteria applicable to specific firms and (2) to design and operate internal accounting systems which will make the resulting corporate social performance measures routinely available. Several difficult issues must be resolved before these tasks can be completed. Chief among these are the choice of performance dimensions to be included in the corporate measurement system, the selection of measures and measurement procedures and development of methods for independent verification of reported data. The firm-level measurement system developed ultimately must be such that reported social performance data would be useful not only for internal decision making, but also for external evaluation of the firm's performance within the framework of macro-level social performance criteria.

Definition of Social Accounting

The purpose of social accounting is to help evaluate how well a firm is fulfilling its social contract. It would accomplish this purpose by providing visibility to the impact of a firm's activity upon society. While the micro-level measurement system provides the information regarding the corporation's social performance, the macro-level performance criteria provide the evaluative framework. In light of this background, social accounting is:

> the process of selecting firm-level social performance variables, measures, and measurement procedures; systematically developing information useful for evaluating the firm's social performance; and communicating such information to concerned social groups, both within and outside the firm.

PROPOSED OBJECTIVES FOR SOCIAL ACCOUNTING

The notion of a social contract offers crucial assistance in objectives formulation by recognizing as two unique roles of a firm (1) the delivery of some socially useful goods and services and (2) the distribution of economic, social or political rewards to social groups from which the firm derives its power. The nature of these two roles warrants further examination.

As a deliverer of socially desirable goods, the firm is cast in the role of an agent of production. In this role, the ultimate test of a firm's success is whether its aggregate contribution to the society is more than its aggregate consumption of the society's resources. Under the traditional classical economics view, a firm's contribution and consumption are presumed to be completely valued in the market place—profits are presumed to be the all-inclusive measure of a firm's net contribution to society.

However, certain types of decisions of an individual firm may affect the actions of other firms or social groups or individuals in ways which are not reflected in the market process. For example, a major bank's decision to close down its branch in the ghetto area may prompt similar actions by other banks operating branches there and, thus, accentuate the economic and social decline of that neighborhood. The adversity caused to this social segment may not be reflected in the bank's net profits. Indeed, the bank's profits presumably will increase as a result of closing down the ghetto area branch. Many such instances are conceivable where the pursuit of private benefits may not result in the optimization of social benefits. Consideration of such external costs and benefits arising from an individual firm's action are necessary for the attainment of a socially optimal allocation of a society's resources. Whether such optimization is arrived through internalization of externalities or through direct government intervention, a common prerequisite to policy making within and outside the firm is information on, and separate consideration of, the externalities which give rise to social costs and benefits [Ronen, 1974].

Objective 1

An objective of corporate social accounting is to identify and measure the periodic net social contribution of an individual firm, which includes not only the costs and benefits internalized to the firm but also those raising from externalities affecting different social segments.

While the first role of a firm under the notion of social contract is that of an agent of production, its second unique role is that of an agent in the resource sharing and benefit distribution processes in society. The resource sharing and benefit policies (e.g., hiring, training, retention and promotion policies; plant location strategies; political philosophies; ethical norms) which a firm adopts have a direct impact upon how the aggregate benefits and sacrifices generated in the society are shared among individuals, communities, social segments and generations. The complexities of making tradeoff decisions among these competing groups are overwhelming, and the absence of theories which deal with interpersonal preferences and aggregate social utility functions are well recognized. Hence, in this second role, the firm's decision process is concerned more with notions of fairness, equity and consistency with social goals than with considerations of optimality.

The social monitoring of individual firm performance in this second role is less direct and more complex than the market-mechanism-based social monitoring of its economic performance. Indeed, the successful attainment of social welfare goals and priorities depends, in a large measure, upon how well embedded they are in the strategies and performance of individual firms—one of the largest organized sectors in modern societies. This relationship between individual firm performance and social welfare is the basis for a second major objective for corporate social accounting.

Objective 2

An objective of corporate social accounting is to help determine whether an individual firm's strategies and practices which directly affect the relative resource and power status of individuals, communities, social segments and generations are consistent with widely shared social priorities on the one hand and individuals' legitimate aspirations on the other.

The foregoing two unique roles—a production agent and a distribution agent—of individual firms in modern society, together with the two corresponding objectives of corporate social accounting, indicate the basic directions, dimensions and challenges involved in measuring corporate social performance. Attainment of these two social accounting objectives is necessary for systematically evaluating how well a firm is fulfilling its social contract.

The two preceding objectives may be viewed as *measurement objectives* of social accounting. Implementing these measurement objectives would ensure that a data base relevant to appraising corporate social performance would be available. However, there remains the task of providing relevant information from this data base to the users of social accounting information. For internal reporting purposes, the firm's management presumably will develop specific reporting objectives consistent with the unique features of the firm's technology, the strategies the firm adopts for fulfilling its social contract and its internal management structure. Obviously, this is not a public policy issue.

However, from the external reporting standpoint, there is need for a public policy on corporate social reporting. The purpose of such a policy is to ensure that social reporting by individual firms would be adequate and relevant for aiding public accountability, evaluation, coordination and monitoring of corporate contributions toward social goals attainment. A further purpose of such a public policy would be to insure that external reporting required of individual firms is cost/benefit-effective from the aggregate social standpoint. In the absence of such a policy, different user groups—the different social constituents of firms—will have different degrees of access to corporate social performance data. Further, an overabundance of data on some aspects of social performance and a paucity of information on other relevant aspects could result. Still further, potentials for biased reporting also exist, e.g., as when a firm reports only favorable aspects of its social performance. Finally, there exists the problem of resolving, without adverse social consequences, conflicts of interest in information needs of the various social constituents. There is thus a compelling need for an explicitly stated *reporting objective* of social accounting:

Objective 3

> *An objective of corporate social accounting is to make available in an optimal manner, to all social constituents, relevant information on a firm's goals, policies, programs, performance and contributions to social goals. Relevant information is that which provides for public accountability and also facilitates public decision making regarding social choices and social resource allocation. Optimality implies a cost/benefit-effective reporting strategy which also optimally balances potential information conflicts among the various social constituents of a firm.*

Of the three proposed social accounting objectives, two relate to the measurement process and the third to the reporting process. All three follow from the notion of a social contract under which the firm has both a productive role and a distributive role in society. While these social accounting objectives provide the basic theoretical framework, implementing these objectives would be facilitated by a set of social accounting concepts discussed in the following section.

PROPOSED CONCEPTS FOR SOCIAL ACCOUNTING

The central notion in the first measurement objective proposed is that of a firm's periodic net contribution to social goals. Traditional accounting income provides only a partial measure of this contribution because its computation is based only on an analysis of historical transactions in the market place. Many of the "transactions" between a firm and the society, e.g., positive and negative externalities, are not handled presently through the market place.

The earlier example of a bank branch withdrawing from a ghetto area provides one example of the nature of such nonmarket transactions between a firm and the society. In this case, the local community is deprived of easily accessible banking services and also perhaps of some employment opportunities. Further, the community would incur additional transportation costs due to more distant commuting for both banking facilities and jobs. Another adverse consequence might be the decline in the value of real estate upon withdrawal of prominent business units from a neighborhood. All of these results may be characterized as the consequences of a nonmarket transaction between the bank and the local community.

Nonmarket transactions also could lead to social benefits—e.g., when a bank decides to open a new branch in a ghetto. Furthermore, nonmarket transactions may involve shifting costs or benefits from one social segment to another. This may not affect the firm's contribution to society as a production agent, but could do so in its distributive role. Affirmative action programs by firms represent transactions whose main direct impact upon society is in the redistribution of income and growth opportunities among different social segments. Social accounting requires recognition of such nonmarket transactions in addition to the traditional market-based financial transactions. Thus, a fundamental concept in social accounting is that of a *social transaction*.

1. A *social transaction* represents a firm's utilization or delivery of a socioenvironmental resource which affects the absolute or relative interests of the firm's various social constituents and which is not processed through the market place.

The significance of recognizing social transactions lies in the fact that their net cumulative effect, along with traditionally determined financial net income, provides the proper measure of a firm's aggregate social impact. For the purpose of bridging the measurement gap between a firm's aggregate social impact and its financial net income, two more concepts are necessary:

2. *Social overheads (returns)* represent the sacrifice (benefit) to society from those resources consumed (added) by a firm as a result of its social transactions. In other words, social overheads is the measured value of a firm's negative externalities, and social returns is the measured value of its positive externalities.

3. *Social income* represents the periodic net social contribution of a firm. It is computed as the algebraic sum of the firm's traditionally measured net income, its aggregate social overheads and its aggregate social returns.

These two concepts are bound to receive considerable attention from both theoreticians and practitioners in social accounting because of the variety of alternative descriptions and measures applicable for these purposes. A proper evaluation of social overheads/returns would require, in the first instance, an identification of the different externalities and social segments affected by each social transaction. A complete enumeration of these would require an impractically elaborate input-output model. Considerable experimentation will be necessary before practical solutions are found in this area.

Secondly, each consequence needs to be "priced" using rates or prices or opportunity costs derived from an appropriate macro-level framework. The problem of developing rates and pricing social transactions of a firm is roughly analogous to, but incredibly more complex than, the problem of developing overhead rates and transfer prices in multidivision organizations [Ronen, 1974].

The problem of developing social overhead/return rates is a derivative of and is coterminous with, the problem of developing an operational definition of social income. The definition proposed above is admittedly vague. As in financial accounting, one approach would be to accept a definition of social income based on a matching of identifiable social costs and identifiable social benefits. While such an approach might be a necessary first step, a more comprehensive and precise definition of social income should be the subject of further research by social scientists.

The next concept, although not yet formally introduced, was used in stating the reporting objective of social accounting. Also, the central notion in the second objective relates to the impact of a firm's activity upon different social groups, with reference for whom the firm is presumed to be a distributive agent. These are the groups with whom the firm has an expressed or implied social contract.

Traditional accounting does not provide formal recognition to these groups. Only the claims of financial equity-holders and the periodic changes in their equity in the firm are measured in conventional accounting. In order to implement the second objective of social accounting, it is necessary to recognize formally in the accounting system all concerned groups. Thus:

4. *Social constituents* are the different distinct social groups (implied in the second objective and expressed in the third objective of social accounting) with whom a firm is presumed to have a social contract.

Formal recognition of social constituents in the accounting system is facilitated through social equity accounts where:

5. *Social equity* is a measure of the aggregate changes in the claims which each social constituent is presumed to have in the firm.

Obviously, social equity claims may not be enforceable under the existing legal system. But measures of social equity would serve as a useful basis for social decision making and for evaluating corporate social performance.

Finally, as a firm's social transactions enhance social well being or consume social resources, formal recognition of these nonmarket events in the firm's accounting system is facilitated by means of a social assets account. A positive externality of the firm (e.g., a decrease in neighborhood crime) would increase the value of its social assets. A negative externality (e.g., pollution) would deplete the firm's social assets. Thus:

6. *Net social asset* of a firm is a measure of its aggregate nonmarket contribution to the society's well being less its nonmarket depletion of the society's resources during the life of the firm.

The net social asset of a firm obviously is not recognizable under the current legal system and does not represent legal title to any future benefits to the firm. However, measures of net social assets would serve as a useful basis for social decision making and for evaluating corporate social performance.

METHODOLOGICAL IMPLICATIONS

Considerable experimentation will be necessary before the objectives and concepts proposed can be translated into a methodology of social accounting. The basic approach implied by the proposed concepts is described below, however, and major problems of implementation are discussed in the next section.

A fundamental step in social accounting would be to identify a firm's social transactions. All decisions and activities of a firm, whether or not they involve a market exchange, would be examined to identify the associated externalities. Such externalities then would be formulated as social transactions.

The process of formulating a social transaction involves identifying three elements. The first element is the *social constituent(s)* affected by the externality being considered.[2] Examples of social constituents are consumer groups, employees, minorities, the local community, investors groups, the general public, groups representing environmental aspects, youth groups and senior citizen groups.

The second element in formulating a social transaction is the specific nature of the *impact* of a firm's action upon the social constituent. In general, such impacts might be either technology-derived or management policy-derived. Thus, product safety and improved service efficiency are illustrative of technology-derived impacts upon consumers. Truth in advertising and sensitivity to customer service needs are illustrative of policy-related variables impacting upon consumers. Other examples of social transactions relevant to various social constituents are pollution-caused damage to health and environment, quality of human resource management, degree of commitment to affirmative action and concern for quality of life and welfare of the local community.

The final, and perhaps most difficult, element is the determination of the relevant social overhead/return *rates* to be used for pricing each social transaction. Since social transactions are not subject to market tests, no automatic process reveals the rates relevant for pricing such transactions. Instead, the rates would have to be developed within a macro social framework. In principle, this issue would be similar to the problem of developing cost and credit transfer rates in integrated multiplant operations. However, the practical problems would pose a serious challenge to any group of experts working on the problem.

---

[2]It is possible that more than one social constituent might be affected by one externality, thus giving rise to multiple social transactions.

An interim solution might be to develop social overhead/return rates at specific industry levels which could be used by individual firms in that industry.

The proposed methodology would require each firm to undertake an audit of its externalities in order to develop a reasonably complete set of social transactions reflecting the firm's ongoing impact upon society which are not subject to the market process. The methodology also requires the valuation of each social transaction using social overhead/return rates. The formal accounting for social transactions then would require determination of a social asset effect on the one hand and social income and social equity effects on the other. Certain transactions may involve an exact tradeoff between one type of social benefit (or cost) and another—both affecting the same social constituent. The accounting for such transactions might not involve a social equity effect. On the other hand, certain other social transactions might involve shifting benefits (or costs) from one social constituent to another, e.g., affirmative action. Accounting for this type of transaction might not involve any social income effect.[3]

To illustrate the approach further, consider the case of a bank. Based on the nature of a bank's function and its operating characteristics, the following social constituents and transactions are plausible.

ILLUSTRATIVE SOCIAL CONSTITUENTS	ILLUSTRATIVE SOCIAL TRANSACTIONS
1. Clients	1. Quality of services which affect thriftiness, savings habits, etc., of clients
	2. Client satisfaction with services
2. Employees	1. Job satisfaction
	2. Opportunities for personal development and professional growth
3. Local community	1. Effect on neighborhood economic development
	2. Effect on education, training, crime prevention, etc., in the neighborhood
	3. Effect on commuter traffic, congestion, pollution, etc.
4. Minority groups	1. Minority hiring, training and utilization
	2. Financial services designed especially to meet minority needs

Clients. The financial earnings of the bank usually are a major indicator of a bank's contribution to its clientele. However, the bank's impact upon them may go beyond that. Through aggressive campaign and management policies, the bank may influence its clientele to achieve greater thrift and more responsible personal fiscal management. Part of the resulting benefits may accrue to

[3]This may not be true if affirmative action programs lead not only to reduced disparities in income and opportunities among social segments, but also to other secondary benefits like greater political stability, fewer crimes, etc.

the bank in terms of greater client loyalty and business, but the aggregate benefit to the client group may exceed that realized by the bank.

Employees. Payroll costs and employee productivity may be reflected by traditional accounting. However, if the job situation leads to personal or professional enrichment, for instance, this positive benefit should be recognized through a social transaction.

Local community. Traditional accounting recognizes only local taxes, utility payments and other such market transaction effects on the community. But the bank's impact upon the community may include greater stability of, and fillip to, the local economy and employment potential. These, in turn, could help lessen crime, enhance educational and training opportunities and, generally, improve the quality of life. On the other hand, the bank's presence might also contribute to traffic problems, congestion and pollution. In all these cases, of course, there is a problem of identifying how much of each effect is attributable to the bank under study.

Minority groups. These may be employees, clients or other social segments. Efforts to reduce disparities in income and employment opportunities are examples of an employee-related social transaction. Client-related social transactions are illustrated by special programs to promote minority enterprises and minority capital formation. In all such cases, those evaluating the social transactions would attempt to recognize the social costs and benefits which are not reflected in the bank's market transactions and, hence, are not recognized by traditional accounting.

PROBLEMS OF IMPLEMENTATION

The objectives, concepts and methodology proposed here hopefully provide a tentative framework for developing pilot empirical applications of corporate social accounting. However several complex problems at the macro and micro levels must be resolved before a comprehensive and generally acceptable approach to social accounting can be developed. These include, at the macro level, the development of generally accepted social goals and social indicators to provide the normative framework within which firm-level performance dimensions and measurement criteria must be developed.[4] It is not the accountant's task to prescribe social goals, programs, or structure, just as it is not his or her task to prescribe a firm's goals, policies or management structure. The accounting theorist would necessarily look to sociologists, political scientists, economists and philosophers, among others, to interpret what is socially desirable and to formulate an operational set of goals—just as he or she relies on econ-

---

[4]Milestones in the "social goals" literature include *Goals for Americans* [The American Assembly, 1960]; *Agenda for the Nation* [Gorden, 1968]; *Toward Balanced Growth: Quantity with Quality* [National Goals Research Staff, 1970); and *Setting National Priorities* [Schultze, et al.]. Milestones in the "social indicators" literature include *Indicators of Social Change* [Sheldon and Moore, 1968]; *Toward a Social Report* [U.S. Dept. of H.E.W., 1969] which is the first attempt to implement the social indicators concepts; and *Social Indicators 1973* [Office of Management and Budget] which provides a substantial volume of relevant social and behavioral information.

omists, behavioral scientists and others to interpret and operationalize a firm's goals and decision/performance system. It is essential that the accountant be familiar with the logic and content of the operationalized social goal set, as he or she is to be guided by it in designing appropriate firm-level social accounting systems. Indeed, he or she might be expected to contribute to the macro-level social goal operationalization process by commenting upon the relative merits and problems of measurement implied by alternative operationalization approaches.

The problem of developing relevant social performance measures is particularly challenging at the micro level. On the one hand, they must follow logically from the firm's strategies and technological realities. At the same time, they must be technically congruent with the macro-level social indicators such that firm-level performance scored as positive using these measures also would imply positive contribution toward social goals. One solution might be to develop a social input/output model in which the coefficients capture all the interrelationships between a given set of firm-level social performance criteria and the macro-level social goal dimensions.[5] However, considerable research will be necessary before data for such models become available.

Another major micro-level problem relates to social overhead/return rates. This is a fertile field for research aimed at better understanding the economics of externalities and the behavioral impact of alternative rates upon firm managements and social constituents. Empirical research testing the feasibility and usefulness of alternative approaches to developing rates in selected performance dimensions would be of immediate benefit to the refinement of social accounting methodology.

CONCLUDING COMMENTS

The proposals in this paper are based on the premise that accounting for a firm's social performance requires a broader definition of a firm's role in society than is reflected in the legal entity notion underlying current accounting practices. Accordingly, the notion of a social contract was introduced which led to the three objectives and five concepts of social accounting proposed earlier. Table 1 summarizes these objectives and concepts. They provide a general framework within which several refinements are possible. More important, they suggest useful directions for further research into the various aspects of social accounting, some of which have been noted earlier. In particular, the concepts of social constituents and social transactions require further debate and empirical testing, and methods appropriate for determining social overheads/returns need to be developed. Alternative versions of the concept of social income are bound to emerge with corresponding implications for measuring social overheads/returns and social equity. In the absence of supporting legal sanctions, the notion of social equity and the determination of its shares attributable to various social constituents will have to be resolved through sociopolitical reasoning. Choices of measures and measurement procedures will have to be resolved based on which alternatives best help meet social accounting objectives. The usefulness and problems of integrating financial accounting and social

[5]Knowledge of this type is assumed in the input/output model presented by Charnes, Colantoni, Cooper and Kortanek [1972].

TABLE 1
Proposed Objectives and Concepts for Social Accounting

Objective 1

An objective of corporate social accounting is to identify and measure the periodic net social contribution of an individual firm, which includes not only the costs and benefits internalized to the firm, but also those arising from externalities affecting different social segments.

Objective 2

An objective of corporate social accounting is to help determine whether an individual firm's strategies and practices which directly affect the relative resource and power status of individuals, communities, social segments and generations are consistent with widely shared social priorities, on the one hand, and individuals' legitimate aspirations, on the other.

Objective 3

An objective of corporate social accounting is to make available in an optimal manner, to all social constituents, relevant information on a firm's goals, policies, programs, perform-ance and contributions to social goals. Relevant information is that which provides for public accountability and also facilitates public decision making regarding social choices and social resource allocation. Optimality implies a cost/benefit-effective reporting strategy which also optimally balances potential information conflicts among the various social constituents of a firm.

Concept 1

A *social transaction* represents a firm's utilization or delivery of a socioenvironmental resource which affects the absolute or relative interests of the firm's various social con-stituents and which is not processed through the market place.

Concept 2

Social overheads (returns) represent the sacrifice (benefit) to society from those resources consumed (added) by a firm as a result of its social transactions. In other words, social overheads is the measured value of a firm's negative externalities, and social returns is the measured value of its positive externalities.

Concept 3

Social income represents the periodic net social contribution of a firm. It is computed as the algebraic sum of the firm's traditionally measured net income, its aggregate social overheads and its aggregate social returns.

Concept 4

Social constituents are the different distinct social groups (implied in the second objective and expressed in the third objective of social accounting) with whom a firm is presumed to have a social contract.

Concept 5

Social equity is a measure of the aggregate changes in the claims which each social constituent is presumed to have in the firm.

Concept 6

Net social asset of a firm is a measure of its aggregate nonmarket contribution to the society's well being less its nonmarket depletion of the society's resources during the life of the firm.

accounting in one combined system need to be explored. Research into questions of materiality, verifiability and bias will receive fresh impetus as corporate accounting systems are broadened to include social performance data. This paper will have served its purpose if it helps to organize the emerging debate on such issues within a logical framework of objectives and concepts.

REFERENCES

Ackerman, R., "How Companies Respond to Social Demands," *Harvard Business Review* (July–August 1973), pp. 88–98.

American Accounting Association, Committee on Nonfinancial Measures of Effectiveness, "Report of the Committee on Nonfinancial Measures of Effectiveness," *The Accounting Review*, Supplement to Vol. XLVI (1971), pp. 164–211.

———, Committee on Measures of Effectiveness for Social Programs, "Report of the Committee on Measures of Effectiveness for Social Programs," *The Accounting Review*, Supplement to Vol. XLVII (1972), pp. 336–396.

———, Committee on Environmental Effects of Organizational Behavior, "Report of Committee on Environmental Effects of Organizational Behavior," *The Accounting Review*, Supplement to Vol. XLVIII (1973), pp. 73–119.

———, Committee on Measurement of Social Costs, "Report of the Committee on Measurement of Social Costs," *The Accounting Review*, Supplement to Vol. XLIX (1974), pp. 98–113.

———. Committee on Social Costs, "Report of the Committee on Social Costs," *The Accounting Review*, Supplement to Vol. XLX (1975), pp. 50–89.

———. Committee on Accounting for Social Performance, "Report of the Committee on Accounting for Social Performance," *The Accounting Review*, Supplement to Vol. LI (1976).

Bauer, R. A. and D. H. Fenn, Jr., *The Corporate Social Audit* (Russell Sage Foundation, 1972).

Bell, D., *The Coming of Post-Industrial Society* (Basic Books, 1971).

Beresford, D., *Compilation of Social Measurement Disclosures in Fortune 500 Annual Reports—1973* (Ernst & Ernst, 1973).

Charnes, A., C. Colantoni, W. W. Cooper, and K. O. Kortanek, "Economic, Social and Enterprise Accounting and Mathematical Models," *The Accounting Review* (January 1972), pp. 85–108.

Dierkes, M. and R. A. Bauer, eds., *Corporate Social Accounting* (Prager Publishers, 1973).

Gordon, K., ed., *Agenda for the Nation* (The Brookings Institution, 1968).

National Goals Research Staff, *Toward Balanced Growth: Quantity with Quality* (U.S. Government Printing Office, 1970).

Office of Management and Budget, Executive Office of the President, *Social Indicators 1973* (U.S. Department of Commerce, Social and Economic Statistics Administration).

Preston, L. E., "Corporation and Society: The Search for a Paradigm," *Journal of Economic Literature* (July 1975), pp. 434–453.

Report of the Study Group on *Objectives of Financial Statements* (American Institute of Certified Public Accountants, October 1973).

Ronen, J., "Accounting for Social Costs and Benefits," in J. J. Cramer, Jr. and G. H. Sorter, eds., *Objectives of Financial Statements* (American Institute of Certified Public Accountants, May 1974), pp. 317–340.

Schultze, C. L., et al., *Setting National Priorities* (The Brookings Institution, annually issued.)

Sethi, S. P., ed., *The Unstable Ground: Corporate Social Policy in a Dynamic Society* (Melville Publishing Company, 1974).

Sheldon, E. and W. E. Moore, eds. *Indicators of Social Change: Concepts and Measurements* (Russell Sage Foundation, 1968).

Shocker, A. D., and S. P. Sethi, "An Approach to Incorporating Social Preferences in Developing Corporate Action Strategies," in S. P. Sethi, ed., *The Unstable Ground: Corporate Social Policy in a Dynamic Society* (Melville Publishing Company, 1974), pp. 67–80.

The American Assembly, *Goals for Americans*, The Report of the President's Commission on National Goals (Prentice-Hall, 1960).

U.S. Department of Health, Education and Welfare, *Toward a Social Report* (U.S. Government Printing Office, 1969).

Evaluating the Effectiveness of Social Programs

ARTHUR L. THOMAS

This article tries to clarify an important dispute. In recent years, various authors have recommended that we accountants take on a new task: evaluation of the effectiveness of social programs (EESP). Indeed, the General Accounting Office and several public accounting firms have already assumed this responsibility.

In 1973, Mildred E. Francis, a biostatistician, published a lead article in the *Accounting Review*[1] claiming that this expansion of our services was inappropriate. Rejoinders by McRae[2] and Granof and Smith[3] followed: Sobel and Francis[4] replied to the latter. Seemingly, the accounting literature has rarely seen parties in deeper disagreement.[5] Much of this conflict results from authors' writing at cross purposes and from different disciplines. Also, Francis, understandably unfamiliar with accounting, made a few errors that her arguments can easily be recast to avoid, but upon which her critics naturally have focused.

Francis' conclusions are too well evidenced and important to our profession to be treated this way. An accountant should restate and amplify her arguments. I'm not a statistician and am ignorant of the social sciences beyond what one learns by casual reading of secondary sources. Therefore, this article merely tries to redirect the EESP debate to its main issues, not to settle them.[6] And

A version of this article was presented at the American Accounting Association 1975 Northeast Regional Meetings. I am grateful to Jacob G. Birnberg, Mildred E. Francis, Michael H. Granof, Sanford C. Gunn, Joseph G. Louderback III and Charles H. Smith for helpful comments on an earlier draft. However, it should be emphasized that their assistance by no means implies agreement with my conclusions.

[1]Mildred E. Francis, "Accounting and the Evaluation of Social Programs: A Critical Comment," *Accounting Review*, April 1973, pp. 245–57.

[2]Thomas W. McRae, "Social Auditing Questioned," *Journal of Accounting*, Dec. 73, pp. 92–94.

[3]Michael H. Granof and Charles H. Smith, "Accounting and the Evaluation of Social Programs: A Comment," *Accounting Review*, October 1974, pp. 822–25.

[4]E. L. Sobel and M. E. Francis, "Accounting and the Evaluation of Social Programs, A Reply," *Accounting Review*, October 1974, pp. 826–30.

[5]This debate has implications that extend beyond these four works. For instance, Robert H. Ashton ("Behavioral Implications of Taxation: A Comment," *Accounting Review*, October 1974, pp. 831–33) objects to a specific proposal for accountants' involvement in behavioral tax research on grounds that parallel one of Francis' arguments. (In the light of the matters summarized below, D. Larry Crumbley's reply ("Behaviorial Implications of Taxation: A Reply," *Accounting Review*, October 1974, pp. 834–37) seems insufficient.) 449

though trying to express Francis' general position vigorously, I'll conclude by exploring what we accountants can legitimately do to assist social programs— and will suggest that genuine disagreement between the parties is much less extensive than they suppose.

WHAT SOME AUTHORS PROPOSE

"[The accountant] sees social scientists stumbling about, seemingly making little progress in improving social well-being, and constantly attributing this lack of progress to their inability to get the 'right' information at the 'right' time. He perceives of himself as having expertise in the collection of and distribution of data and therefore as a vital (almost essential) member of the interdisciplinary teams which are striving to solve our national problems."[7]

Governments spend huge sums to alleviate social problems, yet these problems seem only to worsen. Social program administrators often blame lack of essential information. We accountants are expert in collecting, analyzing, organizing and reporting data.

Likewise, objections similar to Francis' criticism of accountants' attempts to evaluate social program effectiveness are pertinent to some proposals that we evaluate and report social costs and benefits of enterprise activities.

[6]Since only four main works are discussed, and these are short, I shall simplify exposition by avoiding detailed citations. Similarly, I shan't explicitly review Granof's and Smith's or McRae's detailed criticisms of Francis when these either are answered satisfactorily by Sobel and Francis or are implicitly answered in what follows.

For general background to the EESP debate and the proposals summarized in the next section, see American Accounting Association Committee on Measures of Effectiveness for Social Programs, "Report of the Committee on Measures of Effectiveness for Social Programs," *Accounting Review*, 1972 Supplement, pp. 336–96; Richard H. Austin, "The CPA's Social, Civic and Political Responsibilities," *Journal of Accountancy*, Dec. 71, pp. 64–66; W. B. Bolton, "A Critical Look at Governmental Accounting," *CA magazine (Canadian Chartered Accountant)*, May 1973, pp. 35–41; Karney A. Brasfield, "The CPA and Federal Government—Opportunities and Responsibilities," *Journal of Accountancy*, July 71, pp. 71–72; C. West Churchman, "On the Facility, Felicity, and Morality of Measuring Social Change," *Accounting Review*, January 1971, pp. 30–35; David F. Linowes, "Social Responsibility of the Profession," *Journal of Accountancy* Jan. 71, pp. 66–69, "The Accountant's Enlarged Professional Responsibilities," *Journal of Accountancy*, Feb. 73, pp. 47–51 and "The Accounting Profession and Social Progress," *Journal of Accountancy*, July 73, pp. 32–40; John Leslie Livingstone and Sanford C. Gunn, eds., *Accounting for Social Goals: Budgeting and Analysis of Nonmarket Projects* (New York: Harper & Row, 1974); Gerald H. B. Ross, "Social Accounting: Measuring the Unmeasurables?" *CA magazine (Canadian Chartered Accountant)*, July 1971, pp. 46–49, 52–54; Donald L. Scantlebury, "Implementation of Standards for Governmental Audits," *Journal of Accountancy*, May 75, pp. 34, 36, 38, 40 and 42; Philip G. Tannian, "How Public Accountants and Consultants Can Serve Our Cities," *Journal of Accountancy*, June 72, pp. 65–67; the news account on pages 4 and 6–7 of the June 1975 CA *magazine (Canadian Chartered Accountant)*; and the various works that they and Francis cite. For observations that partly parallel those that follow, see Rene Manes, "The Role of the Accountant Vis-a-Vis the New Measurement Constructs: View No. 2," *Accounting Review*, 1974 Supplement, pp. 102–03; and Jacob G. Birnberg and Natwar M. Gandhi, "Toward Defining the Accountant's Role in the Evaluation of Social Programs," forthcoming.

[7]Mildred E. Francis, "Thoughts on Some Measures of Effectiveness of Social Programs," unpublished working paper prepared for Robert E. Jensen, University of Maine, March 1971, p. 34. The April 1973 *Accounting Review* article (footnote 1) is an abridgement of this paper, which contains much valuable supporting material.

One suspects that much money earmarked for social welfare is diverted into political patronage and the salaries of redundant bureaucrats or is otherwise wasted. We accountants are expert in detecting certain misuses of funds. Perhaps even more important, we're expert in *dispelling* suspicions by attesting that statements present fairly how money has been spent.

We perform auditing, managerial accounting and management advisory services for charities, social agencies and community service programs. Some of us have served as volunteers in United Fund and other community efforts, furthered minority group hiring or assisted efforts to protect the environment. Thus, we feel increasing familiarity with social problems and programs.

The turmoil of the 1960s convinced some of our colleagues that their responsibilities to society extend far beyond their traditional duties. Many believe that we are morally obligated to offer our expertise in the broader arena of EESP by

1. Extending our attestations to cover
   a. Compliance of social program administrators and their clients with policies, rules and agreements by which they are bound.
   b. Costs, results and general effectiveness of social programs.
2. Designing information collection and reporting systems for such programs.
3. Helping improve the accuracy of resulting data. Indeed, they judge our doing so to be vital to the success of these programs.

Doubtless such expansion of our responsibilities would be difficult. But isn't it entirely feasible? In our work for the private sector, don't we already do most of what would be required? External and internal auditors regularly test whether firms have complied with government and union contracts and whether employees have respected internal control rules, head office directives and intra-firm agreements. External auditors attest to financial measures of effectiveness and, in reports to management and directors, evaluate management's performance (sometimes even conducting full-scale operational audits). Financial and managerial accountants have developed elaborate, sophisticated systems for processing data. Auditors attest to the propriety and nature of expenditures and to the general quality of descriptive economic statistics. They suggest how the latter may be improved. Finally, auditors and managerial accountants have begun to master the statistical tools needed for EESP and have learned how to serve effectively on MAS teams with many of the experts from other disciplines whose help they need in ministering to social programs.

Why then can't we accountants attest, provide data, enhance accuracy and improve managerial rationality in the public sector, too?

OUR LIMITATIONS

For efficiency of debate, those who reject Francis' replies to this question should consider her arguments in their strongest possible form. Yet her critics have directed much of their fire to easily remedied aspects of exposition. This section tries to fill the resulting gap.

Needs of Social Program Administrators

As we are well aware in managerial accounting, evaluation and planning are inextricably intertwined and shouldn't be divorced. Thus, to say that we accountants are qualified to evaluate social programs is also to imply that we are qualified to help plan them. It therefore is appropriate to ask: What kinds of information do social program planners need? Are we qualified to help provide this information?

Francis contends that the basic reason social programs fail isn't lack of the sorts of data traditionally provided by accountants—costs of providing these programs or the market prices of their results, tests of compliance, cost-benefit, cost-efficiency and cost-effectiveness analyses and other tools of modern management. Instead, most social programs fail for lack of basic knowledge of how related social phenomena work:

1. What people's real needs are.
2. Why the problem being treated exists.
3. What the nature of the environment is in which the problem occurs.
4. What social program outputs actually are.
5. Which of the resulting benefits and detriments should be included in their evaluation.
6. How these should be weighed.
7. What time dimension should be used.

Laity sometimes assume that social scientists have provided a kitbag of answers to such questions. Actually, amazingly little is known; most answers are guesses.

This is why Francis stresses the importance of planning each new social program as an experiment (a claim that her critics have resisted). If social program administrators eventually are to obtain the fundamental information that they need for planning, it's vital that each new program gain additional information through well-designed tests of hypotheses. Equally important, perceiving a social program as an experiment also permits assessing it scientifically to determine whether its intended results are being achieved.[8]

I shall argue that few accountants outside of academia (and precious few even of us) are expert enough in social science methodologies to assist much in such experiments. Indeed, we'll see that our training and experience would hinder us.

Consequences of Our Specialization

Barriers to our attesting, providing data and enhancing data accuracy in the public sector don't result from any personal inadequacies. Instead, Francis claims, they're consequences of our training and experience. As is true of all specialists, by devoting the considerable time necessary to attain expertise in accounting, we've *not* spent the time necessary to become expert in other dis-

---

[8]Though few practitioners take this viewpoint, managerial accounting also involves implicit tests of hypotheses. For instance, the poor motivation caused by using inappropriate depreciation methods or transfer prices in evaluating divisional return on investment may fruitfully be perceived as a consequence of a *failed* experiment.

ciplines. Moreover, becoming accountants has forced most of us to absorb and conform to accounting's intellectual framework and world view—sociologists call this co-optation. Our abilities to assist EESP become limited in two main ways:

1. To be of service, we should be adept in mathematical statistics and familiar with at least one of the other specialized disciplines that planning and evaluation of social programs draw upon. Few of us pass either test.
2. Our training and experience habituate most of us to ways of thought that are of only limited use in EESP.

Unfamiliarity with Other Disciplines

Almost all data for EESP are statistics that, necessarily, are obtained by sampling. Whenever social programs are to be evaluated, someone must decide which statistics and statistical techniques are most appropriate (for instance, often several possible estimators are available; someone must decide which to use). If only for financial reasons, it's also almost always necessary to cope with data that are fallible—for instance, because they

1. Must be time-series data despite the fact that conditions for valid time-series data aren't fully met, or
2. Embody nonsampling errors (for example, biases in estimates or responses, biases due to nonresponse or "observer" errors), or
3. Have been collected for purposes other than the one at hand.

Improving the accuracy of such inherently inaccurate data can only mean such things as improving sampling techniques or developing ways to reduce non-sampling errors.

Of course, statisticians aren't the only people qualified to do this. Yet, even though most members of our profession do have statistical experience, few have had time to add the thorough training in mathematical statistics necessary for real competence here to their already time-consuming training in accounting.[9] If nothing else, mere difficulties of keeping up to date in two literatures usually suffice to ensure this.

Nor is competence in just two disciplines enough. A trained statistician, expert in one social program field (say, criminology), isn't qualified to make necessary statistical decisions in other fields (say, delivery of medical services). Such decisions can validly be made only by specialists thoroughly familiar with the hypothetical causes and effects of the phenomena under consideration, the relevant research literature and the extent and quality of existing statistics. Therefore, besides being thoroughly trained in accounting and keeping up with its literature, an accountant who wishes to evaluate the effectiveness of social programs should also be trained in mathematical statistics and at least one social science and should then keep current with these literatures, too.

[9]Most statistics collected by financial accountants are just attempts to enumerate populations completely or (in the case of allocated data) products of arbitrary transformation functions. And such sampling as auditors perform rarely equips them to face the difficult issues suggested above.

Here's another way to put this last point. In the words of a 1970 AICPA public relations booklet,[10] we accountants are "designers of order." That's to say, we *impose* order upon the jumble of actual business affairs. Anyone who tried to base investment or other business decisions upon the totality of raw facts about even a small firm would soon be overwhelmed by their sheer volume and diversity. Our main task is to make informed decision making possible by analyzing, selecting, classifying and organizing data to make them tractable.

There's no one "right" way to do this. All information is an interaction of raw data from the external world with individual decision makers' ways of perceiving things, decisions to be made, decision models, estimation methods, decision criteria and estimation criteria—and the range of these is vast.[11] Instead, we must tailor our systems of order to the ways that investors and managers structure reality and to our best understandings of their desires, goals and needs. We accountants appear very successful at this, but perhaps not so much because of superior abilities to process raw data as to our usually being good businessmen with clear understandings of how other businessmen think, the types and quality of data available in the private sector and so forth.[12] We are experts in business matters.

We'd have to become equally expert in a host of social programs fields before we could tailor our analyzing, selecting, classifying, organizing and general designing of order to the needs of the new decision makers that we'd be trying to help—expert in agriculture, criminology, demography, public health and welfare administration, just for starters (and to illustrate this range). Otherwise, our services will be as useless (even as counterproductive) as, say, those of an epidemologist or social worker trying to perform traditional *accounting* tasks.

Inappropriate Ways of Thought

With only minor exceptions, we accountants reduce all effects of decisions and other events to sales, profits or net cash flows within the shelter of entity rules that exclude firms' interactions with their environments except as these affect sales, profits or cash flows.[13] Our transformation functions (aggregation

---

[10]American Institute of Certified Public Accountants, "Designers of Order: The Story of Accountancy Briefly Told," *Journal of Accountancy*, July 70, pp. 62–67: also available in pamphlet form.

[11]See, for instance, Arthur L. Thomas, "The Allocation Problem: Part Two," *Studies in Accounting Research No. 9* (American Accounting Association, 1974), pp. 82–83, 105–6, and the works that it cites.

[12]Of course, much of this is unconscious. Just as we learn our particular culture's basic assumptions and ways of perceiving things in early childhood and then thereafter treat them as common sense, so we gain most of our intuitive grasp of appropriate tailoring during our first accounting courses and then internalize it. By the time we graduate, we're aware of its existence only on rare occasions, as when bright first-year students express wonderment at accounting rules.

[13]Human resource accounting tries to add a second dimension—at least by pointing out that excessive short-run concentration on sales, profits and cash flows overlooks things that eventually may harm them. Some authors go on to recommend supplementing conventional financial statements by reporting human resource data in nondollar terms. This would add a true second dimension to these reports. But this and other suggestions for nondollar reporting made by theorists serve for present purposes merely to emphasize the extreme one-dimensionality of most actual accounting practice.

and allocation rules), what benefits and detriments to reflect, how these should be weighed (valued) and what time dimensions to use are, in effect, all given (however arbitrarily). All this simplifies our tasks, greatly reducing the range and difficulty of what we're asked to do. But simultaneously it threatens us with intellectual sedentariness. Privileged usually to ignore issues with which other disciplines must daily cope, we're often ill-fitted to deal with them.

For example, it's a commonplace that we find evaluating activities, such as distribution, that lack outputs readily measurable in sales, profits or cash flows much harder than other aspects of managerial accounting—in fact, it's one of our unsolved problems. We shy away from such assessments and, when forced to make them, worry that our figures are less reliable than we would like. Yet such figures exactly parallel what we've seen EESP requires: either the social welfare that programs create can't be placed on it, except arbitrarily (often because these welfare effects are multidimensional). Or, subtle and very dangerous, counts and valuations can be made, but only on minor aspects of the programs' results (thereby making it likely that programs will be evaluated solely on these minor aspects, much as students sometimes are evaluated *solely* on what easily graded exam questions can measure). Therefore, any claim that we accountants, expert in evaluating business activities, can easily extend our expertise to social programs seems based on a false analogy. If anything, as mentioned earlier, our training and experience would often hinder us:

1. Traditionally, we pride ourselves on our facility at gathering and processing financial and other economic data, but we almost always leave "nonquantifiable" aspects of decisions, social and environmental dimensions of problems and the like to management's judgment. Yet issues that parallel those we ask others to solve are exactly the most crucial ones in social program planning and evaluation.
2. Although Francis erred in claiming that accounting thought is primarily deductive,[14] it is true that most of us are inured to intellectual environments in which one looks to generally accepted accounting principles as one would to axioms or theorems and in which (at least under individual GAAP alternatives) accounting outputs are deterministic. Both modes of thought are inappropriate in the social programs arena, yet all of us received our practical experience and most of our training in them.
3. Finally, and perhaps controversial, we accountants are one of the more thoroughly middle-class groups to be found in society—and have thus internalized standards and simplified perceptions of how other segments of society function that place blinders on us when we try to cope with many problems to which social programs are directed.

Yet, one might reply, granting that we lack important types of knowledge, why can't we contribute to EESP teams composed of experts from various fields, just as we now do to MAS teams? As explained later, perhaps some of us can. But our contributions to MAS teams stem heavily from our general understandings of business, business data and how businessmen think—and few of us have comparable expertise in the public sector. Instead, as we've just seen, most of us would need retraining (even *un*learning) before beginning to be as useful on

---

[14]Francis, 1973, pp. 250–53.

EESP teams. The seeming counterexample of the General Accounting Office is discussed at length by Sobel and Francis and, briefly, in the next section.

Now, as Francis points out, plenty of people able to process data, enhance their accuracy and attest to their quality (and who also have good backgrounds in mathematical statistics and individual social sciences) are already available to social program administrators without asking accountants to reeducate themselves. (For example, government agencies don't need us to attest to the accuracy and integrity of the statistics that they collect and report; casual leafing through statistical journals will demonstrate that trained statisticians are evaluating them now.) Any attempt by us to duplicate their efforts would, at best, be wasteful.

OUR LEGITIMATE ROLES

Yet this is hardly the whole story, nor would Francis claim it to be so. We do have useful skills to offer social program administrators, both individually and in cooperation with others. Some of these skills are exemplified by a GAO audit,[15] cited by Granof and Smith, of the way the Department of Housing and Urban Development managed a grant program designed to help cities combat housing deterioration. Congress intended that this be done primarily by stimulating cities to adopt and carry out housing-code enforcement programs.

The GAO discovered that HUD had failed to exercise its authority to withhold funds (for other federal housing programs) until cities adopted effective local programs and had ignored flagrant instances of cities' (a) failing to approve programs within stipulated periods of time and (b) spending money supposed to be devoted mainly to code enforcement on paving streets and alleys. Cities had also violated HUD guidelines with impunity in other ways gross enough that their detection required no statistical sophistication.[16]

Sobel and Francis quite properly objected to certain generalizations that the GAO erected upon the facts that they described,[17] questioned whether HUD's and the cities' delinquencies might not have advanced Congress' basic objectives more than compliance would have and insisted that in any event what the GAO reported had nothing necessarily to do with the *effectiveness* of this program. Yet, granting this, it's hardly mere middle-class prejudice to insist that, when government agencies or their clients are supposed to operate under rules or agreements, they have moral or legal obligations to comply with them. Failure to do so, no matter how well meant, is anarchic—and should be reported to those who set rules and grant funds. Indeed, political events of the last decade suggest that violations of rules in order to further higher goals are, if anything, even more sinister than traditional corruption due to incompetence and graft.

Thus, it's essential to test the compliance of government agencies and their

[15]Comptroller General of the United States, "Enforcement of Housing Codes: How It Can Help to Achieve Nation's Housing Goal," B. 118754, June 26, 1972.

[16]For instance, in awarding grants to areas already excessively deteriorated by HUD's own criteria. Similarly, the GAO's comparison of the total amount that HUD spent for paving with the similar total of the requests for enforcement grants that HUD wasn't able to fund was deadly, yet required no higher order statistics.

[17]Such as that housing had deteriorated because cities hadn't adopted and carried out effective code enforcement (Comptroller General, ibid., p. 20 and elsewhere).

clients with the guidelines that they're supposed to follow. External and internal auditors are expert at this. Their examinations of internal control are explicitly designed to determine whether employees comply with company rules. They're also experienced in appraising whether firms have honored contracts and whether segment managers have respected company policies and directives, tailored their operations to overall company goals and the like. Surely they're equally capable of testing compliance by government agencies and their clients whenever rules and agreements are specific enough that compliance can unambiguously be distinguished from delinquency (a condition, though, that's less likely to be met in the public than in the private sector). In addition, of course, we can provide our traditional *financial* auditing services to government quite as legitimately as we do to private enterprise.

To generalize, one also should acknowledge that social programs can, and should, be evaluated at various levels of sophistication. Some inquiries demand use of higher order statistical techniques, but others require only natural extensions of what we accountants already do in the private sector. One needn't be a statistician to know when things don't add up. For instance, our local newspaper recently carried the story of a government-financed health insurance program under which some doctors charged fees implying treatment of over 100 patients per day. No training in mathematical statistics is needed to show that this program wasn't being carried out as intended. Similarly, we accountants are quite capable of

1. Investigating cost overrruns on government contracts.
2. Determining whether specific, tangible program objectives have been met (for example, verifying highway construction completion and, with the help of engineers, satisfaction of related quality specifications).
3. Attesting to what government money has been spent for (just as, say, we're capable of determining what portion of a charity's revenues is spent on administration, on public relations and on fund raising).

Therefore, any claim that it would be improper for our profession to expand further into the social programs arena would be unwarranted (nor did Francis so claim).

Instead, the point is that we should confine the services we offer to what we do well and should not (to use the previous illustrations) try to question the general wisdom of the contracts, evaluate whether the new highway meets public needs as well as alternate forms of transportation would or judge the social relevance of the charity.

Perhaps a few accountants are qualified to do the latter things. For ease of exposition, I've spoken of "accountants" as though they were a homogeneous group. Yet, although the great majority of us are limited by training, experience and outlook in ways that seriously restrict the contributions that we can make to social programs, perhaps some aren't. It may be that the latter have been especially active in EESP in the past or will be in the future. In any event, the key to resolving the EESP debate lies in determining the particular skills needed to evaluate specific social programs, regardless of who turns out to possess them, then in finding out whether such skills are already available to government. Only then will we really know who can best contribute, and what, and where.

SUMMARY

Authors vary in what they mean by evaluating the effectiveness of social programs; the spectrum includes

1. Comparison of program benefits and detriments with broad, amorphous social goals, such as preservation of our cities, "fair" income distribution, or law and order.
2. Measurement and comparison of program results with operational objectives specified ex ante—or, more generally, design and evaluation of programs as scientific experiments.
3. Comparison of fiduciaries' actions with their legal or equitable obligations.
4. Measurement and comparison of program costs with ex ante budgets or other standards.

In its efforts to summarize what Francis and her critics have said, this article has deliberately used EESP in all four senses. I invite readers to verify that Francis is primarily concerned with the second sense, whereas her critics are mainly interested in senses three and four. Therefore, usually they're discussing different things and don't really disagree at all. Unfortunately, though, attentive readers of the works cited in this article will also note that individual authors and pairs of authors often inadvertently use the term "effectiveness" in varying senses, sometimes in successive paragraphs. Indeed, much rhetorical force of some EESP literature depends on doing this (for instance, upon making sudden shifts from one of the last three senses to the first sense). This causes confusion.

Evaluation of program effectiveness in the first sense seems unpromising; perhaps it should be left to politicians and newspapers pundits. Francis makes a strong case that few accountants are qualified to evaluate effectiveness in the second sense. Francis' 1971 paper and Sobel and Francis provide specific examples of what can go wrong when unqualified accountants try. Yet, nothing in the EESP debate really hinders our evaluating social program effectiveness in the third and fourth senses.

Therefore, we accountants can legitimately do a wide range of things to assist social programs. CPAs may have especially important roles here because of their reputation for independence and lack of bias. However, the EESP debate underscores the importance of our matching our services to our qualifications, leaving tasks for which we aren't qualified to other experts. We have no reason to feel chafed by such restrictions, for they are the inevitable consequences of professional specialization. To be mortal is to be limited.

V/OTHER CURRENT ISSUES

In this part, various specific issues are examined, including solvency and liquidity, accounting recognition criteria and executory contracts, and intangible assets. Most of these subjects are or have been on the agenda of the FASB. Those which have been examined already may be reconsidered by the FASB for modification and interpretations.

Sections A is devoted to the issue of liquidity and solvency disclosures in financial reporting. Heath and Rosenfield (1979) recommend that more emphasis be placed on conveying information in financial statements pertaining to solvency. In the long-run, solvency and profitability are compatible. Accordingly, financial-statement users should be concerned with solvency. The authors contend that the balance sheet structure for assets and liabilities is based on an outdated notion of solvency assessment, and that the funds statement has failed to reflect solvency.

Section B encompasses accounting recognition criteria and executory contracts. The issues of the timing of revenue recognition criteria and executory fully executory contracts are analyzed. Additionally, accounting for leases, exemplifying executory contracts, is examined. The Report of the Committee on Concepts and Standards–External Reporting (1974) is concerned with the conditions for recognition of income from sales of products, services, and property. The Committee considers the treatment of uncertainty in accounts in determining the alternative points to recognize income from sales. Among the various alternatives examined by the committee is a separation of income recognition from realization in order to provide more timely reporting of earnings events.

Wojdak (1969) discusses the rationale for capitalizing leases among other fully executory contracts, looking to generally accepted accounting principles as a foundation to record fully executory contracts in accounting. Wojdak contends that "the exchange of promises and rights by independent parties upon entering into a contract constitutes an accounting transaction." Dieter (1979) argues that the guidelines set forth in FASB Statement 13 on capital leases are unsuitable, and have been circumvented in practice. Dieter favors a property-right approach that would capitalize all leases as property rights.

Section C deals with accounting for intangible assets. Bierman and Dukes (1975) criticize FASB Statement 2, which calls for expensing research and 459 development costs. The authors suggest that accounting theory does not provide a justification for writing off R & D expenses as incurred.

Tearney (1973) argues that reflection of goodwill on the balance sheet as the excess of the price paid over the net assets received in a business combination is inappropriate. What goodwill stems from, for example, human resources, can be identified and valued, he asserts, if necessary with assistance from appraisers. Accordingly, goodwill should not appear in the financial statements.

V-A / SOLVENCY AND LIQUIDITY

Solvency: The Forgotten Half of Financial Reporting

LOYD C. HEATH AND PAUL ROSENFIELD

The management of a business enterprise is concerned with two broad objectives: to operate the business profitably and to maintain its solvency. Profitability refers to a company's ability to increase its wealth. Solvency refers to its ability to pay its debts when due.

During the first three decades of this century, issues of solvency evaluation clearly dominated financial reporting. Income statements were not in common use, the balance sheet was referred to as *the* financial statement and short-term creditors, particularly bankers, were assumed to be the primary users of that statement. In 1927, Paul-Joseph Esquerré observed:

"It is undeniable that today almost every business balance sheet proceeds on the assumption that it is going to be used to obtain bank loans; and as the banker is presumed to loan only on the security of liquid assets, all the efforts of the statement of financial status are directed towards the proof of that liquidity."[1]

Beginning around 1930, accountants began to shift their attention from issues of solvency evaluation to those of profitability. By 1952 the pendulum had swung completely:

". . . the determination of periodical profit or loss from enterprise operations constitutes the crux of the accounting problem, the central issue around which all other considerations revolve and to which they are unavoidably related."[2]

Since 1952, the focus of financial reporting has remained on profitability. Accounting theorists, accounting educators, groups responsible for promulgating accounting standards, practicing accountants and auditors have been con-

The authors would like to thank Thomas W. McRae, CPA, a manager in the accounting standards division of the American Institute of CPAs, for his invaluable comments and suggestions during the preparation of this article.

[1]Paul-Joseph Esquerré, *Accounting* (New York: Ronald Press Company, 1927), p. 41. See also Hector R. Anton, *Accounting for the Flow of Funds* (New York: Houghton Mifflin Co., 1962), p. 5; A. C. Littleton and V. K. Zimmerman, *Accounting Theory: Continuity and Change* (Englewood Cliffs, N.J.: Prentice-Hall, Inc., 1962), pp. 113–117; and Eldon S. Hendriksen, *Accounting Theory*, 3rd ed. (Homewood, Ill.: Richard D. Irwin, 1977), pp. 56–59.

[2]Maurice Moonitz and Charles C. Staehling, *Accounting: An Analysis of Its Problems*, vol. 1 (Brooklyn, N.Y.: Foundation Press, Inc., 1952), p. 107.

cerned with profitability reporting almost exclusively. With few exceptions, reporting information useful in evaluating the solvency of a company has either been ignored or given a role that is clearly secondary to that of reporting profitability. Financial reporting for solvency evaluation is the forgotten half of financial reporting.[3]

THE RELATIONSHIP BETWEEN SOLVENCY AND PROFITABILITY

Solvency and profitability are clearly related. Long-run solvency depends on long-run profitability. No method of obtaining money to pay debts will be available in the long run to an enterprise that is not profitable. In the short run, however, solvency and profitability do not necessarily go together. An unprofitable enterprise may remain solvent for years because its cash collections continue to exceed its required cash payments. On the other hand, a profitable enterprise in need of cash to finance increasing receivables, inventory and plant may tie itself to an unrealistic debt repayment schedule that could eventually result in its insolvency:

Though my bottom line is black, I am flat upon my back,
My cash flows out and customers pay slow.
The growth of my receivables is almost unbelievable;
The result is certain—unremitting woe!
And I hear the banker utter an ominous low mutter, "Watch cash flow."[4]

THE IMPORTANCE OF SOLVENCY

Investors and creditors, the primary users of general purpose financial statements, need to evaluate the solvency as well as the profitability of companies in which they have interest. Creditors are obviously concerned with solvency. In fact, evaluation of solvency is often referred to as credit analysis, although that term should not be taken to mean that creditors are the only parties interested in a company's solvency or even that creditors are more interested in solvency than other financial statement users. If a company becomes insolvent, equity investors are likely to lose even more than creditors because creditors' rights are senior to those of stockholders in bankruptcy and reorganization proceedings.

Even if a company never reaches the point of insolvency, the mere threat or suspicion of insolvency is likely to result in losses to stockholders. The more obvious consequences are that the market value of their shares is likely to decline and that increased credit costs will tend to reduce profits. But less obvious consequences may be just as serious. Even if there is no imminent threat of insolvency, a company that is short of cash will have to pass up prof-

[3]Some of the material for this article was developed in connection with the preparation of Accounting Research Monograph no. 3, *Financial Reporting and the Evaluation of Solvency*, by Loyd C. Heath (New York: AICPA, 1978).

[4]Herbert S. Bailey, Jr., "Quoth the Banker, 'Watch Cash Flow,'" *Publishers Weekly*, Jan. 13, 1975, p. 34.

itable investment opportunities and restrict cash payments in ways that are likely to affect long-run profitability.

Other financial statment users are also concerned with a company's solvency. Employees, suppliers and customers are concerned because loss of solvency usually means loss of jobs, loss of customers, and disruption of sources of supply. The U.S. government's guarantees of loans to Lockheed Aircraft Corp. several years ago illustrate society's concern over the solvency of at least one major corporation.

EVALUATING SOLVENCY

Solvency is a money or cash phenomenon. A solvent company is one with adequate cash to pay its debts; an insolvent company is one with inadequate cash.[5] Evaluating solvency is basically a problem of evaluating the risk that a company will not be able to raise enough cash before its debts must be paid.

Solvency analysis is not simply a matter of evaluating a company's so-called current assets and liabilities to determine the adequacy of its working capital "cushion." During the last 25 years the emphasis in solvency analysis by sophisticated users of financial statements has shifted from static analysis of working capital position (or "proof of . . . liquidity" as Esquerré called it) to dynamic analysis of cash receipts and payments in much the same way that the emphasis in security analysis shifted from static analysis of balance sheet values to dynamic analysis of net income during the 1930s and 1940s. Today, it is recognized that most of the cash a company will receive within the next years is not represented by assets classified as current (or any other assets now on the balance sheet, for that matter); and most of the obligations it will have to pay during that time are not represented by liabilities classified as current.

Any information that provides insight into the amounts, timing and certainty of a company's future cash receipts and payments is useful in evaluating solvency. Statements of past cash receipts and payments are useful for the same basic reason that income statements are useful in evaluating profitability: both provide a basis for predicting future performance.[6] Information about the due dates of receivables and payables is also useful in predicting future cash receipts and payments and, therefore, in evaluating solvency.

Since cash receipts and payments can never be predicted with certainty, solvency evaluation also involves evaluating a company's capacity to control or adjust cash receipts and payments to survive a period of financial adversity, a concept that has been called financial flexibility.[7] Some of the things included under the concept of financial flexibility are a company's unused borrowing

---

[5]Liquidity is closely related to solvency but it is a narrower concept. The term "liquidity" is usually used to refer to a company's asset characteristics or to its asset and liability structure. As discussed later in this article, a company's ability to remain solvent depends on more than its present financial position as reflected in its balance sheet.

[6]For a specific proposal that enterprises publish statements of past cash receipts and payments, see Loyd C. Heath, "Let's Scrap the 'Funds' Statement," *The Journal of Accountancy* Oct. 78. pp. 94–103, and the monograph referred to in footnote 3.

[7]The concept of financial flexibility is discussed more fully in chapter 2 of the monograph referred to in footnote 3.

capacity and its ability to liquidate assets without adversely affecting the profitability of its remaining assets.

Information about a company's cash receipts and payments is also relevant in evaluating a company's profitability but in a different way. The timing of a company's receipts and payments is irrelevant in the measurement of income except insofar as timing affects the amounts at which assets and liabilities are recorded. The sale of an item for $10,000 cash and the sale of that item for a $10,000 note receivable due in five years with interest at 10 percent are regarded as equivalent transactions in evaluating profitability. They are not equivalent, however, in evaluating solvency because the timing of the cash receipts differs greatly in the two cases. The timing of future cash receipts and payments is the sine qua non of solvency evaluation and the heart of the distinction between issues of solvency reporting and profitability reporting.

EVIDENCE OF NEGLECT

We have neglected solvency. Evidence of that neglect and bias toward the income measurement or profitability point of view can be found in both accounting practice and discussions of accounting problems.

Misleading Balance Sheet Classification

One of the principal methods now used to report information for use in solvency evaluation is to classify assets and liabilities as current or noncurrent. That practice began shortly after the turn of the century in response to the needs, or at least the perceived needs, of commercial bankers. The bulletin that governs current-noncurrent classification today, chapter 3A of Accounting Research Bulletin no. 43, *Restatement and Revision of Accounting Research Bulletins*, first appeared in 1947 as ARB no. 30 and has remained virtually unchanged since that time. That bulletin is defective in many ways. It is based on an outmoded, simplistic, static model of solvency evaluation; it contains incomprehensible definitions of current assets and current liabilities together with lists of assets and liabilities that appear to contradict those definitions; it ignores basic principles of classification; and it not only fails to provide information useful in evaluating solvency but it also provides misleading information.[8] The fact that a bulletin that provides guidance on the major device in financial statements intended for solvency evaluation is so defective and has been allowed to remain in effect for over thirty years with no serious effort to change it is a prime example of how little attention has been given to solvency issues by accounting policymakers.

Misdirected "Funds" Statements

"Where got—where gone" statements, the forerunners of statements of changes in financial position (funds statements), were viewed as tools for use in solvency analysis. William Morse Cole, credited with being the father of funds statements, observed in 1915:

[8]For a discussion of these points, see chapter 4 of the monograph referred to in footnote 3.

"It is obvious that an important result of constructing such a table. . . is the possibility of seeing from it at a glance the changes in solvency."[9]

During the 1920s when H. A. Finney popularized funds statements that explained changes in working capital, providing information for use in solvency evaluation was still the principal objective of those statements. Working capital was considered to be *the* measure of a company's debt-paying ability, and the funds statement was viewed as a way of explaining changes in that measure.

In spite of the fact that financial statement users have shifted their emphasis from working capital analysis to analysis of a company's cash receipts and payments, nearly all funds statements found in practice today are still based on the outmoded and useless concept of working capital.

To make matters even worse, beginning with APB Opinion no. 3, *The Statement of Source and Application of Funds*, in 1964, companies were required to report "significant" financing and investing activities that did not affect working capital as if they did, so that even changes in working capital are not now reported in an understandable way. Duff and Phelps, Inc., an investment research firm, describes the current form of funds statement as "not much more than a miscellaneous collection of plus and minus changes in balance sheet items" and observes that "the predominant emphasis on working capital serves little purpose since working capital is not an important analytical figure."[10] Earl A. Spiller and Robert L. Virgil note that, under APB Opinion no. 19, *Reporting Changes in Financial Position*, "as long as certain types of transactions are disclosed in the required way, apparently any, all, or no underlying concept of funds is appropriate."[11]

The important point is that the original objective of funds statements—that of providing information for solvency analysis by explaining changes in some measure of debt-paying ability—has been lost. Funds statements are now viewed as the residual or "third" financial statement whose function is to report any "significant" information not reported elsewhere.[12]

Rejection of Users' Demands

Some of the strongest evidence of pro-income measurement, anti-solvency bias appears in the accounting profession's response to suggestions by financial statement users that statements of cash receipts and payments would be useful in solvency evaluation because income statements based on accrual accounting conceal the timing of cash movements. Those suggestions have often been interpreted as challenges to the supremacy of the income statement and contemptuously (perhaps fearfully) dismissed. For example, in 1961 J. S. Seidman, a prominent practitioner who was both president of the AICPA and a member of the Accounting Principles Board, stated:

[9] William Morse Cole, *Accounts: Their Construction and Interpretation*, rev. and enl. ed. (Boston, Mass.: Houghton Mifflin Co., 1915), p. 102.

[10] Duff and Phelps, Inc., *A Management Guide to Better Financial Reporting* (New York: Arthur Andersen & Co., 1976), pp. 81–82.

[11] Earl A. Spiller and Robert L. Virgil. "Effectiveness of APB Opinion No. 19 in Improving Funds Reporting," *Journal of Accounting Research*, Spring 1974, p. 115.

[12] For suggestions on how to improve disclosure of some of the information now reported in funds statements, see the Heath article referred to in footnote 6.

"... instead of studying various ways and terminology for presenting cash flow statements, I think the profession is called upon to report to companies, to analysts, to stockholders, and the exchanges that cash flow figures are dangerous and misleading and the profession will have no part of them."[13]

More recently, statements of cash receipts and payments were rejected by the Financial Accounting Standards Board in its exposure draft *Objectives of Financial Reporting and Elements of Financial Statements of Business Enterprises*. The board explained in paragraphs 33 and 34:

"Financial statements that show only cash receipts and payments during a short period, such as a year, [cannot] adequately indicate whether or not an enterprise's performance is successful.

"Information about enterprise earnings (often called net income or net profit) and its components measured by accrual accounting generally provides a better measure of enterprise performance than information about current cash receipts and payments. That is, financial information provided by accounting that recognizes the financial effects of transactions and other events when they occur rather than only when cash is received or paid is usually considered a better basis than cash receipts and payments for estimating an enterprise's present and continuing ability to bring in the cash it needs."[14]

Ruling out statements of cash receipts and payments on the grounds that they cannot "adequately indicate whether or not an enterprise's performance is successful" indicates the board considered only one aspect of a company's performance to be relevant in measuring success, that is, its earnings performance. Apparently the board did not consider a company's success in generating cash and paying off its liabilities to be part of its "performance." Obtaining cash needed to survive and obtaining increased wealth are both necessary parts of an enterprise's performance. Assuring survival and prospering require different kinds of achievement, not simply different amounts of achievement.[15]

The board's argument that enterprise earnings are a "better" indicator of cash-generating ability casts income statements and statements of cash receipts and payments as competing methods of disclosure although they are not. Income statements report the effects of a company's operations on its long-run cash-generating ability; the question of when cash has been or will be received or paid is ignored except as it affects amounts at which receivables and payables are recorded. Statements of cash receipts and payments, on the other hand, report the effects of operations on cash movements during the year; when those movements have affected or will affect income is ignored. Thus, income statements and statements of cash received and payments are complementary, not competing forms of disclosure. They report different things for different purposes. The board's rejection of statements of receipts and payments at the objectives level based on the argument that income statements are "better" indicators of cash-generating ability than cash flow statements indicates an insensitivity to the timing of cash movements and, therefore, an insensitivity to solvency issues.

[13] J. S. Seidman, *Journal of Accountancy*, June 61, p. 31

[14] FASB, *Objectives of Financial Reporting and Elements of Financial Statements of Business Enterprises* (Stamford, Conn.: FASB, 1977).

[15] For a discussion of this point, see Paul Rosenfield, "Current Replacement Value Accounting—A Dead End," *Journal of Accountancy*, Sept. 75, p. 72.

Confusion Between Income Effects and Cash Effects of Operations

Undoubtedly one of the reasons that users' demands for statements of cash receipts and payments have not received more serious consideration is that income measurement so dominates the thinking of many accountants that they do not even distinguish between a company's income and the cash it has generated through operations; they speak of income as if it were synonymous with cash. Thus, they often refer to the retirement of debt and the purchase of plant and equipment "out of profits" when they really mean out of cash generated by operations, and they refer to the income statement as *the* statement of operations even though it shows only one effect of operations. Other effects of operations such as those on cash, on plant and equipment or on capital structure are not, of course, reported in that statement. In fact, before APB Opinion no. 19 became effective in 1971, CPAs routinely stated in their standard reports that a company's financial statements "present fairly . . . the results of its operations" even though only the income effects of operations were reported; no statement was required that even purported to report the effects of operations other than the income effects.

Further evidence of the confusion between the income effects and other effects of operating activities can be found in the common yet confusing and misleading practice of showing income as a "source" of working capital or "funds" on statements of changes in financial position even though this "attempt to tie in these statements with profit and loss misses the major point that these statements are neither segments nor elaborations of income-measuring data, but instead are reports on changes that have occurred in other directions."[16] If accountants are going to provide information useful in solvency evaluation, they must first recognize that net income is not the only effect of operations and that other effects, particularly the cash effect, may be as important as net income.

Effects of Inflation on Solvency

A period of rising prices creates a cash problem and therefore a solvency problem for many companies, because increased amounts of cash are needed to replace higher priced assets. To meet that need, either cash receipts and payments from operations have to be adjusted or additional outside financing must be obtained. Information useful in evaluating the magnitude of a company's need for additional cash to replace higher priced assets is relevant for evaluating solvency under those conditions. Statements of cash receipts and payments, particularly if they are available for several years in which there have been different rates of inflation, and disclosure of the replacement costs of assets held are two types of information that would be useful in estimating a company's need for additional cash to replace assets.

The problem of financial reporting during a period of rising prices has usually been considered only from the perspective of income measurement rather than from the perspective of solvency. The use of replacement prices has been supported on the grounds that it provides a superior measure of income, not that it provides information for estimating a company's future cash requirements. Even when the solvency dimension of the problem has been rec-

---

[16] Maurice Moonitz and Louis H. Jordan, *Accounting: An Analysis of Its Problems*, rev. ed., vol. 1 (New York: Holt, Rinehart and Winston, Inc. 1963), p. 103

ognized, the solution often suggested has been to exclude the excess of the replacement value of an asset over its cost from income to obtain a measure known as "distributable" income—a solution that combines and confuses the income measurement and the solvency dimensions of the problem.[17]

Economic v. Legal Entities

The distinctions between separate legal entities are ignored when consolidated financial statements are prepared; companies within the consolidated group are treated as one economic entity. Legal distinctions between entities, however, are often necessary to evaluate solvency because creditors' rights attach to the separate entities, not to the consolidated entity. From the solvency perspective, a consolidated balance sheet may be misleading because "the pressing liabilities may be in the parent company, but the liquid assets which give promise of meeting these liabilities may be in a subsidiary . . . [where they are] unavailable to the parent. . . ."[18]

Similarly, one subsidiary may have adequate cash available, but the "pressing liabilities" may be those of another subsidiary and legal restrictions may prevent transfer of assets from one subsidiary to another.

Recently the Advisory Committee on Corporate Disclosure to the Securities and Exchange Commission noted this point and made the following suggestion:

"Where there are material blockages to free movements of cash within a consolidated entity (e.g., caused by loan indentures, foreign currency restriction, or other legal constraints which limit a parent's or a subsidiary's movement of cash to another entity within the consolidated group), separate funds statements might be required for the entity in which the blockage had occurred in order to disclose adequately the significance of this blockage to the ability of the consolidated entity as a whole to meet its dividend, debt service, and other commitments from internally-generated cash."[19]

While separate statements of cash receipts and payments for some or all the companies comprising a consolidated entity probably would be useful in the situation described, they are not a complete solution to the problem described because balance sheets, too, can be misleading under those conditions. The point in raising this issue, however, is not to recommend a solution but to point out that consolidated financial statements raise an important issue in the evaluation of solvency that has received little or no attention from accountants.

Consolidated financial statements are usually justified with the argument that they are intended to portray the economic substance of parent-subsidiary relationships rather than their legal form. That argument is specious because a financial statement user concerned with solvency considerations often finds

---

[17] For discussion of this point, see FASB discussion memorandum, *An Analysis of Issues Related to Conceptual Framework for Financial Accounting and Reporting: Elements of Financial Statements and Their Measurement* (Stamford, Conn.: FASB, 1976), ch. 6. See also Rosenfield, pp. 72–73.

[18] Ted J. Fiflis and Homer Kripke, *Accounting for Business Lawyers: Teaching Materials*, 2d ed. (St. Paul, Minn.: West Publishing Co., 1977), p. 604. For discussion of a recent example in which this issue is raised, see Abraham J. Briloff, "Whose 'Deep Pocket?' " *Barron's*, July 19, 1976, p. 5.

[19] *Report of the Advisory Committee on Corporate Disclosure to the Securities and Exchange Commission*, printed for the use of the House Committee on Interstate and Foreign Commerce, 95th Congress, 1st sess., Committee Print 95–29. November 3, 1977. p. 505n.

that the legal form of a relationship *determines* its economic substance, and legal form therefore cannot be ignored. The use of consolidated financial statements, like the problem of financial reporting during periods of changing prices, needs to be looked at from the solvency point of view as well as from the income measurement point of view.

Information on Funding Pension Obligations

A company's obligation to make periodic payments to fund its pension plan often represents a significant cash drain and may be an important consideration in evaluating its solvency. The amount of that obligation cannot be determined by the amount of pension expense reported on its income statement because funding requirements may differ from pension expense reporting requirements.

Current generally accepted accounting principles do not require a company to provide any information about its obligation to provide funding for its pension plan over the next several years. They do not even require it to disclose the amount of its contribution to its pension fund for past periods. APB Opinion no. 8, *Accounting for the Cost of Pension Plans*, is, as its title suggests, concerned almost exclusively with the *cost*, that is, the income effect, of pension plans. It ignores their impact on a company's solvency.

LET'S NOT FORGET SOLVENCY

The solvency perspective that dominated U. S. financial reporting for the first three decades of this century was lost when accountants turned their attention to problems of income measurement during the 1930s. For the past 40 or 50 years nearly all financial reporting issues have been considered almost exclusively from the standpoint of income measurement. Reporting practices that have as their objective providing information useful in evaluating solvency, such as classification of assets and liabilities as current and noncurrent and providing a funds statement, are based on an old model of solvency evaluation that has since been rejected by financial statement users as naive or simplistic.

The solution to the problems discussed here does not lie simply in searching for a new basis of balance sheet classification, in replacing funds statements with statements of cash receipts and payments, in disclosing due dates of receivables and payables, in disclosing replacement costs of assets held, in presenting separate statements of companies comprising a consolidated entity or in disclosing more information about pension obligations—although all those steps would probably help. Those solutions deal only with the current symptoms.

The basic problem is that accountants have forgotten the solvency point of view—not just accounting policymakers but all accountants including management accountants, auditors and accounting educators. The only solution to that basic problem is for them to understand how today's users of financial statements look at solvency issues and to adopt that viewpoint when considering all matters of financial reporting. This does not, of course, mean neglecting the profitability point of view. But unless increased attention is given to providing information useful in solvency evaluation, the accounting profession is likely to find itself subject to increased criticism for failing to provide early warning signals of business failures, of which the Penn Central and W. T. Grant debacles are only two famous examples among thousands that occur every year.

V-B/ACCOUNTING RECOGNITION CRITERIA AND EXECUTORY CONTRACTS

Report of the 1973 Committee on Concepts and Standards—External Reporting

The charge of this Committee is: "To consider the circumstances that might determine when the sale of a firm's product, service, or property is and is not an appropriate event for the recognition of profit (or loss) and to propose a set of concepts or criteria to be applied in making that determination."

In elaborating on the charge, President Sprouse also stated:

> It is anticipated that in considering this issue the Committee will refer to the 1957 revision of *Accounting and Reporting Standards for Corporate Financial Statements*, the report of the 1964 Concepts and Standards Research Study Committee on "The Realization Concept," *(The Accounting Review*, April 1965, pp. 312–322), *A Statement of Basic Accounting Theory*, and perhaps other American Accounting Association documents. Specific reference should be made to any parts of American Accounting Association documents that the Committee considers to be relevant and that the Committee has adopted and/or rejected.

Before considering under which circumstances the sale should be or should not be considered an appropriate event for recognition of profit, one might feel it is necessary to consider directly what is meant by the term "sale." For a merchandising or manufacturing enterprise, the sale usually has been deemed to take place when the goods and the title to the goods are delivered to the customer. The goods are then available either for use or for resale. In a few cases, transfer of title might be delayed and yet a sale is reported. In the case of conditional sales and some leases (Philadelphia plan leases in the railroad industry), the legalisms are ignored on the grounds that these are merely methods of increasing the probability of collection. In still fewer cases, delivery is not insisted upon if the goods are "set aside" for the customer to meet his convenience.

Contrast this with the recent situation in the land development and franchising industries. In the case of land development companies, the "sale" often

"Report of the 1973 Committee on Concepts and Standards for External Financial Reports," American Accounting Association, Supplement to Vol. XLIX 1974, pp. 203–222. Reprinted with the permission of *The Accounting Review*.

has been reported when the buyer and seller enter into a contract for sale. When this happens, the land is not ready for use by the would-be buyer and title has not passed. Title might not pass for an eight-year period and the ability of the buyer to use the land as it was publicized might take even longer because of the lengthy period to construct roads, water and sewage systems, and recreational facilities. In this and in the franchising industry, the "sale" often was what would ordinarily be considered an executory contract. If profit is to be reported before the seller's responsibilities have been largely discharged, it could be only on the basis of the reasoning associated with the percentage of completion method.

Considering these things, it is obvious that there is a great deal of confusion over the meaning and use of the term "sale." Because of this confusion, the Committee decided it could answer the charge better by initially taking the indirect approach of considering realization as the basic consideration; with the sale being thought of as only one possible signal to indicate that realization had taken place, rather than directly considering the appropriateness of the sale *per se*, for the recognition of profit (or loss). Either approach ultimately would lead to the same conclusions, however.

The Committee has found considerable confusion in traditional accounting regarding the essential meaning of realization. Some apparently consider realization as a concept not only concerned with uncertainty, but also essential as a determinant in the concept of income being measured. We feel this fusion of concept and measurement is confusing and detrimental to both. Our initial, basic conclusion is that a distinction between income concept and income measurement is useful and worthy of maintenance. Further, the realization concept should be understood as a means of analyzing and reporting uncertainty. It pertains only to the measurement of income—more particularly to the problems of measurement which issue from uncertainty. Realization does not have relevance to the definition or concept of income—i.e., what types of events and transactions result in income.

As an example, whether specific price level changes should be reflected in the statements as income is a question of concept (some might hold such changes to be necessary adjustments to maintain the physical capital of the firm and, hence, not part of the income stream). Assuming such changes are considered income, then the question is one of timing, i.e., when are they measurable with a sufficient degree of reliability (when has uncertainty reduced to an acceptable level) to justify reflection in the financial statements.

Hence, our charge was not to determine what concept of income should be adopted. Rather, it was to re-examine some of the means used to analyze and compensate for uncertainty in the measurement of income, whatever concept is accepted or adopted. More narrowly, it was to re-examine the appropriateness of relying on the sales event as the critical point at which uncertainty has been sufficiently reduced to warrant the inclusion of profit in the income statement, though, as previously stated, the "sales event" was approached indirectly through other first considerations.

The treatment of uncertainty in accounting should perhaps be divided into two facets. First, there is the analytical process of observing certain selected characteristics of a factual situation for the purpose of assessing the degree of uncertainty which is inherent in the situation. Second, there is the process of designing financial reports so that the accountant's assessment of uncertainty is conveyed in the financial statements.

A general portrayal of some alternative ways of treating uncertainty in accounting is depicted in Figure 1. Obviously, the alternatives presented are not an exhaustive listing of the possible alternatives. Nevertheless, those listed provide a generally appropriate description of the array of alternatives accountants might consider.

Historically, it is difficult to say whether accountants have approached the problem of uncertainty basically through Alternative I, Alternative II, or some combination of the two. Considering the heavy reliance placed on the sales event, at times apparently without consideration to the actual circumstances of the case (such as what happened regarding the reporting of franchise income), one might conclude that accountants have tended to exclude from consideration some of the events and/or variables they deemed to be of marginal significance, and accepted the sales event as a summary indicant of the uncertainty (Alternative I). On the other hand, considering the accepted exceptions to the sales basis (percentage of completion and cash collection methods of recognizing income), one might conclude that accountants have considered several events before selecting one as the most critical point of uncertainty reduction in the given business situation (Alternative II). In a word, the exceptions provide evidence that the sales point has been selected as the "critical" event in most instances, but earlier recognition has been accepted where prediction with sufficient certainty was possible, or later, where it was not. In either case, practice has followed Alternative I or II, or some combination of the two.

In proceeding from "what is the case," to a consideration of "what accountants should be doing," the Committee adopted the position that the uncertainty associated with the financial consequences of business activity is not solely a function of one specific event or variable. The activity of any business unit obviously has many dimensions, several of which are interdependent. Correspondingly, the uncertainty inherent in business activity can be perceived as having many, frequently interdependent, dimensions. The means of analyzing uncertainty inherent in business activity requires an attempt to assess the combined effect of many events and/or variables.

Beyond this point there was a great deal of disagreement among Committee members as to ultimate objectives to be attained and/or the speed with which these objectives ought to be accomplished. A number of the Committee members felt we ought to move to Alternative III and go no further. Some felt we should move to Alternative III but only as a transitional step to Alternative IV. Others felt we should make recommendations which would move us as quickly as

FIGURE 1

	Alternative I	Alternative II	Alternative III	Alternative IV
Accounting Method	Sales Basis	Critical Events Basis	Multiple Events Basis	Multi-dimensional Analysis and Reporting
Variables Analyzed	One, i.e., sale a	One of many a b c . . . n	Many a b c . . . n	Many a b c . . . n
Reporting Technique	Binary: Income is either realized or not	Binary: Income is either realized or not	Binary: Income is either realized or not	Polymeric

possible into Alternative IV, even by-passing Alternative III if possible. Because of these disagreements within the Committee, we felt such differences of opinion also probably exist in the profession, in academic circles as well as among practicing accountants. Consequently, we thought we would serve best the interests of the accounting discipline and the charge given us, if we presented arguments pro and con for these possible alternatives. This should give the reader more complete information on which he can base his decision, as well as indicate areas where further research is needed.

MULTIPLE-EVENTS BASIS—BINARY (ALTERNATIVE III)

Realization Concept

The realization concept developed over the years as the means for dealing with uncertainty. In most instances, it was felt that recognition of profit or loss at the sales point was best since this often was the first point in the long chain of events where prediction of net cash flows was possible within accepted bounds. Exceptions to the sales point have been allowed, as previously indicated, but it should be noted that each of the realization points is an estimate and, as such, is subject to error.

In essence, the realization concept expresses the accountant's requirement that the profit impact of an event (or set of related events) not be too uncertain if that impact is to be reported in the income statement. In other words, the measurement of income must be sufficiently reliable.

Conceptually, the demand for reliable measurement might be expressed as a maximum variance in the probability distribution which describes the profit impact of a set of events (see Figure 2). More practically, the requirement for sufficiently reliable measurement may be approached in terms of reasonable consensus among accountants. Floyd W. Windal has described the measurement requirement as follows[1]:

FIGURE 2

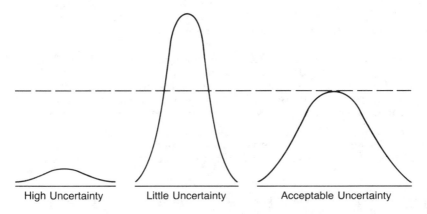

| High Uncertainty | Little Uncertainty | Acceptable Uncertainty |

[1]These definitions were taken from, Floyd W. Windal, *The Accounting Concept of Realization.* Occasional Paper No. 5, Bureau of Business and Economic Research, Graduate School of Business Administration, Michigan State University, 1961, pp. 75–76.

> *Measurement*—objective is, of course, the opposite of subjective. Therefore, in order for an item to be sufficiently objective for recognition, it must appear substantially the same to all accountants examining it. It must not be subject to different interpretations by different people. The quality of measurability seems to satisfy to a large extent the demand for objectivity. If an item can be measured with reasonable accuracy, it assumes a large degree of objectivity.
>
> The requirement of objectivity, and thus measurability, results from the very nature of the accounting process. Accounting is basically a process of quantitative description, and if an item is not objective or measurable it cannot be described quantitatively.
>
> This factor has a broad connotation: an item is considered to be measurable if it can be estimated with a reasonable degree of accuracy . . .
>
> The accountant's judgment necessarily enters into the application of this factor. He must make a decision on the accuracy of his measurement in a particular case . . . his past experience with like items and his technical background give him a good basis for arriving at a sound conclusion.

Although our charge was not directed at a discussion of the realization concept *per se* (at least the word "realization" was not used), we found ourselves constantly bumping into it during our discussions. This is not surprising. "The Concept of realization is an integral part of the process of income measurement"[2] and, we believe, an essential consideration in determining when "the sale of a firm's product, service, or property is and is not an appropriate event for the recognition of profit (or loss) . . ."

The emphasis on realization is an attempt to protect against human frailty which all too often comes to the surface with disastrous results in a world fraught with uncertainty. Most of us are optimistic in good times and pessimistic when things appear dark. Useful income measurement must depend on a pragmatic test of realization, not the hopes and fears of individuals. Most importantly, use of the realization concept identifies basic recordable data which can be used by all of the bona fide interests as an objective point of departure for their interpretations (though as we will see later, perhaps the word "realization" should be dropped and a much different emphasis given to the concept than at present). We feel these statements are in conformity with the intent of the standards of verifiability and freedom from bias as described in *A Statement of Basic Accounting Theory*, with which we agree.

> Verifiability is that attribute of information which allows qualified individuals working independently of one another to develop essentially similar measures or conclusions from an examination of the same evidence, data, or records. This standard does not always require identical results. It may, in some instances, allow variations within known limits.[3]
>
> The standard of freedom from bias is advocated because of the many users accounting serves and the many uses to which it may be put. The presence of bias which may serve the needs of one set of users cannot be assumed

---

[2]1964 Concepts and Standards Research Study Committee, "The Realization Concept," *The Accounting Review*, April, 1965, p. 313.

[3]Committee to Prepare a Statement of Basic Accounting Theory, *A Statement of Basic Accounting Theory*, American Accounting Association, 1966, p. 10.

to aid or even leave unharmed the interests others. . . . Thus, bias should be avoided in external general purpsoe reports.[4]

Regardless of how income is defined, short-run calculations are essential to provide necessary information for those interested in progress of the enterprise. The very essence of the realization concept is directed at this goal of short-term measurement, since there would be no need for the realization concept at all if accountants could wait until the liquidation of the enterprise before making their computations. Some have advocated abandoning the realization concept entirely. Although there is substantial difficulty in the formulation and application of a realization concept, it is difficult to understand how the function of accounting can be performed without one of some sort to aid in effectively dealing with uncertainty, though no implications are intended at this point as to what the concept should mean, or what it should be called.

If it is to be useful, the realization concept must serve as a guide in determining *when* certain asset and liability changes can be appropriately entered in the accounting records and presented in the financial statements.

> The essential meaning of realization is that a change in an asset or liability has become sufficiently definite and objective to warrant recognition in the accounts. This recognition may rest on an exchange transaction between independent parties, or on established trade practices, or on the terms of a contract performance of which is considered to be virtually certain. It may depend on the stability of a banking system, the enforceability of commercial agreements, or the ability of a highly organized market to facilitate the conversion of an asset into another form.[5]

Although we support this statement, it is very broad and therefore needs greater specificity in order to become more operational and useful. The following considerations are the committee's interpretations of what it does (or should) mean.

Over the years, accountants have developed criteria for determining when income is realized. A survey of the literature disclosed that all of the points listed below are considered as necessary prerequisites to the recognition of certain asset and liability changes. Naturally, it is not implied that all of these are invoked in every case. It is simply pointed out here that at some time or another each of the following has been used separately, or in combination with one or more of the others, in determining when certain asset and liability changes were deemed to be realized. The item had to be:

1. earned, in some sense or another,
2. in distributable form,
3. the result of a conversion brought about in a transaction between the enterprise and someone external to it,
4. the result of a legal sale or similar process,
5. severed from capital,

---

[4]*Ibid.*, p. 11.

[5]Committee on Accounting Concepts and Standards, *Accounting and Reporting Standards for Corporate Financial Statements—1957 Revision*, American Accounting Association, p. 3.

6. in the form of liquid assets,

7. both its gross and net effects on stockholder equity had to be estimable with a high degree of reliability.

These criteria seem to justify the following general observations:

1. They appear to be oriented primarily to changes in assets and liabilities, which changes are reflected in the income statement.

2. They appear to be concerned with defining what is to be included within the concept of income, as well as with its recognition (timing and measurement).

3. They imply that the concept of realized revenue is dependent upon the concept of realized *net* income.

4. They appear to be rooted in a "venture" conception of the business enterprise.

5. Many of them are concerned with ensuring objectivity.

6. They are primarily concerned with the *source* and *form* of changes, giving little consideration to *effect* upon the entity.

Admittedly, such listings give an impression of independence and exclusiveness which do not, in fact, exist. However, they do facilitate further discussion since they provide guidelines for determining when uncertainty has been reduced sufficiently.

The Realization Concept Should be Income Statement Oriented

Regardless of how important it may be, the generation of income is not the only activity of an entity. Many changes in balance sheet accounts are not the result of "income transactions," yet they also must be accurately reflected in the financial statements. As a consequence, there is a temptation to hold that the present concept of realization, which is oriented to the income statement, should be broadened to encompass all recordable activities of the entity. However, before such a contention can be supported, it has to be shown that a need exists for including all transactions within the realization concept. Otherwise, such a requirement would be redundant at best; at worst it is confusing and misleading.

1. The realization concept traditionally has been applied to "income type" transactions. To make it apply to "non-income type" transactions would remove whatever operational content it has, or could have. Income is a measurement of the changes in certain types of assets and liabilities. The concept of income tells us what kinds of changes are appropriate to call "income items." The realization concept should tell us "when." (This will be discussed more fully later).

2. A need for extending the realization concept to include "non-income" events could only be shown in those cases where there are reasonable alternative possibilities in timing the recording of the event, since then, and only then, is a guide needed for making a rational choice. When consideration is given to those events not having "income implications" *at the time of entry*, it is difficult to see any rational alternative in timing their entry into the records. For example, there is no choice in timing the recording of money borrowed from the bank. The contracts are signed as soon as negotiations are completed, and the money is made available to the borrower. The entry reflecting the transaction should be made at this time. To make the entry before this is to reflect both a non-existent asset (the borrower does not have the use of the money) and a nonexistent liability (nothing is owed). Making the entry later than at this point results in an understatement of assets and liabilities for the time interval involved. Essentially the same is true for the issuance of capital stock for cash, the purchase of bonds and stocks for investment purposes, fixed asset purchases, or the recording of other financial transactions of the enterprise.

These statements are not meant to imply that measurement of asset and liability changes having only balance sheet effects is not a critical question; it is. But the realization concept should be concerned only with certain balance sheet effects; the effects generated by income transactions. These are determined by the concept of income, not by the realization concept. The Committee has concentrated on uncertainty but it has proceeded on the assumption that income would not be reported until the firm's economic function has been performed, however defined, either completely or partly. Ideally (ignoring measurement problems) income would be reported as the productive processes take place. (However, "productive processes" here is not to be interpreted in the narrow, technical engineering sense. Many efforts are necessary to produce income and "productive processes" should be interpreted to encompass all such efforts). Granted that this has occurred, income should be reported as soon as the level of uncertainty has been reduced to a tolerable level. It may be that this takes place at the time of sale for the industrial firm, but this depends on the circumstances. It is necessary to look for critical events or combinations of critical events to determine the appropriate point at which income should be reported.

Income must always be in existence before the question of realization can arise. Realization is not a determinant in the concept of income; it only serves as a guide in deciding when events, otherwise resolved as being within the concept of income, can be entered in the accounting records in objective terms; that is, when the uncertainty has been reduced to an acceptable level.

Realization would then be tied to some concept of reliable measurability. Holding that income is earned as a result of all the processes which add form, place, and time utility to the products being produced and services provided, and should be recognized as the processes take place, gives an ideal to shoot for in the income determination process. It causes us to look for crucial events, or combinations of crucial events, which will allow recognition at the earliest possible moment while remaining within the constraints of the standards of verifiability and freedom from bias mentioned earlier, (this is what is meant by reducing uncertainty to an acceptable level). Realization is the delimiting factor which tells which of the "income items" in existence are subject to entry in the records and presentation in the income statement.

In a word, certain critical events are necessary to bring income into existence. Certain critical events are necessary for the realization of income. The critical events necessary for realization may be nearly the same as, and occur at nearly the same time as, the critical events giving rise to income, or they may differ and be later, but they can never predate the critical events giving rise to income. An example might clarify the point being made. Assume a customer comes in during 1973 to have a highly specialized machine made to order. We agree to build the machine for $30,000 and the customer advances all the funds immediately. Further assume that we know we will start and complete the machine in 1974, and deliver it in 1975. The cost, without question, will be $20,000; we know what the figure will be to the penny. Some would argue the $30,000 less the discounted value of the $20,000 should be recognized in 1973 as income. Others would argue that the $10,000 ($30,000 less $20,000) should be recognized in 1974 since it has not been earned in 1973 in the sense that no efforts have been made, no assets have been utilized, in carrying out the economic activities of the firm. In other words, these people would argue that the receipt of the $30,000 is a financial transaction. Of course, such questions are critical regarding the nature of income and when it arises, but the question of realization comes up only after decisions are made regarding such questions. Those who argue for 1973 would, having decided that income is in existence, say that income has been realized and, since there are no problems of measurement, that income should be reported. Those opting for 1974, even though no measurement problems are involved, would argue that income is not in existence, thus there is no question of realization.

Concept of Realized Revenue is Dependent Upon the Concept of Realized Net Income

It follows from the previous discussions that all events and transactions whose effects are reflected in the income statement must necessarily fall within the realization concept. With regard to revenue, the necessary objectivity is attained when the present value of gross cash effects of a transaction can be estimated within an acceptable degree of accuracy. The realization concept is also applicable to expenses and losses as well as to revenue; and we feel that revenue should not be considered realized unless the expenses incurred in its production are accurately measurable—that realized revenue is dependent upon realized net income. Or, to state this positively, these statements assert that, even in those cases where revenue satisfied all the criteria of realization, it will not be recorded in the income accounts until the net effects on the stockholders' equity can be accurately determined (although it may be recorded in the asset and liability accounts). This is necessary to fulfill the following:

> In business operations, costs, defined as resources given up or economic sacrifices made, are incurred with the anticipation that they will produce revenue in excess of the outlay. Within this frame of reference, one can then say that costs constitute one measure of business effort, and revenues represent accomplishments coming from those efforts. Appropriate reporting of costs and revenues should therefore relate costs with revenues in such a way as to disclose most vividly the relationship between efforts and accomplishments.[6]

[6]Committee on the Matching Concept, *The Accounting Review*, April 1965, p. 369.

The realization concept is concerned almost exclusively with allocation problems. Many years ago, Professor William A. Paton stated that all expenditures are assets, at least momentarily. The reason many expenditures are placed directly in expense accounts when incurred is for expediency purposes. If it is known that the service utility in the expenditure will have been consumed by the time the books are closed and the statements prepared, it is more expedient to place the amount directly in the appropriate expense account at the time incurred. This doesn't alter the fact that the expenditure results in an asset initially, regardless of how short-lived it might be.

We feel the same thing is true on the other side of the ledger. Regardless of how momentary, the promise of providing goods and services results in an initial liability to the business entity. For example, if a customer buys a shirt for cash, the initial entry should be an increase in cash and an increase in a short-term liability. If transference of the shirt to the customer is considered to be the critical event to the recognition of revenue, when this takes place the liability is reduced and revenue is increased. Since these events usually take place nearly simultaneously, accountants would simply report an increase cash and revenue at the same time, in the above example. On the other hand, if the customer deposited cash in one accounting year for a shirt to be delivered the next, the amount remains in the liability account until the shirt is delivered, under current practice, because the taking of the order is not considered to be the critical event, i.e., income is not considered to come into existence at that time.

Thus, the realization concept to a large degree, is concerned with allocation; i.e., when can assets be allocated to expenses and when can liabilities be allocated to revenues, the answer to one being interrelated with and inter-dependent on the answer to the other, and both depending upon the critical events being satisfied first which give rise to income, regardless of the concept being followed.[7]

Venture Conception of the Business Enterprise. The emphasis which has been placed on revenue is possibly an outgrowth of the venture concept of operations. This probably led to acceptance of the credit-sale basis of revenue recognition. It can be seen that the previously stated criteria relating to (1) conversion, (2) a transaction occurring between the enterprise and someone external to it, (3) legal sale or similar process, and (4) severance from capital, are all tied closely to this credit sale basis for revenue recognition. (More generally they are criteria for judging the uncertainty level.) In fact, the combined requirements in the first three of these leave no alternative to the timing (recognition) of revenue except the credit sale basis, since only at that point can all of them be fulfilled (assuming, again, that an accrual and not a cash basis is to be followed). Further, it seems that the first three of these are directed at ensuring the fourth—severance from capital. Exceptions to any one of the four consequently result in exceptions to the credit-sale basis, and deviations from any one of the first three result in deviations from the severance-from-capital criterion.

[7]The critical event theory was first discussed by John H. Myers, "The Critical Event and Recognition of Net Profit," *The Accounting Review*, October, 1959, pp. 528–532.

This emphasis on the credit sale probably has resulted in neglect of some effects and transactions that might have been reflected in the accounts and statements earlier. The sales point of recognition has become virtually an end in itself. Although its importance in certain circumstances is unquestioned, the credit sale is only one of many possible means of attaining the primary objective of accurate reflection of economic activity. It is not unusual, for example, to read statements that the installment sales method, the percentage-of-completion method, or the procedures involved in recognizing income in farm production, are in conflict with the credit sale basis. Although technically correct by definition, such statements carry connotations which are not altogether good, since they might lead to the erroneous conclusion that income is solely a function of sales effort. Yet, in reality, products are demanded because of form, time, and place utilities added. All efforts are necessary to the final result and, as previously pointed out, the closer accountants can come to making objective measurements as the economic activity (in the broadest sense) takes place, the more useful the results will be.

These so-called deviations are accepted and even encouraged by accountants because they result in a more rational reflection of economic activity.[8] Naturally, revenue (and, consequently, income) is not recognized (or at least should not be) before it is in existence, as stated earlier. But if the goal is to measure economic activity as it progresses, then recognition (timing of recording) is a function of measurement and not a basic or central problem of realization. As soon as objective measurement is possible, realization has occurred and recognition should follow automatically.

As to questions of whether the item has to be in distributable form, severed from capital, and in the form of liquid assets, we see little justification, conceptually or practically, for these criteria being a part of the realization concept.[9] Accepting a given definition of income, whatever it may be, the nature of the asset change is irrelevant. For example, assume a building was accepted in exchange for the products of an entity—products resulting from its primary activity. Certainly this is an income-type event so the only question is whether the income should not be recorded simply because of the nature of the asset received. Many would argue against such recognition. Yet, the entity would only accept the building if it wanted it, if management felt it would be useful in carrying out the entity objectives. If cash were received for the products and then reinvested in the building, few would argue against recognizing revenue (and income) on the sale of the products. One could reasonably assume an intermediate cash transaction even in the direct exchange example and come to the same conclusion. Further, if these requirements were followed any number

---

[8]See, for example:
   a. American Institute of Certified Public Accountants, A.R.B. No. 43, p. 34, and A.R.B. No. 45, pp. 4–5.
   b. W. A. Paton, *Accounting Theory*, The Ronald Press Company, 1922, p. 461.

[9]In this we agree with the 1964 Concepts and Standards Research Committee, "The Realization Concept," *The Accounting Review*, April, 1965, who state, p. 313, "the Committee would stress measurability, and not liquidity, as the essential attribute required for recognition of realized revenue." Also see, Harold E. Arnett, "Recognition as a Function of Measurement in the Realization Concept," *The Accounting Review*, October, 1963.

of procedures presently being followed in practice would have to be dropped, e.g., using the equity method of carrying the investment in certain unconsolidated subsidiaries. "Liquidity" and "distributable form" have been insisted upon, at least partially, to prevent management from depleting its working capital position through the payment of dividends and/or, perhaps, from paying dividends from capital. These are not very good reasons for insisting on these as criteria of the realization concept. There are better ways of measuring uncertainty reduction. Accounting is needed to help management make decisions, not to make decisions for management. If the facts are clearly disclosed as to the nature of the asset increases, management has the information to make enlightened, informed decisions as to dividend declarations and working capital maintenance. Whether or not such decisions are made, is outside the area of accounting. The same things are true regarding the criterion "severed from capital," with one additional point. Certainly capital (however defined) must be maintained before there is income, but reflecting this capital maintenance is a question of matching, not of realization.

Also, the Committee feels, as a general principle, that the entity need not be a party to the market transaction before realized income is recognized, although in many specific cases this might be necessary before reliable measurement is possible. Again, we feel it would be inconsistent to require the entity to be a party to a market transaction as a basis for recording certain transactions or events and not others. For example, adjustments for the changing value of the dollar would not be possible if this requirement were invoked in all cases. Further, many acceptable allocation and estimation procedures in accounting, such as recording depreciation and estimating bad debts, would not be possible under such a requirement. Here, we disagree with the 1964 Realization Concepts Committee.[10]

Consequently, assuming a given definition of income, if Alternative III is to be attained the only question for realization is one of recognition (timing), i.e., when should the income be reflected in the financial statements? This, in turn, is a question of measurement, i.e., in a world of uncertainty at what point can income be measured with sufficient reliability to warrant entering it into the accounts and reporting it in the income statement?

No basic attempt has been made here to determine all the events with which accountants should concern themselves. Such questions are subservient to more basic ones such as: What should be the concept of the accounting entity? What is capital? What is income? The realization concept developed here merely holds that these events should be recognized (reported) as soon as they can be objectively measured, whatever they are, and this means as soon as they are substantiated or capable of being substantiated by an independent, competent investigator. The possibility for such recognition may range all the way from a cash receipts and disbursements basis to a full accretion basis, depending upon the circumstances. In any case, the goal of measuring economic activity as it progresses should be approached as closely as prevailing economic conditions and statistical techniques will allow. Considering an intermediary to that goal, such as the credit sale, as the goal itself, can only result in thwarting the most useful presentations being made to all parties at interest. This does

[10]*Ibid.*, p. 315.

not deny its importance in any given set of circumstances, but its importance is determined by the circumstances, not independently of them.

A step in the right direction might be taken if it becomes accepted that the question of realization is a question of measurement only. Recognition (the timing of recording) would then be subservient to, or better still, a function of measurement. Perhaps an even better way of stating it, is that the realization concept should be dropped, or at least the word "realization." Recognition of income (however defined) would depend on reliable measurement only. This would place emphasis where we feel it belongs, and eliminate many irrelevant arguments.

Measurement Criteria

Having reached this point of asserting that realization should depend only upon reliable measurement, we still need to establish criteria for judging when this can be done. In other words, part of the charge of the committee is to develop criteria to indicate when the sales point is not an appropriate point for income (or loss) recognition. The following general conclusion has been reached.

> *The sales point is an appropriate point for income (or loss) recognition only when income (or loss) cannot fulfill the requirements of measurement at an earlier point. A corollary, of course, is that in some circumstances income (or loss) cannot be recognized until beyond the sales point. Circumstances should determine, however, not arbitrary rules.*

Of course, in those situations, where all reasonably possible recognition points would give nearly the same results, the sales point might be chosen because it is easier and less costly to use. We have no argument with this. Now to the criteria.

We start again with a preceding report.

> Examples of the broad criteria to be considered are "an exchange transaction between independent parties, or on established trade practices, or on the terms of a contract performance of which is considered to be virtually certain. It may depend on the stability of a banking system, the enforceability of commercial agreements, or the ability of a highly organized market to facilitate the conversion of an asset into another form.[11]

As we see it, what accountants attempt to do conceptually is to measure the entity's anticipated net cash inflows (outflows). Even though attempting to apply this concept to practical affairs would be highly subjective, depending as it would upon estimates of the amount and timing of future inflows and outflows and on appropriate discount rates to use, we nevertheless feel it should act as a standard for aiding and directing accountants in what they do.[12] It should always be kept in mind as an ideal goal to shoot for since it would aid

[11]*Accounting and Reporting Standards for Corporate Financial Statements*, 1957 Revision, American Accounting Association, p. 3.

[12]See pp. 220–221 for an illustration calculating the present value of anticipated net cash flows under uncertainty. Such calculations might prove useful under either the Alternative III (Binary) or Alternative IV (Polymeric) methods of treating uncertainty in the determination of net income.

in selecting surrogate measures to use in its place. Not having or not keeping this in mind as a basic goal or standard has resulted in irrational decisions in accounting over the years, we feel, with regard to such things an asset measurement (for example, had accountants concentrated on this objective with regard to franchise accounting, the receivable and income might not have been so badly overstated as they were in many cases).

Of course, more specific criteria are needed. They could be listed for consideration almost without end, but the following are important examples:

1. Credit rating of both buyer and seller.
2. Length of time over which the event takes place.
3. Re-marketability of the item being transferred.
4. Enforceability of the contract.
5. Materiality of the item or transaction in relation to the seller's total business.
6. Extent of past business experience of both buyer and seller.
7. Discreteness and independence of transactions.
8. Necessary expenditures of the seller in order to collect or retain funds involved in the transaction.
9. Business capabilities of the buyer and seller.
10. Unusual uniqueness of the activity or undertaking.
11. Financial terms or arrangements, i.e., easy credit terms, low down payments, extended payment periods.

The interdependence, interrelationships, and relative weightings of such criteria depend on the facts of the particular case, and are likely to vary substantially between cases. Accordingly, the accountant needs to be free to exercise, and must exercise, sound judgment to decide when reliable measurement is possible, and income (or loss) recognition is therefore dictated.

Judgment. Certainly, this still does not indicate exactly how these *specific* criteria are to be used for determining when the sales point is appropriate for income (or loss) recognition. The Committee feels it should not attempt to be too specific for the following reasons.

1. Business events and transactions are becoming increasingly complex and multidimensional in their nature. Our practical experience being limited, it is difficult for us to visualize the number and type of specifics that might arise in a business activity, even if we felt it was desirable to do so.
2. When we hold that income should be considered realized when reliably measurable, we recognize that we are moving along a continuum between absolute uncertainty and absolute certainty. At what point along the continuum the degree of certainty in terms of expected cash flows is reached where income can be thought of as realized, depends upon the circumstances of the particular case, and these can vary in number and relative weighting in an almost unlimited manner. Consequently, we feel that any criteria established, if they are to be effective, need to be relative broad standards which give direction, rather than specific rules that force conclusions regardless of circumstances.

These lead to the following proposition.

Judgment is the foundation of accounting. Criteria established, therefore, should encourage the use of effective judgment, not decrease it.

Judgment is, and must be, the foundation of accounting. The ability to exercise sound judgment is increasing in importance because the increasing complexities of the business world and the events attaching thereto make specific rules inapplicable in numerous real-world settings. Judgment must be emphasized, and efforts increased to make it effective, so accountants can make reasoned and informed decisions as circumstances alter. In carrying out his professional responsibilities good judgment can only exist where there is adequate education, adherence to ethical standards, independence, sufficient experience, and reasonable standards of performance. Anyone can have all of these qualities and exercise bad judgment, true, but good judgment in accounting matters is impossible without them. Present rule-setting practices may encourage practicing accountants to abdicate the proper exercise of effective judgment. And court cases appear to be emphasizing this need for individual judgment in the circumstances.

The first law for accountants was not compliance with generally accepted accounting principles but, rather, full and fair disclosure, fair presentation and, if principles did not produce this brand of disclosure, accountants could not hide behind the principles but had to go behind them and make whatever disclosures were necessary for full disclosure.[13]

As an example, regarding franchise accounting, the Committee feels that adequate criteria were available for practicing accountants to make good judgments regarding the handling of franchise fees. However, it seems they followed a "sales point" rule regardless of the circumstances, and even though this might have been satisfactory under certain circumstances, franchise agreements vary so much on a case by case basis that much over-all bad accounting resulted. In a word, one realization rule of accounting for franchise fees cannot be supported, because all franchise agreements and all participants in franchise agreements are not the same, legally, financially, nor economically. The facts of each case must be weighed to determine whether the point on the continuum between uncertainty and certainty had been reached where reliable measurement was possible and income (or loss) recognition thereby required.

Certainly this emphasis on and responsibility for the exercise of individual judgment has import far beyond the constraints of our charge, in terms of such things as staff training programs of C.P.A. firms, reshaping curricula and teaching methods at universities, and screening for entrance into the profession. Here we simply hold that individual judgment must play a critical role in determining when the sale of a firm's product, service, or property is and is not an appropriate event for the recognition of profit (or loss).

MULTI-DIMENSIONAL ANALYSIS AND REPORTING— POLYMERIC (ALTERNATIVE IV)

In this section we explore two alternative methods for broadening the treatment of uncertainty in accounting statements. In terms of Figure 1, the methods to be discussed relate to Alternative IV (multidimensional analysis and reporting techniques). The specific methods discussed are (1) the separation of the concepts of recognition and realization, and (2) full-scale probabilistic statements.

Separating Recognition and Realization

The traditional realization concept in accounting represents a method for treating the uncertainty that surrounds enterprise performance, but treats this uncertainty in a binary fashion. That is, for reporting purposes, realization is treated as occurring at a single moment in time when the uncertainty imbedded in a financial event is reduced below some acceptable threshhold level. Determining when this threshhold is reached necessitates the exercise of professional judgment. Until this threshhold is reached, uncertainty is deemed to be too high to warrant *any* income reflection of the item in the accounts. After this threshhold is achieved—that it, after uncertainty has been reduced to some acceptable level—then the event is deemed to be realized and is recorded in the accounts and presented in the financial statements.

The treatment accorded uncertainty under traditional realization rules, thus, is an oversimplification of reality in many instances. Uncertainty exists as a continuum in the real world, yet is treated in binary fashion in the accounting records.[14] Insofar as the events under analysis are complex and multidimensional, this simplified accounting treatment may not provide statement users with sufficient detail to facilitate their own analysis of uncertainty and its impact on future results. Furthermore, the threshhold of uncertainty reduction is subjectively derived by the accountant. When the users' views of uncertainty and its impact on periodic performance differ from those of the accountant, the binary reflection of uncertainty levels may not be adequate to allow users to transform the accountant's estimates to accord with their information needs.

An alternative approach is to broaden the realization distinctions made within the accounts themselves. For example, rather than retaining a single threshhold level of uncertainty reduction as a vehicle for income realization, dual uncertainty levels could be introduced. To illustrate, one might accord initial account recognition to an external event when the uncertainty level is still relatively high—that is, a potential income effect may be *recognized* in the accounts earlier than is presently done—but *realization* may be deferred until a somewhat lower uncertainty level is achieved. The net effect of this approach is threefold. First, a differentiation between recognition and realization is introduced into the accounts and reports. Second, because of this differentiation, more uncertainty can be tolerated at the moment of recognition (i.e., the threshhold level of uncertainty can be relaxed), thus fostering a quicker account re-

---

[13]U.S. Second Court of Appeals, Judge Henry J. Friendly in the Continental Vending decision. *U.S. vs. Simon*, 425 F2d 796, (2d Cir. 1969).

[14]Horngren summarizes this position as follows:

The extreme position is that recognition and realization are indistinguishable concepts. That is, "if it can be booked, it's realized." In other words, there is no such concept as unrealized revenue or unrealized income; it is an either/or world.

See Charles T. Horngren, "How Should We Interpret the Realization Concept?", *The Accounting Review*, April, 1965, p. 324.

flection of *potential* income-producing events. Third, the threshhold level of uncertainty required for realization can be made more stringent, thus reducing the possibility of premature and erroneous income realization and reflection in the income statement. In many respects, this approach is an extension of that suggested by the 1964 Research Study Committee on the Realization Concept.[15]

This approach can be illustrated in the following fashion. Consider the case of a franchisor who has "sold" a franchise for $10,000 during the current period. Assume the following: (1) the franchisee paid $1,000 cash and signed a note for $9,000 which bears interest at 10% and is to be paid in 10 equal annual installments (the franchisee expects to repay the note from cash generated by successful operation of the franchise); (2) there has been complete performance by the franchisor of his obligations under the franchise agreement and the cost of these services provided to the franchisee totaled $7,000; (3) the collectability of the note is somewhat uncertain since collectability is a function of the success to be achieved by the franchise outlet; (4) the franchisor lacks sufficient experience with notes of this type to estimate its collectability with a high degree of assurance.

If we assume that the uncertainty still associated with the note is greater than the threshhold level required for balance sheet valuation (and, hence, income realization), then existing practice might defer all costs incurred, assign no value to the note, and treat the cash receipts as a deposit. The potential income impact of this transaction is thus omitted from the accounting records until the uncertainty associated with the note is reduced to at least the threshhold level. This desire to avoid recognizing a value for the note is understandable since uncertainty is high; furthermore, recording a value for the note will often necessitate the recognition of revenue from the transaction—a somewhat objectionable result, given the assumed high uncertainty associated with eventual collection. On the other hand, by failing to assign a value to the note, existing practice will generally not reflect a potential income-generating transaction at the earliest possible moment. Thus, under existing accounting practices, transactions of this type give rise to significant trade-off effects; a liberal valuation rule for the note would tend to suggest revenue realization despite the uncertainties of the situation, while a conservative valuation rule would tend to ignore the potential income impact of a legitimate, arms-length market transaction. Neither approach is particularly appealing.

The bifurcation of the traditional realization concept into separate recognition and realization components suggests one means for alleviating this dilemma. Following this approach, asset value recognition would cease to automatically imply income realization. Accordingly, one could relax the threshhold uncertainty level for attaching a value to the note receivable. That is, since income *realization* will not automatically follow from the assignment of a value to the note, the adverse consequences of overstatement are reduced and values could be assigned under more uncertain conditions than at present. The essential effect of this process would be to accelerate the speed with which certain changes in asset and liability valuations are recognized in the accounts. The fact that valuation changes would be recognized under somewhat more uncertain conditions means that a relatively liberal policy of recognition would be

[15]1964 Concepts and Standards Research Study Committee, "The Realization Concept," *The Accounting Review*, April, 1965, pp. 312–322.

used. Valuation changes would be recognized at the earliest possible moment (i.e., relative to existing practice, we would be willing to tolerate more uncertainty in setting the initial recognition threshhold level) and users would be apprised of impending income flows at a point in time closer to the occurrence of the underlying events that give rise to these flows.

Before a value change would be deemed to be *realized*, however, the uncertainty associated with the change would have to be reduced to a low level. Indeed, the threshhold level to which uncertainty must fall before realization can take place conceivably could be much lower than the existing realization threshhold. That is, if we subdivide the existing realization concept into recognition and realization components, then the criteria for the new realization test could be much more stringent than those currently required for realization. The reason is straightforward. At present, the realization threshhold represents a compromise between our conflicting desires to recognize value changes at the earliest moment and to defer booking income until the probability of its eventual receipt is quite high. But once recognition and realization are separated, this conflicting trade-off is no longer present. That is, the liberalized recognition test is used to reflect value changes as soon as it is feasible to do so. Under this system, realization serves but one purpose—to inform the reader that the probability of receiving recognized value changes is now almost certain. Given this single purpose, it is entirely appropriate to institute a very stringent realization threshhold.

As a result, the separation of recognition and realization is seen to serve a two-fold purpose. First, it accelerates the recognition of probable value changes and thus provides users with the earliest possible recognition of events that are expected to have an eventual income effect. Second, it defers realization of previously recognized value changes until the probability of non-realization is quite low. Since the uncertainty threshholds for recognition and realization differ, the simple binary treatment of uncertainty which exists in current practice could be abandoned.

The primary effect of bifurcating the traditional realization concept into separate recognition and realization components is to broaden the treatment of uncertainty in the accounting records. Under the proposed system when particular transactions extend over a lengthy period, recognition of value changes might take place at one uncertainty level, and these value changes would be deemed to be realized when a different uncertainty level is achieved.

Following this approach, the income statement could appear as follows (although other disclosure possibilities exist):

> Revenue recognized during the period
> *Less: Expenses recognized during the period*
> Operating income recognized during the period
> Less: Income recognized but not realized during the period
> *Plus: Income recognized in prior periods but realized during the period*
> Operating income realized during the period

Once a clear distinction between recognition and realization is introduced into the income statement, it becomes relatively easy to extend this distinction in another direction. Specifically, the 1964 Concepts and Standards Research Study Committee on the Realization Concept suggested a demarcation between operating profits and holding gains. They suggested that holding gains be recognized at the earliest time at which such gains are measurable, that is, when market price movements occur. They further suggested that these gains be treated as realized only when the firm has "validated" the price change by itself engaging in a market transaction that severs the asset or utilizes it in production activities.[16] This procedure, like our suggestion above, also results in a distinction between recognition and realization. Here, the distinction between recognition and realization is dependent not on uncertainty levels, but rather on whether the firm for whom the accounting is undertaken was itself a party to the transaction. If it was, the gain is realized; if it was not, the gain is merely recognized.

Full-Scale Probabilistic Statements

As indicated earlier in the report, the Committee regards the basic problem of realization as dealing with the means of analyzing and reporting the impact of uncertainty on accounting reports. Ultimately, some members of the Committee believe that a more direct assessment of the impact of uncertainty, relying on statistical and other measurement techniques, will be applied. Also, fundamental to accounting reports and their use is the estimation of an entity's anticipated net future cash flows.

For the moment there are too many unresolved issues for the Committee to recommend reports directly incorporating the impact of uncertainty. The Committee believes that the forms of such reporting and the measures of uncertainty to be applied are properly the focus of considerable additional future research. Some of the issues which must be addressed include the following.

1. What will be the form of such a report? Will it emphasize changes in value rather than the traditional revenue-expense categories? How should the changes in value be classified?[17]
2. How shall the future cash flows be predicted? It is assumed that net cash flows for any year will be a random variable operating within some probability distribution. How does one determine the appropriate probability distribution and its parameters? Certain of the cash flows will be dependent on other cash flows of the same and prior periods. This lack of independence complicates the statistical problems considerably. Some of the dependence can be dealt with by focusing on net cash flows. How importantly are the final results influenced by the dependencies? In general, how do the distributions change from one period to the next? Little research on these subjects has been reported. One interesting application to an existing business situation, dealing with some of these problems, was reported by Shank.[18]
3. Even when research suggests a general format of a report and the means of predicting future net cash flows with their associated probabilities,

[16]*Ibid.*, pp. 318–322.

[17]These issues were explored in John C. Gray, *Service Potential Enterprises: A Report of Discounted Cash Flow to Investors*, University Microfilms, Inc., Ann Arbor, Michigan, 1963, pp. 93–95.

[18]John Shank, "Income Determination Under Uncertainty: An Application of Markov Chains," *The Accounting Review*, January, 1971, pp. 57–74.

how specifically should the results be reported? Should the accountant use the cash flow data and the associated probabilities to reduce the probability distributions to a single value, such as the mean or mode, and use these single values in preparing the report? This would probably lead to the simplest possible report, but would force the accountant to choose which single value best represents the total distribution for each year. Another possibility would be to report confidence intervals or ranges in which the true values are likely to lie. Another position would be to prepare reports on the single value basis but provide enough statistical data on the underlying distributions of net cash flow that the user can develop confidence intervals as desired.

No report incorporating the effect of uncertainty can be prepared without answers to the issues and sub-issues raised above. While the Committee feels that considerable research must be done before answers can be offered to these questions, an illustration of one possibility may be helpful.

To keep the illustration within easily describable bounds, an enterprise with a life of three years is assumed. The statements are based on reducing a discrete probability distribution for each year to a single value, the mean, and then the present worth of the means are discounted to find a present value of the future cash flows. As a firm proceeds through its three-year life, the present value of the firm changes because the cash flows draw one year nearer and *also* because the mean or actual cash flow is different from the means used in the discounting process in prior years. Thus, in this simple situation, two components of net income can be distinguished. By assuming that all of the initial investment of the firm is invested in depreciable assets and that they are to be depreciated following the straight line method,[19] a conventional accounting net income based on 100% realization at the point of sale can be determined and compared to the results of the income computed following the method incorporating uncertainty directly.

The basic data used in developing the net incomes is shown in Table 1.

The comparison of the two net incomes is shown on pg. 491.

T_0 indicates the time at which the investment is made and $T_1 - T_0$ indicates the time between T_1 and T_0 or the first year. Note that since the present value of the expected values for each year exceeds the investment by $3,695, there is this amount of income recognized immediately. In effect this is the income earned by the entrepreneural activity of forming the business. In subsequent years the income is attributable to two main factors. The change in present value is basically the normal return on investment for the capital committed to the enterprise at the assumed 10% rate of return. The income attributable to changes in expected value would probably be subdivided in ways useful to management and investors. For example, some of the income may be attributable to changes in the environment which are viewed as being basically beyond the control of management. Other parts of this income might be attributable to specific management actions and might be reported as such.

[19]Note that aside from income tax computations, these assumptions are not necessary to the proposed computations. Thus, in this respect, the proposed computation is simpler than conventional methods.

TABLE 1
Cash Flows from Illustrative Investment
Initial Investment $114,000

		NCF	Prob.	NCF	Prob.	NCF	Prob.	EV
				AT PERSPECTIVE t_0				
End of yr.	1	30,000	(.2)	50,000	(.7)	90,000	(.1)	50,000
	2	40,000	(.3)	70,000	(.6)	80,000	(.1)	62,000
	3	20,000	(.3)	30,000	(.6)	40,000	(.1)	28,000
				AT PERSPECTIVE t_1				
End of yr.	1			55,000	(1.0)			55,000
	2	50,000	(.4)	80,000	(.5)	90,000	(.1)	69,000
	3	30,000	(.3)	40,000	(.6)	50,000	(.1)	38,000
				AT PERSPECTIVE t_2				
End of yr.	1							
	2			75,000	(1.0)			75,000
	3	30,000	(.1)	45,000	(.9)	0		43,500
				AT PERSPECTIVE t_3				
End of yr.	1							
	2							
	3			42,000	(1.0)			42,000

The conventional accounting net income is derived by taking the actual cash inflow for each of the three years and subtracting straight line depreciation of $38,000 for each year.

It must again be stated that the Committee is not recommending at this point this type of reporting. But this is offered as an illustration of one possible means of reporting which would incorporate the impact of uncertainty directly.

CONCLUSIONS

The basic charge of the Committee was to determine when the sales point is and is not an appropriate event for the recognition of profit (or loss) in the accounts and financial statements. The Committee considered this question to be encompassed in the broader problem of dealing with uncertainty, and so approached the charge on this broader scale.

It soon became apparent that the Committee could not reach substantive agreement on any one particular solution to the question of "what should be done" in dealing with uncertainty. A number of reasonable possibilities arose during our deliberations. In the interest of full disclosure and with the hope that research ideas might be generated therefrom, we decided to present these alternatives rather than to choose one position as that of the majority, with accompanying minority reports and statements. In this light we hope the report will be of some usefulness.

COMPUTATION OF NET INCOME ON UNCERTAINTY BASIS
AT T_0 $117,695 $-$ 114,000 = $\underline{\$3,695}$

$T_1 - T_0$ Changes

EV_1	55,000 $-$ 50,000	= + 5,000 × 1.0 =	5,000
EV_2	69,000 $-$ 62,000	= + 7,000 × .909 =	6,363
EV_3	38,000 $-$ 28,000	= +10,000 × .826 =	$\underline{8,260}$
			19,623

PV	50,000 (1 $-$ .909)	= 4,550	
	62,000 (.909 $-$ .826)	= 5,147	
	28,000 (.826 $-$ .751)	= $\underline{2,100}$	$\underline{11,797}$
			$\underline{31,420}$

$T_2 - T_1$ Changes

EV_2 =	75,000 $-$ 69,000	= 6,000 × 1.0 =	6,000
EV_3 =	43,500 $-$ 38,000	= 5,500 × .909 =	$\underline{5,000}$
			11,000

PV	69,000 (1 $-$ .909)	= 6,276	
	38,000 (.909 $-$ .826)	= 3,154	$\underline{9,430}$
			$\underline{20,430}$

$T_3 - T_1$ Changes

EV	(42,000 $-$ 43,500) × 1	$-1,500$
	43,500 (1.000 $-$ .909) =	$\underline{3,955}$
		$\underline{2,455}$

Σ ENI = 3,695 + 31,420 + 20,430 + 2,455 = $\underline{58,000}$

Time	Conventional Accounting Net Income	Net Income Incorporating Present Value and Uncertainty Directly		
		Change in Expected Value	Change in Present Value	Total
T_0	$0		$ 3,695	$ 3,695
$T_1 - T_0$	$17,000	$19,623	11,797	31,420
$T_2 - T_1$	37,000	11,000	9,430	20,430
$T_3 - T_2$	$\underline{4,000}$	$\underline{(1,500)}$	$\underline{3,955}$	$\underline{2,455}$
Total	$\underline{\$58,000}$	$\underline{\$29,123}$	$\underline{\$28,877}$	$\underline{\$58,000}$

A Theoretical Foundation for Leases and Other Executory Contracts

JOSEPH F. WOJDAK

According to the Accounting Principles Board, "The rights and obligations related to unperformed portions of executory contracts are not recognized as assets and liabilities in financial statements as presently understood."[1] Yet, many have advocated the capitalization of long-term leases and other executory contracts such as purchase commitments, employment contracts and the like.[2] "Information about such contracts is clearly relevant to a host of decisions involving stewardship, changes in management, credit extension, and investment decisions."[3] Financial position is affected materially since various asset and liability totals change after capitalization of these contracts. Corresponding changes occur in debt to equity relationships, rates of return calculated on the basis of total assets, and the like. Indeed, recognition of executory contracts as assets and liabilities significantly affects a large number of traditional financial ratios. A great deal more needs to be done in terms of assessing the informational value of capitalized executory contracts. However, it may be that information on assets and liabilities arising under executory contracts is as relevant to statement users' decisions as is information on any other assets and liabilities.

PURPOSE OF PAPER

Before capitalization is proposed, two preliminary tasks should be undertaken. First, the relevance and usefulness to financial statement users' decisions of capitalizing executory contracts must be logically and empirically establilshed. Moreover, very specific capitalization criteria must eventually be developed and simultaneously rules of measurement must be determined. Second, existing concepts of assets, liabilities, etc., must be expanded or refined to accommodate executory contracts.

Joseph F. Wojdak, "A Theoretical Foundation for Leases and Other Executory Contracts," *The Accounting Review* July 1969, pp. 562–570. Reprinted with the permission of *The Accounting Review*.

[1]Accounting Principles Board, "Reporting of Leases in Financial Statements of Lessees," *Opinion No. 5* (American Institute of Certified Public Accounts, September 1965) p. 30. It is interesting to note that governmental units have always recorded executory contracts upon entering into such contracts and before performance has taken place.

[2]See for example Gordon Shillinglaw, "More on Doubtful Areas in Lease Capitalization." *NAA Bulletin* (November 1962), p. 12 and also Committee to Prepare a Statement of Basic Accounting Theory, *A Statement of Basic Accounting Theory* (American Accounting Association, 1966), pp. 32–33.

[3]Committee to Prepare a Statement of Basic Accounting Theory, *op. cit.*, p. 32.

With respect to the first of these tasks, the 1966 AAA Committee to Prepare a Statement of Basic Accounting Theory stated that many executory contracts which "present accounting generally ignores" are relevant, useful, financial information.[4] Accordingly, this Committee recommended the reporting of a number of executory contracts "in dollar terms in the regular framework of the statements."[5]

Given the relevance of executory contracts, this paper takes up the second task. It is maintained that within the context of generally accepted accounting principles a theoretical foundation exists to serve as a basis for recording leases and other executory contracts. In particular, such a foundation permits the capitalization of leases because they represent measurable and recordable assets and liabilities rather than because they are "analogous to" or "like" installment purchases of property. Analogy is a rather weak form of argument.

RELEVANT ASSET CONCEPT

Perhaps the most popular concept today emphasizes that assets are rights to future service potentials or rights to expected future economic benefits. Sprouse and Moonitz state the concept very concisely.

> Assets represent expected future economic benefits, rights to which have been acquired by the enterprise as a result of some current or past transaction.[6]

The long history of the future service potential concept of assets shows that it was utilized by writers such as Sprague, Canning, Paton and Littleton, Vatter, and more recently, the AAA Committee on Concepts and Standards in their 1957 statement.[7] For example, Canning defined an asset as:

> ...any future service in money or any future service convertible into money (except those services arising from contracts the two sides of which are proportionately unperformed) the beneficial interest in which is legally or equitably secured to some person or set of persons.[8]

Interestingly, Canning did feel that his definition would be improved, or more useful to all concerned, if the parenthetical material were eliminated.[9] The implication is, of course, that executory contracts would also be included in the definition of assets.

This paper adopts the Sprouse/Moonitz definition of assets. A slight modification must be made before it can be said to accommodate executory contracts

[4]*Ibid.*

[5]*Ibid.*

[6]Robert T. Sprouse and Maurice Moonitz, "A Tentative Set of Broad Accounting Principles for Business Enterprises," *Accounting Research Study No. 3* (American Institute of Certified Public Accountants, 1962), p. 20.

[7]*Ibid.*, pp. 19–20.

[8]John B. Canning, *The Economics of Accountancy* (The Ronald Press Company, 1929), p. 22.

[9]*Ibid.*

satisfactorily. Needless to say, Professors Sprouse and Moonitz would not necessarily agree with this modification.

ASSET ELEMENTS

There are at least three important elements in this asset definition which may not be entirely obvious:

1. A current or past *transaction.*
2. *Expected* future economic benefits or service potentials.[10]
3. *Rights* to those expected benefits or potentials.

An expanded discussion of the first two of these elements, as they relate to executory contracts, follows. At the time of entering into a contract the parties exchange legal and economic rights. Thus, it seems unnecessary to elaborate further on whether or not rights (third element) are acquired by the parties to a contract.

TRANSACTIONS CONCEPTS

Transactions have always been the basic input into the accounting system. Generally accepted definitions of accounting[11] and the works of numerous individual writers have focused on the importance of transactions:

> The activities of the specific business enterprise, with respect to which the accountant must supply pertinent information, consist largely of exchange transactions with other enterprises. Accounting undertakes to express these exchanges quantitatively. The basic subject matter of accounting is therefore the measured consideration involved in exchange activities. . . .[12]

According to the traditional view, a transaction might be defined as a "a de facto exchange of value between the entity under observation and another party."[13] Most writers would not consider that entering into an executory contract constitutes an accounting transaction.[14]

[10]The phrases "expected future economic benefits" and "service potentials" are taken to be identical in meaning and are used interchangeably throughout the discussion.

[11]For example, in ARB No. 43, accounting was defined as "the art of recording, classifying and summarizing in a significant manner and in terms of money, transactions and events which are, in part at least, of a financial character, and interpreting the results thereof." Transactions were similarly emphasized in the definition of accounting put forth in Paul Grady, "Inventory of Generally Accepted Accounting Principles," *Accounting Research Study No. 7* (American Institute of Certified Public Accountants, 1965) p. 4.

[12]W. A. Paton and A. C. Littleton, *An Introduction to Corporate Accounting Standards,* (American Accounting Association, 1940). pp. 11–12.

[13]William J. Schrader, "An Inductive Approach to Accounting Theory," *The Accounting Review* (October 1962), p. 646. See also Alfred Kuhn, *The Study of Society: A Unified Approach* (Richard D. Irwin, Inc. and The Dorsey Press, Inc., 1963), p. 317, where a transaction is similarly defined as "any exchange of goods between two parties, and the accompanying negotiations,"; or George R. Husband and William J. Schlatter, *Introductory Accounting* (Pitman Publishing Company, 1949), p. 25, who define transactions as "those business experiences in which there is an economic exchange of equal values."

Expanded Transactions Concept—A transaction is basically an exchange of values (economic benefits) and it is suggested that entering into an executory contract constitutes an accounting transaction. Particularly in the case of leases, some writers, notably Rappaport, maintain that an exchange of legally enforceable promises or rights gives rise to assets and liabilities under the transaction concept.[15] Rappaport suggests further "that the prevailing transaction concept be extended to accommodate the recognition of lease contracts and other comparable commitments."[16]

Vatter lends strong support to this position:

> The lease is a complete transaction. The relations established by the contract are positive and specific; even though certain acts are unperformed, the arrangement is incomplete only in the sense that it involves future time. . . . There are definite obligations created by the contract; these, since they can be enforced in the same way as other business commitments, have all the attributes of liabilities.
>
> The counterparts to those liabilities are perfectly valid assets. The lessor's right to compensation is an enforceable money claim, which is unquestionably an asset. The lessee's right to use the property is a claim on service-potentials . . . acquisitions of service potentials establish these assets. . . .[17]

In Vatter's view the execution of a lease contract involves an exchange of property rights giving rise to assets and liabilities under the transaction concept. His analysis seems entirely applicable to other types of executory contracts.

The service potential of an economic good or resource lies in its ability to enhance the future operations of the enterprise, whether that be in the form of increasing the income stream or aiding in the achievement of some other objective. Normally, an enterprise would not enter into a contract unless valuable rights to expected benefits were received under that contract. These rights can be seen in a negative way. A company, which was not able to operate at full capacity because it failed to enter into a contract which would guarantee supply, can easily appreciate the economic benefits which arise under a purchase contract. Likewise, the company which does not produce as a result of a labor strike would hardly argue that the rights received under the labor contract provide no value or benefit. Measuring the value of these rights is, of course, a separate problem, but should not prove to be any more difficult than measuring the value of many other recorded assets.

[14]Husband and Schlatter, *op. cit.* See also Arthur Lowes Dickinson, *Accounting Practices and Procedures*, (The Ronald Press Company, 1913), p. 147, and also William A. Paton and Robert L. Dixon, *Essentials of Accounting*, (The Macmillan Company, 1958), p. 62. In contrast, Professor Schrader (Footnote 13) would agree that entering into a contract constitutes an accounting transaction.

[15]Alfred Rappaport, "Lease Capitalization and the Transaction Concept," *The Accounting Review* (April 1965), pp. 373–76. Others have maintained that entering into or executing a lease agreement constitutes an accounting transaction which should be recorded in the accounts. For example, see Gerald Alvin, "The Execution of the Nonfinancial Lease—An Accounting Transaction?" *NAA Bulletin* (November 1963), pp. 39–46.

[16]*Ibid.*, p. 373.

[17]William J. Vatter, "Accounting for Leases," *Journal of Accounting Research* (Autumn 1966), p. 135.

Additionally, the fact that contract rights can be sold supports the position that they are recordable, economic benefits. Purchase contracts, leases, stock options and the like, can usually be sold. For example, a firm may enter into a purchase contract to receive 100 units of X product at $1 per unit. If the rights acquired under the contract can be sold for $100 (or any other amount) to another party, it is obvious that the purchase contract has economic value or benefit and is, therefore, an asset. Certainly, any contract (or more precisely the rights to service potentials acquired under contract) which can be sold is a recordable asset. In sum, every executory contract changes the total economic rights acquired by the enterprise and changes the total of the economic obligations assumed by the enterprise.

The exchange of promises at the signing of the contract represents an exchange of rights to future service potentials and thus, is a valid point at which to recognize assets and liabilities. Indeed, the exchange of rights at the point of signing a contract may even be more relevant than a subsequent physical exchange of tangible property. Physical possession or physical exchange of economic goods and resources should not be reflected in financial statements unless the corresponding rights to those goods and resources have been simultaneously or previously exchanged. As pointed out earlier, unless the rights are transferred no asset is acquired or no corresponding liability is created.

The subsequent performance and rendering of services under the contract merely change slightly the form of the asset and corresponding liability; perhaps from an intangible to a tangible form. For example, if a long-term purchase contract was negotiated and signed, the right to the service potentials of the goods under the contract could be treated as an intangible asset receivable by the purchase, with a corresponding long-term liability. As the goods purchased under the contract are received, the asset form is converted from being merely goods or merchandise receivable to an inventory account. The corresponding long-term liability becomes a current liability to the extent of the payment required for goods delivered.

EXPECTATIONS/POTENTIALS

The adjectives "expected" and "future" as used in the asset definition adopted here, indicate that there is always some degree of uncertainty as to whether or not economic benefits or service potentials will actually result from economic goods and resources.[18] Thus, to a great extent assets are expectations or potentials.

Expectancy or potential is easily seen to be present in the case of executory contracts where, for example, the delivery of merchandise under a purchase contract is awaited, the receipt of employees' services under a labor contract is anticipated, or there is the expectation of using leased equipment, buildings or land. Uncertainty not only attaches to executory contracts, but also to the benefits to be derived from *all* economic goods and resources. It is not uncommon for conventional assets such as accounts receivable, inventory, investments and the like, to become worthless and provide no economic benefit. Further, there may not be a substantial difference in the degree of uncertainty attaching to the benefits expected from property which is leased as opposed to that which is owned outright. Likewise, there may be as high a degree of un-

[18]Sprouse and Moonitz, *op. cit.*, p. 20.

certainty attaching to the collection of an account receivable as attaches to the delivery of raw material under a purchase contract.

This uncertainty or expectation is very closely related to the traditional concept of the "going concern." Grady described this concept as follows:

> The complexities of present-day business operations, with their high degree of technology, require long-range planning and research. Operating facilities with long-lived usefulness must be acquired, often by incurring long-term debt. Labor contracts with long-term benefits, such as pensions, must be negotiated to assure the necessary manpower for operations. All of these factors support the basic proposition that business managements assume, and properly so, the indefinite continuation of operations.

> . . . It [a going concern] is nevertheless a unifying force behind a whole array of accounting practices and procedures in the so-called "normal" case. "Going concern" implies indefinite continuance. . . . Indefinite continuance means that the business will not be liquidated within a span of time necessary to carry out present contractual commitments. . . . This view makes the concept one of tentative judgment, subject to revision in the future as contractual agreements are changed and plans and expectations with respect to operations shift.[19]

Thus, the accountant cannot be preoccupied with the possibility of contracts being cancelled or with the possibility of firms being unable to perform under executory contracts. Unless there is evidence to the contrary, an assumption should be made that the firm and all business entities with which the firm is contractually related, will in fact carry out all commitments. The accountant has no alternative but to assume that executory contracts will be carried out, executed or performed and that the stipulated economic benefits or service potentials will in fact accrue to all parties under the contract.

On the basis of the preceding discussion a strong case can be made that when parties enter into a contract—the point at which there is an exchange of promises (transaction) giving rise to economic, legal and moral rights and obligations—rights to economic service potentials arise. The point at which this transaction or exchange takes place may thus be used to recognize the acquisition of assets and liabilities arising under a contract, if their value(s) can be measured with a satisfactory degree of objectivity. As with other assets, those arising under executory contracts should not be recorded in the accounts unless they are sufficiently measurable.

LIABILITY CONCEPT

The preceeding discussion lays the groundwork and makes the acceptance of the Sprouse/Moonitz liability definition an easy matter. Adopting the previously discussed interpretation of an accounting transaction the following definition, without further qualification, can be said to include liabilities arising under executory contracts.

> The liabilities of a business enterprise are its obligations to convey assets or perform services, obligations resulting from past or current transactions and requiring settlement in the future. The term "obligations" con-

---

[19]Grady, *op. cit.*, pp. 27–28.

notes a claim or series of claims against the business enterprise, each of which has a known or reasonably determinable maturity date and an independent value which is known or reasonably measurable.[20]

As is the case with assets, the value of a liability also must be known or reasonably measurable before its recording in the accounts is justified.

A number of other basic supporting issues are relevant to this discussion and are taken up in the remaining paragraphs.

POINT OF ASSET ACQUISITION

One of the more important issues underlying this problem deals with when to recognize future service potentials (assets) acquired under contract. Conventionally, accountants have restricted themselves to three dates for asset recognition: (1) date title passes, (2) date the goods or services are physically received, and (3) date cash is paid for the goods or services.[21] There is no reason why asset recognition should be restricted to these arbitrary dates. Rather, as noted by Bedford, goods or services should be recognized as having been acquired as soon as sufficient evidence is available to indicate the goods or services will be used by the enterprise, i.e., when an expected economic benefit is visible. This early recognition of goods and services results in a more complete presentation of accounting information in published reports. Furthermore, an early determination of total assets and liabilities is desirable in terms of giving investors and creditors a more complete picture of financial position. It gives them a more accurate reflection of the total economic services available for use during succeeding periods as well as the total demands on company resources to meet corresponding obligations.

To omit transactions because they do not coincide with one of the above arbitrary dates is to omit "significant information on resources effectively acquired" and results in failure to disclose as fully as possible the anticipated future actions of the enterprise.[22] In addition to leases, Bedford cites another illustrative case where an asset might properly be recognized upon entering into a contract.

> For example, mere discussion of the desirability of acquiring a certain type of machine would not be sufficient evidence to recognize that services in the machine were going to flow into the use of a specific business firm. On the other hand, the placing of an order for the machine might be sufficient evidence, for accounting purposes, to warrant treating the services in the machine as having been acquired.[23]

Goldberg has taken a similar position with respect to executory contracts:

> This suggests that the basis of the event to be recorded is a decision, and that whenever a decision is made which can be translated into suitable

[20]Sprouse and Moonitz, *op. cit.*, p. 37.

[21]Norton M. Bedford, *Income Determination Theory: An Accounting Framework* (Addison-Wesley Publishing Company, Inc., 1965), pp. 114–119.

[22]*Ibid.*, p. 116.

[23]*Ibid.*, pp. 114–115.

measurable terms it can be made the subject of record for accounting purposes. For example, the decision to buy an article may be recorded in the form of a purchase order. . . . In an enterprise with a substantial volume of activities, there is much to be said for incorporating in the accounting system a record of commitments arising from such purchase orders, as well as the more usual record of liabilities arising from the delivery of the goods ordered.[24]

Note that the value of an executory contract must be *suitably measurable* to be admitted to the accounting records. Likewise, Bedford and at least one other current writer have stated the principle that the acquisition of goods and services should be recognized as soon as the acquisition cost is known or measurable.[25] In addition:

> One might contend that acquisition cost is known as soon as the contract for the acquisition is accepted by both parties to a purchase and sale of services, and that this date should be used to recognize services acquired.[26]

Thus, in any proposal for capitalization of executory contracts, adequate recognition must be given to this measurability constraint. In the past, the most important reason for failing to record expectations has been the difficulty of measuring them objectively.[27] It has been shown that the concept of objectivity is at best, a vague and ill-defined concept.[28] The concept must be expanded simultaneously with advances in measurement techniques and new informational requirements of financial statement users.[29] These informational requirements may include capitalized executory contracts.

IMMEDIATE AVAILABILITY OF SERVICE POTENTIALS

Another important question which arises is concerned with whether the immediate availability of the use of the object's service potential is necessary to have acquired an asset. The asset definition being used in this paper does not require immediate availability. Only the expectation of services need be present. The two requirements of future service potentials and rights to those future service potentials can be present whether the object of the contract exists or not.

[24]Louis Goldberg, *An Inquiry Into the Nature of Accounting* (American Accounting Association, 1965), p. 214.

[25]See Robert C. Mogis, "Do Undisclosed Liabilities Distort Financial Statements?" *NAA Bulletin* (February 1961), p. 50, and Bedford, *op. cit.*

[26]Bedford, *op. cit.*, pp. 117–118. Bedford is primarily concerned with income determination rather than financial position. Thus, it is not clear as to whether or not he would consent to capitalizing executory contracts.

[27]R. J. Chambers, "Measurement and Objectivity in Accounting," *The Accounting Review* (April 1964), pp. 264–274.

[28]Harold E. Arnett, "What Does Objectivity Mean to Accountants?" *The Journal of Accountancy* (May 1961), pp. 63–68. See also, Edward J. Burke, "Objectivity and Accounting," *The Accounting Review* (October 1964), pp. 837–849.

[29]Paul E. Fertig, "Current Values and Index Numbers: The Problem of Objectivity," in Robert K. Jaedicke, Yuji Ijiri, and Oswald Nielson (editors), *Research in Accounting Measurement* (American Accounting Association, Collected Papers, 1966), pp. 137–149.

In the case of intangibles, the argument is unsatisfactory that they are not assets because they have no physical existence. The service potential of intangibles derives from the fact that people or institutions will act or refrain from acting in a certain manner which will in turn affect the income stream or other objectives of the enterprise. The service potentials as well as the rights to service potentials of intangibles exists then only in the minds of men. Hence, service potentials can exist prior to and independent of physical existence.

Since Canning had a similar point of view nearly forty years ago his comments are relevant to this discussion:

> Neither the corporeal existence of a material object nor anything necessarily associated with it suffices to make the object an asset . . . What is essential is that there must be some anticipated . . . services to be had . . . as a matter of legal or equitable right, from some person or object . . . One speaks of a motor truck owned by a corporation . . . But neither the legal title in the object nor the existence of the object, nor the two together, constitute the asset. That which is fundamental is that certain anticipated services of the truck will inure to the benefit of the corporation.[30]

In the case of tangible assets another interesting question arises. It is an inescapable fact that one can never be *certain* that service potentials will flow from an object until the services are actually abstracted from the object. It should be emphasized that "service potentials" are not "actual services." The asset definition used in this article does not require that actual services be present, only service potentials. Focus on the word "potential" in the asset definition and it is not inconceivable that the service potential of an uncreated object may be no less real or no less certain than the service potential of a created object.

For example, if a firm signs a contract to lease a building or have a building constructed, can the lessee or purchaser be said to have acquired an asset under the contract if the building has not yet been constructed? It must be conceded that an enterprise cannot *use* the services of a building which does not yet exist. However, the future service potential of the contract is not the building (tangible object of the contract), but rather the services which are *expected* to flow from this building. It might be maintained that whether or not the building is capable of providing services *now* is not relevant to the question of whether an asset exists under the construction contract. A building which is one-fourth completed and one-fourth paid for, would be treated as an asset to the extent of cash payments. Yet, a building in this stage of completion is not capable of providing services *now*. In fact, the future service potential of the building may be unaffected by the fact that the building does not presently exist. The difference between a building which is on the drawing boards and one which is already constructed is that the service potentials are closer to realization in the case of a constructed building, whereas the service potential of the building on the drawing boards is not immediately available. It is suggested that the accountant must, of necessity, assume (unless there is evidence to the contrary) that the object will in fact be created and economic benefits will flow from it. The going-concern concept reinforces this assumption.

[30]Canning, *op. cit.*, p. 14.

CAPITALIZING ALL EXPECTATIONS

The question often posed is: If one would consent to capitalize executory contracts, why not capitalize all expectations? Why stop with the occasion of the contract for recognition of assets and corresponding liabilities? Why not capitalize a company's proposed capital budget or expected future sales and earnings as predicted by a company's president?

First, the act of signing or entering into a written contract is an objective manifestation of the legal, moral and economic commitment of the firm. The contract serves as concrete evidence, particularly when coupled with the going-concern concept as discussed earlier, of the fact that the firm has acquired rights to future economic benefits which are expected to be derived from the object of the contract. This same objective type evidence of service potentials acquired is frequently not present prior to the formation of the contract. Such is the case with capitalizing future sales and earnings or the proposed capital budget mentioned earlier.

Second, the contract also serves as evidence that another, *independent* party has also committed himself to the transaction and has agreed to do whatever is necessary to fulfill the contract for the acquisition of service potentials. In other words, when the other party outside the corporation becomes a part of the contract an exchange of promises and rights (a transaction) has taken place. Prior to the formation of the contract there is only the *intention* of one or both parties to be committed. In the absence of each party's contractual commitment, mere intention might generally be considered insufficient evidence to indicate an exchange has taken place or a transaction has occurred.

In those cases where either or both parties have no intention of fulfilling or are unable to fulfill the contract or there is evidence to indicate that the going-concern assumption is not valid, no asset has been acquired, no liability has been incurred and none should be recorded in spite of the existence of a contract. Of course, legal difficulties can arise where one party has performed. These difficulties are further complicated where performance cannot be reversed. Ignoring these legal problems, in the simple case where no performance has taken place, the asset and corresponding liability amounts should be removed from the accounts when the contract is not to be fulfilled. This procedure is similar to numerous asset write-offs (e.g., bad debts) which currently are permitted.

Generally, with the formation of the contract also comes the establishment of exchange prices for the assets and corresponding liabilities involved in the contract. Prior to exchange of the rights under the contract many assets would not be easily measurable by a particular firm. It should be noted that at some time in the future it may be feasible to incorporate into financial statements, expectations or future transactions which have not been verified by an exchange or by contract. The usefulness of such information in future predictions and decisions would be advocated by some and disputed by others—this is a matter which must be settled by research. However, in the absence of objective evidence to substantiate these expectations and to give some basis for their objective measurement, they cannot be recommended for inclusion in published financial statements.

In the context of the preceding discussion, it might also be asked why accountants should not capitalize economic commitments? The company must, if it is to continue in operation, purchase numerous commonly-used asset services. There are at least two reasons for omitting economic commitments. First, no contract has been formed and no exchange or transaction has taken place. In addition, these services are readily available to all users in the market and information on such economic commitments is probably irrelevant to the decision of most users of financial statements. If these common service potentials were to be purchased via some long-term agreement or contract, their reporting might be relevant since the firm: (1) may have been speculating, which necessitated entering into a fixed commitment at fixed prices, or (2) may be substituting executory contracts for assets as in the case of purchase commitments for inventory or leases for fixed assets. Barring the existence of such a contract, however, the investor or other users would assume that these readily available service potentials or assets will have to be purchased, if the firm is to continue in operation.

EFFECT ON INCOME MEASUREMENT

Recording executory contracts is essentially a balance sheet problem or one of correctly presenting the financial position of an enterprise. The view can be taken that profit is the result of measuring net assets at two different points in time. Accordingly, the recording of most executory contracts will not affect "operating" income in the period first recorded unless, of course, a replacement cost or other current cost is used and changes substantially. Admittedly, the value of the recorded asset and liability can be different but this problem should not arise in the majority of cases. In short, operating income measurement should not be materially affected by capitalizing executory contracts in the accounts and financial statements. In contrast, the measurement of holding gains and losses can be affected significantly. If executory contracts are capitalized some assets and liabilities will be recorded in the accounts one or more periods earlier than they otherwise would have been recorded. Consequently, any price changes on these contracts will similarly be reflected as holding gains and losses one or more periods earlier than they otherwise would have been reflected.

SUMMARY

Executory contract data may be relevant financial information to users of published financial reports and thus the recent literature contains numerous proposals for capitalization of such contracts. In light of these proposals it is especially appropriate to consider how currently accepted asset and liability concepts accommodate leases and other executory contracts. It has been concluded that the exchange of promises and rights by independent parties upon entering into a contract constitutes an accounting transaction. This expanded notion of an accounting transaction coupled with the service potential concept of assets, yields a theoretical framework which accommodates executory contracts. Using this framework, executory contracts qualify theoretically as assets and liabilities which should be recorded in the accounts if objectively measurable.

Is Lessee Accounting Working?

RICHARD DIETER

While the objectives of FASB Statement 13 "Accounting for Leases" appear meritorious, the arbitrary rules, sub-rules, subsequent interpretations and amendments (both official and unofficial) for implementing these objectives have created substantial problems for the independent CPA and for financial management. This article analyzes many of the implementation problems; offers reasons why they have arisen; and finally suggests a solution to the dilemma, primarily with respect to accounting for leases by lessees.

The objective of Statement 13, as described in its Appendix (Basis for Conclusions) was that:

> A lease that transfers substantially all of the benefits and risks incident to the ownership of property should be accounted for as the acquisition of an asset and the incurrence of an obligation by the lessee and as a sale or financing by the lessor.

The Board believed that Statement 13 would remove most "if not all, of the conceptual differences in lease classification as between lessors and lessees and that it provides criteria for such classification that are more explicit and less susceptible to varied interpretation than those in previous literature."

Based on actual results of Statement 13 for over two years, its objectives and the assertion of "less susceptibility to varied interpretation" have not been reached. In fact, there continues to be a significant number of long-term leases that pass substantially all risks and rewards of ownership of property to the lessee and yet continue to be accounted for as operating leases. In addition, while drafters of new leases may have to sharpen their pencils a bit, it is common to find agreements negotiated that provide a finance lease for the lessor and an operating lease for the lessee.

STATEMENT NO. 13—AN OVERVIEW

In studying the lease classification rules of Statement 13, one quickly concludes that the major stumbling block to noncapitalization is in overcoming the test of paragraph 7d. While this paragraph represents only one of four distinct tests that, if met, requires a lessee to capitalize a lease, it is the only new rule that is, in most instances, quantifiable. This rule, commonly referred to as the 90 percent recovery test, requires a lessee to capitalize a lease if the present value, at the beginning of the lease term, of the minimum lease payments equals or exceeds 90 percent of the excess of the fair value of the leased property over any

Richard Dieter, "Is Lessee Accounting Working?" The *CPA Journal*, August 1979, pp. 13–15, 17–19. Reprinted with permission of the *CPA Journal*. Copyright © 1979 New York State Society of CPAs. 503

related investment tax credit retained by the lessor and expected to be realized by him.

The other lessee capitalization rules, referred to in paragraphs 7a, b and c of Statement 13 are not significant hurdles to overcome. For example, paragraphs 7a and 7b require a lessee to capitalize a lease if "the lease transfers ownership of the property to the lessee by the end of the lease term" or if "the lease contains a bargain purchase option." Both of these tests are substantially unchanged from APB Opinion No. 5 and, except for possible varying interpretation of what constitutes a bargain purchase option, few, if any, leases not capitalized under APB Opinion No. 5 (of which there were very few) would not be capitalized under these rules of Statement 13.

The test in paragraph 7c of Statement 13 is also similar to the underlying thrust of APB Opinion No. 5; however, it does differ in that Statement 13 is more specific. It provides that if the lease term (as defined) equals or exceeds 75 percent of the estimated economic life of the leased property, the lessee is required to capitalize the lease. Most practitioners realize that estimates of useful lives of assets are judgmental and, if an estimate is within a given range, they are not apt to object. Accordingly, a building lease of 30 years will commonly not be required to be capitalized under paragraph 7c, because arguments that a building life often exceeds 40 years is easily sustainable and reasonable. Similarly, estimates of economic lives of 12 to 15 years are not uncommon for equipment covered by an eight-year lease. Thus, for all practical purposes, a lessee is able to overcome the numerical test of paragraph 7c and in clear conscience justify it to himself and his independent auditor. There are, however, extremes that have been taken in this regard, particularly by some major retailers. These assertions and the questions raised by the SEC are discussed in this article.

Nevertheless, the 90 percent recovery test remains the focal point of lease capitalization from the lessee's viewpoint. Accordingly, the implementation problems discussed in this article focus on what the issues are, why there are varying interpretations, to what extremes people are willing to go and what they are willing to give up in negotiating leases that do not meet this test.

One of the best approaches to analyze implementation problems that have beset the practitioner is to study carefully specific issues that the FASB has faced or is facing through issuance of official interpretations and amendments to Statement 13. As of May 1, 1979, FASB had amended Statement 13 four times, had issued six interpretations and had in the exposure stage three additional amendments. In addition, the Board has authorized its staff to develop interpretations on two other lease problems.

PART-OF-THE-BUILDING PROBLEM

Certain perceived measurement problems exist in performing lease classification tests for leases involving only part of a building (e.g., floors of a multi-story office building and retail space in a shopping mall). As a result, FASB devised special rules to assist a user of Statement 13 in obtaining objectively determinable costs or fair market values of leased space. It provided without any specificity that, with respect to the lessee:

> If the fair value of the leased property is not objectively determinable, the lessee shall classify the lease according to the criterion of paragraph 7(c)

only, using the estimated economic life of the building in which the leased premises are located.

In practice lessees uniformly asserted that it was never practical to estimate the fair value of a part of a building and thus the 90 percent recovery test was not applicable. Accordingly, only the useful life test was to be applied, and, as discussed previously, this was quickly overcome by applying subjective judgment to estimated useful lives.

Subsequent to the issuance of Statement 13, FASB was asked to clarify when fair value can be objectively determined for a lease involving only part of a building if there were no sales of similar property. The FASB responded by issuing its Interpretation No. 24 in September 1978. It provides that other evidence (e.g., independent appraisal or estimated replacement cost information) may provide a basis for an objective determination of fair value. The Board also acknowledged that (a) it was not imposing a requirement to obtain an appraisal or other similar valuation as a general matter and, (b) a meaningful estimate of fair value "of an office or a floor of a multi-story building may not be possible whereas similar information may be readily obtainable if the leased property is a major part of that facility." This interpretation has had little or no impact on lessee capitalization decisions since Statement 13 continues to be applied literally and information as to fair value remains elusive. Consequently, for the vast majority of leases involving only part of a building or structure, no capitalization is occurring.

RESIDUAL VALUE GUARANTEES

In performing the 90 percent recovery test of Statement 13 a lessee is required to include, in the determination of minimum lease payments, guarantees of the residual value of leased property at expiration of the lease. Lessee guarantees of the residual value, while not uncommon, occur most frequently in leases involving personal property such as automobiles. Since the question of residual value guarantees was not a criterion of lease capitalization prior to Statement 13, it was commonplace to find the residual value guarantee at the end of an automobile lease term equating to the balance of undepreciated cost. Consequently, in performing the lease capitalization tests of Statement 13, many lessees initially found themselves in the unhappy position of having to capitalize most of their automobile leases. Almost immediately after this consequence became known to the car lessors, they set out to amend and rectify lease agreements to overcome the capitalization requirements. This was accomplished primarily through a specific limitation on the amount of the residual value deficiency that a lessee would be required to make up and, in some cases, by limiting the guarantee to situations beyond normal wear and tear.

In addition, the Board assisted lessees in this effort through the issuance of Interpretation No. 19 "Lessee Guarantee of the Residual Value of Leased Property." It dealt with lease provisions that require the lessee to make up a residual value deficiency only in cases where the shortfall in residual value is attributable to damage, extraordinary wear and tear, etc., and whether this type of provision constitutes a lessee guarantee of residual value as that term is used in defining minimum lease payments under Statement 13. The interpretation stated that (1) a residual value guarantee is limited to the specific maximum deficiency the lessee can be required to make up, and (2) a lessee that is required to make up a residual value deficiency attributable to extraordinary wear and tear does not constitute a lessee guarantee of residual value for purposes of defining minimum lease payments.

The practical effect of this interpretation, as it relates to the specified maximum deficiency, can best be demonstrated with an example. Assume a lessee enters into a one-year lease for a current model year Volvo for a monthly rental of $300. The fair market value of the Volvo at the inception of the lease is $10,000. The lessee agrees, at the conclusion of the one-year lease, to make up any residual value deficiency on the car between $3,000 and $8,000. Thus the lessor takes the risk that a one-year-old Volvo would not be worth at least $3,000. In computing minimum lease payments, the lessee would compare the $10,000 to the present value of $3,600 (1 year's monthly payments) and the $5,000 residual value guarantee ($8,000 minus $3,000). The mechanics of the present value computation lead to a conclusion that the minimum lease payments are less than 90 percent of the fair market value of the car at the inception of the lease. While the mechanical test of Statement 13 for capitalization has not been met, it is clear that the lessor has given up very little and yet has been able to achieve an operating lease for the lessee. Thus this interpretation applied literally allows lessees, through a modification of terms that are not economically substantive, to alter substantially the accounting treatment by converting an otherwise capital lease to an operating lease.

CONTINGENT RENT

Statement 13 provides that contingent rentals, from the lessee's viewpoint, are to be charged to expense as incurred, and not considered part of minimum lease payments for the purpose of performing the 90 percent recovery test. Since many leases contain a base rent and an override based on sales, the override rent is excluded from minimum lease payments in determining lease classification. For example, retail space is often leased at a base rate per month plus a fixed or variable percentage of sales over a predetermined amount. Drafters of lease agreements were quick to realize that by a slight reduction in base rent and a minor increase in percentage rent or simply a decrease in the base sales amount, minimum lease payments could be reduced to enable the present value calculation to equal 89 percent of the fair value of the leased property with a miniscule increase in risk to the lessor.

In other circumstances a rental cost is based on the prime interest rate. The following hypothetical example demonstrates the problem. A lease agreement provides that yearly rent will be a function of the prime interest rate times a given principal amount, with a limitation on the absolute amount of rent per year. The limitation would equate to a prime rate of 4 percent. This yearly amount over the lease term would qualify the lease as a capital lease. Nevertheless, the practical interpretation of Statement 13 would be to classify all payments as contingent and consequently the lease would be treated as an operating lease.

Situations such as the above were brought to the Board's attention and in December 1978, it issued an exposure draft of an amendment to Statement 13 providing that:

> Lease payments that depend on an existing index or rate, such as the prime interest rate, shall be included in minimum lease payments based

on the index or rate existing at the inception of the lease; any increases or decreases in lease payments that result from subsequent changes in the index or rate are contingent rentals.

This proposed amendment would appear to correct many of the perceived abuses in using the contingent rental clause based on indexes to avoid capitalization.

IMPLICIT INTEREST RATE IN THE LEASE

Statement 13 provides that when a lessee is computing the present value of the minimum lease payments for the purpose of measuring whether a capital lease exists, it should use its incremental borrowing rate unless "it is practicable for him to learn the implicit interest rate computed by the lessor and the implicit rate computed by the lessor is less than the lessee's incremental borrowing rate." If both these conditions exist, the lessee is required to use the implicit rate. By and large, the lessor's implicit interest rate in the lease is lower than the lessee's incremental borrowing rate. This is due to several factors including the lessor's estimate of the residual value. In addition, in determining an appropriate rate of return the lessor considers the additional tax benefits that flow to the lessor (e.g., cash flow benefits of accelerated depreciation for tax purposes); these benefits are not considered in the lease evaluation criteria of Statement 13. As most practitioners realize today, a lessee request from the lessor for the implicit interest rate will "reluctantly" be declined. In most situations, the lessee will not press the lessor because the direction of the answer is known in advance. As a result, many lessees represent to their CPAs that although they have requested information from the lessor, the lessor has refused to respond. Consequently, when performing the 90 percent recovery test, the incremental borrowing rate is used. As is readily apparent, in a long-term lease, when a present value computation is performed using an interest rate of approximately 10 percent (a rate representative of most companies' incremental borrowing rate today), rentals due after ten years have little or no present value.

This problem was brought to the Board's attention and it has proposed to amend Statement 13 to require the lessee, where practicable, to estimate the interest rate implicit in the lease. In so doing, the lessee is forced into an evaluation of the residual value. This unfortunately raises the issue of how to handle inflation, particularly for leases involving real estate. Should the residual value be viewed as a percentage of original cost based on a depreciable life of 30 or 40 years? Should it take into account trends of the past eight years of significant inflation? Should it take an historical approach that shows real estate values have increased at a rate, in many instances, that exceed normal inflation? The Board has not answered these questions in its proposed amendment.

Through the comment letters the Board has received on its exposure draft of the amendment of Statement 13 entitled "Lessees Use of the Interest Rate Implicit in the Lease" it became aware of the problem of estimating residual values. As a result, the Board has directed its staff to address the question of whether expected future increases in value should be considered in estimating residual values. They have also reached the conclusion to defer a decision on the amendment covering the lessee's use of the interest rate implicit in the lease until that question is solved.

In analyzing how the impact of inflation should be considered in determining residual values many would argue that this judgment should be consistent with the other provisions of Statement 13. For example, the Board had emphasized in Statement 13 that upward revisions of residual value are not acceptable. While this appears to relate primarily to the notion that once property is "sold" (capital lease), additional profit recognition by the lessor should not be permitted prior to end of the lease term, it also seems to preclude giving recognition to inflation. It should also be borne in mind that inflation, in general, is not accounted for under the historical cost framework presently used. Others argue that the interest rate (e.g., approximately 10 percent today) used to discount residual values reflects inflation as that rate far exceeds a pure cost of money and therefore in estimating residual values, inflation should also be considered. They further believe that by not assuming inflation for real estate leases, the lease capitalization test and the use of the implicit interest rate of Statement 13 are avoiding economic reality.

THE RETAILERS' ARGUMENTS

Perhaps in no other industry are the potential effects of lease capitalization as significant to the balance sheet as they are to large retail chains. The majority of these retailers lease substantially all their facilities under long-term leases, particularly in shopping malls and strip centers.

Readers of large retailer's financial statements were given a warning of the magnitude of the impact of lease capitalization by the disclosures required under Accounting Series Release No. 147. Most readers assumed that the "noncapitalized financing leases" disclosed in accordance with ASR No. 147 would become capital leases under Statement 13. How wrong they were! In fact, less than one half, and in some cases only a small percentage of the "noncapitalized finance leases" have been treated as capital leases under Statement 13.

For example, one large retailer reported over 160 leases with a present value of approximately $50,000,000 meeting the SEC's definition of a "noncapitalized finance" lease. Reporting under Statement 13, that retailer reported only 50 leases with a present value of $25,000,000 as capital leases. The major reasons for certain "noncapitalized finance leases" not meeting the capital lease test of Statement 13 were (a) option periods were considered in the lease term for purposes of the ASR disclosures but are excluded in Statement 13's tests: (b) the inability to estimate fair market value where the leased premise was part of large shopping mall; and, (c) the exclusion of leases of a property located in government facilities.

The retailing industry has carefully analyzed the criteria for lease classification under Statement 13 and has sought to take consistent and aggressive positions in interpreting the rules. Recently, the Office of the Chief Accountant of the SEC commented that it would be carefully reviewing the assertions and conclusions reached by the industry since it also was taken back by the lack of capitalization of leased stores and facilities under Statement 13 compared to the disclosures of "noncapitalized finance leases" under ASR No. 147.

The following conclusions reached by several large retailers in implementing Statement 13 have led to many long-term leases being classified as operating leases.

Economic Life

Statement 13 defines economic life as:

> The estimated remaining period during which the property is expected
> to be economically usable by one or more users, with normal repairs and
> maintenance, for the purpose for which it was intended at the inception
> of the lease, without limitation by the lease term.

The conclusion reached by certain larger retailers was that the life of the
property should be measured in terms of a retail enterprise or otherwise. Since
alternative uses (warehouses, etc.) exist, they conclude it is reasonable to assume, for purposes of Statement 13, economic lives of 50 to 75 years. Accordingly, the interpretation leads one to conclude that most real property leases
should not require capitalization in accordance with paragraph 7(c) of Statement 13. Literally applied, retailers with a 50-year lease could argue a life of
75 years and fail the capitalization test of paragraph 7c. Without arguing the
merits of a 75-year life or the apparent inconsistency with the treatment adopted
by nonretailers for economic lives of real property, one wonders whether this
interpretation is consistent with the words "for the purpose for which it was
intended at the inception of the lease." Namely, is it appropriate to consider the
additional useful life as a warehouse that occurs beyond its retail life in determining the economic life under Statement 13?

Part of a Facility

FASB Interpretation No. 24 attempts to rectify a problem of Statement 13,
as covered previously, dealing with leases involving only part of building (space
in a shopping mall) by indicating that other evidence may provide an objective
determination of fair value. One of the factors to be considered is whether the
lessee occupies a major part of the facility. The retailers have concluded that
a major part would be equivalent to more than 50 percent of the available space
which would be an extreme rarity in a shopping mall. Some believe this was
not the intent of the FASB and that a more appropriate interpretation would
be that an anchor tenant would be assumed to have information to estimate
fair market value. This argument appears to have merit, since anchor tenants
are an integral part of the mall and the developer's plans, and it would seem
reasonable that the anchor tenant would often have this information available,
though it may only occupy 10 to 20 percent of the mall space.

LEASES INVOLVING GOVERNMENT FACILITIES

Just prior to finalizing the issuance of Statement 13, FASB added a section
under the rules covering leases involving only part of a building. It read as
follows:

> Because of special provisions normally present in leases involving ter-
> minal space and other airport facilities owned by a governmental unit or
> authority, the economic life of such facilities for purposes of classifying
> the lease is essentially indeterminate. Likewise, the concept of fair value
> is not applicable to such leases. Since such leases also do not provide for

a transfer of ownership or a bargain purchase option, they shall be classified as operating leases. Leases of other facilities owned by a governmental unit or authority wherein the rights of the parties are essentially the same as in a lease of airport facilities described above shall also be classified as operating leases. Examples of such leases may be those involving facilities at ports and bus terminals.

This special exemption had a tremendous impact on the airline industry by allowing them to classify their airport terminal space as operating leases. Many took this exemption also to apply to free standing airline hangars, including maintenance hangars, since the property was on government land and subject to the same considerations as airport terminal space. The SEC raised questions on whether the exemption applied to free standing structures since the exemption provided by Statement 13 was in a subsection covering "Leases Involving Part of a Building." This demonstrated that the SEC was also interpreting Statement 13 literally, although in this case it appeared a bit absurd.

In response to problems such as the one cited in the previous paragraph, the FASB issued an official interpretation—No. 23 "Leases of Certain Property Owned by a Governmental Unit or Authority." The interpretation specifies certain conditions that must be met if the leases in question are to be considered operating leases. One of those is that the lessor has the explicit right to terminate the lease at any time. Since such a right often does not exist, at least certain leases in this area may now require capitalization.

The Board, in response to many comments received that these leases should be subject to the same rules as other leases, gave serious consideration to eliminating the exemption entirely. However, it concluded that further consideration of an amendment should not delay the issuance of the interpretation.

WHERE DOES THIS LEAVE STATEMENT NO. 13?

It now appears likely that Statement 13 will rank fourth in number of interpretations and amendments of an authoritative document, ranking behind only APB Opinion No. 15 "Earnings Per Share," APB Opinion No. 11 "Accounting for Income Taxes" and the all time leader APB Opinion No. 16 "Accounting for Business Combinations." In terms of frustration it may rank higher. These distinctions are not without certain redeeming qualities—countless hours of billable professional time are spent in analyzing lease transactions in light of Statement 13, but one wonders whether this is really productive.

Clearly, from a practitioner's viewpoint, Statement 13 has created practice problems and difficulties by forcing one to rummage through rules, amendments and interpretations when analyzing a lease. Conclusions on lease accounting seem to reach the lowest common denominator in practice, so that most practitioners have concluded that the objectives of Statement 13 and substance over form give way to a literal interpretation of the rules of Statement 13. No white knights are appearing to invoke the Board's objectives, since the Board itself, through its amendments and interpretations has opted, for the most part, to apply the arbitrary rules and percentages literally. To answer the question of why Statement 13 has failed to achieve its objective one must first question the objective itself. From the author's viewpoint, it is questionable whether the objective could ever have been expected to be achieved, since the basis of Statement 13 represented a compromise between capitalizing all leases and capitalizing only those where title passes. Thus, Statement 13 is aimed at a position in between, and the break points are arbitrary. While arbitrary rules may work when the objectives are at the extremes of available options, they rarely work if the position sought is on middle ground.

What then is the solution? Would it not be more workable to require capitalization of all leases that extend for some defined period (such as one year), not on the premise that the lease transfers substantially all the risks and rewards of ownership of the property, but that the lessee has acquired an asset, a property right, and correspondingly has incurred an obligation. Using this criterion the necessity for most of the rules of Statement 13 would be eliminated, and the lessee's balance sheet would give a better picture of its assets and liabilities.

What are the possibilities of such a scenario? It is difficult to predict but certain events seem to indicate that a rethinking of Statement 13 is probable. In March 1979, the Board met to consider the underlying concepts in accounting for leases. The subject matter was placed on the Board's agenda in view of the number of amendments and interpretations of Statement 13 and the inordinate amount of time the Board has spent on Statement 13 problems since its issuance. It is generally acknowledged that with the present complement on the Board, and the hindsight of the Statement's difficulties, if Statement 13 were submitted to the Board in its present form, a majority vote to issue would not be sustained.

At its March 6, 1979 meeting, a majority of the Board expressed "the tentative view that, if Statement 13 were to be reconsidered, they would support a property right approach in which all leases are included as 'rights to use property' and as 'lease obligations' in the lessee's balance sheet."

The other recent development comes out of the Board's exposure draft on accounting concepts. Many believe that the Board deviated from the definition of an economic obligation given in that document when it defined a capital lease. Eventually this inconsistency must be removed. If one uses the definition of a liability in the proposed statement on accounting concepts, it is not difficult to reach the conclusion that all leases represent obligations to transfer enterprise resources and should therefore be reflected on the balance sheet.

Statement 13 has not achieved its goal in terms of the degree of lease capitalization that its drafters believed would be accomplished or in eliminating most of the inconsistencies between accounting for leases by lessors and lessees. This practitioner believes the cause of failure is with the objective the Board used—an objective, as has been demonstrated, not capable of practical implementation. The Board should recognize its obligation to rethink the issue and its objective, taking into account its new definitions of assets and liabilities, and recognize that while compromise in the setting of accounting principles is necessary in many circumstances, a compromise that doesn't work should be discarded.

V-C/INTANGIBLE ASSETS

Accounting for Research and Development Costs

HAROLD BIERMAN, JR., AND ROLAND E. DUKES

The accounting profession has four basic choices available as to the method of accounting for assets:

- Use cost of acquisition.
- Use value estimations.
- Use price level adjusted cost.
- Implicitly assume the value is zero and expense the costs associated with the acquisition of the asset.

In its Statement of Financial Accounting Standards No. 2, "Accounting for Research and Development Costs" (October 1974), the Financial Accounting Standards Board concludes that "all research and development costs encompassed by this Statement shall be charged to expense when incurred." This practice implicitly assumes the expected value of R&D is zero. The Board reached its conclusion as a result of a reasoning process in which several preliminary premises were accepted as true. It may be possible to conclude for pragmatic reasons that the expensing decision reached by the Board is a reasonable practice, but we object to the process the Board used in arriving at the conclusion that R&D should be expensed. Specifically, the following five factors that were offered by the Board as support for its conclusion will be considered:

- Uncertainty of future benefits.
- Lack of causal relationship between expenditures and benefits.
- R&D does not meet the accounting concept of an asset.
- Matching of revenues and expenses.
- Relevance of resulting information for investment and credit decisions.

Following are descriptions of these factors and evaluations of their relevance.

UNCERTAINTY OF FUTURE BENEFITS

The primary justification offered by the FASB[1] for expensing the R&D expenditures is the level of uncertainty associated with the benefits. It is argued that

R&D expenditures have considerable risk where risk is defined as a large probability of failure for an individual project. In reaching its conclusion to expense R&D costs when incurred, the Board states (p. 15) that the "high degree of uncertainty about the future benefits of individual research and development projects" was a significant factor in reaching this conclusion. In elaborating on this conclusion, the Board cites several studies that indicate a high failure rate for research and development projects. Although the Statement is not specific on this point, it appears that because a large proportion of research and development projects are "failures," the Board concludes that all R&D should be treated as failures and expensed. There are several fallacies with this conclusion.

First, it is not clear that the risks and uncertainties of company-sponsored research and development are as formidable as corporate publicists and the references cited by the Board would have us believe. In 1963, Mansfield and Hamburger[2] studied 22 major firms in the chemical and petroleum industries and found that the bulk of the R&D projects carried out by these firms were relatively safe from a technical point of view. Most of the projects were regarded as having better than a 50–50 chance of technical success. In an analysis of 70 projects carried out in the central research and development laboratories of a leading electrical equipment manufacturing company, Mansfield and Brandenburg[3] found that in more than three-fourths of the cases, the ex ante probability of technical success had originally been estimated at .80 or higher, and only two projects had predicted success probabilities of less than .50. After the projects were completed, 44 percent were fully successful technically, and only 16 percent were unsuccessful because of unanticipated technical difficulties.

These findings are consistent with the hypothesis that business firms do not generally begin new product or process development projects until the principal technical uncertainties have been resolved through inexpensive research, conducted either by their own personnel or by outsiders. They are also consistent with the notion that managers are averse to risk and are reluctant to pursue high risk projects when their own reputations and the funds of the company are involved. On the other hand, research and development projects sponsored by the federal government are likely to be more risky than industrial R&D because the federal government bears the financial risk. This point is also made by Scherer.[4]

Second, one has to be careful as to the definition of risk. Because of the historically high profitability of R&D efforts, it may well be that risk defined in terms of expected loss or expected monetary value may be less than many types of plant and equipment expenditures (the different tax treatments afforded the different types of expenditures also affect risk).

[1]Financial Accounting Standards Board, Statement of Financial Accounting Standards No. 2, "Accounting for Research and Development Costs" (Stamford, Conn.: FASB, 1974).

[2]E. Mansfield, "Industrial Research and Development: Characteristics, Costs, and the Diffusion of Results," *American Economic Review*, May 1969, p. 65.

[3]E. Mansfield, *Industrial Research and Technological Innovation* (New York: Norton, 1969).

[4]F. M. Scherer, *Industrial Market Structure and Economic Performance* (Chicago: Rand McNally, 1970), pp. 354–56.

Bailey,[5] who computed the rate of return from R&D expenditures in the U.S. pharmaceutical industry, found a rate of return (pretax) of 35 percent in 1954 and 25 percent in 1961. Bailey explains the decrease in rate of return as being the result of increased R&D expenditures (170 percent increase between 1954 and 1961) as firms realized the high profitability of R&D in this area. Bailey does forecast decreasing returns in this industry after 1962 as a result of more stringent regulations associated with introducing new products and warns of the difficulty of isolating causal relationships. Also, the measurement of profitability of R&D is difficult because there are many factors affecting earnings. But if Bailey is close to being correct, there may be less risk with R&D expenditures (if a large amount of expenditures are made, spread over a large number of projects) than with plant and equipment.

Bailey's findings are reinforced by studies by Minasian and Mansfield. Mansfield[6] found that "among the petroleum firms, regardless of whether technical change was capital-embodied or organizational, the marginal rates of return average about 40–60 percent." He found other industries also high, but not as high as for the period 1946–62. Minasian,[7] in studying firms in the chemical industry (1948–57), found the gross return on research and development to be 54 percent as compared to 9 percent for the physical capital. While Minasian defines this as a social return and not a private return, it is again evident that R&D has been very profitable. Moreover, the expected profitability affects the risk of the expenditure.

This is inconsistent with the definition of risk apparently used by the FASB, which defines risk only in terms of probability of failure. The Board does not consider the reduction in uncertainty that can be achieved by pursuing a portfolio of research and development projects. A simple example will help to illustrate this point. Suppose a firm is pursuing 100 independent R&D projects. For computational ease, we assume each project costs $10,000, that each has a probability of "success" of .10 and a probability of "failure" of .90. Success results in a $200,000 present value accruing to the firm; failure results in no benefits.

Each individual project has 1 chance in 10 of being successful; this is consistent with the point made by the Board that for any individual project the probability that it will generate future benefits for the firm seems dismally low. However, the more important question is, what is the probability of making a profit from the portfolio of projects? Since each R&D project represents an independent event with two possible outcomes, the number of successes in 100 trials is a random variable whose distribution is the binomial distribution. For this example, the probability that there will be one or more successes is equal to .99997.[8] That is, the firm is virtually assured that it will realize 1 or more

[5]Martin Neil Bailey, "Research and Development Costs and Returns: The U.S. Pharmaceutical Industry," *Journal of Political Economy*, January–February 1972, pp. 70–85.

[6]E. Mansfield, "Rates of Return From Industrial Research and Development," *American Economic Review*, May 1965, pp. 310–22.

[7]Jora R. Minasian, "Research and Development, Production Functions, and Rates of Return," *American Economic Review*, May 1969, pp. 80–85.

[8]The probability that there will be 1 or more successes is equal to 1 minus the probability there will be zero successes. The probability of zero success is given as

$$P \text{ (0 successes)} = \frac{100!}{0! \ 100!} \ [.10]^0 [.90]^{100} = .00003$$

successes from a portfolio of 100 R&D projects.[9] This is a substantial reduction in uncertainty when compared to the .10 probability of success attached to individual projects. Moreover, the expected future benefits from the portfolio is $2 million.[10] Thus, while the Board claims a large probability of failure associated with individual projects, it fails to consider the change in the uncertainty (defined in terms of probability of failure) associated with undertaking a portfolio of independent R&D projects.

In the above example, the $20,000 expected future benefit of each project (equal to its probability of success, .10, times the expected future benefit of success, $200,000) is greater than the $10,000 cost of each project. The expected payoff from the portfolio is twice the total cost of $1 million for all 100 research and development projects. To break even, the firm needs 5 or more successes out of 100 projects, and there is .9763 probability of this happening. Thus, rather than .10 probability of success (defined in terms of the individual project), there is .9763 probability of success (defined in terms of the profitability of the portfolio).

Since the firm does not know before it investigates which of the projects will be successful, the appropriate cost of finding the successful projects is the total cost of pursuing the portfolio of projects. Bierman, Dukes and Dyckman[11] discuss this point further with specific reference to accounting for exploration costs in the petroleum industry.

The FASB cites the low probability of success with new products. We argue that this low probability has not been proved. Moreover, it is not a valid measure of risk. The Board needs to define uncertainty and risk more exactly before risk of R&D can be offered as the reason for an accounting treatment. Even if it were agreed that R&D had more risk (a position we do not accept), it is still not clear that this leads to the policy conclusion of expensing the costs of R&D.

There is some uncertainty of future benefits associated with every asset currently recorded on balance sheets. Even the future real benefits that can be realized from holding cash are uncertain, especially during these times of "double-digit" inflation. More analogous to research and development, there is a high degree of uncertainty associated with investments in long-lived plant and equipment, especially in fields where the assets are extremely specialized in nature and where there is rapid technological advance. It is not clear that investments in these kinds of projects are any less uncertain in terms of the probability of making a profit than an investment in a portfolio of R&D projects. If both are uncertain, why should one be recorded differently from the other? It does not appear that using the "degree of uncertainty of future benefits" is

---

[9]If the probability of success for an individual project is .05, .02 or .01, then the portfolio probabilities of one or more successes are .989, .905 and .633, respectively.

[10]The expected present value from the portfolio is the sum of the expected payoffs for the individual projects:

$$\text{Expected present value from portfolio} = \sum_{i=1}^{100} \text{Expected present value of project } i$$

$$= \sum_{i=1}^{100} [(.10)\ (\$200,000) + (.90)\ (0)]$$

$$= 100\ (\$20,000) = \$2,000,000.$$

[11]Harold Bierman, Jr., Roland E. Dukes and Thomas R. Dyckman, "Financial Reporting in the Petroleum Industry," *Journal of Accountancy*, Oct. 74, pp. 58–64.

an appropriate factor or criterion to employ in helping to resolve this issue. So long as the project has a net positive expected future benefit, uncertainty should not lead automatically to a conclusion that cost factors should be expensed.

We argue that at the portfolio level there is the possibility of a substantial reduction in uncertainty vis-à-vis the individual project level. Moreover, expected future benefits will in general be equal to or greater than the total cost of pursuing the research and development portfolio. Thus, the existence of a probability of failure cannot be used to justify the expensing of R&D expenditures.[12]

LACK OF CAUSAL RELATION BETWEEN EXPENDITURES AND BENEFITS

In its Statement the FASB cites (p. 16) three empirical research studies that "generally failed to find a significant correlation between research and development expenditures and increased future benefits as measured by subsequent sales, earnings or share of industry sales." The Board does not specify what conclusion is to be drawn regarding the accounting treatment of research and development costs from the above statement, although it appears to consider this lack of evidence of a direct relationship between research and development costs and specific future revenue as an important factor in its conclusions.

Several points can be made regarding this factor. First, even though the studies cited by the Board were unable to detect a significant relationship between costs of research and subsequent benefits, this does not imply that such a relationship does not exist. That is, when logical deductive reasoning leads to a hypothesized relationship that cannot subsequently be empirically observed, the scientist will generally "suspend judgment" regarding the hypothesis rather than embrace the alternative hypothesis that no relationship exists. It is more appropriate to draw conclusions upon the observation of the phenomena under study rather than upon the inability to observe the phenomena.

Second, considerable research in economics does provide support for the hypothesis that research and development efforts do produce benefits for the firm. Scherer[13] reviews much of this literature when he discusses the relationship between market structures and technological innovation. Subsequent to the Scherer review, several additional studies have contributed to the evidence on the relationship between research and development and various measures of benefit to the firm. Bailey[14] found pretax rates of return from investments in research and development in the vicinity of 25 to 35 percent for the pharmaceutical firms included in his study. He also found that "earnings of the com-

---

[12]An irrelevant argument is offered in paragraph 52 of the FASB Statement. It is stated that companies have the philosophy that "research and development expenditures are intended to be recovered by current revenues rather than by revenues from new product." This philosophy (if it does exist) should in no way affect the accounting for R&D. In addition, in evaluating new projects any sensible method of evaluation will consider the revenue (benefits) associated with the new projects. The current product revenues are irrelevant to the decision to go ahead except to the extent that they supply the cash that is used for the financing of the R&D.

[13]Scherer, especially chapters 15 and 16.

[14]Bailey.

panies over time are clearly related to the number of patents held by the company." The number of patents held by a firm is an often-used surrogate for research output. In a related study, Angilley[15] found pharmaceutical sales to be significantly related to "innovative output," where innovative output was defined in terms of several measures of new pharmaceutical compounds produced by the company. Equally important, he found that his measures of innovative output were all significantly related to the amount of research and development expenditures incurred by the firm. In a more recent study, Grabowski and Mueller[16] investigated the rates of return on investments in physical capital, in research and development and in advertising. They conclude that their result "indicates that R&D does increase the profitability of the firm over competitive levels." For the 86 firms included in their sample, "additional R&D did increase the rate of return on total capital."

Given this brief review of some of the contrary evidence, the FASB's statement (p. 16) that "a direct relationship between research and development costs and specific revenue generally has not been demonstrated . . ." is confusing and somewhat misleading. Clearly, management expects to generate positive returns from R&D. Moreover, the expected profit from large, expensive research and development portfolios is larger than the expected benefits from smaller, less costly portfolios of research and development. An inexpensive plant may turn out to be more profitable than a much more expensive plant, but this outcome does not "prove" that the plants' costs should have been expensed in both cases.

It is probably true that there is a higher variance of benefits arising from the research and development expenditures. But higher variance does not necessarily imply a higher risk is associated with such expenditures (the capital asset pricing model of Sharpe[17] is of relevance here). Applying the capital asset pricing model, the important measure of risk is the covariability of expected return between the individual project and the overall portfolio of securities. Expenditures on R&D to develop new products or improve old ones are likely to be less correlated with market returns than expenditures for expansion into new markets or expanding market capacity. Thus, it seems likely that many R&D expenditures will have relatively desirable risk characteristics compared to expenditures in physical capital.

In sum, it is incorrect to conclude that, because it has been difficult to observe a significant correlation between expenditures and subsequent benefits, future benefits are not generated by research and development expenditures. Moreover, considerable research does exist in which the findings support the hypothesis that research and development does generate substantive future benefits for the firm. While the Board may still determine that the expensing of research and development expenditures is an appropriate accounting policy, it is not clear that the lack of benefits argument is an appropriate supporting factor in this conclusion.

[15]Alan Angilley, "Returns to Scale in Research in the Ethical Pharmaceutical Industry: Some Further Empirical Evidence," *Journal of Industrial Economics*, December 1973, pp. 81–93.

[16]Henry Grabowski and Dennis Mueller, "Rates of Return on Corporate Investment, Research and Development and Advertising," unpublished working paper, Cornell University, 1974.

[17]W. F. Sharpe, "Capital Asset Prices: A Theory of Market Equilibrium Under Conditions of Risk," *Journal of Finance*, September 1964, pp. 425–42.

THE ACCOUNTING CONCEPT OF AN ASSET

The Board appears to be close to requiring the capitalization of research and development when it describes (p. 17) economic resources as those scarce resources for which there is an "expectation of future benefits to the enterprise either through use or sale." While R&D would qualify using this definition, the Board then discusses the criteria of measurability. We argue that the cost of R&D is subject to reasonable measurement. However, the FASB states (p. 17),

"The criterion of measurability would require that a resource not be recognized as an asset for accounting purposes unless at the time it is acquired or developed its future economic benefits can be identified and objectively measured."

Can the economic benefits of an automobile plant be objectively measured at the time it is acquired? This criterion opens the door to the reclassification to expense of many "asset" types of expenditures.

Also, the values of many assets are relatively independent of their costs. A nonregulated pipeline immediately after it has been constructed has value that is independent of its cost. As soon as any cost is incurred, it is a sunk cost and is not price or value determining.

It is probably true that R&D ranks high in variance of relationship between cost and value on specific expenditures. The lack of a one-to-one relationship between benefits and costs tends to argue in favor of a value type of accounting. But if value is excluded from consideration, at least for now, and the choice is between zero (expensing) and cost, lacking other information cost will on the average be a better estimator of value than the zero asset value resulting from the expensing of R&D.[18]

EXPENSE RECOGNITION AND MATCHING

Surprisingly the matching of revenues and expenses of earning those revenues is used as an argument by the Board in favor of expensing R&D (p. 19) because of "the general lack of discernible future benefits at the time such costs are incurred. . . ." The only reason R&D expenditures are made is to benefit future time periods by generating new revenues in those time periods. It is unlikely that R&D will increase the operating revenues of the immediate time period given the time necessary to implement R&D. To argue in favor of immediate expensing is to ignore completely one of the basic principles on which accounting stands—namely, the necessity of matching revenues and expenses. If the Board had chosen to argue that matching was not an important criterion (it wisely did not do so), then its conclusion might be understandable. But to argue that expensing of R&D is consistent with matching is a conclusion that is difficult to comprehend.

RELEVANCE OF RESULTING INFORMATION FOR INVESTMENT AND CREDIT DECISIONS

In paragraph 50 of the Statement, the Board refers to APB Statement No. 4, which indicates that certain costs are immediately "recognized as expenses

[18]For an expansion on this point, see the article by Bierman, Dukes and Dyckman in the October 1974, *Journal of Accountancy*.

because allocating them to several accounting periods is considered to serve no useful purpose." Citing evidence of the high degree of uncertainty associated with research and development and the views of security analysts and other professional investors, the Board states that "capitalization of any research and development costs is not useful in assessment of the earnings potential of the enterprise." The Board concludes that "therefore, it is unlikely that the investor's ability to predict the return on his investment and the variability of that return would be enhanced by capitalization."

There are two points to be made regarding the above reasoning and conclusions. First, the usefulness of accounting data regarding the amount of research and development costs to investors is an empirically testable question. In a study related to this issue, Dukes[19] found that the amount of research and development cost incurred and expensed during the period was significantly related to the security price of the firm. All of the firms in the Dukes study followed the accounting policy of expensing research and development costs, yet results were consistent with investors making capitalization adjustments to research and development costs in estimating the future earnings potential of the firm. That is, the "research intensity" of the firm (more precisely, the research intensity of the industry in which a firm found itself) was a significant explanatory variable in explaining the market value of the firm.

The Dukes study suggests that capitalization may serve a useful purpose in aiding the investor to predict the future return of a security. At a minimum, the study provides support to the Board's conclusion that disclosure of the amount of research and development costs is information relevant to the investment decision.

A second significant issue deals with who would be served by the requirement that research and development costs be expensed. If the results of the Dukes study are accepted, then security price behavior is more closely related to earnings computed with research and development capitalized rather than expensed. It is probably reasonable to expect security analysts and other professional investors to be able to make adjusting calculations to the reported earnings numbers, where sufficient information is supplied to adjust the basic accounting data. One is less confident, however, about the ability of nonexpert investors to make the adjustments. For example, consider an investor who takes the accounting measures seriously and does not adjust the information, analyzing two firms both of which have reported earnings of $2 per share. However, one firm has expended (and expensed) $3 per share on R&D and the other firm has spent zero. The R&D firm would have had $5 per share of earnings if it had not purchased any R&D. The expensing of the R&D expenditures results in the two firms having the same earnings per share, thus implying equal value based on this one measure. These earnings are not comparable and the investor who views them as equivalent will be misled. There is another, related problem. Managers are very concerned with earnings per share, and they assume these numbers are used in the investment decision process. The first firm can stabilize its earnings at $2 per share by varying the amount of R&D it purchases. Thus earnings become a function of decisions to buy or not to buy R&D. It is difficult to see why the decision to buy or not to buy R&D should affect the earnings of

[19]Roland E. Dukes, *Market Evaluation of Accounting Information: A Cross Sectional Test of Investor Response to Expensing Research and Development Expenditures*, unpublished Ph.D. dissertation, Stanford University, 1974.

the current year. A loss firm can reduce its loss by $1 for $1 of R&D it stops buying. This is a relatively easy way to reduce losses. The result of expensing of R&D may distort corporate decision making and lead to faulty measure of income and changes in income through time.

CONCLUSIONS

The primary purpose of this critique is to question the rationale employed by the FASB in arriving at its conclusion. It may well be that requiring all firms to disclose the amount of their research and development costs and to expense these costs is the best feasible solution. Capitalizing of such costs may not be feasible because of attendant lawsuits when the R&D is found to have less value than the recorded cost. But the resulting practice should not then be justified on the grounds that it is good accounting theory.

Virtually every time an accountant records expenditures he or she runs the risk that a later development might, with the aid of hindsight, show that the recording was "wrong." The asset may turn out to be worth much less than cost. The obvious solution for avoiding this sort of situation and resulting criticisms is to expense all costs associated with the acquisition of assets where there is some significant probability that the asset will turn out to be worth less than the cost of the asset. This "conservative" approach to asset measurement is consistent with the Board's recommendation to expense R&D expenditures. The policy decision to expense R&D costs does not appear to be based on sound accounting theory but, rather, appears to be motivated by a desire to avoid the criticism and problems resulting from situations where, after the fact, an asset is found to be worth less than the amount reported by the accountant. It ignores completely the types of errors that arise from a systematic expense overstatement, income misstatement, asset understatement and stock equity understatement. Unfortunately, criticism and lawsuits may force the adoption of such conservative practices. The way to avoid criticism that past earnings and assets have been overstated is to expense all factors associated with assets whose value is uncertain. Such a solution, however, is really a way of avoiding responsibility and is a too easy solution to an extremely difficult problem. The accountant does exercise judgment; he is an estimator and should be willing to face up to the existence of uncertainty, rather than expensing items because their ultimate value is difficult to forecast at the time the cost is incurred.

Theoretically, the accountant should provide the information most useful to society, considering the costs and benefits of the alternative accounting policies. However, the measurement of these costs and benefits is extremely difficult. Currently, all we can do is offer qualitative evaluations of alternatives rather than explicit measures.

However, Dukes[20] has offered empirical evidence of the importance of the disclosure of R&D expenditures. This evidence supports the Board's recommendation that more information relative to the magnitude of R&D expenditures be disclosed. Whatever accounting procedure is finally adopted, the disclosure of the amounts of expenditures by year will enable the analyst using the information to make the adjustments that he sees fit. If one accepts the

[20]Ibid.

hypothesis that capital markets are efficient in the processing of information, disclosure of the amount of the research and development expenditure is an extremely important first step. Given the basic data regarding the amount of the expenditure, an assumption of efficient capital markets implies market prices will reflect appropriate adjustments to the reported accounting numbers. The Dukes study reports findings consistent with this conclusion. However, we are not suggesting that the ability of the market to digest data should be used as a justification for neglecting accounting practices. In the first place, the adjustment process has a cost. Second, there are many other uses of accounting data besides financial analysis for the evaluation of common stock.

When a firm suffers economic difficulty, it is likely that the accounting (book) value of its assets will exceed their economic value. Technological and social change can cause assets to lose value suddenly. It is virtually impossible for the accountant to anticipate and report these value changes and at the same time use cost-based accounting principles of asset and income measurement in a theoretically correct manner. It would be possible to expense all cost factors whose benefit stream has an element of risk, but this would result in reports that were essentially cash flow statements. The income statement prepared in accordance with theoretically correct accrual concepts is an extremely important report. While it is true that later events may indicate that estimated writeoffs of assets were too rapid or not rapid enough, the accountant has an obligation to attempt to estimate the expenses of earning the revenues of a period rather than reporting as expenses the expenditures made during the period. From the point of view of accounting theory, the expenditures for R&D, which are made in the expectation of benefiting future periods, should not be written off against the revenues of the present period. Justification for such practice must be found elsewhere, if it is to be found.

Accounting for Goodwill: A Realistic Approach

MICHAEL G. TEARNEY

Accounting, as a profession, is relatively young; yet in some areas of financial reporting we accountants are outmoded. Goodwill accounting is one area where outdated techniques still exist with the blessing of the Accounting Principles Board. With the exception of amortization,[1] valuing and reporting goodwill arising in business combinations has remained basically unchanged since 1944,[2] and yet one of the primary social responsibilities of any discipline should be to discard old methods and techniques in favor of expanding parameters of work in order to benefit society.

Tremendous strides have been made in the social sciences in the past two decades; many of these changes are concerned with measurement.[3] Since accounting might be viewed as the profession of measurement, we should begin to look beyond the traditional limitations. For example, when goodwill is purchased there is confirmation of its existence, but what factors have been combined to create the favorable conditions formally called "goodwill"? Is it personnel, research and development, production techniques, marketing channels or some combination of them all? Surely goodwill exists in different corporations for different reasons. Certainly more information would be conveyed to financial statement users if accountants tried to identify, measure and report the advantageous circumstances that led to payment for and recognition of goodwill.

This article will attempt to show that the existence and acquisition of goodwill is predicated on some identifiable condition or conditions present within the acquired entity and that failure to recognize these intangibles is a dereliction of duty by the accounting profession. Furthermore, recommendations as well as illustrations for goodwill accounting will be presented.

CONDITIONS FAVORABLE FOR GOODWILL

Goodwill acquired in business combinations represents a payment made by one entity to acquire another's profitability. This payment undoubtedly results from

Michael G. Tearney, "Accounting for Goodwill: A Realistic Approach," *The Journal of Accountancy*, July 1973, pp. 41–45. Copyright © 1973 by the American Institute of Certified Public Accountants, Inc.

[1]APB Opinions Nos. 16, "Business Combinations," and 17, "Intangible Assets," *APB Accounting Principles* (New York: AICPA, 1972), pp. 6637 and 6661.

[2] Committee on Accounting Procedure, Accounting Research Bulletin No. 24, "Accounting for Intangible Assets" (New York: AICPA, 1944). This was the first Institute pronouncement concerned specifically with goodwill.

[3] David F. Linowes, "Social Responsibility of the Profession," *Journal of Accountancy*, Jan. 71, p.66.

negotiations between the entities prior to culmination of the combination. Presumably then, the acquiring corporation has specific reasons underlying its willingness to incur the additional cost. By examining the motivations of acquiring companies one should obtain knowledge of the conditions which typically result in purchases of goodwill.

There are many reasons why one corporation might wish to purchase another. Those most often cited by authors[4] writing on the subject include the following:

1. Accomplishing a particular market objective, 9.8 percent.[5]
2. Saving time in expanding into a new area, 4.3 percent.
3. Acquiring management and technical skills, 5.6 percent.
4. Achieving product diversification, 40.1 percent.
5. Achieving integration, 33.2 percent.

If a firm wishes to expand its sales into new geographic areas, it is usually less risky and costly to acquire an existing company with established marketing channels in the new area than to attempt to develop the distribution channels internally.

Chadbourn, Incorporated, which acquired Hudson Hosiery Company and Charlotte Packaging Corporation in 1969, stated the following in its proposal:

"The proposed mergers will broaden the market penetration of the company into three areas. Management anticipates that the merger with Hudson Hosiery would immediately place the company in greater depth in the "chain-store" market in the United States and into the international market through Hudson GmbH which is operating in Western Europe. Management believes that the Charlotte Packaging merger . . . would bring the company sizable sales in the 'wholesale' market in the United States and that the mergers will also increase the department and specialty store sales of the company."[6]

Litton Industries, now a conglomerate, provides a good example of one company's acquiring another in order to save time in accomplishing an objective. In its early growth, Litton established a research, development and manufacturing position in the office equipment business. In order to create a market position, it considered internal growth from company-sponsored technical developments, but this plan was rejected because it would take eight to ten years to accomplish. Alternatively, Litton decided to acquire an established concern in the market. The result is history: it acquired Monroe Calculating Machine

---

[4] Myles L. Mace and George E. Montgomery, Jr., *Management Problems of Corporate Acquisitions* (Boston: Harvard Universtiy Graduate School of Business Administration, Division of Research, 1962), pp. 9–26; J. H. Hennessy, Jr., *Acquiring and Merging Businesses* (Englewood Cliffs, N.J.: Prentice-Hall, 1966), pp. 6–7; Arthur R. Wyatt and Donald E. Kieso, *Business Combinations: Planning and Action* (Scranton, Pa.: International Textbook Company, 1969), pp. 14–19; and George D. McCarthy, *Acquisitions and Mergers* (New York: Ronald Press Company, 1963), pp. 11–12.

[5] Percentages refer to the percent of 209 New York Stock Exchange listing applications for 1969 dealing with combinations accounted for by the purchase method that indicated the specific reason for acquisition. Of the applications examined, 7 percent either did not disclose a reason or stated a variety of other reasons.

[6] Chadbourn Incorporated, New York Stock Exchange Listing Application No. A-27120 (January 15, 1969), p. 7.

Company, which had 350 company-owned sales branches, and achieved its objective eight years earlier than internal development would have allowed.[7]

Human assets are one of the more important attributes of a successful business. Corporations with inadequate management or engineering personnel will frequently seek out and acquire other concerns with personnel strong in these areas. R. Lee Brummet, speaking of human assets, stated that much of the excess cost over real value of physical assets acquired in business combinations "that we may label as 'goodwill' is in fact a measure of value of human resources."[8] The acquisition of Dyonics, Incorporated, by Rover-Amchem, Incorporated, is an example of one company's acquiring another to fill a personnel void. In its 1969 listing application, Rover-Amchem said the following:

"Notwithstanding the losses which Dyonics has incurred during past years, the acquisition is considered desirable because it will add a company with demonstrated research and development capabilities [personnel] in the area of surgical and hospital equipment to Rover-Amchem's established position in the health care field."[9]

Product diversification and integration are two of the more common reasons for business combinations. Diversification refers to the production or sale of many different products, while integration means production or sale of the same basic product. Integration might be horizontal, i.e., combining two companies selling the same product, or vertical, i.e., two businesses engaged in different stages of production or distribution of a common product. Diversification and integration can be accomplished by internal growth, but external acquisitions result in faster accomplishment of goals.

Among the business combinations accounted for by the purchase method as reported in 1969 New York Stock Exchange Listing Applications, a number of diversified companies stand out. One such company, U.S. Industries, Inc., reported no fewer than nine acquisitions in one year. Corporations acquired by the firm were involved in manufacture of children's dresses, camping and sporting goods, plywood, footwear, polyethylene film, transportation, limousine services, health clubs and spas, and loan offices.[10] All of these acquisitions were made to facilitate growth without considerable delay in time.

The paper boxes and corrugated paper containers industry represents a fully integrated area where integration was achieved primarily by business combinations.[11] This industry consists of the following three basic production stages: (1) growing timber, (2) breaking down timber into several grades of paper and (3) converting the grades of paper into final products. One of the larger concerns in this field is St. Regis Paper Company. In 1969 St. Regis

[7]Mace and Montgomery, *op. cit.*, p. 15.

[8] "Accounting for Human Resources," *Journal of Accountancy*, Dec. 70, p. 63.

[9] Rover-Amchem, Incorporated, New York Stock Exchange Listing Application No. A-28781 (December 1,1969), p. 1.

[10] U.S. Industries, Incorporated, New York Stock Exchange Listing Applications No. A-27500 (March 28, 1969), p. 3; No. A-27555 (April 2, 1969), p. 3; No. A-27596 (April 11, 1969), p. 3; No. A-27911 (May 27, 1969), p. 3; No. A-28253 (August 4, 1969), p. 3; No. A-28404 (September 9, 1969), p. 4; No. A-28441 (September 8, 1969), p. 4; No. A-28655 (October 24, 1969), p. 4; and No. A-28797 (November 24, 1969), p. 4.

[11] Mace and Montgomery, *op. cit.*, pp. 23–24.

acquired two firms to strengthen its integrated operations in the paper business. North Western Pulp & Power Ltd. was acquired to obtain a long-term agreement allowing the cutting of timber[12] and Wade and McArthur Georgia companies to give St. Regis access to 52,000 acres of forest land to supply St. Regis' pulp mills.[13]

It is apparent from the above that, when one entity acquires another and willingly incurs a cost greater than the fair market value of the other's net identifiable assets, the latter company possesses some characteristics important to the acquiring company. These are usually of an intangible nature, e.g., personnel skills, distribution channels, product diversification. Intangibles of this type are frequently the primary motivating factor in the acquisition decision, yet consolidated financial statements not only fail to disclose these assets but also lump them together as one asset called "goodwill."

FAILURE OF FINANCIAL STATEMENTS

Financial statements are prepared as a medium of communication between a business entity and interested parties. Internally developed assets such as personnel skills, marketing channels and goodwill are not disclosed in balance sheets because their value is difficult to determine. Only assets specifically constructed[14] or purchased from outside parties are disclosed in financial statements.

This is why goodwill appears in financial statements only after it has been purchased. Historically, goodwill has become known as the excess profitability of an entity above that considered normal in the circumstances. The cost of goodwill, as specified by generally accepted accounting principles, is the difference between (1) the total cost paid to acquire another entity and (2) the fair market value of assets acquired (usually only those reflected on the acquired company's balance sheet). Thus, goodwill is valued indirectly by assigning it the unallocated portion of the purchase price. The term "goodwill" then represents all of the assets acquired but not specifically identified, regardless of whether or not the purchased company has excess profits.

Goodwill has consequently become a misleading and uninformative term which means different things on different financial statements.[15] In the examples given earlier, goodwill could refer to access to foreign markets (Chadbourn, Incorporated) or to backward integration (St. Regis Paper Company). The point is that the modern conception of goodwill, payment to acquire another's excess income, is no longer valid. In fact, it is not uncommon for one company to pay a premium to acquire an unprofitable firm as Rover-Amchem did when it purchased Dyonics to obtain the services of Dyonics' research and development

[12] St. Regis Paper Company, New York Stock Exchange Listing Application No. A-28831 (November 4, 1969), p. 3.

[13] St. Regis Paper Company, New York Stock Exchange Listing Application No. A-29113 (December 31, 1969), p. 1.

[14] An exception to this general rule concerns patents, where it is acceptable to capitalize the development cost.

[15] Michael G. Tearney, "Compliance With AICPA Pronouncements on Accounting for Goodwill," *The CPA Journal*, February 1973, pp. 121–25.

personnel. The term "goodwill" is an old term that has outlived its usefulness. It conveys absolutely no information to financial statement users about the underlying assets that were acquired in the combination.

A reason often stated for nonrecognition of assets acquired in business combinations, such as human resources, marketing facilities, geographic areas and so forth, is that their value is too subjective to allow allocation of total cost. Using this argument to justify recognition of goodwill rather than other existing valuable assets is analogous to burying one's head in the sand to avoid being seen. Cost assigned to acquired goodwill, in current accounting practice, is as subjectively determined as possible. There is no attempt made to value goodwill directly; rather, goodwill is determined by the "drop-out" method, i.e., whatever is left must necessarily represent goodwill cost. This procedure results in financial statements which fail to disclose any of the underlying assets that prompted the acquisition decision.

A less subjective method that certainly would result in more informative financial statements would be to identify and value these underlying assets. For example, if a particular entity was acquired in order to provide access to previously unavailable geographic areas, this asset, "geographic area," could be readily identified. Its value could be determined by experts in the field, e.g., independent appraisers, based on such criteria as estimated cost to develop the new market and/or increase in income due to earlier penetration of the area. The asset "geographic area" could justifiably be amortized over the estimated time saved by acquisition as opposed to internal growth. Using this suggested approach, rather than valuing goodwill by the drop-out method and then arbitrarily amortizing it over 40 years, would provide financial statement users with more relevant information.

IDENTIFY ASSETS ACQUIRED

Current accounting practices for goodwill, as well as all other tangible and intangible assets acquired in business combinations, need to be updated to allow the preparation of consolidated financial statements that provide users with more information. Accordingly, an investigation should be undertaken of an acquired company's operations to enable identification of all assets purchased in the combination. The implementation of this approach should eliminate the necessity of using the term "goodwill." Whenever an acquired entity does possess excess profitability (theoretical goodwill), the underlying reasons for this excess could be identified, valued and recorded, rather than ignored and arbitrarily labeled "goodwill."

Accountants do not purport to be appraisers but certainly this should not be an excuse to avoid an investigation of an acquired company's assets. Independent appraisers, many of whom specialize in valuing assets acquired in mergers, could be consulted to identify and value "hidden" assets purchased by acquiring an entire going concern.

An intensive investigation to uncover "hidden assets" refers to reviewing acquired companies' accounting records and procedures, operations and negotiations prior to the culmination of the acquisition. In searching for undisclosed tangibles, the accounting procedures used for capitalization v. expensing might provide information regarding valuable assets not disclosed on financial statements. For example, an unfortunate but not uncommon accounting practice is to expense all purchases of small tools regardless of their continuing use. This results in a balance sheet that does not disclose all assets.[16] Once all hidden tangible assets have been discovered, the search begins for intangibles.

Negotiations leading up to a final settlement between the parties to an acquisition probably offer the best evidence of undisclosed intangibles.[17] Prominent assets such as marketing channels and unique personnel skills will likely be mentioned in the minutes of these negotiations. Mention might also be made of the assumed value of the intangibles; if not, a review of past accounting records should disclose amounts incurred in their development.

If a portion of the total cost remains unaccounted for after completion of the above procedures, it probably represents payment made to purchase the acquired firms' excess profitability. The underlying reasons that enable the company to earn additional income should be identified and assigned the remaining cost. Possible reasons for this condition would include favorable location, customer relations, excellent channels of distribution or some similarly advantageous position. Regardless of causes, these reasons should be identified and assigned a portion of cost, even if they have previously been valued at current fair market value. For example, if the primary reason for excess profits is a particularly favorable location and the land has already been currently valued, its proportion of total cost should be increased because the land value to this going concern is more than its fair market value to a nonestablished operation.

The failure of accountants to require identification and valuation of so-called "hidden assets" is not because the task is impossible or impractical, but apparently because of a lack of interest when a generally acceptable and less time-consuming alternative exists—i.e., labeling the entire excess cost "goodwill." Current practices in this area not only negate the informative nature of financial statements but also could result in a disservice to clients. The Internal Revenue Service prohibits the amortization of goodwill for tax purposes, thus providing an incentive to minimize the goodwill cost and maximize the cost of depreciable assets, both tangible and intangible, acquired in business combinations.

A review of past tax court decisions reveals that in many instances assets otherwise called "goodwill" have been identified and amortized. In the *Danco Co.*[18] case the court held that personnel skills acquired in a business combination were valuable assets not includible as goodwill. The court found in a similar case[19] that not only personnel skills but also amounts paid in order to save money in future operations are valid, identifiable assets. In several cases,[20] advantageous location has been considered a separate asset with a value greater

[16] William L. Gladstone, "Tax Aspects of the Allocation of Purchase Price of a Business," *Journal of Accountancy*, Oct. 66, p. 40.

[17] Arthur R. Wyatt, Accounting Research Study No. 5, *A Critical Study of Accounting for Business Combinations* (New York: AICPA, 1963), pp. 63–64.

[18] *Danco Company*, 14 TC 276–290 (1950).

[19] *Ruth M. Cullen*, 14 TC 368–374 (1950).

[20] *Redman L. Turner*, 47 TC 355–363 (1966), and *Maurice A. Mittelman*, 7 TC 1162–1171 (1946).

than the land otherwise would be worth. A decision in one case, *Redman L. Turner*,[21] found that the necessity of immediate occupancy of the premises by the acquirer was an identifiable item (saving of time), which could reasonably be allocated a portion of total cost. Assets such as industrial "know-how," secret formulas and personnel qualifications of business managers have all been considered separate identifiable assets that are not part of goodwill. Apparently saving money (taxes) is incentive enough for a more intensive examination for hidden assets, while the mere disclosure of such assets for informative reasons is not worthy of the search.

An example of the valuation process recommended in this article for all companies acquired under the purchase method of accounting was reported in the January 1964 *Journal of Accountancy*.[22] This case illustrates exactly the same procedures recommended here.

An entire business was acquired for $5 million. The fair market value of all net assets disclosed on the acquired entity's balance sheet was determined to be $2,700,000, leaving an apparent goodwill cost of $2,300,000. Reviewing past and projected earnings revealed the purchase price to be reasonable.

Accordingly, an intensive investigation of the acquired company's operations was undertaken to determine if any hidden assets existed. Several patents and licensing agreements were identified. These assets were valued by capitalizing their expected future benefits. They were considered amortizable over their remaining useful lives. Drawings representing product designs were subsequently identified. The fair market value of drawings was determined by valuing the engineering time, draftsmen's time and overhead applicable to their development. Expected lives of the products represented by the drawings were estimated and used as the period over which amortization was based.

The acquired company was about to market some new models of existing products. Approximately three to five years were needed to design, test and prepare for sale a line of products similar to the new models. Since only a minimum of sales could be expected during the product development period, the new product model rights were considered a valuable asset. The difference between potential profits with and without the new product models was capitalized as the cost of the asset. Typically, this entity's products became obsolete in three years; consequently, the cost was to be amortized over a three-year life.

Another intangible asset identified was the company's unique engineering staff, which had been assembled over a period of years and was specifically suited and trained in the area of primary interest to the entity. The replacement cost of the engineering staff was estimated by using information available on the costs that had been incurred to assemble the department. The cost assigned to the asset "engineering staff" was considered amortizable because similar staffs in the industry consistently turned over in seven years due to pirating of personnel.

A relatively small excess cost still existed after the above valuations. A trademark was subsequently identified and valued. Further investigation revealed the acquired company had excess income because of its high quality

---

[21]*Redman L. Turner*, 47 TC 355–363 (1966).

[22]*John Heath, Jr.*, "Property Valuation Problems and the Accountant," *Journal of Accountancy*, Jan. 64, pp. 57–58.

product and good customer relations. These latter items were assigned the remaining cost and called "goodwill." Certainly a more informative title would have been "high quality product" and "good customer relations."

SUMMARY

Current accounting practices for goodwill as well as for other valuable assets not appearing on an acquired company's balance sheet are not in conformity with available valuation techniques. By substituting the catchall account "goodwill" for many assets purchased in business combinations, such as personnel skills and marketing channels, accountants are not only ignoring the existence of expert appraisers but perpetuating a disservice to clients and the general public as well. It is high time that we accountants recognized our social responsibility in this area.

Valuation techniques have been developed to a point where goodwill no longer need appear on financial statements. All assets acquired in business combinations, regardless how intangible they may be and whether or not they appear on the acquired entity's balance sheet, should be identified, valued and disclosed, thereby removing one of the thorns in the accountant's side.

THE AUTHORS AND THEIR CURRENT AFFILIATIONS

Hector R. Anton
Deloitte, Haskins, & Sells

William H. Beaver
Stanford University

Leopold A. Bernstein
Baruch College, City University of New York

Harold Bierman, Jr.
Cornell University

Richard P. Brief
New York University

D. R. Carmichael
American Institute of Certified Public Accountants

R. J. Chambers
University of Sydney

Richard Dieter
Arthur Andersen & Co., Boston

Nicholas Dopuch
University of Chicago

Roland E. Dukes
Cornell University

Edgar O. Edwards
Rice University

Eric G. Flamholtz
University of California at Los Angeles

Nicholas Gonedes
University of Pennsylvania

David O. Green
Baruch College, City University of New York

Reginald S. Gynther
Coopers & Lybrand, Australia

Loyd C. Heath
University of Washington

John W. Kennelly
University of Texas at Dallas

Baruch Lev
Tel Aviv University

Robert G. May
University of Texas at Austin

K. V. Peasnell
University of Lancaster

Stephen H. Penman
University of California at Berkeley

Kavasseri V. Ramanathan
Harvard University

Lawrence Revsine
Northwestern University

Paul Rosenfield
American Institute of Certified Public Accountants

Richard A. Samuelson
San Diego State University

Aba Schwartz
Tel Aviv University

David Solomons
University of Pennsylvania

George H. Sorter
New York University

Robert R. Sterling
Rice University

Clyde P. Stickney
Dartmouth College

Gary L. Sundem
University of Washington

Shyam Sunder
University of Chicago

Arthur Thomas
University of Kansas

Michael G. Tearney
Drake University

William M. Voss
Ohio University

M. C. Wells
University of Sydney

Joseph F. Wojdak
American Cabinet Corporation

Stephen A. Zeff
Rice University

C
D
E 4
F 5
G 6
H 7
I 8
J 9